Whole Language:
The Debate

moderated by

Carl B. Smith

 Clearinghouse on Reading,
English, and Communication

EDINFO
PRESS

© **1994 by EDINFO Press**
Published by
EDINFO Press and
ERIC Clearinghouse on Reading, English, and Communication
Carl B. Smith, Director
Smith Research Center, Suite 150
2805 East Tenth Street
Bloomington, Indiana 47408-2698

Editor: Warren Lewis
Design and Production: David J. Smith
Cover: David J. Smith

This publication was funded in part by the Office of Educational Research and Improvement, U.S. Department of Education, under contract no. RR93002011. Contractors undertaking such projects under government sponsorship are encouraged to express freely their judgment in professional and technical matters. Points of view or opinions, however, do not necessarily represent the official view or opinions of the Office of Educational Research and Improvement.

Library of Congress Cataloging-in-Publication Data

Whole language : the debate / moderated by Carl B. Smith.
    p. cm.
    Includes bibliographical references.
    ISBN 0-927516-39-X : $24.95
    1. Reading--United States--Language experience approach--
Congresses.   I. Smith, Carl Bernard.
LB1050.35.W46 1994
372.4--dc20   93-33862
                                              CIP

Whole Language: The Debate

Contents

the speakers for Whole Language

Susan Ohanian taught school for 20 years at all levels, grade 1 through college, including high-school drop-outs. After being a staff writer for *Learning Magazine* for some years, she has now gone free-lance. Her award-winning articles have appeared in publications ranging from the *Phi Delta Kappan, Education Week,* and *Atlantic,* to *Washington Monthly, College English,* and *USA Today.* She is a member of the CEE Executive Committee of NCTE and of the Intellectual Freedom Committee. She guests on radio talk shows because she thinks that "educators make a big mistake in talking only to each other and not to the public."

Patrick Shannon is Professor of Education at The Pennsylvania State University, State College, where he is Coordinator of Undergraduate Studies and Professor in Charge of Language and Literacy Education. He is active on editorial boards of professional journals and in committees of professional organizations, among others, the Teacher As Researcher Committee of the IRA, and the Reading Commission of NCTE. He has demonstrated expertise in the fields of literacy, reading, and reading instruction; assessment and testing; and the social implications of education. His most telling work is being done in his paradigmatic revisioning of the socio-political agenda of education in America, addressing questions of control in the educational enterprise, censorship, the rights and powers of teachers and—together with their students—their ownership of education, and education for a democratic society.

the speakers against Whole Language

Michael McKenna is Professor of Education at Georgia Southern University in Savannah. He is a member of the review boards of a number of professional journals in Education, among them *Journal of Reading Behavior* and *The Reading Teacher*. He is a teacher of reading teachers, and his books and numerous research-based articles in scholarly journals are definitive. He is especially interested in the use of computers in reading, and he travels to South Africa to help with the literacy effort there.

John Miller is Dean and Professor in the College of Education at Florida State University, Tallahassee. He has been an elementary and a secondary school teacher, a university professor, and now he bears the burden of administration. His numerous assignments, pages of papers, and many awards have distinguished him as an authority on reading, comprehension, reading instruction, teacher recruitment, use of technology in education, and school restructure. He works as a consultant, trou-bleshooter, and innovator committed to improving the nation's schools and preparing more ethic-minority teachers to take up their work.

Richard Robinson is Professor of Education in the College of Education at the University of Missouri, Columbia, and he holds special responsibility for Continuing Professional Education activities for the Department of Curriculum & Instruction. He has also been an elementary-school reading teacher, including teaching boys in prison. His areas of expertise are teaching reading and reading-teacher effectiveness, reading in the content areas, analysis and correction of reading disabilities, and adult reading (ABE). His scholarship has been published widely in professional journals, from Beijing to Britain.

In 1990, Robinson, McKenna, and some others co-founded the National Reading Research Center, an effort begun partly as a response to a reaction to the strong presence felt of the Whole Language people at the National Reading Conference.

Moderator's Introduction

"And the winner is _____!"
The Context of the Debate

Carl B. Smith
Director, ERIC Clearinghouse on
Reading, English, and Communication
Indiana University, Bloomington, Indiana

F irst you must know that each side in this debate thinks that it has thoroughly trounced the other. My initial impulse is to cheer because the euphoria on both sides of this discussion resembles two pumped-up boxers waiting for the judges' decision after giving fight fans a toe-to-toe battle. Then I begin to wonder about a war in which each side thinks that it has demolished the other. Were they actually on the same battlefield? Or did they kill each other off, and their spirits are now talking to us from the Other Side of the Wall, viewing these matters with disembodied equanimity, no longer burdened by political rhetoric? Then I re-read our debate, snap back from the nether world, and realize that we are hip-deep in political rhetoric on both sides.

This particular face-off between Whole Language proponents and more traditional researchers was sparked when a writer from *U.S. News and World Report* called me up one day asking for "evidence" of whether or not Whole Language works. Thereafter, we generated a preliminary bibliography at ERIC/REC; contestants were picked, and they chose team mates; formal debate resolutions were exchanged, modified, and exchanged again; the first volleys were fired in print; next, the face-to-face shoot-out in San Antone (as editor Warren Lewis, a Texan, likes to describe it) took place at a convention of the National Reading Conference in San Antonio, Texas, in December, 1992; that was followed by further written broadsides; and final victory was declared at last by both sides in the concluding commentaries written by four vested parties. This is the best debate you've ever read: Both sides win!

Evidence for Whole Language

The key word in this debate is *evidence*, but even the idea of "evidence" only unleashes the furies of today's educational politics. That's why almost everyone in education will enjoy reading these pages. Policy makers will find curriculum principles; administrators will find assessment information; teachers will find guidelines for classroom activities.

As Director of the ERIC Clearinghouse for Reading, English, and Communication, I often get calls from people in the media looking for information on teenage trends in reading or evidence of bias in the mass media. We typically answer those requests with a brief printout of ERIC citations and annotations. The reporter from *U.S. News and World Report*, however, did not want "another education bibliography." He wanted a summary of evidence that showed whether or not Whole Language worked. He had heard that entire school systems were mandating a shift to Whole Language. Some of the school systems where he had interviewed personnel had mandated from the top that Whole Language would be the methodology used by all teachers—Houston, for instance. When he asked them for the evidence that led them to require these systemwide changes, he received vague, general statements, ranging from "everybody's doing it" to "research proves that it is effective." But no one offered him specific evidence.

A couple of his school contacts had suggested that he call me at ERIC for the evidence he sought. I told him that I had no handy summary; perhaps he could get the data he wanted from the gurus of Whole Language, those who had a national voice in proposing its adoption. I gave him several names, and he said he would call them.

A couple of days later, the same reporter telephoned again. The Whole Language leaders he had called did not have a summary of evidence that showed that Whole Language worked better than other methods, at least not the hard data that the reporter desired. Two of the three leaders suggested that he call me to get those data. "That's his job," he quoted them as having said.

Even though ERIC does custom searches for clients, those searches pinpoint documents that respond to the descriptor terms that our staff logs onto the database. I convinced him to take a look at the annotated printout that we would develop, and I offered to mark those items that looked promising. If he wanted to see the full text, we could arrange for him to do so.

After he looked at the printout of abstracts, the reporter was back on the line. In the very few comparative studies that appeared in the abstracts, it appeared to him that some data favored traditional methods and some favored Whole Language. There was no clear indication that this new approach was superior to other approaches. "Why, then," he asked, "are these school systems risking the welfare of all their children on an approach that has not shown superior results in scientific studies?"

"I suppose," I replied, "that the adopting schools approve the philosophy behind Whole Language. They believe that using trade books and allowing teachers and students to learn together about things that interest them is more important than following a structured curriculum. They believe in that philosophy, and they are highly motivated by it."

In a cynical tone, he countered: "You're talking salesmanship; you sound like a preacher. I'm asking for scientific evidence. I find it hard to believe that scientists within education are not challenging the widespread use of unproved beliefs. Are there no scientists in the field of education? Are there no reasonable people in this profession?" And he rang off.

Those are the questions that prompted the debate you are about to read. We searched for reasonable people on both sides—those who claim that there is evidence for the effectiveness of Whole Language, and those who doubt its efficacy. Susan Ohanian and Patrick Shannon agreed to stand up for Whole Language as a superior instructional theory. Michael McKenna, Richard Robinson, and John Miller agreed to challenge the claim that the evidence shows that Whole Language works across the broad spectrum of learners. At the outset, the two sides weren't quite addressing the same questions, but we at ERIC thought it was close enough for a match.

Teachers need a management tool

This discussion has significant potential, not because it has technical consequences, such as the validity of types of evidence, but because it may guide teachers towards becoming better instructors. In the complex world of classroom learning, teachers need management tools and guidelines. Teachers' instructional activities involve their students in many aspects of life, both the life of the mind and life within our communities. Without some kind of mental map or set of guiding principles to direct their daily work, teachers might ricochet from one activity to another, leaving students distracted, confused, and disgruntled with schooling.

That's the reason teachers rely on central management tools, such as basic textbooks, Whole Language, individualized education contracts, mastery learning, and so on. Those systems and their learning principles act as compass and roadmap in a classroom filled with many learning needs.

Over the past decade, the term "Whole Language" has risen to prominence, and it now acts as a management tool for thousands of teachers. The leadership establishment in some school districts has mandated the use of Whole Language as the main instructional management device for all teachers in their district. Though these school districts may not be entirely clear what they mean by "Whole Language," they all seem to reject the teaching of skills in behavioral fashion and want to marshal reading and writing around "real literature" in preference to textbook selections. Assorted other principles and beliefs are included with varying frequency.

Conflicting Paradigms

During the past eighty-five years, teachers have given evidence of achievement by using tests of knowledge and tests of skills application. Those tests, sometimes called standardized tests, permitted teachers to present reasonably objective evidence of accomplishment and progress. But if schools now reject those previous objectives and values, then logically they reject the evidence collected under that positivist paradigm. Objective test evidence based on specified knowledges and skills does not match the relative and subjective nature of learning, Whole Language advocates assert.

The issue of conflicting paradigms (mental maps, if you will) presents our debaters with one of their major issues: *Can people occupying two different world views even argue effectively with one another?* The second major issue is no less daunting: *What evidence can Whole Language offer that satisfies the public's demand that all children show accomplishment and make progress towards worthwhile goals?*

Objectivism versus subjectivism has been debated for thousands of years. Though the philosophical debate over the nature of human experience may not be new, our discussion here looks at those two philosophies in the context of concrete educational practice. The past and continuing practice of most schools that use specific objectives, define performances or outcomes, and are assessed by standard criteria, represents one side of this debate's context. The other side is represented by a growing number of schools that choose the relativism of Whole Language which encourages students to explore their world, their own interests, and their relationships with other people. To evaluate that process, Whole Language proponents ask students to assemble portfolios of their work which students and teachers judge according to individual standards.

Benefits for Educators

This discussion is not an esoteric wrangle among purely academic drones. Which language-arts paradigm instructors follow has implications for all the different stakeholders concerned with education—parents, teachers, administrators, and especially the kids.

That is why we chose the debate format: to bring the issue to the attention of a broad audience with the clearest focus possible. The good-news result of this debate would come about if you, reader, could be moved to re-examine your own premises and understandings of the learning process. We hope that the debate causes all kinds of decision makers to do that very thing. Where do we want to go with learning in our schools? How do we develop a reasonable match between our goals and our instructional practices?

The bad news is that the debate format often provokes showmanship more than it does thoughtful inquiry. The audience may tend to become mere cheerleaders in a college-football atmosphere, looking only for catch phrases that incite them either to cheer or to hiss. The voices in this book, however, have mostly resisted the temptation to engage in grandstanding. They have given substantial thought to their work, and their thoughts deserve a substantial reflection and response.

Writer Tom Wolfe predicted that in the '90s Americans will be searching for values, especially spiritual values. In many ways, this discussion focuses more on values than on assessment techniques. This debate reveals some of the politics and some of the values issues that bedevil educators. Who determines policies? Which goals shall we pursue? What standards will be used to assess success? Which learners will receive preference? And a whole lot more.

These kinds of issues will shape the policies of school boards and the implementation strategies of classroom teachers. The question of what evidence the school uses to demonstrate student progress is, therefore, more than a technical discussion of validity and reliability. Our choice of acceptable evidence bespeaks our view of the world in which we work and want to work.

I think of Joan of Arc, the French peasant girl who claimed that heavenly voices spoke to her and called her to lead the French soldiers against the English. The French leaders believed in Divine intervention and that God might speak to them through a woman. Therefore, they followed Joan to victory at Orleans. Later, Joan was betrayed to the English by her own French king, tried as a witch, and burned at the stake because her inquisitors claimed that only the devil would cause a woman to lead an army. Saint to one party, evil witch to another—each side saw Joan's actions through the paradigms of differing sets of values.

Because our paradigms determine the kinds of evidence we shall admit in judging success at school, let us read this debate to help us examine our positions and clarify our values. With a clearer set of values that we can project into our school work, we can determine what behaviors we shall recognize as evidence of progress or success.

With a clearer system of values, we can also better articulate our instructional philosophy, starting from daily classroom activities. If we believe that success is determined by the learner's feeling that he did a good job, then we move classroom activities and the collection of evidence in the direction of the learner's personal perception. If, on the other hand, we believe that success is based on the learner's sense of progress towards common goals, then we move classroom activities and the collection of evidence in the direction of public standards.

Educators usually don't see their work in such starkly polar terms. Though they may see one set of values as their mainstay, they usually recognize strengths in other sets of values.

Battle of Philosophies

In these debate papers and in schools today, we see conflicting philosophies battling for control of policy and instructional practice. According to Whole Language theory, the nature of schooling, that is, the learning experience, is primarily subjective. According to the Positivist theory, schooling is primarily objective. Therein lies the knot of disagreement both over what the school curriculum should be and over the evidence that represents success—a knot that our debaters have tried to untie.

If the school curriculum must follow the individual learner's needs because learning is subjective, then individual, personal responses should be the evidence that teachers assemble to represent this subjective inquiry. Personal reflections in speech and in writing would be the valid representations of this subjective approach.

If, on the other hand, learning and the school curriculum are focused on common, objective experiences, then samples of those experiences/knowledges should be collected by teachers as evidence of common learning. Common knowledge and visible problem-solving techniques, then, would be valid representations of the objective approach.

Since objectivism and subjectivism have been warring philosophies at least since the Ancient Greeks, it is unlikely that we will resolve that philosophical debate here within a few pages. How, then, are we educators to sort out this important disagreement over the values that will guide our policies and our classroom activities?

The turn-of-the-century philosopher William James used the analogy of a mosaic that helps me personally to bridge the gulf between subjectivism and objectivism, and to arrive at conclusions about the objective/subjective nature of learning and teaching. In trying to explain his own philosophy, Pragmatism, James asks us to think of a mosaic that is not cemented with mortar, patterns in stone laid out in sand but not yet fixed in place. Each piece of stone in the mosaic contributes to the overall effect of the artistic image. An individual stone chip, when pulled out of the mosaic, seems unimportant—the pattern is still there. If only a couple of stone chips are removed from the mosaic, we can push the remaining pieces together to reshape the image and still have a coherent picture, though altered slightly.

James uses this analogy to differentiate between objective reality "out there" (the mosaic) and subjective states "inside" (personal interpretations of the mosaic). The objective realities are not merely isolated stone chips: They are parts of a patterned, coherent system. Those hard-as-stone bits of objective reality were arranged systematically by the artist to form the mosaic in the first place; metaphorically, they show us that objective life is coherent in its patterns. Even if our mosaic is missing a couple of stone chips, is missing a couple of experiences that others have had, is missing this or that bit of knowledge that others know, we still see the same coherent image; we still see the objective patterns.

Subjectively, James contends, the individual may use the objective reality in various ways, give it many interpretations, express different feelings about it, and generally manipulate the mosaic for any of a variety of internal, subjective, individual, personal reasons. This subjective state can be referred to as interpretation, personal response, creative imagination, and so on. During learning, the learners decide through these subjective, internal states, whether or not they like the mosaic, what use it has for them, how it could be rearranged for individual purposes, what it means, etc.

The primary bridge between the objective world and the subjective world is language. Language is the intermediary between objective reality and subjective interpretation. The language bridge enables people intrapersonally to make sense of what's "out there" in terms of what's "in here," and interpersonally to share their subjective interpretations of the objective world, no matter what scrambled use they make of their primary reference points.

That, to me, makes language teaching both extremely valuable and great fun. Valuable, because the language-arts teacher helps students refine language usage so that their objective and subjective worlds can be understood and shared. Great fun, because language study is full of surprises and playfulness when students struggle to express their views.

Willam James's Pragmatism does not, I think, tip the winning of the debate in this book either to the one side or the other. What James' analogy does for me is to give me a framework in which to deal with the issues that appear here, particularly the community's demand for objective evidence and the individual's need for subjective expression. The mosaic analogy gives us direction both for the collection of public evidence and for the construction of personal portfolios—both for the objective patterns of common learning, common knowledge, and common goals, and for the subjective rearrangement of the bits and chips of private experience that are individual inquiry, individual interpretations, and individual goals.

As you moderate this debate in your own mind, I invite you to engage in your own active interrogation of the debaters' assumptions, logic, and conclusions, and as you do, to take a close look at your own beliefs about education. We have some important questions to be answered: *"What are the purposes of public evidence in education? How shall we provide public evidence for and about new educational programs that appropriately respond to individual styles and needs?"*

As you will see when you moderate for yourself the debate on these pages, the mental maps/the educational paradigms/the theories of evidence/the belief systems of these discussants demand very different kinds of evidence. We of ERIC/REC and EDINFO Press hope that you find these exchanges stimulating and provocative, but more, we hope that you will come away from this book with your own system of beliefs about teaching, schooling, and learning focused under a clearer light.

Resolutions for Debate

The original resolutions proposed for debate were as follows. The intent of most of them was carried forward throughout the debate, although the statements as specifically formulated did not, in some cases, receive direct attention.

from the Whole Language side

Resolved:

We believe that in our democratic society Whole Language principles and the pedagogy of some advocates offer us a better opportunity than do traditional approaches to develop active, literate citizens who can and will address the question: How do we wish to live together in communities, states, and the nation?

To us, Whole Language principles and pedagogy suggest the following:

Literacy is a cultural, social, aesthetic, historical, emotional, and political, as well as a psychological effort, after meaning.

The contexts in which literate individuals and groups find themselves affect the demands made upon literate behavior and literate abilities to meet and negotiate those demands.

Individuals and groups learn according to their interests and purposes, and they develop "habits of mind," attitudes, and definitions according to what their environment affords. This does not mean that they simply accept what the environment offers.

We ought to recognize these facts and organize environments that afford individuals and groups opportunities to use the cultural, social, aesthetic, etc. aspects of literacy in a variety of environments, for a variety of purposes, in pursuit of a variety of interests in order to develop habits of mind, attitudes, and definitions appropriate in democratic society in and out of schools.

Further Resolved:

Language is a complex system for meaning-making through socially shared understandings which individuals acquire through immersion and intentional use within a language community or social group.

Learning is a social process driven by learners' purposes and intentions which are mediated by their history, culture, and traditions.

Educational science to determine how these principles can be realized is a dialectical process in which knowledge is continuously produced and reconsidered during the educational act (teaching and learning).

Curriculum is the negotiated experiences of teachers and students in classrooms and schools.

Assessment is a means by which students and teachers affirm what they know in order to make decisions about how to support their further learning.

---

from the side opposed to Whole Language

Resolved:

Most educational practices congruent with Whole Language philosophy are unobjectionable to traditional teachers; however, two exceptions are contestable.

1. The contention that skills instruction can be based effectively on the occurrence of teachable moments rather than on systematic direct instruction is without research support.

2. The contention by some Whole Language proponents that direct instruction in decoding is unnecessary because such skills, like those of oral language, will be acquired naturally in meaning-oriented, print-rich contexts, is unsupported by research.

Adams, M.J. (1990). *Beginning to read: Thinking and learning about print*. Cambridge, Massachusetts: MIT Press.

Adams, M.J. (1991). A talk with Marilyn Adams. *Language Arts, 68,* 206–212.

Almasi, J.F., Palmer, B.M., Gambrell, L.B., & Pressley, M. (December, 1991). A methodological analysis of whole language research. Paper presented at the meeting of the National Reading Conference, Palm Springs, California.

Baumann, J.F. (1991). Of rats and pigeons: Skills and whole language. *Reading Psychology, 12,* iii–xiii.

Resolved:

Research comparing Whole Language with traditional practice can be undertaken effectively. Diverse research paradigms are not incommensurable but can serve to illuminate phenomena better by providing multiple perspectives.

Howe, K.R. (1988). Against the quantitative-qualitative incompatibility thesis. *Educational Researcher, 17*(8), 10–16.

Spiro, R.J. (December, 1991). Integrative reconciliation of paradigm conflict in reading: Joining multiple perspectives in reading research, in learning to read, and in preparing reading teachers for practice. Paper presented at the meeting of the National Reading Conference, Palm Springs, California.

Stanovich, K.E. (1990). A call for an end to the paradigm wars in reading research. *Journal of Reading Behavior, 22,* 221–231.

Resolved:

The Goodman model of reading, on which much of Whole Language theory rests, is no longer a viable explanation of reading processes.

Byrne, B. & Fielding-Barnsley, R. (1991). Evaluation of a program to teach phonemic awareness to young children. *Journal of Educational Psychology, 83,* 451–455.

Foorman, B.R., Francis, D.J., Novy, D.M., & Liberman, D. (1991). How letter-sound instruction mediates progress in first-grade reading and spelling. *Journal of Educational Psychology, 83,* 456–469.

Rayner, K. & Pollatsek, A. (1989). *The psychology of reading.* Englewood Cliffs, New Jersey: Prentice-Hall.

Nicholson, T., Lillas, C., & Rzoska, M.A. (1988). Have we been misled by miscues? *The Reading Teacher, 42,* 6–10.

Nicholson, T. (1991). Do children read words better in context or in lists? A classic study revisited. *Journal of Educational Psychology, 83,* 444–450.

Schatz, E.K. & Baldwin, R.S. (1986). Context clues are unreliable predictors of word meanings. *Reading Research Quarterly, 21,* 439–453.

Stanovich, K.E. (1991) Word recognition: Changing perspectives. In R. Barr, M.L. Kamil, P.B. Mosenthal, & P.D. Pearson (Eds.). *Handbook of reading research* (vol. 2, pp. 418–452). New York: Longman.

Vellutino, F.R. (1991) Introduction to three studies on reading acquisition: Convergent findings in theoretical foundations of code-oriented versus whole-language approaches to reading instruction. *Journal of Educational Psychology, 83,* 437–443.

Further Questions:

1. Can the effectiveness of Whole Language ever really be investigated as long as Whole Language remains ill-defined?

2. What is the research base suggesting that Whole Language practices are preferable to traditional approaches?

3. Is it possible that for some students literacy ability is more readily acquired through traditional perspectives and their associated methodologies?

4. Is it possible that some teachers, owing to aspects of personality, might be ill-suited to becoming Whole Language teachers?

5. Edelsky contends that Whole Language, as a "theory in practice," is more than a set of methods, but that it nevertheless entails "congruent practice." Is it not possible to enumerate such practices and to incorporate them selectively to good effect, without accepting and applying them all?

6. Short of defining Whole Language, would an enumeration of "congruent practices" at least serve to define Whole Language practice?

7. How can Whole Language proponents defensibly explain the research base supporting traditional methodologies?

8. What are the specific objections to quantitative research designs used to investigate the effects of Whole Language? Are these objections remediable within the quantitative paradigms?

"Call Me Teacher."

Susan Ohanian
Schoolteacher and Writer,
Schenectady, New York

C all me teacher. I am the sort of person who spends 182 days a year shut up in a room with eight-year-olds—or twelve-year-olds—and not only lives to tell about it but rejoices in the telling. I have taught at every level from grade one through fourteen, including high-school dropouts and engineering students at a technological university. All of these students had one common experience: School had convinced them that they hated reading and writing.

I'm glad I encountered those fledgling engineers early in my career because they showed me the limitations of reading as skill. By every standardized measurement, those engineers-to-be were verbally skilled. Nonetheless, it took not even one week in their presence to figure out that their proficiency was an empty shell. When I asked them to share their memories of "an important literary event" in their lives, they insisted that there had been no such events. After I assigned the topic as homework, pointing out that it was now an important part of their grade, they did manage to come up with some anecdotes about nursery rhymes, Dr. Seuss, fairy tales, and comic books. Out of 87 students, not one offered a memory of an important literary event in his school experience. With the exception of a scattering of comic-book memories, not one of those students who ranked in the superior range of college-entrance examinees talked of an important literary event that had involved himself as an independent reader.

So it became my teacherly goal to find the words that would touch the hearts and minds of students who hated reading. I was determined that they would not leave my class without encountering words that cause a shock of recognition, send shivers of delight down the spine; words that astound, amaze, and leave one yearning for more. I read aloud to my college students—from the newspaper, from essays, from novels—and each day I wrote "wonderful words" on the board, hoping that sooner or later a poetry snippet or snappy paragraph would connect with one student or another. And I didn't need to administer a comprehension quiz to know when a connection occurred.

Over time, different students responded to different words. Joe was the class holdout. No matter what literary jewel I displayed, Joe peppered his scowls with long, drawn-out sighs of exasperation and boredom. Like his classmates, Joe was aliterate, willing to read for information, to pass a test, but unwilling to pick up a book or a magazine for enlightenment or enjoyment. If the printed page was not utilitarian, something directly applicable to engineering, Joe rejected it. On the 32nd day of class, I pointed to a few lines I'd written on the board and announced, "This Chinese lyric is the most beautiful poem I know." Tough, pragmatic, unmovable, scowling Joe stared and stared at the chalkboard. Finally, he stopped staring, straightened up from his permanent slouch in the back row, gave a sigh of surprise, and said, "Hey, not bad." High praise from an engineer-to-be who had been unable to recall any memorable literary event in his life since *Peter Peter Pumpkin Eater.*

I took that lesson from the university to my third-grade classroom. I was determined that no eight-year-old would leave my care unable to testify to powerful connections with wonderful words. I soon discovered that I was in for the struggle of my life. Nobody hated reading like those third-graders hated reading. Small wonder. In a rigorously tested and sorted school, all the certified rotten readers had been lumped together; since first grade they had traveled in a pack, circling short vowels. A number of them had been held back a year, so they had an extra year of hating reading under their belts. I told them that things were going to be different: We weren't going to have workbooks or textbooks. Instead, we would start each school day with 15 minutes of silent reading, and everybody would choose their own books from a beautiful array.

"How come?" they kept whining. How come we didn't do reading the way we were supposed to? How come they didn't get workbooks; every other child in the school got a workbook; where were theirs? Third-graders have a strong sense of how things are supposed to be. Circling vowels *was* reading; filling up a classroom with tradebooks definitely was *not* reading the way it's supposed to be taught. Kids like the busy-ness of workbooks. All that skill work—circling and underlining and matching and filling-in-the-blanks—provides an academic flak jacket, a cover

3

protecting the wearer from the pain and terror that comes from taking risks. Every day for three months, Chris told me just how much he hated my brand of reading. Like his classmates, he scowled, whined, kicked his neighbors, and resorted to those classic third-grade standbys: tears and vomit. I persevered. Once we got independent silent reading out of the way, I read to these children—six, eight, fifteen times a day. They loved being read to; it was having to read by themselves that they hated.

On the 46th day, Chris found words that changed his life forever. I didn't show him the book that changed his life; Jennifer did. I knew the instant when Jennifer discovered something amazing in *Amelia Bedelia.* Her eyes opened wide; she gripped the book tightly; she turned back a page and read it again, mouthing each word as though she could not believe her eyes. Then she burst into a guffaw—covered her mouth quickly and looked up at me. After all, I was a termagant about imposing the rule of *silent* reading. I grinned and winked at her. She grinned and showed the funny page to her best friend. With both of them giggling, Chris insisted, "Let me see," and before he realized what was happening, a book that he was reading to himself was making Chris laugh.

All-of-a-sudden those eight-year-old rotten readers were experiencing a new sensation: scrambling to get their names on a waiting list for a book. Chris came in the next day with a smug, gleeful look on his face. He wanted me to know that he had put something over on me. He announced that he didn't have to wait his turn for my copy of *Amelia Bedelia* because he had persuaded his mother to take him to the city library where he had found another copy. Chris had pulled a fast one, all right. Imagine a rotten reader begging to go to the library!

Emerson once wrote: "A chief event of life is the day in which we have encountered a mind that startled us." College freshman Joe found that event in a 14th-century Chinese lyric poem. Peggy Parish gave my third-graders such an event. She showed my students what language can do, and that led them to discover what they could do with language. They began making their own puns. Suddenly the riddle books I'd tried to introduce in September were a hot item. Surely one good pun-based laugh is worth 10,000 circled short vowels or consonant blends in advancing a child's reading and writing proficiency.

And we didn't use the book as an excuse to do something else. I didn't interrogate my students about main ideas; they didn't make puppets. We used each book as inspiration to read another book. I don't recall ever asking a single question about an *Amelia* book. What is the need for questions when the children's pleasure is so evident? I was amazed and appalled to discover *Amelia* in a basal. The teacher's manual carefully lists the objectives to be taught with the story, including the following crystal clear prose:

> *decode words based on the spelling pattern generalization that a vowel letter followed by a consonant and final e represents a glided (or long) vowel sound.*

Never mind that research shows us that the *final e rule* is true no more than 53% of the time. Even if the rule were 99 and $^{44}/_{100}$% pure, a child who can decode—and enjoy—*Amelia Bedelia*, has no need to practice the *final e rule*. And a child who doesn't "get" the humor won't be helped by the *final e rule*. What he needs is not more rules but more books.

Chris didn't rest on his laurels. He became passionately devoted to Jack Prelutsky's poems, *The Stupids*, Nate the Great, Beatrix Potter, Arnold Lobel, and Steven Kellogg. Chris was so devoted to Potter's "little books" that he wrote out *Peter Rabbit* in longhand in his poetry notebook. When one of his classmates asked him what he was doing, Chris, who professed to hate writing even more than he did reading, explained, "I just like the way the words feel in my fingers." It was a remark akin to Lesley's, a deaf child who kept repeating *scrambled eggs super de dooper de pooper* (her classmates had made an addition to the Seuss text) because, she said, "I like the way the words feel on my tongue."

Lots of people who love books agree that we don't need to assign children skills questions about *Amelia*. Nonetheless, they ask, aren't there some important questions that we need to ask about some literature? I doubt it. For me, the strength of a Whole Language classroom is our belief in the book and the child. I'm sure that sometimes and somewhere there must be some important questions, but as I look back over twenty-odd years of getting books and children together, I just don't recall any. People don't become real readers until they take control: control of the text, control of themselves as readers, and until the joy of the text—not answering questions about it—takes hold of their minds. Any time a teacher asks a question, control of the reading act moves from child to teacher. Sometimes this is necessary, but less is definitely more when it comes to interrogating children about what they are reading.

I often wonder why people have to wait until they leave school to exercise some choice and control over what they read. My husband doesn't read the same books I do, so why should every third-grader in my care read the same books at the same time? We have certain texts in common, but mostly we learn that reading is an independent, solitary act. You do it by yourself; nobody can do it for you. Reading is the place where the individual must take charge if he or she is ever to become a real reader. That superlative essayist Edward Hoagland puts it this way: "Reading a book amounts to being talked to alone by somebody else for a long time." Hoagland observes that books "must be pulled out of the page by the reader, who to some extent recapitulates the labor of the author himself!"

I find that rhetorical analysis of several versions of the same fairy tale provides an intriguing way for students to study text closely and "get into" the wonderful multiplicity and intent of language. A group of first- and second-graders, for example, searched out twenty-nine versions of *Little Red Riding Hood,* trying to locate just what was in that basket. Those children showed me that such a study is never over. Months after we seemed to have completed it, Dougie rushed into the class shouting, "I found another one! My mom took me to a library twenty miles away and we looked and looked. And I found a *Little Red Riding Hood* that nobody has seen yet!" Could the scholar who discovered a new Boswell diary in an attic be any more thrilled than was Dougie with that small book?

Such seemingly simple textual analysis leads some students deeper and deeper into the text. Some students are content to stay with the surface, literal meaning, and that's okay. This kind of research welcomes all students at whatever level of sophistication they can bring to the text. When students can bring their own questions to a text, nobody is left out and nobody fails the questions. Students are excited when I show them that they are conducting the same kind of textual research for which Professor Jack Zipes received a grant. When I show children bits of Zipes's analysis of the contents of Little Red Riding Hood's basket, they are excited to be a part of the community of scholars, people who care about words. They are amazed that professors write thick books about the same kind of research that they themselves are conducting.

Some of my students never achieved control of the text and of themselves as readers. Their failure as readers was not because I didn't ask the right questions; their failure happened because they and I together did not find the right books for them. Bob is the non-reader whose pain is my pain forever. From first-grade onwards, teachers worked hard trying to help Bob overcome difficulties in deciphering letter combinations. By the time he reached my combined 7th/8th-grade classroom, Bob had failed once, and he was a veteran of seven years of reading remediation. Angry, defiant, and obnoxious, Bob spent a good deal of time a) outside my classroom absent with severe asthma and b) inside my classroom screaming and throwing things. Desperate for a solution, Bob's mother enrolled him in a reading clinic at a university. Bob was thrilled, explaining to me that "the professor" knew how to teach him to read. Of course, I expressed enthusiasm. I even hoped that the professor might actually have some secret bag of tricks he could give Bob. The honeymoon lasted about a month. Bob was an intelligent boy. Once he saw that the professor's skills were no different from the skills that for seven and a half years had failed to turn him into a reader, his hurt, disappointment, and rage erupted; and the professor kicked him out. Bob taught me something important: Nobody could teach him to read. We couldn't even help Bob learn to read until he could take control, until he could find a book he wanted to read. This never happened because Bob believed so strongly in the "otherness" of reading: He thought that the teachers, the professor, the skills could do it for him. He never learned to believe in himself or in books.

Keith was fifteen and an eighth-grader when he read his first book—ever. It was Dr. Seuss's *Hop on Pop*, and it was a magic moment. Because my students knew that my definition of reading begins with sitting alone with a book, Keith had spent one and a half years in my class faking his way through 138 *National Geographics*, assorted novels, and a complete set of *World Book Encyclopedia*. One day he started his perpetual whine that "there's nothin' to read" and, in frustration, I shoved the Seuss book into his hands. I still get goosebumps when I recall seeing a beginning reader emerge right there before my eyes. After he'd read the book a few times to himself, running his hands over entire pages as if in disbelief, Keith insisted on reading it aloud to me every day for a week. Then came the magic question—from Keith, not me. "Did this Dr. Seuss write any other books?"

Keith and Bob inspired me to fight the administration, fight the union, fight the state education department for the privilege to forfeit my vested rights in a tenure area, and transfer to the primary grades. I knew in my bones that if Keith and Bob had encountered real books earlier in their school careers, they could have learned to take charge of themselves as readers, instead of relying on somebody else's questions.

A Whole Language teacher takes control of her curriculum so that she can relinquish that control to her students. We can't rely on someone else's canned questions or scope-and-sequence charts because we know that these crutches can cripple our students. Bob and Keith were crippled, not because they couldn't circle short vowel sounds but because they'd circled too many. They spent too much time answering too many questions, and too little time sitting alone with books.

When I asked my 7th/8th grade inner-city toughs to read Ron Jones' *Acorn People*, the characters in this powerful story came alive in our classroom immediately. The story touched us all deeply. We talked about the book—not about rising and falling action or story *schema* or how many ducks were on the pond. We talked about—and laughed and cried about—the lives of the children in the book. We talked about those characters/children the way you'd talk about your neighbor or your brother. Surely it would have been a sacrilege to junk up our powerful feelings with school-type questions. Katherine Paterson speaks passionately of the importance of readers' being free to come to books from their own experience and take from those books what they can and will: "I don't want anyone telling a child what he should get out of one of my books or any book I care about."

Kids who hate school as much as my rotten readers do, rarely pay courtesy calls once they escape. But four years after we read *The Acorn People*, David stopped by. He asked if I'd seen it on TV. "I made my whole family watch it," he said. "The book was better." David grinned at me and added, "I bet you never thought you'd hear me say that about a book. Actually, I never thought I'd say it. But it's true. The book was better."

Qualifications

I feel qualified to participate in this discussion because I have taught reading and writing for nearly twenty years and still have no idea what a schwa is. Whenever I address teachers about teaching reading, I find a way to bring up my deficiency. It's the kind of thing that teachers relate to—gives them that little surge of superiority, I guess. Despite my every attempt to show why the schwa is irrelevant to my life and my students' lives as readers, at least half a dozen generous souls always come forward and insist on explaining what these pesky critters are. Frequently they offer one of those neat little devices for helping students remember arcane things (rather like the "two vowels go walking" chants or the "all cows eat grass" of music-scale fame). Momentarily, schwas seem to make some sort of sense, but before the day is over, I forget again. I suspect that my schwa ignorance is important to me, somehow intertwined with my struggles to maintain a type of professional purity. Okay, so I don't remember the punchline for that "two vowels go walking" stuff either, even though I sure have heard the jingle ringing down a lot of school corridors. I'm reminded of Joan Didion's ironic vow: "I would once and for all get the meaning of the word 'structuralist.'"

Second only to schwas is syllabification. For six years I team-taught with someone who taught kids the sixteen rules for syllabification—and as a free-lance writer I was among that tiny percentage of people in the world who might find that information useful one day; sometimes writers do need to divide words at the end of the line. Even though I heard kids practicing the rules for six years, none of it sunk in. I still rely on my ear, but even though I do get into trouble occasionally it has always seemed easier to use a dictionary than to learn the rules. More to the point, I've never encountered anyone who can tell me just how dividing words into syllables helps a person learn to read. Like so much of the direct instruction paraphernalia, syllabification rules work only for the people who already know how to read. But if you know how to read, of what use is this information (unless you are a free-lance writer, stranded on a desert island without a dictionary, who needs to divide words at the end of a line)?

Need I point out that such information avoidance/ignorance is in no way aligned with soft-headed anti-intellectualism? I confess my schwa and syllabification deficits for the same reason that I confess I hadn't a clue what gerunds are until my students in a Queens high school had to learn them for a departmental exam. I tell these stories, hoping that people might stop and think about how vulnerable we all are, how lacking in information. Daily, we come up against our own ignorance, our constant struggle to learn what we need to know and at the same time to guide our students in that same struggle. We can't teach it all any more than we can know it all. The essence of being a teacher is to decide what

9

is important. For me, in my daily struggle to figure out what is essential, schwas and their ilk have never found a place.

Scope-and-sequence charts are not going to pave the way to heaven—or to literate competency. What an ugly word that is: "competency." What does it mean? Don't you have to ask "competent *for what?*" Rather than asking about competency, I want to know how many soul-tingling thrills of anticipation-of-text students are experiencing in their school career. I want to know how many times a student has closed one book and then echoed Oliver Twist's—and Keith's—inquiry: "Are there any more?" I feel the same way about programs that promise a systematic direct delivery of skills as Garrison Keillor feels about pumpkin pie, and Calvin Trillin about fruitcake: The worst one isn't that much different from the best one.

And I don't offer this information from hearsay, either.

One time I found myself filling in for a "direct instruction" teacher who had become ill half way through the school year. I agreed to do it, figuring that it would be good for me to know what direct instruction was all about. That's when I discovered that I must be tone deaf. I could not hear the vowel distinctions. Oh, I could hear the difference between "O" and "U" well enough, but I'm talking about the difference between "eh" and "uh." The children, all judged to be rotten readers, were definitely better at the system than was I. Of course they had started all this rigma-role in September, and I didn't join them until February. By then, they were terrific at circling the sounds, but they hadn't read a book. They hadn't even seen a book.

I was so upset that the sounding out of words (and non-words) was the total reading program (can you imagine a remedial reading room with no trade books?) that I told the principal I would finish out the year with this program only if all the children could come to me twice a day—once for direct instruction and once for real reading. Then I sat in the federal office until they gave me money to buy trade books.

It isn't only that direct instruction gives children such an odd notion about reading; it presents an odd notion about teachers, too. Teachers become merely the deliverers of someone else's program. When a teacher feels so lacking in control, how can she ever encourage children to take charge?

Getting Things Backwards

I've been informed that participants in this discussion have to argue fair. So what's the fun of that? Eminent researchers have been inflicting academic acid rain on hapless schoolchildren for decades, and now I'm supposed to argue fair? Academics perpetuate repressive orthodoxies that train teachers to become managers of some corporate conglomerate's skills system, and I'm supposed to worry about fairness? My antagonism toward fairness, which I equate with "politeness" and "impartiality," was interpreted by some as an unwillingness always to tell the truth. Perish the thought! I want everyone to know how easy it is for me to tell the truth in academic argument. Why would I need to make anything up when the truth is so much fun? So much more strange and outrageous than anything anybody could invent? I was worried that when people called for fairness they were asking for aloof detachedness. Calm and detached, I'm not. Impartial, I'm not. I care about this issue: I'm partisan about it. If you've ever worked in a restaurant kitchen, you are very careful about dining out. I know too much about publishers' back rooms and how they use their experts-for-hire to remain indifferent—or more than marginally polite—around a scope-and-sequence chart.

Twenty years in classrooms has shown me that we do too many things backwards. Twenty years in classrooms has shown me that understanding does not follow proficiency. The reverse works better: It is more effective to arrange things so that proficiency can follow understanding. Lots of disparate (desperate?) people like to align themselves with *A Nation of Readers*. Not I. The authors of that oft-quoted report recommend giving kids a heavy dose of phonics through second-grade and then cutting off this phonics fix. That's definitely backwards. According to Tagalog folk wisdom, *The fly on the water buffalo's back thinks itself taller than the water buffalo.* Ask any first grader in a typical class what reading is—and chances are he'll tell you about the flies instead of the buffalos. Most kids are so busy collecting little skill bugs that they don't have any notion of what the whole big buffalo looks like. *In the beginning was the Word*, not parts of the word. Better one living word than a hundred dead skills—and skills are dead until they can be built upon a foundation of understanding. After they have a thorough grounding in real books—or, as the jargon of our trade will have it, in authentic texts—students find linguistic analysis and such matters to be fascinating stuff. And such study does make them better readers, no doubt about it, after second-grade.

I do not propose to construct a timeline regarding introduction of linguistic study, but twenty years in classrooms has shown me that the world would be a better place if we would withhold information about such a critter as the apostrophe until children are at least sixteen. I find it as mind-boggling as it is futile that we expose innocent babes of six or seven to the puzzlements of distinguishing between possession and plurality. If we would only wait a while, young readers would figure out apostrophes on their own—and they will know what they figure out in a way that they would never know were we to drill it into them. Better yet, we could try learning from our forebears: Emily Dickinson, for one, didn't bother with apostrophes in her letters at all.

A bit of Haitian folk wisdom tells us: *If you want your eggs hatched, sit on them yourself.* For Whole Language teachers the real issue in helping children learn to read is not which programs or systems a teacher uses or which trade books she puts on her shelves. For Whole Language teachers the real issue is this: Who's in charge? Who's sitting on whose eggs? If children are going to get educated, then the individual teacher in every classroom had better be in charge, and she'd better be willing—and eager—to yield her authority to the children in her care as soon as possible. The only way they are going to succeed as learners is to sit on their own eggs. The most important thing that a teacher—and her students— can learn is that relying on other people's authority is like looking for feathers on turtles. This is a tough message, one not promulgated in many teacher-training institutions. A teacher needs to educate herself so she can trust herself. Then she needs to remember that in teaching reading or anything else, it's better to apologize later than to ask permission first.

In 1969, I wrote my first article about using real books with disaffected readers instead of basals. People wrote me letters, asking me how I "got away with" not using basals. I was stunned. For even that green teacher, being a teacher meant being responsible for what and how you taught. You can't be in a school two weeks without knowing that if the teacher doesn't take charge fast, then somebody else surely will. We need to tag-on a schoolhouse addendum to Yogi Berra's remark: *If you don't know where you are going, you will wind up somewhere else.* Anyone who hangs around schools knows that *if you don't know where you are going, there are plenty of people in the schoolhouse corridors pushing roadmaps that will keep you going in circles.* And plenty of academic traffic cops on duty to make sure you follow those maps. Social anthropologist Clifford Geertz explains why it is so difficult to follow someone else's map. While examining the cerebral territories staked out by social scientists, mathematicians, physicists, and historians, Geertz observed that the facts of scholarly experience do not produce uniform reactions. "Some individuals embrace a clean, well-lighted place, some are repelled by it; some are drawn toward the confusion of everyday, some long for escape from it." What each Whole Language teacher tries to do is figure out where she needs to be, and fights for the right to choose her own maps.

Phonics is not physics. That's why I reject the judgments of people who champion the theoretical over the observable when it comes to reading instruction. Does anybody know where these so-called skills come from? or how we can be sure when we have them? or how many we need? I know that we must quickly push the argument beyond phonics febrility; arguing whether to phonic or not to phonic is really just so much academic swamp gas. But I have to admit that allegiance to *scope-and-sequence charts* puzzles me, probably because for me those weird little objects are no more real than UFOs or crystal power. I am a pragmatist and have put my faith in what I have observed in my own classroom. Early on, my teaching was informed by Frank Smith, James Moffet, and Louise Rosenblatt. Then I came upon three little essays being passed around in the open education underground. David Hawkins's "I, Thou, and It," "Messing about in Science," and "The Bird in the Window" changed my life as a teacher forever. I've read them at least once a year for the past twenty years. They help me remember and renew my faith about what a teacher needs to know to help children develop their understanding of the world around them. These and other Hawkins essays were collected into *The Informed Vision*, (Agathon Press: distributed by Shocken Books), and I mention it every chance I get, hoping publishers can be inspired— or hounded—into bringing it back into print. A new generation needs to hear Hawkins's voice, a voice calling on teachers to be bold.

In the late '60s, Hawkins quietly told us not to answer the behavioral objectivists' questions about skills; instead, he advised, we must question the questions. When you question the questions, you force the issue into a deeper structure, a structure that increases children's capacity to conduct their own learning and to become their own teachers. Whole Language teaching is only very superficially (and perhaps naively) about "loving kids and loving books." Long before Bettelheim, Immanuel Kant gave profound support to the proposition that "love is not enough." The more basic gift is not love but respect, respect for others as ends in themselves, as actual and potential artisans of their own learning, of their own lives. When I celebrate the stories of individual children making connections with individual books, although I know that universal tenets could be promulgated from such stories, I believe in a pervasive sense that you can never share a story or a book; each teacher must dig deeply to find her own stories. She must dig deeply to help the children in her care find their own stories.

Will I offer up a definition of Whole Language? No way. Those consonant blends are frozen forever on the charts, but the children and I must continuously redefine what we need to know. And what we know today may not hold true tomorrow. If there is anything that makes me quarrel with my Whole Language brethren, it is when I get a whiff of the same smugness of rectitude that seems to pervade the direct instruction community. Norman Maclean, author of *A River Runs through It* and *Young Men and Fire,* said that when how you define yourself no longer haunts you, this should tell you that you are dead. Even though I know in my bones that I'm right, I also know that teaching is the most haunting profession I can imagine.

Accountability

I'll close with "accountability," almost as ugly a word as "competency." Since count seems to be the operant term best understood by many educationists, I will tell you that at the end of the school year, Chris and 73% of his classmates scored at or above grade level on the reading comprehension portion of a standardized test, whereas 82% scored below grade level on phonics analysis. Stunning to me, 94% scored above grade level on language arts (grammar, punctuation). I have lots of theories about the latter statistic, but I want to point out that I steadfastly did not "teach" either phonics or punctuation.

You want accountability? I count things that matter: I count book club and stationery purchases; I count reading time and fathers' barroom conversations. In September, I myself had to buy seven of the ten books to fulfill the club's minimum order. Two of the children's three orders were for posters, not books. In January, however, the club offered an *Amelia Bedelia* book, and my students ordered 48 copies. They ordered for themselves, for their cousins, for their neighbors. It was an amazing thing in this lower-middle-class community. I heard reports of half-a-dozen children who had received stationery for Christmas from relatives who were impressed by the numbers of letters the children were writing. By March, these children—who in September had cried and vomited when forced to sit alone with a book for five minutes—were protesting loudly when I called a halt to silent reading after an hour each morning. The school custodian told me about the night at the neighborhood bar when four fathers read aloud student homework about getting hippopotamuses out of the bathtub. But that's another story.

Whole Language and Research: The Case for Caution

Michael C. McKenna
Georgia Southern University

Richard D. Robinson
University of Missouri

John W. Miller
Florida State University

W hole Language as an instructional approach, philosophy, or methodology has great appeal for educators. Emphasizing child-centered classrooms in which students learn by exploring print and constructing a personal knowledge of literacy is an engaging idea. Focusing on meaning rather than the mechanics of decoding seems to capture the essence of what really matters in reading. Demanding authentic assessment strikes a harmonic chord. Insisting that reading and writing will develop as naturally as oral language—if only children are placed in properly supportive environments—seems reassuring. In short, Whole Language has a distinct intuitive appeal that Mosenthal (1989) has associated with the "romantic" view of teaching.

Because Whole Language seems so eminently sensible and inherently optimistic, those who question its "naturalness" and "apparent" efficacy are often viewed as unsensible and pessimistic, as slavish adherents to its antithesis. In other words, those who ask for evidence rather than effusiveness must see literacy instruction quite differently from Whole Language teachers—as the acquisition of skill after skill, arranged in rigid, artificial sequences, taught and practiced in isolation, and learned to overmastery before proceeding. They must view learning to read in large part as a bloodless, mechanical process in which meaning and joy are indefinitely deferred until fluency is attained. We reject this characterization from the outset.

We do not question the efficacy of Whole Language because of a wish to supplant it with any alternative, and certainly not with the one just described. In fact, one of us recently characterized Whole Language instruction as an example of a positive curricular trend toward breaking down the artificial barriers between "subject matter areas," leading to more wholistic instruction (Miller, 1992). Rather, we raise questions because of our commitment to these beliefs:

- Instructional practice should be investigated pragmatically through a variety of methods.

- Widespread implementation of practices should await the results of such inquiry, or, at the very least, that evaluative data should accumulate with implementation.

- The complexity and diversity of children make it unlikely that any practice will be uniformly effective.

In 1990, we detailed some of the questions about Whole Language that have yet to be adequately answered. These include (1) whether Whole Language compares favorably with traditional instruction in fostering reading ability; (2) whether Whole Language practice leads to more positive attitudes toward reading; (3) whether advantages in ability or attitude, if observed, are likely to endure; (4) whether the benefits of Whole Language befall students differentially; and (5) whether Whole Language is better suited to certain teachers' styles than to others (McKenna, Robinson, & Miller, 1990).

Like so many other educational movements (see Slavin, 1989), the advent of Whole Language in schools has largely preceded the careful scrutiny afforded by systematic investigation (Stahl, 1990). To the uninitiated, it may therefore seem reasonable to expect Whole Language proponents to pursue actively answers to questions like the ones we have posed. Their reactions, however (Edelsky, 1990; Goodman, 1992a), suggest that Whole Language is atypical of educational movements in terms of how research informs it. Advocates argue that Whole Language should not be held accountable to the same process of empirical inspection. We, on the other hand, believe that if Whole Language proponents do not establish a credible research base to support their philosophy, it will inevitably fade from favor as have so many other trends.

Lessons from Other Disciplines

Perhaps our position can best be described by means of two analogies, both related to change in American institutions. The first example is that of recent American political trends. The second involves private industry's approach to product research and development. Although neither of these contexts is perfectly analogous to schooling, both shed some useful light on the need for improved evaluative research, both formative and summative in nature, on Whole Language as an instructional approach and philosophy.

A Political Analogy

Consider the major shifts in the American electorate's political ideology over the last 35 years. With the election of John Kennedy in 1960 came a 20-year, bipartisan commitment to social programming, increased governmental support for entitlements, and a major role for government as a service provider. Although specific approaches to implementing this philosophy differed under Democratic and Republican administrations, there was broad support within both parties for the conceptual framework.

In the late 1970s, a complex series of events culminated with the election of Ronald Reagan in 1980. A major philosophical change in the mainstream thought of the electorate had occurred. Unionism lost its potency. The momentum built on diversity and pluralism in society slowed. The notion of government as a broad-based service provider was questioned. In short, a majority of the voting public had tired of the Great Society. It was argued that capital formation, private investment, and the creation of wealth would supply the income needed for social programs. Rather than increasing taxes, taxes would be reduced and the resultant rapid expansion of the economy would be responsible for increasing government revenues.

After a 12-year infatuation with this approach, the American electorate's interest again changed, and one of the more unusual presidential elections in American history occurred. The most heavily supported independent candidate since Theodore Roosevelt participated in the election. All candidates attempted to distance themselves from both the Great Society and "trickle down" economics. Clearly, the interests of the American electorate had again shifted. This shift was marked by the election of Bill Clinton in 1992.

What is the point of this brief political history? To us, it demonstrates the shifting tides of the American voter and the fact that without valid measures of worthiness, most trends are prey to changing fancies. If convincing and substantive data do not exist indicating that a solution has measurable merit, then a change in solutions will occur when the next attractive alternative comes along and the climate is ripe for change. We find this process analogous to change in educational philosophies and the methods they inspire.

It may be argued that this form of change is inevitable and, in fact, not inappropriate. If so, as surely as the synthetic phonics advocates have seen support for their approach erode and the growth of Whole Language occur, so too will come the day that another instructional philosophy, and its congruent methodology, becomes more popular. Hopefully, education will grow as a field of scientific inquiry, and changes will be more related to evidence than to passing interests.

A Business Analogy

Similar to the concern that movements based on their "inherent goodness" lose their appeal when popularity or "correctness" shifts, is a problem that plagues American industry. The difficulty is that people are too concerned with short-term product appeal and sales and not concerned enough with long-term research and development, which is the real road to product superiority. Past president of Xerox, David Kerns, is a well-recognized proponent of this position. He noted that the Japanese, and to a lesser degree other Pacific Rim and Western European countries, have taken a strong research orientation to the development of new products. Meanwhile, American industry has been more closely associated with turning a fast dollar on glamorous products by getting them quickly to market.

American industry once had a reputation as the developer and disseminator of new products for the world while other countries made their income by copying American products. That trend is clearly changing. There are several visible indicators, including the number of patents issued. This important index demonstrates that in recent years Japan and other economic competitors have far outstripped the United States in their commitment to the research and development of new products. A second indicator is dollars spent on R&D as a function of size of the economy. In 1964, Japan spent only 1.4 percent of its GNP compared with our 3 percent in the United States. By 1990, Japan had reached a level of over 3 percent (of a greatly expanded economy) while the U.S. had fallen to the 2.2-to-2.6 range (Okimoto, 1986; Malmgren, 1990). By analogy, educational reformers who disdain empirical evaluation and scientific "product development" for unsubstantiated trends suffer competitively from the lack of long-term product quality that a research infrastructure brings.

Toward a Defensible Position

In essence, our view is that Whole Language theorists as well as reformers in myriad other areas, such as school choice, cooperative learning, and ungraded classrooms, need to develop research plans to evaluate their philosophies and interventions. In the absence of the collection of these data, and careful analysis of them, it seems highly likely that any innovation will be discarded onto the scrap heap of shifting fancy as new and more attractive trends emerge. A recent example is that of leading-edge innovators in open British primary schools, who now find themselves confronting the changeover to a highly regimented national curriculum. Like it or not, criticize it or not, the most likely method for preventing such a fate for Whole Language methodology is to halt the rhetorical harangues and to begin true investigation in earnest.

Our purpose in this initial position statement is threefold. First, we describe what we perceive to be important reasons why research into Whole Language remains problematic. Second, we examine the extent to which existing research from a variety of fields presently informs and supports Whole Language theory. Finally, we begin to discuss the implications of research for present-day classroom instruction. This third goal is more thoroughly pursued in subsequent portions of this debate.

Objections to Research Voiced by Whole Language Educators

Whole Language proponents often dispute evidence provided by research. We have identified four of the reasons, though our list is probably not exhaustive.

1. Problems of definition

Mainstream researchers are often frustrated by the lack of coherent, universally applicable definitions (e.g., Stahl & Miller, 1989). Whole Language advocates readily admit that defining Whole Language is difficult (Newman, 1985; Watson, 1989). Watson suggested that one reason for the difficulty is that individual teachers must construct their own personal definitions. "Teachers," she asserted, "have arrived at Whole Language by way of their own unique paths. Because of this, their definitions reflect their personal and professional growth and their definitions vary" (1989, p. 131). The problem with this stance for those endeavoring to study Whole Language classrooms is this: If Whole Language varies from teacher to teacher, general definitions and generalizable conclusions are exceedingly difficult to make precise.

Researchers have approached this dilemma in a variety of ways. Stahl and Miller (1989), acknowledging the existence of multiple definitions, defined Whole Language broadly in their meta-analysis of comparative studies. This approach was challenged by Edelsky, who charged that they "could not distinguish Whole Language from language experience approaches from activity approaches of the 1950's" (1990, p. 8). More recently, researchers have examined the Whole Language literature for commonalities that might be useful in establishing definitive criteria (e.g., Bergeron, 1990; Moorman, Blanton, & McLaughlin, 1992a). Bergeron constructed the following definition:

> *Whole Language is a concept that embodies both a philosophy of language development and the instructional approaches embedded within, and supportive of, that philosophy. This concept includes the use of real literature and writing in the context of meaningful, functional, and cooperative experiences in order to develop in students motivation and interest in the process of learning (p. 319).*

This definition has already been used to identify Whole Language classrooms by researchers (e.g., Almasi, Palmer, Gambrell, & Pressley, 1991; McKenna, Stratton, Grindler, Rakestraw, & Jenkins, 1992).

2. Problems of paradigms

Quantitative research designs, while not invariably avoided by Whole Language proponents, are not typically employed. Reasons for this tendency vary. Sometimes the dismissal is made on the basis of design problems, such as difficulties with controlling variables (Goodman, 1989, 1992b; Weaver, 1989). When, however, positivist paradigms are used in well-controlled laboratory or clinical settings, the results are often dismissed on the basis of what Stanovich termed "the bogey of ecological validity" (1988, p. 210). When quantitative designs are used to investigate the acquisition of decoding subskills, researchers are criticized for fragmenting the reading process. When the measures used are global, such as comprehension tests, the research is rejected for reasons that are more political in nature (Edelsky, 1990). Requiring students to read and respond to prescribed selections and expecting them to arrive subsequently at similar, predefined reconstructions of meaning, it is argued, are procedures that essentially disempower students, ignore transactional elements of reading, and delegitimize sociocultural differences among readers.

An additional argument, made on the grounds of construct validity, is well worth noting. It is that because reading is multidimensional, reducing reading ability to a single number (such as a comprehension test score) is an inherently questionable practice. Moreover, the practice of aggregating a single indicator of this kind across many students only compounds the problem (Edelsky, 1990). Indeed, numerous mainstream researchers have questioned these practices with regard to the National Assessment of Educational Progress (e.g., Calfee, 1992; Guthrie & Kirsch, 1984). Investigators seeking to compare Whole Language with alternative methodologies thus find themselves in an uncomfortable position: When they examine specific skills, the charge is fragmentation; when they employ global ability measures, the crime is reductionism. A sensible distinction was offered by Pearson (1992) between direct and indirect measures of reading ability. Global measures are inherently indirect, to be sure, but they are not invalid. They form one source of useful evidence in the study of complex phenomena, but they should not be the only source.

Recently, certain researchers and philosophers have argued that the findings produced by one research paradigm should not be automatically rejected but should be used to provide multiple perspectives on the phenomena studied (Howe, 1988; Salomon, 1991; Spiro, 1991; Spiro, Coulson, Feltovich & Anderson, 1988; Stanovich, 1990). Spiro, in discussing the notion of "integrative reconciliation of paradigms," used the metaphor of observing a landscape to underscore the need for more than a single vantage before significant understanding can result. In other words, to appreciate a landscape fully, we might photograph it from several angles, measure what it contains using a variety of instruments, and walk through it a number of times along different paths. Each act contributes information useful to our appreciation, and each has inherent limitations. We should therefore welcome a diversity of data gathered in a variety of ways. Spiro argued that the same is true for research, especially research aimed at exploring processes as complex as reading.

We find it ironic that Stephens (1992) cited Spiro's analogy in support of Whole Language's ostensibly interdisciplinary research base while omitting much of the evidence that multiple paradigms have supplied. Mason and her colleagues, on the other hand, produced a balanced treatment of how research in support of disparate views is indispensable to an adequate understanding of literacy acquisition (Mason, Peterman, Dunning, & Stewart, 1992).

3. Problems of practitioner access

Consistent with Whole Language's constructivist philosophy is a third factor, a belief that teachers must be permitted access to knowledge partly by means of their own professional efforts to construct it through classroom research. Traditionally, as Stephens (1992) pointed out, teachers have been obliged to rely on researchers to distribute and mediate findings. Whole Language philosophy, on the other hand, encourages teachers to reflect on their own practice in order to inform their views of instruction and literacy acquisition. We fully endorse this aspect of Whole Language; we do not, as Goodman recently asserted, dismiss teacher evidence "as only anecdotes" (1992a, p. 356).

However, constructivism raises important epistemological questions. Should practitioners rely only on their own experiences within the classroom? Should their construction of professional knowledge not also include consideration of research produced by others? When teachers choose to publish (that is, to add the products of their research to a publicly accessible database), should their findings be accepted uncritically, without regard to well-established criteria governing the credibility and generalizability of their results? And are teachers who eventually construct positions opposed to Whole Language to be respected for the process through which they have traveled to reach their conclusions?

We contend that the construction of knowledge by practicing teachers is a desirable process. It should, we believe, be facilitated by providing an extensive environment of existing findings that teachers are free to confirm or refute through practice. We object, however, to limiting that environment to findings conducive to a particular kind of conclusion. In a compilation of Whole Language research, for example, Stephens (1991) cited numerous studies that are tangential to Whole Language as well as studies employing quantitative, comparative paradigms. Her inclusive policy suggests that she was receptive to diverse designs and approaches as well as to consideration of an assortment of related issues. Nevertheless, she omitted the Stahl and Miller (1989) meta-analysis and other appropriate research reports. In fact, within the rubric of her four subjective criteria for selection, Stephens included a total of ten comparative studies, all of them generally favorable to Whole Language. Not one of the numerous unfavorable reports was cited. We suggest that Stephens and some other Whole Language adherents in their attempt to remove interpreters from between teachers and research are in fact denying teachers access to research. Stanovich (1988) provided, we think, a cogent depiction of the ideal:

> An adherence to a subjective, personalized view of knowledge is what continually leads education . . . down the well-traveled road of fads, gurus, and uncritical acceptance of so-called authorities . . . . [W]hat science accomplishes with its conception of publicly verifiable knowledge is the democratization of knowledge, an outcome that frees practitioners and researchers from reliance on authority. It is science and the idea of depersonalized knowledge that frees individuals from slavish dependence on authority; and it is subjective, personalized views of knowledge that degrade the human intellect by creating conditions in which it is inevitably subjugated to an elect few whose personal knowledge is not accessible to all (p. 210).

We suspect that nearly all Whole Language writers would endorse these views and that they would react indignantly at any suggestion that a problem to the contrary has emerged. Nevertheless, in their zeal to exclude mainstream researchers from their role as teacher-informers, some Whole Language proponents have adopted that very role. The Whole Language movement is full of university-based gurus.

4. Problems of rhetoric

Less charitable critics of Whole Language have suggested a fourth reason for the research impasse. It entails what they perceive as a rejection of contrary evidence in favor of philosophical assumptions and politics (Stanovich, 1991a). According to Moorman et al. (1992a), "[T]hese assumptions shape the Whole Language version of truth and inhibit discussion" (p. xii; see also Moorman et al., 1992b). This ideological tendency, where it exists, is obviously antithetical to scientific inquiry, in which theory is informed by, and may well change on the basis of, new evidence. We do not believe that such a tendency exists uniformly among Whole Language advocates. We suspect, however, that it is sufficiently prevalent to have initiated (1) the frequent charges that Whole Language philosophy is more dogma than science and (2) the frequent use of religious metaphors to describe the movement (McCallum, 1988; Samuels, 1991).

How Well Does Research Support Whole Language?

In our view, the answer to this important and complex question cannot be an all-or-nothing pronouncement but must be expressed as a matter of degrees. We examine four facets of the question. We contend that available evidence from a variety of sources is generally unsupportive.

1. Comparative studies

Investigations comparing Whole Language with conventional, basal-based instruction in kindergarten and first grade were summarized by Stahl and Miller in their 1989 meta-analysis. Their key findings are as follows:

(a) Whole Language or language-experience approaches appeared more effective than basal reading programs in kindergarten but not in first-grades.

(b) Their effects were stronger on measures of word recognition than on comprehension.

(c) More recent studies show a trend toward stronger effects for basal-reading programs.

(d) Whole Language/language-experience-approach programs appear to produce weaker effects for populations labeled "disadvantaged" than they do with populations not so labeled.

(e) Studies with higher-rated quality tend to produce lower effect sizes (summarized by Stahl, 1990, pp. 141–142).

It is difficult to derive much support for Whole Language from these findings, taken together. This is especially evident when the contribution of the older language-experience studies is excluded. In other words, the review suggests a trend unfavorable to Whole Language, which is a principal reason we cannot agree with Schickedanz, who concluded from this research synthesis that "[w]hole language/language experience approaches are overwhelmingly effective at the readiness/kindergarten level" (1990, p. 128).

Since the appearance of the Stahl and Miller review, two important studies have appeared that amplify these conclusions. In one, a 12-week experiment with preschool children revealed that direct instruction led to greater gains in phoneme knowledge and word recognition than was the case in a far more constructivist setting (Byrne & Field-Barnsley, 1991). Vellutino (1991) correctly interpreted this finding as a caution to anyone tempted to interpret Stahl and Miller as evidence favoring Whole Language in kindergarten. In the second study, first-grade children in classroom settings were observed over an entire school year. The more meaning-centered approach involved 15 minutes of decoding instruction daily, while the more code-oriented setting entailed three times this amount. Children in the latter classrooms demonstrated substantially greater ability to decode both regular and irregular words (Foorman, Francis, Navy, & Liberman, 1991). These studies not only reinforce skepticism about the claims of Whole Language but also they exemplify a welcome new tendency among mainstream researchers carefully to target claims made on behalf of Whole Language.

2. Quality of Whole Language research

Another cause for caution in interpreting the comparative studies is recent questions raised about their quality and about the quality of noncomparative investigations of Whole Language as well. Have these investigations been conducted in a manner that conforms to the research standards prescribed for the paradigms selected?

To answer this question, Almasi et al. (1991) used the literature-generated definition of Bergeron (1990) to identify all studies undertaken in the past 20 years that meet Bergeron's consensus criteria of what Whole Language is. Only 16 studies were found, a result that in itself raises serious questions concerning the breadth of the Whole Language research base. Moreover, only one of these was among the studies examined by Stahl and Miller, who claimed that their approach was "to err on the side of inclusion" (p. 146). This fact further constrains any conclusions to be drawn from their review, particularly inferences favorable to Whole Language.

Almasi et al. then proceeded to gauge the quality of each study by applying established research standards. For the 12 quantitative studies, the criteria of Campbell and Stanley (1966) were employed. For the four qualitative studies, criteria developed by Lincoln and Guba (1985) were used, together with recent considerations raised by other writers on qualitative methodologies. At the risk of oversimplifying this detailed inspection of Whole Language research, we note only that none of the studies met all of the applicable criteria and that only three met even a reasonable proportion of them. Almasi et al. concluded "that the construct 'Whole Language' remains empirically untested."

This finding relates to our earlier discussion of teachers as constructors of professional knowledge, for it suggests that in the case of Whole Language they are left largely to their own devices in order to inform their practice. We concur with the observation of Almasi et al. (1991) that "[t]he practice of relying solely on self-support data for consensus, rather than opening the data up for critical peer review, relegates the central tenets of the Whole Language philosophy to relativism."

3. Support for specific practices

Whole Language advocates have been quick to point out that their perspective is more than a collection of methods, that it is instead "an attitude, not methods" (Rich, 1985, p. 718), "[a] philosophy rather than a methodology" (Clarke, 1987, p. 386), "a theory in practice" (Edelsky, 1990, p. 8), "a set of beliefs, a perspective" (Altwerger, Edelsky, & Flores, 1987, p. 145). But as Stahl (1990) indicated, it is not possible to research the effects of an educational philosophy other than by inspecting the observable teacher practices that issue from it. Indeed, while Altwerger et al. maintained that Whole Language is not practice, they acknowledged that "[i]t must become practice" (1987, p. 145).

Regarding this translation of philosophy into method, Whole Language inherits respectable research bases underlying some of the practices that its adherents espouse. Examples include using writing instruction to benefit reading development (see Tierney & Shanahan, 1991), using predictable books employing repeated phrases and structures (Bridge & Burton, 1982; Bridge, Winograd, & Haley, 1983), and returning to the same book repeatedly (Blum & Koskinen, 1982; Herman, 1985; Herman, Dewitz, & Stammer, 1980; L.J. O'Shea, Sindelar, & D.J. O'Shea, 1985; Samuels, 1979; Taylor, Wade, & Yekovich, 1985).

Whole Language may rightly avail itself of this research base, which serves as powerful justification for much of what one observes in Whole Language classrooms. Nevertheless, this extant support for many of the practices congruent with Whole Language theory clouds the overall research picture concerning Whole Language specifically. Whole Language does not have exclusive claim to these practices, and many of the teachers who embrace them eschew the Whole Language label. For their part, Whole Language adherents likewise frequently suggest that adoption of these practices is insufficient. Moorman et al., from their inspection of the Whole Language literature, concluded that "Whole Language is an all or nothing proposition that teachers must accept as a comprehensive philosophical position from which they are compelled to derive appropriate teaching activities" (1992a, p. vii). Eclecticism, by which teachers might incorporate techniques espoused by other perspectives, is unacceptable (Goodman, 1992a).

At issue is exactly what the comprehensive Whole Language perspective suggests (or demands) about the development of decoding ability. Whole Language adherents themselves have been divided in the matter, and Baumann (1991) did a good job of highlighting the mixed messages conveyed to practitioners. Many adherents, perhaps a majority, favor direct instruction during "teachable moments," when classroom contexts make such instruction relevant to students' current mental foci. (For example, the instant when a student struggles to pronounce *phone* may be a good time to introduce the *ph* digraph.) Others espouse an environmental approach in which students construct knowledge of how print functions in a supportive milieu where opportunities to interact meaningfully with print are optimized.

In light of the division, it is easy to appreciate why Adams's (1990) extensive review of beginning-reading research elicited reactions from the Whole Language community ranging from mildly negative to openly hostile. Many objected to (and we think misinterpreted) such statements as: "[T]here is nothing wrong with giving students well-devised worksheets" (p. 418). Others found within her treatment of the subject that "the evidence supports a Whole Language and integrated language arts approach with some direct instruction, in context, on spelling-to-sound correspondences" (Strickland & Cullinan, 1990, p. 433). Other educators have begun to support similar views (e.g., Gunderson & Shapiro, 1988; Spiegel, 1992; Trachtenburg, 1990).

We suggest that this is the only defensible position open to Whole Language, if it is to be adequately informed by available research. The view that literacy acquisition parallels oral language development in being essentially free of direct instruction "seems to be based as much on faith as on research" (Stahl, 1990, p. 149; see also A.M. Liberman, Cooper, Shankweiler, & Studdert-Kennedy, 1967; I.Y. Liberman & Shankweiler, 1979) and has been characterized by Anderson as Whole Language "in its extreme form" (1988, p. 9). Adams, clarifying her own position, recently offered the following view:

> *For some people, the term emergent literacy alludes to the notion that literacy development is an enormously complex process—that only as its many components mature and merge together can literacy in any real sense "emerge." That is the meaning that I used in the book and tried to develop in depth. But then there are the other interpretations of the term. Don Holdaway defines it as a stage that occurs when the child has begun to recognize letters but still can't sound out words. That's very different. And in a third usage, which is one that I cannot endorse, emergent literacy is linked to the idea that literacy will naturally blossom forth if only the child is surrounded by a rich and joyful world of print (1991, p. 210).*

As researchers examine the constituent practices of the Whole Language perspective, it is natural for dialogue to focus on the issue of how teachers can best facilitate the acquisition of subskills. New research specifically addressed to this issue casts additional doubts about some of Whole Language's more extreme claims (Byrne & Field-Barnsley, 1991; Foorman et al., 1991). Other important questions have also been raised. Whether the occurrence of teachable moments is too undependable to form the foundation of good instruction (Baumann, 1991), and whether

Whole Language classrooms are disadvantageous to children at risk (Pearson, 1989; Williams, 1992), are recent questions that we hope will serve to refine further the efforts of researchers.

4. Challenges to the Goodman Model

The model of reading proposed by Goodman (1967, 1969, 1970) presents a special issue in the more general question of Whole Language research. While we agree with Mason et al. (1992) that research into cognitive models of fluent reading has proceeded along lines separate from the social-constructivist research most often associated with Whole Language, we note the contention of Vellutino (1991) that the Goodman model is central to Whole Language theory. This view is common too within the Whole Language community; Edelsky asserted, in fact, that "Whole Language developed through K. Goodman's (1969) work on a psycholinguistic model of reading" (1990, p. 8).

It is only natural for this model to be important to Whole Language theory in that it postulates a top-down process in which prediction, print-sampling, and context utilization (all meaning-centered actions) are paramount. A meaning-building reader need not process every letter of every word or, indeed, successfully identify all of the words encountered because of the redundancy of language. A reader encountering the sentence, "The beans were in the p_t," might well be able to predict the last word on the basis of context. Such examples are persuasive of the model's contention that words are identified by means of cues provided by context as well as by the letters comprising them. The model accordingly indicates that a reader proceeds by predicting successive words on the basis of context and then confirming or refuting the predictions based on sampling the print that comes into view. In the example above, a reader might first see the initial *p*, next predict that the last word is *pot*, then note the final *t* as evidence supportive of this prediction, and finally conclude that it must be *pot* even though all of the letters still have not been identified. The model is clearly based on risk-taking in the interest of constructing meaning. But what if the last word were actually *pit*? In this case, a student who reads aloud, "The beans were in the pot," while wrong, should not be stopped and corrected since a reasonable prediction has been made.

Is this really how people read? We submit that it is not and that the Goodman Model has been largely repudiated by separate lines of research yielding convergent conclusions.

In one line, studies using eye cameras to track the motion of the eyes during reading have demonstrated beyond dispute (1) that the time required for fluent readers to recognize words in and out of context is nearly the same, and (2) that word length and word frequency—not context—predict much of the variation in eye fixations. (See Adams, 1990; Just & Carpenter, 1987; Rayner & Pollatsek, 1989; and Stanovich, 1991b, for extensive reviews.)

A second line of inquiry has revealed that the amount of information typically available from context (irrespective of certain celebrated, contrived examples) is remarkably small (e.g., Gough, Alford, & Holley-Wilcox, 1981; Schatz & Baldwin, 1986; Shanahan, Kamil, & Tobin, 1981) and often leads to incorrect guesses about word meanings (Pressley, Levin, & McDaniel, 1987). A third, and unrelated, cluster of investigations has revealed that fluent readers rarely expend the effort to make predictions and other inferences as they read (e.g., Corbett & Dosher, 1978; Duffy, 1986; McKoon & Ratcliff, 1986; see also Valencia & Stallman, 1989; Carver, 1992). They find it more effective and more efficient simply to keep reading.

Finally, and perhaps most damaging of all, has been the modified replication of Goodman's (1965) study in support of the model's prediction that context greatly aids word identification. A long-recognized design flaw (see Samuels, 1985) was remedied by Nicholson (1991), who found a far more modest context effect in children from 6 to 8 years old, an effect limited to the poorer readers. Goodman's initial result, and the cornerstone of his model, appears to have been in very large part the product of a flawed research design.

We do not deny that *some* context effect exists. We are not yet prepared to go as far as Fodor (1983) in concluding that word recognition is completely "modularized"—that is, handled through automatic mental subprocesses virtually independent of a reader's meaning-building efforts. On the other hand, evidence from a variety of lines overwhelmingly informs against the Goodman view, and we concur with Nicholson that

Stanovich's (1980) interactive-compensatory model is a far more viable explanation of available evidence. This model indicates that beginning readers and older readers experiencing difficulties will attempt to rely more heavily on context until word recognition becomes more nearly automatic. Even for these populations, however, context effects are far more modest than the Goodman model predicts. Whether this trend suggests instruction that encourages contextual reliance as opposed to that which brings students quickly to automaticity, has been a long-contested and heavily-researched issue. We have tried here to enumerate a few of the reasons for being cautious about adopting the former view.

Implications

The full impact of recent key studies and reviews has yet to be realized. Some of the more successful Whole Language practices may need to be re-examined to explore better why they work. We suspect, for example, that predictable books are useful primarily because (1) they help to ensure early success and (2) they provide for the repetition of words, and *not* because they prepare children to be predictors and context users. Other practices, such as those concerned with the role of direct decoding instruction, will need to be reconsidered with care if recent results are to be accommodated. This is not to say that balance is not possible or desirable. Vellutino (1991) summarized current circumstances as follows:

> *Research findings, on balance, tend to favor the major*
> *theoretical premises on which code-emphasis approaches*
> *to reading instruction are based and are at variance with*
> *the major theoretical premises on which Whole Language*
> *approaches are based. However, the findings do not*
> *preclude the compatibility of certain features of both*
> *approaches (p. 437).*

We heartily agree, and we suggest that many teachers have arrived at similar appraisals. At the same time, they find themselves in a perplexing crossfire of contradictory advice and evidence. The research agenda we set forth (McKenna, Robinson, & Miller, 1990) remains largely unfulfilled. Until more is known, our own advice to practitioners can be summarized in two words: caution and self-reliance. Through even-handed consideration of what has been written, and through careful reflection on their own classroom experiences, teachers appear to be arriving at approaches that work *for them*, regardless of how those approaches may be labelled by others.

Finally, we truly hope that a perspective as promising as Whole Language does not relegate itself to the whims of passing fancy. We hope that when a new and attractive alternative comes along, sufficient data will have been accumulated to defend Whole Language with empirical evidence as well as zeal. The long-term value of research and development should not be dismissed as fogyism. Neither should it be avoided out of a fear that among its outcomes might be slight changes in the initial perspective. Careful validation is the only road to true and lasting change.

References

Adams, M.J. (1990). *Beginning to read: Thinking and learning about print.* Cambridge, Massachusetts: MIT Press.

Adams, M.J. (1991). A talk with Marilyn Adams. [Interview]. *Language Arts, 68*, 206–212.

Almasi, J.F., Palmer, B.M., Gambrell, L.B., & Pressley, M. (1991, December). *Toward disciplined inquiry: A methodological analysis of Whole Language research.* Paper presented at the meeting of the National Reading Conference, Palm Springs.

Altwerger, B., Edelsky, C., & Flores, B.M. (1987). Whole Language: What's new? *The Reading Teacher, 41*, 144–154.

Anderson, R.C. (1988). Putting reading research into practice. *Instructor, 98*(3, pt. 2), 8–10.

Baumann, J.F. (1991). Of rats and pigeons: Skills and Whole Language. *Reading Psychology, 12*(1), iii–xiii.

Bergeron, B.S. (1990). What does the term Whole Language mean? Constructing a definition from the literature. *Journal of Reading Behavior*, 301–329.

Blum, I.H., & Koskinen, P.S. (1982, November). *Enhancing fluency and comprehension through the use of repeated reading.* Paper presented at the meeting of the College Reading Association, Philadelphia.

Bridge, C., & Burton, B. (1982). Teaching sight vocabulary through patterned language materials. In J.A. Niles & L.A. Harris (Eds.), *New inquiries in reading research and instruction: Thirty-first yearbook of the National Reading Conference* (pp. 119–123). Washington, D.C.: National Reading Conference.

Bridge, C., Winograd, P., & Haley, D. (1983). Using predictable materials vs. preprimers to teach beginning sight words. *The Reading Teacher, 36*, 884–891.

Byrne, B., & Fielding-Barnsley, R. (1991). Evaluation of a program to teach phonemic awareness to young children. *Journal of Educational Psychology, 83*, 451–455.

Calfee, R.C. (1992). Authentic assessment of reading and writing in the elementary classroom. In M.J. Dreher & W.H. Slater (Eds.), *Elementary school literacy: Critical issues* (pp. 211–226). Norwood, Massachusetts: Christopher-Gordon.

Campbell, D.T., & Stanley, J.C. (1966). *Experimental and quasi-experimental designs for research.* Chicago: Rand-McNally.

Carver, R.P. (1992). Effect of prediction activities, prior knowledge, and text type upon amount comprehended: Using reading theory to critique schema theory research. *Reading Research Quarterly, 27*, 165–174.

Clarke, M.A. (1987). Don't blame the system: Constraints on "Whole Language" reform. *Language Arts, 64*, 384–396.

Corbett, A.T., & Dosher, B.A. (1978). Instrument inferences in sentence encoding. *Journal of Verbal Learning and Verbal Behavior, 17*, 479–491.

Duffy, S.A. (1986). Role of expectations in sentence integration. *Journal of Experimental Psychology: Learning, Memory, and Cognition, 12*, 208–219.

Edelsky, C. (1990). Whose agenda is this anyway? A response to McKenna, Robinson, and Miller. *Educational Researcher, 19*(8), 7–11.

Fodor, J.A. (1983). *Modularity of mind.* Cambridge, Massachusetts: MIT Press.

Foorman, B.R., Francis, D.J., Novy, D.M., & Liberman, D. (1991). How letter-sound instruction mediates progress in first-grade reading and spelling. *Journal of Educational Psychology, 83*, 456–469.

Goodman, K.S. (1965). A linguistic study of cues and miscues in reading. *Elementary English, 42,* 631–643.

Goodman, K.S. (1967). Reading: A psycholinguistic guessing game. *Journal of the Reading Specialist, 6,* 126–135.

Goodman, K.S. (1969). Analysis of oral reading miscues: Applied psycholinguistics. *Reading Research Quarterly, 5,* 9–30.

Goodman, K.S. (1970). Reading: A psycholinguistic guessing game. In H. Singer & R.B. Ruddell (Eds.), *Theoretical models and processes of reading* (pp. 259–271). Newark, Delaware: International Reading Association.

Goodman, K.S. (1989). Whole Language research: Foundations and development. *Elementary School Journal, 90,* 207–221.

Goodman, K.S. (1992a). Why Whole Language is today's agenda in education. *Language Arts, 69,* 354–363.

Goodman, K.S. (1992b). I didn't found Whole Language. *The Reading Teacher, 46,* 188–199.

Gough, P.B., Alford, J.A., & Holley-Wilcox, P. (1981). Words and contexts. In O.L. Tzeng & H. Singer (Eds.), *Perception of print: Reading research in experimental psychology.* Hillsdale, New Jersey: Erlbaum.

Gunderson, L., & Shapiro, J. (1988). Whole Language instruction: Writing in 1st grade. *The Reading Teacher, 41,* 430–437.

Guthrie, J.T., & Kirsch, I.S. (1984). The emergent perspective on literacy. *Phi Delta Kappan, 66,* 351–355.

Herman, P.A. (1985). The effect of repeated readings on reading rate, speech pauses, and word recognition accuracy. *Reading Research Quarterly, 20,* 553–565.

Herman, P.A., Dewitz, P.A., & Stammer, J. (1980, December). *The development of syntactical chunking in non-fluent readers using the method of repeated reading.* Paper presented at the meeting of the National Reading Conference, San Diego.

Howe, K.R. (1988). Against the quantitative-qualitative incompatibility thesis. *Educational Researcher, 17*(8), 10–16.

Just, M.A., & Carpenter, P.A. (1987). *The psychology of reading and language comprehension.* Boston, Massachusetts: Allyn & Bacon.

Liberman, A.M., Cooper, F.S., Shankweiler, D., & Studdert-Kennedy, M. (1967). Perception of the speech code. *Psychological Review, 74,* 431–461.

Liberman, I.Y., & Shankweiler, D. (1979). Speech, the alphabet and teaching to read. In L. Resnick & P. Weaver (Eds.), *Theory and practice of early reading* (Vol. 2, pp. 109–132). Hillsdale, New Jersey: Lawrence Erlbaum.

Lincoln, Y.S., & Guba, E.G. (1985). *Naturalistic inquiry.* Beverly Hills, California: Sage.

Malmgren, H.B. (1990). Technology and the economy. In W.E. Brock & R.D. Hormats (Eds.), *The global economy: America's role in the decade ahead* (pp. 102–119). New York: W.W. Norton.

Mason, J.M., Peterman, C.L., Dunning, D.D., & Stewart, J.P. (1992). Emergent literacy: Alternative models of development and instruction. In M.J. Dreher & W.H. Slater (Eds.), *Elementary school literacy: Critical issues* (pp. 51–71). Norwood, Massachusetts: Christopher-Gordon.

McCallum, R.D. (1988). Don't throw the basals out with the bath water. *The Reading Teacher, 42,* 204–208.

McKenna, M.C., Robinson, R.D., & Miller, J.W. (1990). Whole Language: A research agenda for the nineties. *Educational Researcher, 19*(8), 3–6.

McKenna, M.C., Stratton, B.D., Grindler, M.C., Rakestraw, J., & Jenkins, S. (1992, December). *Differential effects of Whole Language and traditional instruction on reading attitudes: A modified replication.* Paper presented at the meeting of the National Reading Conference, San Antonio.

McKoon, G., & Ratcliff, R. (1986). Inferences about predictable events. *Journal of Experimental Psychology: Learning, Memory, and Cognition, 12,* 82–91.

Miller, J.W. (1992). The new American school: A preview. *Streamlined Seminar* (National Association of Elementary School Principals), *11*(1), 1–4.

Moorman, G.B., Blanton, W.E., & McLaughlin, T.M. (1992a). The rhetoric of Whole Language: Part one. *Reading Psychology, 13*(2), iii–xv.

Moorman, G.B., Blanton, W.E., & McLaughlin, T.M. (1992b). The rhetoric of Whole Language: Part two. *Reading Psychology, 13*(3), iii–xv.

Mosenthal, P.B. (1989). The Whole Language approach: Teachers between a rock and a hard place. *The Reading Teacher, 42,* 628–629.

Newman, J.M. (1985). Introduction. In J.M. Newman (Ed.), *Whole Language: Theory in use* (pp. 1–6). Portsmouth, New Hampshire: Heinemann.

Nicholson, T. (1991). Do children read words better in contexts or in lists? A classic study revisited. *Journal of Educational Psychology, 83,* 444–450.

Okimoto, D. (1986). Technological follower or developer? In R. Landau & N. Rosenberg (Eds.), *The positive sum strategy: Harnessing technology for economic growth* (pp. 544–591). Washington, D.C.: National Academy Press.

O'Shea, L.J., Sindelar, P.T., & O'Shea, D.J. (1985). The effects of repeated readings and attentional cues on reading fluency and comprehension. *Journal of Reading Behavior, 17,* 129–142.

Pearson, P.D. (1989). Reading the whole-language movement. *Elementary School Journal, 90,* 231–241.

Pearson, P.D. (1992, January). *New directions in learning: A synthesis for the nineties.* Paper presented at a meeting sponsored by Phi Delta Kappa, Atlanta.

Pressley, M., Levin, J.R., & McDaniel, M.A. (1987). Remembering versus inferring what a word means: Mnemonic and contextual approaches. In M.G. McKeown & M.E. Curtis (Eds.), *The nature of vocabulary acquisition* (pp. 107–127). Hillsdale, New Jersey: Lawrence Erlbaum.

Rayner, K., & Pollatsek, A. (1989). *The psychology of reading.* Englewood Cliffs, New Jersey: Prentice-Hall.

Rich, S.J. (1985). Restoring power to teachers: The impact of "Whole Language." *Language Arts, 62,* 717–724.

Salomon, G. (1991). Transcending the qualitative/quantitative debate: The analytic and systematic approaches to educational research. *Educational Researcher, 20*(6), 10–18.

Samuels, S.J. (1979). The method of repeated readings. *The Reading Teacher, 32,* 403–408.

Samuels, S.J. (1985). Word recognition. In H. Singer & R.B. Ruddell (Eds.), *Theoretical models and processes of reading* (3rd ed., pp. 256–275). Newark, Deleware: International Reading Association.

Samuels, S.J. (1991, May). *Concerns about Whole Language.* Paper presented at the meeting of the International Reading Association, Las Vegas.

Schatz, E.K., & Baldwin, R.S. (1986). Context clues are unreliable predictors of word meanings. *Reading Research Quarterly, 21,* 439–453.

Schickedanz, J.A. (1990). The jury is still out on the effects of whole language and language experience approaches for beginning reading: A critique of Stahl and Miller's study. *Review of Educational Research, 60,* 127–131.

Shanahan, T., Kamil, M.L., & Tobin, A.W. (1982). Cloze as a measure of intersentential comprehension. *Reading Research Quarterly, 27,* 229–255.

Slavin, R. (1989). PET and the pendulum: Faddism in education and how to stop it. *Phi Delta Kappan, 70*(10), 752–758.

Spiegel, D.L. (1992). Blending Whole Language and systematic direct instruction. *The Reading Teacher, 46,* 38–44.

Spiro, R.J. (1991, December). *Integrative reconciliation of paradigm conflict in reading: Joining multiple perspectives in reading research, in learning to read, and in preparing reading teachers for practice.* Paper presented at the meeting of the National Reading Conference, Palm Springs, California.

Spiro, R.J., Coulson, R., Feltovich, P., & Anderson, D. (1988). *Cognitive flexibility theory: Advanced knowledge acquisition in ill-structured domains.* (Tech. Rep. No. 441). Urbana-Champaign: University of Illinois, Center for the Study of Reading.

Stahl, S.A. (1990). Riding the pendulum: A rejoinder to Schickedanz and McGee and Lomax. *Review of Educational Research, 60,* 141–151.

Stahl, S.A., & Miller, P.D. (1989). Whole Language and language experience approaches for beginning reading: A quantitative research synthesis. *Review of Educational Research, 59,* 87–116.

Stanovich, K.E. (1980). Toward an interactive-compensatory model of individual differences in the development of reading fluency. *Reading Research Quarterly, 16,* 32–71.

Stanovich, K.E. (1988). Science and learning disabilities. *Journal of Learning Disabilities, 21,* 210–214.

Stanovich, K.E. (1990). A call for an end to the paradigm wars in reading research. *Journal of Reading Behavior, 22,* 221–231.

Stanovich, K.E. (1991a). Cognitive science meets beginning reading. *Psychological Science, 2,* 70–85.

Stanovich, K.E. (1991b). Word recognition: Changing perspectives. In R. Barr, M.L. Kamil, P.B. Mosenthal, & P.D. Pearson (Eds.), *Handbook of reading research* (Vol. 2, pp. 418–452). White Plains, New York: Longman.

Stephens, D. (1991). *Research on Whole Language: Support for a new curriculum.* Katonah, New York: Richard C. Owen.

Stephens, D. (1992). *Whole Language in context* (Tech. Rep. No. 547). Champaign, Illinois: University of Illinois at Urbana-Champaign, Center for the Study of Reading.

Strickland, D., & Cullinan, B. (1990). Afterword to M.J. Adams, *Beginning to read: Thinking and learning about print* (pp. 425–434). Cambridge, Massachusetts: MIT Press.

Taylor, N.E., Wade, M.R., & Yekovich, F.R. (1985). The effects of text manipulation and multiple reading strategies on the reading performance of good and poor readers. *Reading Research Quarterly, 20,* 566–574.

Tierney, R. J., & Shanahan, T. (1991). Research on the reading-writing relationship: Interactions, transactions, and outcomes. In R. Barr, M.L. Kamil, P.B. Mosenthal, & P.D. Pearson (Eds.), *Handbook of reading research* (Vol. 2, pp. 246–280). White Plains, New York: Longman.

Trachtenburg, P. (1990). Using children's literature to enhance phonics instruction. *The Reading Teacher, 43,* 648–654.

Valencia, S.W., & Stallman, A.C. (1989). Multiple measures of prior knowledge: Comparative predictive validity. In S. McCormick & J. Zutell (Eds.), *Cognitive and social perspectives for literacy research and instruction: Thirty-eighth yearbook of the National Reading Conference* (pp. 427–436). Chicago: National Reading Conference.

Vellutino, F.R. (1991). Introduction to three studies on reading acquisition: Convergent findings on theoretical foundations of code-oriented versus whole-language approaches to reading instruction. *Journal of Educational Psychology, 83,* 437–443.

Watson, D.J. (1989). Defining and describing Whole Language. *Elementary School Journal, 90,* 129–141.

Weaver, C. (1989). The basalization of America: A cause for concern. In *Two reactions to the "Report card on basal readers"* [Dialogue] (pp. 4–7, 14–22, 31–37). Bloomington, Indiana: ERIC Clearinghouse on Reading and Communication Skills.

Williams, J.P. (1992). Reading instruction and learning disabled students. In M.J. Dreher & W.H. Slater (Eds.), *Elementary school literacy: Critical issues* (pp. 157–181). Norwood, Massachusetts: Christopher-Gordon.

The San Antonio Shoot-out

Proceedings
of the
National
Reading
Conference

Thursday, 3 December 1992
Hyatt-Regency Hotel, Blanco Room
San Antonio, Texas

Moderator's Comments

Carl Smith (ERIC Clearinghouse on Reading, English, and Communication, Indiana University, Bloomington):

At the ERIC/REC Clearinghouse, we get about 8,000 inquiries per year to which we respond. When an inquiry is specially unusual, our User Services person may turn it over to me.

Not quite two years ago, a reporter from *U.S. News & World Report* was on the line, asking about the phenomenon called "Whole Language." He said: "I understand that Whole Language is being used in many school systems across the country; in fact, some people that I talk to claim that it is sweeping the country," and he asked: "Is that true?"

I said: "I know that the term is used often, that it appears in conferences, etc. etc., but whether it's sweeping the country or not, you'd have to do your own survey to find out. I don't know what that means."

He said: "How would I find that out?" and I gave him some suggestions.

He also said: "Why is it that schools are adopting Whole Language?"

I said: "Rather than answering that question—it's not the function of the ERIC/REC Clearinghouse to speculate on questions like that *[laughter]*—why don't you call some people who are intimately involved in the Whole Language movement?"

So, we did that. We sent this fellow to some of the fathers (and mothers)—the gurus—of Whole Language, and he called them. He asked them for evidence that this thing called Whole Language works. And it appears that at least some of them sent him back to me! *[laughter]*

When he came back to me, I told him that we would run an ERIC search looking for evidence of success of Whole Language in several categories.

He said: "You're not going to just give me a long bibliography, are you?"

And I said: "Yes, I think that's what I'm going to give you." *[laughter]*

He temporarily accepted that, but he was obviously irritated. After he got it—by Express Mail, at his request, at his expense—he called again, and he said: "But this is just a big list of articles, and I can't tell from the abstracts what's good and what isn't."

And I said: "But that's the nature of our database. We do occasionally have summary publications—*synthesis documents*, we call them—in which we try to explain certain phenomena, certain hot topics, or certain trends that keep popping up again and again in our 8,000-per-year inquiries or in the literature."

So he said: "But this is almost useless to anyone outside those who are in the know. Can you tell me, in summary, whether these articles or abstracts that you have sent me do in fact say that there is substantial evidence that the Whole Language *stuff* works?"

I said: "I cannot tell you that because I haven't read all those articles. All I can do is to say that it looks from the reading list that some say it works, and others say it has some weaknesses. There's a balancing effect in effect in that literature, so I can give you that kind of generalization."

He said: "When I asked the gurus of Whole Language if they had any hard data, they said, 'We don't work in hard data'." *[laughter]* And he said: "I pressed them on that because I want test scores or attitudinal scores or I want some sense of how Whole Language is so powerful that school systems will mandate its use." He had just come from Houston, by the way, where Whole Language had been mandated, and then, a year later, had some sort of turmoil in the schools, and they had to back off the mandate and allow different schools to do different things.

He said: "It seems to me that if school systems are mandating these things, then the school systems must be working from evidence, aren't they?"

I said: "You've gotta ask the school systems! I didn't make that decision." *[laughter]*

We were having quite a dialogue, and we went back and forth through this for about three weeks. He would call a school system; they would say: "We just believe in it!" and he would say, "You have changed your school system because you 'just believe in it?' Do you have any evidence, do you have any data?" He constantly kept coming back to that, until he finally said to me—in frustration because I wasn't helping him any, and I was simply trying to explain the position of those who were adopting Whole Language—he said: "I have the impression that I am in the midst of a Baptist convention, . . ." *[laughter]* "and I am a Jew." *[laughter]*

Then he said in frustration and in anger: "Are there no scientists in Education who are exploring this?"

I said: "Yes, there are."

"Well, who are they?"

And I said: "You have them in the bibliography that I sent you!" *[laughter]*

Then he said (directed at me): "Are there no reasonable positions!?" And he hung up. He literally slammed down the phone in frustration.

As a result of that, we began in the ERIC/REC Clearinghouse to discuss this issue. What could we do as a Clearinghouse to pull the ideas together and come up with a summary? Warren Lewis, our Director of Publications, who constantly churns the ERIC database looking for documents that we can publish, and I began to look for a couple of "reasonable people in Education."

We had better luck than Demosthenes had, searching with his lamp in the broad daylight for an honorable man. We found more than a couple of reasonable people—and they're here today—who are going to do something for us, for ERIC/REC, and for the profession. They are putting together a point/counterpoint discussion—not so much a debate-in-print. Debates are all right for the football field and for Presidential debates—or maybe debates are not all right for Presidential candidates, after all; and certainly we don't want to have the kind of debate that the recent Vice-Presidential candidates had, like two boys standing on street corners taunting one another. We're not into that kind of business!

What we want to do is have a reasonable discussion of the issue: Is there evidence that the Whole Language effort works? If so, what is the evidence in support of that conclusion?

The two groups present today have already had their first go at it in the exchange of manuscripts, and ERIC/REC will publish the final document, to include their previous discussion in print and any further exchanges, and also today's discussion, including your own questions and comments.

We will hear first from the folks who feel that Whole Language has data and research evidence to support it, and then we will hear from the folks who feel that there are doubts about that evidence. Those who have resolved that there is evidence for Whole Language are Patrick Shannon and Susan Ohanian. Those who are raising questions and proposing caution about Whole Language and the evidence in support of doing it in such wholesale fashion are Dick Robinson and Michael McKenna. All of these folks have written about Whole Language, and you have probably read what they have written; therefore, we do not need to engage in lengthy introductions. After each of them has had a chance to speak and respond, we'll open the floor to everyone here, and welcome your comments and questions.

"The answer is yes . . . ."

Patrick Shannon (The Pennsylvania State University):

The answer is yes, there is research evidence for the adoption of Whole Language. Thank you very much. *[He makes as if to sit down; laughter and applause.]*

One might wonder about the neutrality of your introduction, Carl, with statements about "gurus," and suggestions that we Whole Language people don't have our own questions about Whole Language, but we'll talk about that at another time. *[laughter]*

Let me start by declaring that Susan and I are not the champions of Whole Language. We cannot and do not speak for the variety of voices and interests and intentions among Whole Language advocates. Today, we speak for ourselves, and we hope that Whole Language advocates will find our voices friendly.

Within the male—even Freudian—forum that is this debate *[laughter]*, Susan Ohanian and I would like to change the title of our opening statement. Although we'd like to declare the title to be "Ours Are Bigger" *[laughter]*, we worry that raging empiricism among us might require veri-fication. *[laughter]* Consequently, we fear that such research would run afoul of the federal government's standards on decency, and reading re-searchers would suffer some of the fate that artists suffered after Robert Mapplethorpe's photography show in Cincinnati. *[laughter]* Although we are confident of victory in this matter, instead we offer as a title: "Look to the Consequences."

We wish to argue that Whole Language advocates follow pragmatism in their view of science and research. Pragmatists are generally skep-tical about the possibility of telling a literally true story of what the world is like. They deny foundationalism, the view that grounded truth and meaning can be determined once and for all.

Pragmatists ask us to give up the idea that we will ever be able to pin down underlying causal entities. They argue that we should give up the search for the God's-eye-view point of view because it's probably impossible to know whether you've found this view, and because it's irrelevant to our needs and practices.

Pragmatists would like to replace the desire for objective knowledge of reality and truth, the desire to be in touch with the reality that is somehow more than the community with which we identify our-selves, and to replace it with a desire for solidarity within that com-munity. Pragmatists believe that we would be better off if we stopped asking questions about the laws of nature, and what is really "real," so that we might devote more attention to the ways of life we are choosing and living when we ask the questions we ask. Pragmatists do not have an answer to the question: How do you know that your conception, or picture, is reality? They don't even pretend to have an answer. Pragmatists do not know whether our current picture or con-ception is closer or farther away from reality than those pictures and conceptions that they've abandoned.

Because all research is a social and an historical product, because all facts are theory-laden, and because there is no incorrigible foundation for science—such as sense impressions or pristine facts—pragmatists doubt that we can actually differentiate between reading reality and reading ourselves. Pragmatists choose some explanations, theories, or stories, and dismiss others, when the former produce their desired community better than do the latter. For pragmatists, choice simply means that one approach is better than another at producing a desired outcome. This is not called "reality"; it's *praxis*—that is, theoretical activity in which the goal is within itself.

Pragmatists stand on the axioms that not everything that "works" is desirable; that not every belief that is "true" is to be acted upon; and that some "objectively" successful approaches will work at cross purposes with our goals. Those that do are irrelevant to our work.

For pragmatists, values and visions of human action and interaction proceed as search for descriptions, theories, explanations, and narratives. Pragmatic choices about what to research, and how to go about it, are conditioned by where we want to go in the broadest of senses. Values, aesthetics, politics, and social and normative preferences are integral to pragmatic research, its interpretation, and its utilization.

The pragmatic method is to try to interpret all notions by tracing their respective practical consequences which are *social*, and not *natural*, in the "verifiable truth" sense of the word. Pragmatic scientists determine how those notions will lead to a desired end.

As pragmatists, Whole Language advocates—and they *are* advocates—start from a set of values, politics, and practices which are most succinctly put by Jerry Harste in three points:

(1) Language is learned through use.

(2) The learner is an informant.

(3) Education is inquiry.

These principles are most elaborately explained by Carol Edelsky and Connie Weaver.

These values require certain sets of social and power relationships among teachers and students, certain content, certain forms of knowing, which lead to a personal, and sometimes social, empowerment through "voice," caring, and human agency.

As pragmatists, Whole Language advocates do not look to science to determine, or to validate, their goals. Rather, they use science to help them develop effective methods for working towards those *valued* goals. Because they employ *praxis*, their practice must have the goals within it; therefore, Whole Language advocates look to language in use by learners, as they inquire after topics of interest in order to induce scientific conclusions about how to help themselves and others who care to help learners to become empowered, both in and out of schools. In short, they look to the consequences of science rather than to its powers to guide their research.

Because Whole Language advocates see science as a language for understanding, because they see themselves as learners, and their teaching lives as inquiry, they understand themselves as empowered to engage in scientific inquiry, to voice their findings, and to make decisions about the adequacy of research to meet their goals. Whole Language advocates look to themselves, to other teachers, and to others who, they believe, share their values as sources for science. They reject all other research because it is not of pragmatic help to them.

Here, we believe, is where the problem arises for many literacy researchers who have been trained in empirical, analytic, or even phenomenological interpretive methods of research. These researchers worry about reality, about objectivity, about the power to explain to others without acknowledging their own values, policies, and practices which drive their work. They are caught up in the power of science to explain what they value, as if that were reality, without really looking to the consequences of their findings on the communities within which we must live. And because they claim their work to be "reality" and "natural," they attempt to privilege their work on all grounds, but their assertion of a foundation of knowledge is an apology for the present domination both in and out of schools.

Whole Language advocates recognize that research does not speak for itself. As pragmatists, they ask us to decide what is useful research by looking at the consequences of the human attempts to use it, and to decide whether this is how we wish to live together.

Thank you.

"Unlike Patrick, we do accept reality...."

Michael McKenna (Georgia Southern University)

[Distributes to the audience copies of the paper by McKenna, Robinson, and Miller—chapter 2 of this book, p. 17 above.]

Unlike Patrick, we do accept reality, and we're trying to discern exactly what it is! I think it important that we begin with a clarification of what our position is because it is extremely easy to infer from the standpoint of instructional practice that we take the antithesis to Whole Language, and that we recommend some sort of bloodless, mechanical approach to literacy instruction in which meaning and joy are indefinitely deferred until fluency is somehow obtained. *[laughter]* Nothing could be farther from the truth.

We do, however, bring a warning to Whole Language because we do see in it many good practices that we think should endure, and the warning is that without an empirical base of evidence, practitioners are eventually going to reject it in favor of the next fanciful trend that comes down the pike.

Why is there such a problem? Patrick has done a good job of outlining some theoretical positions, but we think there are other reasons as well, and we have focused on four of these. This is not an exhaustive list, but it is four problems that we think are crucially important.

1. Problem of definition
2. Problems of paradigms
3. Problems of practitioner access
4. Problems of rhetoric

The first is the problem of definition, defining what Whole Language is—not the easiest of tasks. If you have begun to delve into the literature, you have probably been quickly confused. This is actually exacerbated by the fact that many Whole Language proponents encourage a variety of definitions. In a quotation from Dorothy Watson and her 1989 *Elementary School Journal* article, she says that teachers "have arrived at Whole Language by way of their own unique paths"; because of this, their definitions "reflect their personal and professional growth," and their definitions "vary."[1] In which case, it's extremely difficult to know exactly whether you're in a Whole Language classroom or not.

The real danger in this is that we approach an almost tautological situation in which Whole Language is "whatever I say it is" because it's up to "me" to decide exactly what it is. It's very difficult to research something of that nature.

Recently, because there are commonalities across the definitions, researchers have begun to rely on the literature-generated definition produced by Betty Bergeron in the fall, '90, issue of *JRB*, in which she lists a number of characteristics that Whole Language tends to have, as discerned from the voices of its proponents.[2] So, some researchers are trying to guarantee that they are, in fact, in Whole Language classrooms by making sure that they conform to those characteristics.

---

[1] D.J. Watson, "Defining and Describing Whole Language," *Elementary School Journal* 90: 129–141.

[2] B.S. Bergeron, "What Does the Term 'Whole Language' Mean? Constructing a Definition from the Literature," *Journal of Reading Behavior*, 1990: 301–329.

Some other researchers are resorting to a diabolically clever technique of asking Whole Language advocates to identify outstanding Whole Language teachers so that, there, they have another basis for assuring themselves that they are in Whole Language classrooms.

The second problem is that of research paradigms. Patrick has alluded to those problems, and Whole Language advocates are extremely vocal in their attacks, especially on quantitative designs. In our paper, we enumerated exactly what those objections tend to be—and they do make some good points: There's absolutely no question about that, although we find nothing new in those points.

There *are* limitations inherent in *quantitative* paradigms. We find, therefore, that because no single paradigm is perfect, a very refreshing viewpoint is emerging, namely, that multiple paradigms are desirable. A number of eminent theorists and philosophers, such as Kenneth Howe, Gabby Salomon, Keith Stanovich, and Rand Spiro, have been proposing for the last few years the use of multiple paradigms, if we really have any hope of understanding phenomena.

This includes teachers, and the evidence that they bring to their own knowledge base from instructional practice, which brings us to the third problem, that of practitioner access to knowledge about the effectiveness of instructional techniques. Whole Language theory is an advocacy of empowering teachers to construct their own knowledge base through instruction. We certainly agree with that, but would qualify it, though: Teachers are to be empowered to build their own knowledge base as long as they are also empowered to examine research produced by others.

We find very disturbing a recent, annotated bibliography of Whole Language research that contains *only* studies that are favorable to Whole Language, omitting, not even mentioning, any other study.[3] To us, that is somewhat intellectually dishonest, at best, and it reminds us of an analogy to legal advocacy—the idea that a trial lawyer may put forward evidence that is only favorable to the client and may attempt to impeach or otherwise rule out any other evidence that someone else might suggest.

---

[3] D. Stephens, *Research on Whole Language: Support for a New Curriculum* (Katanoh, New York: Richard C. Owen, 1991).

The fourth problem, one of rhetoric, I pass over, for now. We mention excellent, recent references to this in our paper. [See above, p. 26.] I think you've already heard a pretty good example of Whole Language rhetoric—an excellent example, actually. *[indicating Pat Shannon; laughter]*

I'm going right on to the central question behind this debate, and that is, how well research supports Whole Language practice. This is definitely a complex question; not a simple, straight-forward question. We offer in our paper four perspectives on it. [See above, pp. 27–34.]

The first has to do with comparative studies, and getting to the bottom line of those studies, there is simply no *demonstrable* advantage in Whole Language that has been demonstrated in terms of the effectiveness of reading comprehension on children. Results since the appearance of an important 1989 article[4] keep accumulating: Half of one issue of the 1991 *Journal of Educational Psychology* was devoted to newer studies along the same lines.[5] Longitudinal data based on cohorts in Canada are reported as extremely vexing,[6] and so the issue just gets worse and worse.

Another issue that was raised last year at NRC is the issue of the quality of Whole Language research, not just comparative studies, but any study having to do with Whole Language, both qualitative and quantitative. Janice Almasi and her colleagues at the University of Mary-

---

[4] S.A. Stahl and P.A. Miller, "Whole Language and Language Experience Approaches for Beginning Reading: A Quantitative Research Synthesis," *Review of Educational Research* 59: 87–116.

[5] F.R. Vellutino, "Introduction to Three Studies on Reading Acquisition: Convergent Findings on Theoretical Foundations of Code-oriented versus Whole-language Approaches to Reading Instruction," *Journal of Educational Psychology* 83: 437–443.

T. Nicholson, "Do Children Read Words Better in Contexts or in Lists? A Classic Study Revisited," *Journal of Educational Psychology* 83: 444–450.

B. Byrne and R. Fielding-Barnsley, "Evaluation of a Program to Teach Phonemic Awareness to Young Children," *Journal of Educational Psychology* 83: 451–455.

B.R. Foorman *et al.*, "How Letter-sound Instruction Mediates Progress in First-grade Reading and Spelling," *Journal of Educational Psychology* 83: 456–469.

[6] Reported at the American Psychological Association meeting (Toronto, 1993).

land use the Bergeron definition to identify studies meeting that criterion.[7] One thing that I found somewhat alarming is that they found only sixteen studies, which is not a very hefty research base in and of itself, but they found that none of those studies did a very good job of meeting the research criteria either quantitative—people like Campbell and Stanley—or qualitative—folks like Lincoln and Guba. I conclude on this issue with a quote from their paper, in which they say that "the construct 'Whole Language' remains empirically untested."

The third issue has to do with specific practices of Whole Language. Last month at CRA, I attended a panel discussion of Whole Language, and I posed a question to the panel members of exactly how they would respond if a teacher were to approach them and ask what kind of research evidence underlies Whole Language practice. One of the individuals responded that people forget that many of the practices congruent with Whole Language theory do have respectable data bases. We one-hundred-percent agree with that, and in our paper we enumerate a few of those, and we give the citations that go along with them—*e.g.*, repeated readings and predictable books and reading-writing linkages and so forth.

However, imagine a teacher whose overall approach, which is really a cluster of specific techniques, included *only* techniques that were supported by available evidence: Would that teacher be considered a Whole Language teacher? The answer is no.

The real, kernel issue here is how skills are approached, how decoding instruction is organized, how and when decoding is going to be approached—and this is the one issue according to which the sheep and the goats are fairly well separated. Why not use a cluster of techniques, all of which have been supported by research? It sounds reasonable, but the problems get back to how one views the acquisition of language, how one views models of the reading process, . . .

---

[7] J.F. Almasi *et al.*, "Toward Disciplined Inquiry: A Methodological Analysis of Whole Language Research," paper presented at the National Reading Conference (Palm Springs, December, 1991).

[McKenna, out of time, borrows one minute from his colleague, Robinson.]

One of the issues on which the decoding question hinges is the Goodman model of reading, which has not really had a very good year. This, as everyone in this room well knows, is a top-down, meaning-centered model according to which one postulates print sampling based on predictions and their verification through context utilization.

In our paper, we outline a number of very different paradigms of research histories which have lately converged in their conclusions that the Goodman model is no longer a viable explanation of reading processes. I'm not going to go through those studies here, except to say that they are quite compelling. I would point you for extremely thorough discussions of them to the chapter by Keith Stanovich in the Longman *Handbook of Reading Research,*[8] and also to the book by Rayner and Pollatsek, called *The Psychology of Reading .*[9]

We agree, finally, with Frank Vellutino's summary of all of this, that the Stanovich compensatory model is far better in terms of explaining reading processes for young *and* older kids, than is the Goodman model.[10]

I'm out of time.

---

[8] K.E. Stanovich, "Word Recognition: Changing Perspectives," in R. Barr *et al.*, eds., *Handbook of Reading Research* (White Plains, New York: Longman) 2: 418–452.

[9] K. Rayner and A. Pollatsek, *The Psychology of Reading* (Englewood Cliffs, New Jersey: Prentice-Hall, 1989).

[10] F.R. Vellutino, *op. cit.*

"Who the hell are you?"

Susan Ohanian (Schenectady, New York, Public Schools)

I'm interested in the call for evidence because that is what I would like to bring: evidence for success from a third-grade classroom, and—if I have time—from a seventh grade and also high-school classrooms.

The problem of definition is linked, in my mind, to the problem of excessive orderliness. *[laughter]* I'd like to remind you of something that Anne Tyler wrote about in *The Accidental Tourist*. If you recall, Rose had a kitchen that was so completely alphabetized that the allspice was next to the ant poison. *[laughter]* She and her siblings are in a discussion, an argument over where to put the noodles. Should they be under "n" for "noodles," or "p" for "pasta," and finally Rose decides the point by putting them under "e" for "elbow macaroni." I really worry that a lot of our discussion is about that very point.

An ex-president of ETS listed the virtues of standardized tests as being "accuracy, objectivity, comparability." He says they measure "sheer accomplishment." I brought to you today an example of a letter exchange between me and one of my third-graders. Billy scored

100% on reading comprehension. I bring this because I know there's always that worry that we don't like those tests because our kids don't do very well on them. But Billy scored 100%, and I'd like you to take a look at his writing.

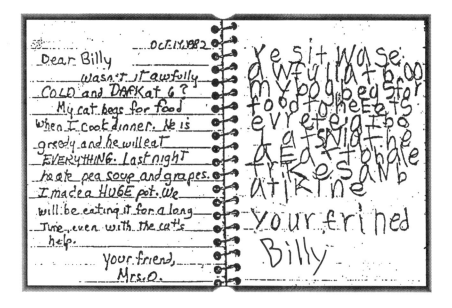

We wrote notes every day. Putting this in context, in my note I was talking about my cats and what they eat for dinner. Billy responds— and I pride myself on being able to read anything that anybody can write, but this took me about a half-an-hour to decode: "Yes, it was awful at six. My dog begs for food, too. He eats everything I do. Last night he ate two whole turkeys and a chicken."

In another context, I could tell you how proud I am that Billy wrote that note. It's the first thing he ever wrote in school. The reading test was the first reading test he ever agreed to take. I begged him to take that test; I said, "You'll show 'em what you can do, and that'll go on your record forever." But, in this context, I contrast the evidence of Billy as a writer with the evidence of Billy as a successful standard-ized-test taker. As a teacher, what would a test on which the child got everything right show me about what I needed to work on with that child in school? What helpful thing could that test possibly tell me? I could show you test results in writing and reading stories from my other students, and the tests do not help me teach them.

But bureaucrats don't like ambiguity. I would offer you that teaching is a smeary surface. We can't go for the quantitative knock-out punch. We have to tell our stories about our children, about ourselves. If you want to *count things*, as a third-grade teacher I can count lots of things.

The first time I put in a book-club order for my students—and I should explain to you that we were in a rigorously grouped school, and I had the "Rotten Readers," *[laughter]*—the first time I put in a book-club order, I myself had to order seven books to make up the minimum order of ten, and two of the childrens' orders were for posters. *[laughter]* But I read to those kids all day. I made them sit with books—and when I say "made," I almost had to tie them in their chairs, at first, to get them to spend five minutes with a book. No excuses! No trips to the nurse! I had to see blood before I let anybody go to the nurse. *[laughter]*

By January, they were complaining when I called a halt at the end of an hour of silent reading. And in January, *Amelia Bedelia* was offered by the book club, and my kids bought 48 copies. They wanted it not just for themselves but for their neighbors, for their cousins; they wanted to spread the good word about that book. This was a working-class neighborhood; it was the first book that many of them had ever owned.

And I might point out that I didn't introduce them to *Amelia Bedelia*. One of the kids chose it to read, and then started laughing during silent reading *[laughter]*, and looked up to me really kinda scared (because I was fierce about *silent* reading), and I kinda winked, and so she poked her neighbor and showed the neighbor, and the news traveled around about that book. There was a long waiting list to get hold of it, and Dougie, who was repeating third grade, pulled a fast one with his own copy that he'd gotten from the public library. He'd pulled a fast one, all right!

If we're going to count things, I might count the empathy that those children showed for each other, for the deaf child in our class who was in public school for the first time, whom the other teachers in our school didn't want to welcome to our school. I wish I could have brought Leslie here; she called me the other night. I wasn't home; she left a message on my machine; she said, "Don't worry; I'm going to write a letter, too." (She knows what letters mean to me.) "I'm going to write a letter, but I want to think about what your face looks like when you hear my voice." Leslie is in her second year of college, now.

Talk about the relatives of these children who bought them stationery for Christmas. Talk to the children about learning to read knock-knock jokes, about being able to see a joke. Yes, there are a lot of definitions of Whole Language, and I'm not really interested in any of them. I just don't think that's what I'm about.

The first year I was teaching, I knew how seriously New York City took the call for emergency credentials because they gave *me* one. *[laughter]* I had a major in Medieval Literature; I had never been near an Education course. I had a very good department chairman who came in once a week and gave me some advice. At one time, I was doing one of those stand-up demonstration lessons, that he had to write up, and it was on Julius Caesar. In the back of the room, one of the toughest kids in the class was reading a newspaper.

Later, when he was telling me about the evaluation, he said that he had leaned over and said to her, "Don't you think you should pay attention to what the teacher is saying?"

And she said to him, "Who the hell are you?" *[loud laughter]*

And I said to him, "Well, when you think about it, who the hell are you? *[more laughter]* You come into my classroom with a briefcase; you don't know anything about that child; you don't know that it's a triumph for her to be reading a newspaper. She had been a chronic absentee. This was the first step." So I say with all due respect to the people who want to count things, "Who the hell are you?"

"Let us not permit ourselves to be forced into bitterly polarized positions . . . ."

Richard Robinson (University of Missouri at Columbia)

Having been a member of NRC for—too long really—since 1969, this is a wonderful turnout that really says something about what we are talking about here. I saw Jim Flood come in; he is the program chairman for next year. I would encourage these kinds of interactive discussions.

I want to read in my six minutes—thanks, Mike, for taking one of my minutes! *[laughter]*—from an article that appeared in our state IRA journal. It is called "Assessing the Tyranny of Whole Language." I think it's something that we all need to think about as members of NRC. Let me read it to you:

> *Let us not permit ourselves to be forced into bitterly polarized positions as we make important educational decisions. There probably is no quicker way for us to lose the support of the public*

and lose the war we wage against illiteracy and ignorance than for us to let differences of opinion escalate into openly partisan battles among ourselves.

The public will not care who wins and loses battles, who gains or regains power. The public does remain rightly concerned [and I think this is true for everybody in this room] about whether children learn to read or not, as evidenced in the U.S. News and World Report, September 14, 1992.

The news magazine's article on Whole Language ends with the observation: "It may be that the best route lies somewhere between the two warring strategies in the nation's classrooms, but that is a message purists on both sides of the reading debate aren't eager to hear." [1]

It is up to those of us in the middle who have supported balance all along to regain our voices and speak out against the unreasoning extremism of the purists from both the right and the left in the literacy debate.

I respect our opponents here for what they have written and what they've presented. I think that what we really need to do is think about where we are headed. If you are aware at all of the history of literacy and reading, you know that what we are doing here today is nothing new. We have been through it in a variety of other situations whether it was phonics, sight words, basals, individualized reading, language experience; and now we're involved in Whole Language.

I would hope that one of the things to come out of an interaction like this is the coming together of people who have a common feeling for children and learning to read. What I'd really like to do is basically suggest some directions towards which we might want to go, some concepts and ideas that we really need to address as a reading community.

The first issue that Mike addressed is the definition of Whole Language. Let me read from our paper: "The concept of Whole Lan-

[1] Richard Burnett, "Assessing the Tyranny of Whole Language," in *The Missouri Reader* 17/1 (Fall 1992): 4.

guage must be defined in terms sufficiently rigorous,"—and I've revised this since I heard David Cohen this morning—"to enable classroom teachers to understand what we're talking about." I thought he made a rather interesting comment, that "people say one thing and in actual classroom observations are doing other things." In our work on teacher expectations, we see that all the time.

[The tape was changed at this point; some of the speech was lost.]

... When it comes to Whole Language, attitude must be investigated less haphazardly both through well-conceived qualitative as well as quantitative designs. How are students reacting to what is going on?

I think a parallel kind of situation is what kind of teachers are able to handle Whole Language classrooms? As I have encountered and worked with Whole Language teachers, I have concluded that there are some very specific kinds of questions that we need to look at. For instance, a literature-based program: How does a teacher organize a literature set, for instance? What is the role of the teacher in an experience like that? How do students select materials? Many of the answers to these questions, I think, we *think* we know, but yet when we observe in classrooms, that is not necessarily what is really happening.

To me, the fundamental question is this: What exactly makes a Whole Language teacher as opposed to a *good*—and I hate to use the word—"traditional" teacher? I'm not sure that one can tell the difference, and so we leave it at that in terms of the questions that we are asking. Hopefully, in a group like this, we can get some discussion and interaction.

Audience Participation

Carl Smith (ERIC/REC):

[To the audience] We invite you, now, to address questions or comments either to individuals or to the panel as a whole.

Edward Fry (Laguna Beach, California):

I'd like to hear an explanation of the question, "Who the hell are you?" *[laughter]* I want to identify myself somewhat as in favor of counting. I don't think that counting negatively impacts children. Medicine went on for many years with anecdotal evidence from both clinical observation and intuition, but the real strides have come from the scientists who work in the laboratory. So, whereas I like heartwarming stories about helping children, I think that our major advances are eventually going to come from the counting.

Carl Smith:

[To McKenna] Michael, do you want to tell him who the hell you are?

Dick Robinson:

You're talking to Susan, aren't you, Ed?

Ed Fry:

That's a good assumption. *[laughter]*

Susan Ohanian:

I think that I reject the medical analogy. I think that that has been used in schools for a long time to great harm to children. I just can't accept that analogy.

Pat Shannon:

I think that I agree with Susan. I don't know what you want me to say other than that. I believe that lots of counting has helped medicine, and some counting has done detriment to medicine. The same thing is true in education. I don't think Susan was talking against all counting; in fact, she suggested some things that we might count to a great benefit of teachers making decisions about what they're going to do in their classrooms.

Unidentified female speaker:

It seems that the idea of empirical evidence is somewhat of a red herring because often times we have empirical evidence for things that we know don't work, say, dividing classes out into ability-based groups: There has been definite evidence that it does cause harm to the children, and yet people aren't willing to change to something new, even when there is evidence that the old might be harmful. So I don't understand the call for evidence when evidence isn't even used.

Mike McKenna:

I think that the evidence on ability grouping is very mixed. In terms of many of the studies that have been done—check some of the Slavin meta-analyses—I think that the results are very inconclusive. Why should this be any different? The jury is still out, essentially.

Jim King (University of South Florida; Shaw Elementary School, Tampa, Florida):

For Dick Robinson: If I understood you correctly, you said that with sufficient rigor that we would be able to communicate clearly to— let's say—first-grade teachers. Teachers would understand better.

Dick Robinson:

Hopefully.

Jim King:

I am currently working in a first grade, and I would like you to explain to me how rigor is going to help me understand my practice better with my kids. Explain the relationship of rigor to my practice.

Dick Robinson:

I'm teaching in second grade, this year, myself. I think "rigor" can be defined in many different ways, but certainly, that a teacher understands what it means to use Whole Language, for instance, in terms of definition. "What is it that we're talking about?" I have a very difficult time, as I look at the literature, in being able to answer that kind of question. So I think that one of the things the community needs to address—and one of the things that Cohen talked about—is the fact that teachers are confused in terms of what they're expected to do. So, in answer to your question, I would hope that we would be able to show them in many different ways, by example, by explanation, by your teaching, by whatever you're doing: Here are some things that we feel are acceptable and we would call Whole Language, or not.

Jim King:

I beg a response.

Dick Robinson:

Sure.

Jim King:

I would humbly suggest that your need to tell me is exactly my problem, and that I don't need that." *[applause]*

JoBeth Allen (University of Georgia):

To follow up on Jim's comment, let me suggest a possible rewording of the exact phrase that he was talking about. I wrote it down. You said: "We need to define Whole Language in terms rigorous enough for classroom teachers to understand what we're talking about." I assume by "we," you meant university people?

Dick Robinson:

No, not necessarily.

JoBeth Allen:

Then who is the "we?"

Dick Robinson:

Teachers, . . . uh . . . whoever [is interested in the subject].

JoBeth Allen:

Maybe this rewording would help. If we said "We in university classrooms need to listen, observe, and reflect in ways rigorous enough that we can understand Whole Language as practiced by Whole Language teachers. *[laughter]*

Dick Robinson:

Even though, one of the difficulties in any discussion like this is that "the devil can quote scripture." We can all come up with examples at polarized ends of practices, examples that are really unfair in the discussion.

We've been working in a school that was defined as being Whole Language, and such practices that I would seriously question as being reflective of Whole Language were in use. For instance, one of my areas is the History of Reading, and I have some charts from the old Lippincott series—they've gotta be over thirty years old—but within the last month I saw a "Whole Language teacher" using these phonics charts as part of a Whole Language program. I question that. I don't think that is a fair use of the term.

What we're seeing is confusion. As Cohen said this morning, what we're seeing during classroom observations is people saying one thing—calling themselves "Whole Language"—and doing diametrically opposite things.

JoBeth Allen:

And you feel that you can decide that?

Dick Robinson:

Yeah, I think so.

Jamie Myers (The Pennsylvania State University):

I have a follow-up comment and question.

Dick Robinson:

To me?

Jamie Myers:

Yeah, to "you folks," yeah. *[laughter]*

You quoted a piece that said that this division—in fact, a *U.S. News* person called it "a war"—between these different factions is a matter of power, a struggle of power. In terms of talking about the rhetorical nature of the opening comments in such ways as would indicate power, it seems to me that the comment is this: Isn't your questioning of evidence an act of power, and this desire to compress what is good or right into one single definition and meaning in terms of a kid's identity or a teacher's action?

That is my comment; my question is: Gentlemen, would you please, for us, define what you consider to be Whole Language, since you've been asking for a clear definition.

Carl Smith:

For the people in the back who can't hear, I'm going to restate Jamie's question or statement. He said that since the reporter in *U.S. News and World Report* talked about a war, and as a struggle for power between two opposing forces, isn't that exactly what the people who are calling for evidence do in assuming that they have the *power* to call for evidence, instead of turning the power over to people who should have it, as the previous person [JoBeth Allen] stated. Is that correct?

Jamie Myers:

Not quite! *[laughter]*

Carl Smith:

But something like that?

Jamie Myers:

It's an *act* of power!

Carl Smith [to Robinson and McKenna]:

Do you want to respond to that?

Dick Robinson:

Go ahead, let them [Shannon and Ohanian] define Whole Language!

Audience:

No, no!

Jamie Myers:

We want *you* to provide us with *your* definition of Whole Language.

Dick Robinson:

I don't have a definition of Whole Language.

Christine Pappas (University of Illinois, Chicago)

You keep acting, though, as if you do.

[Members of the audience speak over one another.]

Jamie Myers:

If you have no conception of it, then how can you evaluate research about Whole Language? You have to have a conception! What is it?

Dick Robinson:

Well, the comment that I have is that the literature presents such a variety of definitions, as Mike said, that any definition that anybody comes up with, not only within but also without the Whole Language community—there seems to be a great diversity of feelings and opinions. You want me to read the definition from Bergeron?

Jamie Myers:

Is it yours?

Dick Robinson:

No, not necessarily! *[he laughs]* I don't have a definition, and that's the reason why I asked the question. Because when I ask people, we get this great variety of definitions. I think that's a vital question. I wish I could be able to say it in twenty words or less.

Judy Buchanan ("Writing Project," Philadelphia):

I'm a classroom teacher, and I'm interested in the example you gave about the charts in the Whole Language classroom. Is it that the existence of the charts means, by definition, that the teacher can't be Whole Language, and she is therefore mislabeling herself? Or is it that you think that she's cheating in teaching, using something that's not in your definition of Whole Language, in order to help the kids learn something? In other words, what's the problem with the charts and the teacher?

Dick Robinson:

Well, you're right; I mean, as Donna Alvermann said, we're all see-ing language—or whatever—from our own perspective. But I have a question in terms of what *her* [the alleged Whole Language teacher] definition of rating is by what she is *doing*.

Judy Buchanan:

So, did you ask her?

Dick Robinson:

Yes.

Judy Buchanan:

What'd she say?

Dick Robinson:

She felt that a sound/symbol relationship, the teaching of phonics in that manner as an isolated skill, was a critical part of initial reading.

Unidentified male speaker:

She said that?

Dick Robinson:

Yeah, that's what she said.

Judy Buchanan:

And so what's your conclusion from that?

Dick Robinson:

That is her definition of reading, or of instruction. She is showing—as Cohen said this morning—not what she *said* but what she is actu-ally doing. A good example is understanding/comprehension. What she did, did not represent what she actually said.

Judy Buchanan:

Of course, it isn't possible to have the whole story here, but this is the same problem: Because of this context, you're giving us a very isolated picture of this incident, but it doesn't prove your point, as far as I can tell, because it seems perfectly plausible to be able to use charts which involve sound/symbol relationships in a so-called Whole Language classroom.

Dick Robinson:

Sure.

Judy Buchanan:

The problem I would posit is one of having to divide teachers into "Whole Language" and "not-Whole Language," . . .

Dick Robinson:

Right.

Judy Buchanan:

. . . and then asking us to choose which we are, and use a label that implies a static state, instead of . . .

Dick Robinson:

That's right, so that you're forced to be at either one end of the continuum or the other. And that is not true! We fall between the extremes. Yet as I work and talk with teachers, I find this division. I find people putting wagons in a circle and saying, "Hey, if you question or if you have any concerns of any sort about Whole Language . . . ," then you're labeled as being a "traditionalist," or being labeled as whatever. I find that unfortunate because in the real world, that does not happen.

Judy Buchanan:

It partly depends on how you ask the questions.

Unidentified female speaker ("I don't want to come up there" to the microphone):

It looks like you're doing the same thing, though, because you're saying that because she does this one thing that might be termed as traditional, she can't be Whole Language.

Dick Robinson:

I'm not necessarily saying that.

Unidentified female speaker:

Well, you implied it.

Another unidentified female speaker:

What *are* you saying, then?

Dick Robinson (to the former unidentified female speaker):

Yeah, OK!

Richard Allington (State University of New York, Albany)

Why is the issue of definition so critical? It seems to me what we know from at least a half-century of counting is that there is enormous variation in classrooms. If you were to take some of the indictments of the basal classrooms—I'm one of those folks who, as a basal author, would say, "Don't blame me for those people misusing that particular vehicle!" In other words, the variations in the basal classrooms in the studies of the '50s, the '60s, the '70s, the '80s showed wide range from teacher to teacher. We have this notion that there is *a* basal classroom, *a* traditional classroom, *a* phonics classroom, and then there's *a* Whole Language classroom. It just seems to me that everything we know from all forms of inquiry that we have engaged in over a half-century suggests that similarly labeled programs, similar materials, are hardly ever introduced in any common pattern when they are introduced over a large number of classrooms.

Dick Robinson (*sotto voce*):

That's not true.

Richard Allington:

So I guess I am not sure why it's important that we end up trying to define what a Whole Language classroom looks like as opposed to some other kind, and supposing that there is such a thing as a Whole Language classroom.

Carl Smith:

Do you have a way, then, of helping us determine the efficacy of a Whole Language program?

Richard Allington:

I would argue that you should treat reading instruction—to use the vernacular of experimental research—not as a dichotomous variable: "us *versus* them," basal or traditional or phonics *versus* Whole Language, or whatever, but as a continuous variable. Rather, we should ask what is it that we see going on? And of the things that we see going on, what seems to be working for children? And beyond that, I would ask: Why do we see what we see?

Carl Smith:

Do any of you want to respond to that or have comments in that direction?

Pat Shannon:

Not really.

Dick Robinson:

As I look back at the history of what has gone on in previous kinds of movements, the good teachers were the ones that drew on the things that seemed to work. What is going to happen, unfortunately, is that instead of coming together and talking, as we're doing here with good questions and interactions, Whole Language is going to pass by the wayside, as has been true of a lot of other things. Teachers are going to take what works for them. They are eclectic people; they know what works in their classrooms. We've seen it in a number of other areas—language experience, phonics, whatever you may look at in the past. They will take what is of use to them and will move on to something else.

I'm from Missouri. *[laughter; audience makes jokes sotto voce about "Show me!"]* I am seeing things going on in classrooms that are almost a complete opposite of some of the very good things in Whole Language that I had hoped teachers were going to adopt. An example: There are a number of programs now, called "Whole Language," in which the children don't do any reading at all. There is one in particular that I know about in which the kids come into class, and the teacher asks them what they saw on the way to school. They write the words down—it looks like something out of the Middle Ages—they write them down, they write sentences with the words, and that is their reading program. I think it's terrible! And yet, as we said, I think there are many good things in Whole Language.

Carl Smith:

I see Jerry Harste standing along the side. He's one of the fellows who came up with the term "Whole Language"—about 14 years ago, Jerry? How do *you* define "Whole Language," Jerry?

Jerome Harste (Indiana University, Bloomington):

As someone who has dedicated his life to clarity and precision . . . *[laughter]*, I feel strongly that the real issue is definitions of inquiry. This would not be a debate if we had a fundamental understanding about inquiry. One of the revolutions that has occurred is that inquiry has changed its stance in education to being a philosophical science. We used to send teachers at the Master's level to take a course in "the Inquiry Department"—we had the notion that inquiry was a problem-solving technique, right? I think that the revolution that has happened is that inquiry has become a philosophical science, a way of viewing the whole of education, so that we can see kids as inquirers, teachers as inquirers. This new view is more in keeping with the goals of NRC.

What the problem here is, is that you [non-Whole Language people] still think inquiry is somehow neutral ground. I mean, if you've been following the '80s *[laughter]*, what the whole bloody damn debate in inquiry has been about is that inquiry is not holy, does not possess some status outside of itself that gets you the truth. You're not addressing the real issue. If you address the real issue, then this isn't a debate.

Carl Smith:

Now, Jerry, what's the real issue, again? State it again!

Jerry Harste:

I think the issue is the views of inquiry.

Carl Smith:

"How we use inquiry, or inquiry is a philosophical . . . ?"

Jerry Harste:

As long as he [Dick Robinson] thinks that inquiry gives you a holy ground on which you can be sure of truth, that it's value-free, that it isn't making a political statement, then his questions make sense. But if what we've been saying here is that we're going to reject all of the debates about inquiry that have taken place in the '80s—I mean, that's what I see the '80s as having done, is to have really said that all inquiry is value-laden, that it is a political statement, that we have to interrogate our values. If you didn't believe that, you shouldn't have damn well stood up and clapped for Donna [Alvermann], but if you believe that, then it seems to me that those questions aren't there. The debate doesn't exist. *[Pause]* Ron [Carver] said that now you know the reason why *he* didn't stand up! *[laughter]*

Betsy Pryor (Revere Local School District, Akron, Ohio):

I am a first-grade teacher, and I would like to suggest to you that if you really want to know if Whole Language works, you should ask the people who are doing it—the Whole Language teachers and learners in the classrooms—because that is where you'll find out that

Whole Language works. That is why Whole Language is spreading across the country because teachers in classrooms are seeing with their own eyes and their own ears and their own hearts that learners are learning to read and write. *[applause]*

Carl Smith:

I see people looking at their watches, so I had better look at mine. We'll let that be the final note. Thanks to the panel, thank you who spoke up, and thanks to all very much for coming!

"People Who Live in Glass Houses...."

Patrick Shannon

The Pennsylvania State University

Responding to the statement, "Whole Language and Research: The Case for Caution," is an easy job for me because I do not share many of McKenna, Robinson, and Miller's reasons for being cautious about Whole Language. However, I consider this job futile because, although this might be an opportunity to have a conversation, I think in this case both sides are more bent on presenting our positions forcefully (so we won't appear to lose) than we are in learning from one another. I hope, however, those who are not so close to this debate can see and learn from the real differences between our positions. We disagree on at least these fundamental issues: our views of reality, of science, and of language; and our differing views point toward different futures both in and out of the classroom.

Most people question Whole Language philosophy and practice because of their own history with language-arts instruction at school. Even if they were unsuccessful in learning the phonics, grammar, and content of traditional lessons, most learned the procedural lessons of reading and writing instruction all too well. For example, they learned that text and teachers are the ultimate authority concerning which knowledge is valuable and which is not. They learned that accuracy is the key to learning, regardless of content, and that error is as much a moral failure as an academic one. They learned that in order to learn something complex, they must master its constituent parts and wait for a test to determine whether or not they know anything of value. Those who were successful at school attribute their success to their capacity to master these procedural lessons as well as the content presented. Those who failed the tests complained about the content perhaps, but they internalized the blame for their failure, believing that they had not worked at it earnestly enough. Prisoners of their own educational history, most people ask sincere questions about the philosophy and practices of Whole Language. That is, they want to enter a conversation with Whole Language theorists who affirm that education need not be humanly stultifying.

Romancing the Metaphor

McKenna, Robinson, and Miller in their statement do not seem to ask sincere questions about Whole Language. Rather, their language and metaphors suggest that they don't believe that Whole Language advocates can hold up their end of a conversation about literacy and literacy education. For example, in their first two paragraphs, they label Whole Language advocates "romantic" and "effusive." Although I believe they intended these labels to be insults (a hypothesis supported by some later labels—"dogma" and "religion"), I think these terms reveal important distinctions between Whole Language and the unnamed view of literacy and instruction that McKenna, Robinson, and Miller would defend. Taking their label "romantic" more seriously than McKenna, Robinson, and Miller themselves did, however, I affirm that *Whole Language advocates are passionate in their commitments, and that they should acknowledge their debt to the so-called romantic educational philosophies of John Dewey and Jean-Jacques Rousseau.*

Although others may have different starting points, I believe that Whole Language has human emancipation as its goal. Whole Language is an expression of resistance against the procedural and content lessons of traditional schooling, and it is action to help teachers and students to take control of their lives through self-exploration, self-expression, and self-understanding. Following Dewey, Whole Language advocates realize that human emancipation cannot remain an intellectual abstraction; rather, they take it as a moral commitment to students, other educators, and themselves which must be demonstrated in what they do and what they say in and out of classrooms. Based on this commitment, they work to establish classroom conditions that offer students and themselves freedom to tell their stories and to control their lives. They plan and act upon the details of what students and others might do together and the cultural politics that those "doings" support. In other words, they don't just *teach*; they evoke a pedagogy in which all activities have the goal of human emancipation embedded within them.

To avoid the possibility of egocentrism and narcissism in their teaching toward self-understanding, Whole Language advocates link self-actualization with social well-being by accepting an implication of Rousseau's theory that each human being possesses all the natural traits of human kind. Therefore, the development of sophisticated self-knowledge and expression prepares individuals to know others in support of public life, enabling each to abhor human suffering, to act against injustice, and to live a caring life—to "love" at least with a social and political love, all others as he or she "loves" him or herself. These links are apparent in Whole Language advocates' emphasis on students' taking the point of view of others during peer conferences and collaborative projects and in the emphasis on developing a community of learners. According to Rousseau, literacy is the springboard from thinking as a child, naturally and egocentrically, to thinking as an adult, politically and socially. *In their commitment to human emancipation, to the putting of philosophy to the practical test, and to the inseparable connection between self and society, Whole Language advocates are romantics.*

Within the political and business metaphors they choose, McKenna, Robinson, and Miller reveal a romanticism of a different sort. They suggest that the social programs of the Great Society were ravaged during the Reagan/Bush Administrations because they had only emotional commitment, but not scientific data, to support their continuation. This political metaphor that implies Whole Language cannot survive close critical scrutiny, rests on three unstated assumptions. First, it assumes that scientific support for Whole Language is lacking. Second, it assumes that legislators, government officials, and even voters (including teachers) are nonpartisan. And third, the metaphor assumes that society (schools) should travel in any direction scientific data might point—as if data speak for themselves.

The first assumption is false. See the lists of research below, pp. 97–98: One, a list of research that has informed Whole Language; the other, a list of research on Whole Language.

The second assumption is naive. If science or data drove governmental and voter decision-making, then how could the government support Star Wars, tobacco producers, or trickle-down economics? The scientific data on these projects are unequivocally negative. For that matter, if data drove political decisions, how could Reagan or Bush have been elected in the first place? *In politics, science is simply a tool manipulated by the powerful to protect privilege.*

The third assumption leads directly to the business metaphor. Here McKenna, Robinson, and Miller raise the club that the Reagan/Bush

Administrations used to beat schools and teachers during the 1980s. They suggest that because business (and schools, by implication) have not been scientific, America is falling behind in a global market economy. They offer David Kerns, former CEO of Xerox and currently a board member of the New American Schools Development Corporation, as an advocate of their scientific position. Mr. Kern's "scientific" approach at Xerox resulted in the elimination of the weakest (the least profitable) elements of the corporation, resulting in the loss of 5,000 jobs in Rochester, New York (where I grew up) and forcing many smaller service businesses into bankruptcy in its wake. Certainly, emotions and compassion were not involved in these "scientific" business decisions. Does Mr. Kern have the same plans for schools? *Can we simply cut off the weakest elements of schooling, as McKenna, Robinson, and Miller's metaphor suggests?*

Through their language and metaphors, McKenna, Robinson, and Miller demonstrate a romance of science. I use this oxymoron to explain that neither side in this debate holds a map to the way things really are; rather, both sides use their imaginations to determine how things ought to be. To support their view of the future through their metaphors, McKenna, Robinson, and Miller demonstrate that they wish science directed all of social life, but they also acknowledge that science does not direct much at all in social life at present. McKenna, Robinson, and Miller imagine that social reality (including literacy and literacy education) can be explained and controlled in the same way as we think about physical reality. They argue that we should be able to enjoy benefits akin to those we've derived through the discovery and control of physical nature. McKenna, Robinson, and Miller base this argument on five assumptions that they derive from physics and chemistry, and then use to question Whole Language and Whole Language advocates:

1. They assume that social reality is directed by discoverable laws, and that theories about these laws are universal—free from temporal and situational constraints. During their discussion about "problems of practitioner access," they chide Whole Language advocates for not recognizing the power that knowledge of their universal laws could place in teachers' hands.

2. They assume that researchers (and teachers, perhaps) can be disinterested in the outcomes and consequences of their efforts to

discover these laws. They believe that researchers can and must divest themselves of all interests and values when conducting these inquiries. Throughout their writing and speaking, McKenna, Robinson, and Miller compare unfavorably the partisanship of Whole Language to the "objectivity" of their own perspective.

3. They assume that the complexities of social reality are only summations of distinct systems of variables that can be analyzed, identified, and reassembled without injury to their theories about social reality. (For example, literacy is simply the summation of reading and writing, both of which are composed of various systems of sub-skills which are composed of . . . and so on.) Accordingly, McKenna, Robinson, and Miller believe that researchers should direct their attention first to the most elemental parts of literacy and literacy education. In their introduction, they lament Whole Language advocates' lack of restraint when changing literacy programs, and they offer a systematic research agenda for Whole Language advocates to follow before they act.

4. They assume that each variable within the subsystems has one precise definition which, once discovered, will hold across time and space. Such precision of definition and devaluing of contexts allows researchers to establish controls in their experiments and to determine causality by manipulating one defined variable or set of variables and measuring the change in defined consequent behavior. In their "problems of definition" section, McKenna, Robinson, and Miller find the lack of precise definition and the deference to situational and human contexts to be the primary impediments to determining the efficacy of Whole Language.

5. They assume that science finds its most exact expression in mathematical logic and deductive reasoning. In their mislabeled "problems of paradigms" section, McKenna, Robinson, and Miller suggest that Whole Language advocates fear statistical analyses and quantitative measurement. (I suggest that McKenna, Robinson, and Miller use the term "paradigm" incorrectly because they call "quantification" a paradigm. However, statistics is a type of logic available to advocates of all paradigms

of science. McKenna, Robinson, and Miller's unstated, but clearly evident, set of assumptions about social reality and science constitutes a paradigm.)

Charles Perfetti's book, *Reading Ability* (1985, Oxford), can serve as an example of this view of reality and science as it pertains to literacy and literacy education. Perfetti marshaled an impressive body of experimental findings in order to support his "verbal efficiency theory of reading." He divided reading into four parts and investigated them separately: lexical access of semantic information, assembly of propositions, integration of those propositions, and construction of text meaning. He manipulated these subparts of reading in various equations to explain reading of familiar and unfamiliar texts. In short, Perfetti looked for a single answer to the question, What is reading?

In contrast, Whole Language advocates find controlled studies like these unhelpful in their efforts to understand literacy and literacy use. For example, Harste, Woodward, and Burke found that experimental designs restricted children's attempts to relate what they knew about written language. In *Language Stories and Literacy Lessons* (1984, Heinemann), they documented that young children demonstrate more of what they know about literacy in some settings than they do in others. They attributed this variation to children's abilities to negotiate adults' language requests in order to make sense of what they are being asked to do. Rather than a single definition of literacy, they found that the definition of literate behavior was negotiated among the participants involved in particular settings.

As Harste, Woodward, and Burke's study demonstrates, Whole Language advocates imagine a different paradigm. That is, they do not share McKenna, Robinson, and Miller's view of social reality, and consequently they do not accept their concerns as compelling. Whole Language advocates believe that people negotiate the meaning and rules of acceptable behavior within particular contexts. For example, literacy is not just a single ability that can be performed equally by all, regardless of context. Rather, to be considered literate by a social group, one must possess and perform reading and writing in ways acceptable to that group. Different groups require different forms of literacy. Think of the differences in what it means to be considered literate at school (puzzling through worksheets and taking standardized exams), at a construction site (trying to make sense of blueprints and notations), at an IRS office (trying to interpret tax codes and laws), or in a publishing house (critiquing a poem and correcting style for clarity and readability). In each place, the rules and meanings of literacy are socially determined. They are, moreover, negotiated across time, not just place. For instance, during early modern times, literacy was regarded as a virtue, not just a necessity, that signified a good person as well as a capable one. At that time, however, people were considered literate if they could sign their names and read a few Bible passages. Today, we consider people who have these abilities only to be nearly illiterate.

Because Whole Language advocates consider social realities to be a social, historical artifact, they recognize that values and interests are necessarily involved in the negotiations in any social situation, including this debate about Whole Language. Although the rules and definitions negotiated in one setting may or may not be generalizable to other settings, studies of social negotiations in specific settings can provide examples of how negotiations might take place in other settings, depending upon the similarity of interests and values of the participants and the context of the settings. In this way, teachers' writing about the negotiations of Whole Language and life in their classrooms becomes compelling reading for other teachers. They do not supply blueprints or laws of behavior; rather, they offer research on how sense was made in their settings and what may be possible in other settings.

Because Whole Language advocates recognize that the meaning and rules of Whole Language are negotiated in each setting, they do not become so frustrated as do McKenna, Robinson, and Miller about the lack of a singular, all-purpose definition of Whole Language. Nor do they find the call for experimental comparative studies compelling. Because Whole Language is never made, but is always in the making in particular settings, researchers who issue those calls or attempt those studies misunderstand the dynamic nature and the purposes of Whole Language. Whole Language does not stand still long enough for slower-moving researchers to calibrate their instruments of study. As researchers, Whole Language advocates seek to determine how participants in particular social contexts (classrooms, families, clubs, etc.) do or do not make sense of each other's actions sufficiently well to accomplish their goals. That is,

Whole Language advocates are pragmatic in their views about science and research. This pragmatism is fundamental to understanding the differences between McKenna, Robinson, and Miller's position and ours and Whole Language's. (See pp. 98–99 for a third list, research on research, for further discussion of science, research, and romance.)

Looking to the Consequences

Pragmatists are generally skeptical about the possibility of telling literally true stories of what the world is like—i.e., discovering its universal laws. They doubt that we can actually differentiate between "out there" in reality and "in here" within ourselves because our values from the past, interests in the present, and imaginations of the future precede and influence our searches for descriptions, theories, explanations, and narratives about the world. Pragmatists suggest that the search for the universal laws of social life be abandoned because it's impossible to know if we've found them, and because they are practically irrelevant to teachers' daily needs and practices. Pragmatists believe that we should stop asking whether our theories are "really real," and, instead, devote more attention to the consequences of our work and questions within the communities in which we live. Pragmatists renounce McKenna, Robinson, and Miller's desire to transcend the community with which they are identified in order to define some grand truth. Pragmatists replace this Faustian quest with a desire for solidarity within the community.

As pragmatists, Whole Language advocates choose what to research and how to go about it, conditioned by their desires for the future. They choose some descriptions, theories, explanations, and narratives about reality, and they dismiss others because the former produce their desired community better than do the latter. Whole Language advocates' pragmatic method is to try to interpret each notion by tracing its own practical consequences to determine whether it will further human emancipation through self-exploration, self-expression, and self-understanding. Their choice is based on the approach that they think is better than another for producing these desired outcomes. *Whole Language advocates do not call their pragmatic approach "reality"; rather, they refer to it as a professional theory, a reflection in action, a praxis—an activity that has its goal within itself. Whole Language advocates stand on the axioms that not everything that works is desirable, not every belief that is "true" is to be acted upon, and that some "objectively" successful approaches will work at cross purposes to expressed goals and therefore are irrelevant.*

This stance explains why Diane Stephens (whom McKenna, Robinson, and Miller mentioned by name) and other Whole Language advocates pick and choose among research findings. Stephens and the others are not trying to hide from "what works," as McKenna, Robinson, and Miller imply; rather, they are attempting to inform educators who have already made a commitment to Whole Language values. No amount of "scientific experimentation" will persuade people either to make this commitment or will dissuade them from having made it. To break the advocates' commitment to Whole Language, critics must demonstrate that Whole Language works against human emancipation, and therefore, is bad for children, society, and themselves.

Whole Language advocates focus on the study and teaching of language in particular ways because of its central role in the negotiations of social life. If the conditions of communities, schools, and classrooms are not only to permit but also to promote human emancipation and individual freedom, then educators and students must understand the properties and possibilities of language within our human, changeable world. That is, language becomes the object and means of inquiry because of its potential to bring about pragmatic results. Language presents us with a dialectic: On the one hand, we see, hear, and otherwise experience life as we do because the language habits of our community predispose us toward certain choices of interpretation. Language supplies our categories of interpretation, our rules for the manner in which those categories can relate to one another, and our points of expression about our interpretations. For example, the language of traditional research and schooling provides teachers with no easy ways to think or talk about how they might support students' language acquisition without textbooks, ability grouping, and lessons. In this way, social negotiations of the past that are encoded in our language set constraining parameters for understanding the world inside the classroom.

On the other hand, language is a tool for negotiating the meanings and rules of our social realities. In conversations, we can synchronize our intentions within the accepted rules of linguistic and social behaviors, but we can also push those rules to explore our intentions more fully to see where they might lead. That is, we can come to know others' interests and intents, and we can crystallize our knowledge of ourselves. Language, then, holds the potential to know others, and also to explore, express, and understand ourselves and what we could become. Of course, it is this very power of exploration that is lost in this forum of written debate about Whole Language. Because we are unwilling (unable?) to synchronize our intentions, we cannot come to know one another, nor can we learn much new about ourselves.

To bring us closer together, both sides would have to recognize the limitations of modernist thought which the Enlightenment brought to us, and the obligations of a postmodern world. We would both have to recognize the legitimacy of other voices, other logics, in the negotiation of reality. That is, Susan, I, and other advocates of Whole Language would have to accept the legitimacy of the scientistic views of McKenna, Robinson, and Miller for what they can contribute, and they would have to deconstruct the hierarchy of authority they've built for experimental study in order to hear the authority of other voices (people) different from their own. As we take steps toward each other, perhaps we will not have to speak so loudly.

Language and Power

Because language allows individuals to communicate across time and space, as well as in face-to-face conversations, all of social reality (past, present, and future) becomes problematic—subject to reinterpretations, imaginations, and different meanings. Think of the various social meanings among Americans of the Columbus enterprise of 1492! Our different language communities and the experiences upon which they are based make the Columbus legacy a stark example of how the past, present, and future are simultaneously negotiated. Through language, entire worlds can be actualized and renegotiated at any moment, if communities can control and expand the patterns of thought and expression that their language forces on them.

Whole Language advocates make a distinction between learning language and learning about language. Whereas learning about language remains largely external, people learn language by acquiring it subconsciously through exposure to everyday language practices within a particular setting and by a process of hypothesis construction in which they receive feedback about their efforts to function linguistically in that setting. Acquisition is intrinsically motivated by an individual's recognition that language is necessary in order to have his or her needs met and to develop social relations. Furthermore, people acquire more than language from subconscious exposure; they learn how to think, act, move, dress, and they learn what to value in order to become functioning members of a socially significant group. Then, as individuals extend their social boundaries beyond family and intimates, they re-engage in the process of acquisition of new languages and new behaviors.

On the other hand, learning about language involves conscious knowledge gained through formal teaching in which language is analyzed to its constituent parts in order to characterize their relationship to each other and the whole. American schools have been organized to teach about language for at least one hundred and fifty years. Although this learning is new for all, it is closest, not by accident, to White middle- and upper-class male language, and therefore, it is easier for some groups to join the school social group than for others. Moreover because of the inequalities of treatment within the history of American schools, some social groups have little intrinsic motivation and few incentives to join the school group. Consequently, learning about language through formal teaching is unequally distributed among those groups who attend public schools.

Whole Language advocates value both the acquisition of language and learning about language. They find that people perform better at what they acquire, although they can analyze and comment more on what they have been taught. Moreover, they recognize that acquisition must precede teaching about language, if the latter is to make sense. Acquisition and learning, then, offer two differential sources of power to language users: Acquirers are usually better than learners at language performance in everyday situations, and learners are typically better than acquirers at explaining, analyzing, and criticizing language use.

Because Whole Language advocates understand language as a means through which individuals gain access to social groups and negotiate meaning in their lives, they value the power of acquisition over the power of learning about language. This is not to say that they find learning about language useless, but they see their primary role as teachers to provide opportunities for students to do language rather than to talk about it. By doing language, students can engage immediately in the ongoing negotiation of social reality in classrooms and community, and they thus learn more about themselves and their place in that reality. Later, when learning about language is combined with acquisition, they can evaluate their place and performance in that reality.

In summary on pragmatic method, Whole Language advocates start from a set of values: the goals of human emancipation, their imagination of a negotiated social reality, the possibilities of language, and the power of acquisition. As pragmatists, they use these values as directives to conduct themselves in certain ways in order to attend to the consequences of their actions at all times. In Whole Language, the ends can never justify the means; rather, the means are indicative of the ends. Accordingly, Whole Language advocates seek certain types of social relationships among teachers and students, certain kinds of content, and certain forms of knowing because they lead to freedom through self-discovery, self-expression, and self-knowledge, to a symbiosis between the individual and society, and to a vigorous sense of human possibilities. They do not look to science to validate these values. Because Whole Language is a set of values, science does not stand above Whole Language. Rather, Whole Language advocates use science to find better ways to support students in their acquisition of, and learning about, language and life.

There's the Rub

McKenna, Robinson, and Miller want science to transcend Whole Language and all social realities. They do not appreciate the Promethean act of Whole Language advocates stealing the fire of science to do with it what they will. Try as they might, McKenna, Robinson, and Miller cannot come to grips with this new negotiated reality. Their first attempt to sidestep this issue is to suggest that Whole Language advocates value only their own research. This is nonsense. Although Whole Language advocates do reject some research beyond their control, they also value and use systematic investigations of language in everyday settings conducted by researchers who appear to share their values. Whether or not it is labeled "Whole Language," this research brings solidarity to the

Whole Language community because its consequences promote human emancipation and offers Whole Language advocates examples of how they might proceed in their own settings.

This research, however, teaches advocates about Whole Language, at best facilitating their abilities to talk about it. It cannot enhance their performance of Whole Language. To improve their own performance, Whole Language advocates must acquire Whole Language by immersing themselves in work based on Whole Language principles so that they may negotiate the meaning of Whole Language within their own social settings, for that meaning cannot come fixed for them in the words and actions of others. Whole Language is always in the making in the experiences of the classrooms. When advocates write and talk about the negotiations and consequences of their work, they inform, and are informed by, the Whole Language community.

As they acquire and learn about Whole Language, Whole Language advocates become researchers in the best sense of that word. They empower themselves to engage in scientific inquiry, to voice their findings, and to make decisions about the adequacy of their own and other research, thereby helping themselves to realize their values. In this process, Whole Language advocates redefine rigor in research. For them, rigor can no longer be determined simply by following some rituals of research method which detach the researcher from the research questions, methods, subjects, and outcomes, as McKenna, Robinson, and Miller claim. Rigor for Whole Language educators develops out of the struggle to connect the researcher in meaningful ways with the purpose for the investigation, those investigated, and the consequences of the investigation. Rigor does not come from detachment, but rather from the researchers' willingness to declare their values, to be open to surprises, to accept responsibility for their actions and the use of their findings, and to be changed by their discoveries.

McKenna, Robinson, and Miller worry about reality, about objectivity, and the scientific power to compare, but without acknowledging the values, goals, and principles that drive their work. They are caught up in the power of their science to explain what they value as if it were reality, but without looking at the consequences of their findings on the communities within which we must live. Because they claim the research that they find compelling to be reality, they attempt to privilege their values on all grounds. *Nevertheless, their romance of science without examination of the use of that science to control individuals' freedom, and their eagerness to protect privilege in and out of schools, is nothing less than an apology for the unequal and unjust educational and social status quo in our society.* These apologies for unjust traditions may be most apparent in McKenna, Robinson, and Miller's concern about the "Goodman Model of Reading."

Desire for a Better Future

Ken Goodman's model of, and research on, reading are both central and irrelevant to Whole Language advocates' work. Following the axiom of pragmatism: that both what to research and how to research are conditioned by a desire for the future, Goodman has conducted thirty years of research to demonstrate that social reality (including language meaning) is contextually based at numerous levels from word to socio-political context, and negotiated among the participants who are always trying to make sense (according to their respective purposes and within their several language communities). Through his research, Goodman intended, and intends, to demonstrate that apparent mistakes during reading are not moral failures of individuals, but miscues of a community trying to make sense of text (and life) through an individual.

Goodman conducted the majority of his work among citizens who have been traditionally disadvantaged at school, often through the passionate applications of what McKenna, Robinson, and Miller call "objective science." At times, Goodman has charged that science is a tool in the political game to protect privilege by setting White, middle- and upper-class, male performance as the norm of reading instruction from kindergarten to college, against which all others are to be judged. The consequences of this science and its political uses are institutionalized in standardized tests, basal reading series, and teacher education programs, all of which inhibit the language of schooled America to imagine and negotiate a different, more just future. Goodman understood, and understands, that different futures in reading programs and society—futures based on justice and equality—require a different set of values and a different conception of human agency to bring about a change for equity and justice. In these ways, Goodman's model and research are central to Whole Language advocates' work.

Goodman's work is irrelevant to Whole Language to the extent that Whole Language cannot be reduced to reading. As peculiar as it may sound, Whole Language has less to do with reading than it does with language, literacy, and power. While many North Americans may learn about reading at school in ways McKenna, Robinson, and Miller describe, they nonetheless acquire literacies commensurate with the demands for communication in the non-school environments to which they have access. What has made idealized White middle- and upper-class male language the norm against which everyone is judged is the access of White middle- and upper-class males to environments of power and privilege. Schools do not teach language and literacy sufficiently to serve this group in any environment in which they may find themselves; rather, school lessons—both in content and process—sanction White middle- and upper-class males' acquisition of the knowledge, confirming to them their right to be in powerful and privileged environments, and reassuring their belief that once they are in those environments, they are likely to be successful. That is, schools teach White middle- and upper-class males that they are subjects in social negotiations of reality in and out of schools.

Schools have different lessons for women, the poor, and language and racial minorities. Because they are held to school standards that are distant for their languages, and because the ways they are held to these standards are arbitrary, these groups acquire the knowledge that they are not good enough to warrant access to powerful and privileged environments, and that they themselves are to blame for their lack of access. As these social categories combine in different ways into different lives, members of these disenfranchised groups learn to see themselves as objects in the negotiations of social realities in and out of school, objects that must defer to others who will direct their lives. Since the turn of the century, schools have used McKenna, Robinson, and Miller's type of science to reinforce these social biases and political injustices.

Whole Language advocates find the consequences of these lessons and this kind of science unacceptable because they work against human emancipation. Moreover, Whole Language advocates attempt to develop classroom environments that will allow all students to acquire the knowledge that they are subjects over (not merely objects within) the negotiations of social realities. They provide invitations for students to act as journalists, anthropologists, geographers, horticulturists, architects, etc. on a simplified level in the classroom so that they learn to believe that they could belong successfully to such social groups when they leave school. This pedagogy enables students and teachers to participate vigorously in the struggle to push privilege aside so that McKenna, Robinson, and Miller's democratic rhetoric might mean more in the future than it did in the past of our founding fathers.

Whole Language is by no means a settled point or position, but Whole Language advocates will be bullied neither by scientists nor anyone else into "objective" and useless definitions. We will resist the will of those who seek not to understand but to dismiss Whole Language because it does not agree with their romance of science or their elitist values. Whole Language advocates ask us to accept personal responsibility for the consequences of our work as we ask and act upon the question: "How do we wish to live together?"

Selected List of Research That Informs Whole Language

Bissex, G. (1980). *GYNS At work: A child learns to write and read.* Cambridge, Massachusetts: Harvard University Press.

Britton, J. *et al.* (1975). *The development of writing abilities (11–18).* London: MacMillan Education.

Carey, R. (Ed.). (1987). *Findings of research in miscue analysis: Ten years later.* Urbana, Illinois: National Council of Teachers of English.

Donaldson, M. (1979). *Children's minds.* New York: W.W. Norton.

Halliday, M. A. K. (1975). *Learning how to mean: Explorations in the development of language.* New York: Elsevier North-Holland.

Harste, J., Woodward, V. and Burke, C. (1984). *Language stories and literacy lessons.* Portsmouth, New Hampshire: Heinemann.

Heath, S. B. (1983). *Ways with words: Language, life and work in communities and classrooms.* New York: Cambridge University Press.

Mehan, H. (1979). *Learning lessons: Social organization in the classrooms.* Cambridge, Massachusetts: Harvard University Press.

Rosen, H. (1983). *Stories and meanings.* Sheffield, England: National Association for the Teaching of English.

Taylor, D. and Dorsey-Gaines, C. (1988). *Growing up literate: Learning from inner-city families.* Portsmouth, New Hampshire: Heinemann.

Selected List of Research on Whole Language

Atwell, N. (1987). *In the middle: Writing, reading, and learning with adolescents.* Portsmouth, New Hampshire: Boynton/Cook.

Edelsky, C. (1991). *With literacy and justice for all: Rethinking the social in language and education.* Philadelphia, Pennsylvania: Falmer.

Five, C. L. (1991). *Special voices.* Portsmouth, New Hampshire: Heinemann.

Hansen, J., Newkirk, T. & Graves, D. (Eds.). (1985). *Breaking ground: Teachers relate reading and writing in the elementary school.* Portsmouth, New Hampshire: Heinemann.

Mills, H., O'Keefe, T. & Stephens, D. (1992). *Looking closely: Exploring the role of phonics in one Whole Language classroom.* Urbana, Illinois: National Council of Teachers of English.

Newkirk, T. (1989). *More than stories: The range of children's writing.* Portsmouth, New Hampshire: Heinemann.

Newman, J. (Ed.). (1989). *Finding our own way: Teachers exploring their assumptions.* Portsmouth, New Hampshire: Heinemann.

Rief, L. (1991d). *Seeking diversity: Language arts with adolescents.* Portsmouth, New Hampshire: Heinemann.

Stires, S. (1991). *With promise: Redefining reading and writing needs for special students.* Portsmouth, New Hampshire: Heinemann.

Wells, G. & Chang-Wells, G. L. (1992). *Constructing knowledge together: classrooms as centers of inquiry and literacy.* Portsmouth, New Hampshire: Heinemann.

Selected List of Research on Research

Aronowitz, S. (1988). *Science as power: Discourse and ideology in modern society.* Minneapolis, Minnesota: University of Minnesota.

Beach, R., *et al.* (Eds.). (1992). *Multidisciplinary perspectives on literacy research*. Urbana, Illinois: National Conference on Research in English.

Bissex, G. & Bullock, R. (Eds.). (1987). *Seeing for ourselves: Case study research by teachers of writing*. Portsmouth, New Hampshire: Heinemann.

Cherryholmes, C. (1988). *Power and criticism: Post structural investigations in education*. New York: Teachers College Press.

Fleck, L. (1979). *Genesis and development of a scientific fact*. Chicago: University of Chicago.

Goswami, D., & Stillman, P. (Eds.). (1987). *Reclaiming the classroom: Teacher research as an agency for change*. Portsmouth, New Hampshire: Heinemann.

Lather, P. (1991). *Getting smart: Feminist research and pedagogy within the postmodern*. New York: Routledge.

Mills, C. W. (1959). *The sociological imagination*. New York: Oxford University.

Popkewitz, T. (1984). *Paradigm and ideology in educational research: The social functions of the intellectual*. Philadelphia, Pennsylvania: Falmer.

Witherell, C. & Noddings, N. (Eds.). (1991). *Stories lives tell: Narrative and Dialogue in education*. New York: Teachers College Press.

Second Negative

Emerging Perspectives
on Whole Language

Michael C. McKenna
Georgia Southern University

Richard D. Robinson
University of Missouri

John W. Miller
Florida State University

I*tem*: Members of the Canadian Psychological Association warn the provincial education ministries about proceeding too quickly with the nationwide implementation of Whole Language. Longitudinal studies of its impact prove their concerns well-founded (Biemiller, 1993; Glasspool, 1993).

Item: Marie Clay, as president of the International Reading Association, approves the formation of a new special-interest group devoted to "balanced" reading instruction. Its founding originated in the cautious skepticism of a group of British educators (Thompson, 1993).

Item: As a result of listening to the comments of Ohanian and Shannon, presented at the annual meeting of the National Reading Conference [see above, pp. 1–15, 48–51, 58–61], a group of researchers organize a new association devoted to the scientific study of reading.

We cite these events as indicators of growing skepticism in this country and others about the unsubstantiated claims for Whole Language. These warnings also indicate the need for a new perspective on beginning-literacy instruction that will permit educators to "transcend the debate" (Adams, 1993) and get on with the business of teaching in ways consonant with what is known about the acquisition of literacy.

Response to Ohanian

We appreciate Susan Ohanian's sincere concern for the welfare of her students and for their growth toward literacy. We appreciate her frustration with the limits of research and its sometimes mixed messages. We appreciate her self-reliance on her own classroom experiences as a means of informing her practice. What we find harder to appreciate are some of the conclusions she has drawn, apparently as a consequence of her concern and frustrations.

One of these conclusions is that she herself claims to have abandoned "counting." We suggest that this is not the case. She does an excellent job in presenting the example of Chris, who succeeded nicely in the classroom environment fostered by Ohanian to reflect a Whole Language philosophy. In the process, she makes clear that while Chris is merely an example, he is typical of the students in her class. She employs, in effect, a single representative case to describe a central tendency among her students. This is a form of counting.

The fact that Ohanian does not cite quantitative indicators, their means, standard deviations, and so forth, does not obscure her actual method. The kind of evidence that she values in judging the effectiveness of a methodology is numerical, and her criterion, though a simple one, is also numerical: that which works best for the majority of her students. To her credit, Ohanian acknowledges that her Whole Language methodology was not universally effective. There are, she concedes, counterexamples, such as Bob. She makes clear, however, that Bob is not typical; thereby, she implies a ratio of success to failure. This implied ratio is yet another instance of the counting that Ohanian says she does not do.

With respect to what we ourselves value as evidence, our position is therefore more closely aligned with Ohanian's than she would probably care to admit. Where we differ is in regard to (1) whether her methodology is demonstrably superior to more structured alternatives, and (2) whether a more diverse set of methodologies would have yielded greater success with some of her more problematic students, like Bob. Let's consider each of these differences.

First, whether Ohanian might have been a more effective teacher using a more structured set of methodologies is a question she answers on the basis of her own experience. She has tried structured approaches, she tells us, and found them wanting. However, the practices that she has apparently rebelled against are those that were popular in an earlier era, a time when sequenced instruction in the minutiae of decoding skills was paramount. She takes pride in not having learned some of the linguistic terminology that often accompanied that kind of instruction. We acknowledge that some measure of gratitude is surely due to Whole Language for helping to rescue American literacy instruction from the grasp of this era and its numbing methods. The approach to literacy instruction that we believe is emerging now is structured but not tightly sequenced, systematic but not dogmatic. We suggest that Ohanian's overall approach to her own classroom instruction would have been enhanced by what we will outline in the next few pages, and that her philosophy of language learning, though probably not completely in accord with ours, would not have been greatly compromised by it.

Second, whether a greater diversity of methods would have met the obviously diverse needs of her students, is another issue on which we disagree with Ohanian. We read with interest of her confrontation with the problem of Bob. Bob represents to experienced, practicing teachers a case in which alternative methods were clearly called for. Ohanian reaches a different conclusion, however. Bob failed not because Whole Language methodology was inappropriate, but because the "right books" were never found. Ohanian's reasoning is circular. She seems to say: "The method failed because it could not be implemented; the method is not, therefore, to blame, and should have been used all along." The true misfortune in this circle of self-authenticating dogmatism is that it rules out philosophically incompatible, though useful, alternatives.

What alternative techniques might have worked with Bob? Two persuasive examples were offered recently by Patricia Cunningham (1992). She tells of her own students, Todd and Eric, who were remedial sixth-graders of normal intelligence and language development. Their chief problem was decoding. Her solution was the use of direct systematic instruction using analogies, together with an analogy-based practice technique involving the dictionary. Cunningham's approach, in particular her reliance on systematic teaching and some degree of decontextualized practice, seems clearly outside virtually any definition of Whole Language, and yet her remarkable success, with the emergence of Todd and Eric as motivated, independent readers, suggests that the extreme Whole Language perspective may be too confining.

Response to Shannon

Like Shannon, we do not presume to speak for educators other than ourselves, but we suspect that many researchers outside the Whole Language community will find much to approve in his remarks. The notion that research is better directed at improving the human condition than at discovering absolute truth, is likely to strike a harmonic chord in the educational research community in general. Unlike Einstein, who confessed a desire to "think the thoughts of God," most of the educational researchers we know are cut from different cloth. Their goals, like Shannon's, are rooted in shared community values and a desire to make life better. They are typically not rooted in the pursuit of absolute knowledge for its own sake. In education, researchers fill a service function to the practitioner—a function not to tell, but to avail, to suggest, to guide, and to encourage.

Good researchers are well-aware of the complexity of the phenomena they study. They are no more prone than Shannon to the kind of reductionist aetiology that he seems to ascribe to them. The general acknowledgment in the research community of this complexity has occasioned the call for multiple research paradigms in the investigation of literacy phenomena. Ironically, Whole Language educators, in their insistence on their own theory only, are often guilty of the very sort of reductionism that Shannon disavows. Consider this evidence, offered by a classroom teacher:

> *A new child was having difficulty with an unknown word. The parent volunteer waited a little bit and then quietly said, "In this class, Mrs. Brountas likes the children to skip the word and go on." The child did, then went back and reread the sentence correctly. "It works! It works!" shouted the parent excitedly. The child said nothing; his broad smile said it all: Whole Language really does work. (Brountas, 1987, p. 60)*

Examples of this nature abound in publications produced by the Whole Language community. In this instance, a causal relationship is asserted between a method that is commonplace in many approaches to instruction and the effectiveness of the Whole Language philosophy.

We suggest, in the pragmatic spirit of building a true community among all literacy teachers and researchers, that Whole Language educators consider the benefits of dialoguing with the other, larger, and more diverse segments of the language-education profession as they strive to reach conclusions. Whatever our individual perspectives on research and instruction, we *all* share many common values and goals, not the least of which is universal enfranchisement through literacy. Open dialogue might well result in better appreciation of the complex relationship between methods and their effects, an appreciation not evident either in the example above or in Shannon and Ohanian's dogmatism. The insularity of Shannon's view, when applied recently to the issue of basal readers, drew the following response from Baumann:

> *Does Shannon as a critical scientist have the exclusive license to ask questions, identify issues, and call for change, leaving those with a different ideological alignment unable to participate in dialogue and change? Further, can a critic's work be analyzed only by those who share the same philosophical perspective as the critic himself? (1993, p. 87)*

These are questions that each reader must resolve, but we suggest that the community of Whole Language practitioners stands to be informed by interaction with the larger research community, just as that community has been beneficially informed by Whole Language. The kind of wagon-circling that Shannon's posture implies seems wholly incognizant of the political realities he ironically acknowledges. Shannon's stance reinforces Pearson's (1989) judgment that the Whole Language movement is politically naive.

Balanced Literacy Instruction

Whole Language theory continues to have a dramatic effect on beginning literacy instruction. In passing through the crucible of real classrooms, however, the Whole Language philosophy adopted by practicing teachers emerges as an alloy. On entering the classrooms of outstanding teachers, by whatever tag they identify themselves, one is now likely to observe instruction that is neither traditional (in the skill-by-skill, part-to-whole sense) nor Whole Language (in the purist, socially-constructivist sense). Rather, it is a happy mixture of the best elements of both, and more.

We are not *prescribing* this balanced approach to instruction, although we do support it. We are *describing* the result of teachers' making their own sense of the issues. The eclectic positions they appear to be reaching are based on a straightforward functional pragmatism: Use what works, use whatever works, and be prepared to use a variety of techniques in search of what will work for each student.

The evidence is ample that this thoroughgoing eclectic pragmatism prevails among all kinds of teachers, Whole Language teachers included. In a nationwide study conducted by the National Reading Research Center, Michael Pressley and Joan Rankin (1993) surveyed some 140 primary teachers identified as "outstanding" by their colleagues. Many of them considered themselves to be Whole Language teachers, and the consensus methodology that emerged did reflect the influence of Whole Language thought: It included the use of outstanding children's literature, daily read-alouds, big books, a print-rich classroom, a focus on process writing, and cooperative/partner reading experiences. But it also included systematic, direct instruction in phonics.

In a second recent study, Sean Walmsley and Ellen Adams (1993) interviewed 71 teachers attending a Whole Language conference. These teachers produced a notably similar list of instructional components. Like the teachers in Pressley and Rankin's sample, however, the Whole Language teachers at the conference used approaches that were broad and included methods at odds with a strict Whole Language philosophy:

> We also learned that these teachers were not "purist" Whole Language teachers, in the sense that they religiously eschew the basal; textbooks for science and social studies; direct instruction of skills; workbooks; and formal, standardized testing. To one degree or another, most of them compromised, either tacking on Whole Language activities to an existing traditional program or supplementing their Whole Language program with traditional materials. And yet, most of these teachers still regarded themselves as Whole Language teachers. (p. 278)

These studies suggest an evolution in American literacy instruction. Whole Language appeals to the need of teachers to make reading and writing meaningful for students. It offers a blueprint for accomplishing this goal in the form of practical strategies and guiding theoretical principles. At the same time, teachers appear to be discovering that the strategies are not always sufficient, and that some of the principles are too narrow to reflect the realities in the classroom. Consequently, new and more productive strategies are being employed, while the principles are being extended and revised to accommodate the realities. The result is what Dixie Lee Spiegel (1992) called the "blending" of Whole Language with systematic direct instruction, and what Courtney Cazden (1992) termed "Whole Language plus." We may be witnessing what the philosopher Hegel would have termed a *synthesis* of two viewpoints: the *thesis* of traditional approaches and the *antithesis* of Whole Language, blended and lifted into a single new perspective superior to both. The following guidelines are consistent with that new synthesis. We offer them in an attempt to summarize the emerging consensus on beginning literacy instruction.

1. Foster a broad base of phonemic and print awareness where it is lacking.

2. Read aloud often and with enthusiasm, presenting to students a wide variety of narrative and expository patterns, styles, and genres.

3. Make available an abundance of high-quality print material, both fiction and nonfiction, and provide plentiful opportunities for students to explore, select, and read.

4. Begin writing experiences early, and encourage children to explore the alphabetic principle through invented spelling. Guide them gently through a systematic transition to regular orthography as this principle is grasped.

5. Lead young literates to realize that reading and writing are, above all, attempts to communicate with others. Give them the balanced understanding that comprehension involves both the meaning that they themselves *construct* from within and the meaning that they *reconstruct* in the attempt to discern what an author intended to convey.

6. Use process writing to distinguish the stages of authorship, from planning and drafting through publishing, and to instill pride in the finished products of literate behavior.

7. Provide systematic (though not necessarily sequential) attention to the acquisition of decoding ability. Conduct unplanned instruction during teachable moments, where feasible, but situate it within the context of a planned program of direct, structured teaching.

8. Integrate literacy instruction with learning across content subjects. Let students write to learn as they learn to write. Help them to improve their reading and writing as they acquire content knowledge, and encourage them to think critically and analytically from the outset.

9. Employ flexible grouping strategies that capitalize on social dynamics and that avoid stagnant, demeaning group identity. Use peer-teaching and collaborative learning as democratically effective approaches to learning.

10. Aim for rapid growth toward automatic word recognition by providing (a) ample time for independent reading of high-quality, high-interest books, and (b) repetition of key words in aesthetically acceptable formats, such as predictable books and repeated readings.

11. Introduce skills in meaningful contexts, but do not be afraid to provide occasional practice in isolation where it is needed (for example, copying spelling words).

12. Assess literacy development in ways that focus on both process and product and also on performance in authentic situations.

Educators at both poles of this controversy will doubtless find something to burn and something to brandish in this list. Our observation is that in actual practice, *all* of these guidelines are being followed in outstanding classrooms. Furthermore, the meld is a happy one. As Dixie Lee Spiegel has observed, "The reality of the world of schooling is that teachers *will* draw what works best for them from both worlds." (1992, p. 43, emphasis in original) Perhaps it is time we attended to what these teachers have forged.

References

Adams, M.J. (1993, April). *Finding the best of both worlds* [panel title]. Paper presented at the meeting of the International Reading Association, San Antonio.

Baumann, J.F. (1993). Is it "you just don't understand," or am I simply confused? A response to Shannon. [letter to the editor] *Reading Research Quarterly* 28, 86–87.

Biemiller, A. (1993, August). *Some observations on beginning reading instruction.* Paper presented at the meeting of the American Psychological Association, Toronto.

Biemiller, A. (1993, December). *Bringing language and basic reading skills together: Some observations on acquiring and using reading skill in elementary schools.* Paper presented at the meeting of the National Reading Conference, Charleston, South Carolina.

Brountas, M. (1987). Whole Language really works. *Teaching K–8,* 18/ 3, 57–60.

Cazden, C. (Ed.) (1992). *Whole Language plus: Essays on literacy in the United States.* New York: Teachers College Press.

Cunningham, P.M. (1992). What kind of phonics instruction will we have? In C.K. Kinzer & D.J. Leu (Eds.), *Literacy research, theory, and practice: Views from many perspectives: Forty-first yearbook of the National Reading Conference* (pp. 17–31). Chicago, Illinois: National Reading Conference.

Glasspool, J. (1993, August). *Enhancing reading instruction for young boys.* Paper presented at the meeting of the American Psychological Association, Toronto.

Pressley, M., & Rankin, J. (1993, December). *National survey of outstanding primary reading teachers: Whole Language experiences and more.* Paper presented at the meeting of the National Reading Conference, Charleston, South Carolina.

Spiegel, D.L. (1992). Blending Whole Language and systematic direct instruction. *The Reading Teacher* 46, 38–44.

Symons, S. (1993, August). A plea for moderation in the whole language movement. Paper presented at the meeting of the American Psychological Association, Toronto.

Thompson, R.A. (1993, April). *Introduction: Balanced reading instruction.* Paper presented at the meeting of the International Reading Association, San Antonio.

Walmsley, S.A., & Adams, E.L. (1993). Realities of "Whole Language." *Language Arts, 70,* 272–280.

Shelley Harwayne

Steven A. Stahl

Jerome C. Harste

Michael Pressley

Whole Language: Now More Than Ever

Shelley Harwayne
(Schoolteacher and Administrator, New York, New York)

As a teacher of writing, I've always believed in the power of point/ counterpoint experiences: Show the children a just-the-facts encyclopedia entry about tarantulas alongside an evocative passage about those furry spiders written by a fine non-fiction writer. Show the children a skimpy, paltry letter from camp next to a juicy, gossipy one. Show the children a tedious bed-to-bed diary entry next to some reflective, insightful journal writing. How can they not get the point? Having seen for themselves, they now have a concrete way to name what they appreciate.

In some ways, reading the artifacts in this debate felt a bit like a point/ counterpoint experience for me. Of course, I'm not at all referring to the quality or style of the writing, but to the content. Reading the materials served as a crystal-clear reminder of what I appreciate in Whole Language teaching and why I will continue to frisk substitute teachers for worksheets when they enter our school.

I read Ohanian and Shannon and was filled with images of real children, real teachers, real classrooms, and real communities. I was engaged, moved, and invested. Their thoughts resonated with the work I do.

The speeches by McKenna, Robinson, and Miller, which I read with as much care, left me feeling detached, a bit removed from reality. They reminded me of why I dropped out of the wrong doctoral program in reading many years ago.

As the director of a New York City public school, I am *not* looking for systematic investigations, improved evaluative research, valid measures of worthiness, or quantitative paradigms. Instead, I'm looking for ways to make every minute in our building count. I'm looking for that "community of learners," the right book for the right child, and ways not just to teach children *how* to read and write but ways of living that will make them *choose* to read and write. I'm looking for ways to make everyone who enters our school passionate about their own literacies. I'm looking for ways to make our schoolhouse the most beautiful, the most nourishing building in the neighborhood. I'm looking for ways to teach reading and writing that will enable children to use their literacies to improve the quality of their inner-city lives.

Several years ago, I ran for the NCTE nominating committee. My position statement read as follows:

> *Garth Boomer has said that the great theorists in English Education are the metaphor-makers, and the people who have most changed classrooms are the storytellers. I think we need to have both holding the reins of English Education. We need people who can take the most profound and complex ideas and capture them in metaphors, and we need people who can talk about classrooms, not in terms of 2.4 reading scores, instructional objectives, and management programs, but in terms of José and Shakira and young Emily.*

Many people must have appreciated the late Garth Boomer's brilliant thinking, and many people must have agreed with my stance because I won the nomination. (I even chaired the committee because I received the most votes. Lots of people must have agreed.)

If I were chair of the nominating committee today, I'd nominate Susan and Patrick as the kind of people we need to hold the reins of English Education.

Why Whole Language?
The proof is in the people.

Come with me. Meet our community. The children are short, tall, rich, poor, dark-skinned and light. They speak Maltese, Burmese, Russian, Albanian, Fon, Chinese, French, Macedonian, Croatian, Spanish, English, Portuguese, Turkish, Urdu, Dutch, Bulgarian, Italian, Korean, Hebrew, Greek, and Hungarian.

Take the tour. Look in every closet, every corridor, every classroom. There are no textbooks, no workbooks, no basal readers. There are no detailed scope and sequence charts of reading skills; no cartons of test-sophistication material; no stacks of inane, fill-in-the-blank worksheets.

Instead, there are children reading real books, real magazines, real newspapers. Even our five-year-olds are chanting jazz refrains, reciting poems, reading signs, and revisiting favorite books.

Meet the teachers. Some are very new, just beginning their careers. Several have been teaching for over twenty-five years. A few were staff developers who decided to return to classrooms. Some are graduate students. Some attended community colleges; others, Ivy League universities.

They're Black, White, Asian-American, Latino.

They're Catholic, Jewish, Protestant, atheist, and agnostic.

They're conservative; they're liberal.

They're meat-eaters; they're vegetarians.

They have loud voices and soft.

They have neat rooms and casual ones.

And yet, they ALL call themselves Whole Language teachers.

And none of these Whole Language teachers has a problem with definition. None is confused in terms of what they're expected to do. None is asking: "What is it that we're talking about?"

All are determined to engage children in authentic acts of literacy. None would ask a child to engage in a reading or writing act that would not make sense to do outside of school. None would put a book in their class library that they wouldn't be proud to display on their coffee table at home. And just as none would teach a neighbor's child to ride a bike by studying pedaling apart from steering and balancing, so too, none would separate out all the skillful acts that go into reading and writing.

Meet the parents, too. Ask them to define a Whole Language classroom. "The children read a lot," they'll say. "They're happy at school. They're allowed to talk and work with friends. There's no boring busywork. And they study big important issues. The children want to know about homelessness, about elections, about saving the planet. And they write a lot, too—even in Math class. They write at home, on vacation, at their grandmas'. They work hard, but they don't seem to mind. They love school."

School-board elections are held every three years in our district. In the previous election, 12,000 people voted. In the recent election, *52,000* people voted! The families support what we're doing. They want it to continue. Whole Language is not a trendy fad in our district.

Who wants hard data, anyhow?

I spent some time in England last summer, teaching at Oxford University. I came across a research report in the British newspaper, *The Independent*, a six-year study conducted at the University of Geneva, entitled, "Gender-related book-carrying behavior: a re-examination." The researchers carefully documented the book-carrying behaviors of 2,602 adults. Lots of data, lots of careful analysis. Their conclusion:

> *If a person is a man then he carries on the side, but if a person carries on the side then that person is not necessarily a man. The relevant question is not why men and women tend to adopt different positions, but why men's carrying behavior is uniform and stable, whereas women's behavior is more varied and changing.*

To this, I must respond simply: Who cares? So, too, when I read the ". . . Case for Caution," by McKenna, Robinson, and Miller, and I hear their plea for more systematic investigation, more empirical data, I again must respond: Who cares?

The teachers I know best are not asking for more systematic investigations. They don't need any outsiders collecting data—their rooms are *filled* with data. Yes, they have questions and concerns. That's why they engage in professional conversations with their colleagues. That's why they conduct serious teacher/researcher investigations in their own classrooms. That's why they join professional organizations and read professional journals.

They do want to read professional articles, but they don't need to see more charts, matrices, and tables. They don't need to hear more about statistical analysis, control groups, and variables. They do want to hear other teachers' stories. They want to hear about other teachers' struggles and successes. They want to know how other teachers cope with constraints of time, space, and money. They listen patiently and professionally to colleagues who have real questions about struggling children, the place of phonics, alternative assessment, national standards, curriculum-building, inquiry studies. Whole Language teachers take their own professional growth very seriously. They search *on their own* for gaps in their instructional programs. They are reflective practitioners, eager to build on what is working, willing to eliminate or revise what is not.

The teachers I know best are not asking for more systematic investigations. In fact, they're calling for fewer quantitative studies. They don't, for example, need batteries of standardized assessment tests to tell them whether their students are growing as readers, writers, and mathematicians. They don't want to administer these tests, send them off to strangers to be graded, and receive sticky labels to be placed on children's cumulative folders. The teachers I know best are *sick and tired* of bureaucratic literacy. They have more important things to do. They could put all that testing money to better use.

Not too long ago at an airport gift store, I noticed a schoolhouse music box. I couldn't resist turning the key—"School days, school days,/ dear old golden-rule days./ Reading and Writing and 'Rithmetic/ Taught to the tune of a hick'ry stick . . . ." We may not have actual hickory sticks in our schools anymore, but standardized tests are serving the same purpose. In some schools, those tests continue to dictate teaching practices, and there is as much pain and punishment attached to them as to those old hickory sticks. Even in our building, where we downplay the yearly plague of tests, we have children who, in the not-so-merry-testing month of May, complain of stomach cramps and develop asthmatic attacks from which they do not suffer at non-testing times. The teachers who have to administer these exams to children who've only been on this planet 7, 8, 9 years, wince as much as if they were witnessing a child being physically abused.

Let's have fewer systematic investigations. Let's have less hard data. Let's drop the tests, and watch teachers across the nation remember why we bother to learn to read. Let's drop the tests, and watch teachers across the nation drop the flash cards and skill-and-drill-sheets and meaningless questions at the ends of chapters. Let's stop labelling kids, and start trusting teachers.

When parents of prospective students visit our school, they ask about our reading scores. I'm quick to remind new parents that those scores are an incredibly tiny, almost insignificant piece of the literacy puzzle. Our students happen to do well on those trivial little passages with words deleted. A computer print-out informs me that "80% of our children read at or above grade level." Is that the kind of hard data some people are looking for? Our scores are unfortunately published in *The New York Times*, in rank-order with other schools' scores. That's when I send the families of my students a letter explaining that reading scores have very little to do with reading. In part, my letter reads as follows:

Ranking high in *The New York Times* list does not guarantee that students see reading as a lifelong pleasure. Those scores do not guarantee that those children long to hang out in bookstores and libraries, sneak books into their beds at night to read by flashlight, or ask for books to be tucked into their camp trunks and vacation suitcases. Those scores do not guarantee that in the future those students will feel comfortable reading aloud in front of their colleagues, their congregations, or their tenants' associations. Those scores do not guarantee that those children will make use of their library cards, belong to book clubs, or read the daily newspaper. Those scores are a very tiny piece of the literacy puzzle.

Whole Language is not a passing fancy.

McKenna, Robinson, and Miller argue that careful validation is the only road to true and lasting change. They suggest that the Whole Language "fad" will disappear without empirical evidence documenting its effectiveness.

I would argue that classroom teachers, the people who make a world of difference in our schoolhouses, will never let the Whole Language movement disappear, and they couldn't care less about empirical evidence. They know that *all* children learn language in whole ways, whether or not the school district encourages Whole Language teaching and learning. They know that *every* writer writes with an individualized process, whether or not the school district encourages the use of the process approach. Those beliefs are non-negotiable, now and forever.

Whole Language teachers will also not let Whole Language disappear because they have too much evidence that says it is working. Whole Language teachers collect many kinds of convincing evidence every day in their Whole Language classrooms that children are growing as language users. Teachers eavesdrop on rich conversations about texts and drafts in progress. (Visitors to Whole Language classrooms marvel at the high quality of student talk). The teachers also observe that children in Whole Language classrooms use language in lots of social ways, both orally and in print. Whole Language classrooms allow for many more social interactions than do the silent, obedient classrooms, controlled by workbook assignments and questions at the end of textbook chapters. (Visitors often comment about how kind and caring the children are. "Don't you have discipline problems here?" they ask). Whole Language teachers also find important evidence in the bulging portfolios that their students compile as they become, in fact, self-evaluators.

Whole Language teachers also know that their views on teaching and learning are on solid ground when they see parents turn out in droves to support them in school-board elections; when state evaluation guidelines are moving towards more holistic assessment; when children save their quarters to buy book-club selections, make frequent visits to public libraries, and, yes, even score high on those mandated standardized reading tests. Children in Whole Language classrooms learn to read; more importantly, they choose to read.

At the risk of sounding touchy-feely—not an acceptable posture in New York City public schools—Whole Language teachers know that Whole Language is effective because their students love school. When the recent asbestos scare delayed the opening of school this semester our students were *not* celebrating in the streets! They were deep-down sad and disappointed that they could not return to those beautiful classrooms, where they are invited to take part in authentic literacy acts which offer real-world pay-off. (An interesting bit of hard data would be a look at the attendance stats of students in Whole Language classrooms compared with those who are not.)

Above all, Whole Language teachers will not let Whole Language fade because this grass-roots movement has enriched and empowered their own professional lives. Teachers are thinking for themselves, no longer relying on red-ink margin scripts to tell them what to say to the children in their care.

For seven years I served as Co-director of the Teachers College Writing Project, a city-wide staff development effort, with university consultants out in the field helping hundreds of teachers throughout New York apply Whole Language to their reading/writing classrooms. Perhaps the most important lesson I learned is that effective curriculum change begins when teachers reflect on themselves as learners. Each year, thousands of Whole Language teachers take part in summer writing institutes and then continue their writing at weekly support groups during the school year. Each year thousands of Whole Language teachers take part in adult reading circles, pulling together to read best-selling novels, poetry anthologies, and professional texts.

These teachers' lives will never be the same, again. They've been touched deeply. They care—truly care—about reading and writing. After having engaged in their own powerful literacy movement, they become determined to offer these same experiences to their students. A teacher who has written a powerful memoir recalling her own foster childhood is not about to teach isolated writing skills to her students! A teacher who has cried with her colleagues over Toni Morrison's *Beloved* is not about to ask children to fill in the blanks on a workbook page!

Whole Language is not the flavor of the month—it is not a passing fancy. Teachers don't casually choose to "do Whole Language" come September, the way that children shop for new, trendy school clothes. Whole Language cannot be tried on like bell-bottoms or platform shoes. Teachers are not looking for the latest way to be cool.

Whole Language doesn't suddenly appear in a building because someone has ordered dozens of journals and shelves of children's literature. Whole Language is not just the blossoms; it's also the roots. Whole

119

Language teachers ground their teaching in philosophical and theoretical beliefs about children and teaching and learning and schools.

Whole Language is not easy to bring in, and it won't be easy to take out. Whole Language will not be cleared from school houses the way chalk dust is pounded out of erasers on the brick wall of the school building. Whole Language will not go up in a cloud of dust because the teachers simply won't let it.

No hodge-podge, please!

We do not need a definition of Whole Language. Perhaps what we need is a definition of eclecticism.

When I interview prospective teachers, I always ask them how they teach reading. If a teacher says, "I use what works, use whatever works," I quickly show them to the door.

Workbooks work. Xerographed activity sheets work. Trivial questions at the end of chapters work. Story-starters work. They're all great behavior-management tools (weapons!). They all keep children at their seats, silent, and busy.

Not everything that works is good. Children who become hooked on phonics get a deceptive picture of what reading is. Children who read watered-down texts get used to them. Poor quality texts become the given. Children who must answer endless, inane questions after reading, get a dangerous view of response to reading.

If "eclectic" means using phonics kits, flash cards, and laminated fill-in-the-blank passages, alongside a shelf of library books, I'm not interested. Loving to read is a high priority in our school building. We can't risk mixed messages. We can't afford to allow even one child to get turned off. From the very first day of school, all students need to understand what it means to read.

If, on the other hand, eclectic means pulling alongside a child, employing lots of ways to discover the student's strengths and weaknesses, having a wide range of high quality texts and genres, offering a multitude of reading strategies, and orchestrating flexible social groupings for reading response, then I'm all for it.

If you were to visit our school, you *would* see teachers pointing out phonic elements, highlighting spelling patterns, marvelling at new vocabulary, but they are *not* being eclectic. They're doing all these worthwhile acts in the name of Whole Language. Nothing is isolated or out of context. Nothing requires pages and pages of workbook reinforcement. Nothing is attached to artificial texts. None of these discrete acts is done in order to prepare children to read. Instead, the students are reading and rereading high-quality texts first, and then, based on the needs of individuals and small groups of students, a thoughtful teacher is pointing out a few fascinating reading/writing concepts.

When I served as Co-director of the Teachers College Writing Project, we asked teachers who were just beginning to study the writing process approach with us, not to be eclectic. We knew we wouldn't be able to help them turn their classrooms into reading/writing workshops if they were combining the process approach with other approaches. "Please don't invite children to choose their own topics during the writing workshop and assign story-starters for homework," we asked. We knew we wouldn't be able to help them turn their classrooms into reading/writing workshops if they were making major alterations on the approach. "Please don't eliminate conferring, red-mark early drafts, or insist on perfect spelling in rough drafts," we asked. "Later on," we suggested, "there will be time to invent and alter methods to reflect your individual personality and needs."

Those kinds of changes are very different from becoming an eclectic teacher of writing. First, the teachers needed to understand the theory behind the process approach, then they could make informed decisions about altering and inventing methods. They could filter out teaching methods that worked against what they understood to be good for young writers.

Teachers who do "a little of this, a little of that," really don't make changes in their teaching. Teachers who twist, squeeze, and stretch new ideas to fit their usual way of teaching, really don't make changes in their teaching. Teachers who visit Whole Language classrooms, and lift a few "cute ideas," really don't make changes in their classrooms.

Cute is not a criterion for Whole Language teachers. Just as you can't be a little bit pregnant, you can't be a little bit Whole Language. My col-

121

league, Joan Backer, suggests that those surface changes alone merely result in "frontal teaching on a rug." Some of us know teachers who are "a little of this, a little of that," right now. Perhaps they are teachers who are in transition, moving towards Whole Language teaching. But, please don't judge what is appropriate or acceptable in a Whole Language classroom by teachers who are just getting started on their journey. Teachers well on their way to fostering a Whole Language environment are *not* teaching with a hodge-podge of techniques. All roads don't lead to Rome when we're talking about literacy.

Whole Language: Rigor in Design, not in Definition

I once heard a teacher voice concern that a visitor thought her Whole Language classroom looked like a birthday party, all year long. My guess is that the visitor didn't have the eyes to see. Perhaps the visitor was so overwhelmed by the beauty of the setting and so unaccustomed to all those joyful social interactions and moments of celebration, that she didn't notice how hard the teacher and the students were working. Whole Language classrooms are scenes of scholarship.

Yes, we need rigor in Whole Language, but not in its definition as the debaters suggest. Rigor belongs, rather, in the life of a classroom and a school. In rigorous Whole Language schools, students, teachers, parents, administrators, members of the community, and support staff work together and they work hard. All members of the school community take their school work seriously.

In Whole Language schools, teachers do teach. When teachers decide to teach and learn alongside their students, it doesn't mean that they become silent or whisper with passive voices. When teachers begin to take their cues from their students, it doesn't imply a laissez-faire classroom. Whole Language teachers are rigorous *inside* their classrooms. They're concerned about not wasting time. They fight interruptions, pull-outs, and the distracting barrage of special events. They have too much regularly scheduled real work to do. Students, too, hardly look up when visitors enter. They, too, have made a commitment to the important work at hand.

Whole Language teachers are also rigorous *outside* their classrooms. They don't "do" Whole Language: They study Whole Language. They take adult learning as seriously as they take children's learning. And, yes, they even pay attention to other instructional perspectives. Their construction of professional knowledge *does* include consideration of research produced by others, even by people with whom they disagree.

Whole Language teachers' day-to-day lives keep them on their toes. They respond to student teachers who sometimes come with bottom-up teaching methodologies. They converse with special-needs teachers who sometimes advocate alternative skills-based techniques. They spend time with new parents who ask, "Where are the workbooks and readers?" or who wonder about purchasing at-home phonics kits. They sort through their daily mail with a critical eye, sifting out inauthentic teaching materials, materials that sometimes are unfortunately mislabeled and misrepresented as Whole Language. Finally, they eagerly read cautionary caveats about Whole Language and transcripts of national debates. They read them, share them, and—with all due respect—they shred them to bits at staff meetings.

Is Whole Language "The Real Thing"? Advertisements and Research in the Debate on Whole Language

Steven A. Stahl
University of Georgia

How I Got Here

My general response to most anything is skepticism. When someone makes an assertion, my response is, "Can you prove it? Where's the evidence?" So, when people were talking about all of the research supporting Whole Language, my response was to ask whether the research base could support the assertions that were being made.

Prior to 1986, I was interested, primarily, in how word meanings affect comprehension. I had conducted a meta-analysis of the effects of vocabulary instruction on reading comprehension, so I was familiar with approaches to synthesizing research literature. I had an interest in beginning reading, largely from my studies with Jeanne Chall, but I had not conducted any research in that area.

In this context, I read a paper by Hans Grundin (1985), a Whole Language advocate, criticizing *Becoming a Nation of Readers* (Anderson, Hiebert, Wilkinson, & Scott, 1985), especially their finding that although Whole Language seemed to be effective in New Zealand and Australia, its effects in the United States were indifferent. Anderson et al. based their conclusion on the U.S.O.E. First Grade studies (Bond & Dykstra, 1967), which found the Language Experience approach generally to be no more effective than currently used basal reading programs. Grundin went back to the U.S.O.E. studies, re-analyzed them, and purported to find that, in fact, what he calls the "precursors to Whole Language" were the most effective of those approaches tested.

It was not the finding that rankled me, although it did surprise me since I was familiar with the original Bond and Dykstra (1967) studies. It was the way that Grundin did his re-analysis. He took each site and ranked the effectiveness of each approach at each site, and then he took a "mean ranking" for each approach. From my perspective after having written a meta-analysis (though I was not then, and am not now, an expert on meta-analysis), this seemed like a strange way of doing things. In the data tables of Bond and Dykstra (1967), Grundin had both order and magnitude information for each site. His approach deliberately ignored the magnitude information.

An example might clear things up: Let's say that at one site, students in the Language Experience approach had an adjusted score of 53, those in a synthetic phonics approach had a score of 52, and those in a basal program had an adjusted score of 50. At another site, students in a synthetic phonics approach had a mean score of 60, those in a Language Experience approach had a mean score of 51, and those in a basal approach had a mean score of 50. (This is very simplified because all sites had mixtures of different experimental approaches.) In Grundin's analysis, the LEA would have a "mean rank" of 1.5 for these two sites, the same as the synthetic phonics approach. Of course, the LEA would have a mean (assuming equal numbers of students at both sites) of 52, and the synthetic phonics approach would have a mean score of 56. The effect of the Language Experience approach might not be significantly different from that of the basal reading program, although that of the synthetic phonics program might be significant. The conclusion of Dykstra (1984) was, indeed, that systematic attention to decoding, regardless of method, in the first-grade year, generally led to greater reading achievement. This was not the only finding of the Bond and Dykstra (1967) study (they also found individual and class differences which suggest that the power of the teacher might be as important as method), but it is one that has been often replicated (Adams, 1990; Chall, 1983; Williams, 1985).

Grundin's approach was not a conventional way of putting together information from different studies, but he had figured out a way of putting those numbers together to produce the results that he desired. I was offended by what seemed to be an attempt to "cook" the data.

Being the skeptic that I am, I tried to do this analysis the right way. The result was the Stahl and Miller (1989) meta-analysis of Whole Language and Language Experience approach research in kindergarten and first grade. In that study, we did a conventional meta-analysis of the Bond and Dykstra (1967) studies, as well as other comparative studies, essentially replicating Dykstra's (1984) and Anderson's et al. (1985) conclusions. We found, as McKenna, Robinson, and Miller summarize, the following:

1. Overall, Whole Language and Language Experience approaches did not produce significantly higher achievement than conventional basal reading approaches.

2. Whole Language approaches seemed to be more effective than conventional approaches in kindergarten, but not in first grade.

3. Whole Language and Language Experience approaches seemed to have greater effects on measures of word recognition than on comprehension.

4. The effects for Whole Language were lower in studies of higher quality and more recent studies, suggesting that the more recent Whole Language approaches were not so effective as the earlier Language Experience approaches.

5. These effects were found on both standardized and "naturalistic" measures.

6. We were unable to find a study in which Whole Language or Language Experience approaches were more effective than a basal reading program in populations described as "disadvantaged," "lower SES," etc.

Is Whole Language a "Research-based" Approach?

When I talk to teachers about Whole Language, they seem to be under the impression that it is well-supported by research. After our review, we concluded to the contrary that the research comparing Whole Language approaches to other approaches is meager, and that existing research on Whole Language does not show that Whole Language approaches (or the earlier Language Experience approaches) produce any better achievement than did conventional basal reading approaches, and they may produce worse results.

Grundin's (1985) paper seems to be a perfect example of the type of science that Shannon prefers. It is pragmatic, in that he found the "right" results, even if he had to do some unusual things with the data. This seems to be a perversion of science and of research in general. Even though we all have prejudices, our allegiance to a set of rules that govern scientific inquiry forces us often to reject those prejudices and conclude that we were wrong.

Knowledge progresses when these prejudices collide. Researcher A finds one thing. Researcher B points out a defect in the design, remedies that defect, and finds something else. Researcher A finds a problem in B's design, etc. until both come up with a finding that seems to be robust. Then, when both Researcher A and B are complacent, along comes Researcher C . . . .

When we did the Stahl and Miller meta-analysis, what we had hoped for was that other researchers would come along and try to prove our conclusions to be wrong, to prove that Whole Language really was a more effective approach to getting students to become better readers. If they did prove us wrong, that was fine with us, because we would have moved the field along. If they didn't, well, that was also fine. We figured, naively, that the weight of research, along with teachers' experiences, would meld Whole Language into existing practice, and education would move forward, as it always has done, through assimilating and accommodating new ideas.

Instead, what we (Stahl, McKenna, & Pagnucco, in press) seem to be finding is that researchers who are looking at Whole Language are largely ignoring the questions we raised. Of the 37 comparative studies that we have looked at as of this writing, only 13 used any measure of reading achievement at all. (Incidentally, only two of those 13 found significant effects in favor of Whole Language, whereas 11 found no significant difference between the methods, compared two at a time.) In contrast, 16 used affective measures (attitude toward reading, orientation toward reading, self-esteem). In the qualitative studies, our impression is also that relatively little reading growth is reported. For example, Five (1991) uses writing heavily to demonstrate growth in the students she has worked with.

This seems to represent a shifting of goals, from achievement to attitude. I have heard teachers say that they want their students to *want* to read, but they are less concerned with how well the students read. This desire is mirrored in the students that they teach. In one of our studies (Stahl, Suttles, & Pagnucco, 1991), we found that students in the traditional classes were very much aware of who the better readers are, but those in the Whole Language groups often had little agreement about who the good readers in their classes were. Whole Language instruction also does not appear to have the effects on attitude that are claimed, either. Of the 16 studies that looked at some affective aspects of reading, only two found significant differences in favor of Whole Language, one found significant differences in favor of the traditional class, and one study found differences in favor of a treated control, which used neither approach. The remaining 13 studies found no difference between the two approaches, similar to our earlier findings (Stahl & Miller, 1989).

Coke Ads and Consumer Reports

If the purpose of research is to demonstrate what you already know is right, then you can never find anything new. From the "pragmatic" view taken by Shannon, then one should simply ignore anything that does not conform with what you were trying to prove. This could be other research studies, or it could be data from classrooms that are being studied.

For example, as McKenna, Robinson, and Miller point out, Stephens (1991) ignored the Stahl and Miller review in her review of research, as well as other studies reviewed by Stahl and Miller in which Whole Language approaches produced results that were not favorable for Whole

Language. This is bothersome, for a good scholar would attempt to make sense of all of the data, not merely the data favorable to one side. If she had castigated our review, for one reason or another, I would have accepted it as part of the process of scholarship, and I would assume that better studies would come about from her criticism. To ignore our study and the others, however, distorts the scholarly record, just as Grundin (1985) distorted the findings from the Bond and Dykstra (1967) study. This is not due only to a decision not to include comparative studies like ours, for Stephens does include Ribowsky's (1985) study. Instead, Stephens chose to include only those studies that she deemed favorable to Whole Language.

That Shannon defends the deliberate disregard of our study and others is one of the more troubling parts of his paper. If we, as a scholarly community, are to have credibility in the intellectual world at large among teachers and other consumers of educational research, we need to be seen as presenting the whole picture. We can be partisan; indeed, how can we be otherwise? But we need to be seen as fair. When one watches a Coke ad on television, we expect to see happy people drinking Coke. We do not expect to see people spitting the stuff out. We do not expect to see people who prefer Pepsi. We know that Coke is selling its product and that it wants us to look at that product favorably. Teachers and others look to researchers, however, as customers look to *Consumer Reports*; they expect us to evaluate instructional ideas as fairly as we can and report our findings as objectively as we can. Although I often disagree with *Consumer Reports* about products that I know about, and find that the things they value are not as important to me as other things, I do know that they are, as much as possible, attempting to evaluate every product they can find on every criterion that they think is relevant.

When you deny the existence of unfavorable research, you tend to leave the impression that all scholars support Whole Language, that Whole Language has strong research support. This impression is, however, misleading. I think we ought to lay the whole case out and trust teachers to evaluate how strong the support is.

What Makes a Case Study an Ad and What Makes It Research?

This deliberate ignoring of information not favorable to one's cause is not limited to ignoring research studies. When one looks at case-study research, such as the research listed by Shannon, the ignoring of unfavorable information can be fatal to the validity of the study. In case-study research, the researcher typically looks at a few cases, the assumption being that close examination of a single case or a few cases can illuminate others. The choice of cases is extremely important. If one chooses only success stories, one can leave the reader with an inflated view of how well a program works. Choosing only success stories is akin to Coke choosing only happy Coke drinkers for its ads. This may be fine for advertising, but it is not research.

The contrast between two studies on Shannon's list should clarify this point. Mills, O'Keefe, and Stephens (1992) described the classroom of Timothy O'Keefe, a first-grade teacher who integrated phonics instruction into his Whole Language classroom. The bulk of the book is devoted to descriptions of a typical day and activities that highlight the role of grapho-phonemic information during literacy activities. The book also includes three case studies, illustrating how three students developed in their command of sound/symbol relationships. These cases were apparently chosen retrospectively, to represent success stories in O'Keefe's class, and to illustrate how students can grow in their phonics knowledge as a result of experiences in a Whole Language classroom.

In contrast, Wells and Chang-Wells (1992) chose three case-study students at the beginning of their collaborative work and followed them through the year in a Whole Language classroom. By choosing their case-study subjects *before* the study began, we have greater assurance that these students are representative of the class as a whole. We also know that the researchers did not choose only those subjects who would prove their point.

I do not mean to criticize Mills, O'Keefe, and Stephens (1992), for they seem to have intended their book not to be research. Instead, their book succeeds well as a way to mediate between what some people have taken to be conflicting goals, but which, in fact, are not: the teaching of phonics and the fostering of the purposefully literate environment of a

Whole Language classroom. Their case studies are intended as advertisements for the success of the program, like the happy Coke drinkers. Stephens (1991) did not include this work (then in progress) in her own review of research. It is Shannon who sees this book as research, not its co-author.

In a similar vein, I see Atwell's (1987) book as a description of how she managed her successful classroom, providing illustrative cases to help teachers envision how such a classroom might work. As such, it works well. If I were teaching seventh- or eighth-grade language arts, I would sit down for a long time with this book. There is much to be learned from it, but it is also not research. It is an advertisement.

Because I do not see these works (and others) as research does not mean that I do not value them. I learned from what worked for other teachers. I would try ideas out, keeping some, not keeping others, as I developed as a teacher. Books such as Mills's et al. and Atwell's allow teachers to try things out, to see how they fit in their classroom. As long as it is kept on that level—teacher-to-teacher—it is fine, but when the stakes get higher, as in the pressures to adopt Whole Language as a district-wide (as in Gwinnett County, Georgia) or state-wide (California) or province-wide (throughout Canada) philosophy, then using these case studies as evidence becomes truly dangerous. I don't consult *Consumer Reports* when I am buying inexpensive items, like a soft drink, but I would consult that periodical when buying an expensive item, such as a car or a dishwasher. Systemwide adoption of a methodology has consequences for a great many students. Major changes should be based on the best research evidence available.

What Would You Say to Keith's Parents?

Case studies are difficult to evaluate. Case studies show that students are making progress, but nearly all students make progress during a school year in all settings, unless you lock them up in a closet. From nothing more than a case study, you cannot know whether the same student would have made more or less progress in different settings. The writing samples that Atwell presents are wonderful, but would these talented writers also have written as well in more traditional creative writing classes? She reports that the low-achieving students "catch fire with enthusiasms" (p. 46), but do they write better than similar students in conventional English classes? We don't know.

As a more troubling example, Ohanian cites the cases of two students, Bob and Keith, as examples of success and failure. Bob was a failure because Ohanian "didn't ask the right questions." His pain is "[her] pain forever." McKenna, Robinson, and Miller ask how many Bobs were in her classes, how many students she failed to reach. This is an important question, because a prospective Whole Language teacher needs to know whether one gets fewer failures teaching like Ohanian than with the old method. By ignoring the failures and trumpeting the successes, we don't know.

But a more important question is what Ohanian did with Bob that he didn't respond to. When it was clear that she wasn't reaching him with her approach, did Ohanian try any other approaches? It seems that when he failed to learn to read, she blamed him for his own failure, ascribing it to his belief in the "otherness" of reading. If he could do it himself, without an "other," however, wouldn't he have done it by now? As a teacher of reading, when I fail to help a child, I keep trying something else until I find something that works. My failures are my own because I couldn't find the right approach, the right book, the right something.

Similarly, did Ohanian try anything else with Keith? Keith seems to be presented as a success. According to Ohanian:

> . . . Keith had spent the 1½ years in my class faking his way
> through 138 National Geographics, assorted novels, and a
> complete set of World Book Encyclopedia. One day he
> started his perpetual whine that "there's nothin' to read"
> and, in frustration, I shoved the Seuss book into his hands. I
> still get goosebumps when I recall seeing a beginning
> reader emerge right there before my eyes. (See above, p. 7)

As Chairman Mao said, "Even the *longest* march begins with a single step." This step may have been a big one for Keith; nevertheless, I would certainly have a hard time justifying a student of Keith's age being unable to read nothing more advanced than *Hop on Pop* after a year and a half in my class. I can give you many more stories about students whom I have taught to read in much less time, with a combination of good skills instruction and high-quality, well-chosen books. Leaving Keith and Bob alone, to emerge as readers on their own, seems to be a risky proposition.

If they could have emerged unaided as readers, would they not have done so already? Why ought we to expect that they might do so now? Further, since it would seem clear that Keith was not emerging as a reader in Ohanian's Whole Language program, does not she have the obligation as a teacher to try other things, any things, to get him to read? In this case, there seems to be a greater allegiance to the program than to the student.

Keith's reading of *Hop on Pop* was certainly a breakthrough for him, but this vignette also illustrates the problems in evaluating Whole Language research. Certainly Keith had grown as a reader during his time with Ms. Ohanian, but did he grow as much as he needed to grow to gain literacy skills adequate to his earning a living? If, at 15, he can read *Hop on Pop*, will he be able at 16 to read a driver's license manual, or the manual for fixing a 1992 Buick? These are important questions not only for Keith but also for society. In many of the studies on Shannon's list, we see the progress of individual students, the "successes" of Whole Language. Although we are not allowed to see the failures, nor know how many there were, we also do not know whether the "success" that these students enjoyed is enough, whether these young people will be able to read and write well enough to accomplish what they want to accomplish as adults.

In all of these success stories, we do not know whether the students made a year's progress in a year's time. I am not trumpeting standardized tests, but we, as a society, do have expectations that our schools will prepare students to be able to do something productive when they finish school, that they will have enough literacy to perform increasingly technical jobs (see Resnick & Resnick, 1977), and that many will be able to go on and succeed with college curricula. These expectations necessitate accountability. I myself am not sure how to measure students' growth in literacy, but I do know that society needs assurance that school children are progressing to the point where they have adequate literacy skills to participate fully in society.

Straw People and Psychoanalysis

Throughout their two papers, Shannon and Ohanian distort the opinions of those who disagree with them, using "straw man" arguments. When they deal with real people, they impute motives and opinions to those who disagree with them. A straw-person argument—let's do be P.C. enough to include Ms. Ohanian—occurs when a clever debater builds up a position or argument that no one holds, and then tears that empty position down in order to appear victorious in the argument. Ohanian sets up a straw person when she tells about a class in which only phonics was taught, and no books were used at all. I don't know any reputable advocate of code instruction, from Adams (1990) to Chall (1983) even to Carnine, Silbert, and Kameenui (1990), who would advocate phonics only, failing to give students the opportunity to savor their skill at real reading. Nor would I expect anyone reasonably to teach *Amelia Bedelia* just to learn the silent e. (I would, however, find it reasonable to teach students silent e words before they read, to help them be able to read the story independently.)

Another straw person is Shannon's imputation that McKenna and his colleagues "assume that social reality is directed by discoverable laws, . . . assume that researchers . . . can be disinterested in the outcomes and consequences of their efforts, . . ." and so on. Then he proceeds to prove that these assumptions are wrong. The problem is that McKenna, Robinson, and Miller—according to my reading—never said any of those things. Shannon read these assumptions into their paper, but never asked them whether they believe that "social reality is directed by discoverable laws," or anything else on his list. I see no attempt by McKenna, Robinson, and Miller either in this debate or in their previous work to discover any law of behavior, only to question whether the research base of Whole Language is adequate for the assertions that are made. In short, they are being skeptics, as good researchers need to be. The straw people of Ohanian and Shannon are stuffed with assumptions about what McKenna and colleagues mean, even though they said no such thing. This goes beyond advertisement to a type of demonizing typical of a mudslinging political campaign, akin to George Bush's use of Willie Horton to brand Mike Dukakis as soft on criminals, even though Dukakis probably had nothing to do with Willie Horton at all.

I am also offended by Shannon's and Ohanian's attempt to psychoanalyze their doubters, especially since I am myself a doubter; to wit:

> *Most people question Whole Language philosophy and*
> *practice because of their own history with language-arts*
> *instruction at school. Even if they were unsuccessful in*

*learning the phonics, grammar, and content of traditional
lessons, most learned the procedural lessons of reading
and writing instruction all too well. For example, they
learned that text and teachers are the ultimate authority
concerning which knowledge is valuable and which is not
. . . . (See above, p. 82)*

I question Whole Language philosophy not because I was personally
enamored with my school education, but because I have worked with,
and observed, teachers—both traditionalists and Whole Languagers—
who can make education exciting and not stultifying, while at the same
time providing the skills and strategies needed for their students to become independent. I question Whole Language philosophy because of
Peg Ballantine and Jackie Littlefield, with whom I worked in South
Berwick, Maine, and Mrs. Teale of Camp Point, Illinois, and Sandy
Mortier of Macomb, Illinois, and a host of other teachers who can combine traditional effort with the development of reading skill and the ability to motivate students to read high-quality literature. I also question
Whole Language philosophy because I spent so many years working with
so many Keiths and Bobs, and I was able to reach them.

The Stakes of the Whole Language Debate

Shannon couches his concern for Whole Language in liberationist
language, with concern for those in our society who have been traditionally poorly served by our school systems. He feels that traditional schooling teaches and tests for middle-class values, making it difficult for
children outside of the cultural mainstream to succeed in them. I know
Patrick, and I know that he is sincere in his concerns; I share many of his
sympathies. Ironically, that is why I am concerned about the rapid growth
of the Whole Language movement, especially in schools that teach economically disadvantaged children, those placed at risk in our society by
a number of socio-economic factors.

Recall that one of our (Stahl & Miller, 1989) findings was that we
could not find a single study in which Whole Language produced higher
achievement with students classified as "disadvantaged," "lower SES,"
and so on. This was not what I expected. I did the analysis only on the
prodding of a reviewer of the paper, who felt that because Whole Lan-

135

guage and Language Experience approaches were advocated for students from non-mainstream backgrounds, that studies of these populations ought to be pulled out and looked at separately. I think that the reviewer thought we would find positive effects in these populations. I know I thought that we would find that the results here would mirror those of the larger study. I did not expect to find the neutral and negative results that we found. Now, as we work on updating the Stahl and Miller analysis (Stahl, McKenna, & Pagnucco, in press), we are finding much the same thing. We seem to be finding positive effects for Whole Language in middle-class populations, but not in lower SES populations.

Our explanation in 1989 still makes sense. Basically, we suggested that Whole Language approaches continue the same type of learning that began long before the child entered school. Children do learn to read through this "natural" approach to reading, by being read to, by practicing and approximating reading through successive attempts, and so on, but that learning is slower and less efficient. If one starts at age six-months or so, the less efficient part is not a concern, for children have more time to learn to read. For a child from a home without a lot of literacy activity, a home in which children are not read to, where there are no magnetic letters on the fridge, and no books and few magazines lying about, Whole Language approaches may, however, be too little, too late. Children from those poor households where literacy is left to the schools, are at a disadvantage in competition with middle-class children whose parents enjoyed greater leisure for literacy and may have inherited a higher view of reading and writing. (To be sure, many poor homes are wonderfully literate; see Chall, Jacobs, and Baldwin, 1990.) Adams (1990) contrasted her son, who had approximately 1,000–2,000 hours of literacy exposure before entering first grade, with other children, observed by Teale (1984), who averaged nearly no reading exposure before going to school. A child with no literacy exposure prior to schooling needs highly efficient instruction to catch up with the more fortunate child. That is what we (Stahl, Osborn, and Lehr, 1990) meant by "different" instruction for children from homes with low literacy.

Delpit (1988), an African-American educator, offered a different explanation for the difficulties of underprepared children in Whole Language classrooms. She suggested that children need to learn the *power code*, or the language used by the power elites, in order to survive in

American society. Children in the mainstream will learn that power code at home, in their interactions with parents and peers. By not teaching this power code to children who grow up outside of the mainstream, where Standard American English is used, Whole Language advocates are impeding them from succeeding within the system.

Neither Delpit nor I denigrate the heritage or language of children from minority culture groups, nor do we deny the need for multicultural education in the truest sense, i.e., for members of *all* culture groups within society. From different perspectives, we both are concerned about the inequity of leaving children from outside the mainstream to figure out what they need to know, without some direct instruction. Marginalized children need public education even more than do mainstream children. Mainstream children, if they don't establish themselves through scholarship or hard work, can always get a job from "Uncle Frank." If poor children fail to develop the reading and writing skills that they need to be productive members of mainstream society, there is generally no "Uncle Frank" to give them a job.

Shannon wants to remake society, to eliminate the system by which Xerox can eliminate thousands of jobs. I will not argue with him on that, but I cannot, as a reading professor, change Xerox. I can teach reading, and I do so in my belief that when people are empowered by the skills of literacy, they are more likely to be able to support themselves and their families.

Alternatives to Whole Language

Unlike McKenna, Robinson, and Miller, I do have an alternative to Whole Language. In a word, it is "eclecticism." This is not a patchwork eclecticism of incompatible methods, a little Whole Language in the afternoon, a little direct instruction in the morning. It is the eclecticism borne of competent teachers' striving to meet the needs of the students in their classes, using all of the methods at their disposal.

Students have different needs as readers; teachers and parents have various goals towards which we want students to develop as readers. As I argued elsewhere (Stahl, 1992a), students need to be able to use reading to learn from text, to perform tasks using directions, and for just plain enjoyment. These different purposes for reading require different sets of strategies, and different ways to attain those strategies. Achievement of these different purposes relies on a set of common processes, including decoding and basic comprehension processes.

One uses different instructional means to achieve these different goals. For example, most children require some instructional intervention to understand the conventions of written orthography. This may involve pointing out, as Tim O'Keefe did for his first-graders (Mills, O'Keefe, and Stephens, 1991), that "Kareem" and "O'Keefe" both have a double e, and mentioning that this doubling makes the /long e/ sound. It also may involve a more structured approach, such as that provided by a basal reading program or a synthetic phonics program or a compare/contrast type of program, such as that discussed by Cunningham (1991). The choice of whether to teach phonics does—and ought to—depend on teachers' knowledge of reading instruction and their knowledge of their students.

Learning to decode words is not the only goal of reading instruction, nor ought it to be the major goal of reading instruction (Stahl, 1992b). Teachers do other things in the classroom to motivate their students to enjoy reading, to comprehend better what they read, to be more strategic in using reading to learn information from text. As teachers juggle the many goals they have for their students, based on their understanding of what they want students to accomplish and what their students need in order to reach these goals, they will incorporate many different instructional methods. They might set aside time for sustained silent reading; they might set aside time for direct skills instruction; they might ask questions of their students' reading; they might provide some explicit instruction in the use of reading strategies as students work through a learning task (Duffy, in press) or provide experiences in which students collaborate to use reading and writing to accomplish specific tasks. In short, sometimes these eclectic teachers look like Whole Language teachers, and may indeed call themselves Whole Language teachers. Often, however, they do non-Whole Language things because their students need that kind of instruction.

Whole Language advocates have openly attacked eclecticism, and they usually seem to be disappointed with even partial moves toward Whole Language. For example, Newman and Church (1990) wrote:

> *Whole language isn't an add-on. It's not a frill. We can't*
> *do a little bit of Whole Language and leave everything else*

untouched. It's a radically different way of perceiving the relationships between knowledge and the knower, between compliance and responsibility, between learner and teacher, between teacher and administrator, between home and school (p. 26).

Similarly, Goodman (1989), in response to a suggestion to blend direct instruction in skills with Whole Language principles, replied:

One cannot reconcile direct instruction with natural learning. Meaningful, predictable, authentic texts are incompatible with carefully controlled vocabulary and decontextualized phonics instruction. Teachers have lived with contradictions, but they don't have to. Whole Language teachers are evolving internally consistent views that enable them to make the instructional decisions necessary to support literacy development (p. 69).

In the view of these Whole Language advocates and others, one cannot have a little Whole Language and a little of something else.

Contrary to Goodman and Newman and Church, however, more teachers are eclectic than they are purely Whole Language. Gambrell (1992) surveyed a small number of teachers in the eastern United States and found that only 4% of the teachers surveyed considered their program to be exclusively "Whole Language," and an additional 10% reported using Whole Language supplemented by basals. Only 1% reported using a children's literature-based program, and another 5% reported using children's literature supplemented by basals. Eighty percent described their reading program as a basal program, and 52% supplemented the basal with children's literature. Although this report represents a significant change from the situation in 1980, very few teachers identify themselves as purely "Whole Language"; surprisingly few teachers resonate to the dominance of the Whole Language philosophy in the professional discourse. Barry (1992), surveying Georgia teachers, found that only 2.7% of the 209 teachers she surveyed considered themselves to be "Whole Language." Pressley (in preparation) surveyed teachers characterized as outstanding and found that, although many identified with the Whole Language movement, the majority also taught phonics explicitly.

This eclecticism is the truest form of pragmatism, of finding out what works and then doing it. It is flexible, for good teachers change their instruction according to the needs of their different classes. Because of the inherent flexibility of teachers of genius, it is too complex to fit them all into a simple advertisement or slogan, but being flexible, eclectic pragmatists is what good teachers were doing before Whole Language, and it is what they will continue to do after the Shannons and the Goodmans and the McKennas and Stahls have left the scene. Our hope is with these teachers because they ignore the debates such as the one presented in this book. Teachers are more concerned with their students than with the politics of instruction. If there is to be an amalgamation between Whole Language and more traditional instruction, it will not come in the academy, for our institutions are set up as stages on which to bandy about ideas, such as we debaters and commentators have done here. Good teachers, on the other hand, respond to the needs of real children, not to abstract ideas, and they will continue to do their flexible, eclectic best to teach. The question is whether we, as researchers, shall support them in their efforts by fair evaluation and high-quality information.

References

Adams, M. J. (1990). *Beginning to read: Thinking and learning about print.* Cambridge, Massachusetts: M.I.T. Press.

Anderson, R. C., Hiebert, E. F., Wilkinson, I. A. G., & Scott, J. (1985). *Becoming a nation of readers.* Champaign, Illinois: National Academy of Education and Center for the Study of Reading.

Atwell, N. (1987). *In the middle: Writing, reading and learning with adolescents.* Portsmouth, New Hampshire: Boynton/Cook.

Barry, M.H. (1992) *A survey of reading approaches.* ERIC Document Reproduction Service, ED 346 437.

Bond, G., & Dykstra, R. (1967). The cooperative research program in first grade reading. *Reading Research Quarterly, 2,* 5–142.

Carnine, D., Silbert, J., & Kameenui, E. (1990). *Direct instruction reading* (2nd ed.). Columbus, Ohio: Charles E. Merrill.

Chall, J. S. (1983). *Learning to read: The great debate* (revised, with a new foreword ed.). New York, New York: McGraw-Hill.

Chall, J. S., Jacobs, V., & Baldwin, L. (1990). *The reading crisis.* Cambridge, Massachusetts: Harvard University Press.

Cunningham, P. M. (1991). *Phonics they use.* New York: Harper Collins.

Delpit, L. (1988). The silenced dialogue: Power and pedagogy in educating other people's children. *Harvard Educational Review, 58,* 280–298.

Duffy, G.G. (in press). Who should own the instructional model? An argument for teacher-as-entrepreneur. In S.A. Stahl and D.A. Hanes (Eds.), *Instructional models in reading.* Hillsdale, New Jersey: Erlbaum.

Dykstra, R. (1984). The effectiveness of code- and meaning-emphasis beginning reading programs. In A. J. Harris, & E. R. Sipay (Ed.), *Readings on reading instruction* (pp. 136–141). White Plains, New York: Longman.

Five, C. L. (1991). *Special voices.* Portsmouth, New Hampshire: Heinemann.

Freppon, P. A., & Dahl, K. L. (1991). Learning about phonics in a whole language classroom. *Language Arts, 68,* 190–197.

Gambrell, L. B. (1992). Elementary school literacy instruction: Changes and challenges. In M. J. Dreher, & W. H. Slater (Ed.), *Elementary school literacy: Critical issues* (pp. 227–240). Norwood, Massachusetts: Christopher-Gordon.

Goodman, K. S. (1986). *What's whole in whole language.* Portsmouth, New Hampshire: Heinemann.

Goodman, K.S. (1989). Whole language *is* whole: A response to Heymsfeld. *Educational Leadership, 46*(6), 69–70.

Grundin, H. (1985). A commission of selective readers: A critique of Becoming a Nation of Readers. *The Reading Teacher, 39,* 262–266.

Mills, H., O'Keefe, T., & Stephens, D. (1992). *Looking closely: Exploring the role of phonics in one whole language classroom.* Urbana, Illinois: National Council of Teachers of English.

Newman, J. M., & Church, S. M. (1990). Commentary: Myths of whole language. *The Reading Teacher, 44,* 20–27.

Resnick, D. P., & Resnick, L. B. (1977). The nature of literacy: An historical exploration. *Harvard Educational Review, 47,* 370–385.

Ribowsky, H. (1985). The effects of a code emphasis and a whole language emphasis upon the emergent literacy of kindergarten children (ERIC Document Reproduction Service ED 269 720).

Stahl, S. A. (1992a). Saying the "p" word: Nine guidelines for exemplary phonics instruction. *The Reading Teacher, 45,* 618–625.

Stahl, S. A. (1992b). *The state of the art of reading instruction in the USA.* Paris, France: International Institute for Educational Planning.

Stahl, S.A., McKenna, M.C., & Pagnucco, J.R. (in press). The effects of whole language instruction: An update and a reappraisal. *Educational Psychologist.*

Stahl, S. A., & Miller, P. D. (1989). Whole language and language experience approaches for beginning reading: A quantitative research synthesis. *Review of Educational Research, 59,* 87–116.

Stahl, S. A., Osborn, J., & Lehr, F. (1990). *Beginning to read: Thinking and learning about print — a summary.* Champaign, Illinois: Center for the Study of Reading.

Stahl, S. A., Suttles, C. W., & Pagnucco, J. R. (1991, April). *The effects of traditional and process literacy instruction on first graders' reading and writing achievement and orientation toward reading.* Paper presented at annual meeting, American Educational Research Association, San Francisco, California.

Stephens, D. (1991). *Research on Whole Language.* Katonah, New York: Richard C. Owen.

Teale, W. H. (1984). Reading to young children: Its significance for literacy development. In H. Goelman, A. Oberg, F. Smith. *Awakening to literacy* (pp. 110–121). Portsmouth, New Hampshire: Heinemann.

Wells, C. G., & Chang-Wells, G. L. (1992). *Constructing knowledge together: Classrooms as centers for inquiry and learning.* Portsmouth, New Hampshire: Heinemann.

Williams, J. P. (1985). The case for explicit decoding instruction. In J. Osborn, P. T. Wilson, & R. C. Anderson (Ed.), *Reading education: Foundations for a literate America* (pp. 205–214). Lexington, Massachusetts: Lexington Books.

New Questions, Different Inquiries

Jerome C. Harste
Indiana University

Questions and questioning have always been associated with education. Susan Langer (1972) put her finger on it, however. Using the example of "Who made the world?" she argued that those who answer, no
matter how diverse the answers ("God," "Nobody"), still share a common
world view. Persons who reject the question, who argue that it is the
wrong one to ask, are harbingers of a new paradigm. Every age has its
questions. To settle on the question is to have the solution in hand. Even
Kuhn (1975) argued that "normal science" is just a paint-by-number af-
fair.

This debate over Whole Language is an argument over what questions to ask. The issue is not settled, for no research *solution* is self-evi-
dent. Different thought collectives ask different questions and have
different verification procedures. At issue is not only Whole Language
but also what constitutes instructional research.

McKenna, Robinson, and Miller believe that research should lend
credence to, and perhaps prove, the superiority of an eclectic position.
Which is better: Method A, Method B, or a combination of the two? Be-

cause they ask the same old question, they apply the same old criteria. Ohanian and Shannon reply, "Nonsense!"

Sometimes it is hard to gain a perspective on an issue when one has one's hand in the cookie jar, and I freely acknowledge that my hand is. Nonetheless, my reading of what has happened in educational research is that in the '70s we learned the value of grounded theory; in the '80s, that all research is political; and in the '90s, that morality and ethics are central to the research process.

Not surprisingly, these shifts parallel shifts in Whole Language over time. For example, over my professional lifetime, research has changed its stance in education. As a graduate student, I—like McKenna, Robinson, and Miller—thought that research was neutral and could be used to settle debates. Sociolinguistics helped me see that "everything is relative," that is, everything is situated in a context. The role of the researcher was to uncover the theory of meaning that was operating in a group.

Critical theorists like Shannon and others helped me see that "everything is political" and that neither researchers nor research methodologies are innocent. Again my notions of research changed. I came to see the role of the researcher as describing the theory of meaning that was in place and then unpacking what happens—both good and bad—when that theory operates.

I still really like research. Education, for me, is synonymous with inquiry. But, feminists and postmodernists have changed my views on what research can be expected to do. I now think that instead of proving the superiority of one method over another, *all research can do is help a learner or a community of learners interrogate their values*, but this is enough to make research valuable.

Changing one's notions of educational research isn't easy. Back in the early days of Whole Language, I must admit that I was attempting to operationalize my theories of language and language learning in classrooms for purposes of demonstrating the superiority of my own ideas. I don't see my role this way anymore. Research can't provide truth. It may lend credence to truth over the long haul, but that's another matter, for it involves 'time' in a geological sense without the stability of rocks as the medium of study. What research can do is help learners put an edge to their learning.

Like Shannon, I think education is about change. Educational researchers have more of a responsibility than just to describe what happens. *I see curriculum research as an attempt to dramatize theory in the classroom and unpack what happens for purposes of interrogating and clarifying one's values.* This is why taking a theoretical stance is important. It anchors difference and hence learning. Because there is no anchor in eclecticism, the likelihood of an eclectic program of research making a difference is nil. The only research criterion for an eclectic program is "What works?" Gas chambers work. So do skill-and-drill bootcamps.

The real issue concerns the kind of world you envision and the kind of person you want to be. McKenna, Robinson, and Miller have as much a philosophical position as do Ohanian, Shannon, and other Whole Language advocates. Their list of characteristics of good reading instruction makes this clear. Importantly, their list is predictable, given their world view of teaching and research. They have yet to discover that effective learners take stances, and that eclecticism is a disease curable by taking a position.

Does this mean that I approve of everything going on in Whole Language? The answer is no, though I do firmly believe that Whole Language is the best thing that has happened in education for a long time. Although one could charge me with imperialism, here is just a partial list of what I see as achievements since Whole Language came on the scene:

Language

- Meaning is now accepted as the core of language.
- We have a new and expanded definition of literacy as well as a new understanding of how the reading and writing process works.
- We have added tons of new words to our professional vocabularies (*miscue, kidwatching, authentic,* etc.) which are being used even by people who don't believe the same things we do. (For those of us who think language is important as it reflects concepts and beliefs, this is not so trivial a matter as those who call it "jargon" would have us believe.)

Learning

- We've learned how to make learning in school fun.
- We have a new respect for children and childhood.
- We have new, important insights into language learning (functionality, text in context, etc.).
- We have a new understanding of the role that language plays in learning (voice, choice, etc.).
- We have a new, expanded understanding of cognition (making connections, storying) and new disrespect for standardized testing.

Curriculum

- We see new possibilities for the language arts curriculum (i.e., expanding communication potential).
- We have a new respect for children's literature.
- We've learned how to inspire writers rather than train spellers.
- We've learned to think about curriculum in terms of uninterrupted engagements as well as in terms of strategy instruction.
- We've come to see knowledge and knowing differently (social, collaborative).
- We've found a forum within which we can talk to like-minded educators in other disciplines.
- We have moved inquiry to the heart of education.

Schooling

- We've provided a solution to the teacher-burnout problem. (More teachers and children want to come to school now than before.)
- We've affected how the publishing industry works. (We've built up Heinemann and, to quote Ken Goodman (1992), "driven basal publishers to see their psychiatrists.")
- Parents are being invited to collaborate in education for the first time.
- We've altered the hierarchical nature of our profession. (Importantly, the new, exciting research questions are coming from classrooms, and teachers, for the first time, are beginning to write their own identities.)

- We've opened the Whole Language Umbrella, and its presence has affected how professional associations conduct business. (Most annual programs now look like WLU put them together.)
- We've begun seriously to affect legislative policy in states like Michigan and Kentucky as well as all of the provinces of Canada.
- We've become more self-conscious about whom education empowers.

As this list suggests—and McKenna, Robinson, and Miller lament—Whole Language is a positivist's nightmare. It is new philosophy and new methods all in one. Shannon hit the nail on the head when he said that "Whole Language has not sat still long enough for researchers to calibrate their instruments."

I suspect it will not sit still in the future, either. I think that the agenda ahead includes at least the following:

a. Whole Language will help educators understand that diversity, not consensus, puts an edge on learning. (This single statement, if understood and taken seriously, could reform the whole of education.)

b. We shall move from Whole Language to Whole Literacy by taking what we know about the role of language in learning and applying it across the curriculum.

c. We shall truly operationalize an inquiry curriculum for ourselves and our children. Said differently, my prediction for McKenna and Company is not only that research in Whole Language is going to get worse before it gets better, but that there is no going home again.

So, where does this leave us? Are there no standards for curriculum research?

I repeat: It depends on your paradigm. Because I am as interested in high-quality research as the next person, below is a working set of standards based on Whole Language insights into the role that language plays in learning and that inquiry plays in education. While some may argue that these standards exist in earlier models of inquiry, too, and that all researchers need do is demonstrate that they have been true to the standards of research for the paradigm they have selected, I find the first argument reductionistic and the second anti-intellectual.

Despite progress already made, I still see the development of a research methodology that truly fits the intent of our discipline as one of the great unfinished agenda items in our profession (Harste, 1992). Given that I believe the only thing that research can do is help a learner or a community of learners interrogate their values, the arguments that follow each standard demonstrate in what ways these new standards obligate curriculum inquirers in new, more responsible ways.

Standard 1. Openness: "Does the research design allow us to learn from surprises?"

Inquiry to be inquiry must be open. This means that the results are unknown. Too often, researchers play a game of "discovery learning" and delude themselves into believing that this is open inquiry.

Openness means that methodology must be able to change to reflect growing understandings of what is being studied. As inquirers come to question their assumptions and values, what wasn't data all of a sudden becomes data, and what was data is no longer of primary interest.

Openness means that there can be no hidden agendas, no prioritizing of knowledge or voice, no attempting to speak for others, no excluding participants from certain parts of the process, no creation—other than self-creation—of identity.

Standard 2. Vulnerability: "Can all participants both confront and support each other in outgrowing themselves?"

The research agenda for the '90s is to make researchers and methodologies speak. Inherent in any study is a set of assumptions and beliefs about how the world works. Research cannot give us truth, cannot tell us what to teach or how best to learn, and cannot—despite its widespread use—tell us a person's developmental level.

Too often in research, the assumptions of the researcher are so embedded in the methodology that they go unexamined. "Subjects" or "informants" are more vulnerable than is the researcher. Confounding the issue is the institutionalization of research method. Assumptions inherent in the methodology become canons that are beyond examination.

Confounding this standard is the difference in power relations in most university-sponsored research settings. Notice how often educational researchers talk of "them" rather than saying "we!"

In collaborative research, not only can we fellow collaborators snap and bite at each other but also one often ends up arguing with oneself . . . and losing the argument! Because the agenda is to interrogate and come to understand underlying values for purposes of improving instruction, the assumptions and beliefs of all participants are the focus of attention. It is, then, an attitude of inquiry, rather than a particular set of methods, that drives the research processes.

All participants in inquiry need to assume that at least one tenet in their existing theories of the world is wrong and that it is their role to uncover which one it is. This is why doubt, rather than certainty, tensions rather than standard deviation, anomaly rather than central tendencies, are key aspects of the procedures that collaborative researchers follow. Put in terms of learning theory, learners have more to learn by focusing on surprises than they have to learn by focusing on predictions based on what they already know.

Standard 3. Reflexivity: "Will the research help us examine what readings we are guilty of?"

"Today," Andy Manning (1992) explained, "inquiry begins with data but is focused on interrogating one's own personal theory of the world." In the past, research began with someone else's Theory (thus the capital T). From the postulates of this Theory a hypothesis was formulated. Methodology was the empirical testing of that hypothesis. The procedures were quite simple: First the researcher gathered data, and then he or she analyzed the data. On the basis of the analysis, the hypothesis was either confirmed or rejected. There were lots of rules in doing experimental research, often requiring years and years of training. But, there were payoffs too. If you followed the rules, the institution of research itself determined the significance of your research and rewarded you.

Assumptions, by their very nature, are invisible, often embedded in the languages and cultures in which we are born. To this end, reflexivity involves the active use of oneself and others as vehicles for outgrowing oneself. Reflexivity is different from reflection. It is much more active. It entails the interrogation of why we use the very constructs we do to make sense of our world.

Why, for example, do Whole Language researchers use meaning as a frame from which to view the reading process? By using this construct, what other readings are made impossible? What are the historical, cultural, and political roots of this construct? Britzman (1992) said it more cleverly, "Each of us must learn to ask, 'What readings am I guilty of?'"

The focus of new research is reflexivity rather than proof. Reflexivity acknowledges that the key to better research is the researcher—not a better test or a better analytical framework or a better statistical measure.

Unless underlying assumptions and beliefs change, nothing different is likely to happen in classrooms. One can, after all, track errors in reading whether one is using a reading inventory or giving a miscue analysis. Unless underlying assumptions and beliefs change, nothing different is likely to happen, despite our use, now, of portfolios in place of standardized tests. A case in point is that, now, you can even buy "standardized portfolios." To change education, one must change the grey matter between the right and left ear. This is reflexivity. There is no other way.

Standard 4. Connectedness: "Does the research begin needed, new conversations in education?"

There are no spectators, only participants, in collaborative research. Criteria for research evolve from the participants themselves as they engage in the process. Knowledge is socially constituted. This means that what we know depends on the company we keep (Wells, 1989). What was fact yesterday is not fact today. Physicists are now talking about quarks and zygotes rather than atoms. Although atoms were a useful concept, nuclear theorists now maintain that this concept restricts thinking. Facts, Fleck (1936) maintained, are best seen as beliefs in social, historical, and cultural time.

Our changing views of knowledge have severely challenged the role of the individual researcher. Even the way we cite people in research is up for grabs. Bibliographies might be more useful if they cited the thought-collective from which the ideas emanated, rather than limited to a list of persons who said things so cleverly that direct reference seems necessary.

With the criteria of connectedness we acknowledge the social nature of knowing, we invite identity through acknowledgment of our intellectual roots. Little is gained by acting as if certain ideas did not stand on the floor of history. If one is to discuss economic theory intelligently, one must deal, for example, with the historical fact of communism: Whether or not the idea of communism is one you like, and whether or not you deem it to have been successful, the fact of communism has forever changed the course of economic theory. Certain thoughts have been thought only because of communism's existence; these thoughts would not have been thought had communism not reared its head.

So, too, in education. Researchers have an obligation to examine the connections of their ideas with other ideas on the floor of history. In that discussion, the power of ideas to move the profession forward is clearer.

In the new, inquiry model, research and learning bear much in common. From what I can tell, they are mirror images of each other, with the single exception that research requires us to make our learning public. It is the artifacts of our involvement in research that allow us to search and re-search our assumptions and beliefs. These artifacts indeed slow inquirers down, providing concrete reference points according to which we can reconstruct and share with one another the mental journeys that we have traveled.

One of the most salient features of inquiry is its relational character. Collaborative inquiry means that a co-dependence exists. Just as true conversation means that what I say lives on in the utterances you make, so collaborative researchers actively use each other to outgrow themselves. There is no delineation of roles. No standing back.

Nor is there a termination point. Because there is no end-point to learning, one merely rests at certain points, taking time to share. These are not so much stopping points as observation points—like on a scenic highway, those turn-out areas where one pauses for a few moments to survey the scenery, reassess one's life, and reflect on the beauty of nature. Presenting to others what has been learned, more often than not begins new conversations and new rounds of inquiry with new collaborators. The journey continues. The road goes ever on.

Standard 5. Community: "Does the research reflect the kind of people we want to be?"

The way we conceptualize curriculum, and the questions we ask about it, will have a critical impact on the kinds of school settings we shape. Instructional research is a moral activity involving commitments to, and beliefs in, people and the role we envision schools playing in a democracy.

Classrooms are not here to silence children, but to hear from them. In a democracy, schools are not to marginalize teachers and students, but to hear all the many voices. It is by hearing all voices that new conversations are begun about the kind of life we want to live and the kind of people we want to be. Strong democratic communities are shaped when we know what contribution each voice makes, when we collectively take new action (Harste & Short, 1989).

Improving the quality of life experienced in schools calls for opportunities for teachers and students alike to experience themselves as learners, engaging together in building, critiquing, and transcending their present realities. Through collaborative inquiry, learners of all ages form, revise, and re-form their understandings of the world, including how it might work more democratically.

Because schools are the means to something else, educational inquiry focuses on change rather than description. Curriculum is a vehicle for offering planned invitations to live a new reality based on what we already know, what we are trying to figure out, and what we believe we might become.

The criterion of community is meant to insure that our research is "educative," to use Dewey's term (1909). Educative experiences have a future about them. Operationally, educational inquirers must take responsibility for what their research does and how it is used. If it doesn't benefit teachers and children, it ought to be abandoned, for it constitutes what Dewey called "miseducation."

Instructional research rooted in the inquiry concept of research will be as infinitely varied as are the lives of learners who inquire there. The key is conversation. Instructional research rooted in inquiry is designed to alter the very way that learners see knowledge as well as the role that language and other sign systems play in knowing, not as experimental conditions, but as direct experiences in conversational living. Education as inquiry means that it all hinges on curricular invitations that encourage new conversations and hence new ways of living lives in classrooms. Said differently, instructional research premised on inquiry encourages openness, vulnerability, reflexivity, connectedness, and community.

Too often we evaluate new programs with old eyes. The time is right to ask new questions. This is not so much up for debate as it is an expression of new reality and a new world order in education.

Bibliography

Britzman, D. (1992). *Personal relevance with a vengeance, or what could go wrong in English education* (Mimeographed; to be released as part of book of proceedings). Invited address given at the Mid-Winter Seminar on Teacher Learning, Teacher Knowing sponsored by NCTE's Assembly on Research and the National Conference on Research in English, Chicago.

Dewey, J. (1909). *Education and experience.* New York: Basic Books.

Fleck, L. (1938). *Genesis of a scientific fact.* Chicago: University of Chicago Press.

Goodman, K. S. (1992). *A socio-psycholinguistic transactional model of the reading process.* Speech given at the Annual Meeting of the International Reading Association, San Antonio, Texas.

Harste, J. C. (1992). Foreword. In R. Beach, J. L. Green, M. L. Kamil, & T. Shanahan (Eds.), *Multidisciplinary perspectives on literacy research.* Urbana, Illinois: National Council of Teachers of English & National Conference on Research in English.

Harste, J. C., & Short, K. G. (1989). *What difference does your theory of language make?* (Mimeographed; to be released as part of a book of proceedings). Keynote address given at the Post-World Congress on Reading, Brisbane, Queensland, Australia.

Kuhn, T. (1975). *The structure of scientific revolutions* (2nd Edition). Chicago: University of Chicago Press.

Langer, S. K. (1972). *Philosophy in a new key* (3rd Edition). Cambridge, Massachusetts: Harvard University Press.

Manning, A. (1992). *Conversations on teacher research.* LEARN Pre-Conference Proposal for the 1992 Annual Meeting of the United Kingdom Reading Association, Mount Saint Vincent University, Halifax, Canada.

Wells, G. C. (1986). *The meaning-makers.* Portsmouth, New Hampshire: Heinemann.

Commentary on the ERIC Whole Language Debate

Michael Pressley
State University of New York at Albany

> . . . *he would never permit himself to fall into the naïve errors of those who try to read some favorite private doctrine into every poet they like of every nation or every age. And Mark abhorred the smug assurance with which second-rate left-wing critics find adumbrations of dialectical materialism in everyone who ever wrote from Homer and Shakespeare to whomever they happen to like in recent times. If the poet is to their fancy, then he is clearly seen to be preaching to the class struggle. If they do not like him, then they are able to show that he was really a forefather of fascism. And all their literary heroes are revolutionary leaders, and all their favorite villains are capitalists and Nazis.*

> Thomas Merton, reflecting on the focus of his teacher at Columbia, the young Mark Van Doren—he taught the literature itself rather than the then fashionable leftist political interpretations. (from "Mentors," in *A Thomas Merton Reader*, Thomas P. McDonnell, editor, New York: Doubleday, p. 233.)

Lynn Gelzheiser and Ruth Wharton-McDonald, both of SUNY at Albany, generously provided commentary on preliminary drafts of this manuscript.

Carl Smith of ERIC requested that I write an integrative, evaluative reaction to the original debate presentations published in this volume. It was clear that he expected I would probably side more with the "against" Whole Language side than with the "for" Whole Language perspective. He was correct in that supposition, with the evidence presented in this volume permitting no other conclusion, at least for anyone who holds traditional scientific values, as I do. Even so, as will become clear, I believe many of the educational practices prescribed by Whole Language enthusiasts deserve a place in school. *I am not against Whole Language, but rather I am unconvinced of its effectiveness, especially relative to alternatives.*

The issues that need to be discussed are so varied that I found it impossible to construct a coherent, seamless response. What I offer instead are replies to important questions that ought to be considered as part of a discussion of Whole Language. I provide answers much as I would in a news conference, not worrying about the formalities of academic citation, with a few exceptions that seem to me to be especially noteworthy. This is consistent with the informality of the other papers. Consistent with them as well, I append a bibliography of articles and books that are pertinent to the issues covered in this commentary.

Before getting to the questions, let me provide a bit of background for those readers who may not be familiar with me or my work, so that they may have some context for evaluating the points I raise here. First of all, I identify myself principally as a research-oriented educational psychologist. I have studied both basic issues relevant to education (e.g., children's ability to use imagery in learning from text, monitoring during reading) as well as large-scale interventions intended to develop many aspects of literacy. Although I am best known for my experimental research, I have used a variety of methodologies throughout my career, from think-aloud analyses to ethnographic interviews. Especially in the last five years, my work has been a blend of quantitative and qualitative research aimed at understanding the structure and dynamics of effective, educator-developed comprehension strategies instruction.

My eclectic perspective both on reading and on reading research is being received well in the schoolplace. One reason is that my points of view are grounded in classrooms: I spend a great deal of time in schools, sometimes formally observing as part of a study, but often less formally, simply continuing a lifelong education about the nature of schooling in America. Although I have never taught primary reading, my vision of beginning reading instruction is not just an abstract one; it is informed, rather, by many concrete experiences in elementary classrooms throughout the United States and Canada and by many interactions with primary teachers from around the world. One Maryland teacher described me as "the professor who sits on the floor and listens to my reading groups." To be certain, however, there is also an abstract side, for I have read and reflected on virtually all of the literature alluded to in the current Whole Language debate—and I wrote some of it as well!

Although I have a bona fide scientific interest in primary reading education, my greatest motivation for working in the area of early literacy is a deep desire for every child to develop to his or her fullest potential. I believe that this maximizes the likelihood that a child can grow up to live freely, happily, and as fully informed and empowered as possible.

Real freedom comes only through full participation in society. For the entire history of the United States, success in conventional schooling, which largely reduces to acquisition of conventional literacy and numeracy, has empowered children of the disenfranchised, so that they can participate more completely in American life than their parents did. If there is one thing that is certain about 20th-century American life, the melting pot worked very well for many groups, and schooling played an important part in the process (e.g., Cremin, 1988). Although school is used to achieve political goals (e.g., Cremin, 1989), Patrick Shannon's assertion that, "since the turn of the century, schools have . . . reinforce[d] . . . social biases and political injustices," (see above, p. 96) is at best a blatant overstatement and, probably more realistically, not consistent with the experiences of most Americans. I doubt that Shannon would receive much support for his claims about schooling and its effects from the children and grandchildren of immigrants who increased their socio-economic level over that of their ancestors, in part through success in American schools, people who achieved much more in the United States than would have been possible in their ancestors' countries. Yes, some schools do better for ethnic minorities and disadvantaged groups than do others—for example, see Bryk, Lee, and Holland's (1993) compelling analysis of education in America's Catholic high schools. Yes, some groups continue to experience difficulties in school—for example, economically disadvantaged African-Americans and Spanish-speaking Americans. Even so, schooling is not the monolithically oppressive force that Shannon suggests it to be. I note especially that exceptionally well-informed critics of American policies toward children, including well-respected scholars who are unambiguously liberal in their political preferences (e.g., Grubb & Lazerson, 1988), do not advance the extreme conclusions about schooling that Shannon and similarly minded social-critical theorists do.

When social-critical theorists report that schooling is an instrument of the privileged for social oppression, they are telling us more about their construal of America than about the state of American schooling. I am aware of social-critical analyses of the institutions of government and church that are similar in many ways to Shannon's remarks in this debate. The themes of gender, race, and class oppression recur—mindlessly so, in my opinion—regardless of the institution under consideration. I take seriously the perspective of Louise Rosenblatt (1978) and others that meaning is a transaction between a reader and a text, with the "text" in the present discussion being school, especially conventional reading instruction. As someone who experienced a strong Piagetian tradition during my graduate school years, I also recognize that a person's beliefs can take over completely in construction of an interpretation, with the result being an egocentric understanding, one sensible only to like-minded individuals. Many social-critical analyses seem to me to be egocentric in this way.

My view of the world is more straightforward and much more empirical than that of the social-critical supporters of Whole Language. My perspective on evidence is that if it looks like a duck, quacks, and waddles, it's a duck—not something else! At the same time, I recognize that some social-critical theorist may argue that race, gender, and class affect bird life as well, with what seems to be a duck actually being a peacock, forced to act like a duck, overcome by oppression unleashed by birds of different colors, genders, and/or higher perches in the pecking order because their plumage draws more dollars in the capitalist marketplace. In general, I ignore these analyses, and, for the most part, I do so in what follows. In particular, my commentary reflects greater respect for the scientific evidence about early reading and primary reading education that has been generated in the past quarter century than did the Whole Language advocates in the San Antonio debate.

Is there compelling evidence that *Whole Language* instruction is more effective than other forms of reading instruction?

No. There is not a substantial body of evidence that would compel a person with conventional scientific values to conclude that Whole Language instruction is more effective than alternative forms of beginning literacy instruction. Those few attempts to study Whole Language instruction scientifically are so muddled methodologically that little can be made of the outcomes. That is why Janice Almasi, Barbara Palmer, Linda Gambrell, and I concluded that Whole Language instruction is largely unstudied (Almasi, Palmer, Gambrell, & Pressley, in press). To the extent that the available research is interpretable, however, there is little in the way of support for Whole Language. For every difference favoring Whole Language over basals or some alternative form of conventional instruction, there is a corresponding failure to find an effect of Whole Language relative to other language-arts teaching. I am reluctant to conclude, however, that Whole Language does not "work" relative to other approaches—that is, I sincerely believe that it has yet to be tested well.

I recognize that assuming Whole Language to be scientifically testable is to assume a lot in the eyes of many Whole Language enthusiasts. They often argue, as Ohanian did in the current debate, that the approach cannot be evaluated because it is expected to affect competencies other than those reflected by standardized measures. Fine, so identify those competencies, and competent reading researchers will find ways to measure them. I am struck that Ohanian, in particular, attributed quite a few behaviors to Whole Language students that potentially could be measured in studies comparing Whole Language and more conventional reading instruction: interpretations of text, affective reactions to literature, number of books read and/or bought, book-sharing events, empathy with classmates, and amount of writing. If Whole Language enthusiasts did make comparisons between the instruction they favor and more traditional approaches—comparisons involving dependent variables like the ones cited by Ohanian—and if Whole Language students did fare better, the case for Whole Language would be much stronger than it is.

It is very disturbing that Whole Language enthusiasts do not run the studies that might inform us better about the intervention they so heartily embrace. To claim, instead, that measurement of Whole Language effects is impossible, is to place the study of reading instruction on a par with the pseudoscientific pursuits of UFOs, out-of-body experiences, and poltergeists. Anyone who wishes to impose their view of curriculum on the nation's students should do better than that, although I recognize that in the politically correct 1990s, the decidedly unscientific, social-critical rhetoric of vocal Whole Language enthusiasts is persuasive in some decision-making circles.

One reason that I urge a commitment to study Whole Language more completely and rigorously is because I am impressed by the claims of many teachers that Whole Language works. On the other hand, I am also impressed that many teachers have told me that Whole Language is failing their students. One Los Angeles teacher recently expressed her concern to me in a public meeting by proclaiming that Whole Language was doing a great deal to usher in "post-literate California," with the majority-educator audience indicating their agreement by applause. The nation needs to know if that teacher's and the audience's perceptions are valid.

Marvin Simner of the University of Western Ontario recently related at the convention of the American Psychological Association the many laudatory comments that the Canadian Psychological Association received from teachers across Canada when the association criticized provincial Ministries of Education efforts to impose Whole Language as an exclusive approach to literacy instruction. Were these teachers telling the CPA about real problems with Whole Language? We do not know, but if the difficulties are real, we should find out. I suspect a great deal could be learned about elementary reading by studying carefully the concerns of teachers who perceive that Whole Language does not work, documenting why they view Whole Language to be failing their students, followed by careful studies evaluating those claims and perceptions as objectively as possible.

In summary on this issue, although I cannot endorse Whole Language based on the evidence currently available, my view is that the issue of Whole Language should be studied much more carefully and completely than it has been in the past. The failure thus far to test Whole Language does not imply that the method does not affect the development of children's literacy; conversely, a recommendation to analyze Whole Language thoroughly ought not to be interpreted as an interest in Whole

Language exclusively. Rather, my perspective is that a variety of alternatives to current primary reading instruction should be investigated intensively as an integral part of deciding how and what to teach American students.

What is my perspective on the definition of Whole Language?

The participants in the debate seem to be operating as classical concept theorists, believing that there has to be a distinctive feature list if there is to be a concept. In fact, there are fuzzy concepts in this world, and Whole Language is one of them. I suspect that I'm in a 99 and $^{44}/_{100}\%$ pure Whole Language classroom when there are both (a) authentic literacy events occurring, including reading and discussion of excellent literature as well as writing, and (b) little or no isolated skills instruction. Although this is a two-feature list, a moment's reflection makes obvious how fuzzy each of the features is: Is it Whole Language if the excellent literature is in a basal? If the writing is "taking dictation" or copying messages from the board? If even one or two children are pulled out for phonics remediation?

One rhetorical tactic that scholars use when they want to derail a discussion is to insist on a precise definition of the concept under consideration, when they know very well that the concept is an ill-defined one. That is how I read some of the attempts to force this Whole Language debate to focus on definition. All of the participants in this debate had prototypical Whole Language classrooms in their mind's eye. Providing a concrete prototype is one way to convey fuzzy concepts. Perhaps future discussions might include videotapes or other presentations of prototypical Whole Language classrooms for the benefit of audience members who might not yet have a vision of Whole Language. Nothing will be gained by continuing the pursuit of an exacting feature list, however, for with fuzzy concepts, the features just cannot be specified exactly.

What are the potentially positive aspects of Whole Language?

Many Whole Language components have been validated as affecting literacy positively in various ways. These components include reading of authentic literature, daily writing, and cooperative literacy experiences.

Moreover, there is no doubt that there are now more of these desirable activities in American schools than when my generation dialogued with our teachers about Dick and Jane, in part because of the Whole Language movement.

Despite some Whole Language claims that components such as daily writing emanated only because of their perspective, there is no doubt that richer scientific analyses of writing, such as those offered by Linda Flower and David Hayes [e.g., Flower & Hayes, 1980], did much to stimulate daily writing in American classrooms. Despite Whole Language claims that increased reading of authentic literature in American classrooms is due exclusively to Whole Language, reading of authentic texts was also stimulated by increased understanding of the need to build students' knowledge, knowledge that can be conveyed in part through experiencing high-quality literature, with much of this work conducted by Richard Anderson, David Pearson [e.g., Anderson & Pearson, 1984] and their associates at the Illinois Center for the Study of Reading.

Even though Whole Language includes effective components, that does not mean that any given mix of them works. For example, in a related area, I know of a number of thinking-skills packages that include many individual strategies that have been validated. Even though the individual strategies work when taught alone, the packages do little for students' thinking (see Nickerson, Perkins, & Smith, 1985), probably because the strategies are taught providing neither guidance about, nor practice in, their coordination. Packages of effective Whole Language components may fail because of an analogous lack of coordination.

An additional complication is that the effective Whole Language ingredients are mixed with ineffective ingredients. McKenna, Robinson, and Miller make much of recent failures to produce evidence in favor of Goodman's idea that readers should rely heavily on semantic context clues for decoding, an important instructional practice in the Whole Language approach. It is not known how much harm such a weak strategy does to the overall Whole Language package, but there is the possibility that effective and ineffective components cancel each other out in some Whole Language classrooms.

Are there effective forms of instruction not included in Whole Language?

As I compliment the Whole Language community for embracing some attractive components, I want to emphasize that there are other effective forms of instruction that Whole Language either ignores or actively opposes. As Marilyn Adams (1990) made so clear in her book, the track record is unambiguous with respect to instruction intended to develop phonemic awareness. That instruction makes a positive difference in long-term reading achievement. Explicit decoding instruction definitely increases the reading achievement of many children as well, again a topic eminently reviewed by Adams (1990). Explicit instruction in the form of one-to-one tutoring, such as Reading Recovery and Slavin's Success for All, promote the literacy of many children who experience difficulties learning to read in classrooms. Wasik and Slavin's (1993) review is extremely informative about tutoring interventions, all of which are more explicitly instructional than classroom life favored by Whole Language enthusiasts. Explicit comprehension strategies instruction is desirable from my perspective, with its validations generally positive to date. Development of a sophisticated repertoire of comprehension strategies for children seems to require more explicit instruction than the Whole Language community endorses (see Pressley et al., 1992).

In summary on this point, there are a number of different interventions and reading instructional tactics that seem effective, at least with some children. Some of these are consistent with Whole Language philosophy, and others are not. Notably, the ones that are not compatible have been developed and researched since the original conceptualization of Whole Language in the 1960s. Well-validated, more explicit primary reading instruction really is more modern than Whole Language, in the sense that its conceptualization is more recent, for Whole Language was conceived in the late 1960s and 1970s (see Pressley, in press, for more about the modernity of explicit instruction compared to Whole Language). Even so, some of the increasingly old-fashioned instruction that is Whole Language should not be forgotten, for it is an attractive part of elementary schooling.

No one could miss that I am not supportive of the Whole Language community. Why am I not, if so much of what they have to offer is valuable?

The case is overwhelming that many in the Whole Language community are attempting to repress data and opinions critical of their point of view. That offends me. I am completely supportive of scientific openness and constructive dialogue between scientists, educators, and other stakeholders in education, including scholars in the field of primary reading. As McKenna, Robinson, and Miller have claimed, Whole Language enthusiasts are differentially attentive to supportive data and ignoring of nonsupportive data. In fact, my reading of the literature is that the Whole Language community uncritically accepts every snippet of data that could be interpreted as consistent with Whole Language (e.g., poorly controlled comparisons of Whole Language with alternative approaches), while disparaging any viewpoint, however well-informed, that is not supportive of Whole Language (e.g., claiming that decoding researchers offer "thalidomide for the mind," as one Whole Language theorist did in a prominent public forum several years ago). Researchers who dare to differ with the Whole Language perspective are labeled as uncaring, political manipulators who engage in repression, much as Shannon implied of his opponents in the present debate.

And there is worse, including on one occasion several years ago, when a prominent member of the Whole Language community declared publicly that the only way to deal with his conventional reading instruction debate opponent would be to "forge a silver bullet, for that is what is needed to kill a vampire." Such rhetoric is not the stuff of the intelligent discussion and reflection that needs to occur as part of evaluating primary reading instruction, but rather is intended to intimidate. When I hear members of the Whole Language community speak of repression, I sometimes wonder if they are not projecting—in the Freudian sense of the term as a defense mechanism—their own tendencies onto the behaviors of others. Whether they are or not, I would be less than candid if I did not indicate that I believe some commentary from the Whole Language community has been intolerably disrespectful of those who hold perspectives different from their own.

I spend a lot of time interacting with the practice community, and that permits another insight with respect to intimidation by some Whole

Language enthusiasts. I have encountered a number of teachers who are under orders from their central offices or principals to comply strictly with Whole Language. Several teachers have told me about how they respond to these directives by smuggling phonics into their classrooms and keeping the materials well-hidden from supervisors, taking very great risks because they are convinced that at least some of their students need more than Whole Language. These are often very well-respected teachers, with years of professional experience. Somehow, the Whole Language community's frequent claims of honoring teachers' decision making seem hollow as I recall such incidents.

In summary on this point, despite the Whole Language community's public embrace of terms like "dialogue" and "emancipation," prominent members of their community seem to prefer a monologue with respect to discussion of Whole Language and primary reading; some Whole Language practitioners prefer a shackling of other teachers to practices compatible with Whole Language philosophy rather than permitting their colleagues to make professional decisions that might conflict with the Whole Language world view. So I return the rhetorical question to the Whole Language camp that they served up to the scientists in this debate: "Who the hell are you?" If you are not academic and professional practice bullies, some of you act like you are; if you are not hypocritical in your commitments to dialogue and emancipation, it certainly seems that some of you are.

Surely, I have more reservations about Whole Language than the rhetorical and political tactics of its supporters. What are my conceptual problems with Whole Language?

First, there is an incredibly heavy emphasis on literature rather than content-area reading in many Whole Language classrooms. Students' individual differences in interest are largely ignored, despite claims of honoring student choice. As a kid, I far preferred science to literature, and I still prefer science to literature! My vision of an emancipated school would be one in which a child, such as I was, could read considerable amounts of science as part of literacy instruction. I wonder if Ohanian's tech students felt emancipated as she forced the literature she loved on them.

A *second* problem is the Whole Language neglect of individual differences in student responsivity to Whole Language instruction, with such indifference likely to impact negatively on the long-term achievement and motivation of many students. We know that students who are doing poorly in the primary grades are at great risk for academic underachievement and long-term declines in academic motivation (e.g., Pearl, 1982). Poor performance in the elementary curriculum and low self-esteem by the end of the grade-school years predict bad things to come. Thus, I was disturbed by Susan Ohanian's discussion of Bob, a middle-school non-reader. For most Bobs, there are potential solutions to their reading problems, although ones that may be too explicit in their instructional emphasis for Whole Language devotees such as Ohanian. There is substantial scientific evidence, both old (see Rohwer, 1973) and new (see Clay, 1991), that some students need more explicit instruction than others. Importantly, some forms of explicit instruction are better than other forms of explicit instruction, and some types of explicit instruction work better with some students than with others. Given that, Ohanian's report of Bob's failure to respond to the explicit teaching that was offered to him is impossible to interpret.

Effective instruction includes alternatives, with many of the effective alternatives for weaker primary-level readers involving intensive, explicit, one-on-one decoding and comprehension instruction, as I discussed earlier. Given the possibility of avoiding long-term literacy problems through instructional changes tailored to students' individual difficulties in school, I view teachers as irresponsible who let students flounder, especially when the decision is an explicit one, principally motivated by a determination to keep all students wedded to one form of teaching. Sadly, I know of occasions when teachers committed to Whole Language refused to provide more explicit instruction to students in need because it would not have been consistent with Whole Language philosophy.

A *third* conceptual concern is with the Whole Language perspective on the determination of human behavior, especially relative to what they claim are the views of the scientific community. Despite Shannon's impression to the contrary, there are many scientific types who believe very strongly in the contextual determination of behavior, with major and influential contextualist theoretical positions offered by Vygotsky, Bronfenbrenner, Bandura, Mischel, Pepper, Baltes, Cole, and others. No one could read my own work, for example, and come away with anything but a sense that I am a dyed-in-the-wool contextualist.

Paradoxically, an important difference between members of the scientific community who are contextualists and the Whole Language theoretical camp is that the Whole Language enthusiasts actually seem to hold an extreme, obsolete, somewhat anti-contextualist view about the naturalness of literacy development: The Goodmans in the late 1960s argued that reading and writing were natural consequences of experience in high-quality literacy environments. Just as Chomsky believed that humans are hard-wired to acquire language when given exposure to it, the Goodmans presumed that humans naturally learn to read and write as a consequence of high-quality, socially-mediated print and literary events (Goodman & Goodman, 1979). In the 1990s, no one with an informed opinion takes seriously the notion that humans evolved to be able to read and write, given print and literary experiences. Reading and writing are clearly piggybacked on to other psychological functions that developed in humans for different purposes. In fact, biologists who have thought hard about this issue are convinced that explicit instruction is required if people are to learn to read and write (see Bertelson & DeGelder, 1989; Liberman & Liberman, 1990).

A *fourth* conceptual concern is with Whole Language advocates' willingness to interpret the views of single teachers. When only the testimony of an individual teacher is considered, it is impossible to know which parts of his or her experiences and perceptions are specific to that teacher's classroom and which parts are shared by others who teach. In my own research on comprehension strategies instruction, I have been clearly demarcating perceptions and experiences common to a number of teachers as well as individual differences between teachers in their perceptions and experiences. A rich portrait of understandings about teaching can emerge from such analyses (see Pressley et al., 1992). Such research requires collaboration with a number of teachers, with respectful attention to both their voices in unison and when they are singing different parts.

Although I urge careful attention to the voices of committed and convinced Whole Language teachers, believing that they can be informative about how to study Whole Language sensibly and sensitively, I am emphatic about not overgeneralizing from individual Whole Language teachers' perspectives about the method's efficacy: I have heard the

167

voices of many other American and Canadian teachers who perceive Whole Language to be ineffective, especially with children who are already at risk for reading failure. (I might add that these perceptions of concerned teachers are consistent with the small amount of data available in evaluation of Whole Language effects on at-risk learners [Stahl and Miller, 1989].) Teachers who are critical of Whole Language deserve to have their experiences and opinions taken into consideration as part of the Whole Language debate, but this is something that definitely has not occurred when only teachers who support Whole Language have been admitted to the conversation.

In short, researchers need to listen respectfully to the reports of more different kinds of teachers than the Whole Language scholarly community has done to date. In particular, exhaustive qualitative analyses of teacher perceptions about Whole Language effects—both positive and negative—might be revealing about what to measure in order to document Whole Language effects. Although any one teacher's perceptions may be idiosyncratic, recurring teacher claims about the effects of curriculum are often going to be based on actual effects.

A *fifth* conceptual complaint is that the voices of children who are likely to be negatively affected by poor reading instruction are missing from Whole Language presentations, or their voices are filtered by Whole Language teachers or by academics supportive of Whole Language. I do not find credible that the persistent complaints about conventional instruction offered by Whole Language teachers and social-critical theorists are the viewpoints of the poor, the disadvantaged, and the excluded. (In fact, I find it offensive when middle-class and upper middle-class professionals presume to speak for the poor!) Were we to begin to hear large numbers of the disadvantaged and excluded—or even provable majorities of teachers and other professionals who are committed *more* to the education of the disadvantaged than to ideologies such as social criticism and Whole Language—describing high-quality, conventional literacy instruction as oppressive, I would begin to take the charge seriously. So long as the indictment of non-Whole Language reading instruction comes from completely committed Whole Language teachers, however, I would assume that it is part of the game of one-upmanship that teachers play in their ideological communities, part of making the case that the instruction they offer is better than the instruction offered by other teachers. As long as the charge comes from university people, I will assume that the rhetoric is part of the game of one-upmanship that university professors play. Social-critical theorists are doing what they can to promote the respectability of their perspectives relative to scientific analyses of reading instruction. To date, these have fared much better in academic circles where one reflects on the relative merits of the scientific analysis of reading and critical theorists' pronouncements.

What might researchers do next?

The critical theorists and I agree that there is reason for concern about the state of schooling at the end of the 20th century. My worries are based on scientific analyses rather than on social-critical assumptions, however. Not only do American students perform poorly on standardized tests but also their inabilities to write, read, and problem-solve at desirable levels also come through both in informal reports from educators and in formal studies of these competencies (see Pressley, El-Dinary, & Brown, 1992).

I do not believe, however, that shifting away from conventional literacy instruction to a Whole Language approach will necessarily improve the situation, not even with respect to reading and writing, as Whole Language enthusiasts argue, based on philosophical positions that they find compelling. Rather, my best guess is that if there really is some optimal form of literacy instruction, the best of Whole Language components, outstanding decoding instruction, and excellent one-to-one remediation will be included in a mix of instructional elements occurring throughout a school day. The intervention will be rich, the alternatives numerous, the possibilities open.

Unfortunately, there is no reasonable conceptual umbrella under which one might integrate the many potential components in an optimal package, no reliable approach to combining attractive and validated elements of instruction to shape an effective whole. In fact, the very real possibility is that a throwing together of effective individual components will result in incoherent instruction. The research community needs to work collaboratively with the practice community to devise integrative instructional models and to test the models, as they are developed.

McKenna, Robinson, and Miller are right in their assertion that excellent research in reading education involves multiple research methods. They are also correct that leading spokespersons for educational research are calling for methodologically eclectic programmatic research. Consistent with those perspectives, my own work in recent years on comprehension strategies instruction has involved a mixture of methods, from large-n experiments to individual case studies, from use of standardized tests as dependent measures to teacher testimonies, from well-controlled, decontextualized studies to fully-contextualized, quasi-experimental investigations.

As I do my multi-method studies of elementary literacy instruction, however, I am struck in particular that none of the luminaries who was cited in the debate as endorsing multiple-method research programs on early reading instruction is carrying out that kind of research program. That is, many more profess multi-method research efforts in literacy than carry out multi-method research programs.

I have experienced great increases in my personal understanding of the nature of effective comprehension strategies instruction because I used multiple methods; the information my colleagues and I have provided to the nation and the profession in recent years is much richer than the conclusions I produced earlier in my career (see Pressley et al., 1992). Thus, I speak from experience in urging other researchers to plan research programs using multiple lenses to examine important aspects of early literacy, including the nature and effects of Whole Language, either as currently construed or as revised.

What next for the practice community?

In the last five years, I have studied intensively comprehension strategies instruction programs devised and implemented by educators. The starting point for these educators was some knowledge of comprehension strategies interventions as studied by reading researchers. The instruction designed by these educators went far beyond the vision of the academics, however. I hope that there are educators who are ready to take a hand in developing instruction that integrates the benefits of Whole Language, phonics, and whatever else might be defensible in the mix. I expect that such educator-designed instruction will be more than the envisionment of either the Goodmans or the decoding researchers, one that captures the best of both viewpoints and more. If there is to be better primary reading instruction than currently exists, educators will be heavily involved in the design and refinement of it. In doing so, however, educators will use some of the powerful building blocks validated by the literacy researcher community. Whatever approach emerges, however, should be evaluated using multiple methods.

As someone who has been a participant in five years of educator/researcher collaborations to evaluate comprehension instruction, I am sanguine that educator/academic collaborations can produce rich evaluations of new, integrative literacy instructional packages. As I call for these collaborations, I am aware that teacher research, rather than researcher/educator collaboration, is heavily favored by some who support the Whole Language approach (e.g., Cochran-Smith & Lytle, 1993). Although teacher research as Cochran-Smith and Lytle conceive of it might appeal to some teachers and some communities of teachers as a means for developing and refining practice (and personally, I hope it appeals to many such communities, for I think it is an approach with excellent potential for improving professional development), teacher research makes little sense as a way of producing information for the nation as a whole. Teachers are not trained to carry out and report systematic scientific inquiries in ways that are acceptable to the many communities who pass judgment on and use educational research. In contrast, researcher/teacher collaborations are powerful because research and teaching expertise can team up to study and report the effects of instruction, with the result being educator-informed use of sophisticated methodologies as part of more comprehensive analyses than either the researchers or the educators could devise on their own. I am puzzled that the Whole Language community can so publicly embrace the concept of collaboration and yet seem so determined to divorce themselves from mainstream educational researchers. This is the kind of thing I mean when I say that there seems to be hypocrisy in some members of the Whole Language community.

Final comments

I really did not find any of the commentary in this volume too reassuring. Although McKenna, Robinson, and Miller were much more on target as far as they went, they did not make much progress toward a vision of the instruction the nation needs. (My personal interactions with them, however, suggest that they have much more vision than comes through in their comments in this volume, which, after all, were tempered because of interaction with a hostile audience.) Mostly polemics and too little evidence, is my summary of the Whole Language remarks in this volume, a summary that applies, sadly, to many other commentaries emanating from the community of Whole Language enthusiasts.

Fortunately, as McKenna, Robinson, and Miller noted, there is an instructional community in this nation that is capable of providing informed, detailed, and articulate commentary about effective primary reading instruction. Joan Rankin and I have spent much of the last year soliciting the insights of outstanding primary reading teachers about reading, teachers nominated by their supervisors because they succeed in getting children to read. I find what these teachers have to say considerably more compelling than the perceptions of any of the participants in this debate. (Joan and I will be reporting our results publicly in the very near future.) I would urge all of the debaters to interact more with teachers like these, and to pay some visits to outstanding primary classrooms— ones in which most of the children learn to read. That is, I encourage the participants to get better grounded about outstanding primary education. Neither reading social-critical theory of education (Shannon), nor re-reading somebody else's inspiring testimonials about teaching (Ohanian), nor analyzing the methods and outcomes of reading research studies (McKenna, Robinson, Miller), suffices to inform about excellent early reading instruction. To begin to know excellent teaching of primary reading, you must know excellent primary reading teachers, and let their minds inform your mind. I would urge all of the participants to sit on the floor in some classrooms in which excellent primary reading instruction is the daily routine. Based on my own personal experience, I believe that if the debaters were to sit on the floor with open minds, their perspectives would broaden.

Finally, lest some reader think that I really am surprised by the hypocrisy in the social-critical camp, I am not. Shannon's viewpoint is closer to Marxism than to any other grand intellectual tradition. Of course, Marxist thinking has co-existed with repression of alternatives at least since 1917. Economic and social philosophies which do not deliver, however, as Marxism has failed to do, are eventually swept away as the dissatisfactions accumulate. If Whole Language harms those who are already disadvantaged, I am confident that eventually it will be swept out of the lives of at-risk children (although regrettably, perhaps not before a great deal of harm is done to individual children). It will die in part because excellent educators are learning about modern advances in explicit instruction that do benefit hard-to-teach students—I am asked about Reading

Recovery, development of phonemic awareness, Success for All, Transactional Strategies Instruction, and other contemporary, explicit instructional programs often enough that I am certain that there is much awareness within the teacher corps about alternatives to Whole Language. If Whole Language is more rhetoric than substance, as social-critical analyses are and Marxism was, excellent educators will find ways to move on to better-validated, more up-to-date instruction. My personal hope for language-arts instruction is an intelligent amalgamation of the strengths of Whole Language with the advantages of other approaches.

Bibliography

Integrative Books on Reading Everyone Should Read

Adams, M. J. (1990). *Beginning to read.* Cambridge, Massachusetts: M.I.T. Press.

Rosenblatt, L. M. (1978). *The reader, the text, the poem: The transactional theory of the literary work.* Carbondale: Southern Illinois University Press.

Foundational Positions on Whole Language and Empirical Reactions to Them

Almasi, J. F., Palmer, B., Gambrell, L., & Pressley, M. (in press). Toward disciplined inquiry: A methodological analysis of whole language research. *Educational Psychologist.*

Goodman, K. S. (1965). A linguistic study of cues and miscues in reading. *Elementary English, 42,* 639–642.

Goodman, K. S. (1967). Reading: A psycholinguistic guessing game. *Journal of the Reading Specialist, 6,* 126–135.

Goodman, K. S., & Goodman, Y. M. (1979). *Learning to read is natural.* In L. B. Resnick & P. A. Weaver, *Theory and practice of early reading,* Vol. 1 (pp. 137–154). Hillsdale, New Jersey: Erlbaum & Associates.

Nicholson, T. (1991). Do children read words better in context or in lists? A classic study revisited. *Journal of Educational Psychology, 83,* 444–450.

Nicholson, T., Bailey, J., & McArthur, J. (1991). Context cues in reading: The gap between research and popular opinion. *Journal of Reading: Writing and Learning Disabilities, 7,* 33–41.

Nicholson, T., Lillas, C., & Rzoska, A. (1988). Have we been misled by miscues? *The Reading Teacher, 42*, 6–10.

Pressley, M. (in press). State-of-the-science primary-grades reading instruction or whole language? *Educational Psychologist.*

Smith, F. (1971). *Understanding reading: A psycholinguistic analysis of reading and learning to read.* New York: Holt, Rinehart, & Winston.

Stahl, S. A., & Miller, P. D. (1989). Whole language and language experience approaches for beginning reading: A quantitative research synthesis. *Review of Educational Research, 59*, 87–116.

Phonemic Awareness and Learning to Decode

Ball, E. W. & Blachman, B. A. (1988). Phoneme segmentation training: Effect on reading readiness. *Annals of Dyslexia, 38*, 203–225.

Ball, E. W. & Blachman, B. A. (1991). Does phoneme segmentation training in kindergarten make a difference in early word recognition and developmental spelling? *Reading Research Quarterly, 26*, 49–66.

Blachman, B. A. (1991). Phonological awareness: Implications for prereading and early reading instruction. In S. A. Brady & D. P. Shankweiler (Eds.), *Phonological processes in literacy: A tribute to Isabelle Y. Liberman* (pp. 29–36). Hillsdale, New Jersey: Erlbaum & Assoc.

Bradley, L. & Bryant, P. E. (1983). Categorizing sounds and learning to read—a causal connection. *Nature, 301*, 419–21.

Bradley, L. & Bryant, P. (1985). *Rhyme and reason in reading and spelling.* International Academy for Research in Learning Disabilities Series. Ann Arbor, Michigan: University of Michigan Press.

Bradley, L. & Bryant, P. (1991). Phonological skills before and after learning to read. In S. A. Brady & D. P. Shankweiler (Eds.), *Phonological processes in literacy: A tribute to Isabelle Y. Liberman* (pp. 37–45). Hillsdale, New Jersey: Erlbaum & Associates.

Calfee, R. C., Lindamood, P., & Lindamood, C. (1973). Acoustic-phonetic skills and reading—kindergarten through twelfth grade. *Journal of Educational Psychology, 64*, 293–98.

Chall, J. S. (1967). *Learning to read: The great debate.* New York: McGraw-Hill.

Cunningham, A. E. (1990). Explicit versus implicit instruction in phonemic awareness. *Journal of Experimental Child Psychology, 50*, 429–444.

Goldsmith-Phillips, J. (1989). Word and context in reading develop-
    ment: A test of the interactive-compensatory hypothesis. *Journal
    of Educational Psychology, 81*, 299–305.

Goswami, U. & Bryant, P. (1992). Rhyme, analogy, and children's
    reading. In P. B. Gough, L. C. Ehri, & R. Treiman (Eds.), *Read-
    ing acquisition* (pp. 49–63). Hillsdale, New Jersey: Erlbaum & As-
    sociates.

Juel, C. (1988). Learning to read and write: A longitudinal study of 54
    children from first through fourth grades. *Journal of Educational
    Psychology, 80*, 417–447.

Juel, C., Griffith, P. L., & Gough, P. B. (1986). Acquisition of literacy:
    A longitudinal study of children in first and second grade. *Jour-
    nal of Educational Psychology, 78*, 243–255.

Lie, A. (1991). Effects of a training program for stimulating skills in
    word analysis in first-grade children. *Reading Research Quarterly,
    26*, 234–250.

Lundberg, I. (1991). Phonemic awareness can be developed without
    reading instruction. In S. A. Brady & D. P. Shankweiler (Eds.),
    Phonological processes in literacy: A tribute to Isabelle Y. Liberman
    (pp. 47–53). Hillsdale, New Jersey: Erlbaum & Associates.

Lundberg, I., Frost, J., & Peterson, O. (1988). Effects of an extensive
    program for stimulating phonological awareness in preschool chil-
    dren. *Reading Research Quarterly, 23*, 263–84.

Stanovich, K. E. (1980). Toward an interactive compensatory model
    of individual differences in the development of reading fluency.
    Reading Research Quarterly, 16, 32–71.

Stanovich, K. (1986). Matthew effects in reading: Some consequences
    of individual differences in the acquisition of literacy. *Reading Re-
    search Quarterly, 21*, 360–407.

Treiman, R. & Baron, J. (1983). Phonemic-analysis training helps
    children benefit from spelling-sound rules. *Memory & Cognition,
    11*, 382–389.

Biological Foundations of Reading Competence versus Whole Language Assumptions

Bertelson, P. & De Gelder, B. (1989). Learning about reading from
    illiterates. In A. M. Galaburda (Ed.), *From reading to neurons* (pp.
    1–23). Cambridge, Massachusetts: MIT Press.

Liberman, I. Y. & Liberman, A. M. (1990). Whole language versus code emphasis: Underlying assumptions and their implications for reading instruction. *Annals of Dyslexia, 40,* 51–76.

Pratt, A. C. & Brady, S. (1988). Relation of phonological awareness to reading disability in children and adults. *Journal of Educational Psychology, 80,* 319–323.

One-on-one Reading Interventions with Weak Readers

Clay, M. M. (1985). *The early detection of reading difficulties: A diagnostic survey with recovery procedure.* Portsmouth New Hampshire: Heinemann.

Clay, M. M. (1991). *Becoming literate: The construction of inner control.* Portsmouth New Hampshire: Heinemann.

Iversen, S. & Tunmer, W. E. (1993). Phonological processing skills and the reading recovery program. *Journal of Educational Psychology, 85,* 112–120.

Pinnell, G. S. (1989). Reading recovery: Helping at-risk children learn to read. *Elementary School Journal, 90,* 161–183.

Wasik, B. A. & Slavin, R. E. (1993). Preventing early reading failure with one-to-one tutoring: A review of five programs. *Reading Research Quarterly, 28,* 178–200.

Multiple-Methods for Studying Comprehension Processing: Research Conducted by Pressley's Group in the Last 5 Years

Brown, R. & Coyogan, L. (1993). The evaluation of transactional strategies instruction in one teacher's classroom. *Elementary School Journal, 94,* in press.

Brown, R. & Pressley, M. (in press). Self-regulated reading and getting meaning from text: The transactional strategies instruction model and its ongoing validation. In D. Schunk & B. Zimmerman (Eds.), *Self-regulation of learning and performance: Issues and educational applications.* Hillsdale, New Jersey: Erlbaum & Associates.

Coley, J., DePinto, T., Craig, S., & Gardner, R. (1993). Teachers adapting reciprocal teaching. *Elementary School Journal, 94,* in press.

El-Dinary, P. B., Pressley, M., & Schuder, T. (1992). Becoming a strategies teacher: An observational and interview study of three teachers learning transactional strategies instruction. In C. Kinzer & D. Leu (Eds.), *Forty-first Yearbook of the National Reading Conference* (pp. 453–462). Chicago: National Reading Conference.

Gaskins, I. W., Anderson, R. C., Pressley, M., Cunicelli, E. A., & Satlow, E. (1993). Six teachers dialogue during cognitive process instruction. *Elementary School Journal, 93,* 277–304.

Marks, M., Pressley, M., in collaboration with Coley, J. D., Craig, S., Gardner, R., Rose, W., & DePinto, T. (1993). Teachers' adaptations of reciprocal teaching: Progress toward a classroom-compatible version of reciprocal teaching. *Elementary School Journal, 94,* in press.

Pressley, M., El-Dinary, P. B., Gaskins, I., Schuder, T., Bergman, J., Almasi, L., & Brown, R. (1992). Beyond direct explanation: Transactional instruction of reading comprehension strategies. *Elementary School Journal, 92,* 511–554.

Pressley, M., El-Dinary, P. B., Marks, M. B., Brown, R., & Stein, S. (1992). Good strategy instruction is motivating and interesting. In K. A. Renninger, S. Hidi, & A. Krapp (Eds.), *The role of interest in learning and development* (pp. 333–358). Hillsdale, New Jersey: Erlbaum & Associates.

Pressley, M., Gaskins, I. W., Cunicelli, E. A., Burdick, N. J., Schaub-Matt, M., Lee, D. S., & Powell, N. (1991). Strategy instruction at Benchmark School: A faculty interview study. *Learning Disability Quarterly, 14,* 19–48.

Pressley, M., Gaskins, I. W., Wile, D., Cunicelli, B., & Sheridan, J. (1991). Teaching literacy strategies across the curriculum: A case study at Benchmark School. In J. Zutell & S. McCormick (Eds.), *Learner factors/teacher factors: Issues in literacy research and instruction: Fortieth yearbook of the National Reading Conference* (pp. 219–228). Chicago: National Reading Conference.

Pressley, M., Goodchild, F., Fleet, J., Zajchowski, R., & Evans, E. D. (1989). The challenges of classroom strategy instruction. *Elementary School Journal, 89,* 301–342.

Pressley, M., Johnson, C. J., Symons, S., McGoldrick, J. A., & Kurita, J. (1989). Strategies that improve memory and comprehension of what is read. *Elementary School Journal, 90,* 3–32.

Pressley, M., Schuder, T., SAIL Faculty and Administration, Bergman, J. L., & El-Dinary, P. B. (1992). A researcher-educator collaborative interview study of transactional comprehension strategies instruction. *Journal of Educational Psychology, 84*, 231–246.

Other References

Anderson, R. C. & Pearson, P. D. (1984). A schema-theoretic view of basic processes in reading. In P. D. Pearson (Ed.), *Handbook of reading research*. New York: Longman.

Bryk, A. S., Lee, V. E., & Holland, P. B. (1993). *Catholic schools and the common good.* Cambridge, Massachusetts: Harvard University Press.

Cochran-Smith, M. & Lytle, S. L. (1993). *Inside/outside: Teacher research and knowledge.* New York: Teachers College Press.

Cremin, L. A. (1988). *American education: The metropolitan experience.* New York: Harper & Row.

Cremin, L. A. (1989). *Popular education and its discontents.* New York: Harper Collins.

Flower, L., & Hayes, J. (1980). The dynamics of composing: Making plans and juggling constraints. In L. Gregg and E. Steinberg (Eds.), *Cognitive processes in writing* (pp. 31–50). Hillsdale, New Jersey: Erlbaum & Associates.

Grubb, W. N., & Lazerson, M. (1988). *Broken promises: How Americans fail their children.* Chicago: University of Chicago Press.

Nickerson, R. S., Perkins, D. N., & Smith, E. E. (1985). *The teaching of thinking.* Hillsdale, New Jersey: Erlbaum & Associates.

Pearl, R. (1982). LD children's attributions for success and failure: A replication with a labeled LD sample. *Learning Disability Quarterly, 5*, 173–176.

Pressley, M., El-Dinary, P. B., & Brown, R. (1992). Skilled and not-so-skilled reading: Good information processing and not-so-good information processing. In M. Pressley, K. R. Harris, & J. T. Guthrie (Eds.), *Promoting academic competence and literacy: Cognitive research and instructional innovation* (pp. 91–127). San Diego: Academic Press.

Rohwer, W. D., Jr. (1973). Elaboration and learning in childhood and adolescence. In H. W. Reese (Ed.), *Advances in child development and behavior* (Vol. 8, pp. 1–57). New York: Academic Press.

The *Whole* Whole Language Debate
*a select annotated bibliography from the **ERIC** database*

*A word about using the **ERIC** database*

"A rose is a rose is a rose," but "Whole Language" is not always "Whole-Language-approach." This particular bit of educational jargon was admitted as a "descriptor" by the conservative gatekeepers of the ERIC database only as late as 1990, some ten years after the phrase, the concern, and the debatable points had become commonplaces in language-arts education and its journals. Previous to its elevation to descriptorhood, however, "Whole-Language-approach" had enjoyed virtual existence as an "identifier" in ERIC. Hence, until the entire ERIC system is retrofitted, you will have to search for "Whole-Language-approach" both in the "ID:" and the "DE:" fields, for it is still electronically remembered as both a descriptor and an identifier.

A machine-readable information database, ERIC makes use of "controlled vocabulary"—a device useful especially to librarians and others interested in precision and search-efficiency. Terms are granted official status in this controlled vocabulary first as identifiers, later as descriptors (proper names remain classified as identifiers). Multiple-term identifiers and descriptors are strung together with hyphens ("Whole-Language-approach"), although one can always eliminate the hyphens and do a "free-text search" which asks the system to find whatever individual words one wants and then allows it to search for them in combination. This Faustean approach gets you more than you want to know, and, probably, a considerable number of irrelevant items, but, at least, you have the feeling that you didn't miss anything.

The ERIC database is constantly changing: Thousands of new items are added each year; every year, several dozen new terms are either added, deleted, or modified in the *ERIC Thesaurus* (the bible of ERIC's controlled vocabulary). Changes in principle in the *Thesaurus*, however, take time to ripple through the vast database in fact. As of the September, 1993, update of the CD-ROM, 221 records still had the term "Whole-Language-approach" listed in the "ID:" field. Eventually, these records will be altered to reflect the upgrading of "Whole-Language-approach," which (to repeat) took place in April, 1990. Until that happens, however, a searcher who limits the search to "Whole-Language-approach" in the "DE:" field will miss out on these 221 documents.

Moreover, older, cognate matters and terms, e.g. "holistic approach" (admitted in 1982) and "language experience approach" (admitted in 1966), which once stood on their own but later came to be thought of in conjunction with Whole Language, offer additional areas of research for the industrious database searcher.

Yet another reason you might miss a desirable item is old-fashioned human error which afflicts ERIC, like it does everything else, because afflicted humans are the ones who tag the items with their "DE:" and "ID:" markers, and some entries that ought to have been tagged "Whole-Language-approach," unfortunately, were not. For all the above reasons, therefore, merely to search under the controlled-vocabulary descriptor, "Whole-language-approach," is to miss a lot that ERIC has to offer.

Another way to pursue Whole Language in the database is to search on the names of its proponents (and detractors)—among the former, for example, Jerry Harste, a theoretician within the Whole Language movement more influential than most. Were one to search the database from 1982 to 1993 only on "Whole-Language-approach," however, one would discover only 3 entries authored by Harste and 4 more to which he was a contributor. If, on the other hand, one searches the database on Jerome (Jerry) C. Harste's name in its possible variations (including his evil twin, Jermome Harste, who exists only in the parallel universe of misprint), one finds 32 items more or less relevant to Whole Language, though not all identified as such.

The present bibliography, then, extensive though it be, does not begin to be exhaustive of all the possible ramifications, nuances, cognates, side-tracks, implications, and praise and blame of Whole Language. We recommend that you think of this list only as a starter. Indeed, because of space limitations, we have presented here only skeletal ERIC entries. To anyone interested in a thorough conspectus of Whole Language as it is represented in the ERIC database, we further recommend that you begin with these few starters, use the ED or EJ numbers to find the full database entries, and then follow the leads that you will find in the "DE:" and "ID:" fields of those entries, whether to narrow or expand your search.

—the Editor

Aaron, Ira E., and others, "The Past, Present, and Future of Literacy Education: Comments from a Panel of Distinguished Educators, Part I," *Reading Teacher 43/*4 (Jan 1990):302-11. [EJ 403 665]
Provides opinions of five eminent educators on a variety of issues in literacy education, including phonics, emergent literacy, reading and writing relationships, Whole Language, and defining literacy.

Abramson, Shareen, and others, "Literacy Development in a Multilingual Kindergarten Classroom," *Childhood Education 67/*2 (win 1990): 68-72. [EJ 423 520]
Whole Language activities promote the English literacy development of young children with limited English proficiency. Teaching strategies for promoting Whole Language development include (1) content-specific instruction, (2) scaffolding, (3) caretaker speech, (4) wait time, (5) peer interaction, and (6) cultural relating.

Activity Book. Comprehension Strategies," *Learning 20/*8 (Apr-May 1992): 31-54. [EJ 449 364]
Provides before-, during-, and after-reading strategies to help students develop reading goals, monitor comprehension, and reflect on what they read. A reading wheel and student pages encourage practice of new strategies. Whole Language and across-the-curriculum strategies are included for building comprehension in other curriculum areas.

Adams, Marilyn Jager, *Beginning To Read: Thinking and Learning about Print* (Cambridge, Mass.: MIT Press, 1990): 494 pp. [ED 317 950]
Drawing on an array of research on the nature and development of reading proficiency, argues that educators need not remain trapped in the phonics versus teaching-for-meaning dilemma and offers instructional alternatives. The book proposes that phonics can work together with the Whole Language approach to reading and provides an integrated treatment of the knowledge and processes involved in skillful reading, the issues surrounding their acquisition, and the implications for reading instruction. Developing the new connectionist theory as it relates to reading and its acquisition, the book underscores the automatic nature of print perception in skillful readers, while contrasting it with the attentive thought required for conceptual learning and understanding. Reviews the history of the debate over approaches to reading instruction as well as the research on their effectiveness. Stresses the importance of preschool language and literacy experiences and includes descriptions of those that will best prepare children for reading instruction.

[**Adams**, Marilyn] "A Talk with Marilyn Adams," *Language Arts 68/*3 (Mar 1991): 206-12. [EJ 422 592]
Interviews Marilyn Adams about her book *Beginning to Read: Thinking and Learning about Print*. Discusses the critical issues of phonics versus Whole Language and what she hopes teachers will gain from the book.

Adams, S. Angela, "Grandma's Gift." (Grand Forks: North Dakota University, 1990): 7 pp. [ED 322 481]
Through an imaginary dialogue with her grandmother, a first-grade teacher reflects on the educational methods which her grandmother used and referred to in her journals and discusses the Whole Language methods used in schools today. A Whole Language classroom is described as a busy place where activity abounds and conversations buzz. Whole Language is a philosophy that the teacher believes in and an encompassing theory blending the use of all language modes. The focus in Whole Language is on the process not the product, on meaning and purpose. Whole Language teachers are empowered through ownership of their teaching. Many of the experiences described in

the classrooms of the 1920s seem similar to what might occur in Whole Language classrooms today, suggesting that effective educational methods will continue to work over long periods of time.

Adler, Louise, and Kip Tellez, "Curriculum Challenge from the Religious Right: The 'Impressions' Reading Series," *Urban Education 27/2* (Jul 1992): 152-73. [EJ 449 493]
Studies curriculum challenges by religious conservatives to the Whole Language-informed "Impressions" reading series in California. Many parents thought the series promoted satanism, witchcraft, and disrespect toward parents. Data from 22 school districts, 4 of which dropped the series, illustrate the complex nature of such challenges and highlight school district planning issues.

Aiex, Nola Kortner, "Using Literature To Teach Reading. ERIC Digest." (1990): 5 pp. [ED 313 687]
Informs teachers who are contemplating using children's literature to teach reading, and provides a brief review of material in the ERIC database on literature-based reading instruction. Includes sections on recent research, basic resources, assessing literature based reading, diverse methods approaches, and practical teaching guides.

Akers, Belle L., "Early Literacy Curriculum: Utilizing Language Experience and Whole Language in Kindergarten." (1988): 54 pp. [ED 315 164]
Reports a study designed to investigate the effects of the use of language experience and Whole Language activities in an early literacy kindergarten curriculum. Attempts to show that participation in a language-enriched environment achieves results similar to those of traditional methods and basal reading programs in regard to the acquisition of literacy skills. After a review of literature on developmental language and Whole Language approaches, an early literacy curriculum was developed for the study population. Through the course of a school year, 16 kindergartners, all of whom were girls attending an all-day class at a private school in San Francisco, were evaluated through observations, samples of work, checklists, and formal assessments. Findings on literacy development showed measurable gains in letter recognition and printing, initial consonant sound recognition, word recognition, and writing. Recommendeds that this model or an equivalent model be implemented in kindergarten classrooms with larger class sizes, in coeducational settings, and with a range of student economic levels so that positive effects of language experience and Whole Language approaches in the early literacy curriculum can be verified.

Albert, Elaine, "Commissurotomy of the Corpus Callosum and the Remedial Reader." (1990): 7 pp. [ED 325 816]
Testimony presented at a congressional hearing on illiteracy (Mar 1986) indicated that good readers use their myelinated corpus callosum fibers (which connect the left and right hemispheres of the brain) at millisecond speeds to coordinate the two brain hemispheres. Students taught using the whole-word recognition method (also called the look/say method and the Whole Language approach) from the start up to age 9 demonstrate effects resembling those caused by the surgical commissurotomy of the corpus callosum. Some researchers feel that there are several external effects that can be used with remedial readers to make up for the corpus callosum which has gone out of the business of decoding print, including: (1) oral reading, (2) using a fescue-pointer, (3) round robin oral reading, (4) sharing a book using a fescue to guide the reader's attention, and (5) confirming correct readings with immediate praise. These researchers also feel that the Whole Language approach, which puts primary stress on gathering meaning has, in the end, destroyed it.

Allen, JoBeth, "Literacy Development in Whole Language Kindergartens. Technical Report No. 436." (1988): 26 pp. [ED 300 780]
Reports an effort to understand how children in Whole Language kindergartens develop as writers and readers. Seven kindergarten teacher/researchers and a university teacher/researcher studied 183 children in the Manhattan-Ogden, Kansas, school district over one school year. Each quarter, teachers recorded all the writing behaviors they had observed in their students. At the beginning and end of the year, they assessed students' ability to recognize letters, sounds, and words, and their ability to read connected text. Results indicated that when children are encouraged to invent texts, they grow as writers, regardless of the reading and writing behaviors they bring to school. Patterns of growth were quite individual and often consisted of the addition of new writing behaviors rather than the abandonment of old behaviors.

Allen, JoBeth, and others, "'I'm Really Worried about Joseph': Reducing the Risks of Literacy Learning," *Reading Teacher 44*/7 (Mar 1991): 458-72. [EJ 421 244]
Reports the findings of three classroom teachers and a university professor from their collaborative study of how Whole Language instruction affects the students that teachers worry about the most. Concludes that elements of time, choice, supported risk taking, belonging, and Whole Language experiences for real purposes make a difference in at-risk students' school life.

Allen, JoBeth, and others, *Engaging Children: Community and Chaos in the Lives of Young Literacy Learners* (Portsmouth, New Hampshire: Heinemann, 1993). [CS 011 326]
Presents results of a longitudinal study of the effects of Whole Language instruction on six first- and second-grade African-American students at risk of failure. The book has three levels of interest: how teachers engage children in genuine literacy, how the process of engaging in a literate community increases learning, and how truly engaging each child was. In the first section, discusses key elements that were studied and why the longitudinal study was undertaken, and gives descriptions of the classroom contexts, researcher perspectives, and the development of the teachers as Whole Language teachers. The next six sections include descriptions of the transactions observed in the classroom. Each of these six sections has a similar format—the child is profiled from the child's own perspective and from the perspectives of the classroom teacher and data sources for each of the next three years. In the final section, develops themes and recommendations. Includes a description of data collection and analysis procedures, and a teacher and writer flowchart.

Allen, Robert, "Developing Parent Inservice Training in the Whole Language Approach for Remediating Elementary Chapter I Students." (Nova University, 1988): 131 pp. [ED 302 833]
Designed to expand the scope of the inservice reading program to help parents understand the Whole Language reading strategies used to remediate students, a practicum conducted a parent survey, carried out parent training sessions, and evaluated the program's success. The practicum focused on 323 parent participants from five Chapter 1 elementary school districts (schools with large numbers of low-income, educationally deprived students). A parent survey and needs assessment were conducted, after which the writer developed and facilitated inservice Whole Language reading training sessions which focused on helping parents better understand Whole Language listening, speaking, reading, and writing strategies. Evaluation indicated that parent understanding of these strategies increased overall 87% for Whole Language writing strategies and 95% for Whole Language reading strategies, with 94% of the parent participants rating the inservice program excellent.

Allred, Ruel A., "Integrating Proven Spelling Content and Methods with Emerging Literacy Programs," *Reading Psychology 14/1* (Jan-Mar 1993): 15-31. [CS 745 591]
Suggests the integration of the methods relating to theories that underlie emergent literacy (such as Whole Language, literature-based instruction, process/conference writing, cooperative learning, and composition-based instruction) with established spelling practices (such as the direct study of a basic core vocabulary, application of proven study steps, and implementation of formal spelling instruction).

Almasi, Janice F., and others, eds., "Literacy: Issues and Practices. 1993 Yearbook of the State of Maryland Reading Association Council. Volume 10." (Maryland: IRA, 1993): 60 pp. [ED 356 465]
Begins with a foreword by Janice F. Almasi that outlines some of the steps that the state of Maryland is taking as a leader in literacy education and literacy assessment, and the eight articles in this edition reflect many of these steps. Contents: "Three Dialogues about Reading Engagement" (John T. Guthrie); "My Classroom Was Literacy Poor!" (Corinne Pritzlaff Weis): "Read to Somebody Everyday: A Shared Reading Program" (Steven P. Chasen and Gail W. Holt); "Blending Reader Response Theories and Reading Comprehension Instruction" (Sandra R. Wallis); "The 'Write' To Learn Mathematics" (Bob. M. Drake and Linda B. Amspaugh); "Intermediate Grade Students' Awareness of the Writing Process" (Natalie Felsher, Judy Ramoy Johnson, and Priscilla P. Waynant); "The Use of Retellings for Portfolio Assessment of Reading Comprehension" (Patricia S. Koskinen, Linda B. Gambrell, and Barbara A. Kapinus); and "The Signing for Reading Success Study Group" (Cynthia T. Bowen, Jean H. Mattheiss, and Robert M. Wilson).

Altwerger, Bess, and others, "Whole Language: What's New?" *Reading Teacher 41/2* (Nov 1987): 144-54. [EJ 360 639]
Suggests that Whole Language is not the whole-word approach, nor merely teaching skills in context, nor the Language Experience approach, nor a new term for the Open Classroom, but rather a point of view about language, literacy, and content learning.

Anderson, Gordon S., "A Whole Language Approach to Reading." (Lanham, Maryland: University Press of America, 1984): 619 pp. [ED 264 540]
Presents an approach to reading instruction based on a socio-psycholinguistic theory of the language learning process. Chapter 1 provides an overview of oral and written language development; identifies language processes, language systems, and cultural setting; and describes a socio-psycholinguistic model of language learning and a teaching-learning model based on socio-psycholinguistic principles. Chapter 2 considers oral language development. Chapter 3 examines the skills and Whole Language models of the reading process, and chapter 4 describes evaluation procedures enabling teachers to assess students' reading development. Chapter 5 reviews the socio-psycholinguistic nature of the reading process from a Whole Language perspective, while chapter 6 describes the socio-psycholinguistic nature of reading and Whole-Language reading approaches, methods, and materials. Chapter 7 explains procedures for organizing a Whole Language classroom, identifies classroom goals, and describes classroom organizational plans. Includes illustrations, bibliographies of literature, and a list of resources for developing individualized reading programs and thematic units.

Anderson, Gordon S., "Handbook for a Self-Programmed Reading Diagnostic/Remediation Approach," paper presented at the Annual Meeting of the National Council of Teachers of English Spring Conference (3rd, Columbus, Ohio, Apr 12-14, 1984). [ED 247 522]
Intended to help reading teachers develop and demonstrate mastery of diagnostic or remediation skills prior to or with application in a real classroom, this handbook

provides simulated materials for use within a course or staff development program to supplement lectures, discussions, readings, demonstrations, and films. Contains (1) a description of the components of the kit, (2) a discussion of the Whole Language reading theory and its application, (3) procedures for using the materials described, (4) procedures for rereading miscue inventory, (5) diagnostic procedures, and (6) instructional procedures.

Anderson, Gordon S.,"A Survey of Teachers' Transition from Skills to Whole Language," paper presented at the Annual Spring Conference of the National Council of Teachers of English (Richmond, Virginia, Mar 18-20, 1993). [CS 011 289]
Examines the concerns, problems, and experiences when teachers change from a traditional skills classroom to a Whole Language classroom. Subjects, 162 of 400 K-12 teachers from several"Ohio Teachers Applying Whole Language" groups, responded to questionnaires (for a return rate of 40%). Results indicated the following: (1) The most important reason given for changing was that they had read the literature about Whole Language and had been influenced to change because they had talked with other teachers about Whole Language. (2) The most difficult problem teachers faced when changing was the lack of books and other materials to support the change. (3) By a ratio of three to one, teachers changed gradually from skills to Whole Language rather than changing abruptly. (4) The most frequent change reported was implementing writing workshops and/or writing journals. (5) Many teachers still used basal readers because they were required to or because other teachers in the district used basals. (6) Most of the support that teachers received came from other teachers. Findings suggest the following guidelines for teachers thinking about changing or who are in the process of change: learning about Whole Language theory and practice before changing, anticipating the problems to be faced, recognizing that change is gradual, and being aware of the need for support.

Andrews, Sharon Vincz, "Creating Whole Language Classrooms: Steps to Becoming Learners Again," paper presented at the Annual Meeting of the International Reading Association (35th, Atlanta, Georgia, May 6-11, 1990). [ED 322 470]
Three basic beliefs support teaching: (1) learning is social and individual; (2) learning must be personally meaningful; (3) learning rests upon a knowledge base that is constructed, not transmitted. The first step to creating an environment which supports learning in meaningful ways is for the teacher and students to become better inquirers into their own ways of learning and knowing and to begin to articulate questions which can direct their thinking during the semester. Transactional replays help to better understand students' resistance to process curriculum in reading and language arts methods classes and the new role for the teacher in relation to students. This strategy involves jotting down notes on conversations during teamwork times and reading them back to the students to begin asking theoretical questions. This reflective process enables the class to see their instructional histories and ways of knowing as educators, their vision of the ideal, and their process of negotiating the current curriculum of the class. New views of learning surface as the community of learners evolves; students begin to see themselves as developing knowledge bases within their groups through the group process. Students are supported in their journeys toward self-knowledge and subject knowledge by group sharing and interaction. Teachers must develop curriculum structures, an audience for all voices, and places to take the risks which support authentic teaching and learning. The roles in the classroom and the curriculum structures created must continue to evolve practically and meaningfully as beliefs about knowledge sources and construction expand.

Antonelli, Judith, "Decoding Abilities of Elementary Students Receiving Rule-Based Instruction and Whole Language Instruction." (1991): 30 pp. [ED 331 002]
Reports investigation of the decoding automaticity of elementary students when receiving rule-based instruction (as a process of applying syllable and structural analysis rules and limited phonics), and when receiving holistic instruction in a Whole Language program (exercises in listening, reading and writing, integrated with classroom instruction when possible). Twenty children in grades one, two, four, and five were selected on the basis of their stanine reading scores on the California Achievement Test and from results indicating average intelligence on the Test of Cognitive Skills. The Sucher Allred Informal Reading Inventory was administered and a comparison of the automaticity of decoding of the two samples was conducted. Results indicated no significant differences, though the mean scores of the experimental group receiving the rule-based instruction were higher than the mean scores of the control group.

Arellano-Osuna, Adelina, "The Empowering of Teachers with Whole Language Literacy Events: A Latin American Experience," paper presented at the World Congress on Reading (13th, Stockholm, Sweden, Jul 3-6, 1990). [ED 324 641]
Examines teachers' beliefs about how reading takes place and how reading processes develop. Subjects, 25 first-, fourth-, and sixth-grade teachers in five different Venezuelan schools, were administered protocols that consisted of a researcher/teacher conference, classroom observation, and an inventory designed to identify beliefs about how reading takes place and how reading processes develop. Results indicated that teachers were divided into three main groups: (1) two were Whole Language oriented; (2) three were eclectic oriented; and (3) 20 were "traditional" skill oriented teachers. A series of seminars and workshops was organized to discuss what the Whole Language approach could offer the teachers for an effective pedagogic practice. Upon completion of the seminars, the "traditional" teachers (and their students) demonstrated that they were comfortable about adopting aspects of the Whole Language approach in their teaching.

Askov, Eunice N., and others, "Adult Literacy, Computer Technology, and the Hearing Impaired." (1989): 42 pp. [ED 353 733]
Considers computer technology's current and potential role in developing literacy in hearing impaired (HI) adults. First, the paper considers findings of adult literacy research including the national impact of illiteracy, functional literacy, communication and thinking skills, the Whole Language approach, the process approach to writing, and functional context instruction. Second, the specific literacy needs and skills of the HI population are reviewed. Considered are the need for improved literacy levels for HI adults, characteristics of HI adults, language development, American Sign Language and English as a Second Language, bilingual instruction, and benefits of literacy programs for HI adults. Third, the use of technology in adult literacy programs is discussed, covering the novelty of technology, advantages and disadvantages of using computer technology, development of computer technology for the hearing impaired, technology implementation in educational programming, and availability and development of computer software. Recommendations include: (1) further research and development applying findings in adult literacy to the special needs of the hearing-impaired population; (2) careful evaluation of the effectiveness of pilot projects; (3) teacher training and technical assistance in computer technology; and (4) communication with ongoing projects and organizations to share information.

Atwell, Margaret, and Adria Klein, eds., "Celebrating Literacy. Proceedings of the Annual Reading Conference at California State University (14th, San Bernadino, California,

Mar 5, 1990)." (1990): 91 pp. [ED 337 744]
Focuses on theories and applications of literature-based education and the use of
holistic methods across the curriculum. Contents: "Windows and Mirrors: Children's
Books and Parallel Cultures" (Rudine Sims Bishop), "Using a Literature-Based
Program with Students with Reading and Writing Difficulties" (Linda Prentice and
Patricia Tefft Cousin), "What It Takes to Have a Literature-Based Reading and
Language Arts Program" (Julia Candace Corliss), "Celebrate Literacy: Cultivate Risk-
Taking" (J. Dixon Hearne and Linda M. LeBlanc), "Building Bridges to Literacy:
Merging Children's Spanish Literature and Social Studies" (J. Sabrina Mims), "The
Westhoff Project: Creating a Whole Language School" (Darlene M. Michener),
"Reading to Learn and Other Study Strategies: Transitions into Junior High/Middle
School" (Olivette Scott Miller and T. Patrick Mullen), "Make Every Kid an Author"
(Susan Abel and Andrea Street), "Would You Rather" (Evelyn Hanssen and Dorothy
Menosky), "Sound Effects Stories" (Adria F. Klein), "The Writing Process and
Cooperative Learning" (Beverly Young), and "Collaboration and Text Revision"
(Margaret A. Atwell).

Au, Kathryn H., and others, "Assessment and Accountability in a Whole Literacy Curriculum," *Reading Teacher 43*/8 (Apr 1990): 574-78. [EJ 408 410]
Discusses a curriculum framework based on six aspects of literacy: ownership, reading
comprehension, writing process, word identification, language and vocabulary
knowledge, and voluntary reading. Notes that this framework is consistent with a
whole literacy approach, and includes an assessment system and provisions for
accountability.

Aufmann, Amy K., and Mary Ann Wham, "Annotated Bibliography of Whole Language
Resources. Literacy Research Report No. 9." (1991): 15 pp. [ED 334 549]
Serving as a guide for teachers interested in implementing a Whole Language
philosophy within their classrooms and as a resource for teachers who have Whole
Language classrooms, this annotated bibliography presents thorough annotations of 12
selected texts published between 1979 and 1992 encouragement and support for the
Whole Language philosophy.

Bailey, Dora L., and Philip Ginnetti, "Adapting Cooperative Learning and Embedding It
into Holistic Language Usage," paper presented at the Annual Meeting of the College
Reading Association (Crystal City, Virginia, Oct 31-Nov 3, 1991). [ED 341 028]
Class collaboration and small group composition illustrate the embedding of cooperative learning theory in Whole Language classroom events. Through this experience all
students participate in active learning. The teacher has a weighty role in decision
making, setting of the lesson, assigning roles, and monitoring segments of cooperative
learning as these are embedded into Whole Language oriented lessons. Students' self-
selected reading choices and writing topics serve as a focus for cooperative learning.
Writing guidance is given in a class collaborated setting as well as in a group collaboration before the students do individual writing. During implementation, the strategies,
story mapping, and the writing process intertwine while students and teacher act
collaboratively and cooperatively. Students are introduced to "fractured fairy tales" by
professional authors, and use simple story maps to focus on the various components of
each story. In the next step, the class collaboratively writes a fractured fairy tale, going
through all steps of the writing process. Then students repeat the process in groups of
four or five before composing an individual piece of writing. This process has been
used successfully by preservice teachers in a field based program and by practicing
classroom teachers.

Baker, Esther J., "Does Inservice Make a Difference? A Way To Measure whether Teachers Are Using What They Learn in Inservice," paper presented at the Annual Meeting of the Washington Association of Supervision and Curriculum Development (Seattle, Washington, Jan 31-Feb 2, 1992). [ED 347 633]
Reports a study to determine the degree to which teachers used an inservice program for the implementation of a primary language and literacy program are presented in this paper. To measure teachers' level of use of the Whole Language philosophy of learning, the Language and Literacy Questionnaire was administered to 112 primary teachers in 6 schools in the Battle Ground, Washington, school district. Findings indicate that 99 percent of the teachers read aloud to their students daily (or nearly every day) and had developed their classroom read-aloud program to the routine level of use. However, they exhibited a low level of use regarding the element of guided reading. Teachers ranked in the 80th or 90th percentiles for 8 of the 10 elements of the Whole Language program.

Balajthy, Ernest, "Can Computers Be Used for Whole Language Approaches to Reading and Language Arts?" paper presented at the Annual Meeting of the Keystone State Reading Association (Hershey, Pennsylvania, Nov 4-8, 1988). [ED 300 766]
Holistic approaches to the teaching of reading and writing, most notably the Whole Language movement, reject the philosophy that language skills can be taught. Instead, holistic teachers emphasize process, and they structure the students' classroom activities to be rich in language experience. Computers can be used as tools for Whole Language experiences in reading and writing, based on principles of holistic language instruction. Classroom reading should center on children's literature rather than basal stories, and software of popular children's literature is available. Teacher feedback for writing should be provided during, not after, the writing process. For this, computer-based revision and editing programs are available for a wide variety of word processing software, giving feedback on grammar, usage, style, and organization. The transition from oral language to print should be as natural as possible, favoring guided language experience over direct instruction in subskills. Several computer programs allow children to write their own stories on the computer, then read the stories back to the children using voice synthesis. Writing should culminate in publishing in order for children to develop a sense of authorship. Desktop publishing is a key computer-based application for developing this sense of authorship in children.

Balajthy, Ernest, "A School-College Consultation Model for Integration of Technology and Whole Language in Elementary Science Instruction. Field Study Report No. 1991.A.BAL, Christopher Columbus Consortium Project," paper presented at the Annual Meeting of the New York State Reading Association (Kiamesha Lake, New York, Oct 1991). [ED 332 155]
A study examined a new collaborative consultation process to enhance the classroom implementation of Whole Language science units that make use of computers and multimedia resources. The overall program was divided into three projects, two at the fifth-grade level and one at the third grade level. Each project was staffed by a team of one college-based consultant, one or two classroom teachers, and two or three preservice teachers enrolled in a college teacher education program. Using a model of collaborative consultation, the team developed and taught science units that were based on Whole Language philosophy. Data were gathered through interviews with team members, observations of actual classroom presentations, and written summaries and evaluations of the project completed by the preservice teacher team members. Results indicated that the team approach, drawing upon the expertise of the classroom teachers, the preservice teachers, and the college consultant, was highly successful, both in

demonstrating new educational methods to experienced classroom teachers and in providing valuable field experience in these methods to preserve teachers.

Balajthy, Ernest, "From Metacognition to Whole Language: The Spectrum of Literacy in Elementary School Science." (1988): 26 pp. [ED 301 865]
Considers the integration of reading and writing into elementary science teaching by way of the implications of two leading theories pertaining to literacy: metacognitive theory and Whole Language theory. Discussion of the implications of metacognition includes attention to the issue of helping to overcome readers' nonscientific preconceptions by teacher modeling of text reading, use of graphic organizers for teaching text structure, and the use of semantic feature analysis for teaching science vocabulary concepts. Discussion of Whole Language centers on a suggestion to redesign research report units to capitalize on student interest and to develop expertise on focused topics, and on a suggestion to use problem-solving journals in the elementary science classroom.

Ballard, Glenda H., "Write Right Now! A Writing Skills Manual for GED Teachers. A Report from the Virginia Adult Educators' Research Network." (1992): 69 pp. [ED 351 538]
Based on a teacher's 14 years of experience in teaching writing, this manual was developed to help General Educational Development (GED) teachers to guide adults to improve their writing ability in preparation for the GED test. The manual is organized in four sections. The first section is a discussion of frequent concerns and problems that writing teachers have. These concerns are based on interviews with GED teachers, research, and the author's experience. The second section is an overview of the process approach to writing, and the third section is a summary of the Whole Language approach to literacy education and its implications for writing. Both the second and third sections begin with a general overview of the technique, proceed with some comments from those in the research field who have knowledge of the techniques, go on to describe a strategy for implementing the approach in the classroom, and conclude with a personal reflection of the author's experience with each approach. The fourth section provides practical activities and ideas for teachers of writing.

Barclay, Kathy, and Elizabeth Boone, *Supporting the Move to Whole Language: A Handbook for School Leaders.* (Jefferson City, Missouri: Scholastic Inc., 1993): 192 pp. [CS 011 408]
Sharing both collective and individual experiences and insights about Whole Language, teaching, and educational change, this book explains Whole Language instruction and its implementation on a school-wide basis. Each chapter moves from research to theory, and from theory to application in classrooms that actually exist. Explains why changes are needed, what those changes will look like in the classroom, and how to make those changes without special funds or staff. Contents: (1) Understanding Whole Language: The 'Whole' Is Greater than the Sum of Its Parts, (2) Seeing Is Believing: What to Look for in a Whole Language Classroom, (3) No One Ever Said that Change Was Easy: Understanding and Fostering Changes in Beliefs and Practices, (4) A Day in a Whole Language Classroom, (5) A Three-Way Partnership: Linking Home, School, and Community, (6) Saying Yes to Accountability: The Assessment and Evaluation of Learning, and (7) Staying Whole: The Importance of Professional Growth and Development.

Barrera, Rosalinda B., "The Cultural Gap in Literature-Based Literacy Instruction," *Education and Urban Society* 24/2 (Feb 1992): 227-43. [EJ 442 370]
Literature-based children's literacy programs usually lack cultural foundation on the

part of teachers providing the instruction. A framework for a cultural base for educators addresses this cultural gap. A series of professional development activities is presented that reflects the theoretical framework and increases cultural sensitivity.

Barry, Martha H., and others, "A Survey of Reading Approaches," paper presented at the Annual Meeting of the American Educational Research Association (San Francisco, California, Apr 20-24, 1992). [ED 346 437]
A study examined the reading approaches used by teachers and how accurately the teachers described the approaches to reading they purported to use. Subjects, 206 teachers in 19 elementary schools from 9 schools districts in a southeastern state, completed a questionnaire. Results indicated that (1) 68.75% of the teachers cited the basal as their primary means of teaching reading, 14.28% reported using the skills approach, 8.93% cited the "Success in Reading and Writing" approach, 2.68% cited the Whole Language approach, and 5.36% cited an eclectic approach; (2) overall, 70.37% of the respondents accurately described the central characteristics of the approaches to reading instruction they purported to follow; (3) all teachers citing the skills approach, 96% of the teachers using basals, 91% of the teachers using the Success in Reading and Writing, and 50% of the teachers using the Whole Language approach accurately described their respective approaches to reading instruction; and (4) the teachers valued oral reading, writing in response to reading, and sustained silent reading.

Bartley, Ninette, "Literature-based Integrated Language Instruction and the Language-Deficient Student," *Reading Research and Instruction 32/2* (winter 1993): 31-37. [EJ 461 041]
Determines whether reading comprehension scores of intermediate-grade language-deficient students improved with use of literature-based integrated language (Whole Language) instruction. Finds a significant gain after 25 weeks of instruction. Suggests that the effectiveness of Whole Language instruction may be significantly enhanced with the use of strategies such as class discussion, oral reading, and direct instruction.

Beach, Richard, ed., and others, *Multidisciplinary Perspectives on Literacy Research* (Urbana, Illinois: National Council of Teachers of English, 1992). [ED 343 082]
Papers presented at the Perspectives on Literacy Conference (2nd, Feb 1990) explore the application of a range of different disciplinary perspectives to studying literacy, drawing not only on newer linguistic and cognitive psychological orientations, but also on cultural anthropology, sociolinguistics, reader-response theory, critical theory, and poststructuralist theory. The collection is organized in four major sections as follows: Difficulties in Adopting a Multicultural Approach; Disciplinary Perspectives and Methodological Approaches; Specific Disciplinary Perspectives on Literacy Research; and Reaction Papers. Contents: a foreword by Jerome C. Harste, (1) "Introduction" (Richard Beach and others); (2) "Multiple Perspectives: Issues and Directions" (Judith L. Green); (3) "Ethnomethodology and the Possibility of a Metaperspective on Literacy Research" (James L. Heap); (4) "Reconciling the Qualitative and Quantitative" (George Hillocks, Jr.); (5) "First, Catch the Rabbit: Methodological Imperative and the Dramatization of Dialogic Reading" (Russell A. Hunt and Douglas Vipond); (6) "Adopting Multiple Stances in Conducting Literacy Research" (Richard Beach); (7) "Modes of Inquiry in Literacy Studies and Issues of Philosophy of Science" (Timothy Shanahan); (8) "A Psychological Perspective Applied to Literacy Studies" (John R. Hayes); (9) "Some Issues Concerning Differences among Perspectives in Literacy Research" (Michael L. Kamil); (10) "Changing Views of Language in Education: The Implications for Literacy Research" (Jenny Cook-Gumperz and John J. Gumperz); (11) "Studying Language and Literacy through Events, Particularity, and

Intertextuality" (David Bloome and Francis M. Bailey); (12) "Literacy Research in Community and Classrooms: A Sociocultural Approach" (Luis C. Moll); (13) "World Knowledge, Inferences, and Questions" (Arthur C. Graesser and others); (14) "Inquiries into the Nature and Construction of Literary Texts: Theory and Method" (Joanne M. Golden); (15) "Articulating Poststructural Theory in Research on Literacy" (Linda Brodkey); (16) "Literacy Research and the Postmodern Turn: Cautions from the Margins" (Peter McLaren); (17) "Multiple Perspectives on Multiple Perspectives" (Diane Stephens and P. David Pearson); (18) "Intuition and Ideology: Exploring the Ecosystem" (Susan Hynds); (19) "What It Means To Be Literate" (Robert Gundlach); (20) "Multidisciplinary Research on Literacy and the Possibility of Educational Change" (Marjorie Siegel); (21) and "What I Learned at This Conference: A Personal Narrative of a Literacy Event" (Ann Matsuhashi Feldman).

Baumann, James F., "Organizing and Managing a Whole Language Classroom," *Reading Research and Instruction 31/3* (spr 1992): 1-14. [EJ 447 088]
Presents definitions of "Whole Language" and classroom organization/management. Describes several plans for organizing and managing a Whole Language classroom. Presents a detailed example demonstrating how to organize and manage a Whole Language primary classroom using a "modified blocked" approach.

Bean, Wendy, and Chrystine Bouffler, "Spell by Writing." (Roselle, New South Wales: Primary English Teaching Association, 1987): 167 pp. [ED 284 266]
Specifically intended to address the teaching of spelling, this description of an elementary school program in Australia deals with many of the pedagogical problems that arise in Whole Language classrooms, and suggests ways for teachers to integrate a process approach to spelling with process writing to create a total language program. Following an introduction on certain teaching challenges—finding conference time with children, providing constructive feedback, and teaching spelling without relying on traditional drill and practice—the first chapter sets up the book's theoretical orientation, that language is a social interaction system. Chapter 2 explores language and spelling development, and reveals that an understanding of how children use strategies to go about learning to spell can lead schools to give up on quota systems and required spelling lists. The focus of Chapter 3 is on creating contexts for writing and the development of standard spelling, while ways of getting started with writing and spelling are presented in Chapter 4. The fifth chapter concentrates on composing as the connection between reading and writing, while the sixth chapter covers editing and different ways of handling the conferencing process. Proofreading and spelling are examined in Chapter 7, where strategies and techniques for teaching standard spelling are discussed. Chapter 8 deals with assessment and reporting of children's writing, and Chapter 9 draws conclusions and discusses changes in classroom management resulting from the Whole Language program.

Bear, Donald R., and Christine O. Cheney, "Literacy Education: An Integrated Approach for Teaching Students with Handicaps," *Intervention in School and Clinic 26/4* (Mar 1991): 221-26. [EJ 427 039]
A developmental model combining both skills and Whole Language instruction in four phases is offered for literacy development in children with mild handicaps. The four phases, common to literacy development in all children, move from pretend reading, writing, and spelling, to the transitional stage of fluency at approximately a third-grade level.

Bembridge, Teri, "A MAP for Reading Assessment," *Educational Leadership 49*/8 (May 1992): 46-48. [EJ 444 314]
When commercially available tests failed to match their Whole Language instructional practices, resource teachers in a Canadian school district developed their own instrument. Assembled over a five-year period, the Multi-Layered Assessment Package (MAP) is a set of procedures accompanied by suggested books, transcripts, and retelling and recording forms. MAP acknowledges the complexity of measuring child development.

Bergeron, Bette S., "What Does the Term Whole Language Mean? Constructing a Definition from the Literature," *Journal of Reading Behavior 22*/4 (1990): 301-29. [EJ 418 066]
Analyzes journal articles pertaining to Whole-Language instruction in elementary classrooms to compile a definition for this term. Finds that definitions and descriptions of Whole Language vary widely throughout the literature and that differences exist between school- and university-based authors' perceptions of the concept.

Berglund, Roberta L., and others, "Teacher Behaviors during Reading Instruction in Australian and American Classrooms. Literacy Research Report No. 3." (1991): 39 pp. [ED 329 930]
Examines, through classroom observations and teacher surveys, the instructional beliefs and practices in reading of second- and third-grade teachers in selected schools in the United States and Australia. Australian participants consisted of 16 second-grade and 11 third-grade teachers in New South Wales; American participants were 17 second-grade and 20 third-grade teachers in Wisconsin. Results were compared to those obtained in a similar study conducted in the mid-1970s to determine whether changes had occurred which might document a shift in reading instruction to reflect a more child-centered perspective where children are actively engaged in the reading process. The data indicate that changes have occurred in both countries regarding the types of questions posed during reading instruction and the amount of praise used. Non-functional student behavior appeared to be reduced as compared to the earlier study. Teacher orientations toward control versus autonomy appear to be related to their degree of acceptance of Whole Language philosophy. The teacher behaviors observed in both countries reflect rather conventional reading practices with the teachers serving as information-givers rather than collaborators and facilitators during reading instruction.

Best, Linda, "Student-Centered College Level ESL Instruction," *Research & Teaching in Developmental Education; 7* /2 (spr 1991): 57-66. [EJ 431 654]
Reviews the challenges that college-level English-as-a-Second-Language (ESL) programs present to instructors and students. Offers suggestions for authentic language experiences in classroom settings. Analyzes the literature on language and literacy, Whole Language, and learning styles. Offers examples of thematic units tailored to elicit authentic language experiences.

Blanton, Linda Lonon, "A Holistic Approach to College ESL: Integrating Language and Content," *ELT Journal 46*/3 (July 1992): 285-93. [EJ 451 715]
A Whole-Language approach for integrating language and content and thereby facilitating students' transition from English-as-a-Second-Language to college mainstream classes is presented as an alternative to traditional as well as new models. Particular focus is on how the model works and the benefits of using such a model.

Blazer, Phyllis C., "Whole Language Annotated Bibliography." (1989): 8 pp. [ED 307 595]
Beginning with a brief introduction which summarizes the characteristics of Whole

Language theory, this 28-item annotated bibliography includes books and journal articles, many of which are 1988 and 1989 publications.

Bloome, David, and others, "Reading and Writing as Sociocultural Activities: Politics and Pedagogy in the Classroom," *Topics in Language Disorders 11*/3 (May 1991): 14-27. [EJ 428 631]
Discusses reading and writing as (1) cognitive processes influenced by social and cultural contexts; (2) sociocognitive processes; (3) a social relationship between authors and readers; and (4) social and cultural activities. Discusses pedagogy and politics in the Whole Language classroom.

Bock, Joan, "Portraits of Six Developing Readers in a Whole Language Classroom," paper presented at the Annual Meeting of the National Reading Conference (39th, Austin, TX, Nov 28-Dec 2, 1989). [ED 318 988]
Investigates how second-grade learners, identified as less proficient, continued their literacy learning in a Whole Language classroom. Subjects, six second-grade Chapter 1 students, were observed during independent reading time twice per week over a period of 8 months. Additional data collection procedures included participant observation, field notes, informal interviews, reading miscue inventories, audio-tape recordings, questionnaires, photographs, and test results. Results indicated that the Whole Language environment supported each of the unique less proficient learners and facilitated optimum growth in reading and writing. Multiple factors contributed to the uniqueness of the subjects: (1) early language experiences; (2) family literacy support; (3) metacognitive awareness of reading and writing processes; (4) instructional methods; (5) social process variables; and (6) physical characteristics of the learners.

Bodycott, Peter, "Developing Reader Critics: Products of Wholistic Learning," *Australian Journal of Reading 10*/3 (Aug 1987): 135-46. [EJ 364 729]
Reports a study that found that children who read, write, and discuss whole texts of their own choice show remarkable insights into literature and its making, and that the insights match those of experienced adult literary critics.

Bolser, Shirley A., "Whole Listening in the Primary Classroom," *Ohio Reading Teacher 25*/3 (spr 1991): 19-27. [EJ434274]
Describes the process of listening within the boundaries of learning. Focuses on Whole Language methods in reading that promote whole listening and can help students improve their listening as well as reading skills.

Bolte, Anne, "Cloze Techniques: Opening Doors to Understanding," *Perspectives in Education and Deafness 8*/2 (Nov-Dec 1989): 6-8. [EJ 408 525]
Discusses applications of the cloze Whole Language technique for teaching reading to deaf students. Techniques described include using cloze questions in shared reading, predicting language in written text, solving cloze exercises with teamwork, working with minimal clues, predicting in patterns, and using cloze techniques for rewriting.

Bolte, Anne, "Our Language Routine: Reading Together and Loving It," *Perspectives for Teachers of the Hearing Impaired 5*/5 (May-Jun 1987): 3-5. [EJ 356 794]
Advocating the Whole Language philosophy as an approach which makes language learning easy and fun for hearing-impaired children, activities involving reading favorite books, shared reading, and rewriting stories wherein new words and sentence structures are introduced in the context of the whole story or poem.

Botel, Morton, and JoAnn T. Seaver, "Phonics Revisited: Toward an Integrated Methodology," paper presented at the Annual Meeting of the Keystone State Reading Association (17th, Hershey, PA, Nov 11-14, 1984). [ED 252 819]

In the context of Whole Language learning, the teaching of phonics can be approached in two different ways. In one situation, the teacher engages children in composing with a purpose and for an audience, during which time the children become aware of graphophonic relationships through their need to spell words. In the o/ther situation, the teacher engages the children in choral reading and language play that proceeds from a carefully chosen or constructed folk rhyme to sentence investigation, to phonic investigation, and, finally, to mastery of the CVC (consonant, vowel, consonant) syllable pattern in single and multisyllabic words. In both situations, the teacher teaches the complex tasks of writing and reading by first engaging children in the task itself and then having them experience differentiating language into its component parts. In the writing task, the differentiation proceeds from the child writing purposefully for an audience to becoming more aware of the graphophonic system through solving the problem of how to spell correctly. In the reading task, the differentiation proceeds from the teacher presenting a chant or folk rhyme chosen or constructed because of its inclusion of words that provide repetition of certain graphophonic patterns. In either situation, the instruction integrates that which is usually taught separately—phonics, spelling, and the study of sentences. This integrated approach is an example of Whole Language learning and it allows more time to be devoted to purposeful reading, writing, and dialoguing in all subject areas.

Bouffler, Chrystine, ed., *Literacy Evaluation: Issues & Practicalities* (Newtown, Australia: Primary English Teaching Association, 1992): 122 p. [ED 350 570]
Recognizing that increasing pressure for greater accountability has accompanied recent economic changes, presents 11 articles on literacy evaluation and assessment: (1) "Evaluation: A Political Issue" (Wendy Crebbin), (2) "Understanding Evaluation" (Kaye Lowe and Bill Bintz), (3) "A Difficult Balance: Whole Language in a Traditional US School" (Penny Freppon), (4) "System-Wide Assessment: Profiling Performance" (John Dwyer), (5) "Assessing the English Language Needs of ESL Students" (Lexie Mincham), (6) "The Primary Language Record: What We Are Learning in the UK" (Myra Barrs), (7) "Assessing Students' Writing: A Hands-On Guide from the Northern Territory" (Vivienne Hayward), (8) "Are Profiles Enough?" (Chrystine Bouffler), (9) "Side-by-Side: Responsive Evaluation in a Whole Language Classroom" (Jan Hancock), (10) "Parents and Assessment" (Ros Fryar and others), and (11) "Developing a Multidimensional Interactive Information Network" (Heather Fehring).

Bradt, Maxine, "Home Literacy the Natural Way," paper presented at the National Conference on Migrant and Seasonal Farmworkers (Apr 29-May 2, 1991). [ED 342 465]
Current research shows that the skills of listening, talking, reading, and writing are learned simultaneously. Children acquire these skills from their experiences of copying adults and interacting with other children. The term "emergent literacy" refers to the combination of the four skills in literacy learning. The Whole Language approach supports emergent literacy by incorporating the skills into children's learning experiences. This approach can be used by teachers and by parents at home. Parents can foster children's literacy by providing them with a rich print and verbal environment at home. This may involve conversing with their children, keeping examples of writing around the home, using wordless books for storytelling, and giving children access to printed materials. The success of a school literacy program often depends on children's literacy learning at home. As a result of recent research which supports natural, rather than formal, language learning, teachers have begun to examine schools' reading readiness programs. Many traditional reading readiness tests measure skills such as

auditory memory and letter recognition, which are abstracted from the reading process. Emergent literacy tests would measure such qualities as children's prior knowledge and ability to associate meaning with print.

Brand, Shirley, "Learning through Meaning," *Academic Therapy 24/*3 (Jan 1989): 305-14. [EJ 388 897]

A Whole Language approach to learning can be successfully used with children with learning disabilities. The approach can alleviate difficulties children have with memory and cognitive problems, anxiety, self-esteem, locus of control, and attentional deficit. Procedures are outlined for implementation of the Whole Language approach in resource room programs.

Brand, Wendy, "Meeting First Graders' Need for Rich, Authentic Literacy Experiences by Moving from a Basal Reader to a Whole Language Orientation." (Nova University,1991): 102 pp. [ED 328 878]

This practicum was designed to allow first graders the opportunity to read and write in a more natural and authentic manner than that permitted by using the basal reading series as the basis for reading instruction. The first-grade reading program was transformed from a basal-oriented approach to a Whole Language approach. Through the use of children's tradebooks, poetry, daily unstructured writing assignments, and flexible reading patterns, the children were able to achieve the skills required by the basal reading tests as well as spend more time in the actual exercises of reading and writing. Results of the practicum were positive. The primary goals and objectives were met. An analysis of the objectives demonstrated that the language arts activities of reading and writing were dealt with more often within the Whole Language environment than in a basal reading classroom. The children enjoyed the process of reading and writing to a greater extent as measured by the amount of time spent reading and writing during free time.

Braun, Carl, "Reading/Writing Connections: A Case Analysis," paper presented at the Colloquium on Research in Reading and Language Arts in Canada (Lethbridge, Alberta, Canada, Jun 7-9, 1984). [ED 266 403]

An addition to the "wholeness of language" debate, reviews theories regarding the reading writing relationship, suggesting that an awareness of the interdependencies and commonalities among various forms of communication may provide insights leading to students learning to read like writers and write like readers. Describes and critiques a study conducted by Braun and Gordon (1983) that explored the effects of narrative writing instruction on reading comprehension. This section highlights the methodological problems (including the failure to provide students with a purpose or an audience for their writing, or the opportunity to revise and edit their work) and misguided assumptions that led to inconclusive results. The critique concludes that (1) research problems must be formulated within the context of a holistic approach to language, (2) research design must provide for observation of the steps in the learning process, and (3) research design must also provide for observation of the cognitive transition from writer-based to reader-based writing. A separate "response," by Robert D. Armstrong is appended to the critique. It elaborates on the previous conclusions regarding the importance of the "wholeness of language" perspective and the means of making the common elements of language competencies available for use.

Brazee, Phyllis E., and Janice V. Kristo, "Creating a Whole Language Classroom with Future Teachers," *Reading Teacher 39/*5 (Jan 1986): 422-28. [EJ 327 879]

Describes how two college professors showed their undergraduate students how a Whole Language classroom works.

Bright, Robin, "Teacher as Researcher: Traditional and Whole Language Approaches," *Canadian Journal of English Language Arts 12/3* (1989): 48-55. [EJ 434 193] Describes an ethnographic study conducted in a grade four classroom during language arts instruction to discover patterns of a traditional approach, a Whole Language approach, or a combination of the two. Compares traditional and Whole Language approaches according to specific dimensions: concept of learning, curriculum, pedagogy, teacher's role, evaluation, and research orientation.

Brown, Cheryl L., "Whole Concept Mathematics: A Whole Language Application," *Educational Horizons 69/3* (spr 1991): 159-63. [EJ 425 226] In whole-concept mathematics, students actually use math and understand the practicality of what they are studying. This learner-centered approach treats students with respect, uses real-life situations, encompasses a variety of learning styles, and involves cooperative learning techniques.

Brown, Jessie, "A Personalized Reading Approach for At-Risk Middle School Students," paper presented at the Annual Meeting of the International Reading Association (36th, Las Vegas, NV, May 6-10, 1991). [ED 336 727] Three studies determined if the Summer Step reading program (a residential camping program implemented on the campus of Camp Baskervill Episcopal Outreach of Pawleys Island, South Carolina, using a personalized, contextualized reading approach) was effective, if children's self-esteem was enhanced by participation in the program, and if the students' attitudes toward reading improved. Sixty-seven boys and 52 girls participated in the reading study; 70 boys and 61 girls participated in the self-esteem study; and 69 boys and 55 girls participated in the attitude study. Approximately 90% of the children were considered high risk students for academic school failure. The residential camping program for adolescent age, predominantly African-American girls and boys lasted 3 weeks for girls and 4 weeks for boys. The emphasis for the reading program was keeping language whole and integrating all of the language processes through the use of the language and experience of the students. Subjects completed pre- and post-tests. A self-concept scale was administered to subjects in the self-esteem study. A Likert test to determine reading attitude was written by the researchers and administered as pre- and post-tests. Results indicated that: (1) students learned the comprehension skills of main idea, contextual vocabulary, detail, and sequencing; (2) students' self-esteem improved; and (3) students' attitudes toward reading improved significantly.

Browne, Dauna Bell, "Whole Language: An Approach to Reading That Fits Native American Reading Styles." (1986): 15 pp. [ED 296 861] This paper presents criteria for a reading program for Native American children based on the theory that these children have learning styles grounded in right hemisphere (brain) dominance. To test this theory the Wechsler Intelligence Scale for Children-Revised was administered to 197 Native American children. Test results are interpreted to indicate a pattern reflecting greater strength in right hemisphere processing. Concludes that lower reading scores of Native American children may be due, in part, to a mismatch between a right hemisphere learning style and a left hemisphere instructional approach. The paper recommends that reading programs for Native American children employ whole-brain learning techniques; visual, auditory, and kinesthetic models for language and thinking; rhythmic and dramatic play; and a holistic method of instruction that recognizes the language, culture, and learning styles that Native American children bring to school.

Bruneau, Beverly J., and Richard P. Ambrose, "Kindergarten and Primary Teachers' Perceptions of Whole Language Instruction," paper presented at the Annual Meeting of the National Reading Conference (39th, Austin, TX, Nov 28-Dec 2, 1989). [ED 316 835]
Explores the perceptions of Whole Language instruction held by a group of teachers of young children. Four questions framed the study: (1) How do teachers of young children define a Whole Language program? (2) What kind of Whole Language activities have the teachers tried in their classroom, and how did teachers feel about the outcomes of the activities they used? (3) What concerns did the teachers have about Whole Language instruction? and (4) What kind of assistance did the teachers believe would be helpful to them as they began to make changes in their literacy program? A survey was designed to assess a general level of knowledge and concerns about Whole Language programs among kindergarten-second grade teachers teaching in a rural or a suburban midwestern school district. Twenty-eight surveys were returned. One finding suggests that most teachers from this small sample accept Whole Language instruction as being an effective means of instruction, but as a supplement to a skills-based approach. It seems imperative that Whole Language advocates address teachers' beliefs concerning how children become literate. Without doing so, Whole Language activities may be viewed as additional instructional experiences which are "fun" but not a means for developing capable literate children.

Bruneau, Beverly J., "Restructuring Practice to Facilitate Children's Literacy Learning: A Case Study of Teacher-Initiated Curricular Change," *Teaching Education 4/2* (Sep 1992): 69-76. [EJ 450 881]
Describes curricular change from a skills-based, basal reader approach to a Whole Language approach to reading instruction from the perspective of a second grade teacher engaged in self-initiated curricular development. A significant concern that emerged was modifying class routine and organization to reflect a different instructional approach.

Bruneau, Beverly, and others, "Parent Communication in a Whole Language Kindergarten: What We Learned from a Busy First Year," *Reading Horizons 32/2* (Dec 1991): 117-27. [EJ 435 634]
Describes how one teacher initiated a Whole Language program and attempted to inform parents about the program. Discusses the importance of maintaining a constant flow of communication to parents and providing variety in the media that are used to carry the communication.

Bruneau, Beverly J., and others, "Parents' Perceptions of Children's Reading and Writing Development in a Whole Language Kindergarten Program." (1989): 22 pp. [ED 314 717]
A study was conducted to determine parents' perceptions of a kindergarten program in the face of change toward a holistic language/literacy curriculum. The participants were the parents of 25 children enrolled in an all day kindergarten class of a university-based child development center. Nine of the parents (all mothers) volunteered to be interviewed individually about parental perceptions of their child's reading and writing development. One theme which was strongly supported was how seriously this group of parents viewed their role in helping their child learn to read and write. One reason for the high degree of acceptance of this approach is that it validates and extends the type of literacy activity that had been occurring in the home. The parents who expressed satisfaction with the Whole Language kindergarten seemed to feel that the emphasis on informal social interactions and development of positive feelings in children about themselves as readers led their children to reading. Some parents voiced

strong concern about helping children with writing through invented spelling and expressed concern about what would happen to their children in first grade. Findings underscore the importance of parents and teachers working together.

Burchby, Marcia, "Literature and Whole Language," *New Advocate 1/2* (spr 1988): 114-23. [EJ 374 833]
Summarizes some of the criticisms which have been directed at basal instruction. Discusses how Whole Language approaches enhance the ability to teach children to read, and engage students in a democratic and democratizing educational experience.

Burk, Jill, and Joyce Melton-Pages, "From Recipe Reader to Reading Professional: Extending the Roles of the Reading Teacher through Whole Language," *Contemporary Education 62/2* (win 1991): 96-101 [EJ 447 939]
Describes the roles of reading professionals in school, focusing on Whole Language learning and noting implications of those roles for administrators and teacher educators; lists recommendations for administrators and teacher educators who wish to support the development of Whole Language instruction.

Burns-Paterson, Abigail L., "First and Third Graders' Concepts of Reading in Different Instructional Settings." (1991): 88 pp. [ED 339 027]
Reports an investigation whether students in Whole Language based and basal reader approaches would have different concepts of reading when asked to define reading. Subjects, 69 suburban New Jersey first- and third-graders and 16 New Zealand first-graders, were asked 3 questions: "What is reading?" "What do you do when you read?" and "If someone did not know how to read, what would you tell her she needs to learn?" The responses of the first-graders were tape-recorded, whereas the third-graders wrote their answers. For each question, responses were placed in one of four categories: vague, educational, decoding, or meaning-centered. Results indicated that Whole Language students gave less vague responses than did those students in basal reader groups. Results further indicated that although many students saw reading as a catalyst for learning and gave "educational" responses, basal reader students were more apt to view reading as solely a school activity, while Whole Language students saw reading as an integral part of their lives. Results also showed that although instructional setting accounted for a few differences, young children think of reading mainly as decoding, and do not see it as a meaning-getting, communicative process.

Busch, Katharine, and Margaret Atwell, eds., "Proceedings of the Annual California State University, San Bernardino, Reading Conference" (13th, San Bernardino, California, May 17, 1989)." (1989): 162 pp. [ED 313 657]
Highlights the active role of the learner. Contents: "Whole Language: Celebrating the Student within the Learning Community through Literature" (Dorothy J. Watson); "Integrating the Curriculum for Better Learning and Teaching" (Stephen B. Kucer); "Non- and Limited-English Speakers in Every Classroom: How Can We Help Them?" (Kathryn Z. Weed and Diana J. Sommer); "Creating Stories about Science through Art, Literature, and Drama" (Linda Prentice and Patricia Tefft Cousin); "The Bilingual Learner and Children's Literature in Spanish: Let the Celebration Begin!" (Joan S. Mims); "Celebrating Poetry" (James H. Rupp); "Beginning Reading: The Next Stumbling Block" (Darlene M. Michner); "Developmental Trends in the Interpretation of Motives, Beliefs and Feelings of Story Characters" (Donna W. Emery); "Study Strategies in Social Studies" (T. Patrick Mullen); "A Longitudinal Perspective of Children's Oral Narratives: Macrostructure, Microstructures and Relationships to Reading Achievement" (Marie Ice); "Illustration and Text" (Margaret Atwell); "Getting the Picture," "New Friends," and "Say It Again" (Katharine M. Busch);

"Becoming a Researcher I: What Do I Want to Know?" and "Becoming a Researcher II: What I Learned—What I Still Want to Know" (Patricia Tefft Cousin); "Getting in Touch with the Past" (Michael Gibson); "Help Me!" (Stephen B. Kucer); "Bilingual Reader Response" (Jaqueline A. Nyerick); "Literature Response Journals" and "Tricksters in Folktales" (Kathy O'Brien); and "Heavens Above" and "Leaf Monoprints" (Linda Prentice).

Busch, Robert F., and Patricia W. Jenkins, "Integrating the Language Arts for Primary-Age Disabled Readers," *Reading Horizons 23*/1 (fall 1982): 41-46. [EJ 271 054] Describes a program of reading instruction for young disabled readers that is based on a theory of the reading process developed by Kenneth Goodman that integrates speaking, reading, listening, and writing activities.

Calderon, Margarita, "Cooperative Learning for Limited English Proficient Students. Report No. 3." (1990): 17 pp. [ED 331 584] Describes cooperative learning strategies, their research base, and the rationale for their use as an instructional process for low English proficiency students (LEPS). The paper examines seven components of effective implementation of cooperative learning with language-minority students, and reports on preliminary work on a 5-year project to examine the effects of the Bilingual Comprehensive Integrated Reading and Composition model of cooperative learning on the reading comprehension, language skills, and writing performance of LEPS. The study is being conducted in the Ysleta Independent School District in El Paso, Texas, and in Santa Barbara, California, under the auspices of the Johns Hopkins Center for the Study of Education for Disadvantaged Students. Topics of this paper include: (1) a rationale for cooperative learning for LEPS; (2) benefits of such learning; (3) cooperative learning in relation to primary language instruction, Whole Language approaches, English as a Second Language and Transition to English programs, sheltered instruction and critical thinking, bilingual settings, and development of cognitive and metacognitive strategies; (4) what cooperative learning is not; (5) instructional models; (6) the philosophy of cooperative learning; and (7) procedures for effective implementation.

Calfee, Robert, "Schoolwide Programs To Improve Literacy Instruction for Students at Risk." (1991): 33 pp. [ED 338 726] Argues that a reformulation of reading and writing in the elementary grades can integrate the following three buzzwords of American education: (1) students at-risk for school failure; (2) the Whole-Language movement; and (3) restructuring. Critical literacy can serve as the centerpiece for empowering teachers and administrators as full-fledged professionals. A schoolwide approach to the literate use of language is described, beginning with anecdotal accounts of two correlated programs, Project READ and the Inquiring School. Project READ is a staff development program to help classroom teachers create a literate environment. In the Inquiring School, the literate-environment model extends to encompass the entire school. The implementation of these projects in a California elementary school illustrates the principles of critical literacy and the proposition that poor children should receive literacy instruction of equal challenge to that provided to students from more affluent backgrounds. It is asserted that virtually all students are capable of a level of critical literacy that allows them to thrive as adults, and that a supportive school context is essential to realizing this goal.

Cambourne, Brian, "The Whole Story: Natural Learning and the Acquisition of Literacy in the Classroom," New Zealand, 1988. [CS 011 352] Based on years of classroom observation, this book presents the thesis that powerful, critical, active, productive literacy can be achieved systematically, and regularly, with large numbers of the school population, if the principles currently known as the Whole Language approach are applied. The book is based on the assumptions that learning to become literate ought to be as uncomplicated and barrier-free as possible, and that once learned, the skills and knowledge that make literacy learning possible ought to endure beyond the classroom. Chapters in the book are: (1) What It's All about, (2) Portraits of Literacy Learning, (3) Prisoners of a Model of Learning? (4) An Alternate View of Learning, (5) Theory into Practice I, (6) Theory into Practice II, (7) Theory into Practice III, (8) Making Connections I: Understanding Reading, (9) Making Connections II: Understanding Writing, and (10) Pulling the Threads together.

Cambourne, Brian, and Jan Turbill, "Assessment in Whole-Language Classrooms: Theory into Practice," *Elementary School Journal 90/3* (Jan 1990): 337-49. [EJ 404 292] Suggests that traditional measurement-based approaches to evaluation are theoretically inappropriate in Whole-Language classrooms. Argues that responsive evaluation can be applied at the classroom level and that the data generated will tell more about children's developing control of language than standardized tests do.

Cantrall, Becky, and others, "Navajo Culture: A Bridge to the Rest of the World," paper presented at the Annual Meeting of the American Educational Research Association (Boston, MA, Apr 19, 1990). [ED 324 163] Describes a Navajo Indian program for making Navajo education more responsive to Native American cultural and educational needs. A survey of existing literature examines American Indian students' historical struggle between cultural identity and Anglo-American assimilation. As Navajo children may lack the schema for tradition- ally defined educational success and competition, schools might reexamine their customary teaching methods. The Greasewood Toyei Consolidated School began emphasizing bicultural education by weaving Navajo culture into the regular curricu- lum. Teachers were empowered to create their own culturally relevant study programs as part of a schoolwide curriculum reassessment. Student-testing and discipline policies were reevaluated. Teachers and assistants attended language workshops that exposed them to the Whole Language approach, a holistic learning method. An evaluation committee determined that the Comprehensive Tests of Basic Skills (CTBS) were inappropriate for Navajo students, and suggested that other achievement measurements be used. Surveys indicated growing use and popularity among teachers and students of the Whole Language approach, prompting additional training and curriculum changes. Greasewood staff developed a school philosophy encouraging further integration of Navajo culture into the curriculum, parental involvement, and the use of the Whole Language approach. As a result, the staff developed an entire new curriculum that balances Indian cultural requirements with state and CTBS testing standards. The document describes further curriculum revision procedures and summarizes new educational objectives for helping Navajo children achieve the balance that is one of the basic tenets of Navajo philosophy.

Carbo, Marie, "Deprogramming Reading Failure: Giving Unequal Learners an Equal Chance," *Phi Delta Kappan 69/3* (Nov 1987): 197-202. [EJ 360 778] Relates individual student experiences to illustrate that many poor readers are dropouts of programs requiring strongly analytic/auditory reading styles. Recommends adopting the Whole Language approach for today's global learners. Uses research findings to outline instructional methods that match students' reading styles.

Carbone, Vincent J., "Improving the Literacy Skills of Delinquent Adolescents through Cottage-Based Whole Language Activities and Experiences." (1991): 59 pp. [ED 335 659]
A practicum was designed to train staff to improve (over an 8-month period) the literacy and reading skills of 60 delinquent adolescent boys residing in a juvenile correction facility. Most of the boys residing at the training school had poor school histories characterized by reading achievement scores several grade levels below their peers and little motivation to improve their skills. A review of the literature indicated that traditional classroom methods of reading instruction would not provide a solution to this problem, and therefore a Whole Language approach to reading was implemented during non-school hours in the transitional residential cottage. The cottage was flooded with reading material suitable to the needs of interests of this population. Results indicated that the youths' attitudes towards reading improved as measured by the Estes Scale to Measure Attitudes Toward Reading. Narrative and ethnographic data suggested substantial practical significance associated with the improved attitudes scores. Collaterally, disciplinary reports were reduced substantially. Includes the Whole Language Experience Skill Checklist.

Carr, Kathryn S., "Literacy in the Workplace: A Whole Language Approach." (1990): 40 pp. [ED 324 441]
The personnel director of a local industry requested reading help from Central Missouri State University for several employees. After several meetings, a workplace literacy program that used the Whole Language approach supplemented by direct instruction in word recognition skills was developed. Two types of tests were written. One, a vocabulary test, required the participant to identify 40 industry- or safety-related words instantly and out of context. The terms were drawn from Occupational Safety and Health Administration forms, technical manuals from the company, and the book entitled "Occupational Literacy" (Rush et al., 1986). The second test used the cloze procedure as a simple and relatively accurate way to assess background knowledge necessary for general comprehension. Participants spent the first day of the program getting acquainted, browsing through magazines and newspapers for interesting articles, learning the VAKT (visual, auditory, kinesthetic, and tactile) method of study, writing journals, and having individual conferences with the instructor to set goals. Days 2-5 were spent reading self-selected materials, continuing word study routines established the first day, and using an informal reading inventory to begin individualized assessment. Ongoing procedures continued and expanded these activities with the aim of enabling participants to meet personal reading goals, build confidence and motivation, increase speaking and writing skills, and increase volume of reading and reading for pleasure.

Carroll, Jacquelin H., and others, "Integrated Language Arts Instruction (Reviews and Reflections)," *Language Arts 70/4* (Apr 1993): 310-15. [EJ 461 023]
Reviews six professional books and classroom materials that could support teachers and other educators in making the transition from integrating reading and writing to a synthesis of language arts with other areas of the curriculum.

Carroll, Jacquelin H., and others, "Whole Language in Upper Elementary Classrooms (Reviews and Reflections)," *Language Arts 69/2* (Feb 1992): 145-51. [EJ 437 487]
Reviews six professional books in three categories: three books written by teachers and other educators writing about their experiences in Whole Language classrooms, two instructional idea books written to help teachers implement specific areas of curriculum (biographies and poetry), and one book on current research. Reviews books and audiotapes suitable for the upper elementary grades.

Casey, Jean, "Monsters and Make-Believe Plus (Software Reviews)," *Writing Notebook 7/3* (Jan-Feb 1990): 32-33. [EJ 402 285]
Reviews Monsters and Make-Believe Plus, a computer program which supports learners in their quest to become skilled language users. Finds it to be one of the most powerful software programs available to implement a Whole Language program.

Caslovka, Arlys, and others, "Teachers Tell the Truth about School Change," *Instructor 101/5* (Jan 1992): 24-27, 32-34. [EJ 443 826]
Provides an overview of several major themes in the education reform movement and how changes brought about by school restructuring affect practicing teachers. Topics include teacher empowerment, site-based management, knowledge-work enterprise, school-university collaboration, professional development schools, Whole Language instruction, and technology.

Catoe, Elizabeth Anne, "Addressing Individual Learning Styles in a Whole Language Classroom." (1992): 34 pp. [ED 346 431]
A study was conducted to determine ways in which student learning styles could be accommodated in a Whole Language classroom. The Reading Style Inventory (RSI) developed by Marie Carbo which follows the Dunn model of learning styles was chosen for the study. The RSI was administered to 10 students in 2 second/third combination grade Whole Language classrooms in Albemarle County, Virginia. The inventories were computer scored and studied by the researcher. Results of the individual profiles showed that a majority of students responded well to global approaches to teaching reading. Several suggestions were made for ways to incorporate Whole Language strategies to match reading styles of students. It is possible for Whole Language teachers to match Whole Language instructional methods to individual reading styles without compromising the philosophies behind either approach.

Chall, Jeanne, "The New Reading Debates: Evidence from Science, Art, and Ideology," *Teachers College Record 94/2* (win 1992): 315-28. [EJ 460 426]
Examines recent debates on the teaching of reading from the standpoint of science, art, and ideology, focusing on the reading theories, research, and practice of the past two decades. The analysis emphasizes the issue of Whole Language versus phonics, noting the effects of Whole Language and phonics on reading achievement.

Chaney, Carolyn, "Evaluating the Whole Language Approach to Language Arts: The Pros and Cons," *Language, Speech, and Hearing Services in Schools 21/4* (Oct 1990): 244-49. [EJ 420 021]
Defines the Whole Language approach and identifies its strengths and weaknesses. An integrated instructional approach is recommended, balancing meaning and exposure to literature with skills instruction and practice.

Changing Schools and Classrooms," *Teacher Magazine 3/8* (May-Jun 1992): 32-37. [EJ 447 931]
Overviews several programs, techniques, and approaches related to improving schools and student learning; includes brief outlines of restructuring, effective schools, cooperative learning, Whole Language, technology, multiple intelligences, the Coalition of Essential Schools, the Accelerated Schools Project, the School Development Program, and the Center for Leadership in School Reform.

Chao, Han Hua, comp., and Carl Smith, ed., "Integrating the Language Arts. Learning Package No. 48." (1990): 51 pp. [ED 333 414]
Originally developed as part of a project for the Department of Defense Schools (DoDDS) system, this learning package on integrating the language arts is designed for

teachers who wish to upgrade or expand their teaching skills on their own. The package includes an overview of the project; a comprehensive search of the ERIC database; a lecture giving an overview on the topic; copies of any existing ERIC/RCS publications on the topic; a set of guidelines for completing a goal statement, a reaction paper, and an application project; and an evaluation form.

Chase, Nancy D., "Hospital Job Skills Enhancement Program: A Workplace Literacy Project. Curriculum Manual." (Atlanta: Georgia State University Center for the Study of Adult Literacy, 1990): 240 pp. [ED 328 666]
Describes a workplace literacy program designed to improve the literacy skills of entry-level workers in the housekeeping, food service, and laundry departments of Grady Memorial Hospital in Atlanta. An introduction describes the goals of the program and the employees served (low-literate adults who relied on word of mouth for most of their information in the workplace). Section 2 gives a rationale for using the Whole Language approach in workplace literacy programs. Section 3 describes the development of the program's curriculum, including a literacy analysis, determining job-specific literacy demands, determining instructional objectives, developing instructional activities and procedures, and assessing the programs. Section 4 describes instructional logistics, such as scheduling classes, recruiting students, and using tutors. Section 5 provides a model for developing hospital-based workplace literacy programs and includes a literacy task analysis and descriptions of instructional sessions.

Cheek, Earl H.,Jr., "Skills-Based vs. Holistic Philosophies: The Debate among Teacher Educators in Reading," *Teacher Education Quarterly 16/*1 (win 1989): 15-20. [EJ 404 573]
Explains the basic tenets of the skills-based and the holistic philosophies of reading instruction. Although the skills-based approach is dominant in both schools and teacher education, debate exists about the most effective approach.

Chew, Charles R., "Whole Language: Not the Sum of Its Parts," paper presented at the Meeting of the Catskill Whole Language Conference (Oneonta, NY, Aug 10-12, 1987). [ED 286 181]
For many years, educators from kindergarten to twelfth-grade have approached the teaching of vocabulary, spelling, grammar, punctuation, and so forth as isolated skills, unconnected with the everyday use of reading, speaking, and writing. Such practices are now viewed with less favor, as researchers and educators approach reading and writing as processes, to be dealt with as a whole. To capitalize on this trend, teachers need to recognize that children come to the classroom knowing something about language use, and that their prior knowledge must be built up and used to help them comprehend and use language experiences. The classroom must also be a literate environment, with plenty of diverse material for children to read, and children must be allowed and encouraged to visit school and public libraries and to browse widely. Additionally, classrooms need not be quiet places for learning to take place because children can learn much about language by discussing their experiences with one another. Teachers must understand that the processes of reading, speaking, and listening have a number of skills in common, such as pre-writing/thinking, drafting, and revising, and that all are valuable to children. The integration of such language arts skills can empower students and build their confidence, and thus improve children and society as a whole.

Christensen, K. Eleanor, "Whole Language in Perspective: A Teacher's Continuum." (1990): 11 pp. [ED 315 725]
Whole Language represents only one of many good concepts about teaching reading to children, but it is not for everybody. Because Whole Language is a philosophy rather

than a specific method, educational practitioners can incorporate different aspects of this philosophy to different degrees. If teachers think of a continuum of theoretical bases underlying the teaching of reading, then they can move along the continuum headed toward an integrated language approach (or Whole Language approach) at their own speed and in their own style. The strength of the Whole Language philosophy—its emphasis on language and language usage, both oral and written, used in real-life situations—cannot help but influence the everyday classroom environment for many children. As teachers consider the continuum of an integrated language approach, the teaching of reading will take a new step forward into the twenty-first century.

Christensen, Lois. M., and Mary Beth Dennis, "Translating Whole Language Child-Centered Teaching Theory into Practice for Preservice and First-Year Teachers, or 'But What Does It Look Like in the Classroom?!'" paper presented at the Annual Meeting of the National Association for the Education of Young Children (New Orleans, Louisiana, Nov 12-15, 1992). [ED 352 181]
The theory and practice of Whole Language teaching should be integral and simultaneous components of preservice teacher education. A number of instructional strategies and class activities can be used to provide preservice teachers with experiences similar to experiences they will provide to elementary school children. Examples of class activities include: (1) writing workshops during language arts and reading methods courses; (2) weekly workshops for collaborative work on assignments, thematic units, and projects; (3) shared reading of literature focusing on techniques of reading aloud and questioning, and exposure to current children's literature; (4) dialogue journals and learning logs in which students summarize the day's learning activities and ideas; (5) learning centers focusing on different topics, activities, and skills, which underscore the advantages of students moving at their own pace; and (6) shared field placements, in which students observe and participate each week in the literacy activities of a primary, multi-age, Whole Language classroom. Specific assignments in language arts and classroom management courses which can help education students understand the Whole Language philosophy include studies of children's authors and illustrators, the design and implementation of learning centers, the creation of child-centered bulletin boards, and the development of a unit using literature as the text.

Christensen, K. Eleanor, "A Study of Teachers' Viewpoints on Whole Language." (1990): 17 pp. [ED 329 907]
Examines preservice teachers' self-ratings of interest/investment in the different contexts of an integrated Whole Language approach, both theoretically and pragmatically. Subjects, 60 graduate students enrolled in reading courses in a small eastern university, completed a self-rating chart dealing with the theory and classroom implications of Whole Language. The chart was completed before any Whole Language topics were presented in the courses. Results indicated that: (1) teachers subscribe either moderately or whole heartedly to the underlying theoretical base of an integrated Whole Language approach and to many of the classroom practices which this implies; but (2) many of these same teachers expressed major concerns about the teaching of Whole Language. Findings suggest that school districts, universities, professional organizations, and publishers need to offer more and better specifics of quality instruction within the Whole Language framework.

Clark, Jack M., "Whole Language Literacy for At-Risk Learners." (Oneouta: State University of New York,1992): 58 pp. [ED 347 025]
This booklet provides strategies for implementing Whole-Language reading and writing in classroom and tutorial settings for at-risk learners, with a focus on migrant

students. The Whole-Language approach integrates reading, writing, listening, and speaking into language arts, social studies, science, and other content areas. Within an environment that fosters support and encourages risk-taking, this approach allows the student adequate time to engage in reading and writing experiences. The first section discusses the processes and conditions of literacy learning in relation to Whole-Language implementation and second language learners, including migrant children. The second section addresses elements of a Whole Language program and provides examples of classroom implementation. Suggestions are also given for English-as-a-Second-Language (ESL) students in developing language through content-area activities. The third section discusses qualities of good writing and provides strategies for engaging students in writing and evaluating their writing. Relevant to migrant children, it stresses integrating ESL reading and writing through a dialogue journal, parent involvement, and setting up "publishing" programs. The fourth section addresses Whole-Language evaluation, by focusing on the learning process as well as on the resulting product. This is accomplished through on-going teacher observations, conferencing, anecdotal records, and examples of children's writings. Examples of evaluation methods are provided. Also included are suggested readings for ESL and other at-risk learners and a Whole-Language literacy bibliography.

Clarke, Mark A., "Don't Blame the System: Constraints on 'Whole Language' Reform," *Language Arts 64/4* (Apr 1987): 384-96. [EJ 348 973]
Argues that if education for language development is to improve, the changes will have to take place in the classroom and that the change needed is to return control of classrooms to teachers. Also argues that for reform to endure, how systems respond to change must be understood.

The **Classroom** Reading Teacher," *Reading Teacher 41/9* (May 1988): 965-79. [EJ 370 165]
Provides a wide range of practical teaching ideas, including tips for using big books, the use of word maps for teaching new concepts, and the use of storybooks to teach counting. Provides an annotated bibliography of summer reading for students and teachers. Discusses the history, content, and future of the Whole Language Approach.

Clewell, Suzanne F., and Shirley A. Wagoner, eds., "Literacy: Issues and Practices. 1990 Yearbook of the State of Maryland International Reading Association Council. Volume 7." (1990): 95 pp. [ED 321 229]
Intended for reading professionals; contents: "Wish Fulfillment and Other Dangers in Reading" (Joan Develin Coley); "Emergent Reading Research: Synthesis and Analysis" (Majorie R. Hancock); "The Role of Affect in the Reading Process" (Mariam Jean Dreher); "Pursuing the 'Wisdom of Practice' in Preservice and Inservice Reading Teacher Instruction: An Electronic Communication Approach" (Mark G. Gillingham); "Passage Dependency and Prior Knowledge: Implications for the Assessment of Reading Comprehension" (Rose Marie Codling); "Adolescents' Exploration of Intimacy through Reading and Writing" (Sheldon Russell); and "Redefining the Role and Evaluation of the Reading Professional" (Jane Brady Matanzo). The following articles focus on classroom practices: "Writing: Magic for a Five-Year-Old" (Deborah Gordon Litt); "Using the Paraprofessional to Extend Whole Language Activities" (Susan Helldorfer); "Using a Language Experience Approach with Reluctant Writers in the Middle School" (Barbara E. Walker); "Teacher Participation in a Primary Screening Project" (Patricia M. Russavage); "'Comprehension System 8': A Teacher's Perspective" (Barbara L. Eddy and Karen A. Gould); and "The Use of Signing to Reinforce Sight Vocabulary: Teachers' Perspectives" (Robert M. Wilson and Cynthia T. Bowen).

Cochran, Judith M., "The Best of All Worlds," *Instructor 98/9* (May 1989): 38-41. [EJ 409 613]
One way to give students the most comprehensive reading instruction is to combine techniques from three approaches to reading: literature based reading instruction, the Whole Language strategy, and the use of basal readers. Lesson plans and student activities which demonstrate this combined approach are presented.

Coley, Joan Develin, "The Good News and Bad News about Whole Language: A Personal Perspective." (1990): 17 pp. [ED 317 956]
The biggest concern with Whole Language instruction lies in ignoring some of the obvious problems in implementation, or denying that there could be any problems at all. Problems mentioned by Maryland reading supervisors involve teacher competence, phonics/spelling/skills instruction, responses of Whole Language advocates when asked what direction educators should take for children who fail when using the Whole Language approaches, assessment, and teacher accountability. It is only because people are trying things that they make mistakes. It is not bad to make mistakes; it is only bad not to admit them or to examine their causes. If Whole Language fails, it will do so because either too many people will do it poorly or it will be done by the staunchest advocates who demand such rigidity that there is no room for the kind of flexibility which research and logic say are essential when educators talk about human learning. The good news about Whole Language methods includes the following points: (1) There is an insistence on authenticity of real texts and on engaging children in real life functional literacy tasks that matter to them. (2) Book reading is up in areas where literature is stressed in the classroom. (3) There is an increasing awareness of the uses of reading and writing together in content instruction. (4) Teachers are excited and show enthusiasm about their reading programs. (5) The kids are excited and enjoy learning and reading in Whole Language classrooms.

Combs, Martha, ed., "National Reading and Language Arts Educators' Conference Yearbook," papers from the National Reading and Language Arts Educators' Conference (Kansas City, MO, Sep 1987). [ED 294 160]
Contents: (1) "Let's Get Creative about Creative Writing in Language Arts Methods Courses" (B. J. Bush); (2) "Journals with A Purpose: Reading, Writing, and Thinking" (K. S. Daves and M. E. Jones); (3) "Making Curriculum Connections: The Centrality of Language Arts" (J. K. Hultquist); (4) "Relationships of Children's Stories to Reading Achievement: A Longitudinal Perspective Grades One to Six" (M. Ice); (5) "Reading Lesson Redesign: Strategies and Guidelines for Modifying Commercial Reading Materials" (S. Macaul); (6) "Multicultural Education for Reading and Language Arts Educators" (L. P. Rivera); (7) "The Developmental Growth of Meaning Vocabulary as Measured by Tests of Listening and Reading Vocabulary" (L. V. Rodenborn); (8) "Literary Gaps Invite Creative Interaction" (J. Watson); (9) "A Report of Attitudes of Secondary Education Students Enrolled in a Required Reading in the Content Areas Course" (R. J. Weimer); (10) "From Product to Process: Reading Assessment from a Whole Language Perspective" (J. W. Woodley); and (11) "The Low Reading Group: An Instructional and Social Dilemma" (L. M. Schell).

Combs, Robin, "Developing Critical Reading Skills through Whole Language Strategies," opinion paper for "Foundations in Reading II" course (Southern Nazarene University, Oklahoma, 1992.) [ED 353 556]
A teacher used classics of children's literature to teach critical reading skills. Although scoring above the national average on the Iowa Tests of Basic Skills (ITBS), the teacher's fourth-grade gifted students exhibited problems with critical reading skills. A

literature unit involving Whole Language strategies using Beverly Cleary's *The Mouse and the Motorcycle* and E.B. White's *Charlotte's Web* was implemented. Students kept literature logues while reading and engaged in classroom discussions using questioning techniques designed to develop critical thinking skills. Vocabulary instruction focused on using context clues in the stories to determine word meaning. Students did research on spiders in cooperative learning groups, assembled a "fact vs. opinion" bulletin board on pigs, and used creative writing to evaluate situations and recommend solutions from a pig's point of views. Students demonstrated higher-level thinking skills and became problem solvers. Students' scores on the ITBS increased remarkably as a class, but bilingual students' increases were a disappointment.

"Common Ground 1989: Suggested Literature for Alaskan Schools, Grades 7-12." (Juneau: Alaska State Department of Education, 1989): 153 pp. [ED 309 447]; and "Common Ground 1989: Suggested Literature for Alaskan Schools, Grades K-8." (Juneau: Alaska State Department of Education, 1989): 130 pp. [ED 314 757]
Intended to assist Alaskan school districts in their own selection and promotion of reading and literature, this guide to literature for use in grades 7-12 has five purposes: (1) to encourage reading and the use of literature throughout Alaskan schools; (2) to promote the inclusion of Alaska Native literature, and minority literature, in addition to the traditional Eastern and Western classics; (3) to help curriculum planners and committees to select books and obtain ideas for thematic units using literature; (4) to stimulate local educators to evaluate the use of literature in their schools and consider ways to use it as core material and as recreational reading; and (5) to accompany the state's Model Curriculum Guide in Language Arts, K-12, supplementing the references to literature, and to promote the reading of literature as an expectation for all Alaskan students. Contents include Criteria for Selection of Books; Questions for Local District Selection; Local Decision-Making Policies; Alaskan Literature; Implementation Ideas; Common Agreement Statements from Professional Associations; Anthologies of Alaska Literature by language groupings; Anthologies of Native American Writers and of Alaskan Writers; Alaskan Poets; Drama/Plays; Poetry; Short Stories; Role of Literature as a Source of History, Values, and Identity; The Right to Read; Library Bill of Rights; Source for Alaskan Literature; Description of Alaskan Associations; and more.

"Comprehensive Instructional Management System—Communication Arts: Whole Language Network, 1991-92. OERA Report," (New York: New York City Board of Education, 1993.) [CS 011 304]
During school year 1991-92, the Whole Language Network (WLN) expanded to include 90 teachers in grades K-6 in 3 school districts participating in the New York City Board of Education's Comprehensive Instructional Management System-Communication Arts project. WLN assisted teachers in using the Whole Language approach and sought to empower teachers to assume a more active role in curriculum decision-making. Evaluation of the WLN during the 1991-92 school year focused on teachers' perceptions and assessment of WLN, the support provided to participants, changing in teaching and assessment practices, and the effects of these changes on students' attitudes and achievement. Results: (1) Large majorities of teachers reported that the WLN was valuable in helping them implement Whole Language instructional strategies. (2) Almost all respondents reported that the instructional materials, support, and meetings and conferences proved valuable. (3) Many teachers reported changes in their approach to teaching. (4) Teachers reported trying a variety of "authentic" assessment techniques. (5) Support provided by school administrators ranged from extremely supportive to lukewarm. (6) Differences in students' pre- and posttest scores

in writing and reading were too small to be educationally meaningful. Recommendations: Greater effort should be directed toward helping teachers incorporate alternative assessment techniques into their classroom; more teachers from the same school should be selected; school supervisors' understanding and support for the program should be increased.

Conn, Sandra, "Textbooks: Defining the New Criteria," *Media and Methods 24/4* (Mar-Apr 1988): 30-31,64. [EJ 369 305]
Describes components of new elementary and secondary school textbook packages and reviews criteria for evaluating textbooks. Topics discussed include the development of teaching aids; curricular considerations; evaluating content-area textbooks; the Whole Language approach to instruction; and the role of librarians and media specialists in subject matter integration.

Connections: A Journal of Adult Literacy. Volume IV. (1991): 66 pp. [ED 333 205]
Contents: "Teaching Moments: Teaching People, Not Lessons" (Patricia Wild); "Whole Language: Implications for the Adult Learner" (Jeri Gillin); "Gatekeepers or Advocates?" (Rosie Wickert); "Writing with Teen Mothers: I Have Something to Say' (Kim Gerould); "Endings Take Time: Moments in the Writing Process" (Lucia Nunez); "Girl Talk" (Patricia Sandoval); "'Teacher, You Decide': Curriculum Development in Workplace ESL (English as a Second Language)" (Johan Uvin); "Adult Dyslexics Speak Out about Dyslexia" (John Gibbons et al.); "Right Brain, No Pain ESL" (Molly Flannery, Robert Browning); "Teaching Lesson" (Marty Kingsbury); "Adult Education: Self-Determination or Self-Delusion?" (Molly Mead); "Integrating Work and Learning in the SFCC (San Francisco Conservation Corps)" (Robert Burkhardt); "Using Bilingual Tutors and Non-Directive Approaches in ESL: A Follow-up Report" (Anthony D'Annunzio); "Teaching Literacy ESOL (English for Speakers of Other Languages): Notes from a Program for Displaced Workers" (Jonathan Skaff); "No More Reading Abuse" (Bridget O'Hagin); and "The Rocky Road from Frustration to Fulfillment: The Saga of a Volunteer" (Kimball Jones).

Connell, James V., ed., "Summary of Research on Implementing Whole Language Learning in Adult Basic Education Settings." (1992)" 70 pp. [ED 355 357]
Reports on a research project that looked at the relationship of Whole Language instruction to adult basic education (ABE) learning. It begins with the background of the three research projects. This section discusses the staff development program that enabled teachers to understand Whole Language, its principles, and its strategies and the research projects that were conducted simultaneously with the staff development program as ABE teachers began to implement Whole Language in the classroom. The next section provides an abstract from the 1990 National Reading Conference symposium presentation "Implementing Whole Language Learning in Adult Basic Education Settings", summarizing three reports. The research reports include: "Implementing Whole Language Learning: Adult Literacy Teachers' Problems and Concerns" (Padak et al.); "An Interim Research Report of the Influence of a Staff Development Process Emphasizing Whole Language Teaching Principles on ABE Teachers' Perceptions of Literacy and Their Literacy Teaching Practices" (Connell et al.); and "Adult Basic Education on Learners' Perceptions of Literacy Learning at the Onset of Implementation of Whole Language Instructional Practices" (Padak). The two final sections highlight eight insights gleaned from the research reports and suggest future research projects.

Cooper, Patsy, *When Stories Come to School: Telling, Writing, and Performing Stories in the Early Childhood Classroom.* (New York: Teachers and Writers Collaborative,1993): 144 pp. [ED 353 586] See Patsy Cooper, "When Stories Come to School:

Telling, Writing, and Performing Stories in the Early Childhood Classroom," *Teachers and Writers 24/3* (Jan-Feb 1993): 1-9. [EJ 457 118]
Offers pre-school teachers, kindergarten teachers, daycare workers, and parents ways to help young children begin to read and write, by placing stories at the very center of the early childhood curriculum. The book includes an in-depth discussion of the crucial pedagogical and developmental roles that stories can play in early childhood education, as well as a practical guide to having children tell their own stories and perform them with their classmates. The book also discusses the use of videos, and the uses and misuses of Whole Language, invented spelling, and the writing process. Contents: (1) Stories in Search of Classrooms; (2) Lessons from Home; (3) What I Had to Learn about Stories in Classrooms; (4) When Young Children Dictate and Dramatize Their Own Stories; (5) Portraits of Young Storytellers; and (6) A Guide to Storytelling in the Classroom.

Cooper, J. David, *Literacy: Helping Children Construct Meaning.* (Buckington, Mass.; Houghton-Mifflin, second edition, 1993): 636 pp. [ED 352 625]
Reflecting dramatic changes in educators' understanding of literacy, this book, a revision of an earlier text published in 1986 under the title, "Improving Reading Comprehension," provides support for preservice and inservice teachers in learning to help children develop literacy effectively. The central feature of the book is a literacy program whose focus is on interactive learning: the book presents and develops a model for creating a program that includes motivation, independent reading and writing, and instruction in reading and writing. Complete unadapted literature (and sample literacy lessons and minilessons for each piece of literature) are included in the book. Each chapter of the book includes strategies and procedures that have been effective with all learners (including second language learners and students with special needs), as well as a graphic organizer preview, an opening vignette to model constructivist teaching in action, a summary, bibliographies of professional references and children's books, and suggested additional readings. Contents: (1) Understanding Literacy Learning and Constructing Meaning; (2) Developing a Literacy Program; (3) Activating and Developing Prior Knowledge; (4) Vocabulary Development in the Literacy Program; (5) Identifying Words as an Aid to Constructing Meaning; (6) Responding and the Construction of Meaning; (7) Writing and the Construction of Meaning; (8) Modeling Strategies for Constructing Meaning; (9) Constructing Meaning across the Curriculum; and (10) Assessment and Evaluation in the Literacy-Centered Classroom.

Cooter, Robert B., Jr., and E. Sutton Flynt, "Blending Whole Language and Basal Reader Instruction," *Reading Horizons 29/4* (sum 1989): 275-82. [EJ 393 419]
Describes a program in a first-grade classroom in a rural school district that integrates holistic and direct instructional ideas by using the basal reader as one part of an otherwise holistic literacy program. Presents the major benefits of and some concerns about the program.

Corey, Kathleen, and others, "A Whole Language Program for Refugee Children." (1987): 19 pp. [ED 290 331]
Preparing Refugees for Elementary Programs (PREP) is a federal program to prepare young refugee children for further learning in the United States. Findings from current research on how children learn to speak, read, and write were used to design the curriculum. All children receive 18 weeks of full-time instruction, during which their parents also study English and cultural and work orientation. The weekly schedule and activities are typical of those in an American school. The largest single block of scheduled time is for English language dealing with familiar topics in school and daily

life. One hour a day is devoted to reading and writing. Eight 30-minute periods a week are devoted to math instruction, and additional time is allotted for recess and enrichment activities. The program uses the natural language approach to oral language development, and Whole Language approaches to literacy development, including shared reading with big books, the language experience approach to reading content, sustained silent reading, dictated stories, dialogue journal writing, and creative writing exercises.

Cothern, Nancy B., "Whole Language Theory-Based Instruction in the Basal Environment: Yes, You Can Do Both!," *Ohio Reading Teacher 26/3* (spr 1992): 9-13. [EJ 442 752] Suggests ways in which teachers may plan and incorporate effectively Whole Language theory into existing programs in which basal materials are established and accepted.

Craddock, Sonja, and Honey Halpren, "Developmental Listening in a Whole Language Classroom," *Canadian Journal of English Language Arts 11/1* (1988): 19-23. [EJ 367 278] Explains the difference between a reading aloud to children program designed to motivate children to read, and a developmental listening program which provides a focus for listening in a Whole Language environment and requires response and evaluation.

Crandall, JoAnn, and Gary Pharness, "Whole Language Approaches in Adult Literacy." (1991): 11 pp. [ED 348 890] After an introduction to the use of the Whole Language approach in adult literacy instruction, this paper describes some techniques or activities used in two adult literacy programs in Vancouver with participants who speak English as a first and as a second language. The Municipal Workplace Literacy Program, operated by the City of Vancouver (British Columbia), is a voluntary and confidential 80-hour program that offers one-half paid release time and serves mostly non-professionals. The Little Mountain Neighbourhood House/Vancouver School Board Tutor Training and Practicum Centre program serves recent immigrants, mostly of Chinese origin but also Indian, Central and South American, Polish, and Russian. Approximately half of the participants have university degrees from their countries of origin; the other half have had little or no formal schooling. Both programs use many Whole Language techniques, including shared reading, transcribed text, sustained silent reading, language experience, and interactive writing for adult literacy learners. Two additional strategies are used as well: an affirmation strategy that has come to be called "Affirmation: The Immigrant's Two Lives and the Cycle of Grief," and a strategy borrowed from the work of novelist Milan Kundera that involves the use of an existential code that inspires and guides the writing. The affirmation strategy uses simple drawings, gestures, translation, and some English to describe the learner's work, relationships, language and cultural connections, education, interests, etc. During the first 20 months of the program, only 2 of the 120 participants dropped out.

Cross, Tracy L., "Content Area Literacy and Reading Comprehension (Have You Read?)," *Reading Teacher 46/8* (May 1993): 708-10. [EJ 462 280] Reviews four books that deal with reading comprehension, phonics in a Whole Language classroom, children's books for mathematics learning, and using nonfiction trade books.

Crux, Sandra C., "H.E.L.P.: A Whole-Language Literacy Strategy That Works!" *Education Canada 31/2* (sum 1991): 16-21. [EJ 433 455] Presents the Holistic Educational Literacy Process strategy for adult literacy education consisting of the following 10 steps: presenting an advance organizer, reading silently, reading aloud, listening to the passage recorded, listening and taking notes, highlighting important points, networking structures, summarizing the passage, revising the written summary, and reflecting and evaluating.

Cullinan, Bernice E., "Whole Language and Children's Literature (Major Figures in Reading)," *Language Arts 69*/6 (Oct 1992): 426-30. [EJ 451 247]
Reflects on the role of literature in reading instruction. Reviews briefly research on Whole Language. Discusses the problems and promises of the Whole-Language approach and the use of children's literature in the classroom.

Cullinan, Bernice E., ed., "Invitation to Read: More Children's Literature in the Reading Program." (Newark, Delaware: International Reading Association,1992): 215 pp. [ED 345 213]
Presents practical and theoretical guidance about using literature to develop literacy. The prologue to the book describes some aspects of Whole Language programs at work, relates research findings that underlie the Whole Language philosophy, and presents scenes of teachers actively using literature in their classrooms. The book is organized into three major sections on genre studies, thematic units, and putting it all together. Chapters: (1) "Books for Emergent Readers" (Charlotte S. Huck); (2) "Act It Out: Making Poetry Come Alive" (Brod Bagert); (3) "Realistic Fiction and the Real World" (Dianne L. Monson); (4) "Interacting with Informational Books" (M. Jean Greenlaw); (5) "Enriching the Arts and Humanities" (Sam Leaton Sebesta); (6) "An Author Study: Tomie dePaola" (Joanne Lionetti); (7) "The Magic of Martin" (Deborah A. Wooten); (8) "Extending Multicultural Understanding" (Rudine Sims Bishop); (9) "Award Winners from Five English-Speaking Countries" (Sylvia M. Hutchinson and Ira E. Aaron); (10) "Organizing a Literature-Based Reading Program" (Dorothy S. Strickland); (11) "Responding to Literature: Activities for Exploring Books" (Linda DeGroff and Lee Galda); (12) "Using Literature with Readers at Risk" (Roselmina Indrisano and Jeanne R. Paratore); (13) "Resources to Identify Children's Books" (Arlene M. Pillar); and (14) "The Censorship Challenge" (Francie Alexander).

Cullinan, Bernice E., ed., "Fact and Fiction: Literature across the Curriculum." (1993): 99 pp. [ED 354 548]
Designed to inspire teachers to explore trade books in new ways, this book presents chapters dealing with historical fiction, diversity education, informational books in the social studies, literature in the math class, and supplementary reading materials for the science instruction. Although each chapter in the book focuses on a specific content area, all show how the areas complement and support one another and how literature helps in the process. Contents: (1) "Making the Past Come to Life" (Linda S. Levstik); (2) "Diversity Education" (Adela Artola Allen); (3) "Factual History: Nonfiction in the Social Studies Program" (Betty Carter and Richard F. Abrahamson); and (5) "Literature in the Science Program" (Dianne Lapp and James Flood).

Cunningham, Patricia M., and Richard L. Allington, "Words, Letters, Sounds, and Big Books: A Beary Good Approach," *Learning 20*/2 (Sep 1991): 91-92, 94-95. [EJ 436 768]
Describes ways that primary teachers can use decoding strategies within a literature-based, Whole Language setting. A three-stage approach involves the book stage (real reading), the word stage (learning words), and the letter/sound stage (learning sounds).

D'Annunzio, Anthony, and Paige E. Payne, "Whole Language Use in the English as a Second Language Classroom. Instruction Guide." (1990): 46 pp. [ED 339 244]
This guide describes the Combined Instructional Approach to adult basic education in

English as a Second Language (ESL) and offers procedures for its implementation. The approach uses literate bilingual tutors with little professional educational exposure to teach beginning reading instruction in ESL. A study of the feasibility of this method involved tutors and students from two groups, Cambodian refugees and immigrants and Spanish-speaking immigrants. Tutors transcribed stories narrated by the students, then followed standard language experience approach (LEA) procedures. Tutors were monitored by a reading specialist and provided with demonstrations and feedback to enlarge their repertoire of LEA skills. Practice in individualized reading was then offered to students. The experiment was found to be successful. The mean pre- to posttest gain for the Cambodian group was three grade levels in 5.5 months, and two grade levels for the Hispanic group in 4 months. Word recognition gains were significant for both groups, and larger for the Hispanic group. Both groups began at the non-English speaking level and achieved the level of a fluent English speaker in the fourth grade. Instructional procedures are outlined in some detail, with special attention given to getting started.

de la Cruz, Beverly Metro, "Implementing a Whole Language Curriculum to Improve Oral Language Competence in an Inner-City Kindergarten." (1989): 124 pp. [ED 313 145] A kindergarten teacher designed and implemented a practicum for increasing the oral language competence of 20 kindergartners in an inner-city public school. Goals were to improve children's receptive and expressive language abilities, social skills, and mastery of kindergarten curriculum objectives, and to increase parent involvement. A Whole Language curriculum was implemented. Instruction focused on themes that included all curriculum content areas. Coordinated curriculum components were designed to maximize student involvement in class activities. Learning centers and cooperative learning strategies contributed to the establishment of a nurturing classroom atmosphere. Parent participation was encouraged through conferences, newsletters, parent education materials, and parent-and-child activities. Primary teachers were trained in Whole Language teaching and learning principles and strategies. Practicum evaluation data revealed that the intervention was effective beyond expectation. The intervention increased the children's receptive and expressive vocabularies, improved their use of appropriate language structures, and contributed to mastery of curriculum objectives. It was evident that the program had a positive impact on teachers.

de los Santos, Lisa A., "Integrating Montessori and Whole Language Philosophies: Methods of Reading in English as a Second Language Classrooms." (1989): 19 pp. [ED 350 092] Following a summary of research pertaining to the Montessori and Whole Language philosophies, this paper examines similarities between the two philosophies. Both philosophies are based on holistic learning, use cross-cultural materials, and stress the teacher's role as a facilitator within the classroom environment. The relationships of the Montessori and Whole Language philosophies to the reading process are then considered. Topics addressed include children's need to be exposed to a variety of teaching methods and the integration of reading and writing in the language arts. A discussion of methods of teaching reading in English as a Second Language classrooms considers the use of touch, sight, and sound; environments that encourage children to develop independence; the use of mixed ability groups; and lessons that involve interpersonal interaction. Describes materials in the Montessori method which teachers can use to teach reading.

de Vleeschower, Mary Jo, "Teaching Teachers for Whole Language Success," *Perspectives in Education and Deafness 11/3* (Jan-Feb 1993): 16-18. [EJ 459 616]

Describes the process of training teachers of students with hearing impairments to use Whole Language teaching methods. The paper discusses success with Whole Language, resistance to Whole Language methods, effects on students, effects on teaching, and advice to other trainers.

DeBoer, June, "The Response of Fifth Grade Low Achievers to Literature-Based Reading Instruction through Whole Class and Heterogeneous Arrangements." (1991): 143 pp. [ED 336 736]
An action research project studied the attitudes and achievement of low-achieving fifth-grade students after participating in a 1-year heterogeneously grouped, literature-based reading program. The project explored the changes in student attitudes towards reading, and changes in students' knowledge in comprehension and vocabulary development. Eight fifth-graders from a Christian school in Michigan were evaluated through a pre- and post-achievement test; a pre- and post-attitude questionnaire, student comments, parental comments and diary, and a pre and post Houghton Mifflin basal grade equivalent skills test required by the principal of the school. Results indicated that the attitudes of low achievers towards reading were more positive after the treatment. The low achievers were more motivated to read, and the reading achievement scores indicated a gain in both vocabulary and comprehension. Results suggest that the attitudes and achievement of the low achievers can increase while participating in a heterogeneously grouped literature-based reading program with instruction that directly instructs them to monitor their own metacognition. Low achievers can benefit from exposure to children's literature to motivate them to read. Through direct instruction of comprehensive strategies, low achievers can learn to monitor their own comprehension. While participating in heterogeneous groups, differences are minimized.

Decker, Barbara C., "Early Literacy Instruction with Computers and Whole Language: An Evaluation of the Writing-To-Read Computer Program with Disadvantaged Minority Children," paper presented at the Annual Meeting of the International Reading Association (36th, Las Vegas, NV, May 6-10, 1991). [ED 335 635]
A study examined the effectiveness of the Writing-to-Read Computer Program in elementary school language arts education. The program is designed to teach children to read through interacting with a computer by learning sound/symbol relationships and by composing stories. First- through fourth-graders from predominantly black, urban schools and from a rural, racially integrated school were tested in vocabulary, reading recognition, reading comprehension, and language subtests of the Metropolitan Achievement Test, and in the reading, language, and spelling subtests of the California Achievement Test. Results indicated that the Writing-to-Read Program produced significant gains in language and spelling which hold up over time. However, it did not seem to influence reading ability. Traditionally, poor language skills have been seen as a detriment to normal development in reading yet the children in this study had strong language scores. Results also suggest that if these children had a Whole Language start in reading instruction beginning in kindergarten, the children's scores in reading would improve dramatically.

DeCotis, John, "Insuring a Quality Education for Your Children: A Guide for Parents." (1989): 27 pp. [ED 336 805]
Offers parents an overview of the elements crucial for a good education, with the intention of motivating them to take an active role in their children's education. Contents: (1) What is an education? (2) Why get a good education? (3) What composes a good education? (4) Is communication important? (5) What can be done at home? (6) Can computers be helpful? (7) Can television be helpful? (8) Can too much pressure be

detrimental? (9) Are private schools a good alternative? (10) What is Special Education and what services does it offer? (11) What are Talented and Gifted programs? (12) Who determines curricula in public schools? (13) What are standardized tests and why are they given? (14) How are public schools accredited? (15) Should schools teach higher order thinking skills or facts and information? (16) Are the fine arts and physical education an essential part of a "good" education? (17) What are developmental education and developmental teaching strategies? (18) What is the "Whole Language" approach to reading? (19) What will the school of the future be like? (20) What is the answer? and (21) Thoughts for the future.

DeGrella, Jeanne Berthelot, "Creating a Literate Classroom Environment." (1989): 19 pp. [ED 312 610]
A literate classroom environment immerses a student in a rich, stimulating, interactive, and purposeful print and language environment which is designed to provide for success in reading, writing, listening, and speaking and the needs of individuals responsible for their own learning in a natural, non-competitive, non-threatening, risk-taking setting. According to researchers, suggestions for teachers to aid in creating a literate classroom environment include: (1) the arrangement of the physical environment; (2) the incorporation of literacy activities such as reading quality literature, sharing books, sustained silent reading, and modeled writing; and (3) procedures to meet individual student needs.

DeGroff, Linda Jo, "Developing Writing Processes with Children's Literature," *New Advocate 2/2* (spr 1989): 115-23. [EJ 386 981]
Suggests methods of using literature to help students select and develop topics, write drafts, confer about their writing, revise, edit, and publish their work. Concludes that students can learn a great deal about writing processes through reading and discussing children's literature.

DeGroff, Linda, "Computers in the Whole Language Classroom," paper presented at the Florida Instructional Computing Conference (Orlando, FL, Jan 1989). [ED 318 452]
Argues that if Whole Language teachers are to use computers in their reading and writing programs, then they will need both software and strategies for using computers that are consistent with their beliefs and goals. For Whole Language teachers, as for other good teachers, it is the teacher's beliefs about curriculum and instruction rather than the technology that will determine the role of the computer in the classroom. This paper explores the place of computers in Whole Language classrooms by considering how computers can facilitate teaching and learning in ways that are consistent with each of the following beliefs commonly held by Whole Language teachers: (1) children learn language through social interaction; (2) children learn by reading and writing whole and meaningful texts; (3) language is used for real purposes and with real audiences; (4) children learn when we emphasize process; (5) children need time and choices for language learning; and (6) language learning involves risk-taking.

DeGroff, Linda, "Is There a Place for Computers in Whole Language Classrooms?" *Reading Teacher 43/8* (Apr 1990): 568-72. [EJ 408 409]
Comments on six points of belief commonly held by Whole Language teachers. Considers how computers can facilitate teaching and learning in ways that are consistent with those points of belief.

Deming, Mary P., and Maria Valeri-Gold, "Computers and the Developmental Learner," *Reading Horizons 32/3* (Feb 1992): 235-38. [EJ 439 183]
Discusses the use of computers in teaching basic writing to college students. Offers computer exercises and activities which foster a Whole Language curriculum.

DeSantis, Diane K., "Restructuring the Curriculum for Active Involvement—Teachers and Students as Learners," revised version of a paper presented at the Annual Spring Conference of the National Council of Teachers of English (Richmond, Virginia, Mar 18-20, 1993). (New Hampshire, 1993.) [CS 011 362]
A fifth-grade teacher researched the experts, observed master teachers, and experimented to find out what worked best for her and her students as she made the transition from the basal to the process approach to teaching the language arts. Taking courses and meeting with others helped support her decision to change. During the process of change, the teacher realized that the basal can be used in a Whole Language way, heavily supplemented with real books, self-selected reading of all types, and oral and written responses. Using the reading/writing process, the teacher tried to incorporate the literary genres that her students were studying by integrating all the areas of the language arts. Portfolios were kept as students finished each genre. Developing the skills of cooperative learning enabled students to become listeners, supporters, and active learners. The teacher selected books based on the students' varied interests and abilities. When students chose the books they were about to read, they followed guidelines from the reading consultant. The teacher readily shared classroom experiences with parents, teachers, principals, board members, and others through frequent communication in newspaper form or invitations to visit the classroom. Performance assessments in language arts included: writing, oral discussions, exhibitions, and portfolios. The teacher constantly observed and evaluated herself and her students. The teacher observed the emergence of active readers, writers, listeners, and speakers—active involvement, active learners, and teacher and students as learners.

Dewalt, Mark, and others, "Effects of Instructional Method on Reading Comprehension," *Reading Improvement 30*/2 (sum 1993): 93-100. [CS745536]
Investigates the relationship between type of reading instruction and reading comprehension. Uses predictor variables including IQ, group, race, and comprehension pretest score to predict comprehension score. Finds that the dependent variable was not significantly related to method of reading instruction, and there was no interaction effect between reading method and IQ in predicting comprehension scores.

Dickinson, Susan, "Creating and Implementing a Model for Motivating Recreational Reading Using a Whole Language Approach for Secondary School Students." (1992): 82 pp. [ED 344 196]
A practicum was designed to increase the amount of recreational reading by secondary school students, and to improve students' attitude toward reading, thus decreasing disruptive behaviors in the classroom. A Whole Language workshop approach was implemented over an 8-month period in two high school English classes, grades 10 and 11, college preparation level, with a total of 104 students. Many of the students had the skills to read but chose not to do so. The workshop was student-centered so that students could become self-directed, choosing reading materials of interest to them. The focus of the curriculum was on reading, thinking, and discussion, and the teacher's role was that of facilitator. Pre- and post-surveys were administered to record changes in student attitudes and improvement in leisure reading. Results showed that students' attitudes toward reading improved; that more students were involved in leisure reading; that fewer disruptions occurred during sustained reading in the classroom; and that students increased the amount of their free time spent in leisure reading. While three of the four practicum objectives were not met, the improvement shown was positive in terms of overall success.

Dolman, David, "Some Concerns about Using Whole Language Approaches with Deaf Children," *American Annals of the Deaf 137*/3 (Jul 1992): 278-82. [EJ 451 570]

Examines the relevance of Whole Language instruction with deaf children and concludes that, although this approach has many values, deaf children often need a more direct approach to acquire English literacy. Educators of the deaf are urged to be wary of adopting general education methods without careful evaluation with deaf students.

Dougherty, Mildred, and others, "Building Decoding and Comprehension Skills into Whole Language," paper presented at the Meeting of the New Jersey Education Association (Atlantic City, NJ, Nov 10, 1989). [ED 317 973]
Nursery rhymes and written phonics used in a meaningful context are valuable teaching methods which can be applied in a Whole Language classroom or in conjunction with a basal reading program. Because nursery rhymes are rooted in oral tradition they lend themselves to oral presentation. They provide forms for the oral beginnings of the best of linguistic skills. Children can easily memorize the rhymes and act them out for the class. The rhymes can then be written down and used as reading material for the students. A simple cut-and-paste activity can help children learn phonics. Each phoneme is named and defined as it is introduced. The children then look through magazines to find examples of the phoneme they just learned and explain what they see in the picture and how they hear the sound in the topic, and they can attach a name to their picture. The contributions are then collected and the entire class reviews the pictures and the corresponding phonemes. The materials used in these activities are at hand and are inexpensive.

Dudley-Marling, Curt, and Don Dippo, "The Language of Whole Language," *Language Arts 68/7* (Nov 1991): 548-54 [EJ 434 263]
Calls for resolution of the ambiguities and contradictions of the language and the practices of Whole Language. Attempts to elucidate conflicting conceptions and practices among Whole Language advocates and thereby make Whole Language even stronger.

Duffy, Gerald G., "Let's Free Teachers to Be Inspired," *Phi Delta Kappan 73/6* (Feb 1992): 442-47. [EJ 439 293]
Drawing on specific examples in elementary school classrooms and flying instruction analogies, shows how teachers can combine tenets of both holistic and direct approaches to reading instruction. Students are more likely to use reading and writing effectively when teachers themselves are empowered to select intelligently from various conceptions.

Dumas, Colleen, "Implementing Whole Language: Collaboration, Communication and Coordination," paper presented at the Annual Spring Conference of the National Conference of Teachers of English (Indianapolis, IN, Mar 14-16, 1991). [ED 343 112]
A parent of a kindergarten child in Texas began observing her child's classroom when she noticed that the Whole Language instructional approach described to parents before the beginning of school was apparently not being implemented as stated. The parent was surprised when her child's teacher suggested, after only six weeks of instruction, that the child be put in a transition program the following year because the teacher believed the child was not ready for first grade. As the year progressed, the parent's frustration and anger grew as indications grew that the child's risk-taking abilities and self-esteem were being destroyed. The child is now progressing well through first grade, and the child's teacher is encouraging invented spelling and creative activities in the classroom. Although communication on the parent/teacher level and the parent/principal level has increased awareness of the importance of children's reading capabilities, more parent education needs to be addressed to make the program successful as a whole.

Duquette, Ray, "Videotape Review: 'Showing Teachers How,'" *Journal of Reading Education 14*/1 (fall 1988): 43-45. [EJ 396 421]
Reviews "Showing Teachers How," a series of 12 videotapes released in 1986 and 1987 dealing with (1) reading instruction using the Whole Language approach in the elementary grades; (2) social studies instruction using trade books; (3) writing instruction; and (4) discussion strategies for current events.

Dyson, Anne Haas, "The Word and the World: Reconceptualizing Written Language Development or Do Rainbows Mean a Lot to Little Girls? Technical Report No. 42." (1990): 36 pp. [ED 318 010]
Current research has fragmented educators' vision of both written language and development. A more integrative vision, one that preserves the integrity of written language as a symbol system, is based on five principles that characterize written language development: (1) the establishment of equivalences; (2) exploration and orchestration of the system; (3) reliance on shifting relationships of form and function; (4) differentiation and integration of symbolic functions; and (5) participation in social dialogue. These principles highlight the dialectical relationship between function and form, between child construction and adult guidance. The articulated vision of development differs in fundamental ways from most current viewpoints, as it does not consider written language as simply an extension of the child's oral language but as the evolution of a distinct symbolic option with links to the child's entire symbolic repertoire. Viewing written language growth in this way may allow for a more open-ended vision of its development, and the developmental principles discussed may suggest some possibilities for negotiation between Whole Language and basic skill proponents.

Edelsky, Carole, "Whose Agenda Is This Anyway? A Response to McKenna, Robinson, and Miller," *Educational Researcher 19*/8 (Nov 1990): 7-11. [EJ 422 237]
Disputes the version of Whole Language presented by Michael McKenna et al. [see EJ 422 236]. Argues that Whole Language is an educational paradigm complete with theoretical, philosophical, and political assumptions and a congruent research agenda. Contends that "paradigm blindness" prevents critics from seeing the legitimacy of Whole Language-generated research.

Edelsky, Carole, ed., "Language Arts Topics and Educational Issues: Information Sheets," Arizona: Center for the Expansion of Language and Thinking (CELT), 1992. [CS 011 336]
This collection of 29 succinct information articles discusses issues relating to language arts, including Whole Language, phonics, student evaluation, spelling, and censorship. Some of contributors to the collection are Ken Goodman, Yetta Goodman, Jerome Harste, Patrick Shannon, and Constance Weaver. Titles of articles are: "Learning to Talk, Learning to Read, Learning to Write," "What Is Whole Language," "What Whole Language Is Not: Common Myths and Misunderstandings," "Some Key Principles of a Whole Language Perspective on Learning and Teaching," "How Whole Language Teachers Develop Phonics 'Know How'," "Research in Support of Whole Language," "Whole Language Is as American as Apple Pie," "Reading in Whole Language Classrooms: Focus on Comprehension," "What about Skills in Whole Language Classrooms?" "Whole Language and the Theological Concerns and Beliefs of Parents," "Phonics Phacts," "Phonics and Dialects of English," "Phonics Is a Flawed System," "Why We Should Not Teach Intensive, Systematic Phonics," "Phonics versus Whole Language: Why Whole Language Teachers Don't Think It Is Much of a Debate," "Why a Whole Language Classroom May Be the Best Place for Your Attention Deficit Disorder Hyperactive (ADHD) Student," "Basal Reading

Programs, Literature-Based Reading Programs, and Literature Programs," "How to Teach Literacy Learners Who Challenge Teachers," "What Does It Mean to Be Literate?" "Adult Illiteracy: Cause? Effect?" "Questions and Answers about Spelling," "What Are Some Tools Teachers Use to Evaluate That Also Help Children Learn?" "Some Aspects of Assessment That We Often Forget" "Who Should Evaluate? What Should Be Evaluated?" "The Mixed Age Primary: What and Why," "Bilingual Learners: Principles That Help; False Assumptions That Harm," "Why Thoughtful Teachers Abhor Censorship," "Statement of the International Reading Association: The Dangers of Censoring Textbooks and Reading Program Materials, and "How Teachers Can Productively Respond to Political Conflicts about Education in Their Communities."

[**Edelsky**, Carole], "A Talk with Carole Edelsky about Politics and Literacy," *Language Arts 69/5* (Sep 1992): 324-29. [EJ 448 430]
Presents an interview with Carole Edelsky in which she discusses the political issues that affect the day-to-day lives of children and teachers in the language arts classroom; political aspects of Whole Language; national political issues and literacy; and political actions teachers can take to improve language arts education.

Edelsky, Carol, and others, "Hookin' 'Em In at the Start of School in a 'Whole Language' Classroom," *Anthropology and Education Quarterly 14/4* (win 1983): 257-81. [EJ 292 638]
Describes how an inner-city sixth-grade teacher with an unusual approach to literacy got children to act according to new expectations before the first day of the school year was over. Discusses the research in relation to other findings on teacher effectiveness.

Edelsky, Carole, and Karen Smith, "Is That Writing—Or Are Those Marks Just a Figment of Your Curriculum?" *Language Arts 61/1* (Jan 1984): 24-32. [EJ 291 277]
Discusses the differences between inauthentic and authentic writing, arguing that most writing in school is inauthentic, because it is written for someone else's intentions. Examples are cited from a classroom with an essentially Whole Language orientation, but which occasionally reverts to inauthentic writing assignments.

Ediger, Marlow, "Reading: Skills versus Ideas." (1991): 10 pp. [ED 339 998]
Debate regarding the teaching of reading as skills versus reading as securing ideas has been in evidence for some time. The "measurably stated objectives" philosophy emphasizes that the act of reading should be divided into specific skills in which the inherent component parts are identified and a highly detailed list of precise objectives are stressed in teaching and learning situations. A psychology of behaviorism harmonizes well with a skills reading curriculum. Toward the other end of the curriculum, an idea-centered curriculum may be emphasized. The excitement and challenge of reading ideas is paramount, and learners seek, select, and read diverse materials, sequencing their own learning. Trade books are much in evidence. A psychology of humanism harmonizes well with a "reading as securing ideas" approach. Holism is involved in that learners are to comprehend subject matter and appreciate literature rather than achieve specific skills, measurably stated, in reading. Specific skills may be emphasized as the need arises, but not as predetermined, precise objectives for learner attainment. Whether behaviorism or humanism is used as the philosophy of reading instruction, teachers need to guide each student to achieve optimally in reading.

El-Amin, Cassaundra, and Mark Richmond, "The Quantitative and Qualitative Analysis of Second Grade Reading Performance Comparing Literature Based and Basal Instruction." (1992): 17 pp. [ED 353 564]
Two separate research methodologies, quantitative analysis and qualitative analysis,

were employed to determine the differences in second-grade children on method of reading instruction. Fifty children in two classrooms from one school in North Carolina were subjects. One of the two teachers employed a literature based methodology, while the second teacher employed a basal instructional format. Quantitative results conformed to that suggested in the literature; specifically, no significant differences were found in achievement between the two groups. Confounding between teacher and methodology was a major weakness in the study; however, the implementation of qualitative analysis yielded substantial additional information with respect to the underlying reasons for outcomes in the two classrooms. The need for confluence of results of qualitative and quantitative methodologies is strongly supported.

Eldredge, Lloyd, "An Experiment with a Modified Whole Language Approach in First-Grade Classrooms," *Reading Research and Instruction 30*/3 (spr 1991): 21-38. [EJ 428 268]

Compares results of a modified Whole Language approach (incorporating daily 15-minute total class phonics instruction) with those obtained from a popular basal approach. Finds that students in the Whole Language classes made greater gains in phonics, vocabulary, reading comprehension, and total reading achievement than students in the basal program.

Engel, Brenda S., "Longfellow School Literacy Project: A Five-Year Study of Outcomes from a Whole Language Program in the Primary Grades." (1991): 183 pp. [ED 344 185]

A two-part study evaluated the effectiveness of Longfellow School's primary-grade Whole-Language literacy project. Part 1 of the study began in the academic year 1984-85 with children in standard English and bilingual classes in grade K-3. Over a 5-year period, a total of 1,021 individual assessments were carried out on 336 students. Data consisted of samples of students' work, classroom observations, and teacher interviews. Part 2 of the study collected additional follow-up data on two cohorts, conducted 13 child studies, analyzed summary data, described the context of learning at the school, and critiqued the instruments used. Results from both parts indicated that: (1) all children in standard classes remaining in the program learned to read and write competently by the time they were in the upper elementary grades; (2) children learned in uneven increments, not according to grade level expectations; (3) children in bilingual classes began school with less knowledge of the conventions of print than those in standard classes but made equivalent gains between kindergarten and first grade; (4) sources of literacy learning varied; (5) questions of morale and self-respect were central to learning; (6) teachers represented a continuum of beliefs and practices; (7) children were exposed to literature on a daily basis; and (8) all teachers changed their beliefs and practices to some extent.

Enoki, Donald Y., "Student Portfolio and Profiles: A Holistic Approach to Multiple Assessment in Whole Language Classrooms," paper presented at the Annual Meeting of the American Educational Research Association (San Francisco, CA, Apr 20-24, 1992). [ED 350 343]

Describes the assessment process in Whole Language classrooms in the Honolulu (Hawaii) School District. The development of alternative measures based on actual student performances was a natural outcome of the teachers' training and implementation of a holistic education/Whole Language program. Multiple and multidimensional assessment emerged from the holistic perspective, resulting in performance-based measures that included authentic samples of students' work. The systematic gathering of selected works led to the development of student portfolios and the student summary profile. Assessment is treated as an integral part of the instructional and learning processes rather than as pre/post measures on test items. Formal and informal measures and process and product measures are being tested in Chapter 1 programs and in Students of Limited English Proficiency programs. Three years of development have led to some significant results in sustained growth in student achievement. Classroom teachers are recognizing the worth of assessment and evaluation as an integral part of instruction. Performance-based measures developed through portfolios can serve as a significant way to measure student growth and development more accurately.

Erpelding, Diana, "Integrating Whole Language with the Basal Reader to Increase the Use of Language and Comprehension of Literature." (1990): 41 pp. [ED 350 578]
Examines whether the integration of Whole Language with the basal reader would increase the use of language and comprehension of literature. Twenty students and one teacher in a split third/fourth grade classroom in a predominantly white, lower socioeconomic school in Ottumwa, Iowa, participated in the study. For 16 weeks, students wrote in journals daily, read silently every day, and were exposed to a variety of Whole Language activities as well as using their basal readers. Students were pre and posttested using a reading attitude survey, a reading inventory, and a curriculum-based assessment. Results indicated that: (1) there was an increase in punctuation, length of sentences, subject verb use and length of written work; (2) all students showed an increase of one grade level in comprehension; and (3) there was a 2% increase in positive attitudes toward reading. Findings suggest that the students benefitted from the combined use of Whole Language and the basal reader.

Esch, Gwendolyn C., "Nurturing Second Graders' Literacy and Language Development through Child-Centered versus Curriculum-Centered Experiences." (1991): 80 pp. [ED 335 705]
A practicum was designed and implemented to foster 24 second graders' literacy and language development via child-centered as opposed to curriculum-centered experiences. The primary goal was to improve students' quality and quantity of writing by allowing extra time, much exposure to more and various non-basal literature, hands-on activities, and experiences geared to their interest level. The second aim was to improve their attitude toward reading by having them cooperatively and actively involved in a uniquely child-centered environment. Pre/post quality and quantity of writing tests and pre/post attitude surveys were administered. Journals, charts, and a log were kept. The number of library books, records, and tapes were increased and changed weekly. Students were assisted in project work, total and small group activities, and field trips. Conferences, mini-lessons, peer tutoring, mapping, brainstorming, and modeling occurred. Students wrote drafts, proofread, revised, and rewrote, while keeping their own writing portfolios and daily language arts sheets. The class newspaper, pen pals, and big book experiences proved rewarding. Total school and parent involvement added support. Results of the quality and quantity of writing tests showed a marked improvement and an increase. Reading attitude surveys revealed a positive dynamic increase.

Espe, Cathie, and others, "Whole Language—What a Bargain!" *Educational Leadership* 47/6 (Mar 1990): 45. [EJ 405 137]
Although the Whole Language perspective requires no money, it does involve "kid watching," or knowledge of individual class members and their interests. As the experiences of two elementary teachers illustrate, educators need only look to their own backyards and to past/present historical events for rich instructional material.

Evans, Deborah J., "Decreasing Overreliance on Basal Readers through Staff Development." (1991): 43 pp/ [ED 335 666]
A practicum aimed to reduce overreliance on the basal reading program in grade 1 of the elementary school. It also endeavored to provide teachers with quality choices to enhance and enrich their reading/writing programs. Five workshops were designed to meet the specific needs of a public school district located on the northeastern seaboard which services 5,000 students. Goals of the practicum were to reduce the time spent on the tests accompanying the basal series, and to offer suggestions for successfully incorporating whole class reading activities and integrating the teaching of reading and writing. The practicum also sought to decrease the number of workbook and skillsheet pages used. Proven strategies were modeled for teachers during the workshops through video tapes and in demonstration lessons. In addition, the teachers were introduced to numerous professional journals, and were encouraged to join professional organizations. Results indicated that all of the teachers decreased the number of tests given and the corresponding amount of time spent on testing. Furthermore, time spent on specific skill instruction decreased while time spent on integrated, meaningful reading/writing activities increased. Results also indicated that teachers are willing to change when meaningful alternatives are modeled for them, and that time, patience, and a supportive environment are required for effective and longlasting change to occur.

Evans, Deborah J., "Increasing Instructional Options for the Teaching of Reading and Writing through Staff Development." (1992): 43 pp. [ED 350 583]
A practicum was designed to increase the instructional options chosen by classroom teachers in order to make meaningful connections between reading and writing for elementary students. Teachers in the target school were experiencing difficulty in translating theory into effective classroom practice. In response to a teacher needs assessment, four key areas of focus were identified and four corresponding workshops specifically geared to teacher grade levels, and including references to the textbook series in use, were developed. The workshops were: (1) What is Whole Language? (2) Integrating Reading and Writing; (3) Whole Class Instruction; and (4) Combining Trade Books with the Basal. Practical handouts accompanied each workshop. A list of trade books that related to concepts and themes in their math series was particularly popular. Classroom visitations and individual meetings were arranged, and professional books, articles and video tapes were also made available. Outcomes were positive, with all the practicum goals being met. All teachers demonstrated the use of several new teaching strategies. Central office administrators became interested and involved in the practicum.

Ezell, Jeanne R., "The Concept of Delivery Applied to Modern Rhetoric," paper presented at the Conference on Rhetoric and the Teaching of Writing (Indiana, PA, Jul 10-11, 1990). [ED 321 267]
Within the field of composition, classical rhetoric was re-discovered in the early 1960s; that interest has been for the most part confined to the first three of the five parts of classical rhetoric—invention, arrangement, and style—with memory and delivery being ignored or, at least, neglected. Recent interest in "the speaking-writing connection," "collaborative learning," and "Whole Language" indicates an interest in delivery. One scholar suggests that teachers can help children consolidate their oral and written resources through exercises that make the functions of speech and writing as similar as possible, such as oral monologues and expressive writing and through using talk as preparation for writing. Teachers who apply collaborative learning to teaching writing have students work in groups, talking throughout their writing processes. Students work together to discover topics and discover what they have to

say about topics. Whole Language combines talking and writing with listening and reading to counteract the fragmenting skills approach to education. Taking delivery back into composition classrooms and considering it along with performance is a fascinating possibility. It is hoped that the interest in delivery demonstrated in the speaking-writing connection, in collaborative learning, and especially in Whole Language will grow. It is an interest in delivery that is more fundamental than the matters of voice and gesture that were so long a part of rhetoric.

Fagan, William T., "Understanding Whole Language as Philosophy and Methodology: A Case of Reductive Bias?" paper presented at the Annual Transmountain Regional Conference of the International Reading Association (8th, Calgary, Alberta, Canada, Sep 30-Oct 4, 1987). [ED 305 600]
Whole Language has become a visible and strong movement in language instruction. Yet there is still considerable disagreement as to what Whole Language entails and there are different degrees of knowledge held by various self-professed Whole Language teachers. Some are at a beginning stage of knowledge regarding Whole Language as philosophy and methodology. This has serious implications for the children entrusted to them. Teachers of Whole Language should have attained an advanced level of knowledge. Seven biases that may interfere with the attainment of knowledge at this level are: (1) oversimplification and overregularization, (2) overreliance on a single basis for mental representation, (3) overreliance on top-down processing, (4) context-independent conceptual representation, (5) overreliance on precompiled knowledge structures, (6) rigid compartmentalization of knowledge, and (7) passive transmission of knowledge.

Farris, Linda, "Teaching through Children's Literature: Whole Language Activities for the Classroom," paper presented at the Annual Meeting of the West Regional Conference of the International Reading Association (Portland, OR, Feb 27-29, 1992). [ED 345 227]
This bibliography lists 106 items of children's literature suitable for use in a Whole Language classroom. Fifteen sections include alphabet books; rhythm, rhyme, and song; science and health; inventions and cures; mystery; fairy tales and folk tales; Native Americans; fun with language; math; friends; jokes and riddles; animals; a mouse thematic unit; and "just because." A concluding section lists books about using children's literature in the classroom.

Farris, Pamela J., and Debra Kaczmarski, "Whole Language, A Closer Look," *Contemporary Education 59*/2 (win 1988): 77-81. [EJ 376 987]
Whole Language learning, which is often defined in abstract terms, is discussed in terms of its rationale, its practical applications, its implications for how communication skills are taught, and its classroom implementation.

Farris, Pamela J., and Carol Andersen, "Adopting a Whole Language Program for Learning Disabled Students: A Case Study," *Reading Horizons 31*/1 (Oct 1990): 5-13. [EJ 418 010]
Presents a case study of a learning disabilities teacher who struggled with the traditional instructional approaches and who adopted a literature-based, Whole Language program. Presents the teachers' reflective comments along with references from the literature of Whole Language researchers and theorists.

Farris, Pamela J., "From Basal Reader to Whole Language: Transition Tactics," *Reading Horizons 30*/1 (fall 1989): 23-29. [EJ 397 681]
Offers suggestions in the areas of classroom management, instructional strategies, and evaluation to assist in making a smooth transition from the basal to the Whole

Language program. Suggests that gradual implementation allows teachers and students to become confident in using this instructional method.

Farris, Pamela J., "Handwriting Instruction Should Not Become Extinct (Views and Other Views)," *Language Arts 68/4* (Apr 1991): 312-14. [EJ 425 354]
Discusses the issue of handwriting instruction through the Whole Language philosophy and direct instruction methods.

Feick, Terry, and others, "Literacy—The Challenge of the Twenty-First Century: A Rural Perspective and A Rural Community Adopts a Literature Based Language Arts Program." (1989): 23 pp. [ED 315 222]
Children from rural backgrounds often struggle with the unfamiliar language and settings in basal reader selections, but the rich knowledge and experience that a rural child brings to the classroom is rarely reflected there. These papers describe a literature based program developed in the Washington Court House City Schools (Ohio) to teach education classes (grades K-12), to think, read, write, speak and listen. Teachers and students read aloud in kindergarten and first grade six to eight times per day and this practice of reading aloud to students continues K-12. Nursery rhymes, poems, songs are written on large charts and the familiar patterns are rehearsed. Daily journals are kept in all grades. Beginning stories and journals are often picture representations and scribble writing, but these fade and writing appears. Spelling is taught under the same non-threatening conditions. Inventive spelling is encouraged. Patterns of correct spelling improve with language experience, not through memorization. Mechanics, usage, and grammar are modeled; teachable moments occur when a child experiences a need for a specific form. Editing skills are developed by conferencing with teachers and peers. High school teachers report improvement in student writing skills. They continue the program using paperback novels and historical novels.

Feldman, Isabel, "A Whole Language Approach to Learning in the School Media Center," in "School Library Media Program Connections for Learning." (Albany: New York State Library, 1991) 105 pp. [ED 346 857]
Theme issue of *The Bookmark* focus on various aspects of school library media programs.

Feng, Jianhua, and George W. Etheridge, "Match or Mismatch: Relationship between First-Grade Teachers' Theoretical Orientation to Reading and Their Reading Instructional Practices," paper presented at the Annual Meeting of the American Educational Research Association (74th, Atlanta, Georgia, Apr 12-16, 1993). [CS 011 350]
Uses survey methodology to determine first-grade teachers' theoretical orientations and students' attitudes toward reading, and structured classroom observations to describe teachers' reading instructional practices. Subjects, 259 of the 428 first-grade teachers (61%) in 94 elementary schools of a large mid-south metropolitan public school system, returned usable survey data. A stratified sample of 15 teachers, five from each orientation (phonics, skills, and Whole Language), were randomly selected for classroom observation and interviews. Results indicated that: (1) the majority of teachers (219, or 84.59%) held a skills theoretical orientation to reading, while only eight (3.10%) held a Whole Language theoretical orientation to reading; (2) 60% of the teachers observed (including all five teachers with a skills orientation) taught reading in a manner consistent with their theoretical orientation to reading; (3) 73% of the teachers observed used basal/skills strategies; (4) all teachers used a variety of instructional strategies to teach reading; (5) all teachers consistently identified their own classroom experiences as the single most important influence in what they believed about reading and reading instruction; and (6) there was no significant

difference in students' reading attitude with respect to teachers' theoretical orientation to reading and reading instruction. Findings suggest that the provision of practical strategies without theory may lead to misimplementation or no implementation at all, unless teachers' beliefs are congruent with the theoretical assumptions of the practice.

Feng, Jianhua, "Whole Language Approach: Is It Really Better?" (1992): 19 pp. [ED 349 548]
Dissatisfied with traditional approaches to beginning reading practices dominated by phonics, basal reading series, and workbooks, and more importantly, influenced by research and knowledge about how children learn to read, teachers/educators launched a grass-roots Whole Language movement in the early 1980s. However, the term "Whole Language" has become broadly defined and loosely used in the professional literature. Because of such diversity in definition and because of inconsistencies within educational literature relating to the concept of Whole Language, it is no surprise that the relative effectiveness of Whole Language is very inconclusive and often controversial. A review of the research on the effects of Whole Language on beginning reading achievement indicates that no consistent conclusion can be drawn regarding its effectiveness. Jeanne Chall proposed that an understanding of how reading develops should help teachers/educators understand the highly controversial issues of what to teach, when, and by what methods. Chall's stage model of reading development may contribute to a better understanding of how reading is acquired and how the total environment, as well as the school environment, may be optimized for pupils at the different stages.

Ferguson, Phyllis, "Whole Language: A Global Approach to Learning," *Instructor 97/9* (May 1988): 24-27. [EJ 374 371]
The Whole Language approach to learning is used to develop reading, writing, and language skills in primary grades and science and social studies skills in intermediate grades. The program is described and its techniques of immersion, theme building, brainstorming, implementation, and flexible grouping are discussed.

Ferrara, Judith M., "Trends in Elementary Writing Instruction in the 1980s." (1990): 37 pp. [ED 333 483]
This bibliographic essay and research review investigates four areas: (1) the characteristics of elementary writing instruction prior to the 80s; (2) the factors which changed writing instruction in the 80s; (3) the characteristics of elementary writing instruction in the 80s: and (4) the place of elementary and pre/in-service textbooks in the teaching of writing. The essay concludes that writing process theory has been practiced across the curriculum in Whole Language or integrated learning classrooms, and suggests that writers, practitioners, and researchers study their evolution, reflect, and share their reflections.

Fields, Marjorie V., and Deborah V. Hillstead, "Whole Language in the Play Store," *Childhood Education 67/2* (winter 1990): 73-76. [EJ 423 521]
Explains the concept of Whole Language instruction by means of examples from a kindergarten unit on the grocery store. Activities include visiting the supermarket, making stone soup, and assembling a play grocery store. Activities teach reading, writing, oral language, phonics, and word recognition.

Finkelstein, Karen S., "Improving Language Arts Skills at the Elementary School Level." (1992): 73 pp. [ED 348 683]
Describes a practicum designed to make a significant difference in increasing students' language expression by assisting teachers with the appropriate techniques to incorporate effectively the writing process in an integrated language-arts curriculum. The

target group consisted of 150 fourth-grade students and five fourth-grade teachers. The implementation period lasted 12 weeks and involved the use of critical thinking skills, analysis, synthesis, evaluation, and graphic organizers. Teachers participated in seven two-hour training sessions designed to assist them in incorporating the writing process into the integrated language arts curriculum. Success of the practicum was based upon the target teachers' required training assignments, performance on the cognitive language arts composition posttest, and the target students' growth in language expression as measured on the Comprehensive Test of Basic Skills and a holistic scoring writing prompt. Results indicated that: (1) the wide variance between language mechanics and language expression scores was narrowed to a one-percentile discrepancy; (2) 52% of the students met the criteria for successful language expression; and (3) all of the target teachers increased their knowledge of the writing process and demonstrated effective strategies for writing instruction.

Fisher, Peter J. L., and Sheila Shapiro, "Teachers' Explorations of Historical Fiction in Literature Discussion Groups." (1991): 26 pp. [ED 353 599]
Reports a study examining the experience of some teachers in a graduate class in literature study who began to explore ways of using literature with their pupils. Subjects, 24 graduate students (9 secondary school teachers and 15 elementary teachers) enrolled in a class on the reading/writing connection, were randomly assigned to 6 groups of 4 students each. Each group read one book about the westward expansion of the United States in four sessions over a two-week period. Discussion sessions were audiotaped and analyzed. Students kept response logs, and after the last class, students completed a survey. Results indicated that: (1) subjects learned about the use of literature and cooperative groups in the classroom; (2) their exposure to literature led to an understanding of the possibilities for its use in social studies; (3) they learned how personal response to literature can be a powerful motivator for reading and learning; (4) role assignments and particular tasks seemed to contribute to literature discussions for these student teachers; (5) they adopted stances to the books which showed their personal involvement with the stories, understanding of characters, events, and themes, the author's craft, and the book as an object in relation to other sources of historical information; and (6) the only disturbing issue was the low frequency with which a critical stance was adopted. Findings suggest that teachers can develop their own literary knowledge in such a way as to be able to extend their students' understandings.

Fitzgerald, Doris F., and others, "Developmentally Appropriate Whole Language the Whole Way: Addressing the Literacy Problem for At-Risk Students." (1991): 13 pp. [ED 342 534]
Describes graduate courses in the Whole Language approach offered by Lander College to 10 rural school districts in South Carolina. The Whole Language approach is seen as a way to meet the educational needs of rural at-risk students. In the first course on the Whole Language approach, 10 early childhood teachers engaged in workshops on the theoretical and research bases for the Whole Language movement. Teachers used journals with invented spelling, a shared literature event, classroom response circles, class books, language experience stories, and a message board. At the conclusion of the course, four of the teachers were successfully operating Whole Language classrooms. Other courses offered to elementary through high school teachers were developed under guidelines from the South Carolina State Department of Education. Teachers in these courses expressed concern about a lack of administrative support for Whole Language and teacher accountability for skills development, driven by published school test scores. As the teachers participated in courses they became

more adept at teaching skills in the context of literature and social conversation. At the secondary level, teachers need to be introduced to the Whole Language approach as an alternative. They also need to work with new delivery systems involving grouping and cooperative learning. There must also be administrative support of changes in methods and delivery systems. At Lander College a Whole Language course has been proposed to improve the language skills of its college students.

Fitzgerald, Jill, and Carol Stamm, "Variation in Writing Conference Influence on Revision: Two Cases," paper presented at the Annual Meeting of the National Reading Conference (40th, Miami, FL, Nov 27-Dec 1, 1990). [ED 331 052]

Reports a study that described the influence of writing conferences on revision knowledge and revision activity for an initially knowledgeable first-grade reviser and a relatively naive one. Subjects, two first-grade students in a Whole Language classroom, were chosen from the 16 students in the class for close study. Data analysis consisted of reading all of the writing and transcripts of interviews and conferences; determining the quality of first and last draft of each composition; coding conference talk; tracing comments between conferences, interviews, and revisions carried out; calculating counts of revisions the children talked about in interviews and revisions they carried out; and reviewing the teacher's observations about the two children's behavior in the classroom. Results indicated: (1) that conference influence was variable, both within and across children; and (2) dramatic differences were noted between the two children in conference influence, with only the initially naive writer profiting significantly from conferences and evidencing clear developmental progress in revision.

Fleisher, Barbara M., and others, "Raising Literacy Levels: A College/Community Agency/Public School Partnership," *Academic Therapy* 25/5 (May 1990): 635-44. [EJ 418 350]

Describes a successful effort at collaboration among a college reading program, a neighborhood self-help agency, and a public school. The three-way partnership was formed to improve the literacy levels of 12 behaviorally disturbed children in the fifth and sixth grades. The project involves Whole Language reading instruction and counseling sessions.

Flemming, Donald N., "Literacy for Learners of Limited English Proficiency: The New Zealand Approach," *TESL Talk* 20/1 (1990): 208-12. [EJ 427 260]

Describes the atmosphere and activities in a primary classroom in New Zealand that affect the literacy development of limited English-proficient children. Key factors are identified, including teacher expectations of success, Whole Language environment, and nurturing classroom climate.

Flennoy, Audrey J., "Improving Communication Skills of First Grade Low Achievers through Whole Language, Creative Drama, and Different Styles of Writing." (1992): 71 pp. [ED 352 599]

Describes a practicum designed to give 12 low-achieving first-grade children more time to improve their communication skills, to promote knowledge development, and to motivate children to become enthusiastic about the reading and writing process. Whole Language, creative drama, and different styles of writing were utilized in the classroom to accomplish the practicum outcomes during a 3-month period. Checklists, questionnaires, and surveys were used in collecting data. Data showed that (1) children chose books when their work was completed; (2) they read orally in groups and independently, and could relate many of their favorite stories because the classroom was encompassed with books; and (3) their writing activities reflected a variety of experiences.

Flickinger, Gayle Glidden, and Emily S. Long, "Beyond the Basal," *Reading Improvement* 27/2 (sum 1990): 149-54. [EJ 412 965]
Describes ways in which teachers who use a basal reading series can go beyond the manual and integrate the Whole Language approach into the language arts program.

Floyd, Sandra N., "Involving Parents in Whole Language Kindergarten Reading Program." (1992): 78 pp. [ED 350 591]
Describes a Whole Language kindergarten at-home reading program. The target group was 27 sets of parents of children in a kindergarten classroom who volunteered to participate. The objectives were to increase the parents' knowledge of Whole Language techniques; increase their level of comfort in using Whole Language techniques at home with their children; and increase the parents' ability to judge critically the quality of children's literature books for instructional use. During a 12-week program, parents in the target group were instructed in Whole Language techniques and given a parent booklet on Whole Language written by the practicum researcher. Following an orientation session, the parents and their children read quality children's literature books at home together and then used Whole Language techniques to extend the reading activities. Critical thinking skills were required of the parents as they filled out weekly questionnaires on each of the books used in the program. The success of the project was documented through the evaluation data gathered, including the weekly returns of Parent Response Forms representing an 85% response rate.

Fluellen, Jerry, "Designing the Holographic Whole Language Program. Opinion Paper," paper presented at the Conference on Teaching African-American Students To Write and Think (Philadelphia, PA, Apr 1990). [ED 330 995]
Describes the use of David Bohm's holographic world view to design a Whole Language program. Characterized by interconnectedness and multidimensionality, Bohm's holographic paradigm joins Eastern and Western belief systems in an old fashion pursuit of wisdom, on the one hand, and a new fashion pursuit of solutions to nonlinear problems in chaotic systems, on the other. These two characteristics, in turn, inform the design of a Whole Language program that combines procedural knowledge (k-w-l, know-want-learn, learning strategy and D. N. Perkins' knowledge as design); declarative knowledge (great world literature); and cooperative learning. The program helps each non-elite middle school student to reach full height as a maker of knowledge others will want to read, hear or see.

"**Focus** on Reading," *Instructor* 98/3 Pt2 (Oct 1988): 1-57. [EJ 386 479])
Reading improvement in school-age children is the focus of the 10 articles within this supplement. Topics include recent research findings, classroom activities, teaching methods, computer-based instruction, literature-based programs, home-based activities, stages of reading development, and reading resource materials.

Foley, Christy L., "Turn Them on to Learning with Two Whole Language Strategies: Guam's Experience—An Overview of Guam's Classroom Realities," *Reading Improvement* 28/1 (spr 1991): 40-43. [EJ 447 110]
Discusses Guam's unique multicultural student and teacher population. Describes two classroom language arts activities (the method of taped repeated reading and "write around") that have met with success and continue to gain momentum in Guam's classrooms.

Ford, Michael, "Whole Language Change: Lessons from Hostile Audiences," *Journal of the Wisconsin State Reading Association 35/*1 (win 1991): 29-35. [EJ 429 707]
Answers the five following common objections to the Whole Language approach: Haven't we tried this all before? What will happen to the child if some teachers use

Whole Language and others don't? Where does the teacher find the time to do all this? Where's the proof that it works? and And what about the future?

Ford, Michael P., and Marilyn M. Ohlhausen, "Tips from Reading Clinicians for Coping with Disabled Readers in Regular Classrooms," *Reading Teacher 42*/1 (Oct 1988): 18-22. [EJ 377 453]
Suggests classroom activities appropriate for disabled readers, including thematic approaches, Whole Language activities, writing in response to reading, incentives and competition, and relaxation techniques.

Foster, Carol, and others, "Classroom Language Instruction Modeled on the Ways Families Talk," *Dimensions 19*/2 (win 1991): 9,11-12,36. [EJ 423 553]
Addresses two questions concerning Whole Language teaching to young children: (1) What is Whole Language? (2) What experiences are appropriate for Whole Language teaching?

Foster, Janet E., "Review of Professional Literature: Mills and Clyde on Whole Language, Plus War Play and Social Skills," *Dimensions 20*/1 (fall 1991): 28-30 [EJ 434 878]
Reviews professional literature on the use of Whole Language programs at all age and educational levels, ways for teachers and parents to respond to children's fascination with war play and war toys, the integration of children's literature into the social-studies curriculum, and the teaching of prosocial skills to preschoolers and kindergartners.

Fountas, Irene C., and Irene L. Hannigan, "Making Sense of Whole Language: The Pursuit of Informed Teaching," *Childhood Education 65*/3 (spr 1989): 133-37. [EJ 385 993]
Discusses Whole Language teaching and learning within a theoretical context. Examines philosophies, materials, and strategies for developing children's literacy skills. Looks at a resurgence of old methodologies and materials with new insights. Offers basic tenets of a holistic approach to language learning.

Fox, Deborah, "ERIC/RCS: The Debate Goes On: Systematic Phonics vs. Whole Language," *Journal of Reading 29*/7 (Apr 1986): 678-80. [EJ 331 222]
Draws on selected ERIC resources to suggest dominant features of two approaches to beginning reading: systematic phonics and Whole Language learning.

Fox, Deborah, "ERIC/RCS: The Debate Goes On: Systematic Phonics vs. Whole Language," *Journal of Reading 29*/7 (Apr 1986): 678-80. [EJ 331 222]
Draws on selected ERIC resources to suggest dominant features of two approaches to beginning reading: systematic phonics and Whole Language learning.

Fradd, Sandra H., and Andrea B. Bermudez, Andrea B., "POWER: A Process for Meeting the Instructional Needs of Handicapped Language-Minority Students," *Teacher Education and Special Education 14*/1 (win 1991): 19-24. [EJ 429 881]
Describes a field-tested instruction and assessment model that fostered development of second-language skills by integrating writing with listening, speaking, reading, and problem solving. The model draws upon elements of process-oriented instruction, Whole Language learning, cooperative learning, cognitive mapping, and reading and writing across the curriculum.

Fredericks, Anthony D., and Timothy V. Rasinski, "Whole Language and Parents: Natural Partners (Working with Parents)," *Reading Teacher 43*/9 (May 1990): 692-94. [EJ 410 147]
Lists 13 Whole Language projects and possibilities selected from many schools which can be used as a source of ideas to stimulate parents' engagement in Whole Language activities. Reports the efforts of 1 school, and describes how parents are involved in promoting reading and writing.

Freeman, Judy, "Reading Aloud: A Few Tricks of the Trade," *School Library Journal 38/7* (Jul 1992): 26-29. [EJ 448 956]
Reading books aloud to students can motivate them to read themselves, but teachers and librarians need to learn new skills to read aloud effectively. Selecting an appropriate book, reading with expression, creating an atmosphere, and using the right questioning techniques to start a discussion all have an impact on successful reading aloud.

Freeman, David E., and others, "California's Reading Revolution: A Review and Analysis," *New Advocate 6/1* (win 1993):41-60. [EJ 454 178]
Examines factors that caused resistance to California's recently mandated approach to reading and language arts instruction that focuses on authentic literacy experiences. Discusses pressures from teachers, administrators, and parents; shifts in student population; and testing. Presents illustrative scenarios from California schools. Suggests ways to counter pressures to return to traditional instruction.

Freeman, Deidre, and Maureen LaMar, Maureen, "ILGWU Worker-Family Education Program Curriculum Guide, 1989-1990." (1989): 87 pp. [ED 313 918]
This teacher's guide for the International Ladies' Garment Workers' Union (ILGWU) educational program provides background information, instructional materials, and instructional techniques for teaching a course in job skills and issues, with emphasis on the development of English language skills. The course is made available to union members and their families. Introductory sections of the guide discuss the classroom setting for the course, student characteristics, monthly teachers' meetings, and the monthly calendar. The remainder of the guide addresses the curriculum itself. Common questions asked by teachers are addressed in question-and-answer format, including how to identify student needs and interests, how to develop and adapt instructional materials, what instructional methods encourage maximum student involvement, and why and how to combine all four language skills areas (reading, writing, listening, and speaking) in one class session. A sample lesson is presented. In the final section, specific program components are discussed in greater detail. These components include writing tasks, a student-produced magazine, use of newspapers, the student council and its activities, development of class picture files, a curriculum library, monthly curriculum material packets, field trips and speakers, library locations and hours, bilingual education and General Educational Development instruction, and grammar instruction. Some classroom and planning materials are included.

Freeman, Ruth H., "Implementation of a Whole Language Approach to Literacy Acquisition." (1990): 26 pp. [ED 320 106]
Describes a comprehensive first-grade language curriculum which views the acquisition of literacy as a Whole Language process. The paper explains how to configure program elements to provide direct instruction, time-on-task, and self-directed learning. The manner, timing, method of instruction, and specifics of the contribution of each component to the program are explained in detail. The methodology of instruction, materials used, and techniques of classroom management which facilitate and support instruction are discussed. Secondary program elements, including projects and units of study, which complete the overall language curriculum, are presented. The paper includes excerpts from the children's work to illustrate the methodology and results.

Freeman, Yvonne S., and Yetta M. Goodman, "Revaluing the Bilingual Learner through a Literature Reading Program," *Reading and Writing Quarterly: Overcoming Learning Difficulties 9/2* (Apr-Jun 1993): 163-82.

Presents alternatives to three misconceptions about bilingual learners to promote the revaluing of these students. Describes traditional views of literacy instruction for second-language learners and suggests a Whole Language literature program as an alternative. Lays out differences between inauthentic, controlled literature-based reading programs and meaningful, authentic programs.

Freeman, David, and Yvonne Freeman, "Whole Language Content Lessons for ESL Students," paper presented at the Annual Meeting of the Teachers of English to Speakers of Other Languages (22nd, Chicago, Mar 8-13, 1988). [ED 295 468]
Whole Language content lessons are recommended as a means for teachers of English as a second language to help their students develop both communicative and academic competence. Whole Language is an approach to teaching that relies on the principles that lessons should: (1) progress from whole to part, (2) be learner-centered, (3) have meaning and purpose, (4) promote social interaction, (5) include all four communication modes (listening, speaking, reading, and writing), and (6) reflect the teacher's faith in the learners. Each of the principles is explained, a content lesson based on these principles is described, and a checklist for evaluating the degree to which any lesson is consistent with Whole Language principles is offered.

Freeman, David E., and Yvonne S. Freeman, "'Doing' Social Studies: Whole Language Lessons to Promote Social Action," *Social Education 55/1* (Jan 1991): 29-32, 66. [EJ 426 384]
Presents a Whole Language model for teaching social studies that is helpful to students learning English-as-a-Second-Language. Outlines Whole-Language principles, and provides a lesson plan that incorporates these principles. Points out that such principles draw upon student experiences.

Freeman, Ruth H., "Becoming Literate in Grade One." (1990): 10 pp. [ED 320 105]
One of the greatest advantages of teaching first-graders to read and write using a whole literacy approach is the flexibility the method provides for meeting the needs of each individual learner. Children use their dictated language as the text and work within small groups. Children can join any group working at an appropriate level or work individually. Several aspects of this flexible, open-ended program contribute to meeting individual needs for progress: (1) children learn to become readers and writers at the same time; (2) children enjoy the mutual support of the peer group; (3) progress is commensurate with development and motivation because of the opportunities for repetition, time on task, and direct instruction; and (4) the management aspect of the program is composed of meaningful reading and writing activities.

French, Martha, "Grammar and Meaning in a Whole Language Framework," *Perspectives in Education and Deafness 10/3* (Jan-Feb 1992): 19-21, 24. [EJ 441 405]
Teaching grammar to deaf and hard-of-hearing students within a Whole Language perspective involves recognition of students' developmental needs and the needs of the task. Strategies for teaching grammar include comparing student work with standard writing; identifying and classifying nouns and verbs; clarifying the roles of modifiers; and building sentences.

Freppon, Penny A., and Karin L. Dahl, "Learning about Phonics in a Whole Language Classroom," *Language Arts 68/3* (Mar 1991): 190-97. [EJ 422 590]
Suggests new bases of information that need to be considered in deciding how to handle phonics effectively in beginning reading and writing instruction. Describes phonics instruction in the classroom of a teacher of a Whole Language kindergarten.

Frew, Andrew W., "Four Steps toward Literature-Based Reading," *Journal of Reading 34/2* (Oct 1990): 98-102. [EJ 413 094]

Outlines a descriptive (not prescriptive) approach for the creation of a literature-based reading curriculum. Describes the 4 steps (behaving with basals, redefining reading, revving up for reading, and letting literature loose) that took the author 14 years of teaching to complete. Argues that literature-based reading programs are fun, enjoyable, rewarding, and well worth the effort.

Ganopole, Selina J., "Reading and Writing for the Gifted: A Whole Language Perspective," *Roeper Review 11/*2 (Dec 1988): 88-92. [EJ 387 275]
Reading and writing instruction for gifted students should address their actual use in meaningful contexts. Reading instruction should emphasize use of authentic materials, modified use of basals, divergent student responses, etc. Writing instruction should emphasize writing as a tool for learning, function before form, and opportunities for sharing student writing.

Garcia, Georgia Earnest, and David P. Pearson, "Modifying Reading Instruction to Maximize Its Effectiveness for All Students. Technical Report No. 489." (1990): 23 pp. [ED 314 723]
Discusses the modification of reading instruction to facilitate the development of comprehension strategies in all children (including those labeled as "at-risk" or "disadvantaged"). Current theoretical views of reading comprehension do not support a discrete skills perspective, but classroom research has documented the influence of basal reading programs on elementary reading instruction. Current views of reading suggest that readers are involved in a recursive search for meaning in which they deploy their own knowledge in concert with perceptions from the text and context to create a dynamic interpretation. In the search for an appropriate instructional model, four delivery models were reviewed: direct instruction, explicit instruction, cognitive apprenticeship, and Whole Language; none, however, were found capable of providing the appropriate delivery system for a comprehension focus. Based on this review, a consensus model of instruction, incorporating features of each model that are appropriate for designing instruction for low-achieving students, is delineated. It includes (1) teacher modeling, to let students in on the secrets; (2) task and text authenticity, to ensure purposefulness; (3) scaffolding, to cope with complexity; and (4) shared decision making, to develop self assessment. This approach to reading instruction requires teachers to move away from the "teacher-proof" model frequently offered in conventional programs to a model in which they make most decisions within their classrooms.

Garofalo, Carol, "LEA—Language Experience Approach: Who Uses It?" (1991): 78 pp. [ED 332 169]
Reports a descriptive study to determine the extent to which the language experience approach (LEA) is used in the kindergarten and first grades of six northwest Bergen County, New Jersey, school districts. Anonymous surveys were mailed to all kindergarten and first-grade teachers in these districts. Forty-five (63%) of the surveys were returned. Results indicated that: (1) the basal reader is still the primary instructional tool of the respondents; (2) 60% of the respondents use class-dictated LEA methods always or often in their programs; (3) teachers with zero to five years of experience placed the least emphasis on the basal reader, the most emphasis on LEA, big books, trade books, and poems, and are apt to use writing-as-process more than any other group except those teachers with more than 21 years of service; (4) writing frequency is greater among the less experienced teachers, and daily writing is significantly greater among the LEA teachers than among non-LEA teachers; (5) for the most part, teachers within any given district used similar programs; and (6) teachers in the Pesce Northern Valley District survey moved more toward Whole Language across the board

than this group. (Seven tables of data are included; 31 references, the survey cover letter, and the survey instrument are attached.)

Gaskins, Robert W., and others, "Using What You Know to Figure Out What You Don't Know: An Analogy Approach to Decoding," *Reading and Writing Quarterly: Overcoming Learning Difficulties 8/2* (Apr-Jun 1992): 197-221. [CS 745 483] Discusses development and implementation of an approach to decoding in which students use words they know to decode those they do not know. Discusses how an analogy approach was implemented in a tutorial setting. Offers guidelines for how the approach can be used in regular classrooms, including Whole Language classrooms.

Genishi, Celia, and Anne Haas Dyson, "Research Currents: On Issues that Divide Us," *Language Arts 64/4* (Apr 1987): 408-15. [EJ 348 976] Presents concerns about children's growth as oral and written language users and how disagreements over teaching strategies can affect this growth.

Gersten, Russell, and Joseph Dimino, "Visions and Revisions: A Perspective on the Whole Language Controversy." (1990): 24 pp. [ED 329 913] Conversations with special educators indicates that many view the Whole Language approach as, at best, a fad and at worst, an assault on what they know about how to effectively teach students with disabilities. In the current atmosphere of increased interest in collaboration between special and general education to better meet the needs of students with handicaps, anxiety over the Whole Language movement is particularly intense. Calls for increased collaboration come at a time when philosophies of optimal reading instruction between special and general education are in stark conflict. Both direct instruction and the Whole Language movement can be distilled into images. Whole Language proponents imagine a classroom where students are genuinely interested in all they read or have read to them. Teachers are always experimenting, and their freedom is reflected in the dynamic classroom atmosphere. Direct instruction presents an image of students learning in a highly interactive situation, one in which they experience consistent success and are provided immediate feedback when they encounter problems. The role of the teacher is, in part, to demystify the process of reading. Use of approaches based on the work of cognitive psychologists can be integrated into either instructional framework to address some of the nagging concerns raised about each model. Special educators should consider seriously the issues and criticisms raised by Whole Language authors. If nothing else, empirical research has enabled reading theorists to move beyond statements of philosophy and toward a serious analysis of what teachers really do with children.

Gevini, Gila, and others, "Abra Cadabra—A New Program for Initial Reading," *English Teachers' Journal: Israel 44* (May 1992): 80-82. [EJ 461 363] "Abra Cadabra," a new computer program for second-language learning for fourth- and fifth-grade students, is described that is based on the Whole Language approach to language acquisition.

Giddings, Louise R., "Literature-Based Reading Instruction: Understanding the Holistic Perspective," *Contemporary Issues in Reading 6/2* (spr 1991): 69-74. [EJ 431 071] Presents a discussion of the ideas that are central to the concept of literature-based reading instruction. Reviews the theory, gives insights from reading research, stresses the importance of literature in the reading program, and offers strategies for literature-based reading instruction.

Giddings, Louise R., "Literature-Based Reading Instruction: An Analysis," paper presented at the Annual Meeting of the International Reading Association (36th, Las Vegas, NV, May 6-10, 1991). See ED 322 475. [ED 333 350] for a similar report.

Reviews the literature relative to the theory and practice of literature-based reading instruction, and seeks to bring clarity concerning the concept of literature-based reading instruction. The paper points out that from a theoretical point of view advocates of literature-based reading instruction draw upon the Whole Language philosophy, psycholinguistics, and cognitive psychology. It notes that proponents of literature-based reading instruction propose that reading should develop naturally and functionally. The paper concludes that instruction should be guided by the needs and interests of learners, beginning with real literature and meaningful print rather than with fragmented language or language constructed for instructional purposes. Although varied studies are reported that support a holistic literature-based approach to reading instruction, the paper suggests that more studies are needed relative to the implementation of literature-based reading programs.

Giddings, Louise R., "Literature-Based Reading Instruction: An Analysis," *Reading Research and Instruction 31*/2 (win 1992): 18-30. [EJ 441 047]
Reviews the literature relative to the theory and practice of literature-based reading instruction. Cites studies that support a holistic, literature-based approach to reading instruction. Suggests that more studies are needed relative to the implementation of literature-based reading programs.

Giddings, Louise R., "Literature Based Reading Instruction: A Whole Language Perspective." (1990): 37 pp. [ED 322 475]
An analysis of the literature helps bring greater clarity to educators concerning the theory and practice of literature-based instruction. There are two common threads in all the interpretations of literature-based instruction: (1) the use of literature as the primary material for reading instruction; and (2) the elimination of the structural support and practices of basal reading systems. Information which provides a theoretical base for literature-based reading instruction focuses largely on the Whole Language philosophy, psycholinguistics, and cognitive psychology. Children become literate, according to the advocates, by being immersed in a literate environment and by being encouraged and supported in encounters with literacy. Studies can be identified to support the trend toward instruction with whole texts and purposeful reading. Proponents of the literature-based instruction movement value whole stories and an emphasis on meaning. Reports indicate that the use of children's literature in the teaching of reading has a positive effect on student's achievement and attitudes toward reading. There is a need for more research on literature-based reading programs and implementation strategies. There appears to be a label, "literature-based instruction," which provides an umbrella for myriad practices. As models are developed, implemented and evaluated, studies should be undertaken so that teachers can receive guidance in using literature to develop proficient readers.

Gipe, Joan P., and others, "Literacy Development of Urban At-Risk Children through Literature-based Reading/Language Arts Instruction," paper presented at the Annual Meeting of the National Reading Conference (42nd, San Antonio, TX, Dec 2-5, 1992). [ED 352 623]
Describes a longitudinal study of the language and literacy abilities of urban at-risk children at several points over a 3-year period. The children were provided with small-group literature-based reading/language arts instruction, and their outcomes were compared with progress in literacy achievement to other, similar groups. Participants in the study were university students enrolled in two methods courses, their two university instructors, and all 300 students in one urban elementary school (K-8) located in a large southeastern city. Data were gathered using both empirical and naturalistic, informal/observational measures. Baseline data gathered during the first

month of the study indicated that the children were in much need of rich literary experiences, and that their attitudes towards reading and writing leaned toward the positive. Observation of the children during the first four months of instruction indicated improvements in children's literacy performance. Data gathered during the remainder of the 3-year study will allow a variety of research questions to be answered.

Glazer, Susan Mandel, "An Interview with Albert Mazurkiewicz (Leaders in Reading Research and Instruction)," *Reading Psychology 9/2* (1988): 159-62. [EJ 390 417] Discusses the use of previous reading research; important historical figures in reading; important research today; and issues that need to be addressed in the future.

Glimps, Blanche Eloise Jackson, and Beverly C. Ashton, "Learning about Minority Cultures and Improving Reading Skills through the Use of Good Literature," paper presented at the Annual Convention of the Council for Exceptional Children (70th, Baltimore, MD, Apr 13-17, 1992). [ED 345 415] Describes the development and implementation of a culture-based literature program to improve the reading skills and understanding of minority cultures in students with mild disabilities. Steps in developing such a Whole Language approach program include: (1) identifying the cultural groups to be studied; (2) choosing both fiction and non-fiction books which reflect the groups in a realistic manner; (3) self-education by the teacher on the cultures of the groups to be studied; (4) and application of appropriate reading activities involving assessing students' prior knowledge, guiding student reading, and evaluating attitude changes.

Gold, Judith, and others, "Whole Language and Teacher/Librarian Partnerships," *Phi Delta Kappan 73/7* (Mar 1992): 536-7. [EJ 441 115] At New York City's progressive Bank Street School for Children, teaching is directed to the whole child's social, emotional, physical, and cognitive development. The school's reading program focuses on a language-experience approach based on student choice. This article shows how collaboration between teachers and librarians has strengthened the classroom-library media center connection.

Goodman, Kenneth S., "Basal Readers: A Call for Action," *Language Arts 63/4* (Mar 1986): 358-63. [EJ 331 248] Explores several concepts relevant to instructional materials that emerged from seminars sponsored by the National Council of Teachers of English and the International Reading Association. Describes how basal readers—so prevalent in instruction—fall short of these concepts, and what can be done to improve instruction.

Goodman, Kenneth S., "Beyond Basal Readers: Taking Charge of Your Own Teaching," *Learning 16/2* (Sep 1987): 62-65. [EJ 361 863] The Whole Language approach to reading instruction integrates, rather than fragments, the reading process. Ways teachers can take reponsibility for their students' literacy by modifying or even putting aside basal readers are suggested.

Goodman, Kenneth S., "Commentary: On Being Literate in an Age of Information," *Journal of Reading 28/5* (Feb 1985): 388-92. [EJ 311 423] Points out that the expansion of written language to serve the full range of functions for all people in an information age is a manifestation of our ability as individuals and societies to create new language forms as they are needed in the context of their use.

Goodman, Kenneth S., "Growing into Literacy," *Prospects: Quarterly Review of Education 15/1* (1985): 57-65. [EJ 320 362] Children growing up in literate societies, surrounded by the printed word, begin to read and write long before they start school. The extent and scope of early literacy development is examined. Theoretical explanations of this development are offered. Implications for schools are presented.

Goodman, Kenneth S., "I Didn't Found Whole Language (Distinguished Educator Series)," *Reading Teacher 46*/3 (Nov 1992): 188-99. [EJ 452 689]
Puts Whole Language and the author's own research into historical, political, and philosophical context. Offers predictions about the future of Whole Language and education in general.

Goodman, Kenneth S., "Look What They've Done to Judy Blume!: The "Basalization" of Children's Literature," *New Advocate 1*/1 (1988): 29-41. [EJ 371 778]
Uses one basalized revision of Judy Blume's "The One in the Middle is the Green Kangaroo" to illustrate how publishers change literature to fit their self-imposed constraints. Criticizes publishers' emphasis on learning words and skills, which causes them to fracture and narrow language, and results in adapted and synthetic texts instead of authentic literature.

Goodman, Kenneth S., "What's Whole in Whole Language? A Parent/Teacher Guide to Children's Learning." (1986): 79 pp. [ED 300 777]
The major purpose of this book is to describe the basis, features, and future of the Whole Language movement. Topics included in the book include: (1) a description of what is known about language and language development; (2) presentation of a Whole Language perspective on literacy development, involving both reading and writing; (3) presentation of criteria that parents and teachers can use in helping children to develop literacy; (4) examples of Whole Language programs already at work; and (5) suggestions for building Whole Language programs and transforming existing programs into Whole Language programs. The book helps Whole Language teachers recognize and define themselves.

Goodman, Kenneth S., "Whole Language *Is* Whole: A Response to Heymsfeld," *Educational Leadership 46*/6 (Mar 1989): 69-70. [EJ 385 285]
Argues in a response to an article by Carla Heymsfield that Whole Language, as a coherent philosophy of language instruction, does not need to be "patched" with skills instruction, and that direct instruction cannot be reconciled with natural learning.

Goodman, Kenneth S., "Whole-Language Research: Foundations and Development," *Elementary School Journal 90*/2 (Nov 1989): 207-21. [EJ 404 268]
Summarizes key characteristics of Whole Language. Theoretical views of learners, teachers, language, and curriculum are explicated. The strong research base for Whole Language is considered. Potential research on Whole Language classrooms is discussed.

Goodman, Kenneth S., "Why Whole Language Is Today's Agenda in Education," *Language Arts 69*/5 (Sep 1992): 354-63. [EJ 448 434]
Discusses changes in textbook publishing, attendance at professional meetings, media coverage, and the response of the "testing community" that demonstrate that Whole Language has become the agenda of education. Discusses the transactional view of writing, social/personal views of learning, teachers redefining themselves and their relations to learners, Whole Language as curriculum, and the new agenda.

Goodman, Kenneth S., and others, "Language and Thinking in School: A Whole-Language Curriculum. Third Edition." (1987): 417 pp. [ED 278 987]
Exploring many possible relationships among language, thought processes, and education, this book is designed to synthesize modern views of language and linguis-

tics, literature and semiotics, and thinking and knowing that are pertinent to education. It develops theoretical positions about language and thinking in school, proposes practical instructional applications for both beginning and experienced teachers, and provides practical means for building and assessing curricula and instruction. Throughout the book, a view of a dual curriculum based on language and thinking is explicated which reflects new theoretical understandings of how and why both written and oral language develop. Contents: (1) language, thinking, and learning: focal points of a dual curriculum; (2) language: why and how; (3) language development; (4) language development in social and historical contexts; (5) coming to know; (6) development of thought with language; (7) structuring in thought: meaning; (8) language structuring: grammar; (9) composing letters to the world; (10) reading and writing: a psycholinguistic view; (11) literacy before school; (12) learning and teaching reading: strategies for comprehension; (13) learning and teaching writing: strategies for presentation; (14) children, literature, and the arts, including a special bibliography of children's books; (15) language and thinking: strategies in teaching; (16) teaching tactics and strategies; and (17) building Whole-Language programs.

Goodman, Kenneth S., and others, *Report Card on Basal Readers* (Katonah, New York: Richard C. Owen Publishers, 1988): 167 pp. [ED 300 794]
Examines the nature of the modern basal reader, its economics, and use. First, the report provides a history showing how the confluence of business principles, positivistic science, and behavioral psychology led to the transformation of reading textbooks into basal readers. Next, the report examines objectives and subjective factors which maintain the dominance in American reading instruction of a small number of very large publishers through their basal readers. The economics and ethics of marketing basals are also examined in the report. Then, the process of producing basals is described, drawing on investigative reporting. That leads to an examination of contemporary basals using a descriptive instrument. Finally, the report offers recommendations for progress in reading instruction within and without the basals. Eight pages of references conclude the report.

Goodman, Kenneth S., ed., and others, *The Whole Language Evaluation Book* (Portsmouth, New Hampshire: Heinemann, 1989). [ED 359 500]
Intended for teachers from kindergarten through adult education and for administrators, this book demonstrates how teachers have fostered environments that facilitate Whole Language evaluation. Discuss strategies used in evaluating students' growth across many curricular areas, including reading, writing, and second language growth; suggest alternatives to standardized tests in mainstream, resource, and special education programs. Contents: "Evaluation of Students: Evaluation of Teachers" (Yetta M. Goodman), "The Art of Teaching: Evaluation and Revision" (Lois Bridges Bird), "'If the Teacher Comes Over, Pretend It's a Telescope!'" (Wendy J. Hood), "Evaluation in a Classroom Environment Designed for Whole Language" (Robert Wortman and Myna Matlin Haussler), "Asi No Se Pone 'Si'" (That's Not How You Write 'Si')" (Rene Galindo), "Whole Language, Texas Style" (John W. Woodley and Carol E. Woodley), "Evaluation: The Conventions of Writing" (Orysia Hull), "When 'Shut Up' Is a Sign of Growth" (Maureen Morrissey), "Guise, Son of the Shoemaker" (Mary M. Kitagawa), "'Well, What about His Skills?: Evaluation of Whole Language in the Middle School" (Karen Sabers Dalrymple), "Everyone's in the Act: Evaluation in a Seventh-Grade Classroom" (Toby Kahn Curry), "Evaluation of Second-Language Junior and Senior High School Students" (Yvonne S. Freeman and David E. Freeman), "Grade Eight Students Cope with Today and Get Ready for Tomorrow" (Richard Coles), "Using Evaluation as an Instructional Strategy for Adult Readers" (Ann M.

Marek), "'...Of Flying to the Stars and Looking at the Dipr': Whole Language Evaluation on the Navajo Reservation" (Susan Howe-Tompkins), "The Evaluation Process—in Process" (Debra Jacobson), "'So Why Don't I Feel Good about Myself?'" (Debra Goodman), "Looking at Invented Spelling: A Kidwatcher's Guide to Spelling, Part 1" (Sandra Wilde), "Looking at Invented Spelling: A Kidwatcher's Guide to Spelling, Part 2" (Sandra Wilde), "'They'll Grow into 'Em': Evaluation, Self-Evaluation, and Self-Esteem in Special Education" (Paul Crowley), "Special Education and Whole Language: From an Evaluator's Viewpoint" (Phyllis Brazee and Susan W. Haynes), "Whole Language, Whole Teaching, Whole Being: The Need for Reflection in the Teaching Process" (Geane R. Hanson)

Goodman, Kenneth S., and Frederick V. Gollasch, eds., *Language and Literacy: The Selected Writings of Kenneth S. Goodman. Volume I: Process, Theory, Research* (Boston: Routledge & Kegan Paul, 1982): 305 pp. [ED 261 358]
Encompassing his work in the psycholinguistics of reading, this book presents Kenneth Goodman's major papers focusing on miscue analysis, the theoretical model of the reading processes derived from it, and relevant research perspectives. Contents: introduction, (1) the reading process, (2) theory and practice in the reading process, (3) the reading process as a psycholinguistic guessing game, (4) the linguistics of reading, (5) the decoding process, (6) psycholinguistic universals in the reading process, (7) universal features in the reading process, (8) what researchers know about reading, (9) miscues as windows on the reading process, (10) theory and reality of miscue analysis in reading, (11) a linguistic study of cues and miscues in reading, (12) analysis of oral reading miscues as applied psycholinguistics, (13) influences of the visual peripheral field, (14) learning about psycholinguistic processes by analyzing oral reading (with Yetta Goodman), and (15) linguistically sound research in reading. A final chapter by Brian Cambourne evaluates the Goodman reading model. The appendix contains the Goodman Taxonomy of Reading Miscues.

Goodman, Kenneth S., and Yetta M. Goodman, "A Whole-Language, Comprehension-Centered Reading Program. Program in Language and Literacy Occasional Paper Number 1." (1981): 27 pp. [ED 210 630]
Intended for reading teachers and school administrators, this paper proposes a Whole Language, comprehension based approach to reading instruction that is rooted in the humanistic acceptance of the learner as problem solver and that builds on strengths and minimizes preoccupation with reading deficiency. Following an introduction and rationale for this holistic approach, the paper outlines the key principles of the approach relating to the reading process, teaching and learning, and instructional materials. The paper then examines the myths of reading readiness, controlled vocabulary, phonics, and mastery learning. The next section of the paper details the essentials of an in-school program that draws on the learning taking place outside school, beginning with preschool and progressing through beginning reading, developmental reading, and an alternative to remediation. The conclusion of the paper reexamines the strengths of a holistic reading program.

Goodman, Yetta M., ed., *How Children Construct Literacy: Piagetian Perspectives.* (Newark, Delaware: International Reading Association, 1990): 136 pp. [ED 316 833]
Designed to contribute toward providing opportunities for young children to enlist their own powerful intelligence in the construction of their understanding of reading and writing, this book is a collection of six studies presented at the International Reading Association's Eleventh World Congress. An introductory chapter, "Discovering Children's Inventions of Written Language" (Yetta M. Goodman), discusses the prehistory and history of Piagetian studies and presents an overview of the chapters.

237

Other chapters include: (1) "Literacy Development: Psychogenesis" (Emilia Ferreiro); (2) "Literacy Development and Pedagogical Implications: Evidence from the Hebrew System of Writing" (Liliana Tolchinsky Landsmann): (3) "The Language Young Children Write: Reflections on a Learning Situation" (Ana Teberosky); (4) "A Passage to Literacy: Learning in a Social Context" (Clotilde Pontecorvo and Cristina Zucchermaglio); (5) "Applying Psychogenesis Principles to the Literacy Instruction of Lower-Class Children in Brazil" (Esther Pillar Grossi); and (6) "Children's Knowledge about Literacy Development: An Afterword" (Yetta M. Goodman).

Goodman, Yetta M., "Roots of the Whole-Language Movement," *Elementary School Journal 90/2* (Nov 1989): 113-27. [EJ 404 262]
Gives a history of the Whole Language movement. Looks at the early use of the term "Whole Language." Explores influences from philosophy, psychology, linguistics, and education on development of Whole Language. Discusses influences from early educational movements in the U.S., England, and New Zealand.

Goodman, Yetta M., and others, *Reading Miscue Inventory: Alternative Procedures.* (New York: Richard C. Owen Publishers, 1987): 238 pp. [ED 280 009]
Expanding on the original "Miscue Inventory," this book examines various miscue analysis procedures and discusses how they provide teachers with effective methods for understanding and measuring students' reading processes. The chapters are divided into three parts, focusing on miscue analysis and the reading process, miscue analysis procedures, and miscue analysis and curriculum development. Respectively, chapters discuss (1) the importance of miscue analysis for reading professionals, the historical development of miscue analysis procedures, a recommendation for self-monitoring the reading process, and a student whose oral reading is used as an example throughout the book; (2) the reading model developed by Kenneth Goodman; (3) the collection, organization, and marking of miscue analysis data; (4) questions used in miscue analysis; (5) an alternative procedure for miscue analysis; (6) three more alternative procedures including information on miscue selection for coding, question usage, scoring the retelling, forms for miscue coding and retelling, and calculation of statistical information; (7) three models of reading instruction and the essentials of a whole language reading program; and (8) how the information gained through miscue analysis might be used as the basis for a reading program. Appendixes include a summary of procedures, Gordon's miscue analysis, blank forms used in various procedures, and previous miscue analysis formats.

Goodman, Yetta, and others, "A Two-Year Case Study Observing the Development of Third and Fourth Grade Native American Children's Writing Processes." (Tucson: Arizona Univeristy, College of Education, 1984): 432 pp. [ED 241 240]
To gain an understanding of the development of the composing process, researchers observed, categorized, analyzed, and collected the writing of 10 Papago third and fourth graders in the Indian Oasis Public School District of Arizona over a period of two years. Of 30 children originally chosen to represent lower, middle, and upper development levels, 6 became the focus of in-depth study. Researchers collected data from observation; videotapes; interviews with parents, children, and teachers; and debriefing notes. They also studied 300 English language texts (over 17,000 words) produced by the children in regular classroom settings to determine the status and development of the orthographic features (spelling, punctuation), syntactic features (clauses, phrases, terminable units), and semantic and pragmatic issues including textual cohesion, contractions, dialect, metalinguistic knowledge, and overt behaviors accompanying writing (such as revision, subvocalization, rereading, interruptions, resource use, stop and think). The report describes the findings and the educational

environments in the children's classrooms. It includes detailed analyses of the development of the writing process of each of the six children studied in depth. The analyses include information regarding the children's background, samples of the children's work, excerpts from the interviews, and descriptions of the various aspects of the writing process.

For a short version, see **Goodman**, Yetta M. and Sandra Wilde, "Writing Development in Third and Fourth Grade Native American Students (Social Context, Linguistic Systems, and Creation of Meaning). A Research Report. Program in Language and Literacy Occasional Paper No. 14." (Tucson: Arizona University College of Education, 1985): 64 pp. [ED 278 017]

Gordon, Richard K. and Ana M. Serrano, "Approaches to Teaching Language Arts in a Bilingual Multicultural Setting," paper presented at the Annual Meeting of the Association for Teacher Educators (73rd, Los Angeles, California, Feb 13-17, 1992). [ED 354 481]
A study of Whole Language teaching in urban heterogeneous classrooms was undertaken to identify teacher student classroom discourse patterns. Using the Gutierrez Index of Coding Schema, researchers identified three discourse scripts in the 14 bilingual and multicultural classrooms in southern California under investigation. These are the recitation script, the responsive script, and the responsive-collaborative script. Indicates that most teachers favored the responsive script when providing Whole Language instruction. There were educationally significant differences between experienced and novice teachers on selected variables of the scale. There were insignificant correlational results on the type of discourse pattern that teachers used and the standardized California Achievement Tests language subsection.

Gothard, Heather M. and Suzanne M. Russell, "A Tale of Two Teachers (or How Our Children Led Us into Whole Language)," *Childhood Education 66*/4 (sum 1990): 214-18. [EJ 417 095]
Presents two kindergarten teachers' accounts of the use of the Whole Language approach to children's learning in class. Describes the reading of a children's book to a public kindergarten class and the subsequent literacy related activities.

Graves, Marilyn, and Jan Senecal, "Let's Celebrate Whole Language (A Practical Guide for Parents)," paper (in the form of an 8-panel brochure) presented at the Annual Meeting of the National Council of Teachers of English (79th, Baltimore, MD, Nov 17-22, 1989). [ED 312 614]
Developed by experienced professionals, this brochure is designed to let parents know what the Whole Language Approach is, how it is being used in the classroom, and how parents can apply Whole Language in the home.

Green, Max, "Spelling within One School's Whole Language Framework," *Australian Journal of Reading 11*/1 (Mar 1988): 11-21. [EJ 373 312]
Shows that an elementary school's spelling program evaluation led to the formulation of a spelling policy reflecting the school's Whole Language approach to learning.

Greene, Beth G., "Integrating Processes in the Language Arts (ERIC/RCS)," *Language Arts 70*/4 (Apr 1993): 323-25. [EJ 461 025]
Presents annotations of 12 books, conference papers, and other materials concerning the reading/writing connection, literature-based reading, and Whole Language.

Griffith, Priscilla L., and Janell P. Klesius, "The Effect of Phonemic Awareness Ability and Reading Instructional Approach on First Grade Children's Acquisition of Spelling and Decoding Skills,' paper presented at the National Reading Conference (40th, Miami, FL, Nov 27-Dec 1, 1990). [ED 332 160]

A study examined the relationship between reading instruction and the development of decoding and spelling skills and the writing fluency of children with varying levels of phonemic awareness. First grade children from two classrooms in a rural Florida school district who began school high and low in phonemic awareness received either Whole Language or traditional basal instruction. The Whole Language curriculum included the shared book experience and extensive writing activities; the traditional basal curriculum included explicit phonics instruction, but very little writing. Results show that high phonemic awareness children outperformed low phonemic awareness children; there was no significant difference between instructional approach in the performance of children on any of the measures. Effect sizes indicated that children who started school high in phonemic awareness were at an advantage in the Whole Language classroom. Children who started school low in phonemic awareness were given an advantage by being placed in the traditional classroom, although the magnitude of that advantage was not as strong as was the advantage to high phonemic awareness children of being in the Whole Language classroom. Children in the Whole Language classroom became more fluent writers; children in the traditional classroom became more accurate spellers in their compositions.

Griffith, Priscilla L., and others, "The Effect of Phonemic Awareness on the Literacy Development of First Grade Children in a Traditional or a Whole Language Classroom," *Journal of Research in Childhood Education 6/*2 (spr-sum): 85-92. [EJ 460 128]
Examined the acquisition of decoding and spelling skills and the writing fluency of first graders who received either Whole Language or traditional basal instruction. Children with high phonemic awareness outperformed those with low phonemic awareness on all literacy measures, regardless of the instructional method used.

Griffith, Priscilla L., and Janell Klesius, Janell, "A Whole Language Flight Plan: An Interview with Three Teachers," *Reading Horizons 4/*30 (Jan 1990): 5-14. [EJ 402 257]
Provides suggestions to teachers planning to implement a Whole Language program, based on interviews with three Whole Language teachers. Focuses on support for the Whole Language program; decisions about curriculum and evaluation; development of vocabulary and comprehension; strengths and weaknesses of the Whole Language approach; and preparation for Whole Language instruction.

Grindler, Martha, and Beverly Stratton, "The Reading/Writing Connection in Whole Language," *Ohio Reading Teacher 26/*1 (fall 1991): 11-14. [EJ 437 420]
Discusses the part reading and writing play in the Whole Language approach. Offers 11 recommendations to help teachers provide a functional approach to language development.

Grindler, Martha C.; Stratton, Beverly D., "Whole Language Assessment," *Reading Improvement 29/*4 (win 1992): 262-64. [EJ 455 613]
Describes systematic assessment procedures as alternatives to standardized testing that yield more descriptive records of children's reading abilities. Notes that the assessment procedures are consistent with the contemporary understanding of reading which indicates that prior knowledge and the ability to use predictive skills greatly influence comprehension.

Grindler, Martha, and Beverly Stratton, Beverly, "The Reading/Writing Connection in Whole Language," *Ohio Reading Teacher 26/*1 (fall 1991): 11-14. [EJ 437 420]
Discusses the part that reading and writing play in the Whole Language approach. Offers 11 recommendations to help teachers provide a functional approach to language development.

Grisham, Dana L., "The Integrated Language Arts: Curriculum Enactments in Whole Language and Traditional Fourth Grade Classrooms," paper presented at the Annual Meeting of the American Educational Research Association (74th, Atlanta, Georgia, Apr 12-16, 1993), California, 1993. [CS 011 350]
Presents results of a study of how teachers' attitudes and beliefs affect their enactment of literature-based curriculum materials, whether student attitudes differ in accordance with the teacher's orientation, and whether student achievement in reading and writing differ between Whole Language and traditional classrooms. Two Whole Language and two traditional teachers in four suburban fourth-grade classrooms in southern California were chosen. Teachers were observed for over 100 hours over a year. Pretest and posttest reading and writing attitude measures and reading achievement tests were administered. Writing samples were taken at three points. Analysis of teacher, principal, and student interviews present the insider's view of the classroom. No statistically significant differences were found in reading. On attitude measures, classes were split between one Whole Language and one traditional teacher. Students in the traditional teachers' classes significantly outscored those in Whole Language classes on writing measures.

Grisham, Dana L., "Teacher Epistemology and Practice: Enactments in the Elementary Language Arts Classroom," paper presented at the Annual Meeting of the National Reading Conference (42nd, San Antonio, TX, Dec 2-5, 1992). [ED 355 472]
Investigates how literature-based reading/language arts materials were being used in two "exemplary" third/fourth grade combination classes, the influence of teacher epistemology on classroom instruction, and whether teachers were enacting the Whole Language emphasis mandated by the state. One of the two participating teachers had over 20 years experience and the other had 3 years experience in a large southern California urban school district. Data sources included classroom observations and videotapes of the language arts segments of the school day 2 days per week for 3 consecutive weeks; interviews with six students from each class; and reading and writing attitude measures. Results indicated that: (1) each teacher had coherent theories of how reading should be taught, and used theory to guide her practice; (2) both teachers appeared to be integrating the language arts as envisioned by California's English/Language Arts Framework, but the textbook was the preeminent authority; (3) fewer worksheets and workbook assignments were given, and more authentic skills-based assignments were generated, than has been shown to be the case in past studies; (4) both teachers felt free to construct curriculum for their students; (5) reading and writing attitudes of the students were generally positive; and (6) collaborative learning was common in both classes, but there was still much lecturing and recitation. Findings suggest that both of the teachers studied have epistemological stances that are far from a constructivist epistemology of teaching and militate against the tenets of Whole Language.

Groff, Patrick, "Teachers' Opinions of the Whole Language Approach to Reading Instruction," *Annals of Dyslexia 41* (1991): 83-95. [EJ 455 879]
First- and second-grade teachers (n=275) were surveyed concerning their knowledge about and attitudes toward the Whole-Language approach to reading instruction. Findings suggest that many teachers are not persuaded that the Whole-Language approach to reading instruction is to be preferred over other methods such as intensive phonics instruction or basal reader instruction.

Gross, Patricia A., "Interactive Reading on the Secondary Level," paper presented at the Annual Meeting of the National Reading Conference (41st, Palm Springs, California, Dec 3-7, 1991), Pennsylvania, 1991. [CS 011 345]

Reports a study of two teachers and four secondary-level English classes that examined how traditional methods of teaching literature were replaced by more interactive and integrated approaches to text, based primarily on Whole Language philosophy. Intervention aspects were purposefully kept open-ended to accommodate each teacher's understandings and preferences. Built-in, weekly, three-way meetings among researcher and teachers allowed for the necessary interaction through which grounded theory could become operative. Quantitative data included surveys, teacher tests, student work samples, and gradebook records of student scores. Teachers read literature regarding interactive teaching methods, and, for five weeks, ongoing coaching sessions and researcher participant observations enabled teachers and students to experiment with interactive methods in terms of reading. A ninth-grade teacher dropped inhibiting methods she had developed over the years, and she invited and weighed suggestions, adapting them to her needs and those of her students. She recognized the extent to which she had dominated the entire teaching/learning situation and noted the consequent negative effect on students. An eighth-grade teacher identified control as the major issue in her classroom. Her students liked and admired her intense desire to get them to learn, but they resisted her regimentation and disciplinary methods. The students thrived with the changes. Overall, student marking period grades increased appreciably. Findings suggest that interactive methods of reading allowed for greater expression of student voice and choice of content and method of studying literature. Teachers revitalized themselves and their classrooms.

Gross, Patricia A., "Shared Meaning: Whole Language Reader Response at the Secondary Level," paper presented at the Annual Meeting of the National Reading Conference (42nd, San Antonio, Texas, Dec 2-5, 1992), Pennsylvania, 1992. [CS 113 346] Reports a study the results of which underscored the potential of Whole Language philosophy as a framework for secondary English teachers and students as they move away from strictly traditional methods. Research methods included case study, grounded theory, and qualitative inquiry. Participants included two veteran teachers who taught in a predominantly White, suburban high school with 1,000 students in grades 7 through 12. Data collection spanned one year and included interviews with the teachers, anecdotal field notes, lesson plans, assignments, student work samples, and teacher learning logues. By the end of the second semester, one teacher who taught seventh and eleventh graders regretted having stalled in using dialogue journals. Though she had primarily held to traditional ways of insisting upon required readings of common texts, she had found students read more willingly and more carefully when engaged in dialogue journal activities that enabled them to verbalize opinions in writing and then share ideas with peers. The other teacher, who taught eighth and twelfth-graders, used three forms of dialogue journals and quickly recognized the potential for students to grapple with words and ideas. The teachers approached change warily, yet found the results edifying. The students reacted strongly to restraints imposed by required readings and study guide questions; they much preferred the freedoms of selecting their own reading, exploring their own ideas, and consulting with one another to construct meaning.

Gross, Patricia A., and John Shefelbine, "Whole Language Teacher Education in Multicultural Contexts: Living Our Own Models of Learning," paper presented at the Annual Meeting of the National Reading Conference (41st, Palm Springs, California, Dec 3-7, 1991), Pennsylvania, 1991. [CS 011 344] Reports a study in examination of the reactions and responses of new and veteran teachers throughout a full semester graduate in-service course that introduced Whole Language theory through experiential learning. The 30 K-8 teachers in the course came from seven schools of a large inner-city school district where 70% of the students lived below the poverty level. Two-thirds of the teachers were African-American or Hispanic. The class environment revolved around variability, variety, choice, flexibility, and multicultural awareness. Data included teacher learning logues, an "examination" that solicited what teachers understood and liked or did not understand and disliked about Whole Language, application projects, and classroom visits after the course ended. The teachers came to trust the class, each other, and themselves as they experienced a range of writing tasks and shared their difficulties in analyzing the journal articles which they read. They expressed an excitement about learning, sharing, and grappling with issues and they underwent a series of reactions to interactive and cooperative learning methods. All attempted some Whole Language activities with their classes and reflected upon the strengths and weaknesses of Whole Language. Findings suggest the need for more avenues of professional collaboration for teachers to discuss professional issues, integrated and interactive activities for teachers to learn through experience and with one another, and opportunities for teachers to engage in spiral learning in conjunction with practice.

Grundin, Hans U., "A Commission of Selective Readers: A Critique of *Becoming a Nation of Readers*," *Reading Teacher 39*/3 (Dec 1985): 262-66. [EJ 326 494]
Criticizes the report of the Commission on Reading for its biased selection of research and its poor synthesis on Whole Language approaches.

Guide for Native Language and Content Area Literacy Programs for High School Haitian Creole-Speaking Students." (1992): 55 pp. [ED 353 823]
Consists of a series of sample lesson plans designed for teachers and supervisors delivering instructional services to students with limited English proficiency and native language literacy in Haitian bilingual programs. The guides contain 14 sample lesson plans; five native language instruction sample lesson plans and nine content area (social studies, mathematics, science) sample lesson plans. Materials are based on the principle of promotion of dual literacy, and are designed to capitalize on students' prior knowledge. The guide also encourages use of the Whole Language approach in both native language and content area components. Lessons are designated for one of two student skill levels: (1) limited or no formal education; and (2) some basic native language literacy skills, comparable to a student in grades 3-5. An introductory section outlines the guiding principles of instruction on which the plans are based. Each lesson plan contains a topic, instructional materials needed, specific performance objectives, class activities, sample questions, and in some cases, a passage or poem in Haitian Creole.

Gunderson, Lee, and others, "The Effects of Teacher Modeling on Primary Writing," paper presented at the Annual Meeting of the National Reading Conference (38th, Tucson, AZ, Nov 30-Dec 3, 1988). [ED 309 403]
To investigate differences in students' writing development due to teacher modeling, a study examined students enrolled in Whole Language classrooms in grades 1 and 2 in two separate school districts. Students enrolled in independent classrooms where teachers did not provide writing models were in a school in a lower middle class neighborhood of Vancouver, British Columbia. Approximately 65% of the students were from families in which English was the second language (ESL). Modeling classrooms were in a school in a middle class neighborhood of Richmond, British Columbia, a suburb of Vancouver. Approximately 30% of the students were ESL. Teachers in independent classrooms asked students to write on the first day of class. Students read their writing to the teachers who responded positively. Teachers also kept notes about students' writing. As students began producing more mature texts,

teachers kept a chronological log of their conferences. Teachers in the modeling classrooms asked students what they would like to write, then wrote the sentence(s). Often students emulated the teacher's model. In addition, teachers wrote comments containing the essence of what students indicated they had written. For both types of classes, students' writing for first and second grades was photo-copied. Each writing product was analyzed for number of words, number of t-units (independent clauses with all attendant modifiers), quality, and topic choice. Quality was measured on a nine-point experimental scale developed to reflect writing structure and quality. Findings revealed that both strategies produced eager, competent writers.

Gunderson, Lee, and Jon Shapiro, "Whole Language Instruction: Writing in 1st Grade," *Reading Teacher 41/4* (Jan 1988): 430-37. [EJ 371 822]
Reports extensive observations of a Whole Language program in two first-grade classrooms that support Whole Language instruction. Outlines the advantages and disadvantages of the approach for both students and teachers.

Gunn, Cathy, "Whole Language Bibliography," *Writing Notebook 7/3* (Jan-Feb 1990): 9-10. [EJ 402 279]
Annotates (1) 28 professional books which deal with the Whole Language approach in the area of reading and writing; and (2) eight books to use as computer-related resources.

Gunn, Cathy, "Computers in a Whole Language Classroom," *Writing Notebook 7/3* (Jan-Feb 1990): 6-8. [EJ 402 278]
Describes strategies which teachers can model to help their students become cognitively aware of language. Suggests that teachers model writing and reading strategies at the same time they demonstrate word processing functions.

Gursky, Daniel, "After the Reign of Dick and Jane," *Teacher Magazine 2/9* (Aug 1991): 22-29 [EJ 433 793]
Examines the philosophy of the Whole Language approach to teaching and learning. Whole Language stresses that language should remain whole and uncontrived and children should use it in ways that relate to their own lives. Answers are not so important as learning processes in the Whole Language approach.

Gutknecht, Bruce, "Learning about Language Learners: The Case for Informal Assessment in the Whole Language Classroom," *Reading Improvement 29/4* (win 1992): 210-19. [EJ 455 603]
Maintains that continued over reliance on traditional skills-based assessment of reading abilities provides the Whole-Language teacher with little, if any, useful information for instructional planning. Suggests informal assessment procedures that focus on the language learner and provide a rich information source on which to base instructional decision making.

Gutknecht, Bruce, "From Basic Skills to Whole Language in Reading Instruction: Can We Get There from Here?" (1989): 14 pp. [ED 319 017]
Reading instruction based on the acquisition of basic skills has produced a basic level of literacy in children, but such minimal levels of literacy are no longer sufficient for students required to deal effectively with complicated literary and informational material encountered in upper elementary, middle, and high school texts. Research in the cognitive processes of readers has produced models of the reading process that show reading as a search for meaning in which the readers bring their experiential background and their language systems to their understanding of the author's message. Recognizing the limitations of basic skills instruction, school systems across the nation are implementing a shift in both instruction and materials to the Whole Language

approach. In short, Whole Language reading instruction begins in the mind of the reader, not with the letters on the page. Using a "top-down" or transactive/interactive approach, teachers should use meaningful, predictable stories and ask literal and interpretive level questions, involving children in comprehension strategies. Reading should not be taught as a fragmented series of subskills, because real language does not exist in isolated bits and pieces.

Gutknecht, Bruce, "All the King's Horses and Men, Basic Skills, and Whole Language," 15 pp. (1990). [ED 319 016]
Like Humpty Dumpty after the fall from the wall, language does not work effectively when it is not whole. For many students, the reading problems they begin to experience in the third or fourth grade are caused by the basic-skills manner in which beginning reading is taught. Recognizing the limitations of basic-skills instruction and the genre of reading instructional materials that focus on a skills-acquisition model of the reading process, school systems across the nation are implementing a shift in both instruction and materials to what is known as a literature-based, Whole Language approach. New directions for reading and writing instruction will enable students to meet the challenge of higher literacy expectations. Literature-based, Whole Language reading instruction must begin with the understanding and acceptance of the purpose of reading. Reading instruction must be implemented in the context of the other language/communication processes—spelling, listening, and writing.

Haese, Kari K., "Putting Whole Language, Literature-Based Reading into Practice," *Journal of the Wisconsin State Reading Association 35/2* (spr 1991): 17-21. [EJ 432 425]
Presents three patterns of literature-based reading instruction and illustrates their role in the moving from a traditional reading program toward a Whole Language, literature-based reading program.

Hafer, Jan, and others, "Sowing the Seeds of Literacy," *Perspectives in Education and Deafness 10/1* (Sep-Oct 1991): 7-10 [EJ 439 401]
A book-centered, Whole Language approach to literacy education is proposed for young children with hearing impairments. Through the context and vocabulary of a selected book, children work on gross and fine motor skills, language, speech, audition, writing, cognitive skills, and social skills.

Hahn, Elizabeth B., "Environmental Education (Research into Practice)," *Reading Psychology 10/1* (1989): 89-92. [EJ 393 490]
Describes reading center activities designed to make reading fit into the real world and the real world fit into reading. Uses a Whole Language approach both to promote ideas that are novel to students and to promote excellent children's literature.

Hajek, Ellen, "Whole Language: Sensible Answers to the Old Problems," *Momentum 15/2* (May 1984): 39-40. [EJ 301 723]
Advocates the use of the Whole Language method in writing instruction to emphasize communication rather than mechanical correctness in writing. Discusses the following Whole Language techniques: having children see themselves as authors, using predictable books, encouraging inventive spelling, and using and displaying student work.

Hale, Marilyn, "The Literacy Project at Sir William Osler High School: Year 1, 1990-91." (1991): 54 pp. [ED 353 549]
A formative evaluation was conducted during the first year of a Whole Language literacy project at Sir William Osler High School, Ontario, Canada, which serves students who have been diagnosed as functioning below grade level. Interviews were

conducted to collect descriptive information from the six Osler staff members involved in the project, the school administrators, and the central administrators responsible for the support and implementation of the project about the various aspects of the literacy program. Results indicated that: (1) the general objectives addressed by the Osler staff members were both cognitive and affective in content; (2) specifically, the staff addressed reading and writing; (3) the general objectives of the school administrators were more global in nature; (4) teachers used an eclectic approach in choosing teaching strategies; (5) staff and school administrators attended staff development activities; (6) all three groups agreed that the TSA (Teacher Specially Assigned) was instrumental in getting the project off the ground; and (7) the role of the TSA in the next year was seen differently by staff members when compared to school administrators and program staff.

Hale, Marilyn, "The Literacy Project at Maplewood High School: Year 1, 1990-91." (1991): 53 pp. [ED 353 550]
A formative evaluation was conducted during the first year of a Whole Language literacy project at Maplewood High School, Ontario, Canada, which serves students who have been diagnosed as functioning below grade level. Interviews were conducted to collect descriptive information from the five Maplewood staff members involved in the project, the school administrators, and the central administrators responsible for the support and implementation of the project about the various aspects of the literacy program. Results indicated that: (1) there was a consistent broad objective held by teachers and school administrators involved in the literacy project; (2) the students involved in the project were in grades seven and eight with a reading ability level of approximately grade two and often little or no writing ability; (3) teachers used an eclectic approach in choosing teaching strategies; (4) the strategies that did not work were varied; (5) some problems arose with peer evaluation; (6) all staff members and school administrators attended staff development activities; (7) the English Language Centre was the major resource used by teachers and school administrators at Maplewood; (8) the objectives will be continued for the second year; (9) there was some uncertainty whether the students in the program in the second year would also include those in grade nine; and (10) most teachers wanted the role of the TSA (Teacher Specially Assigned) to be the same the second year.

Hall, Nigel, *The Emergence of Literacy* (Portsmouth, NH: Heinemann, 1987) [ED 282 179]
Focusing on the relationship between learning oral language and learning about written language, this book discusses the emergent literacy (EL) of children growing up in a Western, print-oriented society, as well as findings of research conducted during the past 15 years on how children make sense of the way in which literacy works in their culture. Chapter one discusses recent views about and research on EL that represent explicit claims about literacy as a language process, while chapter two outlines the linguistic and social background of EL, detailing the emergence of both oral language and literacy in context. Chapter three focuses on two aspects of EL: the understanding of environmental print and the understanding of continuous text, usually in the form of stories. Chapter four reviews findings of many investigations regarding emergent writing abilities and discusses whether young children have a commitment to writing, understand anything about when and why people write, and know about how people write. Chapter five examines the contrasting views of J. Downing and J. Harste with regard to how children approach reading instruction, while tests and procedures designed to assess emerging literacy in the context of nursery and infant classrooms are discussed in chapter six. The final chapter discusses EL and schooling, focusing on the situations created within schools for teaching children to become literate and

whether literacy continues to emerge with the same ease that it did before the transition into school.

Halpern, Honey, "Ideas for Collaborative Work in Whole Language Classrooms," *Canadian Journal of English Language Arts 12*/3 (1989): 56-60. [EJ 434 194] Discusses collaboration between teachers and students and among students. Presents classroom strategies that use the principles of collaboration in the Whole Language class.

Halpern, Honey, "Classroom Scene: Contemporary Canadian Children's Literature for the Intermediate Grades: A Whole Language Approach," *Reading Canada Lecture 5*/4 (win 1987): 268-73. [EJ 371 760] Presents effective methods for the discussion, sharpening, and enrichment of readers' responses. Includes methods to teach students how to choose a good book, an individualized and/or group reading and response program, and journal writing techniques. Provides a bibliography of Canadian children's literature for intermediate grades.

Halpern, Honey, "Contemporary Canadian Children's Literature for the Intermediate Grades: A Whole Language Approach," paper presented at the Annual Meeting of the Transmountain Regional Conference of the International Reading Association (7th, Vancouver, British Columbia, Canada, May 29-31, 1986). [ED 281 161] Teachers must make sure that the right book gets to the right child at the right time in order to develop positive reading habits. However, once a book is selected, students should be encouraged to think about what they are reading and use the story to evaluate and enrich their personal knowledge. Two classroom programs that use the Whole Language approach to reading are (1) an individualized and/or group reading and response program and (2) journal writing as a response to literature. For students who work well independently, the first program uses varied project ideas that do not represent the easiest option—such as preparing a television commercial to try to get others to buy the book, writing a letter to a character in the book, designing a book jacket, finding and playing music to accompany a scene from the book, or making a time line with illustrations of events. In the second program, the students keep a structured journal as they read a novel. In the journal, the students should be encouraged to detail their personal responses, research topics introduced in the novel, describe themes and characters, include creative writing of their own, and write a letter to the book's author. Writing and having someone read and respond can generate an English program that achieves cognitive and affective results.

Hamayan, Else V., "Teaching Writing to Potentially English Proficient Students Using Whole Language Approaches. Program Information Guide Series, Number 11, Summer 1989." (1989): 18 pp. [ED 337 038] Innovative methods and strategies are described for teaching writing to potentially English proficient (PEP) students (also known as "limited English proficient"), who may or may not be literate in their native language, using holistic natural approaches. The approaches are based on the premise that students acquire language (speaking, reading, and writing) naturally when they engage in self-motivating activities that are stimulating, interesting, and meaningful to them. The guide is the result of work done at the Illinois Resource Center as well as in programs funded by the U.S. Department of State for Southeast Asian refugee students. Assumptions underlying current and innovative approaches to teaching writing are outlined and holistic natural approaches, such as language experience stories, dialogue journals, diaries, and creative writing are described. Considerations for implementing holistic language approaches are also described, including the need for intensity and constancy, using holistic approaches in a non-holistic curriculum, and monitoring student progress.

Hamman, Vincent E., "Teachers' Awareness of Reading Terms," *Reading Improvement* 29/3 (fall 1992): 174-78. [EJ 452 726]
Identifies elementary classroom teachers' awareness of Whole Language and basal reading terms. Finds that teachers were more aware of basal reading terms. Finds that university/college course was the highest reported source of awareness with each of 30 survey terms.

Hammond, Jennifer, "Oral and Written Language in the Educational Context," paper presented at the World Congress of the International Association of Applied Linguistics (Sydney, New South Wales, Australia, Aug 11-16, 1987). [ED 301 880]
Argues that, despite the usefulness in emphasizing the similarity between the linguistic systems underlying oral and written language, that the Whole Language approach fails to take into account the real and significant differences that exist between oral and written language and the different purposes for which they are used. Children need explicit guidance and support in making the shift from oral to written language. A classroom exercise in which students gather and discuss a topic involving their own experiences and then are asked to write about it exemplifies the problem. The implicit assumption is that oral and written language is the same and all students have to do is write down what they said. However, the children do not see any difference in purpose for the oral and written activities. There is no sense of the purpose of writing as forming a context-free and permanent record of events. In developing effective literacy programs an extra step is required. A lesson could begin with oral discussion, then provide children with information about what a successful text, written for a particular purpose, actually looks like. Only after such information would the children attempt to write texts themselves.

Hancock, Marjorie R., "Putting It All Together: A Selected Bibliography of Whole Language," *Illinois Schools Journal 70/2* (1991): 31-42. [EJ 429 502]
Presents a selected bibliography of 44 entries concerning Whole Language theory, research, practice, and evaluation. Annotations are followed by subheadings indicating the primary foci of the book or article. These sources will help practitioners make the transition from traditional to Whole Language instruction in reading and writing.

Hanlin, Jayne Ilene, "Give the Classics a Front-Row Seat," *Learning 20/5* (Jan 1992): 54-57. [EJ 440 398]
A fifth-grade teacher describes that by reading classic literature aloud to her students each day, she helped them along the road to literature-based learning. Discusses the advantages of the Whole Language approach.

Hansen, Joe B., and Walter E. Hathaway, "A Survey of More Authentic Assessment Practices," paper presented at the Annual Meeting of the National Council on Measurement in Education (Chicago, IL, Apr 4-6, 1991). [ED 333 039]
Information was gathered to determine the extent to which more authentic education assessments, including Whole Language assessments, are being implemented, and to identify which organizations conduct authentic education assessments. Materials used by the surveyed organizations were collected and catalogued into a compendium of authentic assessment techniques. A conceptual framework was developed for characterizing the stage of development an organization attained with respect to authentic assessment; this framework ranged from the initial policy decision through making the assessment operational. A questionnaire was mailed to individuals representing 433 educational organizations and businesses in the United States, Canada, and several other countries. Representatives were asked what they were doing to answer the call for more authentic assessment and, more specifically, how they were addressing the

call for more Whole Language assessment. A total of 110 organizations responded positively to either of the two questions administered, a response rate of 25.4%. Of these, 106 respondents indicated that they were attempting more authentic assessment, with 75 attempting Whole Language assessment. Forty-one organizations submitted materials to be catalogued. In general, assessments were in the developmental stage, with relatively little full implementation.

Hanson, Richard, and others, "Reading/Writing Relationships: Implications for Teachers," *Journal of the Wisconsin State Reading Association 35/*1 (win 1991): 57-63. [EJ 429 711]
Outlines four ways in which reading and writing are related. Identifies eight actions teachers should take to enhance literary development in their classrooms. Suggests two initiatives that teachers might take to enhance literacy in homes, schools, and communities.

Harker, John, "The Whole Truth about Whole Language (The Reading Connection)," *Canadian Journal of English Language Arts 12/*1-2 (1989): 54-56. [EJ 390 389]
Examines the Whole Language movement from both historical and research perspectives. Concludes that teachers should not rely on one methodology or philosophy to further children's reading, and that teachers' interactions with students supercede the importance of any particular method.

Harman, Susan, and Carole Edelsky, "The Risks of Whole Language Literacy: Alienation and Connection," *Language Arts 66/*4 (Apr 1989): 392-406. [EJ 390 404]
Discusses the acquisition of literacy, particularly its acquisition through the Whole Language approach, as possibly having unanticipated repercussions in the lives of the learners. Proposes four constructive ways of noticing, respecting, and using these repercussions of change in a Whole Language classroom.

Harns, Charles M., "Whole Language Training Module: For Training Teachers and Tutors of Adult Reading Students." (1992): 37 pp. [ED 349 428]
Presents a 3-hour workshop in Whole Language theory and practice to be used for inservice training of a small group of tutors or teachers of adult reading students. Suggested group size is 6-15 people. Part I explores the background and concepts of Whole Language from the point of view of the psycholinguistic model of the reading process. Participants are immediately asked to participate in an interesting activity that brings to the surface the importance of the reader's background knowledge in the process and the importance of using whole and meaningful text to help the reader use all the cue or clue levels in the act of reading. Part II presents one broad approach often used in Whole Language-oriented teaching: process writing. Presents several specific strategy lessons consistent with Whole Language thinking

Harp, Bill, "When You Do Whole Language Instruction, How Will You Keep Track of Reading and Writing Skills? (When the Principal Asks)," *Reading Teacher 42/*2 (Nov 1988): 160-61. [EJ 381 763]
Discusses several ways to evaluate reading and writing skills in a Whole Language classroom, including evaluation checklists, holistic evaluation of writing, and miscue analysis. Provides a literacy development checklist for reading and writing.

Harp, Bill, ed., "Assessment and Evaluation in Whole Language Programs." (Norwood, Massachusetts: Christopher-Gordon,1991): 251 pp. [ED 331 043]
Intended for practioners, this book discusses many of the critical questions being asked about the role of Whole Language in schools. Examines the growing research base that supports Whole Language and offers practical and realistic suggestions for tackling the many thorny issues involved in the assessment and evaluation of students. Contents:

(1) The Whole Language Movement (Bill Harp); (2) Assessment and Evaluation (John Bertrand); (3) Principles of Assessment and Evaluation in Whole Language Classrooms (Bill Harp); (4) Reading Evaluation—Miscue Analysis (Dorothy Watson and Janice Henson); (5) Whole Language Assessment and Evaluation Strategies (Ward Cockrum and Maggie Castillo); (6) A Collage of Assessment and Evaluation in Primary Grade Classrooms (S. Jeanne Reardon); (7) Holistic Assessment in Intermediate Classrooms: Techniques for Informing Our Teaching (Yvonne Siu-Runyan); (8) Whole Language Assessment and Evaluation in Special Education Classrooms (Hilary Sumner); (9) Assessment and Evaluation in Bilingual, Multicultural Classrooms (Dorothy King); (10) Record Keeping in Whole Language Classrooms (Jean Church); (11) Reporting Progress to Students, Parents, and Administrators (Ron Hutchison); and (12) Whole Language Assessment and Evaluation: The Future (Jerome Harste and William Bintz).

Harp, Bill, "Why Don't You Ask Comprehension Questions? (When the Principal Asks)," *Reading Teacher 42*/8 (Apr 1989): 638-39. [EJ 386 939]
Discusses literature and research concerning comprehension questions, particularly in the context of the Whole Language Movement. Notes that there are other ways for students to demonstrate their text comprehension, such as literature logs, small group discussion, and individual or group projects. Suggests several implications for the classroom.

Harp, Bill, "When the Principal Asks: 'Why Are Your Kids Singing during Reading Time?'" *Reading Teacher 41*/4 (Jan 1988): 454-56. [EJ 371 826]
Argues that music and singing readily fit the needs of the Whole Language approach to reading instruction. Provides a five-step method for using music to teach reading.

Harper, Joan, "The Teacher-Librarian's Role in Literature-Based Reading and Whole Language Programs," *Emergency Librarian 17*/2 (Nov-Dec 1989): 17-18,20. [EJ 405 655]
Argues that language programs should result not only in competent language use but also in reading for enjoyment. The advantages of a Whole Language approach in achieving this goal are discussed. Strategies for incorporating this approach into traditional programs by developing literature-based reading units as extensions of basal readers are suggested.

Harste, Jerome C., "The Future of Whole Language," *Elementary School Journal 90*/2 (Nov 1989): 243-49. [EJ 404 271]
Comments on the future of Whole Language, predicting that the movement will continue to expand with an increased understanding of the role that language plays in learning, a growing respect for alternate ways of knowing, and a renewed interest in curriculum.

Harste, Jerome C., *New Policy Guidelines for Reading: Connecting Research and Practice* (Urbana, Illinois: ERIC Clearinghouse on Reading and Communication Skills and National Council of Teachers of English, 1989). [ED 311 393]
Intended to help teachers, researchers, curriculum developers, and administrators develop improved policy in reading instruction and research, this book challenges several widespread assumptions about effective reading instruction and concludes with 20 policy guidelines which can be used to evaluate existing reading programs and redesign them to aim at higher levels of comprehension. Contents: (1) "Reading, Reading Instruction, and Reading Research," discussing the relationship among the three; (2) "Supporting Practical Theory," dealing with trusting teachers, supporting inquiry, taking risks, building upon what we know, and supporting self-evaluation; (3)

"Effective Change Projects," discussing the characteristics of school reading programs exemplifying effective school change and dynamic, research-based instruction; (4) "The Agenda Ahead"; and (5) "Guidelines for Improving Reading Comprehension Instruction," encapsulating available information about the conditions that are likely to improve the teaching of reading in our schools.

Harste, Jerome C., "What It Means to Be Strategic: Good Readers as Informants," paper presented at the Annual Meeting of the National Reading Conference (36th, Austin, TX, Dec 2-6, 1986). [ED 278 980]
A study was conducted to identify strategies used by successful readers in comprehending and interpreting various kinds of texts. Seventy-three graduate students were asked to keep a journal (unedited and freely written) of what they were thinking as they were reading Umberto Eco's novel "The Name of the Rose." Selected journal entries were divided into 771 introspective commentaries that were marked by a shift in topic or attention on the part of the reader between and among "reader," "text," or "context" codes, plus the extended discussion of what the reader made of such shifts in attention. For purposes of coding response types, a "reading strategy" was defined as a cognitive choice—visualize, compare, criticize, etc. Adjusting rate, underlining, and taking notes were defined as a "reading technique." Results suggest that mentally good readers spend about 69% of their time off the page attempting to make connections, recasting what they have read in terms of what they currently know, criticizing themselves and the author's performance, and/or extrapolating what they have read to see what it might have to say about everything from ethnography to the meaning of life. Findings support the contextual embeddedness of all reading and interpretation and how instructional tasks can bolster the use of reading as a tool for learning.

Harste, Jerome C., and others, *Language Stories & Literacy Lessons.* (Portsmouth, New Hampshire: Heinemann, 1984). [ED 257 113]
As a result of a program of research about cognitive processes involved in learning to read and write among 3-, 4-, 5-, and 6-year old-children, this book attempts to get teacher-researchers to think through the implications of recent insights into literacy and literacy learning. The first section examines instructional assumptions; proposes a new view of language development; presents a language lesson from a 3-year old; suggests a new perspective concerning the relationship between literacy and race, sex, and socioeconomic status; and examines literacy assumptions. The second section presents key patterns in language and language learning that were seen in the language stories of the children, and examines the organization of the writing, the intentionality of the children as language users, the generativeness of language, risk taking as being central to cognitive processing, writing as a form of social action, the text as the basic unit of language, how language is learned, and new patterns in literacy. The third section deals with the conceptual implications and the methodological implications of literacy and literacy learning. Research task directions and a bibliography are appended.

Harste, Jerome C., and others, "The Young Child as Writer-Reader, and Informant. Final Report." (Bloomington: Indiana University Department of Language Education, 1983). [ED 234 413]
The second of a two-volume report, this document focuses on the study of written language growth and development among 3-, 4-, 5-, and 6-year-old children. The first section of the report introduces the program of research by examining its methodological and conceptual contexts. The second section provides illustrative and alternative looks at the young child as writer-reader and reader-writer, highlighting key transactions in literacy and literacy learning. The third section pulls together and identifies how the researchers' thinking about literacy and literacy learning changed as a result of

their research and offers an evolving model of key processes involved in literacy learning. The fourth section comprises a series of papers dealing with the spelling process, children's writing development as seen in letters, rereading, and the role of literature in the language pool of children. The fifth section contains taxonomies developed for studying the surface texts created by children in the study. Extensive references are included, and an addendum includes examples of task sequence and researcher script, "sample characteristics" charts, and sample characteristics summary statements. (FL)

Harste, Jerome C., and others, "Creating Classrooms for Authors: The Reading-Writing Connection." (1988): 403 pp. [ED 320 168]
Intended for practitioners, this book presents a curricular framework for classroom reading and writing experiences that help students understand how reading and writing relate to reasoning and learning. The two sections of the book are organized around three major components of curriculum and how each component was realized in three Indiana classroom settings—inner city, suburban, and small town/city. The first section summarizes current knowledge about reading, writing, and reasoning as it relates to curriculum learning. Although the major curriculum components overlap, they involve: (1) how to begin an authoring cycle; (2) creating a conducive context for exploring literacy in the classroom; and (3) using this frame for communicating and extending curriculum. Full lesson plans for the 32 strategies discussed are included in Section Two. Three feature articles in the book offer readers the opportunity to hear directly from the teachers involved in classrooms using the authoring cycle as a curricular frame. The intent of these feature articles is to present key insights as well as various portrayals of how to begin.

Harste, Jerome C., and Kathy G. Short, "What Educational Difference Does Your Theory of Language Make?" paper presented at the International Reading Association World Congress (Queensland, Australia, Jul 11-13, 1988) and at the Annual Meeting of the International Reading Association (34th, New Orleans, LA, Apr 30-May 4, 1989). [ED 311 397]
Good language users monitor and understand their own involvement in the learning process. They understand how language is used to make and reshape their world. Everyone needs to be allowed to test his or her personal theories of the world against practice and vice versa. Given the nature of society, it is important that conceptions of literacy begin with the notion of voice and the importance of hearing everyone's voice. Empowerment begins when each individual is able to name the world as he or she sees it. In naming the world through language, differences are noted and transformative conversations begin. From listening to new voices new anomalies can be identified, new conversations can be started, and potentially new behaviors can be explored. Classrooms organized on a theory of literacy that values hearing individual voices must be judged by a different set of performance criteria than has traditionally been the case. Strong communities are not formed on the basis of likeminded individuals, but rather on differences, where the different voices making up the community are heard and listened to. It is by hearing different voices that the resources available in a community of learners become known as well as transformed. Classrooms which place a priority on understanding the role that language plays in enhancing learning become communities of learners, as various examples of children's writing illustrate. New criteria for a good theory of language include (1) allowing each person to have a voice; (2) beginning needed conversations; and (3) providing a mechanism whereby those conversations can continue.

Hatch, J. Amos, "Out from between a Rock and a Hard Place: Whole Language in Tennessee," *Reading Improvement 30*/3 (fall 1993): 161-65. [CS 746 237] Describes the ways key issues in Whole Language implementation were handled in Tennessee's pilot program. Offers a framework for encouraging teachers to look closely at the advantages of Whole Language without squeezing them between a rock and a hard place. (See ED 336 724]: The Whole Language Pilot Project in Tennessee was designed to respect teachers' judgments, to assume that their current practices are effective given the circumstances in which they work, and to offer Whole Language principles and practices as alternatives for teachers' consideration. The major vehicle for helping teachers understand Whole Language possibilities was a series of monthly teleconferences broadcast over satellite television during the 1989-90 school year. Participation in the pilot project was voluntary, and 40 schools chose to sign on as pilot schools. Faculties from other schools also viewed the broadcasts, bringing the total number of educators participating in the year-long project to over 1,300. The project's approach concerning basals was to help teachers conceptualize a continuum of possible uses for their basals, then to encourage them to reflect on the outcomes they desire and to select from possible uses based on what they wish to accomplish. The project suggested to teachers that there are many advantages to moving in the direction of using more flexible (rather than structured) classroom time and a wide variety of options for grouping children. The project offered teachers a broadened perspective on skills instruction and evaluation that attempted to balance principles of Whole Language with concerns for skill mastery. A continuum of strategies (incidental teaching, unit teaching, strategic teaching and direct teaching) was presented to teachers. Teachers were encouraged to make active decisions based on their best professional judgment about what was taught, when, and how. Treating Whole Language learning among professional educators as a transaction rather than as a one-way transmission reduces the chances of placing teachers between a rock and a hard place.

Haycock, Ken, "Whole Language Issues and Implications," *Emergency Librarian 17*/2 (Nov-Dec 1989): 22-24, 26. [EJ 405 565] Defines the Whole Language approach as an attitude about how children learn as well as a teaching strategy that transcends specific curricular areas and extends far beyond language arts. The implications for publishers, teachers, librarians, and curriculum developers are discussed.

Hayes, Bernard L., and Kay Camperell, eds., "Developing Lifelong Readers: Policies, Procedures, and Programs." (1992): 159 pp. [ED 352 609] Selected papers from the 1991 annual conference of the American Reading Forum are presented in this yearbook. The papers, which deal with issues regarding ways to develop and strengthen a society of active readers, address policies, procedures, and programs for the beginning child reader, the beginning adult reader, and a range of readers in between and beyond. Contents: "Developing Problem Solving Environments to Prepare Teachers for Instruction of Diverse Learners" (Victoria J. Risko); "Reasons 'Effective' Strategies Are Not Used: Student's and Teacher's Explanations" (Richard J. Telfer and others); "Are Teachers Using Whole Language to Teach Reading: A National Perspective" (Patricia K. Smith); "Reading Recommendations for a Multi-Cultural Tomorrow" (Kathleen Evans and Terry Bratcher); "Lifelong Reading by Teachers as Bibliotherapy" (Don Lumpkin); "Scenes from a Classroom: Literature for Thinking about Teaching—An Annotated Bibliography" (Marilyn Eanet); "Caldecott Medal Books (1938-1991): Some Observations" (Sylvia Hutchinson and Ira E. Aaron); "Promoting Readership within Public Schools: Survey of Administrators and Recommendations for Practice" (Emilie P. Sullivan and others); and "Assessing Job-Related Basic Skills: Job Trails as an Example" (Eunice N. Askov and Bernice P. Sheaffer). Panel presentations in the yearbook are: "Developing Lifelong Literacy: Some Stories Inspired by Roger Schank's 'Tell Me a Story'" (Wayne Otto and others); "The Portrayal of Ethnic Characters in Newbery Award Winning Books" (Cindy Gillespie and others); "Kindergartner's Use of Theme-Based Integrated Texts" (Marino C. Alvarez and Judith Vaugh); "Evaluation of Statewide Workplace Literacy Computer-Assisted Instruction for Commercial Drivers: R.O.A.D. to SUCCESS" (Emory Brown and Eunice N. Askov); and "An Innovative Program for Meeting the Literacy Needs of a Non-Majority-Culture Community" (Mary Beneditti and others).

Heacock, Grace Anne, "The We-Search Process: Using the Whole Language Model of Writing to Learn Social Studies Content and Civic Competence," *Social Studies and the Young Learner 2/3* (Jan-Feb 1990): 9-11. [EJ 420 701]
Demonstrates teaching citizenship through student involvement in current issues. Presents We-Search—a process using the Whole-Language approach for group research projects in a Fairbanks, Alaska, third grade class. Highlights class projects, including one concerning transportation of plutonium across international borders. Emphasizes how We-Search fosters civic competence.

Heald-Taylor, Gail, "Whole Language Strategies for ESL Students. Language and Literacy Series." (1986): 83 pp. [ED 280 287]
Outlines learning strategies in language arts for children in kindergarten to third grade learning English as a second language (ESL). They are designed for the Whole Language or Natural Approach. Although reading and writing are the key language components emphasized, listening, speaking, drama, and visual arts activities have been included. The key strategies highlighted are dictation, literature in language learning, process writing, themes, and evaluation. An introductory section gives an overview of the method and the strategies used. A section on the organization of strategies into a classroom timetable follows. Separate sections outline activities using the different strategies, and for each activity, general information and implications for ESL students are presented.

Heller, Mary F., "The Promise of Whole Language Instruction," *Kansas Journal of Reading 7* (spr 1992): 41-48. [EJ 428 332]
Contains a vignette of a second-grade classroom in which a Whole Language approach is used to teach reading and writing. Defines and describes Whole Language theory, practice, and goals. Offers guidelines to facilitate the process of changing from the basal to the holistic approach.

Henney, Maribeth, "Literature-Based Theme Units," paper presented at the World Congress on Reading (13th, Stockholm, Sweden, Jul 3-6, 1990). [ED 325 840]
With the current emphasis on Whole Language, the use of children's literature as the basis for reading instruction is widespread. Theme units have been suggested as one way to provide stimulating opportunities for children to explore and learn. Whole Language based literature theme units emphasize process more than product. Units are designed to encourage students to use information from literary, scientific, and historical bodies of knowledge of the past and present, and to speculate about the "what-ifs" of the future. Units may be organized in various ways, for example, by topic, genre, author, literary devices, vocabulary and language; and by having students read a whole text and then discuss it. A variety of resources and materials can be incorporated into unit study. Teachers first need to consider the content they wish to convey and the type of unit to be taught, and then plan appropriate activities to achieve

their goals. Literature-based theme units are a way to immerse children in reading and enable them to use this reading in interesting, meaningful, relevant activities.

Henney, Maribeth, "Can a Whole Language Approach Be Effectively Implemented in a University Level Course?," paper presented at the Annual Plains Regional Conference of the International Reading Association (18th, Wichita, KS, Oct 17-20, 1990). [ED 325 841]
Because so many elementary schools are employing Whole Language instruction, it is essential that graduates from university elementary education programs be prepared to teach in this way. Twenty-five junior and senior elementary education majors enrolled in a block program of 3 courses: reading methods, language arts methods, and a field practicum experience 2 mornings a week for 10 weeks in elementary classrooms. The reading and language arts methods courses were combined and taught as one course for a period of 3 hours twice a week. The course was organized so that students were given a firsthand experience with Whole Language. All language arts were involved in an integrated way, although specific areas were also dealt with from time to time. Activities were self-chosen, based on students' interests. There were many positive results from this course. First and foremost, students learned Whole Language theories, processes, problems, and alternatives through direct experience. Probably the greatest shortcoming was that students did not learn as much content about how to teach reading and language arts as they might have in a more structured lecture-recitation class. Revisions to the course were made as a result of these initial experiences in teaching university classes with a Whole Language base.

Henry, Jean, "Holistic Teaching Strategies for Hispanic Students." (1991): 40 pp. [ED 351 892]
In an effort to support Spanish and English-as-a-Second-Language (ESL) literacy education and to help preserve the dignity and identity of the Hispanic community in central Pennsylvania, a literacy program was established and staffed by volunteers and paid employees. Beginning with two students and a volunteer tutor, the class has grown into a multilevel and intergenerational group. Program services include outreach, placement, family reading consultation, and transportation assistance. The primary program objectives are to develop an ESL curriculum appropriate for this population, to develop and refine teaching strategies using a holistic, Whole-Language approach to second language instruction, teach at least 20 Hispanic students to improve their English speech, reading, and writing skills using the curriculum, produce a collection of Hispanic stories in English, and strengthen links between the Hispanic community and community services. The project report presented here includes a summary of program structure, notes on instructional materials used, attendance patterns, the new student orientation process, lesson plan structure, classroom teaching methods (poetry, public speaking, jazz chants, and cooperative work), and anecdotal information.

Heymsfeld, Carla R., "The Remedial Child in the Whole-Language, Cooperative Class-room," *Reading and Writing Quarterly: Overcoming Learning Difficulties 8*/3 (Jul-Sep 1992): 257-73. [CS 745 624]
Considers theory, research, and techniques associated with Whole Language and skill-based approaches to reading (including issues related to teaching phonics and reading comprehension) to see how children needing remedial work can best be served. Examines ways that group activities and cooperative learning can support remediation.

Heymsfeld, Carla R., "Filling the Hole in Whole Language," *Educational Leadership* 46/6 (Mar 1989): 65-68. [EJ 385 284]

Because both Whole Language and traditional skill-based instruction have strengths, educators should use a combined approach that includes direct instruction in phonics and reading comprehension skills along with Whole Language instruction.

Hiebert, Elfrieda H., and Charles W. Fisher, "Whole Language: Three Themes for the Future," *Educational Leadership* 47/6 (Mar 1990): 62-64. [EJ 405 142]
Whole Language and skills-oriented instruction to find that students in Whole Language classes spent more time on cognitively complex literacy tasks. Educators need to balance the use of narrative and expository text, integrate subject matter areas, and use a variety of instructional grouping strategies.

Hill, Sara, ed., and others, "[Special Issue on Classroom Instruction]. Information Update." (1989): 17 pp. [ED 321 107]
This newsletter issue focuses entirely on classroom instruction in adult basic education (ABE) and English-as-a-Second-Language (ESL) programs. The first article, "Whole Language and Adult Literacy Education" (Kazemek), describes 10 principles of holistic language education and how they may be translated into actual classroom practice. The practices include sustained silent reading; sustained silent writing; prepared oral reading as a social activity; language experience texts; reading, reread- ing, and retelling published texts; strategy instruction; and informal assessment. The second article, "Building a Community of Learners (Schneider), describes how such a community is created at the ABE learning centers at the New York Public Library. "Teachers Talk about Writing" (Slivka) contains a discussion by four ABE teachers from Region 3 of the New York City Board of Education on how they facilitate writing in their classes. "Parallels in Literacy and Second Language Acquisition" (Hill, Rabideau) argues that ABE and ESL teachers can learn from one another and provides examples. "Teaching Writing through the Arts" (Denis) explains how a drama and playwriting teacher from New York City Public Schools uses theatre games and writing exercises that build writing confidence and interest, including talk sessions, oral storytelling, monologues, two-character plays, free associative plays, team writing, and a sound effects writing exercise.

Hillerich, Robert L., "Whole Language: Looking for Balance among Dichotomies," paper presented at the Annual Meeting of the Colorado Council of the International Reading Association (Denver, CO, Jan 31-Feb 2, 1990). [ED 315 746]
Like so many slogans, "Whole Language" is a dangerous term because its meaning varies with each educator. Whole Language is not a method of teaching, nor is it a program; it is a philosophy or viewpoint. Nine major characteristics of a Whole Language approach as culled from a variety of sources, with most agreed upon by a majority of authors, are: (1) fun in reading; (2) oral language as a bridge to print; (3) risk taking; (4) use of rich literature; (5) developmental versus preconceived sequence; (6) integrating the language arts; (7) reading whole texts versus excerpts; (8) meaning- ful use of language versus isolated drill; and (9) reading is a natural act. While bits and pieces of method associated with the philosophy have been supported by research, little research has been done on the total. Educators are obviously in a state of flux. Educators must make every effort to ensure that the effective elements are here to stay, especially: the encouragement to modify curriculum to fit kids instead of trying to fit kids into preconceived molds; the emphasis on children doing a lot more real reading and writing; and the practice of children doing both reading and writing as communi- cative acts rather than devoting the majority of time to skill exercises. If children are to become independent readers, the skills they do learn need to be used in real reading. Educators need to recognize that both skill and interest are essential.

Hinnenkamp, Barbara, "Reading and Writing with a Special Needs Student: A Case Study." (1991): 9 pp. [ED 326 846]
In the 1988-89 school year, a teacher introduced Whole Language learning to teach reading and writing in her classroom while documenting and then evaluating its effect on a 12-year-old special needs student named Debbie. According to formal testing, Debbie was functioning in the moderately handicapped range of ability, and her speech and language skills were commensurate with her ability. Debbie participated in a variety of reading and writing activities throughout the year, including: individual reading class, group reading activities, independent reading, group writing activities, independent writing, group spelling class and four thematic units of study. Four data collection procedures were used to document changes in Debbie's reading and writing over the school year: 2 reading miscue inventories, 14 running records of her reading, samples of Debbie's writing throughout the year, and a retelling of stories before and after the thematic unit. Comparative results indicated that Debbie did change and grow as a reader and writer, a fact that clearly demonstrated the effectiveness of Whole Language learning to promote language learning and literacy growth of special needs students.

Hobson, Eric, "Where Do College Students Come From? School/ University Articulation in Writing Theory," *Freshman English News 19/3* (fall 1991): 26-28. [EJ 437 371]
Charges that postsecondary educationists pay scant attention to developments outside their circle (such as the Whole Language movement), and thus are hindered in teaching the newest generation of college students. Discusses the Whole Language movement, its importance, its relationship to freshman composition theory, whether it challenges contemporary college-level-based composition theory, and what the future holds.

Hobson, Eric; Shuman, R. Baird, "Reading and Writing in High Schools: A Whole-Language Approach." (1990): 97 pp. [ED 317 987]
Arguing that students should be encouraged frequently to listen, to speak, to read, and to write in all areas of the curriculum and to begin asking the questions that reveal the dependence that exists between various bodies of knowledge, this book is based on the Whole Language theory. The book is designed not only to help students learn such specifics as grammar, usage, and mechanics in real and natural ways, but also to provide teachers with opportunities to make linkages with the community and to involve parents and other citizens in school activities. Chapters 1 and 2 discuss how people learn and what the Whole-Language approach is. Chapter 3 presents the skills of decoding (listening and reading); chapter 4 considers the skills of encoding (speaking and writing). The last chapter offers final comments about communication skills.

Hodges, Carol A., "Assessing Early Literacy." (1988): 28 pp. [ED 35 130]
Criticisms leveled at readiness tests in general by a variety of early childhood groups and at reading tests in general by reading researchers certainly appear to be valid for traditional paper and pencil reading readiness tests. These reading readiness tests have not kept pace with advances in early literacy instructional techniques, such as those represented by the Whole Language approach. They assess isolated skills that may have very little to do with whether or not a child is able to gain meaning from print in the environment or can understand the purposes and functions of print. While other tests, such as the Linguistic Awareness in Reading Readiness (LARR) test, the Concepts About Print (CAP) test, and the Test of Early Reading Ability (TERA) represent significant advancements in assessing some of the concepts deemed important in early reading, they, too, have disadvantages which make their use impractical in most cases. Systematized observation, performed by responsible

teachers who have a knowledge of reading and writing processes, the developmental process, and observational and record keeping procedures and analysis, represents one very useful tool for assessing growth and development in early reading and for providing information for making the daily instructional decisions that must be made by classroom teachers.

Hoffman, Paul R., "Spelling, Phonology, and the Speech-Language Pathologist: A Whole Language Perspective," *Language, Speech, and Hearing Services in Schools 21/4* (Oct 1990): 238-43. [EJ 420 020]
Discusses properties of Whole Language theories applied to spelling development and examines interrelated processes between spelling and speech sound production. Speech-language pathologists are encouraged to serve as resources to teachers in spelling instruction and to utilize Whole Language strategies that relate speech production to reading and writing in phonological therapy.

Hoffman, James V., "Am I Whole Yet? Are You? (Leadership in the Language Arts)," *Language Arts 69/5* (Sep 1992): 366-71. [EJ 448 435]
Discusses the author's experiences in learning about the Whole Language approach. Suggests that Whole Language is not so much about method or philosophy as it is about power. Offers five suggestions for administrators and teacher educators to help teachers explore the possibilities of Whole Language.

Holland, Kathy W., and Lee Ellis Hall, "Reading Achievement in the First Grade Classroom: A Comparison of Basal and Whole Language Approaches," *Reading Improvement 26/4* (win 1989): 323-29. [EJ 408 392]
Compares the effects of basal and Whole Language approaches on the reading achievement of first grade students. Finds no statistically significant differences in reading achievement between classes taught with a basal approach or with a Whole Language approach.

Hollingsworth, Paul M., and D. Ray Reutzel, "Whole Language with LD Children," *Academic Therapy 23/5* (May 1988): 477-88. [EJ 370 470]
Use of the Whole Language theory can improve the reading and writing of the language-learning disabled. This paper describes resource room characteristics necessary to create a Whole Language-learning environment and outlines instructional practices consistent with Whole Language theory, such as reading aloud, language experience approach, predictable story books, etc.

Hollingsworth, Paul M., and others, "Whole Language Practices in First Grade Reading Instruction," *Reading Research and Instruction 29/3* (spr 1990): 24-26. [EJ 410 032]
Examines the degree to which Whole Language practices have become a part of reading instruction offered by first-grade teachers in six school districts. Finds that teachers spent less than 10 percent of the reading instructional time engaged in practices which could be considered in agreement with Whole Language theory.

Hollingsworth, Sandra, and others, "Listening for Aaron: A Teacher's Story about Modifying a Literature-Based Approach to Literacy To Accommodate a Young Male's Voice. Research Series No. 206." (1991): 27 pp. [ED 333 361]
A case study showed how a third-year teacher modified the socialized culture of literature-based literacy instruction she found in her second-grade classroom and teacher education program to reach particular children who were having difficulty learning to read and write. Aaron, the subject of the case study, was a second-grade African-American student who could neither read nor write at the beginning of the study. At the start of the school year, the teacher incorporated a program for systematic, whole-class phonics/spelling instruction. She insisted that the children take

responsibility for their own learning, for sharing their knowledge with others in cooperative tasks, for resolving conflicts, and for organizing and helping her run the classroom. Still, Aaron's "voice" could not be heard in the classroom. As a result of discussion with peers, the teacher included supplemental systematic instruction in linguistic analyses and phonemic awareness, in groups small enough to command teacher attention to individual children. At the end of the year, Aaron was promoted to the third grade, saw himself as successful, was anxious to tackle new material, felt his depression lifted, experienced less conflictive situations with his peers, and was able to read and write full, large letters and stories. Findings suggest that, regardless of socialized norms, the ethics of teaching require providing all children with the means of accessing literature independently.

Hollingsworth, Sandra, and others, "Learning to Teach Literature in California: Challenging the Rules for Standardized Instruction. Research Series No. 200." (1991): 26 pp. [ED 332 202]
A longitudinal study, involving five beginning teachers, revolved around questions about how teachers' own emerging theories of literacy instruction are shaped by their interactions with other theories and perspectives and through their own work with students who are learning to read, write, and understand text in schools. Trained in the Whole Language or process approach to literature, the teachers in this study found it difficult to implement that approach with inner-city African-American, Latino, and Filipino students. The purpose of the study was both to inform teacher education policy and to provide teacher educators with ideas for better supporting beginning teachers. Triangulated data sources which documented the new teachers' learning consisted of audiotaped transcripts of monthly collaborative meetings and bimonthly videotaped classroom observations of literacy lessons as well as audiotaped open-ended interviews with the teachers. These teachers' experiences suggest at least three areas for reform in literacy education: reconsidering programmatic attention to beginning reading; integrating knowledge of literacy and school cultures; and redefining the boundaries of teacher education. All of the teachers found that sticking to the popular and policy-imposed "rules" for using original literature in any form was inappropriate for many children. The stories told by these teachers suggest that it may be beneficial to support beginning teachers internally as they are learning to teach literature. Without this support, the difficulty in learning to teach a literature-based, Whole-Language program designed to give all children access to literacy may lie with the institutional rules in schools and not with the new teachers.

Homan, Susan P., and others, "A Holistic Reading and Language Arts Approach for the Intermediate Grades," *Reading Horizons 30/2* (Jan 1990): 15-24. [EJ 402 258]
Describes an integrated reading/language-arts program designed to meet the needs of Chapter 1 sixth-grade students. States that one of the basic tenets of the program is that children learn best by actively participating in language activities, not just reading about language skills.

Hood, Wendy, "Whole Language: A Grass-Roots Movement Catches On," *Learning 17/8* (Apr 1989): 60-62. [EJ 407 871]
Describes a Whole Language support group that evolved from the efforts of two teachers to implement the Whole Language approach to reading. A list of Whole Language support groups for teachers and of networking newsletters is included.

Horn, Evelyn D., "Whole-Language Principles Applied to a Remedial Reading Course, X100 at Indiana University at South Bend," Indiana, 1992. [ED 354 480]
Presents a syllabus and proposed course outline for X100, a skills-based college

remedial reading class (at Indiana University at South Bend) keyed to the Whole Language literature. Reviews two sourcebooks for information regarding the use of Whole Language at the secondary level and lists viable Whole Language strategies to be used specifically in X100. Summarizes comments and observations of local Whole Language practitioners as well as some comments from a former X100 student. discusses the logistics of carrying out a Whole Language program in X100. Discusses possible evaluation tools to use in a Whole Language classroom.

Hornstein, Stephen, and others, "Whole Language Goes to College." (1992) 11 pp. [ED 341 960]
Based on the belief that teacher educators can no longer be satisfied to teach about Whole Language without teaching through Whole Language, this article presents five major premises of Whole Language and then describes several strategies by which this philosophy has been implemented in university classrooms. The premises are that learning happens best: (1) when it occurs in "wholes" rather than in disjointed, decontextualized parts; (2) when learners perceive and participate in authentic uses of what is being learned; (3) when the social nature of learning is valued and taken advantage of; (4) when learners have control over what, when, and how they learn; and (5) when learners have the opportunity to reflect on their learning. The article next describes five activities which stem from the premises just listed: (1) walking journals (written dialogues among a group of people); (2) literature circles and text sets (a group of people coming together to read and discuss a related set of books); (3) author's circles (small groups who give feedback on each other's writing); (4) expert projects (self-chosen student projects); and (5) community engagement (projects designed to help students use the community as a resource for creating knowledge and meaning).

Horton, Linda Green, "A Whole Language Unit for Ninth Graders," *English Journal 75/8* Dec 1986): 56-57. [EJ 345 197]
Outlines a student-conducted literature course that uses several classic novels ("My Antonia," "The Pearl," etc.) as the basis for group discussion, writing, and oral performance activities—all directed toward extracting "meaning" from the books selected.

Houghton, Brenda L., "Developing a Spelling Program for Low-Functioning Second Grade Students." (1990): 64 pp. [ED 324 117]
A 10-week practicum intervention was designed to improve second graders' spelling skills. A target group of five students who had exhibited difficulty in staying on-task and were performing a half-year below grade level was selected. Practicum goals were that 60 percent of target children would: (1) score at least 80 percent on spelling tests in the 9th and 10th weeks; (2) recognize, at least 80 percent of the time, a misspelled word that had been taken from a spelling list and used in 10 sentences; and (3) demonstrate more positive attitudes toward spelling. The intervention consisted of the implementation of a spelling program that focused on the interweaving of traditional methods of teaching spelling, modality-based instruction, the use of computers, and a Whole Language approach. Students used spelling words in journals, creative stories, sentences, and poems. Computer activities designed to aid visual memory of spelling words and heighten student motivation were made available. Comparison of pre- and posttest evaluation data indicated that students' achievement in spelling and attitudes toward spelling improved. All practicum goals were attained and exceeded. It is concluded that the success of the program shows that spelling must have a meaningful and motivational purpose in students' daily work.

Hudelson, Sarah, "Write On: Children Writing in ESL." CS: ERIC Clearinghouse on Languages and Linguistics, Washington, D.C. (1989): 120 pp. [ED 309 653] Focuses on the writing development of young English-as-a-Second-Language (ESL) learners in order to provide teachers with an overview of research and theory about ESL children's writing from the perspective that research and theory may and should form practice. Recent research on children's first and second language writing is reviewed, including the influence of native language reading and writing ability on ESL writing development. The application of these research findings to instructional strategies and the need for classroom assessment and documentation of children's progress as writer's are considered. The following topics are highlighted: (1) the Whole Language approach; (2) the use of peer review in the classroom; (3) the elements that ESL students bring to writing; and (4) the connection between reading and writing.

Huebsch, Winnie R., "Utilizing Tradebooks in the Elementary School: Considerations and Implications for Change." paper presented at the Annual Meeting of the International Reading Association (36th, Las Vegas, NV, May 6-10, 1991). [ED 334 559] Since 1987, the school district of West Allis-West Milwaukee (Wisconsin) has reviewed and revised its elementary reading program based on the philosophy that spoken, read, and written language must flow naturally from the child, be used in meaningful ways to communicate real needs, and involve tradebooks. Numerous inservice presentations and meetings generated a rich flow of dialogue that has eased much of the discomfort which attends any major educational change. The basal reader has become but one component of a varied literature program. Increasingly, reading instruction has moved towards "whole-class" instruction. Trade books were chosen by a committee (with input from many staff members) and gradually introduced into the curriculum. Distribution and financial constraints remain the greatest challenges to the success of the tradebook program. Mandated district testing needs to become more consistent with the principles of Whole Language, literature-based instruction if it is to reflect appropriately the reading/language arts growth of the students in the district.

Huggins, Laura J., and Marie C. Roos, "The Shared Book Experience: An Alternative to the Basal Reading Approach," 19 pp. (1990). [ED 319 018] Reflects research evidence to suggest that (1) literature has a positive effect both on reading achievement and attitude toward reading; and (2) the use of a literature-based program is an effective alternative to the traditional basal reading approach. The majority of studies concluded that the literature-based approach produced higher reading achievement and fostered more positive attitudes toward reading than the basal-reading method. Students of all ability levels, given the opportunity to experience reading as a visual and thought process, take a more active role in their own learning. Students not only learn to read, they also develop a love for reading and become life-long readers through the process of using a literature-based approach. Research evidence also supports the use of a shared book experience. Most teachers are required to use a basal reading series. One literature-based, Whole Language-oriented basal series is "Impressions." "The Story Box in the Classroom" is a kit which provides numerous strategies for shared reading. In literature-based programs, the secret of success is fostering the right learning environment, one in which a natural intimacy between teacher and students develops and one in which reading is pleasurable and meaningful.

Hughes, Sandra M., "The Impact of Whole Language on Four Elementary School Libraries," *Language Arts 70/5* (Sep 1993): 393-99. Reports on an exploratory comparative study of the impact of Whole Language on four elementary school libraries. Finds that librarians were excited about the impact of Whole Language, and that they wanted to talk to someone about it. Concludes that Whole Language empowers librarians.

Hurst, Betina S., "Design and Implementation of a Staff Development Program in the Elementary School." (1991): 71 pp. [ED 337 872]
Outcomes of a staff development program based on the Whole Language philosophy that was implemented in a rural Florida elementary school are presented in this practicum report. Two surveys of 29 and 35 faculty, respectively, indicated needs for faculty cohesiveness, a unified purpose, and an update of language- arts teaching skills. A staff development program based on the Whole Language philosophy and a combination of the development/improvement and training models was then imple- mented. Voluntary participation in weekly meetings provided teachers with informa- tion on Whole Language strategies and access to research material. Pre- and post-tests comprised of a survey and the Theoretical Orientation Reading Profile (TORP) measured gains in teacher agreement with Whole Language philosophy and reliance on peer discussion/sharing. Outcomes included a change in language- arts philosophy, improved group unity, and increased willingness to utilize the method in the future.

Hyde, Diana DeShazo, "Supporting First Graders' Growth as Writers through Whole-Language Strategies." (1990): 51 pp. [ED 322 507]
Reports a practicum that sought to increase the opportunities for 17 first-grade students to write for real, human reasons and in natural circumstances. They were to use writing as a natural and acceptable outlet for expression, and to conceive of their writing as an extension of themselves. Each day a name was drawn to take home a stuffed bear, which served as a motivation companion for writing; the next day, the bear was brought back and the student wrote a story of his/her adventures with the bear. The student then sat in the Author's Chair, put on the Author's Cap, and read his/her story. This promoted voluntary involvement in literacy activities in students' free time, and increased writing output. Students also, in a collaborative learning venture, put together a whole-class book every month. There was increased oral reading to the students in different registers of language. Checklists were kept in each student's personal writing folder. The actual writing period was expanded to allow for all components of writing to take place. At the end of implementation, 14 of the 17 students were writing at least one page a day (many were writing more than that); the quality of students' writing had risen noticeably; students were collaboratively putting together one book a week; and the use of "book language" was common.

Hyde, Diana DeShazo, "Evaluating Student Learning in Language Arts in the Primary Grades through Whole Language Assessment Techniques." (1992): 108 pp. [ED 345 206]
Reports a practicum that sought to measure and document real learning in natural circumstances through the use of Whole Language assessment techniques involving observation checklists on which skills for the language arts (writing, spelling, reading) were listed. Skills were measured using descriptor words such as "stable," "evident," and "not evident" in order to plot a student's progress in literacy development in a positive way. A reading behavior form was also included. This classified students into one of three learning groups, according to the answers given to a list of seven ques- tions; emphasis was on behavior and learning style. These alternative assessment forms were collected in a simplified seven-page booklet format for each student. Not only could students' skills be assessed quickly through check marks in the appropriate columns but also their style of learning was included in the booklet. Results indicated that teachers who used the Observation Checklist preferred this type of assessment to

the report card format, and found instructional decisions easier to make when using these forms.

Hyslop, Nancy, and Carl Smith, comps., "Writing Strategies for Gifted Children. Learning Package No. 45." (1990): 44 pp. [ED 333 411] and "Ways To Evaluate Writing. Learning Package No. 47." (1990): 52 pp. [ED 333 413]
Originally developed as part of a project for the Department of Defense Schools (DoDDS) system, these learning packages were designed for teachers who wish to upgrade or expand their teaching skills on their own. The package includes an overview of the project; a comprehensive search of the ERIC database; a lecture giving an overview on the topic; copies of any existing ERIC/RCS publications on the topic; a set of guidelines for completing a goal statement, a reaction paper, and an application project; and an evaluation form.

Ingle, Laura A., "Improving Students' Language and Parental Classroom Involvement through the Use of a Computer and Multi-Media Applications." (1992): 71 pp. [ED 350 605]
A parental involvement program was developed and implemented in a prekindergarten class setting. The program focused on using a "talking" computer to bring the adults into the classroom to work with the students. The program featured child-generated, parent-transcribed, computer-reproduced Whole Language stories for use at home and school. Parents were taught how to use the computer and the software and were encouraged to work with their children and other students during the school day. Results indicated that the program was significantly successful, with dramatic increases recorded in the number of classroom volunteers. It fostered a new sense of community among the parents, leading to a greater degree of cooperation and mutual support. Parent and student attitudes proved positive and parent/child interactions in the classroom increased.

Instructional Media: Comunication Skills. Advisory List." (1992): 25 pp. [ED 340 064]
This annotated bibliography of instructional media in communication skills presents annotations of 112 books and videotapes for students in grades from pre-kindergarten through grade 12, and of 38 books and videos for teachers. The material in the bibliography for students consists mostly of poetry collections published in 1990 and 1991. The materials for teachers in the bibliography deal with writing instruction, literature instruction, the Whole Language approach, and classroom management.

Israel, Mindy, "The Application of the Whole Language Approach to Reading Instruction to Children in Kindergarten." (1992): 120 pp. [ED 340 013]
The Whole Language approach to reading instruction has been gaining the support of many educators and teachers, and the aim of this thesis is to show how this movement has gained its momentum. The first chapter of the thesis deals with the history of the Whole Language movement and provides an overview of the research literature that supports the concepts inherent in Whole Language approaches. In the review of the literature, the thesis examines in depth Piaget's cognitive developmental theories and Goodman and Smith's psycholinguistic view of reading. The second chapter of the thesis discusses the application of the research in practice as it applies to children in kindergarten. The thesis explains in detail additional methods specifically applying to Whole Language, such as Don Holdaway's shared-book experience. The third chapter examines the needs in the field and where the field is heading in the future. The thesis discusses the need for additional research, along with the needs for teacher education and new testing methods, concluding with a discussion of how kindergarten teachers feel about the Whole Language approach in their classrooms.

Jacobson, John, and others, "Reading Instruction: Perceptions of Elementary School Principals," *Journal of Educational Research 85*/6 (Jul-Aug 1992): 370-80. [EJ 453 780]
Survey examined 1,244 elementary principals' understanding of current issues in elementary reading instruction and information sources they used to learn about issues. Principals reported awareness of current reading issues, including Whole Language. They did not have enough confidence in their understanding of issues to give a reasoned rationale for taking one particular side.

Jamar, Donna, and Jean Morrow, "A Literature-Based Interdisciplinary Approach to the Teaching of Reading, Writing, and Mathematics," paper presented at the Annual Plains Regional Conference of the International Reading Association (18th, Wichita, KS, Oct 17-20, 1990). [ED 324 652]
Using literature as a natural catalyst in an interdisciplinary approach, teachers can effectively bring the basics of reading, writing, and mathematics together to provide a learning atmosphere that promotes risk-taking as a natural and necessary part of learning. Integrating these areas throughout the curriculum enables students to develop a sense of purpose in content area classes. Such a sense of purpose will also help students recognize the connections between what is learned in school and what is used in real life. For students to realize a practical application of reading, writing, and mathematics, materials must be interesting and relevant.

Jardine, David W., and James C. Field, "Critical-Interpretive Explorations of Innovative Language Arts Practices at the Elementary School Level," *Canadian Journal of Education 16*/2 (spr 1991): 206-09. [EJ 438 629]
Describes a proposed research project in which two university-based researchers and four elementary school teachers will investigate problematic features of Whole Language instruction in monthly reflexive conversations. One hypothesis is that problems with Whole Language practice are indicative of a more broadly based cultural malaise.

Jervis, Charles K., "A Model for Integrating Non-Traditional Skills and Instruction from Literature and Art into Science Classroom Activities." (1992): 23 pp. [ED 352 242]
Presents a model that incorporates traditional art skills into the high school science classroom. Science, art, and English teachers are provided with a scheme by which science works can be incorporated into art or English classes and literary and art analysis skills can be applied in the science class. Using this model, students read, analyze, critique, and investigate the presentation of scientific information in literary works, and they use artistic skills to present their observations or interpretations of scientific phenomena. Based on these works, scientific information is organized into a variety of formats, both the traditional science report and non-traditional creative arts products such as essays, videos, poems, photographs, and drawings. A lesson plan based on the Robert Frost poem "Design" is provided which demonstrates essential aspects of the analysis and assignment scheme, along with examples of student products.

Jett Simpson, Mary, "Organizing the Whole Language Reading Class: Readers' Workshop and Focused Study Reading Workshop," *Journal of the Wisconsin State Reading Association 35*/1 (win 1991): 49-55. [EJ 429 710]
Describes the Reader's Workshop and the Focused Study Reading Workshop. Offers them as a way to accommodate the characteristics of individuals, to respect the knowledge of readers who are at earlier stages of reading development, to establish a system which teaches problem solving, and to provide for active child involvement and ownership in the reading process.

Jochum, Julie, "Whole Language—Writing: The Critical Response." (1989): 4 pp. [ED 307 631]
Writers of all ages and abilities come to the act of writing with three critical needs: (1) they need a commitment of time; (2) they need ownership over their topics; and, most important, (3) they need a response to their personal revelations. Sharing and responding to student writing can take place in writers' circles and writers' conferences. In a writers circle, students gather in small groups and share their writing processes or products and receive responses from their peers. The most effective writers conferences are brief and focus on what the writers are communicating rather than on the perceptions of the respondent. The writer is the informant as open-ended questions are used to expand or to focus the conference.

Johns, Jerry L., "Helping Readers at Risk: Beyond Whole Language, Whole Word, and Phonics," *Journal of Reading, Writing, and Learning Disabilities International* 7/1 (Jan-Mar 1991): 59-67 [EJ 428 566]
Five generalizations for reading instruction with disabled and normal readers are presented: (1) caring, positive relationship between teacher and student; (2) the role of rereading and daily reading; (3) appropriate materials; (4) interest as a springboard to learning; and (5) the unification of instruction.

Johns, Jerry, "Reflections on Whole Language, Whole Word, and Phonics." (1989): 6 pp. [ED 312 613]
The reading profession's current emphasis on Whole Language may have helped to raise the recurring debate between meaning-based (Whole Language) and phonics-based (code emphasis) approaches to teaching reading. As some researchers have linked Whole Language with whole word, phonics advocates have come forth with renewed vigor to offer a series of claims and counterclaims. What has failed to occur in this debate is any movement away from the simplistic claims for improving reading instruction. Some teachers have already discovered ways to combine the strengths of several approaches to reading. Teachers who remain committed to their primary mission of developing literacy among their students will not get caught up in the power struggle between phonics and Whole Language. They will continue to apply what works—no matter what those in the reading profession choose to call it.

Johns, Jerry, and others, *Adult Literacy: Instructional Strategies*. Focused Access to Selected Topics (FAST) Bibliography No. 70., ERIC/REC, Indiana, 1993. [CS 011 332]
Noting that adult literacy will continue to be a focus as the changing needs of society are addressed, presents annotations of 40 journal articles and ERIC documents dealing with instructional strategies in adult literacy. Annotations in the FAST bibliography date from the period 1989-1992 and are divided into three areas: overview; Whole Language approaches; and computers and technology.

Johns, Jerry, and others, "Whole Language in the Elementary School. Focused Access to Selected Topics (FAST) Bib No. 67." (1993): 5 pp. [ED 356 459]
After defining Whole Language as a philosophy of literacy instruction based on the concept that students need to experience language as an integrated whole, this ERIC "FAST Bib" presents an annotated list of 35 ERIC documents and journal articles consisting of critiques of and responses to the Whole Language approach in the elementary school. The materials, which were published between 1988 and 1992, are divided into six sections: (1) Overview; (2) Critiques; (3) Recent Research; (4) Elementary Applications; (5) Applications to Special Populations; and (6) Teachers' Roles.

Johns, Kenneth M., and Connie Espinoza, "Mainstreaming Language Minority Children in Reading and Writing. Fastback 340." (1992): 45 pp. [ED 356 626]
Designed for regular classroom teachers in whose mainstream classes language-minority children are enrolled, this guide offers background information and sugges-tions for helping these students become proficient in English reading and writing and for involving them as resources for global and cultural awareness in majority-language classmates. The first chapter discusses specific barriers to language acquisition among language-minority students: (1) reductionist concepts of language and learning implicit in the mainstream curriculum; (2) cultural differences; and (3) inadequate communica-tion among adults in the children's lives. The second chapter examines the reading and writing needs of this population, including instructional materials, classroom environ-ment, topics, and nonverbal communication. The third chapter describes useful classroom techniques, all within the Whole-Language approach to teaching, including: using literary works; providing substantial oral language experiences; providing time for silent, sustained reading; encouraging use of student journals; incorporating technology; and promoting cooperative learning. Concludes that meeting the needs of language-minority students in a mainstream classroom is possible if teachers recognize the barriers to educational opportunity facing the children, understand that they are better prepared than they realize to work with this population, use cooperative learning strategies, and see the children as cultural resources.

Johnson, Betty, and Eric Stone, "Is Whole Language Restructuring Our Classroom?" *Contemporary Education 62/2* (win 1991): 102-04. [EJ 447 940]
Discusses Whole Language learning in Indiana classrooms, its philosophical origin and appropriate educational environment. Offers a set of beliefs about Whole Language teaching and presents guidelines to help schools restructure their thinking about the curriculum and learning climate.

Jordan, Cynthia, and Lana J. Smith, "Planning for Whole Language across the Curriculum (In the Classroom)," *Reading Teacher 45/6* (Feb 1992): 476-77. [EJ 437 440]
Provides a sample Whole Language matrix that systematically organizes the multitude of activities and strategies of an integrated curriculum. Discusses how this matrix may be helpful for teacher planning and documentation for administrators and parents.

Kachur, Amy, "Making a Change toward Whole Language," *Ohio Reading Teacher 24/2* (win 1990): 20-25. [EJ 432 435]
Explores the challenge of making the transition from a traditional basal-oriented language-arts program to a literature-based program. States that initiating a literature-based reading program requires an appreciation and grasp of the Whole Language philosophy.

Kahn, Jessica, and Pamela Freyd, "A Whole Language Perspective on Keyboarding (Online)," *Language Arts 67/1* (Jan 1990): 84-90. [EJ 406 683]
Discusses the use of keyboarding skills in elementary classrooms and stresses the importance of establishing writing environments that help children to understand writing as communication.

Kamii, Constance, ed., and others, *Early Literacy: A Constructivist Foundation for Whole Language. NEA Early Childhood Education Series.* (Washington, D.C.: National Education Association,1991): 158 pp. [ED 335 703]
Considers early literacy education and Whole Language from the perspective of constructivist theory (which states that human beings acquire knowledge by building it from the inside in interaction with the environment) and research. More specifically, the book intends to show that the Whole Language movement is part of a larger

revolution in thinking about learning and teaching, and to enable Whole Language advocates to explain, evaluate, and improve upon their beliefs and practices on the basis of a scientific, explanatory theory about how children acquire knowledge. The first four chapters of the book describe constructivism and the research supporting it, while the rest of the book deals with classroom practices and related issues such as assessment. Contents: (1) "What is Constructivism?" (Constance Kamii); (2) "Literacy Acquisition and the Representation of Language" (Emilia Ferreiro); (3) "Principles of Spelling Found in the First Two Grades (Francois Siegrist and Hermina Sinclair); (4) "Spelling in Kindergarten: A Constructivist Analysis Comparing Spanish-Speaking and English-Speaking Children" (Constance Kamii and others); (5) "Learning to Read in New Zealand" (Brian Cutting and Jerry L. Milligan); (6) "Shared Book Experience: Teaching Reading Using Favorite Books" (Don Holdaway); (7) "Modeled Writing: Reflections on the Constructive Process" (Maryann Manning and Gary Manning); (8) "Reading to Know" (Barbara A. Lewis and Roberta Long); and (9) "An Approach to Assessment in Early Literacy" (Brenda S. Engel).

Kaminski, Robert. "Legends for Sale, Poems for Free: Whole Language Activities Can Be Inspired by Risk-Taking and Scene Changes," *Emergency Librarian 19*/2 (Nov-Dec 1991): 21-24. [EJ 436 318]
Describes two classroom activities that were developed to promote a Whole Language approach to listening, speaking, reading, and writing. One involved fifth grade students who wrote legends that other students paid to read and evaluate, and the other involved an eighth grade English class who gave free poetry readings in a coffee house setting.

Kaminski, Lindalee, "Improving Social Studies Achievement: An Interdisciplinary Approach." (1989): 88 pp. [ED 327 457]
A high percentage of students in a second-grade class with low socioeconomic characteristics demonstrated exceptionally low achievement in social studies. The problem was addressed by the implementation of an interdisciplinary program to increase basic skills in all areas of the curriculum. Activities designed to increase the target group's understanding of social studies concepts while practicing skills in reading, language arts, mathematics, and science were incorporated into all subject areas using a Whole Language approach. An emphasis on critical thinking and daily news events allowed for student growth in inferential comprehension and the formation of attitudes about the world. The results indicated a significant increase in social studies achievement for all target group members (N=16). Students also demonstrated positive affective changes as their concern and interest in the news increased.

Karch, Barbara, "A Whole Language Approach for Kindergarten," *Gifted Child Today (GCT) 13*/6 (Nov-Dec 1990): 56-59. [EJ 421 427]
A kindergarten teacher recounts her classroom experience introducing children to reading via the Whole Language approach, which is based on the belief that children learn to read and write naturally by listening, watching, speaking, and writing. Classroom photographs and samples of student work illustrate the article.

Karges Bone, Linda, "Classic Book Units for G/C/T Youngsters," *Gifted Child Today (GCT) 14*/1 (Jan-Feb 1991): 8-9. [EJ 424 475]
Use of classic book units with gifted elementary students is described as an interdisciplinary approach to stimulating student interest. Sample activities are offered from a unit on Mark Twain's "Huckleberry Finn," with linguistic, artistic-creative, scientific, mathematical, and socio-leadership activities, classified as application, synthesis, analysis, knowledge application, and evaluation according to Bloom's Taxonomy.

Karnowski, Lee, and DeAn Krey, "Preparing Pre-Service Teachers for Whole Language Classrooms," *Journal of the Wisconsin State Reading Association 35/*1 (win 1991): 73-76. [EJ 429 712]
Describes the reorganization of teacher education methods courses at University of Wisconsin-River Falls. Lists Whole Language tenets, large group session topics, and sample integrations for prekindergarten through middle school grades. Asserts that the experience demonstrated the benefits of the Whole Language philosophy.

Karolides, Nicholas J., ed., *Language Learning*. (1985): 36 pp. [ED 278 999]
Explores classroom methods for enhancing language acquisition. Contents: (1) Forests and Trees: Conservation and Reforestation" (Joyce S. Steward); (2) "Using Literature to Teach Language" (Richard D. Cureton); (3) "Language Learning through Sentence Combining" (Nicholas J. Karolides); and (4) "ERIC/RCS Report: Evaluating Language Development" (Fran Lehr).

Kasten, Wendy C., and Barbara K. Clarke, "Reading/Writing Readiness for Preschool and Kindergarten Children: A Whole Language Approach. FERC Research Project Report." (1989): 87 pp. [ED 312 041]
Details a year-long study of the emerging literacy of preschoolers and kindergarteners in two southwest Florida communities. Using a quasi-experimental design, investigation focused on two preschools and two kindergarten classes that implemented certain strategies associated with a Whole Language philosophy, including daily shared reading experiences and weekly opportunities to write freely. The classes and matched comparison groups were pretested and posttested with qualitative and quantitative measures, including the Goodman Book Handling Task, a story retelling inventory, the Metropolitan Early School Inventory (ESI), and the Metropolitan Readiness Test. Findings indicated that the preschool experimental classes performed significantly better than comparison groups on the Goodman Book Handling task, the story retelling inventory, and on subtest C of the ESI. Kindergarten experimental classes performed better than their comparison groups on the Goodman Book Handling task, subtests B, C, E, and F of the Metropolitan ESI, and the Metropolitan Readiness Test. Experimental subjects not only knew more than their comparison peers on meaningful aspects of reading, but exhibited enthusiasm for books and stories, and were observed developing attitudes toward literacy that are not measurable.

Kasten, Wendy C., "Bridging the Horizon: American Indian Beliefs and Whole Language Learning," *Anthropology and Education Quarterly 23/*2 (Jun 1992): 108-19. [EJ 448 043]
Explores the relationship between the principles of Whole Language teaching and Whole Language learning, especially for elementary school students, and the culture of many Native American students, listing seven points of compatibility. The experience of the Miccosukee Indian School in Miami (Florida) illustrates the use of Whole Language.

Keefe, Charlotte Hendrick, and Donald R. Keefe, "Instruction for Students with LD: A Whole Language Model," *Intervention in School and Clinic 28/*3 (Jan 1993): 172-77. [EJ 458 487]
A Whole-Language instructional approach is presented for use with students with learning disabilities. Teacher behaviors are outlined, including demonstrating, expecting success, and responding to students. Learner behaviors are also discussed, such as using language in natural situations, making approximations in their learning, taking responsibility, and engaging with the learning process.

Keefe, Donald, and Valerie Meyer, "Teaching Adult New Readers the Whole Language Way," *Journal of Reading 35/*3 (Nov 1991): 180-83 [EJ 434 199]
Provides a brief summary of Whole Language theory and offers suggestions for its application in adult education settings. Maintains that when instructional techniques rooted in Whole Language theory are used with adult beginning readers, learning is more meaningful and success can be dramatic.

Kepler, Lynne, "Hands-On Whole Science. Shining Science: Shed Some Light on the Science of Summer," *Instructor 101/*9 (May-Jun 1992): 42-44. [EJ449375]
Presents summer science activities for elementary students that focus on sunlight and other natural and artificial light sources (e.g., fire, flashlights, and fireflies). Related activities which involve Whole Language use of language arts, art, and math are included. A reproducible page teaches children Morse Code using a flashlight.

Kersting, Frank, and Janice Ferguson, "Narration in Reading Remediation." (1988): 21 pp. [ED 299 536]
A case study examined the whole/part application of the language experience approach to reading as used for students whose reading development is severely delayed. The subject, a third-grade female student reading on the first-grade level as determined by the Woodcock Reading Mastery Tests-Revised (Woodcock, 1987), participated in a reading remediation program. The method used was the narrative technique and other remediation procedures such as word attack and sight word practice, and oral and silent reading in the SRA series. At the end of 6 months of instruction, the subject's reading level had improved to the grade level of 2.6. These results suggest that the language experience approach could prove to be a viable technique in reading instruction for prereaders, readers, and illiterate adults. The literature on narration provides a systematic format for developing stories that resemble reading texts. The stories can be used to teach story frame and improve semantic, syntactic, and comprehension skills. Applied seatwork can be assigned which strengthens the individual's skills in those areas. As an individual develops more competency in narration, reading ability in inferencing and structure should improve.

Kiefer, Barbara, comp., "Toward a Whole Language Classroom. Articles from *Language Arts*, 1986-89." (1990): 79 pp. [ED 326 881]
A collection of articles originally printed in *Language Arts*, the membership journal of the elementary section of the National Council of Teachers of English, this book responds to the thousands of teachers looking for ways to incorporate student-centered, collaborative learning strategies into their classrooms. The articles draw heavily upon the experiences of reflective teacher-researchers who have adapted approaches based on the Whole Language philosophy to meet the unique learning styles of their students. Contents: (1) "What Am I Supposed To Do While They're Writing?" (Mary K. Simpson); (2) "The Writer's Inside Story" (Carin Hauser); (3) "First Grade Thinkers Becoming Literate" (Carol S. Avery); (4) "'What Did Leo Feed the Turtle?' and Other Nonliterary Questions" (E. Wendy Saul); (5) "Children's Response to Literature" (Janet Hickman); (6) "Building Castles in the Classroom" (Karen L. Erickson); (7) "Connecting to Language through Story" (Marni Schwartz); (8) "Storytelling and Science" (Kathleen Martin and Etta Miller); and (9) "Children's Narrative Thought, at Home and at School" (Richard Van Dongen).

King, Dorothy F., and Kenneth S. Goodman, Whole Language: Cherishing Learners and Their Language," *Language, Speech, and Hearing Services in Schools 21/*4 (Oct 1990): 221-27. [EJ 420 018]
Applies Whole Language techniques to children with cultural and linguistic differences

and provides guidelines for enabling speech-language pathologists to assume a role of active involvement. Whole Language can provide a context for involvement in the areas of bilingual education and other language and dialect learning and for conducting assessments and interventions.

King, Caryn M., and Rita M. Bean, comps., "Literacy Instruction: Practices, Problems, Promises. Proceedings of the Annual Conference and Course on Literacy (37th, Pittsburgh, Pennsylvania, Jun 1990)." (1990): 100 pp. [ED 329 900]
Opening remarks by Rita M. Bean; four keynote addresses: "Toward Uncommon Sense Literacy Learning; Integrating Reading and Writing" (John Mayher); "Literacy Learning in At-Risk First Graders" (Diane DeFord); "Developing Motivated Readers: What Schools and Parents Can Do" (Dixie Lee Spiegel); and "Alternatives to the Regular Education Initiative" (James Kauffman). Next are five essays on the theme of Literature: Its Potential in the Classroom, written by local authors, librarians, and other professionals from the literacy community (Sally Alexander, Patricia Harrison Easton, Susan Kaufold, Elizabeth Segel, and Karen Waggoner). These essays are followed by papers from five workshops: "Assessing Readers and Writers in Primary Whole Language Classrooms" (Deborah Wells); "A Novel Way to Teach the Novel" (Joanne L. Ridge); "Developing Intertextual Comprehension: Students Reading Multiple Texts" (Douglas Hartman); "Using a Process Approach in Remedial Reading Instruction" (Rebecca Hamilton and others); "Risk Factors in Early Reading" (Danielle Zinna); "Literacy Development: An African American Perspective" (Shirley A. Biggs); "Fostering Emerging Oral and Written Language through Projects" (Jeanette Allison Hartman); "Cutting Edge Strategies for Tutors of Adult Learners" (Beverly Ohemeng); and "A Review of 'Perspectives: From Adult Literacy to Continuing Education'" (Alice Scales). Closing remarks by Thomas LaBelle conclude the document.

Kinzer, Charles K., and Donald J. Leu, eds., "Literacy Research, Theory, and Practice: Views from Many Perspectives. Forty-First Yearbook of the National Reading Conference." (1992): 543 pp. [ED 351 671]
Contents: "Family Uses of Literacy: A Critical Voice" (D. Madigan); "Intergenerational Literacy: Impact on the Development of the Storybook Reading Behaviors of Hispanic Mothers" (D. Eldridge-Hunter); "Portfolio Assessment: Teachers' Beliefs and Practices" (J. Flood and others); "Psychometric Properties of the Reader Retelling Profile: A Case Study" (K. E. Meredith and others); "The Validity and Utility of Portfolio Assessment" (P. Dewitz and others); "An Examination of 'The Simple View of Reading'" (L. G. Dreyer and L. Katz); "An Exploration of Meaning Construction in First Graders' Grand Conversations" (L. M. McGee); "Intertextuality: Searching for Patterns That Connect" (K. G. Short); "One Writer's Construction of Text and Self: The Role of Voice" (G. Kamberelis and W. McGinley); "Children's Metacognitive Knowledge about Reading and Writing in Literature-Based and Conventional Classrooms" (L. B. Gambrell and B. M. Palmer); "Implementing Whole-Language Instruction for Young Children: Cases of Teacher Development and Change" (B. J. Bruneau); "Reading without Ability Grouping: Issues in First-Grade Reading Instruction" (D. P. Hall and P. M. Cunningham); "A Case Study of Academic Literacy Tasks and Their Negotiation in a University History Course" (M. L. Simpson and S. L. Nist); "Predicting the Location of Answers to Textbook Search Tasks" (M. J. Dreher); "Dynamics of Change: Speculation on a Forthcoming Model of Response to Literature" (K. Armstrong); "Non-Traditional Learners' Written and Dialogic Response to Literature" (V. J. Goatley and T. E. Raphael); "Circles within Circles: The Uses of Storytelling within a Seminar for Preservice Reading Teachers" (S. J. Moore

and R. V. Lalik); "Collaborative Research on Teacher Study Groups: Embracing the Complexities" (C. Klassen and K. G. Short); "Incident at Paradigm Springs: Fieldnotes on Writing from a Critical Stance" (J. Konopak); "Literature, Literacy, and Resistance to Cultural Domination" (L. Spears-Bunton); "Persons and Society in Reading: Connections to Liberalism and Beyond" (B. Kachuck); "A Content Analysis of Basal Readers: Teaching Suggestions for ESL/LEP Students Learning to Read English" (J. S. Schumm, and others); "Flexible Scaffolds: Shared Reading and Rereading of Story Books in Head Start Classrooms" (C. A. Elster and C. A. Walker); "Examining Content Area Reading Beliefs, Decisions, and Instruction: A Case Study of an English Teacher" (E. K. Wilson and others); "Effects of Word-Related Variables on Vocabulary Growth through Repeated Read-Aloud Events" (C. B. Leung); and "Matthew Effects in Learning New Words while Listening to Stories" (T. Nicholson and B. Whyte).

Kirby, Maxine R., "Improving Literacy Experiences of At-Risk Kindergarten Children through a Teacher Education Workshop." (1989): 90 pp. [ED 318 173]
The goals of this practicum were to help teachers of at-risk kindergarten children become more knowledgeable of developmentally appropriate practices for 5-year-olds, and to research, define, and translate appropriate literacy development theory into practical application strategies for teachers. A needs assessment survey was developed and administered to six kindergarten teachers. Subsequently, a staff development program was conducted, teachers were monitored and assisted, and follow-up meetings were held. In the staff development workshop, three strategies were proposed to increase literacy development: the Whole Language approach, shared reading, and a modified language experience approach. Based on workshop information presented, teachers were to select and implement at least one appropriate literacy development strategy. The teachers chose to use an adapted Whole Language approach. Analysis of practicum evaluation data indicated that both teachers and students benefited from the program.

Klesius, Janell P., and others, "A Whole Language and Traditional Instruction Comparison: Overall Effectiveness and Development of the Alphabetic Principle," *Reading Research and Instruction 30*/2 (win 1991): 47-61. [EJ 424 276]
Examines the differences in the effectiveness of Whole Language and traditional instruction in end-of-the-year reading, writing, and spelling achievement for children with varying levels of incoming phonemic awareness, reading, and writing ability. Finds that neither program was more likely to close gaps between children high or low in these incoming abilities.

Koebler, Saundra, comp., and others, "Literacy through Literature. Proceedings of the Annual Conference and Course on Literacy (38th, Pittsburgh, Pennsylvania, Jun 1991). (1991): 102 pp. [ED 347 503]
Focuses on the use of literature programs in the development of literacy skills and the attainment of broader educational outcomes. Contents: "Acting Meaning: The Play of Reading" (Shirley Brice Heath and Shelby Anne Wolf); "Remembering Pennsylvania" (Lois Lowry); "Families and Literacy: Building Social and Cultural Continuity" (Vivian L. Gadsden); "The Secret of the Lifetime Reader or the Clue in the Classroom" (Elizabeth Segel); and "The Secret of the Life-Long Reader or the Clue in the Classroom" (Margaret Mary Kimmel). Session presentations are: "Helping Parents and Teachers Develop Positive Dispositions toward Reading in Preschool Children" (Donna DiPrima Bickel); "Rights without Labels: A Mainstreaming Project" (Nicolette Armstrong and others); "Literacy through Experimental Verse: Selected Works of e. e. Cummings" (Albert C. Labriola); "Enriching Early Literacy with Long-Term Projects"

(Jeanette Allison Hartman); "The Heartwood Project: An Ethics Curriculum for Children" (Eleanor Gettleman and others); "Liberty, Learning, and Literacy: Promoting Higher Order Thinking in the Social Studies Classroom" (Caryn M. King and William E. McDonald); "Teaching after the Summer Institute: Where I've Been and Where I'm Going" (Mimi Botkin); "Reaching Back, Moving Forward: An Intergenerational Approach to Literacy and Literature" (George R. Skornickel, Jr.); "Promoting Literacy through Bibliotherapy" (Lelia Allen); "The Ethnic Mosaic: Multicultural Books for All Our Children" (Joan Brest Friedberg); and "Writing Workshops for Children" (Karen Waggoner). The three graduate student papers are: "Whole Language Makes Learning Fun, Even in High School" (Shandel Gilbert); "Ownership" (Marion E. Gosson); and "World War II: Through the Eyes of Literature" (Elizabeth Tihey Harbist and Edith P. Jones). The five middle school papers, briefly introduced by Patricia Thomas, are: "Being Black In America" (Sahara Bey); "Untitled" (Edward Caldwell); "When I Grow Up" (Brandy Fleming); "My Scariest Experience" (Maurice Harvey); and "Untitled" (Erica Hatcher).

Koepke, Mary, "The Power to Be a Professional," *Teacher Magazine 2/9* (Aug 1991): 35-41. [EJ 433 795]
Describes experiences of a fifth-grade teacher who converted her classroom to a Whole Language teaching and learning environment. In her child-centered classroom, she emphasized student empowerment and decision making, cooperative learning, and flexibility. Her top priority was for students to participate and learn critical thinking and problem-solving skills.

Koplowitz, Bradford, "Lois Lenski and the Battle between Fact and Fiction," *Journal of Youth Services in Libraries 5/1* (fall 1991): 95-103. [EJ 436 246]
Discusses Lois Lenski's children's books, focusing on the realism that predominates in her work through the use of real-life observation as opposed to imagination alone. Ways to use her work as part of a Whole Language approach to teach reading as well as science, geography, and social studies are suggested.

Korkeamaki, Riitta Liisa, and Mariam Jean Dreher, "Finland, Phonics, and Whole Language: Beginning Reading in a Regular Letter-Sound Correspondence Language," *Language Arts 70/6* (Oct 1993): 475-82. [CS 746 128]
Reviews the typical approach (synthetic phonics) to teaching reading in Finland. Suggests that teachers in English speaking countries can learn from problems Finnish teachers face, and vice versa. Finds that, despite a highly regular writing system, Finnish teachers report that a heavy phonics emphasis does not solve their reading instruction problems.

Korngold, Blanche, and Judith Zorfass, "FULFILL: Framework for Uniting Learners by Facilitating Instruction in Language and Literacy. Final Report." (1991): 171 pp. [ED 340 025]
A project was designed to help mainstream teachers in Grades 1-3 facilitate language learning in all students, but especially in those who have language disorders. A naturalistic study followed teachers participating in the project to examine what factors promote change in teachers' knowledge, beliefs, and practice. The overall approach to language arts learning and teaching fostered by the project was a constructivist one resembling the Whole Language approach. Three elementary schools in Eastern Massachusetts, and a set of 10 teachers underwent intensive training and were studied over a 3-year period. Results documented the changes teachers made with respect to the organization and climate of the classroom (finding some of the most consistent changes here), and to reading and writing instruction. Results further depicted, in mini-case studies, the way each teacher changed over the 3-year period. In addition, results

identified three sets of factors (teacher, intervention, and contextual) that had an impact on the change process. Results indicated that complex change in knowledge, beliefs, and practice was not a result of particular factors, but rather resulted from a dynamic interaction among factors—the teacher's abilities and desires interacted with elements of the intervention, and contextual influences interacted with the scope of the intervention. Results further indicated that the presence or absence of the critical factors (dissonance, individualization, chemistry, and coalescing) contributed to extensive, moderate, and minimal change in teachers. Findings suggest that training teachers to use a Whole Language approach would be most effective.

Kretschmer, Robert E., "Psychological Processes: Processes in Reading and Writing. What We Know and Need To Know about Learner Competencies of Hearing Impaired Adolescents and Young Adults." (1989): 31 pp. [ED 353 730]
Examines the reading and writing processes of persons with hearing impairments, particularly those leaving school and in transition from school to work. The reading/writing act is viewed from three perspectives: (1) cognitive science or information processing; (2) text organization and its functions; and (3) the processes whereby individuals are socialized to print. The reading/writing process is seen to be highly interactive and heavily dependent upon and reflective of the reader's knowledge level and processing capacities. Text structure and organization including grammar, sentential structures, and textual or discourse structures are briefly considered in relation to learning requirements and subject differences. Finally, reading and writing are thought of as existing within the context of social interactions and the culture at large. Affective aspects of literacy are also briefly reviewed. The research on the literacy skills of hearing-impaired individuals is summarized. Educational implications include the value of a Whole Language process approach to literacy and of advance organizers such as semantic mapping.

Kucer, Stephen B., "Understanding Literacy Lessons: Do Teachers and Students Talk the Same Language?" paper presented at the Annual Meeting of the National Council of Teachers of English (79th, Baltimore, MD, Nov 17-22, 1989). [ED 321 228]
Examines the relationship between teacher and student understandings. Subjects consisted of 26 third-grade students, of whom six were chosen for case studies, in a school in a large metropolitan area. All students were Latino, bilingual, and from working class homes. Modified cloze lessons were taught, and three types of data were collected with regard to the lessons: video tapes and field notes of the lessons observed, literacy artifacts, and teacher and student interviews. The focus of the data analysis was to discern how the various participants in the lesson (students, teachers, and ethnographer) understood the activity and the degree to which these understandings were shared across participants. Field notes indicated that the only issue which emerged was that at times the children had difficulty in using the information presented after the blank to judge the meaningfulness of their responses. Literacy artifacts indicated that 93% of all student responses were meaningful. Student and teacher interviews indicated there was a large degree of misunderstanding between the teacher and the case-study students. It was the nature of school as an institution in general, and the lack of authenticity in the lesson in particular, which accounted for the discrepancy between teacher and student understandings.

Kucer, Stephen B., "Authenticity as the Basis for Instruction," *Language Arts 68/7* (Nov 1991): 532-40. [EJ 434 261]
Reports on research that investigated students' perceptions of the purpose of certain Whole Language strategy lessons. Concludes that, even in Whole Language lessons, authenticity may be missing. Helps educators think more deeply about what literacy

lessons should be like for students and how instruction can help develop students' strategies while maintaining the integrity of the whole.

Ladestro, Debra, "Making a Change for Good," *Teacher Magazine 2/9* (Aug 1991): 42-45. [EJ 433 796]
Describes middle and high schools in Upper Arlington (Ohio) that use the Whole Language approach to teaching and learning. The schools emphasize student-centered education, cooperative learning, and student involvement in decision making. The curriculum is fully integrated, with writing used as a learning tool in all subject areas.

Lake, Veronica A., "Valentine Book Buddies," *Learning 20/6* (Feb 1992): 80-83. [EJ 443 816]
Describes one educator's Whole Language approach to elementary school reading. Her class activities focus on books and friends during February to help celebrate Valentine's day. Two student pages offer friendship-oriented student activities.

Lamb, Holly, and Diane L. Best, "Language and Literacy: The ESL Whole Language Connection." (1990): 11 pp. [ED 324 915]
Proposes that through the use of Whole Language techniques, an English-as-a-Second-Language (ESL) teacher can incorporate holistic language situations into the ESL classroom and advance the student's acquisition of a second language. Whole Language techniques such as spontaneous conversation, brainstorming with semantic maps, dialogue journals, and writing folders are described. Student work samples provide illustrations. It is concluded that by including a Whole Language system in the ESL classroom, a teacher can teach all four language skills (listening, speaking, reading, and writing), thereby maximizing the use of instructional time and exposing students to a large amount of language in many different forms.

Lamme, Linda Leonard, "Authorship: A Key Facet of Whole Language," *Reading Teacher 42/9* (May 1989): 704-10. [EJ 388 677]
Traces the importance of authorship in literacy development, and shows how authorship can become one focus of a Whole Language classroom.

Lamme, Linda Leonard, and Pam Lee, "Crossing the Moat: From Basic Skills to Whole Language in a Kindergarten Curriculum," *Childhood Education 66/5* (1990): 295-97. [EJ 418 847]
Interviews a Florida kindergarten teacher who uses the Whole Language philosophy to help elementary students learn skills through ongoing reading and writing activities. Thematic units are used to encourage teacher facilitation and peer teaching.

Lamme, Linda Leonard, "Exploring the World of Music through Picture Books, *Reading Teacher 44/4* (Dec 1990): 294-300. [EJ 418 090]
Describes how children's picture books with musical themes allow readers to explore the world of music, the use of these books can enrich a Whole Language curriculum, and how picture books with musical themes can be integrated into various curriculum plans.

Lamme, Linda Leonard, "Illustratorship: A Key Facet of Whole Language Instruction," *Childhood Education 66/2* (win 1989): 83-86. [EJ 401 265]
Presents early childhood teachers with Whole Language ideas for helping young children establish a sense of illustratorship; these include studying favorite authors or illustrators, teaching children to recognize salient features of book illustrations, establishing a sense of audience, displaying children's drawings and writing, and publishing children's work.

Lamme, Linda Leonard, and Linda Ledbetter, "Libraries: The Heart of Whole Language," *Language Arts 67/7* (Nov 1990): 735-41. [EJ 417 962]

Describes examples from Florida elementary schools that show what happens when librarians and teachers collaborate in language-arts curriculum and instruction. Outlines practices that enhance the development of selecting books and using libraries.

Lamme, Linda Leonard, "Exploring the World of Music through Picture Books," *Reading Teacher 44*/4 (Dec 1990): 294-300. [EJ 418 090]
Describes children's picture books with musical themes as explorations of the world of music and the use of these books to enrich a Whole Language curriculum. Explains that picture books with musical themes can be integrated into various curricula.

Lamme, Linda Leonard, and Cecilia Beckett, "Whole Language in an Elementary School Library Media Center. ERIC Digest." (1992): 4 pp. [ED 346 874]
Examines changes that are involved in an elementary school library media program when the school's instructional methods move from a basic skills to a Whole Language approach. These changes are discussed in terms of three curricular foci—theme studies, process writing, and literature-based reading—and new demands that are placed on the collection and the school librarian. Because the Whole Language approach relies heavily on children's literature instead of textbooks, large numbers of trade books are required, and librarians must work cooperatively with teachers to ensure that the necessary resources are available in the media center when needed. Flexible scheduling in the school media center is important to the success of theme studies as it allows children to seek answers to questions as they arise. Since Whole Language generates an enormous demand for books, videos, cassettes, and computer programs, library media specialists can expect dramatic changes in collection use as well as changes in their role. Not only must library media specialists become very familiar with the library collection, but they must also serve as a resource to students and teachers during the planning and execution of theme studies, a teacher of information skills, and an instruction leader.

Landry, Maureen D., "Developing Literacy among Kindergarten Children through the Implementation of Child Centered Activities Based upon Reading Recovery Principles." (1991): 90 pp. [ED 335 641]
A practicum provided child-centered activities for 20 kindergarten children during regular school hours. Goals for the practicum were to: (1) develop literacy; (2) increase social interaction between the teacher and the child through verbal and body language communication which weaves reading and writing into the relationship; and (3) obtain a shared commitment to literacy with the assistance and help of the parents and school staff. Child-centered activities utilizing the regular classroom facility and based upon reading recovery principles were used. Results showed a significant shift in students' attitude and performance towards reading, writing, and language. Results suggest that child-centered activities which wove reading, writing, and language behavior into the learning process developed literacy.

Larrick, Nancy, "Give Us Books!...But Also...Give Us Wings! (Concepts and Themes)," *New Advocate 4*/2 (spr 1991): 77-83. [EJ 424 220]
Discusses problems associated with literature-based reading programs that use children's literature in the same way basal readers are used. Encourages teachers to allow students the freedom of exploring and learning from the book without generating drill and vocabulary lessons from it.

Laughlin, Mildred Knight, and Claudia Lisman Swisher, "Literature-Based Reading: Children's Books and Activities To Enrich the K-5 Curriculum." (1990): 165 pp. [ED 339 993]
Helps teachers and media directors to use children's literature to enrich elementary reading programs and to pursue sound educational objectives as they share the books

and stories. Provides activities designed to expand and enrich the opportunities for children to become literate. It is a tool which addresses the need for children to read widely in order to practice their literacy and begin to form ideas and judgments. Contains three chapters by level: (1) kindergarten, transitional, and first grade activities; (2) second- and third-grade activities; and (3) fourth- and fifth- grade activities. Each chapter presents several units on topics including: visual literacy, predicting, patterns in literature, sequencing, characterization, plot line, vocabulary, discovering and using information books, exploring poetry, analyzing contemporary realistic fiction, learning from biographies and autobiographies, enjoying modern fantasy, and introducing classics. Each unit presents student objectives, gives an annotated list of recommended books for use with that unit, details a group introductory activity, and outlines numerous follow-up activities related to the recommended reading.

Lawhon, Rachel, "Emerson Was Right: 'The Secret of Education Is Respecting the Pupil,'" *Perspectives in Education and Deafness 9/4* (Mar-Apr 1991): 14-15. [EJ 429 874]
A teacher at the Model Secondary School for the Deaf (District of Columbia) recounts how she learned to use the Whole Language approach to writing instruction, to encourage student writing and conduct teacher/student conferences, and to stimulate students' reading interests.

Lehman, Barbara A., and others, "Teacher Perceptions and Practices for Using Children's Literature in Elementary Reading Instruction," paper presented at the Annual Meeting of the National Reading Conference (40th, Miami, FL, Nov 27-Dec 1, 1990). [ED 329 937]
Investigates three questions regarding: (1) teachers' views about the role of children's literature in the reading program; (2) how teachers implement literature-based reading programs in their classrooms; and (3) the congruence between teacher perceptions and teacher practice regarding literature-based reading instruction. Subjects, 192 teachers, completed two-part questionnaires designed to assess teacher perceptions of and identify classroom practices in literature-based reading instruction. Results indicated that the teachers who participated in the study agreed widely on certain beliefs and practices: that teachers should develop their own literature programs; that children's literature should be the major component of elementary reading programs; that children should be taught to think critically about books; and that these children should independently read books of their own choosing every day. Second, teachers disagreed considerably on other practices and beliefs, including the importance of reading many books versus studying one books in-depth; the importance of recommended grade level reading lists; how children should be grouped for instruction; and how to assess children's learning in literature-based reading. Results indicated a congruence between teacher perceptions and teacher practice regarding literature-based reading instruction. Results also indicated that certain other variables were related to teachers' beliefs and practices, including teaching location and teacher experience.

Lehr, Susan, "Creating Classroom Contexts for Readers: Linking Children with Books," *Reading Horizons 30/3* (spr 1990): 195-208. [EJ 408 318]
Discusses how teachers can structure contexts in which reading excites children and links them effectively with books in a variety of genres. Argues that literature is a vehicle for facilitating intellectual growth and critical thinking.

Leigh, Gregory R., and others, "Basic Education Needs of Adults Who Are Hearing Impaired." (1992): 108 pp. [ED 348 500]
Examines the extent to which people in Australia with impaired hearing were receiving some form of literacy assistance and whether requests for service were fulfilled by

providers of Adult Literacy and Basic Education (ALBE) services. A questionnaire was sent to a sample of 71 providers. In addition, telephone interviews were conducted with 100 hearing impaired people by persons competent in hearing impaired communication. The interview schedule focused on seven specific areas: background information; hearing impairment information; educational background/history; current educational requirements; previous experience with adult education; awareness/knowledge about current adult education options; and basic ALBE information. In addition, hearing impaired respondents were asked to provide a self-assessment of literacy and numeracy skills. Among the conclusions and recommendations that were drawn regarding the future ALBE service delivery, several are representative: (1) there is underrepresentation of hearing impaired people in ALBE services; (2) literacy skills are important to this group; (3) there is a low level of awareness about services and programs; (4) service provision program access should be facilitated through oral communication, sign communication, and signed communication; and (5) programs should be based on Whole Language principles and strategies highlighting semantic processing of text and metacognitive skills.

LeNard, Judith, and Linda Delk, "Three R's and a Very Big C: Reading, 'Riting, Replication and Change," *Perspectives in Education and Deafness 10/3* (Jan-Feb 1992): 8-11, 16 [EJ 441 403]
A group of Ohio teachers of deaf students received in-depth training in the use of Whole Language strategies, focusing first on writing strategies, followed by reading instruction and integration of reading and writing. The training plan involved group instruction, reading materials, observations, individual conferences, teacher/trainer dialogue journals, and extracurricular activities.

Lerner, Janet W., and others, "Critical Issues in Learning Disabilities: Whole Language Learning," *Learning Disabilities Research and Practice 7/4* (fall 1992): 226-30. [EJ 455 828]
This article presents an interview with two experts in Whole-Language instruction (Patricia Tefft Cousin and Margaret Richeck) and then offers a commentary section that provides another perspective of the Whole Language method, concluding that children with learning disabilities need many types of instruction.

Levande, David I., "Teacher-Reported Factors Influencing Reading Instruction," *Reading Improvement 27/1* (spr 1990): 2-9. [EJ 411 518]
Reports on what factors teachers say have influenced their beliefs and instructional practices concerning reading. Finds that both subskills-oriented and Whole Language teachers identified their classroom experiences as teachers as the single greatest influence on their beliefs about reading and reading instruction.

Levande, David I., "Theoretical Orientation to Reading and Classroom Practice," *Reading Improvement 26/4* (win 1989): 274-80. [EJ 408 386]
Investigates whether teachers behave in ways consistent with their theoretical orientation to reading during reading instruction. Finds that a majority of the teachers did not teach reading in a manner consistent with their self-reported theoretical orientation.

Levin, Jill, "Expanding Prospective Teachers' Beliefs about the Reading Process To Enable Changes in Classroom Practice through the Use of Whole Language." (1992): 92 pp. [ED 347 506]
A practicum designed to help prospective teachers explore instructional approaches that differ from their intrinsic beliefs about how reading should be taught is described in this report. Particular emphasis was placed on using the Whole Language approach,

as opposed to the more traditional basal reader or skills oriented approaches to reading. All student participants were placed in kindergarten, first, second, or third grade classrooms for implementation purposes. The practicum involved: (1) administration of pre- and post-surveys of teacher beliefs as related to classroom practices; (2) development of a pre- and post-questionnaire of Whole Language terminology; (3) requiring students to use literature-based lessons in their classrooms; (4) teacher-made materials; (5) introduction of cooperative learning; (6) use of big books, dictated stories, and experience charts; (7) observation of students in field placements; and (8) organization of several oral presentations as a means of sharing ideas. Analysis of the data revealed that student participants used more holistic strategies in their classrooms and exhibited enthusiasm and inquisitiveness about Whole Language and its potential effectiveness. Post-survey results indicated that prospective teachers changed their attitudes toward the Whole Language approach and were more willing to reflect on how changes in classroom practice can be developed to meet the needs of beginning readers.

Levstik, Linda S., and Ruby Yessin, "'I Prefer Success': Subject Specificity in a First Grade," paper presented at the Annual Meeting of the American Educational Research Association (Boston, MA, Apr 16-20, 1990). [ED 322 207]
Research on restructuring domain-specific knowledge suggests that inferences made by a learner are based more on what and how concepts are structured and organized in particular domains than on the age of the learner. In this view, it is possible for children to operate more expertly in a particular area than could be explained by global stage or the "expanding environment" theories. Therefore, it is crucial to understand how domains are structured and organized in classrooms, and the ways in which children respond to those structures. This paper discusses the nature of history instruction in a nontraditional first grade classroom and is based primarily on class-room observation. The class operates from what the teacher identifies as a Whole Language perspective in which cross-disciplinary thematic units are the focus of instruction. The teacher teaches from what is labeled a "perspective of care." Historical content is specifically structured to emphasize personal response, ways of "finding out," and the development of ethical/moral sensibilities. Among the conclusions drawn are that history, can be shaped to particular forms and structures in the classroom based on the teacher's conception of history, and that even very young children can begin to develop the interest and understanding that lead to mature historical thinking.

Lieberman, Jan, "Literature in Concert: Oral Interpretation Harmonizes with the Whole Language Curriculum," *Emergency Librarian* 19/2 (Nov-Dec 1991): 8-9. [EJ 436 315]
Discusses the development of oral interpretation skills to promote literature in the classroom as part of the Whole Language curriculum. Describes the benefits of listening to adults read aloud and telling stories are discussed, and the importance of listening skills and audience etiquette.

Lim, Hwa-Ja Lee, and Dorothy J. Watson, "Whole Language Content Classes for Second-Language Learners," *Reading Teacher* 46/5 (Feb 1993): 384-93. [EJ 459 174]
Describes a summer school English-as-a-Second-Language classroom that uses a content-rich Whole Language curriculum. Highlights experiences that were successful in facilitating literacy development, including reading experiences, writing experiences, talking and reading, and talking and writing. Discusses the effectiveness of the instructional experience.

Lindsey, Melinda, "The Curricular Experiences of Low Achieving First Graders in a Whole Language Program." (1989): 23 pp. [ED 319 007]
A study was conducted to investigate the curricular experiences of the low achievers, including the quality of the programs they participated in and the congruence between their classroom and pullout programs. Three lower-middle-class first graders in the Pacific Northwest participated in the study: John spent the entire day in the classroom; Ginny was pulled out of the classroom 15 minutes daily to receive remedial help in reading comprehension in the Chapter 1 program; and Michael was pulled out of the classroom 25 minutes daily to receive help in reading comprehension and word attack from the special education teacher in a resource room setting. The reading programs implemented for each of the students were investigated primarily through classroom observation, informal conversations with teachers, summaries of journal entries, and children's written work. Portions of the core classroom program were judged to be of poor quality in both student responses and teacher-student interactions. It is likely that this negatively affected the achievement of the at-risk students. The experiences of Ginny and Michael in their respective pullout settings appear to be qualitatively different from their classroom experiences. Text difficulty was controlled by orthographic features rather than by meaning; instruction was teacher-directed rather than learner-controlled; materials were teacher-selected rather than student-selected; expected student responses differed; and student-teacher interactions were sustained longer. (Nineteen references are attached.)

Linek, Wayne M., "Grading and Evaluation Techniques for Whole Language Teachers," *Language Arts 68/*2 (Feb 1991): 125-32. [EJ 421 171]
Identifies the need to resolve inconsistencies between the Whole Language teaching approach and school, district, or state grading and evaluation policies. Suggests attempting to bring the inconsistencies to light while also undertaking individual, group, and criteria comparison. Discusses data collection techniques which can help achieve these ends.

Linn, Jeffrey B., "Whole Language in the Social Studies," *Social Science Record 27/*2 (fall 1990): 49-55 [EJ 434 972]
Argues that a Whole Language approach can help bring social studies to life for students. Explains that the arrangement of terms into a web or map that shows the terms' interrelationships and is one way of using the Whole Llanguage approach. Provides guidelines for thematic instruction and a list of potential themes.

Literacy/Alphabetisation, 1991-92." (1992): 154 pp. [ED 350 394]
Journal of the Movement for Canadian Literacy, this document consists of the four issues comprising Volume 15. Number 1 contains "Literacy for Participation in the Economy" (Bill Fagan); "Environmental Print" (Pat Rigg); "'I Need Help'" (Nan Nichols); and reviews of "Alpha 90: Current Research in Literacy," "Leadership for Literacy: The Agenda for the 1990s," and "NewsAble." Number 2 consists of "Lettuce Patch Learning" (Irene Jensen); "La Magie des Lettres" ("The Magic of Letters") (Elise Mennie); "Spelling Tricks: Whole Language in Practice" (Mary Norton); "'Special Ed' Teachers in Literacy" (Michele Tessier); and reviews of "Taking Care: A Handbook about Women's Health" and "A Literacy Celebration." Contents of Number 3 are "Learning Disabilities—An Official Definition" (Learning Disabilities Association of Canada); "Adult Learners and Learning Disabilities—What Do We Know?" (Johanne Jasmin); "To Label or Not To Label" (Patricia Hatt); "Diagnosing and Teaching Adults with Learning Disabilities" (Ricki Goldstein); "Programming with Adults Who Have Learning Disabilities" (Fred A. Reekie); a review of "Adult Literacy Resource Materials"; "Learner Action Group of Canada—Mission Statement"; and "A

National Literacy Strategy for Older Canadians" (Andrew Aitkins). Number 4 contains "Organizing Adult Literacy and Basic Education in Canada: An Update" (John Macdonald); "Response to Organizing Adult Literacy and Basic Education in Canada" (Ann Slater); "Women and Literacy Research: Contradictions and Context" (Betty-Ann Lloyd); "Helping Kids Learn: Family Literacy in Arviat, Northwest Territories" (Martha Main); "The Learner Action Group of Canada" (Alan Kobe); and a review of "The Land that We Dream of: A Participatory Study of Community Based Literacy."

Livingston, Carol, and Nancy Taylor, "Networking as Community—The Nature of Curriculum: Whole Language," paper presented at the Annual Meeting of the American Educational Research Association (San Francisco, CA, Apr 20-24, 1992). [ED 348 649]
Considers the status and potential of researcher/practitioner collaboration toward higher literacy through a restructured curriculum based on the Whole Language philosophy. Specifically, it examines the status, contribution, and potential of the dialogue in a Whole Language topical session on the School Renewal Network, an electronic networking community of researchers and practitioners. Four sections correspond to the following four focus questions: (1) What has happened thus far regarding Whole Language? (2) How has thinking and practice about reading and language instruction for students changed? What has been the effect on your colleagues and school? (3) What has been the effect on you, your school, and your colleagues in regard to Whole Language and participation in the network's interactive community? and (4) How can the network help you/your colleagues to improve literacy instruction and experience for students? In this regard, how could the research/practitioner community be strengthened? The first section presents descriptions of the six schools in the Whole Language group and a discussion of the development and current status of Whole Language in those schools to date. The second section describes in more detail the individual and institutional changes in each school. The third section describes the content of the papers distributed through the network and the nature of the participant interaction during a 2-day meeting. This section also presents testimony of the network's impact on the Whole Language group participants, their colleagues, and their schools. The fourth section integrates the major recommendations for research drawn up at the meeting with a brief review of the extant research literature on Whole Language organized around three major issues: a justification, documentation, and balance. A number of questions are then provided concerning development and change as they pertain to Whole Language.

Looby, Theresa N., and James S. Turner, James S., "Improved Reading Achievement of Sixth Grade Students When Using a Whole Language Approach in Conjunction with a Basal Reading Program." (1987): 22 pp. [ED 290 124]
Investigates whether basal reading instruction combined with Whole Language development instruction would help a group of sixth graders improve in reading skills as measured by the Metropolitan Reading Test. Subjects, 82 students from a metropolitan area in the Southwest, were given pretests and posttests which measured performance in word recognition and comprehension. Results indicated that word recognition was increased and comprehension growth was affected when language development was included in the reading program. The groups receiving language development showed higher gains in word recognition and comprehension. Findings also indicated that gender and ethnic background were not contributing variables. Findings suggest that the language development approach was effective in improving reading achievement.

Lopez, Eileen B., "Dialogue Journal Writing in Kindergarten and First Grade Classrooms." (1990): 63 pp. [ED 324 115]
An assistant principal for elementary instruction implemented a 10-week practicum intervention designed to use teacher in-service sessions to encourage the provision of daily opportunities for journal writing to kindergartners and first graders. In-service sessions offered: (1) an overview of highlights of related research; (2) approaches to the evaluation of student writing samples; (3) discussion of writing sample collection and evaluation; and (4) discussion of student progress in writing. Parents of participating students were invited to attend an evening orientation session in the week of the second in-service session. Included in the orientation were suggestions about activities parents could use at home to reinforce and support Whole Language instruction. Practicum effectiveness was assessed through classroom observations, reviews of student journals, comparison of students' pre- and post-samples, and a parent survey. Data indicated that students were provided with daily journal writing oportunities and that teachers wrote responses twice weekly. Students showed significant gains in developmental writing levels. Parental reactions to students' journal writing and invented spellings were positive. Related materials, such as surveys used and graphic analyses of pre- and post-intervention writing samples, are appended.

Lore, Rosemary, and Ed Chamberlain, "Language Development Component Compensatory Language Experiences and Reading Program 1989-90. Final Evaluation Report." (1990): 128 pp. [ED 328 882]
Intended to improve language and reading skills of selected underachieving students, the 1989-90 Compensatory Language Experiences and Reading Program (CLEAR) of the Columbus, Ohio, public schools served 5,135 pupils in grades 1-8. Implementation of the program was accomplished through daily instructional activities to strengthen and extend regular classroom instruction without pursuing the basic reading textbooks. Instructional techniques and use of materials based on Whole Language principles, skill-centered objectives, and computer assisted instruction were applied to fit individual needs. Three different reading treatments were evaluated: regular, Whole Language, and computer assisted instruction. The program was evaluated through administration of the Comprehensive Tests of Basic Skills as pretest and posttest. Results indicated that: (1) 57.7% of the 2,755 pupils in the overall sample gained more than 3.0 normal curve equivalent (NCE) points in the total reading category and there was an average gain of 5.6 normal curve equivalent points across grades and treatment groups; (2) 64.7% of the pupils in the overall sample of 2,533 students for the reading/oral comprehension category gained at least 3.0 NCE and the average gain was 7.2 NCE across grades and treatment groups; (3) 72.8% of the students were promoted or passed their target courses; and (4) 80% of the students in the Whole Language program reached an appropriate text reading level for promotion to the next grade. The program will be totally restructured during the 1990-91 school year.

Loucks-Horsley, Susan, ed., "The Reading-Writing Connection: A Whole Language Approach. An Annotated Resource List. Linking R&D to Practice Series No. 9603." (1988): 9 pp. [ED 296 308]
The 31 references cited in this resource list from 1980 to 1987, intended for researchers, curriculum developers, and teachers, were selected to help make sense of the reading-writing connection and to help answer three questions: (1) What is the Whole Language approach? (2) Why should I teach reading and writing together? and (3) How can I teach reading and writing together?

Lovitt, Zelene, "Rethinking My Roots as a Teacher," *Educational Leadership 47/6* (Mar 1990): 43-46. [EJ 405 136]
If Whole Language classes are to be student-centered and teacher responsive, teachers must relinquish several commonly held assumptions regarding student performance levels and abilities, testing practices, lesson planning, and classroom control. In the process, they will gain the freedom to achieve their own potential and enhance their students' potential.

Lowe, David W., and others, "Whole Language for At-Risk Readers," *Preventing School Failure 37/1* (fall 1992): 14-18 [EJ 457 529]
Identifies the student at risk in reading, defines Whole Language philosophy, and gives examples of Whole Language instructional strategies that address the needs of the at-risk reader. These strategies include teacher modeling of reading and writing, student choice of reading materials, providing time to read, and developing thematic units.

Luckhart, Anne F., "Improving Congruency of Resources/ Activities/ Assessment in Intermediate-Level Language Arts Programs with Current Knowledge of Literacy Development." (Nora University, 1991): 147 pp. [ED 322 508]
This practicum was designed to improve the congruency of resources, activities, and assessment strategies in intermediate-level language arts programs with a holistic process-oriented perspective on literacy development. Taking place in a large public elementary school in Vancouver, Canada, the practicum's goals were: (1) to implement "literature-based" programs in several classes; (2) to nurture lifelong reading habits by improving students' attitudes toward reading and increasing the number of books read; and (3) to foster among teachers a commitment to a holistic approach to literacy development and to instructional practices congruent with this perspective. Literature-based language arts programs were implemented, emphasizing student choice of texts; more varied and creative personal responses to literature; a broader range of assessment practices including portfolios, response journals, self-evaluations, and individual development profiles; integration with other subject areas; liaison with the library and librarian; parent education; and enrichment activities using a variety of media. The following activities were conducted: class newsletters were sent home, implementation of a daily Home-School Book in which students shared their school activities and experiences; creation of bulletin board displays to advertise the holistic approach to literacy development; provision of a literature review to school staff; presentations to parents and teachers on program organization and instructional practices; and development and administration of the evaluation components of the practicum. Results were positive from students, teachers, and parents.

Luke, Allan, "Curriculum Theorizing and Research as 'Reading Practice': An Australian Perspective," paper presented at the Annual Meeting of the American Educational Research Association (San Francisco, CA, Mar 27-31, 1989). [ED 307 585]
Whole Language approaches to the teaching of reading and writing have received broad support by United States advocates of "critical pedagogy." This paper outlines a case study of the Australian implementation of Whole Language inservice courses for the teaching of literacy in elementary schools. Drawing from post-structuralist theory and critical linguistics, it models a discourse analytic approach to curriculum research. Argues that a critical analysis of curriculum projects depends on a "situated reading" of extant relationships between the state and schooling.

Macginitie, Walter H., "Reading Instruction: Plus ça Change...," *Educational Leadership 48/6* (Mar 1991): 55-58. [EJ 422 857]
Unless educators can learn from past extremes, the current emphasis on literature and Whole Language instruction may undermine phonics and other necessary principles.

Fortunately, a reborn emphasis on writing will assist the development of accurate decoding and stress the phonemic structure of language. Educators must embrace "best" trends and jettison excesses.

MacGowan-Gilhooly, Adele, "Fluency before Correctness: A Whole Language Experiment in College ESL," *College ESL 1/*1 (Mar 1991): 37-47. [EJ 432 955]
Describes a college English-as-a-Second-Language curriculum model based on a Whole Language approach that is presented to stimulate others to review and revise their own curriculum.

MacGowan-Gilhooly, Adele, "Fluency First: Reversing the Traditional ESL Sequence," *Journal of Basic Writing 10/*1 (spr 1991): 73-87. [EJ 425 335]
Describes an ESL department's Whole Language approach to writing and reading, replacing its traditional grammar-based ESL instructional sequence. Reports the positive quantitative and qualitative results of the first three years of using the new approach.

Malicky, Grace V., "Myths and Assumptions of Literacy Education," *Alberta Journal of Educational Research 37/*4 (Dec 1991): 333-47. [EJ 438 293]
Critiques two overstatements about literacy: the illiteracy problem is much worse than many people think, and it is getting worse; and literacy development is both the cause and the solution to many social problems and will lead to economic development. Explores issues in literacy education such as skills versus processes, standardized testing, learning disabilities, and the Whole Language approach.

Malicky, Grace, and Charles Norman, "Whole Language: Applications to Special Education," *Canadian Journal of English Language Arts 11/*3 (1988): 19-25. [EJ 385 179]
Examines three children in remedial contexts to show how Whole Language principles can be used to guide diagnosis and instruction for special needs children. Notes that remedial programs should embed instruction in meaningful events in the students' lives, rather than focusing on component parts in reading and writing.

Malicky, Grace, and Charles A. Norman, "The Reading Concepts and Strategies of Adult Nonreaders," *Journal of Reading 33/*3 (Dec 1989): 198-202. [EJ 402 133]
Explores the nature of illiteracy for adults who have made no or minimal progress in learning to read or write. Finds further support for using the Whole Language approach and the language experience approach for adult beginning readers.

Mallak, Joan E., "A Comparison of the Whole Language Philosophy of Instruction with the Basal Reading Program. Grades K-2," 59 pp. (1991). [ED 332 161]
Reviews the practices and purposes of the new basal reading serieses and the Whole Language philosophy. Explores the possibility of a comprehensive adoption of either program or a combination of both. Indicates the desirability of using the Whole Language philosophy and shaping a classroom that is real, natural, and functional. Recommendations focus on the importance of the teacher's incorporating the necessary skills and sound/symbols within the literature lesson.

Mambo, Marjorie, and Susan Wheatley, "Curriculum Design: Whole Language through Music and Art." (1992): 80 pp. [ED 351 263]
Reports a project that involved the development of an integrated art and music curriculum model for elementary grades. In this discussion, an example of one integrated unit is described for each of grades one through six. The curriculum units are centered around literary or musical themes that incorporate a variety of interdisciplinary experiences. The themes for each grade that were chosen for the pilot project were: Grade 1, Trains; Grade 2, African animal tales; Grade 3, Native American

cultures; Grade 4, Venice in Italy; Grade 5, The Far East; and Grade 6, American folk genres. The students involved in the project seemed to learn a great deal from their experiences through the integrated units.

Manning, Gary, and others, "Reading and Writing in the Middle Grades: A Whole Language View." (1990): 66 pp. [ED 314 731]
Opines that reading and writing in school should be natural and enjoyable for children, and its ideas are based on the Piagetian theory that knowledge is constructed by each individual and the psycholinguistic view that learning takes place best when viewed as holistic and when instructional materials for children are authentic and purposeful. Describes the constructive nature of children's thinking, reading, and writing, and the natural development of these processes. Chapter 1 discusses a model of literacy learning and the role of teachers in creating sound literacy programs for their pupils. Chapters 2 and 3 present instructional ideas that support the literacy development of middle grade students. Chapter two centers on developing readers; some of the topics covered include reading aloud, literature sets, reading conferences, book talks, strategy lessons, and reading journals and logs. Chapter 3 focuses on developing writers and discusses various aspects of the writing workshop, writing outside the workshop, and assessment of writing—only those ideas which are consistent with a Whole Language view of literacy development have been included. Chapter 4 comments on specific questions about the Whole Language approach to reading and writing.

Manning, Gary, and Maryann Manning, eds., "Whole Language: Beliefs and Practices, K-8. Aspects of Learning Series." (1989): 243 pp. [ED 309 387]
Includes the ideas of many of the leading authorities on Whole Language and contains chapters on the meaning of Whole Language, the skills movement, reading and writing development, and teacher autonomy. Contents: "Whole Language: What's New?" (Bess Altwerger and others); "Language Arts Basics: Advocacy vs. Research" (Peter Hasselriis and Dorothy J. Watson); "Examining Instructional Assumptions: The Child as Informant" (Jerome C. Harste and Carolyn L. Burke); "Demonstrations, Engagement and Sensitivity: The Choice between People and Programs" (Frank Smith); "'Burn It at the Casket': Research, Reading Instruction, and Children's Learning of the First R" (Anne M. Bussis); "Early Phonics Instruction: Its Effect on Literacy Development" (Maryann Manning and others); "Reading Comprehension: From Cardboard Keys to Meaningful Text" (Barbara A. Lewis); "When Was 1864? Reading Comprehension—Making It Work" (Maryann Manning and others); "Authentic Language Arts Activities and the Construction of Knowledge" (Maryann Manning and others); "Early Spelling Development: What We Know and What We Do" (Gary Manning and Maryann Manning); "Social Interaction and Invented Spelling" (Constance Kamii and Marie Randazzo); "Kid Watching: An Alternative to Testing" (Yetta M. Goodman); "Literature as the Content of Reading" (Charlotte S. Huck); "Shared Book Experience: Teaching Reading Using Favorite Books" (Don Holdaway); "One-On-One Reading" (Roberta Long and others); "Fifth Graders Respond to a Changed Reading Program" (Cora Lee Five); "All Children Can Write" (Donald H. Graves); "Is That Writing—Or Are Those Marks Just a Figment of Your Curriculum?" (Carole Edelsky and Karen Smith); "Write? Isn't This Reading Class?" (Marie Dionisio); "Dialogue Journals: A Tool for ESL Teaching" (David L. Wallace); "The Author's Chair" (Don Graves and Jane Hansen); "Beyond Basal Readers: Taking Charge of Your Own Teaching" (Kenneth S. Goodman); "Restoring Power to Teachers: The Impact of 'Whole Language'" (Sharon J. Rich); "A Reflection on Reflective Practice in Teaching Reading and Writing" (Bernice J. Wolfson); "In the Process of Becoming Process Teachers" (Gary Manning and others).

Manning, Maryann Murphy, and others, "Reading and Writing in the Primary Grades. Analysis and Action Series." (1987): 82 pp. [ED 306 558]
Argues that reading and writing in school should be natural and enjoyable for children, this book is based on the Piagetian theory that knowledge is constructed by each individual and the psycholinguistic view that learning takes place best when viewed as holistic and when instructional materials for children are authentic and purposeful. The book describes the constructive nature of children's thinking, reading, and writing, and the natural development of these processes. Chapter 1 discusses a model of literacy learning and the role of teachers in creating sound literacy programs for their pupils. Chapters 2 and 3 present instructional practices, consistent with the Whole Language approach, that support natural literacy development of young children. The last chapter presents final comments.

Manning, Maryann, and others, "Writing Development of Inner City Primary Students: Comparative Effects of a Whole Language and a Skills-Oriented Program," 37 pp. (1990). [ED 336 745]
Compares the writing development and ideas about writing of students in a Whole Language program with students in a skills-oriented program from the time they entered kindergarten to the end of the second grade. Subjects were 22 inner-city students who completed second grade out of an original kindergarten cohort of 50 minority students who had been randomly divided into a Whole Language group and a skills-oriented group. Subjects were interviewed regarding their views about writing at the end of each year, had their spelling ability assessed at the end of first and second grade, and had their writing assessed in a variety of ways throughout the 3-year period. Results indicated that students in the Whole Language group did the following: (1) were better writers; (2) viewed themselves as writers of real texts and had confidence in themselves as writers; (3) outperformed the skills-oriented students on measures of spelling achievement. Findings suggest that Whole Language should be considered as an alternative to skills-oriented instruction in inner-city schools. [See ED 324 642 for a similar report]

Manning, Maryann, and others, "Effects of a Whole Language and a Skill-Oriented Program on the Literacy Development of Inner City Primary Children," paper presented at the Annual Meeting of the Mid-South Educational Research Association (New Orleans, LA, Nov 8-10, 1989). [ED 324 642]
This study compared the effects of Whole Language practices with the effects of a skills-oriented program on the reading achievement of a group of children from an inner-city, low socioeconomic school from the time they entered kindergarten to the end of second grade. Subjects were 22 children, all of a minority race, randomly placed in one of the two groups. Assessments were made at the end of each school year of children's ideas about reading, their reading behaviors, and their reading achievements. Results showed that by the end of second grade, children in the Whole Language group were better readers than those in the skills-oriented group in all areas.

Maquire, Mary H., "Understanding and Implementing a Whole-Language Program in Quebec," *Elementary School Journal 90*/2 (Nov 1989): 143-59. [EJ 404 264]
Describes the development and implementation of a Whole Language program in Quebec, a unilingual French province. Focuses on the meaning of educational change at various levels of Quebec's educational system. Presents perspectives and competing ideologies on Whole Language.

Marek, A., and others, "A Kid-Watching Guide: Evaluation for Whole Language Classrooms. Program in Language and Literacy Occasional Paper No. 9." (1984): 54 pp. [ED 277 978]

Divided into four sections, this monograph focuses on effective evaluation in the Whole Language classroom. The first section discusses the Whole Language philosophy and classroom, and lists the beliefs that proponents of this approach hold about Whole Language teaching and teachers, language, and language learners. The second section addresses evaluation concepts centering on observation and interaction with students as they are engaged in the functional use of language, and emphasizes that student growth in a Whole Language classroom must be evaluated in a context sensitive to (1) opportunities for flexibility of language use, (2) students' values and attitudes about language, and (3) students' knowledge about language. In addition, three essential focuses of the evaluation process are described: observation of the students, interaction with students in using language, and analysis of students' products. The third section contains evaluation questions based on these emphases, while the final section provides supplemental evaluation tools for Whole Language teachers. These tools are organized around areas relating to specific language uses, such as oral language experiences, bookhandling, print awareness, and reading and writing experiences.

Marley, Bernard M., and Linda G. Marley, "Big Foot to the Rescue or Story Starters: A Component of Whole Language," paper presented at the Annual Conference of the Indiana State Council on Reading (Indianapolis, IN, Mar 29-31, 1990). [ED 321 295] The creative writing process, like any writing process, begins with a prewriting activity. Story starters are one such activity which teachers can use to begin the creative writing process with their students. For example, large cartoon-like characters made on an opaque projector can be used to initiate discussion. The second step requires a drafting of ideas into story form. Thirdly, the youngsters use their peers in revising their stories. The writer is responsible for responding to the criticism and for making the essential corrections. Next, students rewrite their stories and proofread. They are encouraged to use a dictionary or get help from a peer. Noise levels may be louder than usual, but learning is taking place. Once all corrections have been made, the publishing process begins. Given paper with an outline of the cartoon-like character on it, students write the final copy within the drawn character. They illustrate the paper and make covers for their books. Completed books are shared with the class.

Martin, Rodney D., "Empowering Teachers to Break the Basal Habit," paper presented at the Annual Meeting of the International Reading Association (36th, Las Vegas, NV, May 6-10, 1991). [ED 334 568] Certain events between the late sixties and the eighties were major influences in empowering Australian reading teachers to break the basal habit. During the late sixties a growing number of elementary classroom teachers and principals were showing an interest in classroom practices that focused on children's individual progression. During the early seventies, a number of "alternative education" or "non-graded" schools emerged, and teacher training institutions began to adapt courses to reflect contemporary trends. During the mid-seventies schools became progressively more literature-based, and made use of new books such as Don Holdaway's "Core Library." During the late seventies, curriculum evaluation became the responsibility of the school. In addition, the value of standardized tests was becoming widely questioned. Finally, during the eighties, a study of a New Zealand teacher training system resulted in the development and implementation of the Early Literacy Inservice Course. By the mid-to-late eighties, individual publishers could no longer market basal readers; evaluation became increasingly dependent on the teacher's observations, records, and samples of work; and publishers, teachers, and academics began to collaborate to develop a broad range of valid materials for the classroom. Some reasons why teachers were so willing to break away from dependence on basal texts include the empowerment of teachers through the political acceptance of alternatives, training, a grass roots movement, and cooperative effort.

Martin, Beverly A., "Common Threads: A Whole Language Text for Intermediate ESL Readers. ESL: Reading In a Skills Curriculum. Northampton Community Coll., Bethlehem, PA. Adult Literacy Div." (1990): 124 pp. [ED 327 072]
Designed for adult students of English as a Second Language who are reading at approximately an intermediate level. Ten chapters address a variety of topics relating to daily life in the United States, including: travel and transportation; the nuclear and extended family; holiday traditions and customs; the education system; college life; the workplace and its rules and expectations; life changes and adjustments; moving to a new community; wedding customs, traditions, and etiquette; buying on credit; compromise; making major purchases; health and hospital care; child care alternatives; and working parent concerns. The following essential language, cognitive, and life skill areas are targeted in each chapter: schema development; vocabulary enrichment; word study skills; constructing meaning; metacomprehension; language enrichment; and life skills. Chapters contain two readings and include, for each, pre-reading activities and exercises, a preview of the reading, the passage, comprehension questions, and additional exercises and activities.

Mason, Jana M., ed., "Reading and Writing Connections." (Champagne-Urbana, Illinois: University of Illinois, 1989): 310 pp. [ED 308 471]
Reflects the value of demonstrating connections between reading instruction and writing and shows practitioners that writing can be blended with reading instruction and how writing activities can be used not just to augment reading but also to establish and bolster emergent reading. Contents: (1) "Speech to Writing: Children's Growth in Writing Potential" (Martha L. King); (2) "Forms of Writing and Rereading from Writing: A Preliminary Report" (Elizabeth Sulzby and others); (3) "Movement into Word Reading and Spelling: How Spelling Contributes to Reading" (Linnea C. Ehri); (4) "Connections in Learning to Write and Read: A Study of Children's Development through Kindergarten and First Grade" (Lee Dobson); (5) "Reading and Writing Attempts by Kindergartners after Book Reading by Teachers" (Jana M. Mason and others); (6) "Reading and Writing Development in Whole Language Kindergartens" (JoBeth Allen and others); (7) "Writing and Reading : The Transactional Theory" (Louise M. Rosenblatt); (8) "Connecting Writing: Fostering Emergent Literacy in Kindergarten Children" (William H. Teale and Miriam G. Martinez); (9) "Research to Practice: Integrating Reading and Writing in a Kindergarten Curriculum" (Alice J. Kawakami-Arakaki and others); (10) "Preschool Children's Reading and Writing Awareness" (Janice Stewart and Jana M. Mason); (11) "Success of At-Risk Children in a Program that Combines Writing and Reading" (Gay Su Pinnell); and (12) "Acquisition of Expository Writing Skills" (Taffy E. Raphael and others).

Mather, Nancy, "Whole Language Reading Instruction for Students with Learning Disabilities: Caught in the Cross Fire," *Learning Disabilities Research and Practice 7/* 2 (1992): 87-95. [EJ 443 022]
Reviews the history of Whole Language versus code-emphasis approaches to reading instruction. The paper concludes that students with severe learning disabilities may learn to read in a Whole Language, mainstream classroom, if provided with supplemental instruction, a variety of instructional techniques, and appropriate intensity and duration of services.

Matthews, Marian K., "Gifted Students and Whole Language: A Descriptive Study of Four Classrooms," paper presented at the Annual Meeting of the American Educational Research Association (San Francisco, CA, Apr 20-24, 1992). [ED 351 834]

Looks at the provision of differentiated language-arts instruction for gifted students by means of Whole Language instruction approaches in regular classes. Two classrooms in each of two elementary schools were identified as exemplary Whole Language classrooms and each contained several students identified for school gifted programs. One classroom in each of grades 1, 2, 4, and 5 was represented. Participant observation was conducted at least once per week for approximately a semester. Additionally, interviews with the classroom teachers, the principals, the reading/language arts coordinators, the teachers of the gifted, and the targeted students were conducted. The benefits of the Whole Language approach for these students were analyzed in terms of: student choice of reading materials, responses to reading, and writing projects; use of time; social interaction; and appropriate teaching. Analysis indicated: all teachers and classrooms provided examples of some exemplary practices but none provided all those components advocated by either Whole Language experts or educators of the gifted; the classroom that provided the most exemplary Whole Language practices also provided the most differentiation of learning experiences for gifted students; and both students and teachers had difficulty articulating what appropriate challenges and differentiated language experience meant to them. It is concluded that, although Whole Language instruction is a positive approach, it does not preclude the need for differentiated gifted programming.

Mazely-Allel, Marianne, "Holistic Language at the High School Level," *Contemporary Education 62/2* (win 1991): 120-21 [EJ 447 942]
Holistic teaching in secondary school English helps avoid subject matter isolation and fragmentation. It involves exposing students to forthcoming information, covering subject matter, and following up on information presented. It engages the whole student, creating effective communicators who think critically and comprehend written and spoken messages.

McCarthy, William G., ed., and others, "Whole Language Learning for Elementary School Teachers, Children, and Parents." (1989): 69 pp. [ED 320 103]
Designed to disseminate theoretical ideas and practical strategies concerning Whole Language so that learning for children and practice for teaching may be enlightened and improved. Contents: "Whole Language Learning" (William McCarthy and Alicia Sutton); "Planning the Program and Organizing the Classroom" (Marilyn Brummett and others); "Whole Language Learning through Theme Building: Self Concept Enhancement and Building of Self Esteem" (Caroline Cass); "Motivating the Emerging Writer" (Deborah Flurkey); "Music and Language, Partners in Communication" (Jane Conner and William McCarthy); "The Highlighting of Context as a Powerful Strategy for Beginning Readers and Beginning Teachers" (Sharon Andrews and Carol Turner); "Reading and Publishing Books" (Marilyn Brummett); "The Writing and Reading Connection in the Intermediate Classroom" (Patricia Gannon Smith); and "Evaluation and Record Keeping in Primary and Intermediate Grades" (Deborah Flurkey and Patricia Gannon Smith).

McCarty, Teresa L., "Language, Literacy, and the Image of the Child in American Indian Classrooms," *Language Arts 70/3* (Mar 1993): 182-92. [EJ 459 198]
Describes how educators at one Navajo community school are transforming assumptions about schooling for indigenous groups from a deficit model to one that views bilingualism, biculturalism, and multiculturalism as assets to be tapped. Bases the discussion on a long term ethnographic study of the changes brought about through the implementation of bilingual Whole Language pedagogy.

McCaslin, Mary M., "Whole Language: Theory, Instruction, and Future Implementation," *Elementary School Journal 90/2* (Nov 1989): 223-29. [EJ 404 269]
Comments on three areas of general concern in the Whole Language movement: developmental theoretical underpinnings; "do's and don'ts" of Whole Language instruction; and the future implementation of Whole Language teaching and learning.

McCloskey, Mary Lou, ed., "Turn-On Units: English as a Second Language Content Area Curriculum in Math, Science, and Computer Science for Grades K-6." (1992): 171 pp. [ED 347 090]
Thematic units, the basis of organization for this guide, work in many ways toward the dual goals of language and content area instruction. The thematic units presented here address topics of high interest to limited English-proficient (LEP) students, including robots; using a computer data base; activities with plants; building terrariums; architecture; and cooking. In order to provide LEP students with an active role in the learning process, the units incorporate many opportunities for them to play games, participate in movement activities, enter into role playing, create art works and constructions, cook and manipulate materials. To bridge the gap between the classroom and the real world, the units incorporate field trips and other activities that provide LEP students with motivational experiences to facilitate their learning of the new culture as well as the new language. To help LEP students toward full literacy, the units use a Whole Language approach, including many experiences with rich literature, and opportunities to develop writing skills. In addition, the units are planned to incorporate the language, math, and science objectives of the Georgia Basic Curriculum. Each of the units in the guide includes an introductory statement of purpose, learning objectives, key concepts, a brief outline of activities, grade levels for which the unit is intended, and a list of suggested resources. Each unit addresses a range of several grade levels. Georgia Basic Curriculum objectives for each activity are displayed on a grid. Each activity includes recommended grouping and teacher role, a list of materials needed, detailed procedures, suggestions for evaluation, and possible extensions of the activity.

McCoy, Linda Jones, and Victoria Hammett, "Predictable Books in a Middle School Class Writing Program," *Reading Horizons 32/3* (Feb 1992): 230-34. [EJ 439 182]
Describes Whole Language activities (including using predictable books and rewriting of literary and poetic patterns) used for teaching reading and writing in a Kansas middle school.

McCoy, Linda Jones, "Integrating Predictable Book Techniques with Basal Reader Instruction," Kansas, 1993. [CS 011 294]
Noting that teachers have expressed a need for more information on how they can incorporate Whole Language into their classrooms, describes ways of combining Whole Language techniques in a program that continues to use the basal reader. Offers a brief view of the basic steps often used to incorporate predictable books into a basal program. Describes a year-long project in which a college reading-methods instructor volunteered to teach (using predictable books and basals) on a daily basis with a group of 15 first-graders. Presents sample lessons (emphasizing fluent reading, writing, and other language skills) written by graduate students of the college reading-methods teacher. Presents two teaching plans—one to use when the basal reader is the major method of instruction and the other to use when the basal is used as a supplemental book. Concludes that observational data in the classroom supported the combination of predictable books and the basal reader approaches to reading instruction.

McCracken, Robert A., and Marlene J. McCracken, Marlene J., "Stories, Songs, and Poetry to Teach Reading and Writing: Literacy through Language." (1986): 157 pp. [ED 276 987]
Focusing on the development of literacy, this book discusses the teaching of reading and writing through stories, songs, and poetry. It is argued that, to develop literacy, teachers must know what to teach, how to teach efficiently, and how to assign practices through which children learn. The book is organized into three general parts. The first two chapters provide a statement of beliefs about literacy as natural learning and about reading readiness. Chapters 3 and 4 describe the reading process as apprehension and prediction and discuss ways to begin the teaching of reading. Chapter 5 centers on phonics as a skill to be learned through spelling and writing and applied in reading. The ideas expressed in this chapter are considered a fundamental part of teaching children about language and print. Chapters 6 through 9 address beginning writing and relevant research. The final chapter addresses the role of parents and nonteachers in reading instruction.

McDermott, Peter, and Julia Rothenberg, "The Role of Literature and Writing in Social Studies Methods Texts: A Case for Change in Teacher Education," paper presented at the Annual Meeting of the New England Education Research Organization (Portsmouth, NH, Apr 1991). [ED 337 399]
Five current social-studies methods textbooks were examined to determine how writing and literature are presented to prospective teachers. The results of the examination show that only one of the methods textbooks offered a positive and informative explanation of how literature can be used to learn the social studies. Three of the textbooks were viewed as recognizing the importance of writing, although only two offered sufficient information and examples of how it might actually be used for learning. The conventional approach to teaching social studies offered by current methods textbooks perpetuates a textbook oriented teaching that does not serve the purposes of social studies in these changing times.

McEachern, William Ross, "Supporting Emergent Literacy among Young American Indian Students." (1990): 3 pp. [ED 319 581]
Links the development of listening comprehension to the emerging reading comprehension of young American Indian students, and suggests ways that teachers can use locally produced materials to enhance young students' emergent literacy. Reading comprehension is the key to literacy, and prior knowledge supports listening and reading comprehension. However, most commercial reading materials used in schools do not reflect American Indian students' exprience of the world. Since there are many culturally distinct American Indian groups, producing commercial materials for all Indians is not a viable alternative. Studies have shown, however, that culturally relevant instructional materials increased listening comprhension among American Indian primary students. Such findings indicate the effectiveness of teachers' efforts to produce instructional materials locally. Such efforts might involve inviting community storytellers into the classroom and transcribing oral presentations for use as reading materials, or encouraging children to develop stories based on their own experiences. Teachers must also recognize the linguistic diversity of their students, who may use English as first language, second language, or dialect. Students' linguistic backgrounds must be considered when designing a language-arts program.

McGee, Lea M., and Richard G. Lomax, "On Combining Apples and Oranges: A Response to Stahl and Miller," *Review of Educational Research 60*/1 (spr 1990): 133-40. [EJ 414 301]
Criticizes Stahl and Miller, who compared the effectiveness of Whole Language/

language experience programs versus basal reader approaches, for misrepresenting concepts related to emergent literacy and inadequately defining Whole Language, the lack of equivalence between the two nonbasal approaches, and problems with conclusions concerning decoding.

McInerney, John, "Polishing the Whole Act," paper presented at the Annual Indiana University Fall Language Arts Conference (Bloomington, IN, Nov 10, 1988). [ED 304 664]
"Whole Language" is not a set of practices to teach reading; it is a set of beliefs, a philosophy about learning which derives from the notion of keeping learning whole and intact rather than fragmenting it into discrete bites. Many kinds of activities can be implemented according to Whole Language theory: (1) having students make up the rules for the class which are collected and sent home to parents; (2) having students write down one thing remembered from the previous day's lesson (but not grading or collecting it); (3) using pasted-together sheets of paper for students to write a continuing story which is shared with other students; (4) having one student each day write a sentence about something interesting to them which is put onto a "class calendar" and also serves as the class handwriting assignment; (5) tape recording trade books and student-written stories; (6) having students bring in newspaper clippings of global events and posting them on a map of the world; (7) evaluating each student's reading individually by listening to them read; and (8) transferring one student's story onto an overhead and having the class edit it.

McIntyre, Ellen, and Marianne Davis, "Reading Interactions in a First-Grade Whole Language Classroom," *Contemporary Issues in Reading 6/2* (spr 1991): 75-82. [EJ 431 072]
Relates a teacher's observations in a Whole Language classroom of first graders enabling each other to read. Suggests reading techniques that foster this collaborative learning.

McIntyre, Ellen, "Young Children's Reading Strategies as They Read Self-Selected Books in School," *Early Childhood Research Quarterly 5/2* (Jun 1990): 265-77. [EJ 413 822]
Investigates strategies that beginning readers use as they read self-selected texts in the reading centers of first-grade Whole Language classrooms. Patterns of reading behavior show general movement from a focus on pictures to a focus on print. Strategies were recursive, not developmentally linear.

McKenna, Michael C., and others, "Whole Language: A Research Agenda for the Nineties," *Educational Researcher 19/8* (Nov 1990): 3-6. [EJ 422 236]
Examines the current rift in perspective between Whole Language arts and traditional language arts instruction by analyzing the basis of each view in research and theory. Suggests research developments that might alleviate the present impasse. Describes the need for new hypotheses, a variety of designs, improved instrumentation, and collaborative investigations.

McKenna, Michael C., and others, "Whole Language and the Need for Open Inquiry: A Rejoinder to Edelsky," *Educational Researcher 19/8* (Nov 1990): 12-13. [EJ 422 238]
Replies to Carole Edelsky's response [see EJ 422 237] to the authors' article on the schism between proponents of Whole Language and traditional language arts instruction. Defends the questions posed by the authors' research agenda, and suggests that diverse research methodologies can be employed in tandem to address them. Calls for collaboration among researchers.

McKinsey, Laura, "Integrating Whole Language and Outdoor Education," *Journal of Outdoor Education 25* (1990-91): 19-22. [EJ 431 791]

Compares the philosophies of Whole Language instruction and outdoor education. Both incorporate other subjects in a theme approach, use meaningful materials, are student-centered, and are process-oriented. An outline of a teaching unit based on the story "Sarah Plain and Tall" integrates Whole Language and outdoor education.

McMahon, Susan I., "Book Club Discussions: A Case Study of Five Students Constructing Themes from Literary Texts. Elementary Subjects Center Series No. 72." (1992): 61 pp. [ED 353 572]
Investigates the development of theme as five fifth-grade students read children's literature, recorded their responses in logs, and discussed their ideas in small, student-led peer groups. The five students met together as one group over the course of 5 weeks as they read historical fiction focused on Japan during World War II. Data included student logs, transcripts of their discussions, field notes, and student inter-views. Results indicated: (1) student thinking about themes presented by texts varied over time; (2) instruction played a key role in the development of response; (3) students needed multiple means through which to express their response and develop-ing ideas about theme; and (4) teachers need not dominate student interactions to insure they comprehend text and develop a sense of relevant themes. Findings suggest that students' ideas, as represented through their logs and discussions, develop as a result of increased opportunities to read, write, think about, and discuss the ideas presented in texts and that instruction should include such opportunities within reading programs.

McNeilly, Patricia, "Old Teachers Can Learn New Tricks," *Ohio Reading Teacher 24/4* (sum 1990): 34-38. [EJ 432 607]
Describes her transition from traditional reading instruction to a Whole Language approach. Discusses journal writing and dramatization as two effective teaching strategies.

McVitty, Walter, ed., and others, "Getting It Together: Organising the Reading-Writing Classroom." (1986): 130 pp. [ED 278 043]
Emphasizing the importance of developing a social classroom climate, this book addresses the organization of the reading/writing classroom. Nine sections: (1) present a statement of principles based on this concept of classroom organization (J. Steinle); (2) discuss scheduling the school day as an important area of teacher planning (P. Sloan and D. Whitehead); (3) suggest ways of managing classroom resources and space to create conditions similar to those in which children master oral language (H. Brown); (4) discuss the theoretical and practical bases for providing personalized learning for all children through appropriate grouping techniques (L. Unsworth); (5) suggest some desirable outcomes of a teacher's contract with a learner, and outline the history of and rationale for contracting (A. Fleet); (6) describe cooperative classroom learning activities that involve peer tutoring (Knox Grammar School staff members); (7) address the issue of parents as home tutors of literature, citing results from recent naturalistic research supporting the notion (M. Kemp); (8) define team teaching, describe its benefits, present a number of case studies, and provide practical guidelines for implementing it (M. Mannison); and (9) focus on the use of teacher-made learning centers as a means of fostering independent learning while providing stimulating Whole Language activities (L. Unsworth).

McWhirter, Anna M., "Whole Language in the Middle School," *Reading Teacher 43/8* (Apr 1990): 562-65. [EJ 408 408]
Describes Whole Language reading workshops used in eighth-grade classrooms. Notes that workshops consist of three components: time to read, ownership through self-selection, and opportunities to respond to the reading through dialogue journals.

Melvin, Mary P., "Boxes, Bottles, Bags, and Brochures (In the Classroom)," *Reading Teacher 43/4* (Jan 1990): 351-52. [EJ 403 679]
Uses boxes, bottles, bags, brochures, and other print materials to design more interesting and more effective Whole Language lessons.

Mersereau, Yvonne, and others, "Dancing on the Edge," *Language Arts 66/2* (Feb 1989): 109-18. [EJ 385 112]
Describes an alternative elementary school where teachers work together to offer dance as a complement to writing and the study of literature in a Whole Language approach. Encourages teachers to add new ideas to their curriculum, to use individual talents, and to collaborate with other teachers.

Meyer, Valerie, and others, "Case Study—Norman: Literate at Age 44," *Journal of Reading 35/1* (Sep 1991): 38-42. [EJ 431 148]
Describes how three tutors helped an adult progress from being a nonreader to being a competent and enthusiastic reader, using an approach rooted in Whole-Language research and practice.

Meyerson, Maria J., and John C. Van Vactor, "The Reading Theoretical Orientation of Teachers Who Instruct Special Needs Students," *Reading Psychology 13/3* (Jul-Sep 1992): 201-15. [EJ 448 397]
Investigates the reading orientation of teachers who instruct students with special needs by using the Theoretical Orientation in Reading Profile. Finds that teachers in the study were not strongly associated with any one theoretical orientation but tended to be eclectic. Finds also that the teachers clustered primarily into two orientations: Whole Language and skills/phonics.

Mickelson, Norma, and Anne Davies, "A Whole Language Program in the Intermediate Grades: Questions and Answers." (1987): 23 pp. [ED 290 146]
Focusing on a Whole Language program for the middle grades in Canada's Northwest Territories, this interview transcript consists of responses by Anne Davies, a teacher from Yellow Knife, in the Northwest Territories, and currently a doctoral student, to questions posed by Norma Mickelson, a professor at the University of Victoria in British Columbia. Davies claims that the Whole Language program is still evolving, but is already a viable alternative to traditional approaches in intermediate grade classrooms. Davies begins by asserting that very few modifications are necessary to use the Whole Language approach with older students, then describes a typical day in the classroom, which includes (1) reading; (2) sharing; (3) journal writing; (4) editing; (5) written reactions to reading; (6) logic exercises; (7) Whole Language content area instruction; and (8) quiet time. Davies next describes her holistic evaluation methods, which are based on observation. Davies' discussion then turns to using microcomputers in middle grade classrooms, including use of language arts software and interactive games. Finally, Davies talks about the role of the Whole Language teacher, interaction with administrators, the teaching philosophy, and the atmosphere in Whole Language classrooms.

Midvidy, Nancy, "Teaching beyond the Basal Program," *Reading: Exploration and Discovery 13/1* (fall 1990): 19-26. [EJ 431 087]
Provides examples of how holistic procedures can be implemented by teachers who want to supplement the required basal. Demonstrates how students' reading ability, language acquisition, and communication skills can be strengthened as teachers activate prior knowledge, provide language-rich environments, consider reading/writing connections, and focus on thinking.

Miller, J. Kenneth, and Jerry L. Milligan, "A Comparison of the Whole Language Approach with a Basal Reader Approach on the Decoding and Comprehending Ability of Beginning Readers." paper presented at the European Conference on Reading (6th, Berlin, West Germany, Jul 31-Aug 3, 1989). [ED 313 693]
Examines whether children learn phonic decoding skills by reading without direct phonic instruction; compares the effects of a Whole Language first-grade reading program with the effects of a traditional basal reading program; determines whether there was a difference in decoding and comprehending abilities across levels of ability. Subjects, an experimental group of 33 low socioeconomic first grade students in two classrooms who completed the year-long program and a control group of 33 low socioeconomic students in two other elementary schools matched by sex and reading readiness, completed a Nonsense Word Test to assess decoding ability and a Deletion test to assess their ability to comprehend increasingly more difficult prose. The control group used the Scott Foresman Basal Series. Testing occurred upon completion of the school year. Comparison of the test results indicated that: (1) students in the Whole Language classrooms scored as well in decoding ability as those students who received direct phonics instruction; (2) as a group, students in the Whole Language classrooms scored higher on the Deletion Test than the control group (indicating greater comprehension of increasingly difficult prose); although (3) subjects scoring in the middle and lowest on a reading readiness test accounted for much of the difference in the overall difference in the mean scores on the Deletion Test. Findings suggest support for the Whole Language approach.

Miller, James G., and others, "Whole Language—Inside and Outside!" *Pathways to Outdoor Communication 1*/1 (fall 1991): 14-15. [EJ 434 894]
Describes a teacher's efforts to compile an anthology of poems written by fourth-grade students. Whole Language activities progressed from poetry reading and group writing to individual writings based on outdoor themes. Presents examples of students' poetry.

Miller, Janet A., "Theoretical Orientation of British Infant School Teachers," paper presented at the Annual Meeting of the College Reading Association (34th, Nashville, TN, Nov 2-4, 1990). [ED 327 823]
A study examined the theoretical orientation of infant school and infant department teachers in England. The Theoretical Orientation to Reading Profile (TORP) was used to determine the teacher's orientation to reading instruction. TORP applies a Likert scale response system to a series of statements about how reading should be taught. Subjects included 146 teachers and head teachers from over 40 different schools. Three teachers scored within the lower range indicating a phonics orientation. One hundred nineteen scored within the middle range of the scale which indicated a skills orientation. Twenty-four responded within the high range of the scale indicating a more Whole Language orientation. These results indicated that the majority of the teachers who participated in the study appeared to hold a skills orientation to reading instruction, rather than a Whole Language orientation. Nevertheless, many teachers indicated preferences for several of the practices associated with Whole Language. Their "middle of the road" orientation, in addition to the traditional autonomy of individual schools and teachers in determining instructional methods and materials in England, apparently results in the use of a wide variety of approaches to beginning reading, including reading schemes, trade books, thematic units and an integrated day which incorporates a number of language-related activities which support emergent literacy.

Milligan, Jerry L., "Understanding the Current Great Debate in Reading," paper presented at the Annual Meeting of the Washington Organization for Reading Development (Spokane, WA, Oct 28-29, 1988). [ED 301 867]

The debate between the Whole Language approach and the word-centered skills approach to beginning reading instruction is likely to continue into the next decade, so it seems crucial that educators at all levels understand thoroughly the views held by the participants. Advocates of the Whole Language approach believe effective readers see meaning as they read and that reading skills are learned by reading. Whole Language proponents use more global observation assessments and are concerned with giving background to readers. Advocates of the word-centered skills approach want to provide readers with the skills necessary to decode meaning from individual words. Thus they focus on developing sight vocabulary and phonics, break language into smaller units to aid readers in developing skills, assess progress by demonstrating proficiency for each skill, and control the readers' exposure to new vocabulary.

Milligan, Jerry L., and Herbert Berg, "The Effect of Whole Language on the Comprehending Ability of First Grade Children," *Reading Improvement 29/3* (fall 1992): 146-54. [EJ 452 721]
Assesses the effectiveness of Whole Language instruction over the course of a school year. Finds that middle and low progressing experimental subjects and experimental males at each of three ability levels attained significantly higher mean scores on a cloze test than did their counterparts in the control group (who used basals).

Mills, Heidi, and Jean Anne Clyde, "Children's Success as Readers and Writers: It's the Teacher's Beliefs That Make the Difference," *Young Children 46/2* (Jan 1991): 54-59. [EJ 426 220]
Discusses the effects of teachers' beliefs and practices on teachers' perceptions of students' abilities and potential for success. Uses the example of a child referred from a traditional kindergarten, where he did poorly, to a Whole Language child development center, where he excelled. Urges teachers to examine the impact of their beliefs on their practices.

Mills, Heidi, and others, "Looking Closely: Exploring the Role of Phonics in One Whole Language Classroom." (1992): 85 pp. [ED 341 955]
Addresses the issues of phonics in Whole Language classrooms and phonics plays in reading and learning to read; rooted in the language stories and literacy lessons of teachers' observations of at-risk children learning to read. Begins with an introduction to one Whole Language teacher's classroom and to his philosophy. The second chapter describes a typical classroom day so that readers can have a sense of how children learn about letter-sound relationships across the day. The third chapter looks at the growth of three children over the course of a year. The fourth chapter makes explicit the role of the teacher, so that teaching and learning about grapheme-phoneme relationships from a Whole Language perspective might be more easily understood.

Mills, Heidi, and Timothy O'Keefe, "Accessing Potential: Lessons from an 'At Risk' Six-Year-Old." (1990): 11 pp. [ED 323 542]
A case study of an at-risk student in a Whole Language "transition first grade" (representing an extra year between kindergarten and first grade) classroom chronicles her transition from an anxious and withdrawn student to an enthusiastic learner. Although it took nearly a month for the student to relax in the classroom, she then responded eagerly to writing experiences. Although a quiet person, she developed a real desire to communicate. During writing/journal time, she began to engage the adults and other children in written conversation. During quiet reading she could often be found reading one of the big books using a pointer. She also participated in a class project on plants. The student grew temendously during her transition first grade year because: (1) her experiences were grounded within a genuine social context; (2) she

was treated as a learner; (3) she was encouraged to use art, language, and mathematics in concert to construct meaning; and (4) the teacher collaborated with the students when making curricular decisions.

Mills, Heidi, and Jean Anne Clyde, eds., *Portraits of Whole Language Classrooms: Learning for All Ages,* (Portsmouth, New Hampshire: Heinemann, 1990) [CS 011 356]

Highlighting typical days in a variety of Whole Language classrooms, describes learners of all ages, beginning with a home day-care setting through preschool programs and elementary classrooms to a junior high and high school. Describes a special education site and an English-as-a-second-language classroom, and concludes in a laboratory school staffed by graduate students in a university reading methods course. Teachers' descriptions of classrooms life and their personal reflections presented in the book encourage readers to take a reflective stance and consider the beliefs that underpin their practice. Contents: (1) "Literacy Learning in a Home Day-Care Setting" (David J. Whitin and Phyllis E. Whitin); (2) "A Natural Curriculum" (Jean Ann Clyde); (3) "Teachers and Children: Partners in Learning" (Heidi Mills); (4) "A Day with Dinosaurs" (Timothy O'Keefe); (5) "Supporting Literacy Development: On the First Day in First Grade and throughout the Year" (Vera E. Milz); (6) "Teachers and Students as Decision Makers: Creating a Classroom for Authors" (Gloria Kaufmann and Kathy G. Short); (7) "Mind Games: Discovering Poetry through Art" (Margaret Grant); (8) "Making Learning Real for Intermediate Kids" (Eric Stone); (9) "Units of Study in an Intermediate-Grade Classroom" (Thom Wendt); (10) "Learning together in the Resource Room" (Patricia Tefft Cousin and Alane Lancaster); (11) "Whole Language and the ESL Classroom" (Lia Ridley); (12) "Language Learning through Family History" (Phyllis E. Whitin); (13) "Learning on the Job: Whole Language in a Middle School Remedial Program" (Betty Ann Slesinger); (14) "'I Have Never Read Five Books before in My Life': Reading and Writing Naturally in High School" (Donelle Blubaugh); (15) "We Call It Good Teaching" (Diane Stephens and others); and (16) "Whole Language: Starting New Conversations" (John McInerney and Jerome C. Harste).

Monson, Robert J., and Michele M. Pahl, "Charting a New Course with Whole Language," *Educational Leadership 48*/6 (Mar 1991): 51-53. [EJ 422 856]

Enlarges the phonics/Whole Language debate by focusing on the classroom teacher's evolving role. Whole Language instruction involves a fundamental change in a teacher's belief system concerning classroom culture. A complex paradigm shift is needed from teachers' transmission of knowledge to students' transaction or engagement with constructing meaning.

Moore, Carol, "Increasing Reading Fluency for Learning-Disabled and Remedial Readers." (1990): 82 pp. [ED 323 519]

A practicum addressed the problem of lack of fluency of learning-disabled and low-achieving students (N=24) retained in the first grade by using predictable books written in a natural manner emphasizing the children's natural language. Two evaluation procedures from the Reading Miscue Inventory were used to determine the degree to which students reduced miscues that altered the meaning of the text. Retelling of the story gave the reader an opportunity to enhance the construction of meaning. Strategies based upon a holistic view of the reading were implemented to provide students with the ability to sample, predict, and confirm as they made use of the knowledge, within a pragmatic context, of the syntactic, semantic, and graphophonic cueing systems, each interacting in order to process print. Results indicated decreased levels of miscues, taken individually and in sentence context, and a shift in attitude from a subskills or skills view of reading to a more holistic and personal view of reading. Fluency was increased as measured by the goals set for the study.

Moore, Alex, "A Whole Language Approach to the Teaching of Bilingual Learners. Occasional Paper No. 15." (1990): 23 pp. [ED 332 500]
A case study is presented that details the English learning experiences of Mashud, a Bangladeshi boy who emigrated to England. Although Mashud was fluent and skilled in his native Sylheti language, he had a great deal of difficulty learning English. He attempted to spell phonetically and showed little understanding of grammar or punctuation. In writing assignments, Mashud consistently produced formulaic moral tales. Mashud's teacher hypothesized that Sylheti, as an oral language, had emphasized learning moral lessons and formulaic repetition of information rather than creative writing skills. Instead of discouraging his Sylheti-based linguistic attempts, the teacher employed individualized discourse and autobiographical writing tasks to expand Mashud's English knowledge and writing ability. Mashud showed marked improvement in these areas, illustrating the importance of individualized, Whole Language approaches to educating bilingual students.

Moore, Sharon Arthur, and David W. Moore, "A Whole Lot More about Whole Language (Professional Resources)," *Reading Teacher 43/8* (Apr 1990): 594-95. [EJ 408 413]
Describes five Whole Language professional resources that present many insights into Whole Language theory along with specific ways to implement it in the classroom.

Moore, Sharon Arthur, and David W. Moore, "Whole Language—Yet Again (Professional Resources)," *Reading Teacher 45/2* (Oct 1991): 156-7. [EJ 432 497]
Reviews five professional resource books on Whole Language instruction and mentions three additional books on the topic. Suggests these books to educators who are interested in obtaining information and support for child-centered instruction.

Morrice, Connie, and Maureen Simmons, "Beyond Reading Buddies: A Whole Language Cross-Age Program," *Reading Teacher 44/8* (Apr 1991) 572-77. [EJ 425 369]
Describes a cross-age reading program used to refine and extend the Whole Language and process writing goals that are part of the school curriculum plan. Discusses the observation of students and evaluation strategies.

Morrison, Constance, "A Literary, Whole Language College Reading Program," *Journal of Developmental Education 14/2* (win 1990): 8-10, 12. [EJ 427 546]
Describes a Whole Language approach to teaching reading comprehension using novels, essays, and short stories. Considers the shortcomings of lab classes and reading textbooks; curriculum goals and criteria; the use of ability groupings, testing, and placement; textbook selection; and teaching strategies emphasizing verbal interaction, writing, higher-level reasoning and critical thinking skills.

Morton, Johnnye L., "What Teachers Want To Know about Portfolio Assessment," 8 pp. (1991). [ED 336 728]
Based on questions asked by teachers in classes, workshops, and conference sessions, provides brief answers to eight of the most frequently asked questions about portfolio assessment: (1) What is a portfolio? (2) What should be put in the portfolio? (3) How much should be put in the portfolio? (4) How do I find time for portfolios? (5) Are checklists available? (6) How can I give letter grades if I use portfolio assessment? (7) How do I start a portfolio? (8) How can I communicate to parents and administrators? Concludes by stating that portfolio assessment is an evolving concept and that teachers must continue to experiment, talk to other teachers who use portfolios, and read professional journals in a continuing effort to develop meaningful, acceptable literacy assessment.

Mosenthal, Peter B., "The Whole Language Approach: Teachers between a Rock and a Hard Place (Research Views)," *Reading Teacher 42*/8 (Apr 1989): 628-29. [EJ 386 933]
Discusses the difficulties teachers face with the current dual emphasis on teaching from a Whole Language curriculum while teaching cultural literacy and evaluating with standardized tests. Asserts that researchers need to focus on the complementarity between these approaches.

Moss, Barbara, "Ten Tips for First-Time Whole Language Users," *Ohio Reading Teacher 24*/3 (spr 1990): 38-42. [EJ 432 485]
Provides 10 tips based on research, observations, experiences, and comments from practitioners which will help teachers get through the first year of implementing a Whole Language approach. Offers a 15-item list of resource companies and their addresses that might assist teachers and educators who wish to investigate this area further.

Moss, Barbara, "Planning Effective Whole Language Staff Development Programs: A Guide for Staff Developers," *Reading Horizons 32*/4 (Apr 1992): 299-315 [EJ 442 766]
Discusses some principles, considerations, and cautions for those conducting staff development programs in Whole Language. Discusses factors necessary for effective implementation of Whole Language programs.

Moustafa, Margaret, "Recoding in Whole Language Reading Instruction," *Language Arts 70*/6 (Oct 1993): 483-87.
Explains new research findings about how children learn letter/sound correspondences, relates the findings to Whole Language reading instruction, and outlines a theory for how children acquire the letter/sound system without direct instruction in phonics. Describes recent findings on phonological processes involved in learning letter/sound correspondences and discusses relevant findings on children's cognitive processes.

Myers, John W., "Making Sense of Whole Language. Fastback 346." (1993): 45 pp. [ED 356 453]
Based on the premise that Whole Language is a philosophy or perspective, rather than a set of practices, this fastback develops a definition of Whole Language, presents an information processing model of language processes, and discusses theory-practice relationship and assessment as they relate to Whole Language. Sections of the fastback are: Making Sense of Whole Language; A Holistic View of Language: What Research Says; Theory into Practice: Whole Language Arts; and Whole Language and Assessment. The pamphlet concludes that: (1) theory determines practice; (2) integrated language activities are more powerful than separated ones; (3) Whole Language arts cut across the curriculum; and (4) instructional goals should drive the assessment of language arts skills.

Nadler, Diane Leboe, "Teaching Reading to Chapter One Pre-First Grade Students Using a Literature Based Approach." (1989): 76 pp. [ED 323 518]
A literature based reading program was developed to improve reading comprehension skills of 14 students in a Chapter 1 pre-first grade class. Instead of using a basal reader for instruction, the students were exposed to trade or literature books, The reading strategies that were pre- and posttested were recognition of a sight vocabulary, recognition of the letters of the alphabet, and recognition of family rhyming words. The results indicated a marked improvement in reading comprehension as well as increased student self-esteem from success in reading.

Neal, Kathy S., and Barbara Everson, "Memories and Written Remembrances: Creating a Link between Prior Knowledge and Children's Literature," paper presented at the Annual Meeting of the College Reading Association (34th, Nashville, TN, Nov 2-4, 1990). [ED 327 838]
Reading comprehension is much more than a decoding of the printed words on the page; it is, rather, a complex interaction between readers and their personal past experiences as they relate to the text. A connection between the text and past experiences of the readers can stimulate expectations about the text. Facilitating these links presupposes a careful review of appropriate children's literature. Two books particularly suited to calling up memories in the reader are "Wilfrid Gordon McDonald Partridge" by Mem Fox and "When I Was Young in the Mountains" by Cynthia Rylant. Teachers can generate a list of words representing key concepts from such books. Students then make their own predictions about the story's plot. After reading the story, these predictions are compared with the author's intended message. Students choose one of their own memories to use as a focus for personal narratives. These writings are first shared in peer-response groups and then the teacher responds to the writings. An analytical scale is used for assessing the writing. Such a scale guides a purposeful dialogue between student and teacher and eases the student through the process of revision.

Newman, Harold, "Utilizing Psycholinguistic Insights in Teaching via the Basal Reader," paper presented at the Annual Meeting of the New York State Reading Association (16th, Kiamesha Lake, NY, Nov 2-5, 1982): 13 pp. [ED 227 471]
Ideas of educational psycholinguists Frank Smith and Kenneth Goodman can be combined with the ideas presented in current basal reader manuals to help teachers teach reading more effectively. Since reading and speaking are parallel processes, teachers may invite children to "read" with them, hearing the melody of language as they point to interesting or dramatic sentences in the text. Assisted reading, in which the child reads the same text after the teacher, is another useful device. Basal reader authors and psycholinguists agree on the need to continue to refine and enrich oral language competency. Even though we read for meaning more than for word identification, basal readers emphasize word identification as the foundation of comprehension. Basal readers stress phonics, but Smith and Goodman argue that teaching phonics makes it harder, not easier, for children to learn to read. Smith's view of the relativity of comprehension, however, is affirmed by the writers of most basal reader manuals. Both psycholinguists and basal reader authors recognize that reading involves using visual clues to predict meaning. The Directed Reading Activity, a series of steps used in basal readers to promote children's predictive strategies, is the best way not only of teaching reading skills but of stimulating student interest. Research also indicates the usefulness of miscue analysis and the questionable value of recall tests.

Newman, Judith M., "Whole Language: A Changed Universe," *Contemporary Education* 62/2 (win 1991): 70-75. [EJ 447 936]
Examines how changes in the view of the universe led to Whole Language learning, a collaborative process in which the social contexts of language are taken seriously. Suggests that Whole Language is not a teaching method but a belief and discusses how to transform teaching into a learning experience.

Newman, Judith M., ed., *Finding Our Own Way: Teachers Exploring Their Assumptions* (Portsmouth, New Hampshire: Heinemann, 1990).
Intended for teachers, the articles in this book examine some of the uncertainties and problems that practicing teachers encountered when moving from a traditional to a holistic perspective in their teaching. Reports the questions, conflicts, changes that are

part of becoming a learner-directed teacher. Contents: "Finding Our Own Way" (Judith M. Newman); "Learning in a Whole Language Classroom" (Albert Layton); "A Teacher Learns How" (Pat Kidd); "'Herb's Revenge'—Writing Our Own Play" (Christine Clark); "Learning from Christopher" (Chris Trussler); "Why Teachers Must Be Writers" (Murray Wickwire); "Simply, 'Margot'" (Beth Valentine); "Who Should Have Control?" (Evelyn Bent); "But You Haven't Done Any Research" (Janet Ripley); "Looking Back" (Fred Williams); "Creating a Climate of Affirmation: Education beyond Fear" (Marion Anderson); "That First Year Back" (Florence Kanary); "Looking for Mistakes That Make a Difference" (Roberta Jones); "Side by Side" (Margot Shutt); "What Denise Tried to Show Me" (Linda Christian); "Celebrating Growth" (Nancy Anthony); "Why Didn't This Chicken Cross the Road?" (Brian MacDonald); "Dear Mrs. Gillon" (Jan Gillin); "A Belief System under Siege" (Michael Coughlan); "Fear, Risk, and Change: Reflections on a Year as Learner" (Beverly R. Boone); "Time for Change" (Sumitra Unia); "I Don't Know Enough French!" (Janice L. Clarke); "A Letter to the Principal" (Linda Cook); and "The Key" (Fred Williams).

Newman, Judith M., ed., "Whole Language: Theory in Use." (Portsmouth, New Hampshire: Heinemann,1985): 204 pp. [ED 300 778]
To show how Whole Language theory can be put into practice, this collection of articles, many written by practicing teachers, suggest ways that teachers can help students become active participants in their own learning. Contents: (1) "Insights from Recent Reading and Writing Research and Their Implications for Developing Whole Language Curriculum" (Judith M. Newman); (2) "What Teachers Are Demonstrating" (Meredith Hutchings); (3) "Andrew and Molly: Writers and Context in Concert" (Wayne Serebrin); (4) "Using Children's Books To Teach Reading" (Judith M. Newman); (5) "From Sunny Days to Green Onions: On Journal Writing" (Sumitra Unia); (6) "To Judith: A Look at a Child's Writing Development through His Letters" (Judith M. Newman); (7) "Learning To Spell" (Olga Scibior); (8) "The Message Board: Language Comes Alive" (Reta Boyd); (9) "What about Reading?" (Judith M. Newman); (10) "Text Organization: Its Value for Literacy Development" (Susan Church); (11) "Conferencing: Writing as a Collaborative Activity" (Judith M. Newman); (12) "It Makes You Feel Needed: Students as Teachers" (Judy Mossip); (13) "Activity Cards" (Winniefred Kwak and Judith M. Newman); (14) "Mealworms: Learning about Written Language through Science Activities" (Judith M. Newman); (15) "The War of the Words" (Susan Church); (16) "Yes, They Can Learn" (James Boyer); (17) "Danny: A Case History of an Instructionally Induced Reading Problem" (Susan Church and Judith M. Newman); and (18) "Yes, That's an Interesting Idea, But...: On Developing Whole Language Curriculum" (Judith M. Newman).

Newman, Judith M., and Susan M. Church, "Myths of Whole Language (Commentary)," *Reading Teacher 44*/1 (Sep 1990): 20-26. [EJ 413 063]
Looks closely at 19 myths about Whole Language teaching, learning, and assessment, especially the myths "not to criticize teachers but to help all teachers examine their pedagogical assumptions" and "to learn from the contradictions found."

Newton, Debra Lee, "Whole Language: What Is It?" (1992): 33 pp. [ED 354 494]
Presents guidelines to promote implementation of Whole Language. Uses Donald Ely's (1990) conditions for change as a framework. These conditions are: dissatisfaction with the status quo, the existence of knowledge and skills, availability of time and resources, participation, commitment, leadership, and presence of rewards and incentives. After a brief description of Whole Language, the report presents individual case information on two reading specialists, a school teacher, and a reading coordinator

who were involved in the process of changing to Whole Language. Based on analysis of the cases, it appeared that while Ely's conditions were still present, they required a slightly different interpretation and some modification, and the report then lists and discusses 10 conditions specifically for Whole Language implementation that emerged from the analysis.

Nicholson, Tom, "Reading Wars: A Brief History and an Update," *International Journal of Disability, Development and Education 39/3* (1992): 173-84. [EJ 459 558]
Summarizes the debate among major theorists of the Whole Language approach (Kenneth Goodman and Frank Smith) and their critics (e.g., Philip Gough). Concludes that the Goodman/Smith theoretical position has not stood the test of time, though some of their instructional recommendations may be valid for other reasons.

Nicholson, Tom, "Reading is Not a Guessing Game—The Great Debate Revisited," *Reading Psychology 7/3* (1986): 197-210. [EJ 342 370]
Reviews the debate on the importance of decoding in reading, focusing on the positions taken by P. Gough and K. Goodman. Argues that the debate is settled, with Gough's view having more explanatory power in terms of helping to understand the success of the good reader and the plight of the poor one.

Nigohosian, Elsie T., "Meeting the Challenge of Diversity: Applying Whole Language Theory in the Kindergarten with ESL Korean Children." (1992): 98 pp. [ED 352 818]
Reports a study that investigated how the core experiences of a Whole Language kindergarten influenced four Korean immigrant children to acquire English language and literacy. Core experiences examined include reading aloud and response, shared reading and writing, independent reading and writing, and inquiry activities. Information gathered for the case studies from anecdotal records, portfolios, and interviews was analyzed to arrive at generalizations and identify some universals about language learning. Results suggest that when the Korean learners of English as a Second Language (ESL) were immersed in a literate environment and engaged in speaking, reading, and writing experiences that were integrated, meaningful, and functional, they learned to speak, read, and write English. These experiences provided the children with an opportunity to observe demonstrations and engage in real speaking, reading, and writing processes using authentic materials and resources. Because the curriculum was child-centered, the children could choose experiences appropriate to their strengths and interests. As a result, they were motivated to learn in a risk-free environment. Recommendations are offered to administrators and to ESL and regular classroom teachers.

Nistler, Robert J., and Grace M. Shepperson, "Exploring New Directions for Staff Development: Teachers in Charge of Change," paper presented at the Annual Meeting of the National Reading Conference (40th, Miami, FL, Nov 27-Dec 1, 1990). [ED 329 895]
After a decision was made at a Texas elementary school to adopt a Whole Language philosophy toward literacy instruction, a study was designed to address three research questions: (1) What levels of concerns are raised by teachers in the areas of "self," "task," and "impact"? (2) What responses do these concerns elicit from university researchers and other participants? and (3) What changes occurred among participants during their involvement in the initial phase of this project? Data sources included: audio tapes of weekly inservices with 2 university researchers, 23 teachers, and the school principal; teacher journals; participant responses to questionnaires; field notes of classroom observations; and collaborative interactions with teachers. Initial inservices were designed to help participants identify current practices in order to facilitate their assimilation of new knowledge at later stages of the program. Activities

promoting individual reflection and talk among teachers provided opportunities for new understandings and beliefs to be confirmed or rejected, with the eventual goal of establishing a common knowledge base. Other inservice meetings were designed to guide individual exploration into Whole Language instruction, to identify instructional themes/topics and accompanying children's literature by grade levels, and to provide an opportunity for participants to report on the themes and supporting literature they had compiled. In their journals, essays, concern surveys, and conversations, the voices of teachers confirmed the efficacy of the following change factors: change is a process, not an event; change is a highly personal experience; change involves developmental growth; and change is best understood as it directly affects classroom practice, students and preparation time.

Norris, Janet A., "Facilitating Developmental Changes in Spelling," *Academic Therapy 25/* 1 (Sep 1989): 97-108. [EJ 400 614]
Spelling should be recognized as a developmental process that is child-initiated and discovery-based. Through use of an integrated Whole Language approach, children can be provided with opportunities to acquire spelling as a natural language process by beginning at their own developmental level and refining their internal knowledge of word representation.

Norris, Janet A., "From Frog to Prince: Using Written Language as a Context for Language Learning," *Topics in Language Disorders 12/*1 (Nov 1991): 66-81. [EJ 439 628]
Presents strategies, including communicative reading strategies, to facilitate holistic language learning in young children with language and learning disorders. Strategies include pairing oral and written language and using preparatory sets, semantic maps, flowcharts, and theme building. An example of narrative discourse demonstrates how adults can mediate such learning.

Norris, Janet A., and Jack S. Damico, "Whole Language in Theory and Practice: Implications for Language Intervention," *Language, Speech, and Hearing Services in Schools 21/*4 (Oct 1990): 212-20. [EJ 420 017]
Presents theoretical principles of the Whole Language approach and its historical interdisciplinary influences. Suggestions for implementing Whole Language intervention with language-disordered children are presented, such as using theme building to achieve long- and short-term objectives, using scaffolding strategies, and using developmentally appropriate interactions.

Northup, Lynne, "Person of the Day: Cultural Literacy in the Elementary Classroom," *Social Studies and the Young Learner 4/*3 (Jan-Feb 1992): 17-18. [EJ 449 319]
Describes teaching method in which a person of the day is featured on a calendar and used as the basis of that day's social studies class. Explains that the strategy introduces authors, artists, inventors, and others and provides matching activities. Suggests the method can incorporate aspects of cultural literacy into social studies, fine arts, Whole Language, and mathematics skills.

Nurss, Joanne R., "Hospital Job Skills Enhancement Program: A Workplace Literacy Project. Final Evaluation Report." (1990): 103 pp. [ED 328 665]
A workplace literacy program was designed to improve the literacy skills of entry-level workers in the housekeeping, food service, and laundry departments of Grady Memorial Hospital in Atlanta. Classes were held twice per week for 36 weeks at the hospital on job time. Literacy was defined as reading, writing, oral communication, and problem solving. Materials were developed on the basis of a job literacy audit that included interviews with and observation of workers, interviews with supervisors, and

analysis of written materials pertinent to the job. The Whole Language approach was used by one full-time instructor, one part-time instructor, and several volunteers who taught 66 participants (primarily black women with an average of 10.5 years of employment at the hospital). Students were assessed before and after instruction by a Cloze reading test, using passages from job materials; a writing sample yielding a writing process score; and role-playing of a job situation scored for oral communication. Statistically significant gains were obtained for reading, writing, and oral communication. Participants believed that the program increased their academic skills (61 percent), improved their oral (39 percent) and written (34 percent) expression, improved their job knowledge (29 percent), increased their confidence (27 percent), and refreshed their basic education (24 percent). Supervisors believed the program benefited workers, especially in oral communications.

Ohanian, Susan, comp., "Energize Your Math Program!" *Instructor; 101*/8 (Apr 1992): 44-46, 48-49. [EJ 446 607]
Presents strategies used by elementary teachers from around the country to promote mathematics learning in the classroom. Their ideas include using manipulatives, participating in cooperative learning, keeping math journals, collecting portfolios, and reading literature that relates to math concepts in real life.

Ohanian, Susan, "Readin' 'Rithmetic—Using Children's Literature to Teach Math," *Learning 18*/3 (Oct 1989): 32-35 [EJ 412 467]
Describes techniques using literature to help students develop a number sense and to enliven math classes. Books and activities are suggested that address concepts of pattern and order, counting, estimation, factorial analysis, and exponents. Techniques incorporate open-ended discussions that leave room for emotion, intuition, creativity, and humor.

Ohanian, Susan, "Success Stories," *Learning 17*/4 (Nov-Dec 1988): 52-57. [EJ 394 491]
Spotlights the outstanding accomplishments of a remedial reading teacher, whose conviction that children could learn that reading could be fun led her to use storytelling as a jumping-off point for building literacy based on listening, speaking, reading, and writing.

Ohanian, Susan, "Who's Afraid of Old Mother Hubbard?" *New Advocate 3*/1 (win 1990): 39-48. [EJ 402 231]
Refutes the sequential, building-block theory of cultural literacy that advocates mastery of a prescribed body of cultural knowledge. Argues that teachers must help students find joyful encounters with words which will knock their socks off and inspire them both to search for understanding and to reach for another book.

Ohlhausen, Marilyn M., and others, "Viewing Innovations through the Efficacy-Based Change Model: A Whole Language Application," *Journal of Reading 35*/7 (Apr 1992): 536-41. [EJ 440 913]
Describes the Efficacy-Based Change model which takes into account the complexity of the change process for individual teachers. Notes that the model is being tested and refined within a variety of settings, including a staff development project designed to support a group of teachers as they explore ways to provide Whole Language services to other teachers.

O'Keefe, Tim, "Whole Language Teaching Today," *Instructor* 102/4 (Nov-Dec 1992): 43-49. [EJ 458 485]
Presents an excerpt from the journal of a second-grade teacher who reflected on the daily challenges and possibilities of learning in a child-centered, meaning-based

classroom free of workbooks and standardized testing; an interview with author Nancie Atwell, a language specialist and veteran teacher; and suggestions for books and journals.

Oldfather, Penny, "What Students Say about Motivating Experiences in a Whole Language Classroom," *Reading Teacher 46*/8 (May 1993): 672-81. [EJ 462 276]
Describes insights about students' motivation for literacy learning based on a student-researcher collaborative inquiry in a fifth- and sixth-grade Whole Language classroom.

Oldfather, Penny, "Sharing the Ownership of Knowing: A Constructivist Concept of Motivation for Literacy Learning," paper presented at the Annual Meeting of the National Reading Conference (42nd, San Antonio, TX, Dec 2-5, 1992). [ED 352 610]
"Sharing the ownership of knowing" (a constructivist concept of motivation for literacy learning) is a dynamic classroom interaction in which a teacher's constructivist epistemological stance facilitates students' sense of their own construction of meaning and the integrity of their own thinking. Sharing the ownership of knowing was one of several interactive processes identified within the classroom of a constructivist teacher who was the subject of a qualitative study of student motivation. The study was initiated in a small academic community in a southern California school. As a participant-observer, the author of the study shared the thinking and experience of 31 students in a student-centered Whole Language fifth- and sixth-grade classroom. After analyzing the data, the participant-observer identified connections between self-expression, constructivism, and epistemological empowerment. The concept of epistemological empowerment is a dimension of students' motivation for literacy learning that may be present in social constructivist classrooms as the teacher shares the ownership of knowing. Those who are epistemologically empowered may become more engaged as literacy learners when they become aware of their own construction of meaning.

Oldfather, Penny, "Students' Perspectives on Motivating Experiences in Literacy Learning. Perspectives in Reading Research No. 2," (Athens, Georgia and College Park, Maryland: National Reading Research Center, 1993.) [CS 011 319]
A longitudinal study examined students' perceptions of their learning and motivation in a Whole Language classroom setting. Subjects, 14 fifth- or sixth-grade students who collaborated in the inquiry as co-researchers, were interviewed in-depth. The mixed fifth- and sixth-grade classroom at the Willow School in southern California repre-sented the school's diversity. Students were actively engaged in an integrated, thematic, real-world curriculum. The classroom buzzed with readers and writers who shared the teacher's contagious sense of excitement about learning. In using literacy activities for self-expression, students experienced a direct connection between their learning activities and who they are, how they think, and what they care about. The richness of experience promoted by the curriculum nurtured students' thinking and feeling, moving them to express themselves and to be engaged in the literacy process. Students said that having choice was one of the main reasons they felt so motivated to learn. The students appreciated the teacher's enthusiasm, humor, and fun-loving presence. Findings suggest questions and answers for teachers to use in considering how their classrooms might honor students' voices more fully. This classroom provides one model of how teachers can share control and responsibility with their students.

Olds, Henry F., Jr., "Reading, Writing, and Restructuring: A Case for Renewal," *Writing Notebook: Creative Word Processing in the Classroom 9*/3 (Jan-Feb 1992): 19, 42. [EJ 440 964]

Discusses the need for fundamental restructuring of language-arts instruction. Discusses the benefits of the Whole Language approach and the current problems with testing, use of instructional time, and the lack of teacher support.

Oppelt, Shirley, "Improving Reading Skills of Fourth Grade Students through a Literature Based Reading Program." (1991): 58 pp. [ED 332 164]
A practicum developed and implemented an integrated reading program to raise reading vocabulary and comprehension scores and reading attitudes in a fourth-grade classroom. A classroom of 23 students was used to implement the program. A standard diagnostic test was used to record pre- and post-test scores in vocabulary and comprehension, and a reading attitude survey test was used to analyze students' attitudes about recreational and instructional reading. The program consisted of a reading and writing workshop daily with emphasis on learning skills through experiences with whole text. Built-in time for reading aloud, reading silently, self-selection of reading materials and stressed process writing was provided. Results indicated a 14% increase in vocabulary and a 20% increase in comprehension skills. The most noticeable improvement was in the students' attitudes toward reading. Findings suggest that this program can provide a vehicle to facilitate and increase learning achievement.

Option '90 Inter-TAC Institute on Curriculum and Instruction (Washington, D.C., Mar 29-30, 1990)." (1990): 183 pp. [ED 330 450]
The materials collected in this document were submitted to a conference focused on issues relevant to Chapter 1 programs. A wide variety of resources was presented to participants. Resources for teachers related to mathematics cover the topics of teaching reform; curriculum and instruction; problem solving; and estimation. Resources on reading involve strategies for teaching advanced skills; critical and creative thinking; problem solving; and semantic mapping. Writing resources concern critical thinking skills; lessons in descriptive writing, the writing of fiction, and letter writing; problem development and solution; and Whole Language philosophy.

Orr, Patricia B., "Improving Critical Reading Skills by Use of Multiple Methods/Materials Individualized Instruction." (1989): 47 pp. [ED 323 507]
Describes an individualized multiple methods/materials approach to the teaching of reading to improve the critical reading skills of seventh grade students in a middle school in Georgia. The core of the program was the use of novels selected with the particular interests of adolescents in mind. Sixty-four students in the developmental and accelerated reading classes participated in the 10-week program, which allowed for self-selection of books, self-pacing in reading rate, and uninterrupted time to read. A management system was formulated to allow for independent work by the students. Student/teacher conferences were built into the program. Critical reading skills were taught by a variety of methods and materials, including teacher instruction, worksheets geared to the individual books, and independent practice using reading kits and other individualized practice material. Pre- and posttests of critical reading skills, while showing higher scores for 70% of the students, did not show the gains projected at the start of the program. However, student reaction to the program was excellent: greater enthusiasm for reading was immediate and sustained; student self-management worked well; and creative book projects were devised and well received.

Osburn, Bess, "Lesson Plans, Behavioral Objectives and 'Whole Language': Can They Work Together?" (1983): 16 pp. [ED 262 376] Using a Whole Language approach in teaching the language arts presents a realistic structure and setting for reading and writing, allowing students to practice reading skills in such a way that they actually encounter and engage in the skills, rather than focusing on mastering one skill at a time. On the other hand, the recent accountability movement suggests that teachers must be able to assess the child's growth and their own teaching with specific, measurable objectives. To meet those requirements, a lesson plan is needed that provides for teaching reading skills using Whole Language activities while assessing the child's growth and the teacher's teaching with specific objectives. University reading practicum students responsible for teaching reading-disabled students were instructed to write such lesson plans. In one university reading practicum, students teaching reading-disabled children write a lesson plan for each session with a child. The basic format of the plan includes three parts (goals and objectives, procedures, and evaluation of the lesson), with lessons planned around eight requirements. This approach to lesson planning gives practicum students a guide to planning reading lessons while using Whole Language materials, and the most important aspect of the procedure is that it does not detract from the process of enjoying good literature.

Otto, Beverly White, and Monica Iacono, "Implementing Changes in Reading Instruction." (1990): 24 pp. [ED 323 526]
Describes teachers' perceptions and experiences in implementing Whole Language activities in their kindergarten and elementary classrooms. Ten teachers who were part of a pilot Whole Language program participated in the study. Throughout the 1989-1990 school term, data were collected through teacher questionnaires distributed every six weeks. The focus of the questionnaires was on teachers' selection of Whole Language activities and their evaluation of the success of the activities in their classrooms. Teachers' perspectives on student responses to changes in learning activities and parent responses to the curriculum were also examined. Teachers reported increased frequency in using specific Whole Language activities throughout the year, while continuing to use some subskill activities. The management of time and the necessity for creating their own teaching materials were frequently mentioned as problems in implementing Whole Language activities. Assessment of progress was frequently mentioned as a source of difficulty. During the course of the year, teachers voiced fewer concerns and problems and enthusiastically described their children's involvement in Whole Language activities.

Otto, Wayne, "Hoping to Hear from You Soon in Hope, BC.," *Journal of Reading 32*/8 (May 1989): 734-37. [EJ 388 549]
Responds to letters from readers in response to recent "Research" columns. Deals with the issues of learning disabilities, Whole Language approach, the "skills" perspective, junk food textbooks, and punctuation.

Otto, Wayne, "Research—Almost on the Road Again," *Journal of Reading 30*/1 (Oct 1986): 90-93. [EJ 339 961]
Offers a humorous perspective on being a proponent of the Whole Language approach to reading instruction in the face of those who favor phonics and specific skill instruction.

Pace, Glennellen, "Stories of Teacher-Initiated Change from Traditional to Whole-Language Literacy Instruction," *Elementary School Journal 92*/4 (Mar 1992): 461-76. [EJ 441 942]
Through the stories of nine innovative teachers, factors that promote or impede grassroots change efforts in elementary school are examined, especially in terms of teachers' attempts to shift from traditional textbook, teacher-centered language, and literacy curriculum to a learner-centered, Whole Language approach. Identifies three major sources of tension.

Pace, Glennellen, "When Teachers Use Literature for Literacy Instruction: Ways That Constrain, Ways That Free," *Language Arts 68*/1 (Jan 1991): 12-25. [EJ 419 866] Identifies key premises from Whole Language theory relative to (1) language and language acquisition; (2) reading and writing processes; (3) teaching and learning; and (4) curriculum. Notes that these premises provide direct assistance to teachers in planning literature-based instruction. Discusses questions and underlying principles using classroom events.

Pahl, Michele M., and Robert J. Monson, "In Search of Whole Language: Transforming Curriculum and Instruction," *Journal of Reading 35*/7 (Apr 1992): 518-24 [EJ 440 911] Suggests ways that transactional learning can be reflected in staff development practices. Addresses issues raised during attempts to implement a Whole Language staff development program. Contends that what unites Whole Language teachers is a unique but common orientation toward instruction and curriculum and that this orientation can be reflected in Whole Language staff development programs.

Pai, Nani, and others, "Multicultural Perspectives on Literature, Instruction, and Research (Reviews and Reflections)," *Language Arts 70*/3 (Mar 1993): 225-29. [EJ 459 202] Presents reviews of eight professional resources for those interested in multicultural children's literature or in instruction and research in classrooms with students of diverse backgrounds.

Palmer, Barbara C., and others, "An Investigation of the Effects of Newspaper-Based Instruction on Reading Vocabulary, Reading Comprehension, and Writing Performance of At-Risk Middle and Secondary School Students. Final Report." (1989): 171 pp. [ED 315 732] A study investigated the effects of using daily newspapers to supplement normal classroom instruction with at-risk secondary school students. Subjects, 627 at-risk 8th-through 12th-grade students in 41 intact classes, were assigned to one of three conditions of newspaper usage over an 18-week period. The first group received newspapers three times per week and were given related instruction using a Whole Language approach. The second group received newspapers three times per week without related instruction. The third group served as the control and received no newspaper supplement to normal classroom instruction. Analyses of pretest and posttest scores indicated: (1) students who received newspapers with instruction improved their reading vocabulary, reading comprehension, and writing performance more than students who received newspapers without instruction and students who received no newspapers; (2) secondary school males benefited most from newspaper usage; (3) benefits of newspaper usage increased with time; and (4) 1-day training (which had been given to the teachers of all the students) did not produce uniformly effective classroom use of newspapers among all teachers.

Pappas, Christine C., and others, "Collaborating with Teachers Developing Integrated Language Arts Programs in Urban Schools (Focus on Research)," *Language Arts 70*/4 (Apr 1993): 297-303. [EJ 461 021] Illustrates the concerns and problems that two teachers have tackled and are currently addressing as they change their teaching to an integrated language program. Considers issues and dilemmas that emerge when teachers begin to share power with their students. Covers some parallel power issues that arise in the collaboration between university-based and school-based teacher researchers.

Pappas, Christina C., and others, "An Integrated Language Perspective in the Elementary School: Theory Into Action." (1990): 344 pp. [ED 315 775]
An integrated language perspective on teaching in the elementary school is outlined in this book. The text provides the theory on which the perspective is based and provides many examples of how it may be translated into practice. Chapter one provides the general principles of the integrated language perspective. Chapter two describes the characteristics of children and teachers in the integrated language classroom. Chapter three shows how to plan thematic units, while chapter four demonstrates how to implement these units by presenting eight prototypes in action at various grade levels and school settings. Chapter five provides a model of written genres and explains more about the reading and writing processes. Chapter six covers a range of "kid watching" procedures and techniques. Chapter seven goes into more detail about how to integrate language across various curricular areas. Chapter eight discusses in much greater detail many of the activities and routines mention in earlier chapters. Chapter nine deals with evaluation and accountability, while chapter ten provides suggestions for changing present programs in elementary schools along the integrated language perspective.

Pardo, Laura S., "Accommodating Diversity in the Elementary Classroom: A Look at Literature-Based Instruction in an Inner City School." (1992): 27 pp. [ED 353 575]
Examines how a teacher accommodated diversity in a fifth-grade classroom in an inner-city school during a 2-year project involving literature-based reading instruction with small student-led response groups called Book Clubs. The Book Club project operated in the classroom using the four components of literacy instruction—reading, writing, discussion, and instruction. The teacher took field notes three or four times per week and kept a personal journal. Some groups were audio-taped and video-taped, and university-based researchers took field notes on a regular basis to provide data about group activity. Four issues that arose during the 2-year study were: (1) grouping students heterogeneously so that they could function cooperatively to discuss literature; (2) choosing appropriate literature, in terms of reading level, interest level, and availability; (3) giving students a voice in this process as the teacher struggled to help students take ownership of the learning process; and (4) working around the constraints of teaching in a public school system. Findings suggest that accommodating the diversity in the students by dealing with these issues as they arose brought successful literacy experiences to many of the students during their year in Book Club.

Parker, Margaret, and Juan Barroso VIII, "Strategies for Teaching and Testing Reading," *Hispania 69/*3 (Sep 1986): 720-22. [EJ 344 010]
Describes a method of intensive guided reading instruction in a second language which reduces frustration, ensures success, and implements the processes of reading instruction set forth by Kenneth Goodman and elaborated by others.

Partridge, M. Elizabeth, and others, "The Effects of Daily Opportunities To Draw and Write on Kindergarten Children's Ability To Represent Phonemes in their Spelling Inventions," paper presented at the Annual Meeting of the National Association for the Education of Young Children (Denver, CO, Nov 7-9, 1991). [ED 341 482]
This quasi-experimental study measured the effects of daily opportunities to draw and write on kindergarten children's ability to represent phonemes in their spelling inventions. All students involved in the study had previously been tested using the Gesell School Readiness Screening Test and placed in developmentally appropriate kindergarten programs. A total of 88 kindergarteners in 4 classes (2 developmentally younger and 2 developmentally older) participated in the study. Children in the experimental groups received daily opportunities to draw and write, while those in the control group received weekly opportunities. During the study, both treatment and both

control groups continued their regular program of study: a Whole Language approach which included shared-book activities, language experience activities, and exposure to the writing process. Results indicated that kindergarten students' daily participation in discussions about books, and in language and writing activities, was effective in enhancing their phonemic representations in spelling inventions. When compared with kindergarten children who participated in writing activities only once a week, subjects in the experimental group who wrote daily scored significantly higher in their invented spelling ability.

Partridge, Susan, "Whole Language and the Learning Disabled." (1991): 16 pp. [ED 337 748]
There is much more to a learning disabled (LD) child's successful learning than part-to-whole or whole-to-part instruction. Among the many factors to be considered are his/her learning style, interests, abilities, aptitudes, health, and parental support. Instructional programs for learning disabled children should be based on the students' uniqueness just as it should be for all other children. Educators should be aware of the research done with LD children and should challenge any findings which are not found to be so in their experience with LD children. Parental support should be sought and successes should be shared with colleagues. Experience with children of all ages shows that in order to include all children, teachers must beware of letting the instructional pendulum swing too far in any one direction. There is a place for both whole-to-part and part-to-whole instruction for LD students, as those students favoring Whole Language instruction can profit by some part-to-whole instruction and those favoring part-to-whole instruction can profit by some Whole Language instruction.

Pathways of Language Development. (Hawthorn, Victoria: Australian Council for Educational Research, 1990): 251 pp. [ED 325 849]
Prepared by teachers for teachers, this practical classroom guide offers a process of monitoring language development and planning for development within a Whole Language framework, supported by a compendium of appropriate practice to be drawn on when needed. The guide (1) emphasizes the interdependence of reading, writing, talking, and listening; (2) highlights the close similarities between learning to talk and learning to write and read; (3) emphasizes the complex process of language development; (4) demonstrates that monitoring and assessment of each student's language development can be a natural part of classroom management; (5) suggests ways of observing and evaluating students' development, recording and analyzing data and planning appropriate learning; and (6) provides support for teachers in describing students' progress in language development for communicating with other teachers, students, and parents. The guide's framework offers a useful way of looking at Whole Language through five interdependent strands which serve to organize the range of indicators of language development, most of which represent more than one of the four major modes of reading, writing, talking, and listening. The guide is designed so that teachers can adapt it for use with their classes or individual students, in accordance with their own organizational and teaching styles.

Patterson, Leslie, ed., and others, "Teachers Are Researchers: Reflection and Action." (Newark, Delaware: International Reading Association,1993): 242 pp. [ED 356 452]
Focuses on the language-arts teacher/researcher; offers a testament to teachers' expanding participation in collecting data and building theories about teaching, learning, curriculum, and assessment. Contents: "Reflection, Inquiry, Action" (Leslie Patterson and Patrick Shannon); "Historical Perspectives" (Katherine P. McFarland and John C. Stansell); "Finding and Framing a Research Question" (Ruth Shagoury Hubbard and Brenda Miller Power); "Hard Questions about Teacher Research" (Marne

B. Isakson and Robert M. Boody); "Meeting the Challenge of Research in the Elementary Classroom" (Karen Smith); "Learning through Whole Language: Exploring Book Selection and Use with Preschoolers" (Jean Anne Clyde and others); "Living through War Vicariously with Literature" (Caryl G. Crowell); "Talking and Thinking: Making What We Read Ours" (Adele Fiderer); "Sow a Thought, Reap an Action" (Jan Hancock); "A Look at the Process" (Mary Ann Nocerino); "Renewing Inspiration through Research" (Carol Minnick Santa); "Finding a Voice: One Girl's Journey" (Phillis E. Whitin); "A Case Study of a Writer" (Katie Wood); "A Year with Reading Workshop" (Dawn M. Cline); "What Students' Written Reflections Reveal about Literacy" (Kathleen Stumpf Jongsma); "Into the Woods: The Impact of Prereading Activities" (Lee Patton); "Connecting to the Classics" (Jeanine S. Hirtle); "Teacher and Student Perceptions of the Value of the Computer for Writing" (Mari M. McLean and Christine M. Gibson); "Teacher Research for Teacher Educators" (Kathy G. Short); "Explorations in Reflective Practice" (Diane Stephens and Kathryn Meyer Reimer); "The Importance of Reflection in Decision-Making" (Laura G. Heichel and Tristan M. Miller); "Promoting Reflection through Dialogue Journals" (Sharon Lee and Nancy T. Zuercher); "Collaboration and Inquiry in a Teacher-Education Classroom" (Kathryn Mitchell Pierce); and "Passing on the Joy of Literacy: Students Become Writing Teachers."

Patterson, Retie Y., "Implementing an Integrated Approach to Reading To Develop Critical Thinking Skills among a Group of First Graders." (Nova University, 1992): 143 pp. [ED 348 659]
The practicum reported in this paper addressed the high percentage of children receiving below average grades in an average first- grade reading comprehension class by implementing an integrated approach to reading. Various screening devices, a survey of kindergarten teachers, the Dolch Basic Sight Word Test, the Analytical Reading Inventory (Woods and Move, 1985), the Health Reading Level Test (D. C. Health, 1989), and an Interest Inventory (Miller, 1978) were employed to discern specific behaviors among the children. Based upon these findings a Literature Based Instruction classroom was organized and implemented to provide relevant learning strategies and experiences. The children were exposed to an active constructive process. It required them to think before, during, and after reading, a process that involved the interaction of the reader, the material being read and the content of the material. The results indicated a significant achievement level for the target group. It was concluded that children can be introduced to the world of reading by way of an invitation to join in the sheer joy of playing with the gift of language. If, in the real world, reading, writing, speaking, and listening are highly integrated activities, then the literacy activities that take place in classrooms should be similarly integrated.

Paulet, Robert O., "The Whole Language Approach: Will It be Used in Quebec and Manitoba?" *English Quarterly 17/4* (win 1984): 30-36. [EJ 316 569]
Explains the Whole Language teaching strategy. Shows what to expect in classrooms of Whole Language advocates. Describes curriculum guides based on the approach.

Paulin, Mary Ann, "The Teacher-Librarian and Whole Language Programs," in "School Libraries in a Diverse World: Providing the Personal Touch. Proceedings of the Annual Conference of the International Association of School Librarianship (20th, Everett, Washington, Jul 22-27, 1991)." (1992): 235 pp. [ED 350 005]

Pearson, P. David, "Reading the Whole-Language Movement," *Elementary School Journal 90/2* (Nov 1989): 231-41. [EJ 404 270]
Characterizes the Whole Language movement in terms of its philosophical, political, and curriculum assumptions and consequences. Praises the movement for the good it

has done; points out problematic features of the movement; evaluates the likely legacy of the movement.

Peck, Jackie, "Reader Stance: Whose Choice Is It?" paper presented at the Annual Meeting of the National Reading Conference (42nd, San Antonio, Texas, Dec 2-5, 1992,) Texas, 1992, 13 pp. [ED 353 574]
A recurring theme within the prolific body of research on reader response is that of reader stance. Although several prominent theories of reader response spr from different perspectives, they share one common property: Each describes reader response in terms of two opposed domains with particular responses falling somewhere on a continuum between them. A composite of three models offers the shared features of each model appearing at the poles of the continuum. Efferent reading, the participant role, and interpersonal context all share public rather than personal tendencies and lean toward convergence of thought. Aesthetic reading, the spectator role, and intrapersonal context share personal and divergent qualities. Ironically, this composite configuration of similarities among theories also reveals a most glaring confusion of terminology. In Whole Language classrooms, reading focuses on authentic whole texts which nurtures development of aesthetic stance; conversely, instruction that overemphasizes attention to surface features such as letter/sound correspondence impedes its development. The impact of teacher questioning on students responding implies the need for cautious examination of current practice to develop informed practice. Open-ended questions engender deep, personal connections between reader, writer (the text), and the rich social context of the classroom.

Peetoom, Adrian, "Whole Language and the Bible," *Language Arts 66/3* (Mar 1989): 318-22. [EJ 386 903]
Argues that the Bible should be reinstated as an elementary school text, and that while doing so is controversial, it is compatible with a Whole Language approach to teaching.

Pesce, Regina T., "First Grade Reading Instruction: Current Trends in the Northern Valley Regional District." (1990): 52 pp. [ED 320 118]
A study was conducted to determine the current trends in reading materials and methods used to teach first grade students to read in the Northern Valley Region of Bergen County, New Jersey. Twenty-one first grade teachers responded to a survey which consisted of open-ended questions asking about goals and incentives, multiple choice questions on demographics, and questions on the kinds of teaching materials commonly found in primary classrooms. Results indicated a moving away from using the traditional basal and phonics program toward a Whole Language approach. Another trend is that those who have been teaching less than 10 years are more likely to use a Whole Language approach, as are teachers with more education. Results also showed that the majority of reading materials and methods are chosen by the teacher and that administrators who get involved in choosing reading materials usually choose basal and phonic programs. The paper concludes with recommendations made to administrators and teachers on the basis of this research.

Phillips, Laura A., "'Weaving a Web' of Literacy: A One-Year Evaluation of the Implementation of a Literature-Based Whole Language Approach," paper presented at the Annual Meeting of the American Reading Forum (11th, Sarasota, FL, Dec 12-15, 1990). [ED 327 840]
A study investigated the effectiveness of a program to improve the reading/vocabulary skills of an ability-grouped fifth grade class of "low achievers" (N=15) through the implementation of a literature-based Whole Language approach. Students were read aloud to from quality children's literature. From these books, spelling and vocabulary

lists were developed and administered 30 minutes a day, 4 days a week during the scheduled classroom reading period. By means of a thematic web, additional skills and subject matter were interwoven so as to provide students with a less fragmented curriculum. The Iowa Tests of Basic Skills were administered in the spring prior to the program and again in the spring of the following year. Results indicated gains of: (1) one year and four months in vocabulary; (2) one year and five months in reading; and (3) seven months in spelling. While the positive statistical findings related to the project were encouraging, the classroom teacher was much more excited by the day-to-day response from the students. For the first time, this group of "low achievers" became aware of the function of print, the nature of written language, and the structure of narrative text. They began to value books, independently selected books appropriate for their reading level, and were eager to share books with each other and the teacher.

Phillis, Debra L., "The Teacher as "Enabler": Heterogeneous Whole Language and Self-Esteem." (1991): 15 pp. [ED 348 688]
A teacher who had directed a K-12 language arts program at the Alamo Navajo Reservation in Magdalena, New Mexico employed problem-solving skills that involved the affective domain as well as the sensory-motor areas important to education even in older children. This teacher's classrooms are heterogeneously grouped. A thematic approach is used across the curriculum to learn through language. Third- and sixth-grade students write across the curriculum: spelling, reading skills, math, and language arts texts are integrated to complement the social studies curriculum, for example. Reading, reflection, and revision play an important role in the writing process approach used in the classroom. Oral exercises include "raps" made with spelling words, and reading aloud utilizing "beat" techniques. Groups of students follow developmental progression, and an interactive, thematic approach to multicultural literature insures affective/cognitive development. Various research indicates that it is by hearing written language read aloud that the emergent reader-writer constructs surface structure. Group reading and writing projects should include creative parallel activities that involve motor skills. Working in small groups, students read and write with reflection, integrating concepts as they move towards a larger understanding.

Piazza, Stephen, and Charles Suhor, comps., "Trends and Issues in English Instruction, 1990—Six Summaries. Summaries of Informal Annual Discussions of the Commissions of the National Council of Teachers of English." (1990): 15 pp. [ED 315 793]
Information on current trends and issues in English instruction, compiled by the directors of six National Council of Teachers of English commissions, is presented in this report, the seventh annual report by the commissions. The commissions and their directors are as follows: (1) Reading Commission (Constance Weaver); (2) Commission on Literature (John Pfordresher); (3) Commission on Media (William V. Costanzo); (4) Commission on Composition (Sharon Crowley); (5) Commission on Language (Jesse Perry); and (6) Commission on Curriculum (Linda Shadiow). Some of the subjects discussed in the document include Whole Language, concerns about the widespread increase of legislative actions regarding teaching, narrow concepts of literacy, the literary canon, literature instruction and evaluation, the dangers of "performance goals," teacher education, teacher as researcher projects, the role and use of mass media and new technologies in the classroom, writing assessment and the politics thereof, language arts textbooks and their assumptions about teaching and learning, the use of computers in the classroom, ability grouping, and local curriculum development.

Piazza, Stephen, and Charles Suhor, comps., "Trends and Issues in English Instruction, 1991. Reports on Informal Annual Discussions of the Commissions of the National Council of Teachers of English." (1991): 25 pp. [ED 335 699]
Information on current trends and issues in English instruction, compiled by the directors of six National Council of Teachers of English commissions, is presented in this report, the eighth annual report by the commissions. The commissions and their directors represented in the report are: (1) Commission on Reading (Patrick Shannon); (2) Commission on Composition (Sharon Crowley); (3) Commission on Language (Jesse Perry); (4) Commission on Literature (John Pfordresher); (5) Commission on Curriculum (Richard Adler); and (6) Commission on Media (Barbra Morris). Some of the subjects discussed in the report include concerns about the widespread increase of legislative actions regarding teaching, narrow concepts of literacy, current teaching practices in literature classrooms at all levels, cultural literacy and how it impedes the acquisition of literacy, writing instruction as a political act, the misuse of the term "Whole Language," appropriate use of computers in English classrooms, changing approaches to evaluation and assessment, active learning, teacher education, media education, media use in the schools, writing assessment and the politics thereof, language arts textbooks, the use of computers in the classroom, ability grouping, and local curriculum development.

Pickering, C. Thomas, "Whole Language: A New Signal for Expanding Literacy," *Reading Improvement 26/2* (sum 1989): 144-49. [EJ 398 843]
Describes "Whole Language" as a new term for literacy instruction that emphasizes application of reading and writing in meaningful contexts. Argues that the theoretical base for Whole Language is closely related to key ideas of language experience and psycholinguistics, but that Whole Language represents a new paradigm.

Pils, Linda J., "Soon Anofe You Tout Me: Evaluation in a First-Grade Whole Language Classroom," *Reading Teacher 45/1* (Sep 1991): 46-50. [EJ 431 098]
Presents a variety of literacy evaluation strategies devised and implemented by a teacher who is making the transition to Whole Language.

Pinnell, Gay Su, "Reading Recovery: Helping At-Risk Children Learn to Read," *Elementary School Journal 90/2* (Nov 1989): 161-83. [EJ 404 265]
Describes the implementation and evaluation of an early intervention program, Reading Recovery, designed to help young, at-risk children become writers. Research evaluation results in New Zealand and in the United States and a case study of a five-year-old child are presented.

Piper, Terry, and George Labercane, "Mutual Negotiation and the Teaching of Writing in a Multicultural Setting," *Journal of Teaching Writing 9/1* (spr-sum 1990): 11-20. [EJ 424 318]
Argues that teachers can help students develop writing competence by stressing social aspects of language and learning. Describes the mutual teacher/student negotiation observed in two elementary schools. Shows that student writing can improve through the creation of a community of children supportive of one another's language efforts.

Platt, John S. and others, "Understanding and Educating Migrant Students," *Preventing School Failure 36/1* (fall 1991): 41-46. [EJ 444 507]
Describes characteristics of migrant students that place them at risk educationally and reasons for low special- education delivery rates are examined. Offers guidelines for educational intervention, with the goal of increasing migrant children's economic options and opportunities. Recommends three methodologies: learning strategies, cooperative learning, and Whole Language.

Polin, Linda, "The Other Half of Whole Language," *Writing Notebook: Creative Word Processing in the Classroom 8/2* (Nov-Dec 1990): 32-33. [EJ 418 110]
Notes that the "other half" of Whole Language is the enjoyment of expressed meaning, speaking and listening, and performing and experiencing performance. Describes interactive multimedia technology that can provide opportunities for students to experience theater and poetry as audiovisual productions.

Pollack, Hilary L., "Veteran Teachers and Whole Language Instruction," *Journal of the Wisconsin State Reading Association 35/1* (win 1991): 37-41. [EJ 429 708]
Describes the positive experiences of veteran teachers who have switched from basal reading to the Whole Language approach.

Pomerance, Anita, "A Collaborative Adult Literacy Training Workshop for Tutors and Students: The Student-Tutor Orientation. Center for Literacy, Inc., Philadelphia, PA. (1990): 29 pp. [ED 324 469]
A pilot tutor training project, the Student-Tutor Orientation (STO), was designed to meet the need for making Whole-Language concepts of reading and writing instruction accessible to tutors as well as students through hands-on experience and for establishing a collaborative tutoring relationship in which students share in decision making. Together, tutors and students at a literacy program in a large Northeastern city learned the new concepts and strategies such as the language experience method. Use of materials relating to student goals and interests was emphasized, with instruction on how to make difficult but interesting texts accessible through such strategies as student listening and duet reading. Writing was stressed from the beginning, using invented spelling if necessary. After a year's use, in which 11 STOs were given and 97 tutor-student pairs trained, the approach seems to be superior to the agency's former training methods in several respects. Retention of tutors after training and hours of service surpassed those of a comparable series of the Center for Literacy's training a year ago. Tutors expressed increased confidence, and tutors and students reported more goal-related materials used and more writing done. Staff members requested STOs for their areas, stating that they felt the STOs produced better tutoring. Students were enthusiastic about their progress and their gains in self-esteem.

Prenn, Maureen C., and Patricia A. Scanlan, "Teaching as We Are Taught: A Model for Whole Language Inservice," *Reading Horizons 31/3* (Feb 1991): 189-98. [EJ 421 219]
Explains that five characteristics of a Whole Language environment (time, ownership, process, conferences, and resources) affect teachers' and students' experiences in a Whole Language inservice course.

Prillaman, Susan, "Whole Language and Its Effect on the School Library Media Center," *North Carolina Libraries 50/3* (fall 1992): 161-64. [EJ 453 248]
Examines the evolution of the Whole Language curriculum, its current theory and practices, and its effect on the school library media center. The similarity between Whole Language and the Montessori approach to literacy is discussed, and the role of the media specialist in a Whole Language library media center is described.

Project G.L.A.D. A Program of Academic Excellence. Language Acquisition to Literacy in a Multilingual Setting." (1991): 57 pp. [ED 340 219]
Project GLAD (Guided Language Acquisition Design), a model of inservice teacher training in which teachers learn to modify instruction to promote acquisition of English as a Second Language, is outlined. The model uses the Whole Language approach to language learning. Its development was guided by research in Whole Language theory; integration of content and language within the curriculum; the role of the first language in learning; the value of culture; second language acquisition; neurological organiza-

tion and brain hemisphere functions; effective reading and writing instruction; classroom environment; heterogeneous instructional grouping; and language functional environment. The teacher training is accomplished with a team of two instructors who model peer coaching. Instruction includes several days of training in theory and research, observation of demonstration lessons each day for one week, a week of classroom practice, feedback and coaching, and the opportunity for further instruction to become a trainer.

PROUD Adult Readers 1-4. People Reading Their Own Unique Dictations [and] A Guide for Teachers and Tutors." (1992): 129 pp. [ED 353 403]

Consists of a guide for teachers and tutors and four "readers" for adults. These readers are intended to eliminate the problems associated with book-centered, one-to-one tutoring, such as the following: (1) uninteresting, irrelevant materials focusing on single reading skills rather than reading as communication; (2) materials that lack learner-centered activities; or (3) materials that reinforce low self-worth attitudes. The guide explains the purpose of the readers and has sections on language experience, choosing the appropriate reader, and the use of the readers. It also offers points to remember when using the readers and suggests other uses for the material. Each of the four books consists of stories and follow-up activities designed to teach reading to adult students. The stories, written by students using the language experience ap-proach, range from a few sentences to a few pages. Skill exercises presented after each story include fill-in-the-word, word and plural formation, word search, and compre-hension questions. Stories are illustrated with cartoons. The materials are progressively more challenging, so that the teacher can select the appropriate level for each student or may start the student in book one and progress from book to book.

Pryor, Elizabeth Gibbons, "Whole Language Rhetoric: Clarifying Misconceptions," *Ohio Reading Teacher 25*/1 (fall 1990): 15-22. [EJ 432 646]

Explores four misconceptions about the Whole Language approach; attempts to replace them by grounded realities associated with Whole Language.

Quintero, Elizabeth, and Ana Huerta-Macias, "All in the Family: Bilingualism and Biliteracy," *Reading Teacher 44*/4 (Dec 1990): 306-12. [EJ 418 093]

Discusses the goals of Project Family Initiative for English Literacy (FIEL) and the rationale for the model on which it is based. Describes the curriculum and the content of the five-step lessons. Provides an example of one family's literacy growth within the project.

Rabin, Annette T., "Selecting Literature for the Whole Language Classroom: What Factors Should We Consider?" paper presented at the Annual Meeting of the International Reading Association (36th, Las Vegas, NV, May 6-10, 1991). [ED 334 553]

Although Whole Language teachers say they no longer consider readability evaluation (in the sense of measuring word and sentence length) in the selection of literature for their classrooms, they do have criteria for matching the readers or prospective readers in their classroom to literary materials. Teachers in Whole Language classrooms see the following factors as being important to the readability of the literature which they select: (1) print size; (2) illustrations; (3) repetition; (4) vocabulary; (5) predictability; and (6) interest. Nonfiction reading materials can also be evaluated for typographic clues (bold type or italics), presence of graphs and charts, and a variety of other aids to comprehension and clarity.

Rafferty, Cathleen D., and others, "Developing a Reading/Writing Curriculum for At-Risk High School Students" paper presented at the Annual Meeting of the National Reading Conference (41st, Palm Springs, CA, Dec 3-7, 1991). [ED 343 087]

A study analyzed teacher and student perceptions of a literature-based reading/writing curriculum for at-risk high school students. Eighteen students, (3 girls, 15 boys) ranging in age from 15 to 18 years, began English 9, a redesigned one-semester literature-based make-up course for students who failed ninth-grade English. Prior to the study, the course consisted of repeating the same kind of instruction that resulted in student failure in the regular classroom. Eight students were interviewed mid-way through the second semester. Data also included field notes and interviews with teachers concerning courses taken after the students completed the make-up course. Results indicated that although students had been placed in English 9 for various reasons, almost all responded favorably to the redesigned curriculum, which used a literature-based reading/writing approach taught in a relaxed and democratic classroom atmosphere. Most English 9 students and their subsequent English teachers concurred that through these means, the students had acquired both the motivation and literacy skills necessary to succeed in the academic school environment.

Raines, Shirley C., and Robert J. Canady, "Story Stretchers for the Primary Grades: Activities To Expand Children's Favorite Books." (Mr. Rainier, Maryland: Gryphon House,1992): 257 pp. [ED 355 469]
Third in a series of "story stretchers," means to extend children's enthusiasm for stories and to better connect children's books and teaching ideas with other areas of the curriculum. The book contains 18 units or themes with 5 focus books per unit. Each focus book has read-aloud suggestions for the book and five story stretchers per book. Thus, there are 90 read-aloud suggestions and 450 story stretchers for 90 different children's books. For each of the book's 18 themes, the books selected are "stretched" into different centers, activities and areas of the curriculum, including art, creative dramatics, games, classroom library, mathematics, music and movement, science and nature, special projects, special events and the writing center. The units, or themes, are as follows: (1) I am Me, I am Special, Look What I Can Do!; (2) Families; (3) Friends; (4) Feelings; (5) Celebrations; (6) I Care about My World, the Environment; (7) Weather; (8) Machines and Things; (9) Animal Life; (10) Life in the Sea, Real and Imagined; (11) Pets, Dogs, and Cats; (12) Another Time and Place; (13) Native American Legends and Folktales from Other Countries; (14) Mysteries, Secrets and Adventures; (15) Bears in Tall Tales, Funny Tales, Stories and Poems; (16) Fun with Words; (17) Poems, Chants, Rhythms and Rhymes; and (18) Tall and Funny, Funny Tales.

Raines, Shirley C., "Professional Books," *Childhood Education 67/3* (spr 1991): 194-97. [EJ 430 355]
Reviews (1) A Middle School Curriculum from Rhetoric to Reality, by James A. Beane; (2) Enquiring Teachers, Enquiring Learners, by Catherine Twomey Fosnet; (3) How Children Construct Literacy, Yetta M. Goodman, ed.; (4) The New Literacy, by John Willinsky; and (5) The Everyday Guide to Opening and Operating a Child Care Center, by Daniel F. Kingsbury and others.

Ramsey, Wallace, "Infusing Clinical Reading Instruction with Whole Language," paper presented at the Annual Meeting of the National Reading and Language Arts Educators' Conference (2nd, Kansas City, MO, Sep 27-28, 1985). [ED 266 411]
Emphasizes a Whole Language approach in the reading clinic at the University of Missouri (St. Louis) because disabled readers need to practice their skills simultaneously in speaking, listening, and reading. At the clinic, teachers are encouraged to learn and use several approaches to teaching reading. However, the language experience approach is emphasized because it is the least known by graduate students. Teachers encourage children to share real experiences, as well as vicarious ones, and

then stimulate thorough oral discussion of any shared experience before attempting to recreate a real story. The child's story is recorded in standard English, without attaching labels of correctness or incorrectness. Follow-up activities are designed to improve more specific skills. A balanced approach to word recognition is taken, with the use of context, sight words, phonics, and morpheme analysis emphasized in proportion to their usefulness in reading and to the child's particular learning style. Teachers report a positive jump in the level of interest in reading and a marked increase in willingness to participate, with measurable and significant growth recorded for most children.

Ramsey, Cynthia, ed., and Trinidad Lopez, eds., "ESL: The Whole Person Approach." (1989): 151 pp. [ED 311 738]
Provides a model for training teachers of limited English proficient (LEP) students of Hispanic origins to eliminate sex bias in English-as-a-Second-Language (ESL) materials and teaching approaches. Although the guide aims primarily at the educational and personal empowerment of LEP Hispanic girls, it is also intended to assist in removing sex bias from the bilingual multicultural curricula in which ESL is taught to both female and male Hispanic students. The guide may also be used as a model for developing materials and activities suitable for use with other racial, ethnic, or linguistic groups. An introductory section describes the purpose, goals and objectives, target population, and defines ESL. Part 1 consists of three essays on multicultural education, a humanistic approach to language teaching for sex equity, and feminism in this cultural context (Chicana feminism). The second part outlines two workshops. The first workshop provides an orientation to the component parts of the Whole Person Approach to ESL teacher training, and includes 12 related activities. The second workshop familiarizes participants with criteria for the Whole Person Approach to ESL, and includes four activities.

Raphael, Taffy E., and Cynthia H. Brock, "Mei: Learning the Literacy Culture in an Urban Elementary School," paper presented at the Annual Meeting of the National Reading Conference (42nd, San Antonio, TX, Dec 2-5, 1992). [ED 352 611]
A case study described Mei, a second-language learner from Vietnam, in terms of her participation in a literature-based reading instructional program, Book Club. The context of the case study was an urban neighborhood K-5 school in a large midwestern city district. Data were collected about Mei from third through fifth grades using reading logs, journal entries, audio- and video-tapes of Mei's Book Clubs, field notes, and interviews with Mei, her teachers, and her family. Three target Book Clubs representative of the entire data set were selected and analyzed. Results indicated that: (1) the amount of Mei's participation increased from a fifth of the overall contributions in her fourth grade four-member Book Club, to a third of the overall contributions in her five-member Book Club during the spring of fifth grade; (2) there was an increase in Mei's self-confidence, in terms of increased initiations of new topics and persistence in getting her topics discussed by her peers; and (3) changes in substantive features of Mei's discourse over time were shown in both the increased depth and level of her comments. Findings suggest that Book Club is a valuable social context for second language learners to experience meaningful and authentic opportunities to learn to use academic discourse to discuss texts.

Raphael, Taffy E., and others, "Teaching Literacy through Student Book Clubs: A First-Year Teacher's Experience. Elementary Subjects Center Series No. 41." (1991): 33 pp. [ED 336 743]
Describes the experience of a fourth- and fifth-grade, first-year teacher's participation in the Book Club Project of the Center for the Learning and Teaching of Elementary

Subjects. The Book Club included the use of high-quality children's literature, opportunities for response to literature in multiple ways, and instruction that focused on different ways to develop an appreciation for experiences with literature. The paper first describes the four components that make up the Book Club program: reading, writing, discussion (i.e., student-led small-group and whole-class), and instruction. Focuses on a 6-week folktale unit, using the unit as the context for discussing the issues faced by the teacher in moving toward a literature-based instructional approach, the needs of the students, and how their instructional support helped facilitate their growth with both comprehension strategy use and with response to the literature they read. Students' growth is described in terms of "what to share" during their student-led discussions and "how to share it." Transcripts of students' small group discussions or Book Clubs are used to provide a window into their interactions around the literature selections read, while samples of students' writing and drawings are used to reflect individual responses. In addition, transcripts and writing samples are used to describe progress in question-asking, seeking clarification, overall participation, use of personal experiences, and links to other texts.

Rasinski, Timothy V., "Holistic Approaches to the Remediation of Difficulties in Reading Fluency." (1989): 12 pp. [ED 314 720]
Holistic approaches to remedial reading can be effective in promoting the reading growth of poor readers. Learning to read is most effective when it occurs in a context of functional and meaningful literacy activity. In order to create such a context students need to be engaged with real texts in a search for meaning. Repeated readings, taped readings, the Neurological Impress Method, and phrase-cued texts help readers deal with real texts. Each of these approaches, and variations and combinations that can be developed by creative and insightful teachers, offer remedial teachers proven techniques for developing fluency in holistic and meaningful ways.

Rasinski, Timothy V., ed., and others, "Reading Is Knowledge: Thirteenth Yearbook of the College Reading Association, 1991." Kansas: College Reading Association, 1991
This 1991 yearbook contains five sections: (1) Knowing about College and Adult Literacy; (2) Knowing about Home and Community Literacy; (3) Knowing about Literacy Instruction; (4) Knowing about Teacher Education in Literacy; (5) and Knowing about Teacher Education in the Content Areas. Contents: "Program Evaluation: The Politics of Developmental Reading" (Donna L. Mealey); "Do College Students Who Plan before Writing Score Better on Essay Exams?" (M. K. Gills and Mary W. Olson); "College Students' Reading Assessment: Are We Surveying or Diagnosing?" (Cindy Gillespie); "Activating Implicit Theories of Reading: A Metacognitive Approach" (M. Cecil Smith); "Language Experience in a Family Literacy Project" (Elinor P. Ross); "Home Literacy Practices of Parents Whose Children Are Enrolled in a Whole Language Kindergarten" (Timothy V. Rasinski and others); "Parental Involvement through Workshops" (Nancy B. Masztal); "Case-Based Instruction and Learning: An Interdisciplinary Project" (Marino C. Alvarez and others); "Reading Perceptions of Urban Second Graders" (Elizabeth G. Sturtevant and others); "Join the Club! A New Approach to the Traditional Reading Clinic" (Rebecca F. Carwile and Karen L. Parker); "Second Grade Urban Students' Attitudes toward Reading" (Wayne M. Linek and others); "Video-Based CASE Analysis to Enhance Teacher Preparation" (Victoria J. Risko and others); "A Descriptive Study of the Reflective Statements of Preservice Teachers" (Barbara J. Walker); "Do As I Say, Not As I Do—Teacher Education" (Linda A. Packman); "Developing a Meaningful Early Field Experience for Reading Methods Courses" (William Earl Smith); "Perceptions of Preservice and Inservice Teachers Regarding Test-Taking Procedures and Test-

Wiseness Programs" (Jerry L. Johns and Susan J. Davis); "Whole Language Collaboration Project: Three Case Studies to Represent Change" (Grace M. Shepperson and Robert J. Nistler); "Whole Language and Changing Language Arts Instruction: A National Survey" (Patricia K. Smith and others); "Theoretical Orientation of British Infant School Teachers" (Janet A. Miller); "A Model for Teaching Content Area Reading Strategies to Preservice Teachers" (Victoria G. Ridgeway and others); "Attitudes toward Teaching Reading in the Content Areas: A Correlational Study" (Cindy Gillespie and Nancy Clements); "Exchanging Places: College to High School Classroom" (Judy S. Richardson); and "Making Links: Reading across the Curriculum Workshops for Content Area Faculty" (Anne R. Friedman).

Rasinski, Timothy V., and others, "Home Literacy Practices of Parents Whose Children Are Enrolled in a Whole Language Kindergarten," paper presented at the Annual Meeting of the College Reading Association (34th, Nashville, TN, Nov 2-4, 1990). [ED 327 822]

A study focused on families whose children were successful but not exceptional students in kindergarten. Subjects were eight parents (all mothers) whose children had been enrolled the previous year in a kindergarten program that maintained a Whole Language curricular orientation. The children (four girls and four boys) were highly successful in kindergarten though none had been deemed exceptional in the progress they made in learning to read and write by the teacher, parent, or third-party observers who were part of the research team. Parents were interviewed during the two months immediately following the children's completion of kindergarten. The parents were asked a set of questions concerning their approach to literacy learning and their satisfaction with the kindergarten's holistic curriculum. Interview results indicated several home-based literacy activities including the following: reading aloud; taking dictation from child; developing interest in words, through games, etc.; writing; and providing an informal and functional literate environment. Two conclusions were drawn from the study: (1) the home literacy activities described are similar to those described in that work and tend to validate the conclusions derived from previous work; and (2) the literacy activities in the home were highly congruent with those found in the Whole Language kindergarten.

Rastall, Peter, "Whole Language and Phonetic Spelling," *Reading Improvement 30*/1 (spr 1993): 35-40. [EJ 462 354]

Describes a phonetic spelling scheme called "Rational Spelling" that is claimed to be easy to learn and use, and that could be used to encourage students to read and write freely at an early age.

Raupp, Magda, and others, "Key Strokes: A Guidebook for Teaching Writing with Computers." (1987): 83 pp. [ED 333 761]

This guide is the result of three projects that have been working to address the problem of intergenerational illiteracy in writing. While writing skills are limited among the general population, they are even more limited among limited-English-speaking students (both school-aged and adult learners). The guidebook is a self-help manual for teachers interested in helping such students write better. The guide offers ideas on how to help students manage the writing process; provides strategies for helping students generate ideas, develop audience awareness, and compose; and gives hints on encouraging students to revise papers they have already begun. The guide provides general information on the writing process as well as specific suggestions, examples, strategies, and procedures for an effective writing program. An introductory section provides an overview of research findings in writing. Implications for teaching writing are examined in section II. Subsequent sections focus on aspects of writing instruction.

Reeves-Kazelskis, Carolyn, and Richard Kazelskis, "Effects of an Expanded Language Experience Approach on Oral Cloze Performance of Kindergarteners," paper presented at the Annual Meeting of the Mid-South Educational Research Association (Little Rock, AR, Nov 7-11, 1989). [ED 312 615]
A study explored the effects of an expanded Language Experience Approach (LEA) on listening comprehension skills of kindergarteners. During a 2-year period, two exerpiments were conducted with different groups of kindergarteners. The second experiment replicated the first experiment and was conducted to determine if an expanded LEA would produce different effects with kindergarteners who were more representative of the population than were those in the first experiment. In both experiments, the experimental (expanded LEA) and the control (traditional LEA) conditions were implemented by the same two teachers. A total of 44 kindergarteners were involved in the first experiment (22 experimental and 22 control) and a total of 47 kindergarteners were involved in the second experiment (23 experimental and 24 control). The two LEA conditions differed only in the kinds of follow-up activities associated with each of the conditions. The results of both experiments favored the use of an expanded LEA. The oral cloze results of experiment 1 revealed significant differences between the experimental and control groups on beginning ($p<.05$), medial ($p<.01$), and total cloze ($p<.01$) scores. In experiment 2, the experimental and control groups differed significantly ($p<.05$) on beginning, medial, and total cloze scores. Significant differences in final cloze scores of the experimental and control groups were not found in either of the experiments. Results indicated that the use of an expanded LEA is likely to be more effective than the traditional LEA in facilitating development of listening comprehension skills.

Reiff, Judith C., *Learning Styles. What Research Says to the Teacher series.* (Washington, D.C.: National Education Association,1992): 42 pp. [ED 340 506]
Reviews several approaches for describing learning styles and the instructional implications of an emphasis on learning styles for teachers. Several reasons for the importance of understanding individual learning styles are provided; such understanding leads to: (1) reduction of teacher and student frustration; (2) higher student achievement and an improved self-concept; (3) accommodation of a variety of learners in a classroom; (4) the versatility that is crucial to learning; and (5) improved communication with administrators, parents, counselors, and other staff. Cognitive, affective, and physiological learning styles are considered. Approaches for describing cognitive styles include brain theories, conceptual tempo, field dependence/field independence, mind styles, modalities, and multiple intelligences. Approaches for describing affective styles include conceptual systems theory and psychological types. Finally, approaches for describing physiological styles revolve around elements of learning styles which have been classified into four kinds of stimuli: environmental, emotional, sociological, and physical. Six approaches for incorporating instruction that takes learning styles into account in the classroom are: (1) pedagogical intelligence; (2) Carol Hall's Living Classroom; (3) Whole Language; (4) Foxfire activities; (5) the 4MAT System; and (6) the DICSIE (Describe, Interact, Control, Select, Instruct, Evaluate) Model. Concludes that teachers pass through several stages in their understanding of children's learning styles, and emphasizes that administrative support, staff development, peer coaching, parent education, and personal determination and commitment are crucial in a positive learning styles classroom.

Reimer, Kathryn Meyer, "Literature Based Classrooms: Three Perspectives. Draft," paper presented at the Annual Meeting of the National Reading Conference (40th, Miami, FL, Nov 27-Dec 1, 1990.) [ED 350 576]

A study attempted to delineate the parameters of practice that are referred to as literature-based reading instruction and explored the perspectives of the teacher, the students, and the researcher about the use of literature in three different literature-based classrooms. Six teachers (third grade or above) were identified, teachers who were highly respected within their systems, had a number of years of teaching experience, and used literature as the basis for their reading programs. Three of the teachers were part of the field testing of interviews, surveys, videotaping, and document data collection, data analysis, and pattern confirmation. The other three teachers' classrooms became the sites for more intensive observation, interviewing, and analysis. Results indicated that three anchoring points existed on the spectrum of classroom practice in literature-based instruction: (1) literature used as the text in a basal curriculum; (2) literature as the basis for an individualized reading program; and (3) literature as the key to integrating the curriculum throughout the day. Results also indicated that students took on the language of the teacher and seemed to move toward the teacher's perception of what was occurring in the room. Findings suggest that it was the power, control, and autonomy the teachers sensed they had that freed them to use literature—and to differ widely from each other in their use of literature.

Renegar, Sandra L., "Reading and Music: Take Note." (1986): 9 pp. [ED 315 735]
Music can exert a positive effect on a reading program both in complementary skill development and as a means of forcing task attention. These positive effects have been documented in research. Both music and reading require skills such as auditory and visual discrimination, reception, and association; eye-motor coordination; interpreta-.tion; word meanings in and out of context; and language reception. The integration of music and reading provides an excellent instrument for the Whole Language approach. Thus, music is a natural ally of the reading teacher both as a motivational tool and a vehicle for instruction.

Reutzel, D. Ray, and Robert B. Cooter, "Whole Language: Comparative Effects on First-Grade Reading Achievement," *Journal of Educational Research 83/5* (May-Jun 1990): 252-57. [EJ 414 234]
Results of this study supported the belief that Whole Language strategies and routines used in first-grade classrooms will yield scores on traditional standardized achievement tests of reading that are comparable or superior to those resulting from the use of basal reader programs.

Reutzel, D. Ray, and Paul M. Hollingsworth, "Whole Language and the Practitioner," *Academic Therapy 23/4* (Mar 1988): 405-16. [EJ 367 478]
The Whole Language philosophy of teaching reading and writing is outlined and related to children's acquisition of oral and written language. A typical Whole Language classroom is described, along with the roles of the teacher and students. A chart contrasts Whole Language theory with more typical methods of literacy education.

Reuys, Stephen, "A Quest for Meaning in Adult Basic Education," *Adult Learning 3/7* (May 1992): 22-23. [EJ 442 471]
A holistic philosophy that learning should be driven by a quest for meaning is manifested in adult basic education by such varied approaches as process writing, Whole Language, problem posing, alternative assessment, mathematics as problem solving and critical thinking, and family literacy.

Reyhner, Jon, ed., "Teaching American Indian Students." (1992): 366 pp. [ED 355 058]
Consists of 18 essays that discuss teaching methods and resource material promoting productive school experiences for American Indian students. The first section of the

book introduces the notion of empowerment of Indian students through multicultural education, foundations of Indian education, the history of Indian education, tribal and federal language policies, and a successful bilingual program. Section 2 discusses the importance of adapting teaching methods and curriculum to Indian culture and to the learning styles of Indian children. It also offers recommendations for promoting a positive working relationship between teachers and parents. Section 3 describes language and literacy development, the role of the first language in second language development, and the characteristics of American Indian English. Section 4 addresses the importance of Indian students' exposure to literature relevant to their culture and background. It provides suggestions for Whole Language teaching strategies, teaching strategies to enhance students' reading comprehension, and an overview of literature written by American Indians. Section 5 makes specific suggestions for teaching social studies, science, mathematics, and physical education to Indian students.

Reyhner, Jon, ed., "Teaching the Indian Child. A Bilingual/ Multicultural Approach. 2nd Edition." (1988): 331 pp. [ED 301 372]
This collection of 20 essays by 21 authors presents teaching methods and resource material promoting productive school experiences for American Indian students. The chapters are organized into five sections. The opening chapter of section 1 emphasizes that teachers must understand and respect the cultures and backgrounds of their students, an attitude essential to a bilingual and multicultural approach to Indian education. Other chapters in this section (1) outline the historical background of Indian education; (2) discuss tribal language policies and the ingredients of a successful bilingual program; and (3) examine multicultural education goals and the value of cultural relativism for minimizing ethnocentrism and eliminating racism. Section 2 (1) describes the stages of oral language development and the role of the first language in second language development; (2) provides practical suggestions for teaching English as a second language; (3) discusses necessary elements for reading comprehension; and (4) presents a Whole-Language approach to language arts. A section on teaching Indian literature discusses the inadequacies of basal reading textbooks, examines the use of storytelling in the classroom, provides a motif bibliography, and lists sources of culturally appropriate books for different grade levels. Section 4 makes specific suggestions for teaching social studies, science, mathematics, and physical education to Indian students. The final section discusses the parents' role as first teachers, a positive working relationship between parents and teachers, theories concerning self-efficacy, and means to empower Indian students.

Rhodes, Lynn K., and Curt Dudley-Marling, "Readers and Writers with a Difference: A Holistic Approach to Teaching Learning Disabled and Remedial Students." (Portsmouth, New Hampshire: Neinemann, 1988): 329 pp. [ED 293 117]
Intended for teachers of learning disabled or remedial learners at all levels, this book presents a holistic perspective on reading and writing instruction, focusing on meaningful, purposeful literacy applications. The book begins with a general discussion of learning disabled and remedial students and then introduces readers to a holistic theory of reading and writing development. This is followed by a thorough discussion of an observational approach to reading and writing assessment and a consideration of the problem of writing meaningful goals and objectives from a holistic perspective. In the main body of the book, a large number of instructional strategies that have been found successful in encouraging literacy development are provided. Contents: "Planning Instruction"; "Prereading Instruction"; "In-Process Reading Instruction"; "Post-Reading Instruction"; "Composition: Choices and Instruction"; and "Transcription: Choices and Instruction." In addition to specific instructional strategies, teachers

are encouraged to surround students with print and encourage the discovery by students that reading and writing are meaningful, purposeful, and personally worthwhile. The final chapter presents a discussion of collaboration on a literacy program with parents, teachers, and administrators. Also included is an extensive list of predictable trade books for children.

Rhodes, Lynn K., and Nancy L. Shanklin, Nancy L., "Miscue Analysis in the Classroom (Assessment)," *Reading Teacher 44*/3 (Nov 1990): 252-54. [EJ 416 393]
Discusses the procedures for using the Classroom Reading Miscue Assessment which was developed by Denver area Coordinators/Consultants Applying Whole Language to help teachers efficiently gather miscue data.

Ribowsky, Helene, "The Effects of a Code Emphasis Approach and a Whole Language Approach upon Emergent Literacy of Kindergarten Children," 28 pp. (1985). [ED 269 720]
Reports results of a year-long, quasi-experimental study investigating the comparative effects of a Whole Language approach and a code emphasis approach on the emergent literacy of 53 girls in two kindergarten classes in an all-girls parochial school in the Northeast. Subjects in the experimental class received instruction in Holdaway's Shared Book Experience Program, a Whole Language approach, while subjects in the comparison class received instruction in Lippincott's Beginning to Read, Write, and Listen Program, a code emphasis approach. Emergent literacy—the concepts about reading and writing resulting from a child's first encounters with printed material—was divided into three subsets: linguistic, orthographic, and grapho-phonemic literacy. Posttest results for each of these literacy sets indicated a significant treatment effect favoring the Whole Language group. The results corroborated Holdaway's research, which indicated a high level of success with the Shared Book Experiences in comparison with a code emphasis approach. The study showed a naturalistic learning model to be structured and viable within a school instructional environment that was informal, relaxed, and supportive.

Rich, Sharon J., "Restoring Power to Teachers: The Impact of 'Whole Language,'" *Language Arts 62*/7 (Nov 1985): 717-24. [EJ 326 518]
Explores the cooperation and resistance that teachers often encounter as they begin to use a Whole Language approach in their classrooms, and discusses Whole Language as a teaching attitude—returning the freedom of learning to students, but still with requisite responsibilities for providing students with all the options from which they may choose.

Rich, Sharon J., "Whole Language: The Inner Dimension," *English Quarterly 18*/2 (sum 1985)" 23-37. [EJ 327 822]
Describes the Whole Language concept and its manifestations in teaching. Argues that Whole Language teaching can be seen as a political activity since it returns power to the children and the teacher.

Richards, Janet C., and Joan P. Gipe, "Whole Language Teaching and Mandated District Objectives Are Compatible," *Reading: Exploration and Discovery 13*/1 (fall 1990): 8-18. [EJ 431 086]
Demonstrates that a first-grade teacher in a classroom covers district objectives for reading and language arts within the context of a Whole Language philosophy. Illustrates the teacher's recognition of the needs of the students, and that the teacher encourages them to participate in making decisions about what activities are included in the unit. (See ED 347 165 for a similar report.)

Richards, Janet C., and others, "Teachers' Beliefs about Good Reading Instruction," *Reading Psychology 8/1* (1987): 1-6. [EJ 353 679]
Identifies two statistically significant prediction equations involving independent dynamics that are based on information provided by 225 primary teachers regarding (1) 14 predictor variables and (2) their orientations toward three instructional emphases: graphophonics, skills, and Whole Language.

Richardson, Marcia, and others, "Evaluation of Whole Language and Traditional Language Arts Instruction Using a Cloze-Procedure Test for Reading Comprehension," 22 pp. (1991). [ED 339 012]
Reports a study investigating whether there was a relation between methods of language arts instruction and reading comprehension as measured by the cloze-procedure. Subjects, 88 third-grade students in four classes (two "traditional" and two "Whole Language") at two elementary schools in South Dakota, had their reading comprehension tested six months into the school year using a 35-item Cloze procedure. The two traditional teachers and the two self-taught Whole Language teachers had identified themselves on a self-report measure of teaching strategies. Data from the comprehension test were analyzed using a t-test. Results indicated no significant difference between the reading comprehension of students instructed using traditional (basal reading) and Whole Language methods of instruction. Includes the teacher survey instrument, the checklist of classroom items normally found in a Whole Language environment, a sample cloze-procedure passage, a sample of verbatim and acceptable answers, and a table of data.

Richardson, Paul, "Language as Personal Resource and as Social Construct: Competing Views of Literacy Pedagogy in Australia," *Educational Review 43/2* (1991): 171-90. [EJ 429 571]
Assesses the debate between the process writing/Whole Language approach to literacy education and genre-based writing instruction. Explains that the former stresses ownership and voice and the latter identifies and linguistically describes the genres used in school and proposes a curriculum model for teaching writing.

Richmond, Mark G., and others, "The Role of the Writing/Reading Connection in Reading Instruction in the Jones County, MS, School System," paper presented at the Annual Meeting of the Mid-South Educational Research Association (Knoxville, Tennessee, Nov 11-13, 1992,) Tennessee, 1992. [ED 345 487]
Reports a study of the degree to which teachers employ or perceive that they employ writing/reading strategies in their classrooms, and their perceptions regarding the degree to which their school system should support that effort. A pilot sample of 15 practicing teachers was drawn from a demonstration school in southwest Louisiana. Subjects, 71 K-8 teachers from the Jones County School System in Mississippi, completed a questionnaire. A random sample of eight teachers was drawn for classroom observation. Two instruments designed to assess teachers' perceptions of their Whole Language awareness were administered to the pilot group study for validation purposes. Results of both studies indicated that there was an apparent gap between theory and practice relative to the implementation of a writing/reading basis for literacy development. Teachers appeared to regard their practice at a much higher level than is borne out by observation of environment and practice, and teachers tended to view the school system as needing to provide more support for their ventures into Whole Language methodology.

Riley, Margaret C., and Donna L. Coe, *Whole Language Discovery Activities for the Primary Grades*. (New York: Prentice-Hall, 1992). [CS 011 347]
Presents for the K-3 teacher hundreds of ready-to-use individual and group activities

for developing reading, writing, listening, and speaking skills, all correlated with other curriculum areas and organized into nine monthly sections. Includes teaching strategies, individual and group games, activity sheets, quizzes, writing exercises, and vocabulary builders. Each of the monthly sections provides (1) three forms of literature (a Caldecott book title with a synopsis, a poem, and a traditional song) corresponding with monthly themes; (2) language, math, social studies, and science activities developed through the thinking levels of Bloom's taxonomy for each literature form; (3) a "skill correlation chart" correlating the activities with key concepts in language, math, social studies, and science; (4) display ideas for the monthly book, song, and poetry selections; and (5) reproducible open-ended "think sheets" to facilitate recording ideas in individual, small group, and large group activities. Includes an introductory discussion of Whole Language and Bloom's taxonomy, sections on management and evaluation to help teachers integrate instruction to fit other literature selections, and a parent section to promote home support and encouragement.

Rickert, Colleen, "Support Groups for Reading Supervisors (Reading Supervisors)," *Journal of Reading 33*/8 (May 1990): 642-43. [EJ 410 008]
Describes a Coordinators Applying Whole Language (CAWL) group that provides a way for reading coordinators in a number of school districts in a metropolitan area to support each other. Argues that reading supervisors can influence classroom reading and writing instruction among local school districts.

Ridley, Lia, "Enacting Change in Elementary School Programs: Implementing a Whole Language Perspective," *Reading Teacher 43*/9 (May 1990): 640-46. [EJ 410 138]
Describes how one resource person demonstrated and discussed Whole Language teaching methods in five elementary and middle schools to start the process of educational change.

Rigg, Pat, "Whole Language in TESOL," *TESOL Quarterly 25*/3 (fall 1991): 521-47. [EJ 435 954]
Presents key aspects of the Whole Language perspective; describes examples of Whole Language principles in practice in elementary, secondary, and adult English-as-a-Second-Language programs. Reviews recent Whole Language research on second-language development.

Robb, Laura, "A Cause for Celebration: Reading and Writing with At-Risk Students," *New Advocate 6*/1 (win 1993): 25-40.
Describes a remedial program for seventh- and eighth-grade students who failed a state literacy test and were reading below grade level. Outlines the successful program, based on a reading-aloud program, responding to stories, writing, paired reading and questioning, connecting vocabulary to individual stories, and reading to kindergarten and first-grade children.

Robbins, Patricia A., "Implementing Whole Language: Bridging Children and Books," *Educational Leadership 47*/6 (Mar 1990): 50-54. [EJ 405 139]
Reading and writing at one New Hampshire school district are considered integrated processes. Writing generates an enthusiasm for reading, and reading generates the impetus for writing. Whole Language instruction has produced high reading comprehension scores, an increase in book-reading quality and quantity, and a dramatic drop in special education students.

Roberts, Robbie B., "Writing Abilities of First Graders: Whole Language and Skills-Based Classrooms," paper presented at the Annual Meeting of the Mid-South Educational Research Association (Lexington, KY, Nov 13-15, 1991). [ED 341 981]
Compares the writing abilities of children in a Whole Language classroom with those

of children involved in a skills-based classroom. Subjects, 37 African-American students in two heterogeneous first-grade classrooms in a low socio-economic area school in the inner-city of a large Alabama city, completed a reading/writing assessment (a sample of the Stanford Achievement Writing Test for second-grade students) after 7 months of instruction. One group of subjects consisted of 19 students who had been instructed using a Whole Language curriculum; the other group consisted of 18 participants who had been instructed using a traditional curriculum emphasizing skill mastery. Writing samples were analyzed according to content and the ability to express thought. Total words and t-units (number of thoughts) were also compared between the groups. Results indicated that, on all tools of assessment, the Whole Language group scored significantly higher than the skill-oriented group.

Robinson, Richard D., and Jeanne M. Jacobson, "The Multi-Faceted World of the Reading Teacher or This vs. That vs. Empowered Choices," *Reading Horizons 30/*1 (fall 1989): 39-40. [EJ 397 683]
Discusses the pros and cons of traditional vs. non-traditional teaching methods. Explores non-traditional methods such as Whole Language, student developed materials, combining writing with reading, informal testing, teacher collaboration, and professional education and development.

Robinson, Richard, "An Interview with Dr. Donna Wiseman (Leaders in Reading Research and Instruction)," *Reading Psychology 14/*2 (Apr-Jun 1993): 165-70. [CS 745 755]
Presents an interview with Donna Wiseman. Discusses current programs and activities of Whole Language, criticism of leaders in Whole Language for being above any question or criticism, the existing research base for Whole Language, and the future of the Whole Language movement.

Robinson, Helja, "Anna's Worlds: Whole Language Learning in a Bilingual Context." (1989): 30 pp. [ED 324 102]
Shows that bilingualism can be an enriching part of children's lives. A young child named Anna, living in a bilingual environment in which English and Finnish were spoken, was observed and her speech recorded. This discussion focuses on aspects of Anna's acquisition of language. Initial discussion works toward a definition of bilingualism and describes the social experiences of the bilingual child and the effects of bilingualism on the child. Daily observation and recording of the child's speech revealed that the majority language, which, after a move from Finland to the United States, changed from Finnish to English, emerged quickly from a receptive stage and moved to a productive stage. While Anna was able to conduct role-play exclusively in English 4 weeks after entering nursery school in Mississippi, emotional attachment to certain Finnish words was evident. Extensive examples of Anna's code-switching, keeping the languages separate, self-correcting behavior, literacy learning, learning to count, concept acquisition, and second language maintenance, are provided. Concluding remarks focus on the role of the teacher with bilingual students in the classroom.

Robinson, H. Alan, "Whole Language and Whole Language Instruction: A Definition, paper presented at the Annual Meeting of the Nassau Reading Council (Long Island, NY, Apr 16, 1988) and a shorter version presented at the Annual Meeting of the International Reading Association (33rd, Toronto, Canada, May 1-6, 1988). [ED 297 270]
What Whole Language is and is not, what Whole Language instruction is and is not, and whether "subskills" can be integrated into a Whole Language approach are topics worthy of consideration. Whole Language is natural language within a given context and in relation to a given situation. Isolated bits of language used for exercise rather than for real communication are not natural language. Language which is not a unit,

which does not have a sensible beginning and ending, and which does not serve to communicate within a meaningful context for a given purpose is not Whole Language. Whole Language instruction includes the teaching and learning of skills and/or strategies within a setting in order to accomplish a goal that cements, extends, and expands learning. It is not the planned teaching of skills in a sequence over time. It is frequently coupled with an integrated or thematic approach to learning. This approach is consistent with a Whole Language approach but is not mandatory. The role of the Whole Language teacher includes developing strategies for dealing with fragments of language, such as objective and standardized tests. Subskills instruction can be subsumed in a Whole Language approach to reading instruction if the subskills are recognized as reading purposes and major organizational strategies. Learning and functioning through language is the process as well as the goal of Whole Language instruction.

Roos, Marie C., "Integrated Literacy Development and Computer-Based Instruction," paper presented at the Annual Meeting of the American Association of Colleges for Teacher Education (San Antonio, TX, Feb 25-28, 1992). [ED 341 032]
Noting that recent developments in computer technology facilitate the integration of media in literacy development, this paper reviews 18 items of courseware designed to promote literacy development within a Whole Language framework. The reviews are divided into four sections dealing with the following topics: (1) idea processors and the contributions of graphic organizers to information processing in the content areas; (2) media integration systems and the capacity to synthesize interdisciplinary content; (3) desktop publishing as a vehicle for producing sophisticated report formats; and (4) courseware in reading and literature designed to promote integrated literacy development. Concludes that these programs are useful both across the curriculum to facilitate information processing and in conjunction with thematic, literature-based, or content area units of study to enhance higher-order thinking.

Roos, Marie C., and others, "The Effect of an Introductory Reading Course on Pre-Service Teachers' Theoretical Orientation to the Teaching of Reading," paper presented at the Annual Meeting of the International Reading Association (38th, San Antonio, Texas, Apr 26-30, 1993), Texas, 1993. [ED 356 470]
Reports a study that tested the usefulness of the Theoretical Orientation to Reading Profile (TORP) in terms of its accuracy in measuring preservice teachers' change in theoretical orientation to reading as a result of having taken a reading methods course. Subjects, 27 upper-division elementary education majors (the experimental group) and 15 upper-division students enrolled in an elementary level curriculum course (the control group) took the TORP as pre- and posttests. The reading methods course taken by the experimental group was literature-based and Whole Language in orientation. Results indicated an increase in the posttest scores in the direction of a skills/Whole Language orientation, suggesting a movement away from a subskills or phonics perspective on the continuum to either a skills or Whole Language theoretical orientation. Findings suggest that the reading-methods course influenced students' pretest beliefs about reading instruction as measured by the TORP.

Roosen, Joan, "Reflections of a Teacher," *Young Children 47*/5 (Jul 1992): 80-81. [EJ 447 660]
Presents a teacher's reflections on the need to know about, and talk with parents and other teachers about, the benefits of using a child development-based, Whole Language, thematic approach to teaching in the primary grades.

327

Rorschach, Elizabeth, Anthea Tillyer, and Gail Verdi, "Research on ESL Composition Instruction: The Fluency-First Approach," paper presented at the Annual Meeting of the Teachers of English to Speakers of Other Languages (26th, Vancouver, British Columbia, Canada, Mar 3-7, 1992.) [ED 350 848]
An experimental English-as-a-Second-Language (ESL) program at City College (New York) is reported. The federally funded project investigated the effectiveness of an instructional method entitled "Fluency First" and based on Whole Language theories of learning. It requires large amounts of reading and writing, collaboration with peers, and self-examination of learning processes. Participants were 24 students of varying ages and language backgrounds. The report consists of an overview of the approach and program, tabulation of quantitative data on ESL student achievement from 1983 to 1991, presentation of a case study of the seven Latin American students, a discussion of participating teachers' responses to the program, and a brief assessment of the implications of the research for other ESL programs, particularly in the areas of faculty development, curriculum design, and instructional material development.

Rosaen, Cheryl L., and Danies J. Cantlon, "Coherence in Literature-Based Thematic Units. Elementary Subjects Center Series No. 53." (1991): 37 pp. [ED 340 042]
Analyzes and compares two elementary literature-based thematic curriculum units. A broad set of framing questions developed by a team of researchers representing six subject areas was used with a particular focus on the extent to which the two units would likely promote understanding and appreciation of literature and the extent to which writing was used to enhance such understanding and appreciation. Each unit was examined for its coherence, which included appraisal of the theme's potential, how the theme was developed throughout the unit to enhance and support literary understanding and appreciation, the kind of knowledge promoted, and the ways in which activities and writing assignments were complementary. Results showed that (1) because the "Survival Tales" unit focused discussions and writing activities, it fostered a deeper understanding of the literature than does the "On the Edge" basal unit whose theme is not developed as coherently; and (2) the "Survival Tales" unit provided multiple opportunities for interaction using the four language modes in authentic reading and writing tasks, giving students a chance to make personal, social, and academic/metacognitive connections. Results indicated that teachers need to choose resources for literature-based units well and consider seriously the power of the theme for developing literary understanding and appreciation.

Roser, Nancy, "A Partnership for Change: A University Perspective," paper presented at the Annual Meeting of the World Congress on Reading (13th, Stockholm, Sweden, Jul 3-6, 1990). [ED 323 504]
A small-scale collaboration between members of a school of education and a public school district (involving some reading/language arts faculty and students from the University of Texas on the one hand and the curriculum director, volunteer reading teachers, media specialists, and elementary teachers in a school district in San Antonio, Texas on the other) illustrates how schools of education and public schools may forge partnerships to create new forms of teacher education and conduct inquiry about teaching and learning. The collaborative efforts centered on moving toward a literature base for the elementary language arts curriculum and illustrate Gary Griffin's seven critical features of an effective clinical teacher-education program. Griffin's framework proposes that the program must be embedded in a school context, and that the collaborative effort should be context-sensitive, purposeful and articulated, participatory, knowledge-based, ongoing, developmental, analytic, and reflective.

Rosberg, Merilee A., "The Reading/Writing Connection: Using Student Teachers," based on a paper presented at the Annual Meeting of the Iowa State Reading Association (Des Moines, IA, Apr 6-8, 1989). [ED 308 476]
The student teacher, practicum, or field-experience student can fit readily into a Whole Language classroom even if he or she has not been trained to use the process. The teacher needs to take time to discover the student associate's strengths and abilities; time taken to examine these abilities and to consider how they might be mutually complementary with the teacher's interests is quite worthwhile. Student teachers should be involved in planning lessons from the very beginning, as are the students in a Whole Language classroom. The continuance of a literate environment in the classroom can be ensured by using the skills of the student teacher to enhance and expand the community of learners in the classroom.

Roskos, Kathy, "A Naturalistic Study of the Ecological Differences between Whole Language and Traditional Individualized Literacy Instruction in ABE Settings." (1990): 89 pp. [ED 329 769]
Examines differences between a prescriptive individualized approach to literacy instruction in adult basic education (ABE) settings. Six ABE classrooms participated in the study with four continuing traditional literacy instruction and two providing Whole Language-oriented literacy instruction. Average attendance per session was 12 adults. The classroom served as the unit of analysis, with a total of 60 hours of observation conducted by a trained observer over the 6-month implementation phase of the year-long project. The findings revealed substantive differences between the two modes of instruction along various dimensions of educational climate. Interpreted broadly, the findings suggest that Whole Language-oriented instruction is more andragogical in nature, more supportive of higher-order thinking with print, and a more compelling form of literacy acquisition for adult learners. Implications for ABE policies and practices were identified.

Ross, Elinor Parry, "Moving toward a Whole Language College Classroom," *Journal of Reading 35/*4 (Dec-Jan 1991-92): 267-71. [EJ 435 525]
Describes changes made in the teaching of a college preservice education course in children's literature and reading methods that reflect principles of the Whole Language approach. Discusses integration of curriculum, social context, classroom environment, evaluation, writing, purposeful learning, and opportunities to choose.

Ross, Elinor P., "How to Use the Whole Language Approach," *Adult Learning 1/*2 (Oct 1989): 23-24, 27, 29. [EJ 396 202]
Techniques for using the Whole Language approach include read-aloud sessions, student story dictation, practice in using decoding skills, word banks, and exercises that stress the connection between reading and writing. The method considers individual needs and interests, offers relevance, and builds on adults' experiences.

Routman, Regie, "Teach Skills with a Strategy," *Instructor 101/*9 (May-Jun 1992): 34-37. [EJ 449 373]
Describes how to teach skills strategically in Whole Language classrooms. Discusses differences between skills and strategies and notes how to move from skill to strategy. A section on teaching phonics examines phonics charts and personal phonics booklets; suggests an order for teaching phonics.

Routman, Regie, "Transitions: From Literature to Literacy." (1988): 352 pp. [Ed 300 779]
Intended to provide support, encouragement, and ideas for teachers wanting to make the transition from skill-oriented basal texts to literature-based Whole Language programs, this book describes a successful existing program and offers suggestions on

how any elementary classroom can benefit from such a transition. Contents: (1) "My Turning Point: Catalysts for Change"; (2) "Why Change? A Need for Active Literacy"; (3) "The Reading Program: Teaching Reading with Children's Books"; (4) "Using Predictable Books: What You Need To Know"; (5) "Literature Extension Activities: Meaningful Independent Work"; (6) "The Writing Program: How To Begin It and Keep It Going"; (7) "The Reading-Writing Process: Moving into Grade 2"; (8) "The Literature-Writing Program: Continuing in Grade 3"; (9) "Parent Involvement: Communication"; (10) "First Year Journals: Entries from Two Teachers"; (11) "Everyday Concerns: Organization and Classroom Management"; (12) "Evaluation: Evaluating the Process As Well As the Product"; (13) "Making Changes: The Need for Teacher Support"; (14) "Any Questions?" (15) "Postscript: Transitions"; (16) "Resources for Teachers"; and (17) "Recommended Literature" (classified by grade and literary style, and by level of difficulty).

Rowe, Barbara Anne, "Phonics Phoenix: A Lesson in Literacy in Small-Town Mississippi," *Policy Review 51* (win 1990): 74-77. [EJ 411 306]
Describes the successful use of the beginning reading program called "Sing, Spell, Read, and Write" (SSRW) in Aberdeen, Mississippi, elementary schools. Using a Whole Language rather than basal reading approach and emphasizing phonics and total immersion, SSRW has been instrumental in dramatically improving achievement test scores and in combating illiteracy.

Ruddell, Robert B., "A Whole Language and Literature Perspective: Creating a Meaning-Making Instructional Environment," *Language Arts 69/8* Dec 1992): 612-20. [EJ 452 767]
Argues that Whole Language is a philosophy that places meaning-making at the center of learning and instruction. Suggests that literature and a literature-based program play a critical role in the classroom and in developing student motivation. Suggests that the teacher is the critical facilitator for meaning making in an interactive Whole Language environment.

Rupp, James H., "Whole Language in the Elementary ESL Classroom," paper presented at the Annual Meeting of the Teachers of English to Speakers of Other Languages (20th, Anaheim, CA, Mar 3-8, 1986). [ED 273 121]
The Whole Language approach to literacy, which has been highly promoted in the Albuquerque, New Mexico, public schools, is based on recent psycholinguistic research on the reading process, and it views learning to read as a developmental process moving from the whole to the parts. It is done in an encouraging, positive environment that is as risk-free as possible, where children are asked to use their background and experience and be active partners in the process. Many similarities exist between the Whole Language approach and the teaching of English as a second language (ESL), where the four language skills are taught as an integrated whole. In both, the teacher's role includes facilitating and modeling language use and creating an environment where it is almost impossible not to learn. An elementary school ESL program has incorporated the Whole Language approach into a variety of ESL activities, including: the morning message on the board that can contain almost anything and serves as a vehicle for reacting, discussion, and other group activities; squiggle writing, in which students are given written squiggles from which they develop a picture and story; and use of resource materials for students to do research on a given topic that is also incorporated into other class activities. The techniques have proven successful and may suit some instructional styles and situations.

Sabin, Barbara J., "The Conflict between Instruction That Characterizes Chapter 1 Programs and Instruction That Results from the Whole Language Philosophy." (1989): 38 pp. [ED 334 548]
Explores the conflict between instruction that characterizes Chapter 1 programs (which appear to advocate segmentation, isolated skills instruction, and other curricular incongruencies with the core reading classroom) and instruction that results from Whole Language philosophy. The paper maintains that the conflict may be due to a misinterpretation of Chapter 1 guidelines by state and local agencies. It examines the inadequacies of Chapter 1 reading programs resulting from the currently held unstated philosophy created by its guidelines, and discusses the nature of effective reading instruction based on Whole Language philosophy that could occur in Chapter 1 programs dependent on a reinterpretation of Chapter 1 guidelines.

Sacco, Margaret T., "Enhancing Multicultural Literature by Using the Whole Language Approach in Diverse Settings while Facing the Censorship Challenge," paper presented at the Annual Spring Conference of the National Council of Teachers of English (Richmond, Virginia, Mar 18-20, 1993), Ohio, 1993. [CS 213 970]
The Whole Language approach offers many opportunities for enhancing and effectively using multicultural literature in diverse settings. Recently many English teachers have departed from the traditional canon, including in their reading lists literature by writers who represent various ethnic and cultural groups. However, censorship has become a very strong threat to those teachers considering the use of multicultural literature in the classroom. Teachers can become paralyzed by the fear of censorship, thus preventing the opening up of the canon. Diversity strengthens and enriches a culture, however, so that readings concerning different ethnic and cultural perspectives should be encouraged. One excellent means of introducing such works into the curriculum is a Whole Language approach. Social studies students, for example, might read a novel concerning apartheid in South Africa. Teachers can promote the reading of these books by preparing booktalks, short talks about books which entice readership. Through various means, teachers must strive to incorporate multicultural perspectives into their classrooms. Includes an annotated bibliography of 12 works of young adult fiction, all useful for teaching multicultural perspectives.

Sainz, JoAnn, "Critical Literacy: How Can the Limited Proficient Adult Be Academically Supported and Enabled To Gain the Necessary Knowledge in Reading/Writing Communication Skills To Successfully Complete a Degree Program for Integration into the Workforce?" paper presented at the Conference of the National Association for Adults with Special Learning Needs (Aug, 1991). [ED 346 755]
Few jobs with any prospects for advancement are expected to be available to poorly skilled students, especially limited English proficient individuals with insufficient reading skills. The consensus is that continuing to allow a disproportionate number of minority or disadvantaged students to pass through the education system without meeting high standards of achievement means they are likely to end up in dead-end jobs or on welfare. Recent findings from the field suggest that one of the barriers to better programs for underachievers is that educators are skeptical about students struggling with basics being capable of higher order thinking and problem solving. Among the topics examined in this paper are the following: defeatist attitudes for the older poor reader or non-reader; types of approaches to teaching beginning reading; opposing arguments about teaching methods; inherent problems with low-level reading skill instruction; mental processes that occur while reading; profiles of at-risk adult students; the underdeveloped basic skill of listening and speaking; the failure of traditional methods of teaching beginning reading to adult at-risk students; and the link between higher literacy skills, college programs, and jobs.

331

Salvage, G. Joyce, and Phyllis E. Brazee, "Risk Taking, Bit by Bit," *Language Arts 68/5* (Sep 1991): 356-66. [EJ 431 037]
Argues that typical language arts instruction for special education children is misguided because it emphasizes identifying and remediating deficiencies in individual children. Offers a model for teaching at-risk children that applies Whole Language principles and practices to meet the needs of special education students.

Salzer, Richard T., "TAWL Teachers Reach for Self-Help," *Educational Leadership 49/3* (Nov 1991): 66-67. [EJ 435 750]
The Whole Language Movement may be the most widespread and fastest growing grassroots curriculum trend in U.S. education. Although a few Teachers Applying Whole Language (TAWL) groups are affiliated with school systems, the majority are supported entirely by teachers from different school districts meeting together voluntarily to advance their own professional development.

Sammon, Susan F., "A Correlation Study: The New Jersey College Basic Skills Placement Test and Degrees of Reading Power Test." (1988): 52 pp. [ED 296 288]
A study investigated whether a positive correlation existed between scores obtained by incoming freshman on the recently developed Degrees of Reading Power Test (DRP) and the required Reading Comprehension subtest of the New Jersey College Basic Skills Placement Test (NJCBSPT). The subjects, 217 William Paterson College freshman enrolled in a lower level developmental reading course and 91 enrolled in a higher level course, were pretested with the NJCBSPT in the summer of 1987 before course enrollment. Placement in developmental reading courses was made based on scores obtained with this test. Pretesting with the DRP took place the first week of class and posttests were conducted at the end of the semester. Results indicated that the new test, DRP, does correlate positively with the current state test, NJCBSPT, in its present format. For this sample, sex was a factor on the DRP, with males significantly outperforming females across levels. Students who completed a basic skills course which emphasized comprehension strategies taught through the reading of a variety of whole texts (content area selections, news stories, and novels) made significant gains as measured by comprehension tests such as DRP and NJCBSPT. The direct-instruction-via-Whole-Language-materials model appears to be effective.

Samuels, S. Jay, and Alan E. Farstrup, eds., "What Research Has To Say about Reading Instruction. Second Edition." (1992): 363 pp. [ED 340 011]
Maintaining the balance between theory and application of the 1978 edition, this book's second edition keeps up with changes in the reading curriculum by adding chapters on text structure, metacognition, and home background not found in the first edition. Chapter titles are: (1) "The Role of Research in Reading Instruction" (Wayne Otto); (2) "Home and School Together: Helping Beginning Readers Succeed" (Lloyd O. Ollila and Margie I. Mayfield); (3) "Whole Language Research: Foundations and Development" (Kenneth S. Goodman); (4) "Assessing Literacy: From Standardized Tests to Portfolios and Performances" (Elfrieda H. Hiebert and Robert C. Calfee); (5) "The Role of Decoding in Learning to Read" (Isabel L. Beck and Connie Juel); (6) "Reading Fluency: Techniques for Making Decoding Automatic" (S. Jay Samuels, Nancy Schermer, and David Reinking); (7) "Developing Expertise in Reading Comprehension" (P. David Pearson, Laura R. Roehler, Janice A. Dole, and Gerard G. Duffy); (8) "Improving Reading Instruction in the Content Areas" (Stephen Simonsen and Harry Singer); (9) "Text Structure, Comprehension, and Recall" (Barbara M. Taylor); (10) "Metacognition and Self-Monitoring Strategies" (Ruth Garner); (11) "Teaching the Disabled or Below-Average Reader" (Jeanne S. Chall and Mary E.

Curtis); (12) "Reading and the ESL Student" (Joanne R. Nurss and Ruth A. Hough); and (13) "Teaching Adults to Read" (Thomas G. Sticht and Barbara A. McDonald).

Sanacore, Joseph, "Administrative Guidelines for Supporting the Whole Language Philosophy," 28 pp. (1990) [ED 324 665]
Administrators need to realize that Whole Language is a multidimensional belief system, that everyone involved in its implementation must become a learner, and that this process requires risk taking in a supportive environment. Principals can provide support by working cooperatively with teachers during every phase of implementation. The following guidelines are suggestions that can be added to individuals' repertoires and used when needed: (1) Form study groups for the purpose of sharing information. (2) Develop a firm belief in emerging literacy. (3) Treat independent reading as an important activity rather than as a frill. (4) Encourage the teaching of vocabulary through reading immersion. (5) Support teachers' demonstration activities that reinforce the role of context for expanding word knowledge. (6) Focus on informal evaluation that is well-matched with instruction. These guidelines are only a sampling of the many ways in which educational leaders and teachers can take risks while they promote worthwhile strategies and activities for children.

Sanacore, Joseph, "Intra-class Grouping with a Whole-Language Thrust," *Reading and Writing Quarterly: Overcoming Learning Difficulties 8/3* (Jul-Sep 1992): 295-303. [See EJ 320 414]
Presents five grouping patterns for Whole Language classrooms, intended both to provide children with flexibility and complement other approaches to organizing instruction. The negative effects of long-term ability grouping has been discussed often in educational literature, and recent research has identified several areas of concern, including a need for more variety in intra-class instructional grouping. Whole Language educators are apparently so dissatisfied with the traditional, rigid three-group plan that they may be avoiding most small group patterns. The challenge to Whole Language teachers is to organize a variety of groups, including Shared Reading, Shared Meetings, Literature Circles, skill groups, and strategy groups. These patterns provide children with flexibility while they prevent the self-fulfilling prophecy of "once a problem reader, always a problem reader." They also complement other ways of organizing instruction, including whole class and individual activities. Unless varied grouping is incorporated into classrooms, the Whole Language movement may never demonstrate its full potential for helping children grow as readers and writers.

Sanacore, Joseph, "Success in Literacy through Early Intervention." (1990): 16 pp. [ED 314 713]
Helping children gain an early sense of success in literacy is vital to their growth since it creates a foundation for future success. Because of learning difficulties demonstrated in early development, which may be triggered in part by changing modern lifestyles, teachers need to be sensitive to the issue of preventing learning problems from becoming serious disabilities. Demonstrating sensitivity to the child's emerging literacy and prior knowledge are steps in the right direction, and these can be aided by informal evaluation (which replaces standardized testing with observation, interaction and analysis) and a Whole Language method of language instruction. These approaches can help children be successful during their school careers and throughout their lives.

Sanacore, Joseph, "Needed: A Better Balance between Narrative and Expository Text." (1990): 14 pp. [ED 317 968]
Providing young children with a better balance between narrative and expository text makes sense. Initially, children develop fluency through familiar narrative structures

333

and themes. As the children achieve reading fluency, however, they benefit from increased exposure to expository text. Supporting this thrust are varied approaches and resources, including installing a classroom library, reading aloud, and using magazines. Maintaining a balance of narration and exposition also means not overdoing one type of text to the deemphasis or preclusion of the other, regardless of the teaching-learning context. The challenge to educators, especially those supporting a Whole Language philosophy, is to encourage a balance of discourse types as children engage in authentic literacy events throughout the school year.

Sanacore, Joseph, "Schoolwide Literature-Based Practices: Cooperative Leadership Is an Asset." (1993): 16 pp. [ED 354 488]
A literature-based approach across the curriculum helps students to personalize content-area curricula, to enjoy reading a diversity of subject-matter materials, and to improve attitudes toward reading. Teachers, supervisors, and administrators can cooperatively support literature-based practice across the curriculum by creating a positive professional attitude, designing thematic units, and incorporating team teaching to provide a realistic context for complementing and transcending traditional textbooks. These approaches also increase the chances of promoting students' long-term reading habit. Carrying out successful literature-based practice, however, depends on genuine sharing among colleagues. Unless cooperation becomes the norm, such worthwhile ideas as using literature across the curriculum will not have the beneficial impact that they deserve.

Sanacore, Joseph, "Emerging Literacy: An Important Whole Language Concern." (1992): 20 pp. [ED 346 441]
Emerging literacy is a vital concern not only for Whole Language enthusiasts but also for all concerned with helping each child extend his or her individual literacy development. By avoiding a traditional, behavioristic, reductionist, readiness-oriented classroom, the primary school teacher provides a greater opportunity for creating a natural learning environment. Such an environment supports children's emerging literacy by highlighting developmentally appropriate activities related to the importance of play. This play-oriented context sends a message to children that the teacher understands and respects who they are and also values what they can do. With this foundation established, the teacher can extend play in specific ways to promote children's individual literacy learning. Sociodramatic play, dramatic activities, shared reading, reading aloud, and immersion are only a sampling of the creative ways in which a caring, knowledgeable teacher can support children's individual literacy learning. These and other developmentally appropriate activities must be a major part of the primary school classroom so that children are free to grow and develop in natural ways.

Sandel, Lenore, "Exploring the Solar System: A Literature Unit within a Whole Language Context." (1992): 7 pp. [ED 346 440]
A useful framework for literature-based instruction is the curriculum related literature unit which provides a total resource for content area teaching. Such a unit could be based on the science curriculum, "Exploring the Solar System," and could be developed thematically through topics of space or the solar system. The teacher's initial step is to create a collaborative graphic plan or organizer for a satellite display synthesizing the students' prior knowledge, reading text, literature, and curriculum goals. This organizer or mapping becomes the key to the selection of books and planning of literature activities. A unit can be organized to include science, math, social studies, and language arts content through development of research reports, time lines, distance calculations, creative writing, and drama and art projects. Class activities and sug-

gested books demonstrate how, in the music classroom, music appreciation and skills are taught and learned in this unit design in concert with the arts of language and other curriculum areas. Whether the point of departure in developing a teaching unit at any level is a specific subject, book title, or current interest, webbing the unit themes within all areas of language and learning emerges as a Whole Language approach in instructional concert, interweaving impressive and expressive language within the context of literature.

Sandel, Lenore, "Head Start to Full Start: A Progression of Gains in Fulfilling Children's Preschool Needs," paper presented at the National Working Conference on New Directions in Child and Family Research: Shaping Head Start in the 90s (Alexandria, VA, Jun 24-26, 1991). [ED 338 342]
Examines literature on early intervention programs for disadvantaged and culturally diverse children from the 1960s to the present. The focus is on Project Head Start and its history, follow-through support programs in the primary grades, and current research on emergent literacy. The background of Project Head Start is provided, and follow-through support programs are discussed, the aims of which are to emphasize the same goals as Head Start and adjust learning experiences that reinforce the early gains. The importance of continuity between Head Start programs and primary grade experiences is emphasized. Parent involvement is described as an effective element in the development of a child's early relationships, interests, and language. Current literature on emergent literacy and the role of experience in a child's development are considered. Theoretical principles of emergent literacy curricula, activities, and objectives are stated. The correlation of the Whole Language approach and emergent literacy with the cumulative research on child development and learning has cogent potential for application with programs and social policy.

Sarratore, Janet, and Beverly W. Bell, "Enhancing the Language Arts: Using Creative Dramatics." (1989): 10 pp. [ED 308 559]
Creative dramatics can be used effectively by the elementary teacher to help motivate students to become involved in various language arts activities. Dramatic play, pantomime, story dramatization, imagination exercises, creative movement, improvisation, and other structured activities encourage students to relate new experiences to old. As they increase their range of associations to familiar words and objects, students confront genuine purposes for acquiring the skills of reading, writing, speaking and listening.

Sawyer, Diane J., "Whole Language in Context: Insights into the Current Great Debate," *Topics in Language Disorders 11/3* (May 1991): 1-13. [EJ 428 630]
Discusses the history of U.S. reading instruction; instructional approaches and learning processes; the Whole Language view of literacy acquisition; promoting literate behavior through reading to or writing with children, shared reading, and guiding children's reading/writing; and use of the Whole Language approach with learning-disabled students.

Scala, Marilyn A., "What Whole Language in the Mainstream Means for Children with Learning Disabilities," *Reading Teacher 47/3* (Nov 1993): 222-29 [CS 746 349]
Describes how a teacher of children with learning disabilities worked with three regular classroom teachers to teach mainstreamed children in whole language classrooms. Shows how students' reading abilities, self-esteem, and motivation improved as the lines were blurred between abled and disabled, teacher and specialist, and right and wrong.

Schafer, Virginia, "The Effects of Teaching a Whole Language Philosophy to Second Grade Students," 122 pp. (1989). [ED 309 400]
Reports a study investigating differences in reading achievement of students taught according to Whole Language philosophy compared to students taught using a basal textbook. Subjects, 20 second-grade students taught using a Whole Language philosophy and 17 second-grade students in the same school using basal textbooks, were given pre- and posttests to determine their reading achievement. Pretests indicated no significant differences in reading achievement between the two groups, and posttests given four months later also indicated no differences in reading achievement. Includes three tables of data, 62 references, the pretest, sample lesson plans, and statistical computations.

Scharer, Patricia L., "Perceptions and Practices: An Exploration of Literature Discussions Conducted by Teachers Moving toward Literature-Based Reading Instruction," paper presented at the Annual Meeting of the National Reading Conference (42nd, San Antonio, TX, Dec 2-5, 1992). [ED 352 636]
A study explored the changing role of the elementary teacher within the context of book discussions as teachers move from basal instruction to literature-based reading instruction. As part of an earlier study, two upper-grade teachers consistently expressed concern during interviews and group discussions with their colleagues about how to foster both literary appreciation and literacy achievement through book discussions. Three additional classroom book discussions were videotaped one year after videotapings were made in connection with the earlier study. Both teachers were interviewed before and after the book discussions concerning how they planned, organized, facilitated, and evaluated the discussions. Results indicated that although both teachers had goals of fostering child-centered discussions supporting higher-level thinking, one teacher seemed unable to adjust her instructional stance in ways that would foster a more student-centered discussion, while the other teacher appeared to value students' interpretive and critical thinking and was also able to orchestrate classroom conditions to foster such talk during book discussions. Findings support the argument that teachers may claim to value creative, interpretive responses but concentrate mainly on literal responses in the discussions they actually conduct.

Scharer, Patricia L., and Deana B. Detwiler, "Changing as Teachers: Perils and Possibilities of Literature-Based Language Arts Instruction," *Language Arts 69*/3 (Mar 1992): 186-92. [EJ 439 169]
Presents a case study of a sixth-grade teacher trying to increase her use of literature for language arts instruction. Shows the challenges and successes of attempting to get better at teaching.

Scheffler, Anthony J., and others, "Examining Shifts in Teachers' Theoretical Orientation to Reading," *Reading Psychology 14*/1 (Jan-Mar 1993): 1-13.
Examines direction, durability, and dynamics of affected shifts in teachers' theoretical orientation to reading after a two-day Whole Language workshop. Finds that teachers moved away from initial beliefs as to how reading should be taught and retained this distance, but did not move with consistency toward an alternative orientation.

Scheu, Judith, and others, "Literature-Based Language Arts Programs: Present and Future (Reviews and Reflections)," *Language Arts 69*/7 (Nov 1992): 557-63. [EJ 451 376]
Discusses six professional resources and three classroom resources that can help practitioners decide what they should be doing and what they need to understand to function in a literature-based language arts classroom.

Scheu, Judith, and others, "Teaching and Learning of Nonfiction (Reviews and Reflections)," *Language Arts 68*/6 (Oct 1991): 502-07. [EJ 432 547]
Reviews 13 professional materials that explore the uses of expository texts and informational materials designed to be used with elementary and middle school students in the classroom. Discusses a book that provides a Whole Language perspective on language learning and teaching.

Schickedanz, Judith A., "The Jury Is Still Out on the Effects of Whole Language and Language Experience Approaches for Beginning Reading: A Critique of Stahl and Miller's Study," *Review of Educational Research 60*/1 (spr 1990): 127-31. [EJ 414 300]
Refutes Stahl and Miller, who compare the effectiveness of Whole Language/language experience programs versus basal reader approaches. Criticizesthem for their lack of longitudinal data, alternative interpretations, and information concerning the broad goals of Whole Language approaches.

Schierloh, Jane McCabe, "Using Classic Novels with New Adult Readers," *Journal of Reading 35*/8 (May 1992): 618-22. [EJ 442 708]
Suggests that teachers can use adapted or abridged classic novels with Adult Basic Education (ABE) students and enrich them by reading aloud short passages from full-length novels. Offers guidelines for selecting novels and excerpts.

Schiffer, Edward W., "Using Whole Language Materials in the Adult ESOL Classroom." (1989): 96 pp. [ED 327 063]
A practicum explored the use of instructional materials based on the Whole Language approach to second language learning in adult English-as-a-Second-Language (ESL) instruction. The approach was implemented in a beginning ESL classroom at an adult education center that had previously used publisher textbooks, which were not thought to provide adequate English language input. The materials selected for Whole Language instruction were texts designed for adult basic education and written in Whole Language. Classroom and homework exercises were also developed for use with a national newspaper. Other media (television, movies, songs, and pictures) were used for additional Whole Language exposure. Quantity and quality of both written and oral language learning and assignment completion among the 17 students were evaluated. Results indicate that the use of Whole Language materials promoted language acquisition at a faster rate than the use of commercial ESL materials.

Schindley, Wanda, "Banning the Excerpts: The New Fanatic Faction in the English Profession," *English Journal 80*/4 (Apr 1991): 73-74. [EJ 424 306]
Argues that excerpts from the literary canon and from contemporary nonfiction should be included in secondary education textbooks of the future, contrary to the opinion of militant Whole Language supporters.

Schleper, David R., "When "F" Spells "Cat": Spelling in a Whole Language Program," *Perspectives in Education and Deafness 11*/1 (Sep-Oct 1992): 11-14. [EJ 454487]
Describes the use of invented spelling in educational programs for students with deafness. Students use a variety of spelling strategies, such as visual, kinesthetic, sounding out, handshape in sign language, and functional spellings. Methods of encouraging risk taking in spelling are discussed, and the changing use of spelling tests is noted.

Schleper, David R., "Whole Language Works...and I've Got Proof!" *Perspectives in Education and Deafness 11*/3 (Jan-Feb 1993): 10-15. [EJ 459 615]
Reviews research on the use of Whole Language with students with hearing impairments and identifies recurring themes, such as Whole Language is effective for

students from a variety of backgrounds and age levels, and literacy development of deaf students exposed to a literate environment parallels that of hearing students.

Schneider, Susan, "Integrating Whole Language with a Sheltered English Curriculum: A Longitudinal Evaluation of At Risk Language Minority Students," paper presented at the Annual Meeting of the National Reading Conference (Miami, FL, Nov 27-Dec 2, 1990). [ED 332 520]

A study evaluated two El Paso, Texas bilingual education program types, including a state-mandated transitional model (n=18 schools, 5,607 students) and a bilingual immersion program (n=19 schools, 4,717 students). Both programs are designed so students will exit after grade 4, but some continue in grades 5 and 6. Student characteristics are similar across programs. Transitional programs have tended toward the audio-lingual approach, and immersion uses recent language-acquisition methods and the Whole Language approach and teaches reading and content areas in English. More recently, a language-arts approach has been encouraged, but not widely embraced, in the transitional program. Longitudinal data on student progress in the two program models and process data for three years has been gathered, and teachers were surveyed twice. Analysis of the data indicates that as in previous years, the immersion students performed better on standardized tests than transitional program students, with the gap narrowing in reading and math in the upper grades. Regardless of program, the students make the same average grades and are promoted at a similar rate. It is concluded that the bilingual immersion program can provide needed first-language instructional support and development as well as a richer, faster, more complete exposure to English.

Schnelle, Linda, and James D. Riley, "Guided Story Invention." (1991): 16 pp. [ED 342 006]

Guided story invention is a strategy for Whole Language instruction. The strategy stimulates construction of story and storylike passages, and incorporates: (1) student knowledge of story structure; (2) the reading and writing of meaningful text; (3) a focus on meaning as a function of teacher coaching; and (4) encouragement of self-monitoring of reader understanding. Preparation is the first major component of the strategy. The teacher guides the discussion of students' experience in writing stories and knowledge of structure. The second major component, story invention, incorporates group writing, a model story situation, and questions to guide story invention or to elaborate the model situation. At the point of group writing, the teacher may serve as secretary, to record sentences for student discussion groups, after first choosing a sentence that will motivate further response. In the model situation illustrating the strategy, groups start with the same sentence, but with details altered. Students are then asked to respond to questions about characterization and setting, and each group continues the sequence, choosing sentences after a discussion period. The final component, reconstruction/extension, includes the two aspects of reviewing the process of story invention and children's independent application of that process. Adherence to the principles underlying guided story invention is essential to success of the teaching process.

"School Health Program. Kindergarten." (1991): [ED 346 058] (For Grade 1, see ED 346 059; for Grade 2, see ED 346 060; for Grade 3, see ED 346 061.)

In order for individuals to make informed decisions about their health, they must have support, information, and skills to help them understand what promotes their health and what they themselves can do to enhance health. The major goals of the Northwest Territories (Canada) school health program are: to provide factual information on the human body; to enable students to develop skills that, along with factual information, will allow them to make informed choices related to health; to enhance students' self-esteem through self-understanding; to enable students to develop attitudes which lead to positive lifestyle behaviors; and to promote lifestyle practices which are conducive to lifelong health. This guide contains instructional strategies, lesson plans, reproducibles, and teacher background materials for kindergarten classes. The material is organized around six units: mental and emotional well-being, growth and development, alcohol and other drugs, nutrition, safety and first aid, and dental health. This guide also contains an introduction to the complete program, including scope and sequence charts outlining the major topics at each grade level. A discussion of the language development approach (using Whole Language) for students who are not proficient in English is also included.

Schory, Maria Emmi, "Whole Language and the Speech-Language Pathologist," *Language, Speech, and Hearing Services in Schools 21*/4 (Oct 1990): 206-11. [EJ 420 016]
The Whole Language approach to literacy parallels the acquisition of oral language, which enables speech-language pathologists to assume leadership roles in such literacy programs. Aspects of Whole Language programs are discussed, including language, both oral and written; assessment and planning; service delivery; intervention; and the oral language-reading relationship.

Schroeder, LaVern, "Custom Tailoring in Whole Language Evaluation," *Journal of the Wisconsin State Reading Association 34*/4 (fall 1990): 45-55. [EJ 434 224]
Clarifies the term "emergent literacy" and reviews significant informal assessment techniques, record-keeping systems, and reporting measures appropriate for emergent literacy. Discusses guidelines for Whole Language assessment. Suggests areas of evaluation to be considered for inclusion in a locally developed emergent literacy assessment system. Outlines steps to follow in developing local assessment measures.

Schulz, Elizabeth, "Nourishing a Desire to Learn," *Teacher Magazine 2*/9 (Aug 1991): 30-34. [EJ 433 794]
Describes the experiences of first-grade teachers who use the Whole Language approach to teaching and learning. Learning involves students participating in activities they find meaningful and sharing knowledge with their peers. Students must exercise initiative in learning, and they are responsible for making choices.

Schuman, Davida R., and Juliette Relihan, "The Role of Modeling in Teacher Education Programs," *Reading Horizons 31*/2 (Dec 1990): 105-12. [EJ 419 764]
Presents four strategies (journal writing, directed listening-thinking activity, use of big books, and language experience approach) which are components of many Whole Language classrooms and can be used by teacher educators to model teaching methods beginning teachers can use in their classrooms.

Schwab, R. G. Jerry, and others, "Implementing Innovative Elementary Literacy Programs. Program Report." (1992): 84 pp. [ED 350 596]
Describes the implementation processes of dramatically improved literacy programs in elementary schools which are leading the move to restructure literacy education in the Northwest (Alaska, Idaho, Montana, Oregon, and Washington). The first document in the collection, "Strategies for Improving School-Wide Literacy Programs: A Regional Depiction" (R. G. Jerry Schwab and others), is a depiction of the goals, innovations, implementation strategies, and barriers and facilitators of change in 41 elementary schools noted for their progress in literacy education. Following the depiction, the collection presents three case studies of individual schools' development of innovative teaching and social organization: "Adventures at Alki Elementary: A Case Study of School-Wide Literacy Change" (Sylvia Hart-Landsberg); "Transformation on the

Tundra: A Case Study of School-Wide Literacy Change" (R. G. Jerry Schwab); and "West Orient's Dramatic Performance: A Case Study of School-Wide Literacy Change" (Sylvia Hart-Landsberg).

Schwartz, Susan, and Mindy Pollishuke, "Creating the Child-Centred Classroom," 100 pp. (1991). [ED 329 893]

Provides practical implementation strategies for, and a clear outline of, the theory behind the child-centered classroom, which involves an understanding of the concepts of Whole Language and active learning. Teachers are to use the ideas to build their own beliefs and understandings, and to develop their own philosophy regarding the child-centred classroom. Suggests practical classroom strategies that as a base from which to begin, a springboard from which to experiment, to modify and to adapt to fit teachers' and students' individual needs and strengths. Despite many references to planning and implementation in all curriculum areas, the book is not intended to form a comprehensive guide for all subjects; rather, recommends activities as a sampling of possibilities that teachers might find helpful. Chapter titles: (1) Whole Language and Active Learning: A Philosophical Model (2) The Physical Set-Up of the Classroom (3) Timetabling (4) Classroom Atmosphere (5) Whole Language (6) An Integrated Child-Centred Curriculum (7) Learning Centres (8) Record Keeping, Student Evaluation and Parental Involvement.

Sebesta, Sam, "Literacy for Batman's Child," paper presented at the Annual Meeting of the International Reading Association (35th, Atlanta, GA, May 6-11, 1990). [ED 317 985]

The wealth of information gleaned from reading research both past and present needs to be applied to a practical eclectic reading methodology. First, an emergent instruction model needs to be created that takes into account the immediate interests and needs of the learner. This model should recognize that learning is a transaction, with the learner sharing in the transaction in a way that direct instruction does not. Second, the eclectic approach of the future must respect the centrality of the teacher. It cannot prescribe or script what they are to do and say. Despite the differences in approaches, many effective instructors teach in balanced, individualistic ways and represent the central figure in a child's education—the constant, stable adult on whom learning depends. Third, educators need to re-think children's interests. The possibilities for using realia and technology to initiate, not just reflect, interests in school are enormous, not to be confined to what a child has seen on TV or in the neighborhood. Fourth, aesthetic response to literature reading instruction needs to be considered, otherwise reading instruction will produce a condition called "aliteracy": an aliterate is a person who can read but who does not choose to do so. Finally, more attention needs to be devoted to the questions of what is functional reading for a child and how educators can increase what a child does with functional reading.

Seda, Ileana, "Rich Literacy Curricula: Undocumented and Unstandardized," paper presented at the Annual Meeting of the National Reading Conference (39th, Austin, TX, Nov 28-Dec 2, 1989). [ED 322 486]

Concerns the reduced and limited curricula which tests may represent. Observations were made at 18 different elementary and middle school classrooms in four school districts in central Pennsylvania during the language arts instructional period. All of the teachers were involved in promoting a holistic approach to literacy. Through hours of observation and conversations with the teachers, several themes were recurring: high levels of performance displayed by low ability learners; inadequacies of report cards; and teachers' frustrations about reducing children's learning to a letter grade. A major theme with teachers was how to educate parents and the public about the learning that was occurring in the classroom. Results indicated that teachers were effectively mediating learning activities so their students could become actively involved and owners of their learning. These rich curricula are undocumented because they do not explicitly inform the general public about the highly skilled, sophisticated performances and growth students display through the daily activities they perform. They are unstandardized because there is no handbook with a script for the teachers to repeat back to their students. The main reason for a lack of public knowledge is there is no formal outlet to report learners' performance and learning growth, except grades and test scores which do not capture the richness of the curricula.

Sensenbaugh, Roger, "Reading Teachers and Their Students (ERIC/RCS)," *Reading Research and Instruction 31/2* (win 1992): 98-101. [EJ 441 053]
Presents annotations of nine articles from the ERIC database that discuss the pedagogical relationship between reading teachers and their students. Includes articles that deal with Whole Language instruction, student motivation, instructional grouping, questioning techniques, and the characteristics of effective teachers.

Seufert, Darlene, "An Annotated Bibliography of the Literature Dealing with Language Experience in the Primary Classroom." (1988): 49 pp. [ED 298 505]
Examines the literature concerning language experience in the following areas: (1) the rationale for incorporating language arts in the primary classroom; (2) whether using language experience aids the child in developing reading strategies; (3) the achievement scores of children using language experience; (4) whether language experience develops oral language skills; (5) whether language experience aids in increasing sight vocabulary; (6) whether self-authored stories increase reading comprehension; and (7) how a child using language experience views him/herself and reading. The items in this bibliography date from 1966 to 1988 and include journal articles and documents in the ERIC database. For the purposes of this bibliography, the terms "language experience approach," "integrated language arts program," and "Whole Language" are interchangeable.

Shanahan, Timothy, "New Literacy Goes to School: Whole Language in the Classroom," *Educational Horizons 69/3* (spr 1991): 146-51. [EJ 425 225]
The Whole Language approach considers it essential to make learning active, to be respectful of teachers and learners, to allow students to develop ownership and control of their language and learning, and to use a variety of subjects together holistically.

Shanklin, Nancy L., "Whole Language and the Writing Process: One Movement or Two?" *Topics in Language Disorders 11/3* (May 1991): 45-57. [EJ 428 633]
Describes development of the Whole Language movement and the writing-process movement. Outlines 10 principles shared by both movements, such as the role of prediction, function before form, and integrated use of cuing systems. Implications for language specialists working with language-disordered students are addressed.

Shannon, Patrick, "The Struggle for Control of Literacy Lessons," *Language Arts 66/6* (Oct 1989): 625-34. [EJ 397 620]
Examines skills-based, interactionist, and Whole Language positions on literacy instruction, focusing on the issue of control. Discusses how these three approaches are reflected in both Canadian and American basals. Argues that students must be treated as active learners, adding a political and sociological dimension to the Whole Language approach.

Shapiro, Holly Rose, "Debatable Issues Underlying Whole-Language Philosophy: A Speech-Language Pathologist's Perspective," *Language, Speech, and Hearing Services in Schools 23/4* (Oct 1992): 308-11. [EJ 457 502]
Challenges two assumptions underlying Whole Language philosophy: spoken language

is directly comparable to written language, and skilled readers rely on contextual information more than on the printed word. Speech-language professionals are urged to engage in some instructional practices associated with Whole Language but also advocate methodologies inconsistent with Whole Language.

Shapiro, Jon, and James Riley, "Ending the Great Debate in Reading Instruction," *Reading Horizons 30*/1 (fall 1989): 67-78. [EJ 397 687]
Proposes an end to the debate in reading instruction between the proponents of data-driven approaches and proponents of concept-driven approaches by offering two major principles of reading instruction. Explores characteristics of each approach and the danger of overemphasizing either aspect of reading.

Shapiro, Jon, and Lee Gunderson, "A Comparison of Vocabulary Generated by Grade 1 Students in Whole Language Classrooms and Basal Reader Vocabulary," *Reading Research and Instruction 27*/2 (win 1988): 40-46. [EJ 368 655]
Compares the vocabulary generated from writing samples of 52 first-grade children in two Whole Language classrooms with vocabulary contained in the basal reader program. Concludes that Whole Language instruction does not limit children's exposure to systematic repetition of important vocabulary.

Shapiro, Jon, and Donna Kilbey, "Closing the Gap between Theory and Practice: Teacher Beliefs, Instructional Decisions and Critical Thinking," *Reading Horizons 31*/1 (Oct 1990): 59-73. [EJ 418 016]
Examines the relationship between instructional practices which teachers use and current theories of literacy development. Shows that the "fit" between current theories of literacy development and the traditional basal approach is inadequate. Addresses the role of critical thinking in transforming teachers' perspectives about the reading process and how they teach reading.

Shapiro, Jon, "Sex-Role Appropriateness of Reading and Reading Instruction," *Reading Psychology 11*/3 (1990): 241-69. [EJ 413 059]
Studies the attitudes toward reading as a sex-role appropriate behavior in classrooms using basal reading instruction or the Whole Language approach. Suggests that the nature of instruction has a significant effect on boys' view of the sex-role appropriateness of reading and writing.

Shaver, Judy C., and Beth S. Wise, "Literacy: The Impact of Technology on Early Reading," paper presented at the Annual Meeting of the American Reading Forum (11th, Sarasota, FL, Dec 12-15, 1990). [ED 327 832]
In reflecting on an overview of research on microcomputers in the public schools, a researcher found that early programs were largely based on a programmed instruction model. Computers were primarily used to provide for simple repetition of low-level decoding tasks. The emphasis of Whole Language literacy is in direct contrast to this approach. Rather than teaching the various aspects of communication as separate entities, Whole Language focuses on the integration of the communication skills of listening, speaking, writing, and reading. The computer can be a valuable tool for helping to immerse children in an environment in which print is filled with meaning. A computer-based program, "Writing to Read," was developed by IBM to enhance writing and reading skills of kindergarten and first grade students by increasing students' understanding of sounds, words, and sentence structure. Based on the success nationally of the "Writing to Read" program, 20 "Writing to Read" programs funded by state grants in Louisiana were evaluated to determine their effectiveness. Results revealed similar statistics to those found nationally: (1) increased gain scores on word recognition and vocabulary; (2) improved writing samples; (3) increased ability to

remain on task; (4) greater self-confidence; (5) fewer retentions; and (6) enthusiastic support from teachers and parents. An IBM "Writing to Read" lab was installed in a local Chapter 1 school in a low socioeconomic area. Results after the first full year of operation are similar to results achieved state-wide.

Shaw, Ellyn A., "Impressions of Whole Language Reading Instruction from the Land Down Under," *Journal of the Wisconsin State Reading Association 35/*1 (win 1991): 43-48. [EJ 429 709]
Discusses a teacher's perspective on the Whole Language approach to reading instruction, based on her observations of Australian students. Examines the theoretical frameworks, the materials used for instruction, the time allotted for instruction, the role of the teacher, the lesson format, and student motivation.

Shaw, Patricia A., "A Selected Review of Research on Whole Language," *Journal of the Wisconsin State Reading Association 35/*1 (win 1991): 3-17. [EJ 429 706]
Identifies quantitative research regarding Whole Language. Includes studies on preschool literacy, literature and basal reading, at-risk first-grade children, Whole Language and traditional approaches to beginning reading, students' writing ability, Whole Language and older students, and implementation. Concludes that Whole Language may be more effective at different stages of reading development.

Shepperson, Grace, and Robert J. Nistler, "Whole Language Collaboration Project: Implementing Change in One Elementary School," *Reading Horizons 33/*1 (1992): 55-66. [EJ 452 779]
Describes a long-term inservice program aimed at restructuring one elementary school's literacy program. Focuses on observed changes that occurred as teachers became active participants in staff development sessions designed around effective change principles.

Shepperson, Grace M., and Robert J. Nistler, "Whole Language Collaboration Project: Three Case Studies to Represent Change," paper presented at the Annual Meeting of the College Reading Association (34th, Nashville, TN, Nov 2-4, 1990). [ED 329 894]
In response to the restructuring of a school's literacy program, a study was designed to address three research question: (1) What levels of concerns are raised by teachers in the areas of "self," "task," and "impact"? (2) What responses do these concerns elicit from university researchers and other participants? and (3) What changes occurred among participants during their involvement in the initial phase of this project? Data sources included audio tapes of weekly inservices involving 2 university researchers, 23 teachers, and the school principal; teacher journals; participant responses to questionnaires; field notes of classroom observations; and collaborative interactions with teachers. Findings from the initial phase of the study are reported through three case studies. They represent change that occurred in teachers who had been initially perceived as traditional, average and expert regarding Whole Language literacy instruction. In their journals, essays, concern surveys, and conversations, the voices of teachers, as represented by Doris, Jackie, and Jean, confirmed the efficacy of the following change factors: change is a process, not an event; change is a highly personal experience; change involves developmental growth; and change is best understood as it directly affects classroom practice, students and preparation time.

Shields, Jennifer, and Sheena Matheson, "Whole Language and Then Some!" *TESL Talk 20/*1 (1990): 213-23. [EJ 427 261]
Discusses the merits of the Whole Language approach in the context of teaching Canadian Native children to read and write in English. Ways of adapting and supplementing the Whole Language approach for their specific needs are suggested.

Short, Kathy G., and Carolyn L. Burke, "New Potentials for Teacher Education: Teaching and Learning as Inquiry," *Elementary School Journal 90/2* (Nov 1989): 193-206. [EJ 404 267]
Discusses teacher education by focusing on beliefs about learning that are built on recent understandings about language. Considers changes that teacher educators have explored in their classrooms and programs.

Siegel, Janna, "'Whole'-ier Than Thou!" (New Mexico, 1993) [ED 356 467]
No trend in education has been more exalted than Whole Language, which has a following of teachers, researchers, and specialists who are almost fanatical in their observance. The debate is between two types of direct instruction: The "atomistic" approach encourages teachers to break down reading into its component parts; the "holistic" approach preaches that teachers should teach reading in context of a child's natural language and interests. Teachers ought to take an integrative approach that includes the best of both worlds. Suggestions for reading teachers include: (1) Use a variety of methods. (2) When students have problems, find the method with which the child has the most success. (3) Try new things. (4) Teach the reading of nonfiction. (5) Demonstrate that reading and writing are tools for communication. (6) Keep up on their own reading and writing. Teachers should not, howevver, do the following: Embrace any one method to the exclusion of others; close their minds to new, innovative, or even older methods of instruction; hoard their ideas; give up on any student having trouble reading; or assume that they know whether or not their students are learning. Teachers need to remember that reading is not the most important skill in the world: A child is not doomed to failure just because he or she cannot read.

Siera, Maureen, and Martha Combs, "Transitions in Reading Instruction: Handling Contradictions in Beliefs and Practice," *Reading Horizons 31/2* (Dec 1990): 113-26. [EJ 419 765]
Describes experiences of two first-grade teachers who were beginning to make a transition from basal reading to a more holistic approach. Suggests that, although teachers are in transition from basals to more holistic approaches, some incompatible and contradictory elements will exist.

Sierra, Judy, "Whole Language and Oral Traditional Literature, or, Pigs, Puppets and Improv," *Emergency Librarian 19/2* (Nov-Dec 1991): 14-15, 17-18. [EJ 436 317]
Discusses the development of oral language skills for elementary-age children, highlighting the use of well-known folk tales such as "The Story of the Three Little Pigs" to involve a group in an oral language experience. The use of puppets is described, and props and resource materials are suggested.

Simich-Dudgeon, Carmen, "English Literacy Development: Approaches and Strategies that Work with Limited English Proficient Children and Adults." (1989): 12 pp. [ED 318 274]
Reviews selected research studies and practices on the teaching of literacy to limited English proficient (LEP) students suggests that there is considerable variation in the way literacy is defined. Several methods currently being used to develop LEP students' literacy skills are reviewed. Many LEP students continue to be taught reading skills through phonics rather than the Whole Language or language experience approaches. Initial research on grammar-based approaches indicates that they are not as effective as others. Striking similarities appear in the success of both adults and children being taught by the various approaches. Effective LEP adult literacy programs reflect learner needs, educational backgrounds, and abilities, almost invariably integrating a basic skills focus with instruction in life or survival skills needed for daily functioning. The

following guiding principles for facilitating English literacy with LEP students were suggested by G. Wells (1987): (1) responsibility for selecting tasks, deciding on means for attaining goals, and evaluating outcomes; (2) language should be seen as a means for achieving other goals; (3) writing, reading, speaking, and listening should be seen as complementary processes; and (4) an important place should be accorded to the sharing of personal and literary stories at all stages.

Sinatra, Richard, "Integrating Whole Language with the Learning of Text Structure," *Journal of Reading 34*/6 (Mar 1991): 424-33. [EJ 422 603]
Presents ways that the learning of text structure can occur naturally for adolescents in a Whole Language framework. Offers five global contexts in which conceptualization, communication, collaboration can occur to help students use language and understand how text is organized. Six suggestions provide teachers with a place to start as they move into Whole Language instruction: (1) Provide only meaningful experiences for the language learner. (2) Provide situations in which children read to learn as they learn to read. (3) Provide a language learning setting that acknowledges the uniqueness of each individual learner. (4) Provide experiences that guide, support, monitor, encourage, and facilitate learning. (5) Provide opportunities for expression (writing) and comprehension (reading) through the idea of authors as readers. (6) Based on an understanding of Whole Language learning, speak to those who do not understand.

Slaughter, Helen B., "Indirect and Direct Teaching in a Whole Language Program," *Reading Teacher 42*/1 (Oct 1988): 30-34. [EJ 377 455]
Investigates the teacher's role in a Whole Language classroom. Asserts that explicit written guidelines concerning the teacher's role in directing and supporting student learning should be available for novice teachers in training and for experienced teachers who want to shift from a conventional approach to a Whole Language approach.

Slaughter, Helen B., and others, "Contextual Differences in Oral and Written Discourse during Early Literacy Instruction," paper presented at the Annual Meeting of the American Educational Research Association (69th, Chicago, IL, Mar 31-Apr 4, 1985). [ED 260 380]
An ethnographic study of kindergarten through grade two classrooms was conducted of various sociolinguistic contexts in which young students were developing oral and written language competencies. Nonparticipant observations were conducted in both regular classrooms and Chapter I small group classroom settings. The observations were analyzed from a variety of perspectives spanning a range from Whole Language to a more conventional language arts approach to instruction. A coding system was developed to assist in the analysis of protocol data regarding literacy events, oral language interaction, and evaluation occurring in classroom settings. The data indicated that for the most part literacy lessons must have functional meaning for the child if positive learning is to occur. Includes an overview of the major aspects of a Whole Language approach to instruction, the responses of low-achieving students to Whole Language activities, recommendations for improving the literacy learning of young students, and definitions and discussion of selected codes for analysis of protocol data.

Smith, Kenneth J., and others, "The Debate Continues," *Phi Delta Kappan 74*/5 (Jan 1993): 407-10. [EJ 457 2020]
In the February 1992 *Kappan* (see EJ 439 292), Frank Smith advocated formal reading instruction be abolished and teachers merely read to students and turn them over to authors. This article argues that the scientific study of learning is essential. This

country can ill afford to rear generation of illiterates who have learned lazy, inefficient work habits from being taught that learning is effortless.

Smith, Carl, comp., "Trends and Issues in Reading Education. Learning Package No. 11." (1990): 47 pp. [ED 333 377]
Originally developed for the Department of Defense Schools (DoDDS) system, this learning package on trends and issues in reading education is designed for teachers who wish to upgrade or expand their teaching skills on their own. The package includes a comprehensive search of the ERIC database; a lecture giving an overview on the topic; the full text of several papers on the topic; copies of any existing ERIC/ RCS publications on the topic; a set of guidelines for completing a goal statement, a reaction paper, and an application project; and an evaluation form.

Smith, Carl B., ed. *Alternative Assessment of Performance in the Language Arts: What Are We Doing Now? Where Are We Going? Proceedings of a National Symposium* (Bloomington, Indiana, Aug 27, 1990)," 315 pp. (1991). [ED 339 044]
Presents the complete proceedings (written presentations as well as transcriptions of oral presentations and group discussions) of a national symposium on alternative assessment in the language arts. Oral presentation titles: "Current Issues in Alternative Assessment" (Roger Farr); "Whole Language and Evaluation: Some Grounded Needs, Wants, and Desires" (Jerome Harste); "State Policy and Authentic Writing Assessment" (Diane S. Bloom); and "Alternative Assessment in Columbus, Ohio: What We're Doing Now (Not Much); What We're Going to Be Doing (A Lot More)" (Bert Wiser and Sharon Dorsey). Written presentation titles are: "Alternative Assessment in Language Arts" (Roger Farr and Kaye Lowe); "Assessing Whole Language: Issues and Concerns" (William P. Bintz and Jerome C. Harste); "State Policy and 'Authentic' Writing Assessment" (Diane S. Bloom); and "Alternative Assessment in Reading and Writing: What We're Doing and What We'd Like To Do in Columbus Public Schools" (Bert Wiser and Sharon Dorsey). Group session titles are "What Are the Implications for Instructional Materials in Alternative Assessment?" "What Are the Connections between the Theory and Politics of Alternative Assessment?" "What Are the Theoretical Issues Involved in Alternative Assessment? What Are the Practical Issues Involved? How Can These Issues Be Addressed Together?" "What Are the Implications for Curriculum Planning When Implementing Alternative Assessment?" and "How Do Societal Concerns Influence the Development of Alternative Assessment?" Includes transcriptions of the comments by six representatives of educational publishers concerning the future of assessment; and, from the concluding session, "Setting the Future Agenda" (Carl B. Smith); and "Aprés Symposium: Thoughts on What Happened and Next Steps" (Marilyn R. Binkley). Includes four appendices entitled: "Portfolio Assessment: A Survey among Professionals" (Jerry L. Johns and Peggy VanLeirsburg); "Literacy Portfolios: A Primer" (Jerry L. Johns); "How Professionals View Portfolio Assessment" (Jerry L. Johns and Peggy VanLeirsburg); and "Research and Progress in Informal Reading Inventories: An Annotated Bibliography."

Smith, Patricia Gannon, "A Practical Guide to Whole Language in the Intermediate Classroom," *Contemporary Education 62/2* (win 1991): 88-95. [EJ 447 938]
Discusses the role of the intermediate Whole Language teacher, including maintaining a proper environment, emphasizing meaning, encouraging risk taking, providing sufficient learning time, focusing on students, encouraging collaboration, using whole pieces of language, using the best literature, teaching skills in context, evaluating, and integrating different aspects of the curriculum.

Smith, Frank, "Learning to Read: The Never-Ending Debate," *Phi Delta Kappan 73/6* (Feb 1992): 432-35, 438-41 [EJ 439 292]

Methods such as phonics or Whole Language can never ensure that children learn to read. Children must learn from people—from teachers initiating them into the readers' club and from authors' writings. Children's relationships with teachers, each other, and the learning task itself are supremely important. Observation, not testing, gauges student progress.

Smith, Michael Sloane, "A Study of the Socialization of Student Teachers with a Whole Language Perspective." (1990): 232 pp. [ED 329 903]
To date there has been no research done on teacher education programs that use Whole Language as a vehicle for instilling reflective forms of pedagogy. This study is an initial effort to develop a research base in this area. The study examined the socialization process of teachers who adopted the teaching perspectives of the Whole Language approach in a variety of placement sites. Subjects, six white female elementary student teachers, were specifically chosen for their high degree of commitment and a well-informed understanding of the philosophy of Whole Language. The primary methods used for data gathering were interviews, observations, and examinations of relevant documents. Results indicated: (1) the basic tenets of Whole Language philosophy are in line with those tenets of reflective pedagogy that many educators are attempting to promote; (2) the subjects' teacher education program was responsible for moving them towards their Whole Language perspectives but was deficient in many areas; (3) subjects faced many constraining factors during the student teaching experience, including interactive, personal, institutional, and cultural factors; and (4) all the subjects continued to support verbally their original beliefs about Whole Language, even though they were forced to conform to the existing curriculum.

Smith, Michael S., "The Difficulties of a Curriculum Helper in an Urban School," paper presented at the Bergamo Conference (Dayton, OH, Oct 16-19, 1991). [ED 357 090]
Describes the experiences of a teacher and a curriculum helper in designing and implementing a fifth grade language arts curriculum at an inner city, magnet school in Indianapolis (Indiana). The report describes the work in three phases: (1) making explicit the problems with the previous language arts curriculum; (2) formulating a plan for a language-arts curriculum to replace the old one; and (3) implementing the new plan. The first section describes the teacher's difficulty in designing an approach that would both teach the conventions of grammar that students needed to survive academically and connect with students' backgrounds and interests. A section describing the curriculum plan development discusses a Whole Language approach and a learner-centered design. Problems included the students' lack of experience with a learning situation in which they are given choices and must take responsibility for their learning. The paper also describes the use of the "Authoring Cycle," and how evaluation methods were designed and implemented and their ups and downs. A conclusion notes the difficulties of designing a Whole-Language approach, the challenges to giving up attachments to skills-oriented and teacher-directed instruction, and the importance of students being ready to experience more independent learning.

Smith, Michael S., "So You Want To Be a Whole Language Teacher: Constraining Factors That Beginning Teachers Face," paper presented at JCT Conference (Dayton, OH, Oct 14-17, 1992). [ED 357 002]
Six student teachers who were committed to the tenets of Whole Language were studied to determine how they manifested their Whole Language perspectives in light of the enabling and constraining factors they faced in their specific field sites. Results indicated that the six student teachers were forced to alter their teaching behaviors significantly due to constraining factors. The impact of context on teacher's behavior is examined in general, and the categories of constraining factors that cut across all of the

six student teachers' experiences are outlined. Constraining factors are categorized in four levels: (1) interactive factors; (2) institutional factors; (3) cultural factors; and (4) personal factors. For each level, anecdotal examples of the six teachers' experiences illustrate the constraining factors involved: working with the curriculum, cooperating teachers, university supervisors, student behavior problems, lack of resources, and personal limitations.

Smith, Michael S., "Manifesting a Whole Language Perspective: Novice Teachers in Action," paper presented at the "Creating the Quality School" Conference (Norman, Oklahoma, Mar 30-Apr 1, 1992), Missouri, 1992. [CS 011 381]
Reports an interpretive field study in examination of how beginning teachers with a Whole Language perspective manifested their beliefs. Using the methods of purposeful sampling, four student teachers who were both committed and knowledgeable concerning the tenets of Whole Language were observed and interviewed during the student teaching experience. Results indicated that each of the student teachers maintained her Whole Language philosophy. Five categories emerged depicting the beliefs and teaching practices of these student teachers: (1) existing school practices, (2) knowledge and learning, (3) curriculum, (4) concept of teacher, (5) concept of student. Findings suggest that the student teachers' beliefs and teaching practices matched very closely with the dimensions outlined by those calling for reflective teaching, and that teacher preparation programs interested in developing reflection in future teachers might consider Whole Language philosophy.

Smith-Burke, M. Trika, and others, "Whole Language: A Viable Alternative for Special and Remedial Education?" *Topics in Language Disorders 11*/3 (May 1991): 58-68. [EJ 428 634]
Explores the assumptions of traditional remedial and learning disabilities education and summarizes empirical evidence challenging this approach; examines the assumptions underlying Whole Language and the teacher's role in a Whole Language context; presents data on the efficacy of Whole Language instructional programs; and discusses the potential benefits of Whole Language for special populations.

Smutny, Joan Franklin, ed., "Illinois Council for the Gifted Journal, 1992." (1992): 85 pp. [ED 347 752]
Contents of this annual issue of the Illinois Council for the Gifted Journal: "How Can I Tell If My Preschooler is Gifted?" (Susan Golant); "Early Childhood Education for the Gifted: The Need for Intense Study and Observation" (Maurice Fisher); "Assessing Gifted and Talented Children" (James Webb); "Early Assessment of Exceptional Potential" (Beverly Shaklee and Jane Rohrer); "Teacher Assessment of Preschool and Primary Giftedness" (Jane Wolfe and W. Thomas Southern); "Characteristics of Gifted Children and How Parents and Teachers Can Cope with Them" (Annemarie Roeper); "The Needs of the Young Gifted Child (A Short and Incomplete Overview)" (Annemarie Roeper); "The Whole Child and the Gift—Nurturing Our Very Young Gifted Students" (Dorothy Massalski); "Integrating the Gifted Child into Family Life" (Caryl Krueger); "Family Factors in the Adult Success of High-IQ Children" (Rena Subotnik and James Borland); "The ABC's of Curriculum for Gifted 5-Year-Olds: Alphabet, Blocks and Chess?" (Susan Kaplan); "Teaching Thinking Early" (Anne Crabbe and Pat Hoelscher); "Greater Gifts Than These" (Susan Belgrad); "Creating a Nurturing Classroom Environment" (Laura Requarth); "Education of Young Gifted Children" (Peggy Snowden); "Intuition is for the Learning" (Don Rapp); "Cooperative Learning: A Wolf in Sheep's Clothing" (Susan Linnemeyer); "Reaching All Students in a Heterogeneous Classroom through Whole Language" (Margaret Bryant); "Gifted Education: To Be or Not to Be?" (Kathy Hagstrom); "From Ownership to 'Allship':

Building a Conceptual Framework for Education of the Gifted and Creative" (LeoNora Cohen). Two additional articles are: "My Life and How it Grew" (Julian Stanley) and "What the Gifted Need: Toward a General Unified Plan for Gifted Education" (Jessie H. Sanders and Leonard H. Sanders).

Snow, Mary B., and others, "Assessing a Whole Language Program: A Five-Year Study," paper presented at the Annual Meeting of the National Council of Teachers of English (79th, Baltimore, MD, Nov 17-22, 1989). [ED 333 342]
A longitudinal study evaluated the Cambridge Lesley literacy Project as implemented in the Longfellow School in Cambridge, Massachusetts. Five years of data on the progress of all children from kindergarten through third grade in both the Spanish bilingual program and the standard program were gathered during twice-weekly visits to the "literacy center." Three instruments were used to gather the data: "Concepts about Print," "Language Development Reading Test," and "Visual Cue Writing Sample." Two brief profiles of very different learners demonstrated that the important element in documenting students' progress that they learn to read and write and how they learn to read and write, not when and in comparison to whom. Results, reported for only one cohort over a five-year period, indicated that: (1) given a generally supportive, developmental learning environment, children become competent readers by grade five or six, reading at levels appropriate to their ages; and (2) individual students' progress toward competence is dramatically uneven.

Sorenson, Nancy L., "Holistic Evaluation of Literacy Development: Framing the Process," *Reading Research and Instruction 32*/4 (sum 1993): 66-75. [CS 746 251]
Proposes a framework for holistic evaluation of literacy development that is based on principles from Whole Language theory. Argues that evaluation should be longitudinal, contextual, and evaluative.

Spann, Mary-Beth, "Kindergarten Clinic: When Spelling Is Thinking," *Instructor 101*/7 (Mar 1992): 50 [EJ 445 265]
Discusses the use of invented spelling to help kindergarten students learn to spell. It provides a natural foundation for building spelling abilities by making students think about words and generate new knowledge. Suggests activities and guidelines for a developmentally sensitive spelling program.

Spann, Mary-Beth, and others, "Primary Place. Whole Language—Starting Out and Staying Strong," *Instructor 102*/1 (Jul-Aug 1992) 80-82. [EJ 450 843]
Addresses the needs of primary grade teachers, focusing on Whole Language. It offers strategies from various primary teachers on such issues as classroom supplies, Whole Language displays, literature-based activities, charts, graphs, language logs, and end-of-the-day journals.

Spann, Mary-Beth, and others, "Whole K Catalog," *Instructor 101*/3 (Oct 1991): 48, 50. [EJ 436 814]
Several elementary teachers present school-tested ideas for student assessment and activities for teaching writing. The article describes how one school conducted student assessment using a new checklist system and portfolios. Information is presented on schools that integrated literature, art, life skills, math, and role playing to teach writing.

"Spelling: Successful Teaching and Learning." *Scope 5*/4 (May 1990): 5 pp. [ED 320 142]
Focusing on the Whole Language and the direct instructional approaches, this pamphlet summarizes research on teaching and learning spelling. The pamphlet notes that the goal of the Whole Language approach to spelling instruction is to produce competent, independent spellers who learn through use and express their progress as

increasingly successful approximations to mature practice. The pamphlet lists seven aspects of the traditional method of direct instruction which are based on recent research.

Spiegel, Dixie Lee, "Blending Whole Language and Systematic Direct Instruction," *Reading Teacher 46*/1 (Sept 1992): 38-44. [EJ 449 773].
Reviews some of the benefits of the Whole-Language philosophy. Discusses the importance of systematic direct instruction, defining it and presenting arguments for including it in the classroom. Urges building bridges between Whole Language and more traditional approaches.

Spiegel, Dixie Lee, "Adaptability and Flexibility of Literature Resource Materials (Instructional Resources)," *Reading Teacher 43*/8 (Apr 1990): 590-92. [EJ 408 412]
Discusses the importance of the adaptability and flexibility of instructional resource materials. Highlights one quality resource for young readers, "Bookshelf, Stage 1," and another for intermediate level students, "Reading beyond the Basal Plus."

Spiegel, Dixie Lee, "Content Validity of Whole Language Materials (Instructional Resources)," *Reading Teacher 43*/2 (Nov 1989): 168-69. [EJ 398 815]
Offers a five-point checklist that educators might use to determine the content validity of materials labeled Whole Language. Recommends "The Whole Language Sourcebook" and the "Story Box" program as high content validity materials.

Squire, James R., ed., *The Dynamics of Language Learning: Research in Reading and English* (Urbana, Illinois: ERIC Clearinghouse on Reading and Communication Skills, Urbana, 1987). [ED 280 080]
Focuses on future directions for English and reading research; contents: (1) "Reading and Writing Relations: Assumptions and Directions" (James Flood and Diane Lapp); (2) "The Cognitive Base of Reading and Writing" (Stephen B. Kucer); (3) commentaries by Alan Purves and Julie Jensen; (4) "Thought and Language, Content and Structure in Language Communication" (Diane Lemonnier Schallert); (5) "The Design of Comprehensible Text" (Robert C. Calfee); (6) commentaries by Judith Langer and Robert J. Tierney; (7) "The Shared Structure of Oral and Written Language and the Implications for Teaching Writing, Reading, and Literature" (Miles Myers); (8) "Oral Language, Literacy Skills, and Response to Literature" (David K. Dickinson); (9) commentaries by David Dillon and Roselmina Indrisano; (10) "Research into Classroom Practices: What Have We Learned and Where Are We Going?" (Bryant Fillion and Rita S. Brause); (11) "Classroom Practices and Classroom Interaction during Reading Instruction: What's Going On?" (M. Trika Smith-Burke); (12) commentaries by Arthur N. Applebee and Dolores Durkin; (13) "An Examination of the Role of Computers in Teaching Language and Literature" (Bertram C. Bruce); (14) "Technology, Reading, and Writing" (Lawrence T. Frase); (15) commentaries by Johanna DeStefano, and Edmund J. Farrell; (16) "Organizing Student Learning: Teachers Teach What and How" (Jane Hansen); (17) "Assessing the Process, and the Process of Assessment, in the Language Arts" (Peter Johnston); (18) commentaries by Jerome C. Harste and P. David Pearson; (19) "Constructing Useful Theories of Teaching English from Recent Research on the Cognitive Processes of Language" (M. C. Wittrock); (20) "Themes and Progressions in Research in English" (John T. Guthrie); and (21) "Retrospect and Prospect" (James R. Squire).

Staab, Claire F., "Teacher Mediation in One Whole Literacy Classroom," *Reading Teacher 43*/8 (Apr 1990): 548-52. [EJ 408 406]
Describes one morning's reading and writing activities in a first grade classroom to provide an example of how one whole literacy teacher mediates children's learning.

Stahl, Steven A., "Riding the Pendulum: A Rejoinder to Schickedanz and McGee and Lomax," *Review of Educational Research 60*/1 (spr 1990): 141-51. [EJ 414 302] Considers the effectiveness of Whole Language/language experience programs versus basal reader approaches. The politicization of Whole Language teaching and the use of the nonbasal approaches in kindergarten versus first grade are the focal themes.

Stahl, Steven A., and Patricia D. Miller, "The Language Experience Approach for Beginning Reading: A Quantitative Research Synthesis." (1988): 45 pp. [ED 294 139] Examines the effects of the language experience approach (LEA) on beginning reading achievement in five projects conducted as part of the United States Office of Education first grade studies and 32 additional studies comparing basal reading approaches to LEA. Using two methods of quantitative synthesis (vote-counting and meta-analysis), analyses indicated that, overall, LEA approaches and basal reader approaches were approximately equal in their effects, with the following exceptions: (1) there were indications that LEA approaches may have been more effective in kindergarten than in first grade; (2) LEA approaches appeared to produce stronger effects on measures of word recognition than on measures of reading comprehension; and (3) more recent studies showed a trend toward stronger effects for the basal reading program relative to LEA methods. Findings suggest that Language Experience has an important function early in the process of learning to read, but that as the child's needs shift, LEA becomes less effective.

Stahl, Steven A. and Patricia D. Miller, "Whole Language and Language Experience Approaches for Beginning Reading: A Quantitative Research Synthesis," *Review of Educational Research 59*/1 (spr 1989): 87-116. [EJ 399 815] To examine the effects of Whole Language and language experience approaches on beginning reading achievement, a quantitative synthesis was performed on two databases: 5 first-grade studies of the United States Office of Education and 46 additional studies comparing basal reading approaches to Whole Language and language experience approaches.

Stahlschmidt, Agnes, "The Whole Language Approach [and] Support for the Whole Language Approach—What the Library Media Specialist Can Do," *School Library Media Activities Monthly 6*/4 (Dec 1989): 30-31. [EJ 404 206] The first article describes the Whole Language approach as an outgrowth of individualized reading and the language experience approach, which encourages students to read books about their own interests, regardless of their reading levels. The second suggests ways in which media specialists can contribute to the planning and implementation of Whole Language programs.

Stanek, Lou Willett, "Whole Language for Whole Kids: An Approach for Using Literature in the Classroom," *School Library Journal 37*/9 (Sep 1991): 187-89. [EJ 433 304] Discusses the use of literature in the Whole Language approach. Examples show the integration of a second grader's experiences with the curriculum; integrating the language arts in the middle school via study of the author as well as the book; and the integration of literature into the study of history.

Stanek, Lou Willett, "Whole Language: A Movement out of Sync," *School Library Journal 39*/3 (Mar 1993): 110-12. [EJ 461 493] Discusses the Whole Language philosophy of curriculum; focuses on the need for cooperation between librarians and teachers. The need for adequate teacher training is discussed, curriculum planning is considered, negative marketing tactics of publishers are described, and suggestions for successful programs are offered.

Starr, Kevin, "Whole Language and the Essential Elements of Effective Instruction: Sheathe Your Daggers!" (1989): 16 pp. [ED 304 657]
Numerous parallels exist between two instructional approaches sometimes thought to be incompatible: Whole Language and Madeline Hunter's "Essential Elements of Effective Instruction." The biggest parallel between Whole Language and the Hunter model is in the area of meaning: true Whole Language instruction depends on making learning meaningful and the Hunter model stresses that meaning is the single most important factor contributing to successful and rapid learning. Other parallels include: (1) avoiding the teaching of skills in isolation; (2) emphasizing demonstration and explanation as important teacher actions; (3) stressing creativity and spontaneity; and (4) underscoring the active character of learning. Six parallel aspects of student motivation also exist, including feeling tone and level of success.

Stasko, Mary I., "Increasing Reading Comprehension and Vocabulary Retention Skills by Using the Whole-Language Approach." (1991): 69 pp. [ED 331 013]
A practicum addressed the high percentage of students who were experiencing difficulty with reading comprehension and vocabulary retention in a fifth-grade Drop Out Prevention class by implementing a supplemental Whole Language program. Subjects were 19 fifth-grade students. An informal reading inventory, an attitude survey, and academic grades were used as pretest measurements. The students were instructed in reading through the use of a 13-week Whole Language program. In addition to any supplemental reading done by the students, each week the students were required to read five short stories or one book. The weekly Whole Language activities were centered around the reading done by students. Students worked on Whole Language activities for at least one hour per day. Results indicated that there was an increase in reading comprehension, vocabulary retention and attitudes towards reading and academic grades. Concludes that the use of Whole Language instruction was effective in increasing reading comprehension and vocabulary retention skills.

Stasz, Bird B., and others, "Writing Our Lives: An Adult Basic Skills Program," *Journal of Reading 35*/1 (Sep 1991): 30-33. [EJ 431 146]
Describes a two-year literacy project: an innovative adult basic skills class designed and orchestrated by the students themselves, where Head Start mothers and college-student volunteer tutors worked together. Attributes the project's enormous success to combining the Whole-Language approach with oral history and the writing process, resulting in the publication of four books.

Steele, Jeannie L., and Kurt Meredith, "A Districtwide Staff Development Program for Transitioning from a Basal to a Whole Language Literacy Program: The Teacher Educator's Role as a Partner in the Change Process." (1993): 24 pp. [ED 356 189]
Describes Project MILE (Moline Improvement in Literacy Education), a school/university partnership program between the University of Northern Iowa and Moline (Iowa) Public School District No. 40. The project called for a long-term collaborative effort in order to develop a complex and sophisticated level of university involvement with a single school district, which would allow for observation of successes and failures and provide opportunities for refinement of training efforts based on feedback. The project combined the prescriptive and catalytic models of organizational intervention, as teacher educators served as consultants to bring new information and strategies to the school teaching and administrative staff and as facilitators for staff-directed instructional, organizational, and curricular change. The project specifically sought to train faculty members in implementation of a language learning program based on a Whole Language philosophy. Offers a brief overview and rationale of the 5-year project, an outline of the intervention model implemented, details regarding the

methods for implementing the project; discussion of methods for establishing trust (ascribing a heightened sense of professionalism to the teaching staff, attributing greater respect for faculty decision making, and empowering faculty to set their own course for literacy learning), and a review of successes and shortcomings of the model.

Steele, Jeannie L., and Kurt Meredith, "Comprehensive Language Learning Philosophy and Goals," paper presented at the Annual Meeting of the National Reading Conference (39th, Austin, TX, Nov 28-Dec 2, 1989). [ED 326 876]
Contains a statement of the Moline School District's language learning philosophy and goals, and articulates the district's philosophy of providing students with language learning skills necessary to become life-long learners. The document includes specific objectives and anticipated student outcomes for the following: life-long learning, life experiences, parental involvement, home/school/community cooperation, classroom environment, teachers as implementors and facilitators, language learning as a natural communication process, variety of teaching strategies, inclusion of literature and media, child-centered learning, and non-threatening natural assessment.

Stephens, Diane, "Toward an Understanding of Whole Language. Technical Report No. 524." 1991): 46 pp. [ED 326 843]
This report discusses Whole Language, portraying it as a philosophy of education with three basic premises: (1) learning in school ought to incorporate what is known about learning outside of school; (2) teachers should base curricular decisions on what is known, they should possess and be driven by a vision of literacy, they should use observation to inform teaching, and they should reflect continuously; and (3) teachers as professionals are entitled to a political context that empowers them as informed decision makers. The report begins with a brief discussion of each of these premises and then surveys research that has been conducted on classrooms and practices that are consistent with a Whole Language philosophy.

Stephens, Diane, "Whole Language in Context." (1992): 16 pp. [ED 341 964]
Whole Language is a response to the increased knowledge base about language, literacy, and learning. Whole Language educators believe that teachers should have direct access to this knowledge base and be supported in their efforts to use it to inform instructional decisions. This response stands in contrast to more traditional responses in which university educators use the knowledge base to develop instructional innovations and then try to sell teachers these innovations/methods. Debates pro and con Whole Language are really debates about power and control, and a commitment to teaching as informed, reflective practice necessitates rethinking the roles of university and public school educators as well as reconceptualizing the relationship between them.

Stewig, John Warren, and Sam Leaton, eds., "Using Literature in the Elementary Classroom. Revised and Enlarged Edition." (1989): 144 pp. [ED 308 542]
Focuses on the wealth of language learning possibilities that open up when teachers surround children with attractive and well-written books and know how to use them in imaginative ways. It reflects the current movement in elementary education toward child-centered teaching and integrating the language arts. Contents: (1) "Reading to Learn about the Nature of Language" (A. Barbara Pilon); (2) "Using Picture Books for Reading Vocabulary Development" (Alden J. Moe); (3) "The Tradebook as an Instructional Tool: Strategies in Approaching Literature" (Helen Felsenthal); (4) "Book Illustration: Key to Visual and Oral Literacy" (John Warren Stewig); (5) "Reading Leads to Writing" (Richard G. Kolczynski); (6) "Creative Drama and Story Comprehension" (Mary Jett-Simpson); and (7) "Literature across the Curriculum" (Sam Leaton Sebesta).

Stice, Carole F., and John E. Bertrand, "What's Going On Here? A Qualitative Examination of Grouping Patterns in an Exemplary Whole Language Classroom," *Reading Horizons 32*/5 (Jun 1992): 383-93. [EJ 445 690]
Describes a classroom in which the teacher has developed a sense of community through her emphasis on Whole Language instruction. Describes the organizational patterns of both the teacher's and the children's activities in this exemplary Whole Language classroom. Documents instances of collaboration and student choice.

Stice, Carol F., and others, "Literacy Development in Two Contrasting Classrooms: Building Models of Practice toward a Theory of Practice." (1991): 241 pp. [ED 340 004]
A 1-year-long naturalistic study examined the differences and similarities in the literacy experiences of second grade at-risk children in 2 different types of classrooms: 1 traditional and 1 Whole Language classroom. The purpose was to develop models of the 2 contrasted classrooms. The study sought to shed light on the probable causes accounting for the differential literacy development taking place through comparing and contrasting the activities of the 44 inner-city children and 2 teachers participating in the study. Results indicated that the Whole Language philosophy created a classroom where children were encouraged to think, make choices, problem solve, and collaborate on learning in ways that are very different from a traditional classroom. Results further indicated that the Whole Language teacher spent more time actually teaching during the reading/language arts block than did the traditional teacher. Results also showed that children's "off-task" behavior usually had a literate basis in the traditional classroom.

Stice, Carole F., and Nancy P. Bertrand, "Whole Language and the Emergent Literacy of At-Risk Children: A Two Year Comparative Study." (1990): 82 pp. [ED 324 636]
Reports results of a two-year-long pilot study of the effectiveness of Whole Language on the literacy development of selected at-risk children, comparing the performance of nearly 100 first and second graders in Whole Language and traditional classrooms. Findings showed that children from the Whole Language classrooms performed as well as their counterparts from traditional classes on standardized achievement tests in reading. Informal, qualitative measures of literacy development indicated that, compared to children in traditional classrooms, children from the Whole Language classrooms: (1) read for meaning better, corrected more of their mistakes, and retold more fully the stories they read; (2) wrote so much that they did as well or better than their traditional counterparts on spelling, with little or no direct instruction in spelling; (3) appeared more confident in their reading; and (4) appeared to possess a wider variety of strategies related to reading. The study concluded that children in the Whole Language classrooms appeared to feel better about themselves as readers, writers, and learners; seemed to know more about the reading process, and appeared to learn the mechanics of reading and writing as well as or better than their traditional counterparts without high levels of direct skill and drill instruction; and appeared to be on their way to becoming more independent learners than the children in the traditional program. Concludes that Whole Language (in the hands of trained and committed teachers) appears to be a viable alternative to traditional instruction for young children at-risk.

Stratton, Beverly D., and others, "Discovering Oneself," *Middle School Journal 24*/1 (Sep 1992): 42-43. [EJ 449 953]
Describes an approach in which students develop a book about themselves that combines photography and word processing skills. The project is based on the Whole Language model of teaching literacy that develops reading, writing, listening, and speaking skills.

Strickland, Kathleen M., "Changes in Perspectives: Student Teachers' Development of a Reading Instruction Philosophy," paper presented at the Annual Meting of the Association of Teacher Educators (Las Vegas, NV, Feb 5-8, 1990). [ED 331 037]
A study compared the philosophies developed in undergraduate methods courses with philosophies influenced by example under a cooperating teacher in an elementary school classroom. Subjects for the first part of the study were 14 undergraduate students enrolled in a methods course. The subjects for the second part of the study were 12 students who had recently completed the same methods course and were participating in their field experience at a suburban public school three days a week for five weeks. Data were collected through administration of the Theoretical Orientation to Reading Profile (TORP) at the beginning and end of the semester, several reaction papers written by students, and observations and conversations with the cooperating teachers. Results indicated that students were influenced by the philosophies of their university professors, and many were open to new ideas and philosophies. As indicated in the second half of the study, however, many students left methods courses with no orientation or philosophy. The amount of influence cooperating teachers had on students varied. Although the influence on behaviors or methods of classroom management was evident during observation, very few students were influenced philosophically by what they saw happening in the classroom. Students with a Whole Language philosophy used terms such as "believe" and "know" when discussing what they were doing in the classroom, indicating that they had an understanding of the reasons behind the way they were approaching literacy.

Strickland, James, "Computers and Composition in the Context of a Whole Language Philosophy," paper presented at the Annual Meeting of the Conference on College Composition and Communication (43rd, Cincinnati, OH, Mar 19-21, 1992). [ED 343 131]
A Whole Language philosophy can guide the use of computers to enhance the teaching of composition and provide cautions against their misuse. A Whole Language classroom is student-centered. When computers are introduced into a classroom, the technology tends to draw attention to itself, making the machine the center of the lessons, forcing students to learn a new vocabulary, and learn a new way of performing old tasks. In contrast, in a Whole Language classroom, the computer helps in the curriculum rather than shapes it. Computer-assisted instruction at one time promoted drill-for-skill programs, and recently idea-processors, spell-checkers, and style-checkers, creating on-line versions of five-paragraph essays, focusing attention on error detection. However, a Whole Language classroom with computers is language rich, looking at language as exciting and dynamic, a means of bringing groups together, fostering collaborative learning and communication between and among discourse communities.

Strickland, James, ed., *English Leadership Quarterly* (1991): 65 pp. [ED 344 245]
Contents: "CEL: Shorter and Better" (Myles D. Eley); "Toward a New Philosophy of Language Learning" (Kathleen Strickland); "Whole Language: Implications for Secondary Classrooms" (Barbara King-Shaver); "Whole Language: Moving to a Whole New Neighborhood" (Bill Newby); "Student Writers Set Their Own Goals" (Sharon Wieland); "Assessment in a Whole Language Environment: Teaching Students to Document Their Own Writing Progress" (Edgar H. Thompson); and "Returning Vocabulary to Context" (Carol Jago). Articles in number 2 deal with learning labels and include: "Unmasking Psycho/Biological Labels for Language Acts" (Cornelius Cosgrove); "'Skills Kids' and Real Literature" (Sharon Wieland); "Track-ing or Sidetracking?" (Carole Bencich); "Flor: A Learning Disabled Child in a Whole

Language Classroom" (Deborah Wells); "Room to Talk: Opening Possibilities with the 'At-Risk'" (Suzanne Miller); "Do You Teach LEPs or REAL Students?" (Darlynn Fink); and "A Silent Calling: Why I Chose This Career" (Ron Goba). The changing literature classroom is the focus of number 3 and includes: "Teaching Literature, Canon Formation, and Multiculturalism" (William F. Williams); "Feminism and the Reconstitution of Family" (Jody Price); "When Whole Language Learners Reach Us: Challenges for a Changing Secondary Literature Classroom" (John Wilson Swope); "Writing about Literature with Large-Group Collaboration: The We-Search Paper" (Esther Broughton and Janine Rider); "Tying Reader Response to Group Interaction in Literature Classrooms (Edgar H. Thompson); and "Mr. C. Didn't Do It This Way" (E. Carolyn Tucker). Articles in number 4 discuss Whole Language, literature, and teaching and include: "Putting an End to 'Cliffs Notes' Mentalities" (Pamela Kissel); "Placing Whole Language in a Workshop Setting" (William Murdick and Rosalie Segin); "The Business of Television" (Rick Chambers); "Student Teacher Education Program" (Joellen P. Killion); "Using Computers to Foster Collaborative Learning in the Creative Writing Classroom" (Theresa M. Hune); "Sentence Combining: A Spoonful of Sugar" (Jace Condravy); "Taking Johnny Back" (Carol Jago); and "Leadership as Shared Vision" (Joseph I. Tsujimoto).

Suhor, Charles, "ERIC/RCS Report: Orthodoxies in Language Arts Instruction," *Language Arts 64*/4 (Apr 1987): 416-20. [EJ 348 977]
Presents the opposing viewpoints on grammar study, phonics and Whole Language instruction, and the role of information in English language arts.

Sulentic, Margaret Mary, "Whole Language for High-Risk Students. A Descriptive Study." (1989): 94 pp. [ED 323 490]
A study was conducted to determine the appropriateness of a particular Whole Language program, entitled "Project Victory," designed specifically for a group of high-risk, seventh-grade students in a predominately urban intermediate public school. Subjects were 20 students identified as high-risk by their school district on the basis of the Iowa Tests of Basic Skills performance scores. Project Victory consisted of a 3-hour morning block of language instruction based on the philosophical theory of Whole Language. The program integrated the language processes of reading, writing, speaking, listening, and thinking and focused on functional, relevant literature such as magazines, newspapers, and trade books. Curriculum and instruction were based on the specific language needs of the student. Both formal and informal evaluation procedures were used to assess the program. Observations revealed a change in student' attitudes and students appeared more inclined to work cooperatively as the year progressed. Emerging patterns of free reading material choices also became apparent. Students also appeared calmer, more trusting, and more willing to take risks in the classroom as the year progressed. It was observed that students learned positively from their mistakes. An increase in parental involvement was also noted. Based on the positive results of the study, further research on curriculum and instruction for high-risk students based on the theory of Whole Language is needed.

Sumara, Dennis, and Laurie Walker, "The Teacher's Role in Whole Language," *Language Arts 68*/4 (Apr 1991): 276-85. [EJ 425350]
Searches for some precision in the discourse of Whole Language with respect to the role of the teacher as expressed in words such as *empowerment, control, predictability,* and *authenticity*. Observes and interprets the practice of two successful Whole Language teachers to refine understandings of these concepts as they are enacted in classrooms.

Summaries of *1991-92 EDCORE Grant Winners*. (1992): 65 pp. [ED 344 715]
This document includes a pamphlet and report pertaining to International Paper Company's EDCORE (Education and Community Resources) grant program. The pamphlet describes the program which awards grants in communities where International Paper Company's employees live and work. It highlights three EDCORE grants in Louisiana, Wisconsin, and Maine. The accompanying report contains information on 1991-92 EDCORE grant winners. One hundred forty-seven grants totalling $549,167 were awarded in school districts in the states of Alabama, Arkansas, California, Louisiana, Maine, Mississippi, New York, Oregon, Pennsylvania, South Carolina, Texas, and Wisconsin. Grant descriptions are organized alphabetically by state, and within state by the International Paper Company Facility which is in partnership with local school districts. Grants fall into the categories of John Hinman Teacher Fellowships, School Projects, and Open Opportunity Grants. Each grant description contains the title, the teacher or coordinator, the school, the amount awarded, and a brief summary of the project. Grant topics include: (1) Whole Language instruction; (2) enhanced science programs; (3) geography instruction; (4) cooperative learning; (5) student publishing; (6) higher level thinking skills; (7) community involvement; (8) enhanced mathematics instruction; (9) reading programs; (10) environmental education; (11) outdoor education; (12) writing instruction; (13) educational technology; and (14) programs for at-risk students.

Summer Program Options. *Summer Program Academic Resources Coordination Center.* (1992): 31 pp. [ED 350 123]
This directory, compiled by the Summer Program Academic Resources Coordination Center (SPARCC) in Loudonville, New York, describes 19 summer programs that demonstrate a variety of delivery systems used to meet the educational and social needs of migrant students. SPARCC was a migrant education grant that developed and helped implement model summer migrant education programs in New York, Florida, and Virginia. Program profiles contain the following information: (1) the delivery models used in the program such as all-day summer school, Saturday or weekend programs, camping trips, and correspondence courses; (2) the state in which the program is located; (3) project description, including specific objectives and activities; (4) date and time schedule of project; (5) number of students participating; (6) student qualifications for program participation; (7) staffing requirements; and (8) contact person and telephone number. Includes information on using the Whole Language approach and other curricula in a summer program format.

Swain, Sherry Seale, "Inside My Writing Classroom," *PTA Today 18*/1 (Oct 1992): 16-18. [EJ 455 163]
Describes the process approach to writing instruction, examining the literature-based approach to reading and the Whole Language learning approach. In Whole Language classrooms, reading, writing, listening, and thinking are interwoven. The article offers ways for parents to support such approaches at home and school.

Swan, Ann M., "Getting a Good 'View' of Whole Language," *Ohio Reading Teacher 25*/4 (sum 1991): 31-34 [EJ 437 380]
Discusses the issues of language, learning and teaching, and kids and teachers in a Whole Language classroom.

Swan, Ann, "Getting a Good View of Whole Language," *Ohio Reading Teacher 26*/2 (win 1992): 11-12. [EJ 442 698]
Discusses the Whole Language philosophy and its view of language, learning, teaching, view of the relationship between students and teachers, and the holistic approach.

Swiniarski, Louise B., "Voices from Down Under: Impressions of New Zealand's Schooling," *Childhood Education 68/4* (sum 1992): 225-28. [EJ 450 538] Presents conflicting views of New Zealand's schooling from teachers' perspectives and examines some of the reforms, including Whole Language, and reflections of New Zealand's educators. Discusses some of the implications for U.S. schooling.

Swoger, Peggy A., "Scott's Gift," *English Journal 78/3* (Mar 1989): 61-65. [EJ 388 461] Describes the effects of using the writing workshop approach on Scott, a student with learning disabilities, and the phenomenal progress he made. Maintains that students' giant leaps occur because students are little learning machines when they are learning what they themselves need to know.

Tanner-Cazinha, Diane, and others, "New Perspectives on Literacy Evaluation (Reviews and Reflections)," *Language Arts 68/8* (Dec 1991): 669-73 [EJ 435 629] Reviews five professional books that examine a variety of theoretical, social, and cultural issues related to assessment in schools and classrooms. Concludes that traditional literacy evaluation is more often a barrier than a help.

Targovnik, Nina R., "An Invitation Extended To Critically Examine Whole Language: The Silent Student Speaks," (1993): 16 pp. [ED 354 496] Reacting to Whole Language zealots who are not willing to hear new viewpoints or engage in a dialogue with people who differ from their paradigm of education, a graduate student-teacher-researcher who is in general agreement with Whole Language principles responds to a series of conversations in which she was a listener but not a participant. The gist of each of the 12 conversations is given and discussed in turn. Her conclusions are that: (1) while her silence in these conversations was generally tolerated, those who advanced Whole Language felt there was no place for silence; (2) there is one basic philosophy of Whole Language that all must learn; (3) there is a "right" way for teachers to act in Whole Language classrooms; (4) Whole Language "zealots" have proclaimed that content areas are dead; (5) Whole Language advocates have proclaimed traditional tests as the work of the devil; (6) textbooks of all sorts are condemned; (7) Whole Language enthusiasts insist that aliterates are worse off than illiterates; (8) the idea that students need to manipulate texts and to become intimately involved in the writing process is a common "buzz phrase" of the Whole Language camp; (9) Whole Language advocates seem not to acknowledge that some students do not learn to read by merely reading; (10) Whole Language enthusiasts often ignore other voices or do not give others a chance to voice their opinions; (11) Whole Language advocates find that women have a unique way of thinking and feeling which is not valued by the schools, workplace, or society; and (12) Whole Language enthusiasts do not listen to people espousing non-politically correct views.

Taylor, Denny, "Teaching without Testing: Assessing the Complexity of Children's Literacy Learning," *English Education 22/1* (Feb 1990): 4-74. [EJ 411 503] Discusses the "Biographic Literacy Profiles Project," a seminar for teachers and administrators which focused on developing an alternative to current assessment methods in elementary language arts. Shows how the process of changing assessment patterns can reflect the same integrative, holistic goals that teachers have for working with children. Discusses possible consequences of making this paradigm shift in assessment.

Tchudi, Stephen, "The Interdisciplinary Island. Whole Language, Holistic Learning, and Teacher Education," *Holistic Education Review 5/1* (spr 1992): 30-36 [EJ 445 255] Describes a Whole Language, interdisciplinary summer program for school and college teachers. From hands-on exploration and reading and writing about self-selected topics, participants learned to understand theory and practice of Whole Language instruction and to explore implications for their own teaching.

Temple, Charles, and others, "The Beginnings of Writing. Second Edition." (1988): 270 pp. [ED 308 547]
Emphasizing the constructive role teachers pay in children's literacy development, this book provides a clear and richly illustrated description of children's writing development from preschool through approximately fourth grade. The book, divided into the three sections covering beginning writing, spelling, and composition, consists of the following chapters: (1) "A Child Discovers How to Write"; (2) "The Precursors of Writing"; (3) "Features of Children's Early Writing"; (4) "What Children Do with Early Graphics"; (5) "Invented Spelling"; (6) "Learning Standard Spelling"; (7) "Making Progress in Spelling"; (8) "The Functions and Forms in Children's Composition"; (9) "Writing in the Poetic Mode"; (10) "Approaching the Transactional Mode"; and (11) "Writing: The Child, the Teacher, and the Class." The epilogue is entitled "Playing with Literature and Language: Amy's Story."

Teschner, Richard V., "'Provided There Is an Adequate Exposure to This L2 in the School and Environment and Sufficient Motivation to Learn It': The Applicability (at times *pace* Cummins) of Majority-Language Immersion Programs to Limited- or Non-English-Proficient Spanish-L1 Grade-School Populations in the United States-Mexican Border Area." (1988): 39 pp. [ED 302 087]
The El Paso, Texas, Independent School District's district-wide program in majority-language (English) immersion is examined to determine the source of its success. The program's similarities to and differences from the Canadian immersion model are explored. The program's superior results in comparison with the same district's transitional bilingual education programs are looked at in terms of James Cummins's discussions of bilingual education. Concludes that the immersion program's superiority over the transitional programs can be explained largely in terms of its maximal use of English and its Whole Language approach. The bilingual immersion program approach is recommended not as a panacea, but as a superior educational alternative.

Thomas, Grace Gilliard, "Increasing Literature Interests in First Grade Retained Students in a Chapter I Reading Lab by Matching Reading Approaches to Their Reading Styles." (1990): 179 pp. [ED 321 243]
Addresses the problem of all students not learning to read in the same manner when the instruction was limited to only one approach, that of the basal reader with its phonics emphasis. The Reading Style Inventory, the Swassing-Barbe Modality Index, and the Bradway Quick Check were administered to the students attending the Chapter 1 reading lab. Reading techniques found in the Whole Language philosophy were used which accommodated the students' reading styles. Parental involvement in the reading process was also included. Ten-high quality paperback books were used as part of the reading instruction and were given to the students to begin a home library of readable books. Motivational activities and rewards were used and stressed throughout the 8 months to increase students' interest in books. Results of the practicum were positive. The goal was achieved for all the students participating in the practicum. Results indicated on a teacher-made interest survey that their interest in literature and the amount of time they read alone, with a friend, and with a parent had all increased substantially.

Thompson, Richard A., "A Critical Perspective on Whole Language," *Reading Psychology* *13*/2 (Apr-Jun 1992): 131-55. [EJ 448 369]
Argues that reading educators need to appraise objectively the Whole Language instructional philosophy in relation to what is known about reading methodology.

Discusses the Whole Language philosophy, its history, the "whole sentence method," and Whole Language weaknesses. Advocates developing a "balanced reading program," which would emphasize skills instruction as well as Whole Language ideas.

Thompson, Linda W., "The Use of Literature in a School: An Inquiry." (1985): 19 pp. [ED 305 630]

Examines the practitioner's perspective of literature and how literature is being used in the classroom. Teachers, librarians, and administrators at a suburban school serving over 700 children from kindergarten through fifth grade were interviewed, and professional journals directed toward practitioners, published curriculum guides, and books about children's literature written for teachers were examined. Findings indicated that the observed classroom and curricular uses of literature focused on helping students develop a love of reading and developing reading proficiency by reading, but that these activities emphasized developmental curriculum the least. The lower grades, using a Whole Language approach, showed more evidence of a developmental curricular focus. Findings indicated that the commonly occurring literature curriculum objectives of exposure to different literary genres and the recognition of the use of literary forms and devices were not evident in the classroom and that professional materials had limited influence on the practitioner.

Thomson, Brenda, and Lynn D. Miller, "Pilot Study of the Effectiveness of a Direct Instructional Model as a Supplement to a Literature-Based Delivery Model; Traditional Teaching to Whole Language: A Focus on Instructional Routines." (1991): 33 pp. [ED 352 602]

A study examined the effects on 80 first graders' reading achievement when direct instructional phonics is incorporated as a supplement to a Whole Language approach. Two first-grade classrooms used the Houghton-Mifflin Integrated Literature Program, and two other classrooms supplemented the program with direct phonics instruction. Subjects completed a school readiness inventory and word recognition and fluency pretests, and were given posttests on word recognition, fluency, and the Houghton-Mifflin Student Progress Survey. Results indicated that the direct instruction group: (1) did significantly poorer in the school readiness inventory; yet (2) scored as well on the word recognition and fluency posttests as the other group; and (3) scored higher on the student survey. A second study of teaching and learning of reading in seven upper elementary reading resource rooms was conducted using the premises of grounded theory research. One finding of the study is relevant to a possible explanation of teachers' willingness to consider new instructional ideas: an underlying routine seemed to bind together the more obvious routines into stable interlocking networks. Traditional teachers who resist a Whole Language orientation often raise concerns associated with routines. In order "to do" Whole Language, a traditional teacher must relinquish the notion that a transition to a Whole Language orientation simply means a change of materials and the inclusion of a few new procedures. For major changes to occur efficiently teachers need to appreciate that change in one routine may strongly impact others.

Thrash, Blanche Carter, "Whole Language and the Media Center." (1992): 43 pp. [ED 346 828]

Investigates the services provided by elementary and middle school media centers to support Whole Language instruction, and to determine how the media program contributes to the goals, resources, and teaching strategies of the Whole Language movement. The population for the study included all 81 elementary and 15 middle schools in the Atlanta, Georgia, City School System. Data were collected in 1991-92 using a mailed survey questionnaire and analyzed using descriptive statistics. Responses from 78% of the media specialists surveyed indicated that: (1) media center services to support Whole Language instruction included storytime, library displays, assisting pupils with research, book fairs, creative writing activities, and book reviews; (2) resources provided by the media program for Whole Language included media committee minutes, media memos, professional articles, Whole Language bibliographies, and a handbook of services; (3) cooperative planning between the classroom teachers and media specialists infused library skills into Whole Language instruction; and (4) assisting pupils with research was a priority. This research study helps bring attention to the significant role the media center plays in the Whole Language movement. It is concluded that Whole Language affords the library media center the opportunity to provide educational leadership and promote research and learning.

Thursby, Ann, "A Teacher-Training Design for a Multicultural Setting." (1992): 198 pp. [ED 355 762]
Investigates the need and appropriate design for an inservice training program for teachers in a multicultural educational program in the Philippines called "Preparing Refugees for Elementary Programs," or PREP. The PREP program provides classroom instruction to Indonesian refugee children 6.5 to 11 years of age and is administered at the Refugee Processing Center in the province of Bataan. Program objectives included flexible and systematic procedures for identifying and meeting evolving staff training needs, experiential learning and Whole Language instruction, and development of problem-solving skills. The report outlines the program and reviews relevant literature, then discusses the group-oriented Filipino culture and its implications for such a program, especially for the Whole Language approach to teaching. A description of the adult learner follows, focusing on adult development within different cultural contexts and implications for teacher training. Methodology used for designing the teacher training program is then described, including formulation and field testing. Results of field testing are reported in some detail, including tallies of participant responses to program components and emphases and recommendations for improved training design in 1990 and 1991. The trainers' manual for the proposed program forms a larger portion of the report, and a final section provides an overall summary of the project and conclusions. An article on evaluating teachers using the Whole Language approach is appended.

Tibbetts, Katherine A., and others, "Development of a Criterion-Referenced, Performance-Based Assessment of Reading Comprehension in a Whole Literacy Program," paper presented at the Annual Meeting of the American Educational Research Association (San Francisco, CA, Apr 20-24, 1992). [ED 344 931]
Describes the development of a criterion-referenced, performance-based measure of third grade reading comprehension. The primary purpose of the assessment is to contribute unique and valid information for use in the formative evaluation of a whole literacy program. A secondary purpose is to supplement other program efforts to communicate and reinforce objectives for student performance and instructional practices. The Kamehameha Schools/Bishop Estate is a private non-profit educational institution in Hawaii. One of its largest and oldest projects is the Kamehameha Early Education Program (KEEP), which is designed to improve the literacy skills of native Hawaiian children by improving the quality of instruction they receive. KEEP hires and trains teacher consultants for public elementary schools to provide training and support. An innovative student assessment was developed to determine student outcomes supplementing a portfolio approach with a criterion-referenced test with performance-based constructed response items. Assessment development was a collaborative effort of educators, students, and evaluators that was field-tested in 1991.

361

The prototype assessment directly taps curricular objectives in a format that is congruent with instructional practices.

Toliver, Marilyn, "Try It, You'll Like It: Whole Language (In the Classroom)," *Reading Teacher 43*/4 (Jan 1990): 348-49. [EJ 403 676]
Offers suggestions to incorporate holistic reading and writing activities into existing curricula and classroom structure to create a print-rich environment in which children use reading and writing in meaningful ways.

Tovey, Duane R., and James E. Kerber, eds., "Roles in Literacy Learning: A New Perspective." (1986): 187 pp. [ED 264 535]
Refining and better understanding the roles parents, teachers, administrators, and researchers play in helping children learn to process written language is the focus of this book. Part 1 considers the role of the parents and includes the following articles: "Learning to Read: It Starts in the Home" (David B. Doake): "Let's Read Another One" (Diane L. Chapman); and "Literacy Environment in the Home and Community" (Yetta M. Goodman and Myna M. Haussler). Part 2 considers the role of the teacher in the following articles: "Teaching and Language Centered Programs" (MaryAnne Hall); "Guiding a Natural Process" (Don Holdaway); and "Nourishing and Sustaining Reading" (Margaret Meek Spencer). The articles in part 3 discuss the role of the child: "Apprenticeship in the Art of Literacy" (Anne D. Forester); "Children's Quest for Literacy" (John McInnes); and "Children Write to Read and Read to Write" (Diane E. DeFord). The articles in part 4 consider the role of the administrator: "Emergence of an Administrator" (Marilyn D. Reed); "Removing the 'We-They' Syndrome" (G. William Stratton); and "Cultivating Teacher Power" (Moira G. McKenzie). The role of the researcher is covered in part 5 in the final articles: "Theory, Practice, and Research in Literacy Learning" (Robert Emans); "Reading Research at the One Century Mark" (Edmund H. Henderson); and "The Researcher, Whole Language, and Reading" (William D. Page).

Trenholm, Dorothy S., "What Is the Effect of Traditional Language Teaching Method versus Whole Language Teaching on Learning Sentence Structure?" (1992): 22 pp. [ED 353 552]
Examines the effect of a Whole-Language-type program for learning sentence structure with high school students in a dropout prevention program. Subjects, 60 students in a Chicago, Illinois public school dropout prevention program, were randomly assigned to a control or experimental group and were administered a diagnostic pre- and posttest on parts of speech and sentence structure. The experimental group was taught by the Whole Language/TDSSP (TreneD Sentence Pattern Paradigms) method in which one subject-verb paradigm was taught for each of 6 weeks. Results indicated that the treatment made a statistical significance. A review of the literature on Whole Language occupies the greater part of this paper, preceding the description of the study.

Trute, Joy W., "Improving Basic Language Skills of Limited English Proficient Kindergarten Children." (1990): 84 pp. [ED 315 183]
A kindergarten teacher implemented a 10-week practicum study designed to enhance the English acquisition of 38 limited English proficient kindergarten children. Primary goals of the study were to: (1) narrow the learning gap between the English speaking children and the limited English proficient children; and (2) develop language skills the children would need in first grade. To attain these goals, pretests and posttests were designed and administered to assess students' English comprehension. Test items were related to prescribed kindergarten objectives. In addition, Whole Language experiences were developed; literature was selected; sixth-grade peer teachers were recruited; and

communication with students' families was established. Practicum evaluation data indicated that outcomes were positive. Students improved in their English comprehension. Many staff members expressed interest in Whole Language strategies and came to observe classroom activities.

Tunnell, Michael O., and James S. Jacobs, "Using 'Real' Books: Research Findings on Literature Based Reading Instruction," *Reading Teacher 42*/7 (Mar 1989): 470-77. [EJ 385 147]
Reviews several studies which support the success of a literature-based approach to literacy with various types of students (limited English speakers, developmental readers, remedial readers, etc.). Describes several common elements found in different literature-based programs, including the use of natural text, reading aloud, and sustained silent reading.

Turnbull, Carol, "Three Dimensional Teaching," *Canadian Journal of English Language Arts 12*/1-2 (1989): 57-58. [EJ 390 390]
Examines several factors limiting the implementation of the Whole Language approach, including mystification of the concept, lack of parent involvement, and overzealous implementation. Discusses ways to avoid these problems.

Uhry, Joanna K., and Margaret Jo Shepherd, "The Effect of Segmentation/Spelling Training on the Acquisition of Beginning Reading Strategies," paper presented at the Annual Meeting of the American Educational Research Association (Boston, MA, Apr 16-20, 1990). [ED 331 020]
Investigates whether instruction in spelling would affect acquisition of the alphabetic strategy by beginning readers. Subjects, 28 beginning first- and second-graders of average or above-average intellectual ability in Whole Language classrooms, participated in small group training for two 20 minute periods a week for 6.5 months. Experimental subjects were given segmenting/spelling tasks, while controls were trained to read letters, words, and text. Both groups used computers. Results indicated that trained subjects made significant early gains in using alphabetic strategy and were significantly better than controls by the end of the study at reading regular and irregular nonsense and real words, and at oral passages, but not at silent comprehension. Findings suggest that spelling may affect reading through the mapping of sounds onto letters.

Uhry, Joanna K., and Margaret Jo Shepherd, "Segmentation/Spelling Instruction as Part of a First-Grade Reading Program: Effects on Several Measures of Reading," *Reading Research Quarterly 28*/3 (Jul-Sep 1993): 218-33. [CS 745 804]
Notes that experimental subjects were trained to segment and spell phonetically regular words, while controls were trained to read letters, words, and text. Finds that trained subjects made significant gains and were better than controls at posttest in measures of reading nonsense words, real words, and oral passages, but not of silent reading comprehension.

"**Using** Fairy Tales for Critical Reading. Bonus Activity Book," *Learning 19*/8 (Apr 1991): 23-42. [EJ 427 873]
Uses the Whole Language approach to encourage young readers and prereaders to become critical listeners and viewers by comparing different versions of familiar fairy tales ("The Three Little Pigs" and "Beauty and the Beast"). Class activities, educational games, posters, and student activity pages are included.

Usova, Constance J., and George M. Usova, "Integrating Art and Language Arts for First Grade At-Risk Children," *Reading Improvement 30*/2 (sum 1993): 117-21. [CS 745 541]

Describes an intensive integrated art and language-arts instructional program for first-grade at-risk children. Notes a combination of Whole Language, language experience, and basal reading approaches. Finds a marked improvement in reading, writing ability, and language ability.

Valdez, Alora, "Classroom Management Beliefs and Practices in an Early Childhood Classroom: A Case of Mrs. W.'s Conflict of Interest," paper presented at the Annual Meeting of the American Educational Research Association (72nd, Chicago, IL, Apr 3-7, 1991). [ED 340 513]
A year-long interpretive case study was conducted to examine a second-grade teacher's beliefs and practices concerning classroom management during Whole Language instruction. The study was designed to determine whether the teacher's beliefs concerning classroom management matched those discussed in the early childhood literature and also whether they matched her practices. If it were determined that her beliefs and her practices were not congruent, the effect of this incongruence on her and her students would also be assessed. From data analysis it was concluded that the teacher held strong beliefs about classroom management and that they were similar to those discussed in the early childhood literature, which emphasizes the indoctrination of self-direction in students. Yet her practices appeared to be similar to those discussed in the classroom management literature, which emphasize the teacher's establishment and maintenance of order through academic work. Because of this discrepancy, her students were not becoming self-directed, and this caused her frustration. The teacher felt that she might have to become less nurturing if she became cognizant of the differences between her classroom management beliefs and practices. With time, however, she used her newly found awareness to come up with concrete ways to make her beliefs and practices work for her and not against her.

Valencia, Sheila W., "New Assessment Books (Assessment)," *Reading Teacher 45/3* (Nov 1991): 244-45. [EJ 432 662]
Reviews two recent professional publications concerning alternative assessment: "Portfolio Assessment in the Reading-Writing Classroom" and "Assessment and Evaluation in Whole Language Programs."

Valeri-Gold, Maria, and James Olson, "Using Research-Based Whole Language Strategies to Empower At-Risk College Readers," *Research & Teaching in Developmental Education 7/2* (spr 1991): 81-91. [EJ 431 656]
Describes the following research-based Whole Language instructional strategies: predictions as a prereading activity, "webbing" words or ideas around a specific topic, shared writing, journal writing, vocabulary development, clustering synonyms as a way of approaching new vocabulary, context clues, analogies, definition maps, and reading short stories and novels aloud.

Van Arsdale, Minerva, and others, "Teachers Writing about Books That Made a Difference (Have You Read?)," *Reading Teacher 46/2* (Oct 1992): 162-64. [EJ 451 259]
Presents reviews by elementary school classroom teachers of books that have had a significant impact on their teaching and the philosophical underpinning for their actions. Includes reviews of four books on literature, literacy, language arts, Whole Language, the holistic approach, and assessment.

Varble, Mary Ellen, and Veronica Stephen, "Integrating a Whole Language Approach in Secondary Schools." (1991): 6 pp. [ED 353 540]
Deals with how to integrate a Whole Language approach in secondary schools. Following a short outline of the differences between Whole Language principles and skills-based precepts, key tenets of Whole Language are briefly discussed. The next

section of the issue deals with principal-teacher partnerships, and these are followed by brief descriptions (under the school name and address) of three secondary school teachers who use Whole Language in their English classes.

Varble, Mary Ellen, "Analysis of Writing Samples of Students Taught by Teachers Using Whole Language and Traditional Approaches," *Journal of Educational Research 83/5* (May-Jun 1990): 245-51. [EJ 414 233]
Second-graders taught by the Whole Language approach produced better writing samples, for content and meaning, than did second graders taught by the traditional approach. No differences were evident in the use of mechanics. Sixth-grade samples evidenced no difference between the two approaches.

Vassallo, Philip, "Putting Children before Grown-ups," *American School Board Journal 179/3* (Mar 1992): 42, 44. [EJ 441 141]
In the Children's School, a pilot project in New York City's south Bronx neighborhood, a unique program for kindergarten to third-grade students features the Whole Language approach. This philosophy puts children first and provides an environment that gives children varied choices for learning.

Vaughn, Sherry Curtis, and Jerry L. Milligan, "If They Learn To Read by Reading, How Do We Get Them Started?," paper presented at the Annual Transmountain Regional Conference of the International Reading Association (7th, Vancouver, British Columbia, May 29-31, 1986). [ED 301 868]
Psycholinguistic theoretical information provides the framework for the argument that talking books, taped books, shared book experiences and composing activities that include real text prepared for a specific audience provide an environment conducive to beginning reading. Six assumptions underlie the learning-to-read process: (1) children learn to read by making attempts to understand whole text that is meaningful to them; (2) children learn to read by reading often; (3) the process of learning to read must be enjoyable; (4) children improve their reading proficiency by reading materials somewhat beyond their current capacity; (5) children, even nonreaders, can read most materials of interest to them provided they are given sufficient background; and (6) reading and writing are reciprocal processes.

Veatch, Jeannette, "Whole Language and Its Predecessors: Commentary," paper presented at the Annual Meeting of the College Reading Association (Crystal City, VA, Oct 31-Nov 3, 1991). [ED 341 035]
Since the rise of the Whole Language movement, Sylvia Ashton-Warner's key vocabulary, individualized reading, and experience charts have been notable for their omission from the many books available on Whole Language. Whole Language strength is notable in at least four major areas: (1) its learner-centeredness; (2) its scorn of commercial behavioristic material, such as basals and workbooks; (3) its demand for integration of all curriculum, especially the language arts; and (4) its salutary insistence on authenticity in teaching methodology. Omission of key vocabulary, individualized reading, and experience charts from current practice is puzzling, since each is compatible with the four characteristics of Whole Language. One explanation for this omission is that divergence is not considered "pure" Whole Language. Also, the expansion of the Whole Language movement has taken place since 1970, but the three activities were popular before 1970. The publication dates of entries in the bibliographies of five major Whole Language texts were analyzed. Results indicated that 92% of the citations bore dates after 1970. Particularly noteworthy is one page from one of the bibliographies which reveals an ignorance of the disputes that have roiled the field of reading for decades by including only one reference to "phonics," the only subject

other than Whole Language mentioned. Findings suggest that proponents of Whole Language have chosen to ignore, or were ignorant of, approaches and activities popular before 1970 that were compatible with their philosophy.

Villaume, Susan Kidd, and Thomas Worden, "Developing Literate Voices: The Challenge of Whole Language," *Language Arts 70*/6 (Oct 1993): 462-68. [CS 746 126]
Suggests that the essence of Whole Language is students developing literate voices. Discusses a seven-month partnership in which the authors participated in, and reflected on, literature discussions with small groups of fourth graders. Explores how literate voices are developed in real classrooms.

Von Lehmden-Koch, Cheryl A., "Attitudes of K-6 Teachers towards Invented Spelling," Ohio, 1993. [CS 011 305]
Reports a study that determined attitudes of elementary teachers of grades K-6 towards the use of invented spelling. Twenty-nine teachers in two rural school districts in northwest Ohio completed a questionnaire designed to investigate the extent of Whole Language use, spelling strategies taught, and attitudes towards invented spelling. Results: Teachers in the primary grades (K-3) were more accepting of the use of invented or phonetic spelling than the teachers in the intermediate grades (4-6). Teachers were not pleased with the way they actually taught spelling—they taught spelling differently than they thought it should be taught.

Vivian, Diane M., "A Thematic Literary Unit: Using Literature across the Curriculum in an Elementary Classroom." (1990): 15 pp. [ED 316 867]
"Think Big" is a thematic literary unit, using literature about elephants in a holistic way and attempting to cross the curriculum into the content areas of science and math. It is a way of expanding the basal reading series and providing appropriate and supportive instruction in a cooperative, more interactive learning environment. To assess what students already knew and to stimulate interest, students were informally given an elephant facts test and brainstormed about elephants. After reading non-fiction books about elephants, the factual information was confirmed and reviewed by use of cloze procedure, semantic mapping, and reviewing the initial brainstorming words and phrases. Students participated in literature groups to discuss and retell fiction stories. Students spent time daily in writing workshops which provided for practice and sharing of their written responses to literature. They made up their own stories about elephants and collected elephant jokes and riddles. Students responded to the books about elephants that they read at home in a variety of ways. Math skills were used to generate new meaning for the concepts of size and weight used in the elephant fiction and non-fiction materials. During science, students compared and researched the size of mammals. Reading, writing, and literature were used as a vehicle through which learning occurred.

Wagner, Betty Jane, "ERIC/RCS Report: Integrating the Language Arts," *Language Arts 62*/5 (Sep 1985): 557-60. [EJ 322 101]
Reviews materials from the ERIC system and other sources on providing natural learning situations in which reading, writing, speaking, and listening can be developed together for real purposes and real audiences in the self-contained elementary class-room.

Wagner, Betty Jane, "Whole Language: Integrating the Language Arts—and Much More. ERIC Digest." (1989): 4 pp. [ED 313 675]
In response to a current grass-roots movement among teachers, this ERIC digest provides an overview of the Whole Language approach. The first section outlines what Whole Language is, and the second section enumerates what Whole Language is not.

The third section discusses what happens in Whole Language classrooms, and the final section discusses theory and research supporting Whole Language.

Wakefield, Alice P., "An Investigation of Teaching Style and Orientation to Reading Instruction," *Reading Improvement 29/*3 (fall 1992): 183-87. [EJ 452 728]
Examines whether teachers who have a webblike, multidimensional ordering style preference are more likely to view Whole Language as a valuable approach to language arts instruction than are teachers with a more methodical, step-by-step orientation to learning. Finds that a relationship exists between learning style preference and orientation to reading instruction.

Waldon, Mary Ann, "Whole Language Approach Applied (Research into Practice)," *Reading Psychology 9/*3 (1988): 259-65. [EJ 391 845]
Presents numerous Whole Language activities used by kindergarten teachers, including experience charts, dictated stories, student-written "books," and recipe writing.

Walmsley, Sean A., and Ellen L. Adams, "Realities of '"Whole Language,'" *Language Arts 70/*4 (Apr 1993): 272-80. [EJ 461 018]
Interviews a group of New York teachers to investigate the issues that teachers confront as they make the transition to Whole Language and attempt to sustain it. Discusses the amount of work involved in Whole Language instruction; relations with other faculty members, administrators, and parents; organization of instruction; defining Whole Language; and evaluating students.

Walmsley, Sean A., "James Moffett Reconsidered: Ahead of His Time, Again?" *English Education 25/*2 (May 1993): 120-27. [CS 745 505]
Discusses the achievement of James Moffett in the field of language-arts instruction, particularly by studying his seminal work *A Student-Centered Language Arts Curriculum, K-12,* and the changes made in the four editions of the book from 1968 to 1992. Claims that Moffett continues to be ahead of his time in his field.

Wangberg, Elaine G., and Mary K. Reutten, "Whole Language Approaches for Developing and Evaluating Basic Writing Ability," *Lifelong Learning 9/*8 (Jun 1986): 13-15, 24-25. [EJ 335 472]
Describes a Whole Language approach to the development of literacy and a Basic Writing Scale developed to evaluate growth in writing ability and to diagnose strengths and weaknesses in the writing of illiterate adults.

Waterman, David C., "Whole Language: Why Not?" *Contemporary Education 62/*2 (win 1991): 115-19. [EJ 447 941]
Explores the evolution of Whole Language learning, examining educational reform since the 1950s. Presents descriptions of Whole Language learning, noting confusion about its definition, and debating whether it is a reaction to poor reading and language arts teaching or response to criticisms of teaching since the 1950s.

Watson, Dorothy J., ed., *Ideas and Insights: Language Arts in the Elementary School.* (Urbana, Illinois: National Council of Teachers of English, 1987): 246 pp. [ED 287 173]
Intended to provide elementary school language-arts teachers with new and interesting teaching activities, this book contains over 100 teacher-tested classroom activities that are based on the Whole Language approach to learning. Chapters discuss the following: (1) a world of language in use; (2) literature points the way (including themes and organization, literature and experience, and extended literature); (3) making sense by reading (including predictions and expectations, reading awareness and control, invitations to read, and music, drama, and reading); (4) writing for self-expression; (5)

learning to write by writing; (6) writing for an audience (including developing a sense of audience, and messages, notes, and letters); (7) reading, writing, listening, and speaking across the curriculum (including language arts across the curriculum, and reading and writing newspapers); (8) kids helping other kids: the collaborative effort (including cooperative learning, and games and holiday activities); (9) home is where the start is; and (10) valuing and evaluating learners and their language.

Watson, Dorothy J., "Defining and Describing Whole Language," *Elementary School Journal 90/2* (Nov 1989): 129-41. [EJ 404 263]
Considers the need for a definition of "Whole Language" and difficulties involved therewith. Characteristic experiences in Whole Language learning communities are discussed.

Watson, Dorothy J., "Action, Reflection and Reflexivity: Thinking in the Whole Language Classroom," 17 pp. (1990). [ED 322 474]
Whole Language has to do with beliefs about language and learners that lead to beliefs about curriculum and instructional procedures. The term emerged as a label for the way language is thought to be learned: as a cohesive organization of systems working together as one—as a whole. Whole Language also refers to the learner as being whole—as sound and healthy, rather than flawed and in need of fixing. Whole Language means that learners and teachers are at the center of curricular gravity; all materials and resources are used only if they are appropriate, authentic, and lead to student reflection and reflexivity. Invitations originate from the authentic life of the classroom and are issued by teachers, students, by appropriate and compelling resources and materials, and even from the acts of reading and writing themselves. Invitations to action that can lead to reflection and reflexivity come from students' abilities, interests and needs, and such invitations have to do with: listening and telling stories, reading real literature, writing with real intent, discussing and sharing with others, and solving difficult problems. Reflection involves the personal and systematic exploration of possibilities. Reflexivity involves independence, initiative, and creativity, and is characterized by restructure or extension of the present performance and the forging of new ideas or questions. When teachers serve as facilitators, give invitational demonstrations, and ask their students to do only those things that they are willing to do themselves, high-quality thinking and learning take place.

Watson, Dorothy J., and others, "Two Approaches to Reading: Whole-Language and Skills," paper presented at the Annual Meeting of the International Reading Association (29th, Atlanta, GA, May 6-10, 1984. [ED 247 546]
A study was conducted to observe and describe two reading instruction procedures stemming from two different theoretical influences. Two teachers, one skills and one Whole Language oriented, were selected on the basis of peer and administrator recommendation, among other qualifications. Their stated instructional base and theoretical orientations were measured using the Theoretical Orientation to Reading Profile (TORP). Data were collected from video tapes and their transcriptions and from teacher journals. The results were analyzed using these questions as guides: On what unit of our language and linguistic system did the teacher focus the children's attention? What aspects of reading were emphasized? Was the reading material contingent on the student, teacher, or material? and, What attitude toward reading specific text did the teacher encourage? Findings showed that in every category of observable data the teachers adhered closely to their theoretical model, and that, in diametric opposition to the instructional position of the skills teacher, the Whole-Language teacher focused children's attention on the largest unit of language suitable for the situation, encouraged the children to construct meaning sensible to them and

their lives, permitted deviations from text in allowing miscues, involved children in planning, utilized library books and other texts, and encouraged children to "think about and feel" what they read.

Weaver, Constance, "Alternatives in Understanding and Educating Attention-Deficit Students: A Systems-Based Whole Language Perspective. NCTE Concept Paper Series. Concept Paper No. 3." (1991): 53 pp. [ED 337 755]

The prevailing concept of Attention-Deficit Hyperactivity Disorder (ADHD) is a medical one: those exhibiting significant problems in maintaining attention and restraining impulses are said to have a "disorder," which implies some sort of malfunction within the individual. What is needed is a "both/and" perspective: a perspective that simultaneously acknowledges the validity of the social criticisms of the origin and consequences of ADHD, and at the same time acknowledges and attempts to alleviate the very real difficulties of children. A general systems view of ADHD sees causes as multi-dimensional and multi-directional—a view compatible with and contributing to a Whole Language philosophy. The forthcoming "Diagnostic and Statistical Manual" (version IV) will list the defining characteristics of ADHD under two relatively separate behavioral dimensions: inattention-disorganization, and impulsivity-hyperactivity. It is not easy even for trained clinicians to distinguish ADHD from other problems. Research indicates that medication complemented by cognitive or behavioral therapy is more effective than any of the treatments alone. There are numerous strategies effective in educating ADHD children that reflect a systems perspective by adjusting the environment and environmental demands to meet the needs of students. Because Whole Language theory reflects a "both/and" stance toward responsibility for learning and a conviction that teachers need to work with children to help them control their behavior, Whole Language teachers may be particularly effective with ADHD students.

Weaver, Constance, *Reading Process and Practice: From Socio-Psycholinguistics to Whole Language.* (Portsmouth, New Hampshire: Heinemann, 1988): 483 pp. [ED 286 157]

Based on the thesis that reading is not a passive process by which readers soak up words and information from the page, but an active process by which they predict, sample, and confirm or correct their hypotheses about the written text, this book is an introduction to the theories of the psycholinguistic nature of the reading process and reading instruction. Each of the 12 chapters includes questions for journals and discussion, and extensive learning activities. The chapters deal with the following topics: (1) beliefs about reading; (2) what language means, and why it matters in the teaching of reading (including schema theory and contrasting models of reading and reading instruction); (3) how words are perceived; (4) how context aids in word identification; (5) why word-identification views of reading (such as phonics and basal reader approaches) are inappropriate; (6) how a socio-psycholinguistic view of reading is relevant to reading instruction; (7) how the acquisition of literacy parallels the acquisition of oral language; (8) how a Whole Language approach can be implemented (chapter contributed by Dorothy Watson and Paul Crowley); (9) how reading can be taught in the content areas (chapter contributed by Marilyn Wilson); (10) how to assess readers' strengths and begin to determine their instructional needs; (11) how to help those with reading difficulties; and (12) coming whole circle (chapter contributed by Dorothy Watson).

Weaver, Constance, "Understanding and Educating Attention Deficit Hyperactive Students: Toward a Systems-Theory and Whole Language Perspective." (1992): 32 pp. [ED 344 376]

Argues that Attention Deficit Hyperactivity Disorder (ADHD) should be viewed as a dysfunctional relationship between an individual with certain predispositions and an environment which generates certain expectations, demands, and reactions. The paper presents a model in which: ADHD behaviors result from a combination of inherent neurological factors interacting with environmental circumstances and demands; relevant aspects of the individual's inherent biochemical nature may have been determined by either hereditary or environmental factors or both; ADHD behaviors may be alleviated most effectively by attending to both the individual and the environment; and ADHD students will succeed best when teachers and schools try to meet the needs of these students rather than merely trying to fit them into a rigid system, while considering the usefulness of medication. The paper then presents a systems-theory approach to educating ADHD students. Ten ways that Whole Language classrooms may be particularly beneficial for ADHD students are discussed. The paper also describes additional ways of providing the kinds of structure that ADHD students need, an example illustrating a Whole Language approach to behavior problems, and low-cost but high-efficiency support services that the school might provide to ADHD students and their teachers.

Weaver, Constance, "Whole Language and Its Potential for Developing Readers," *Topics in Language Disorders 11/3* (May 1991): 28-44. [EJ 428 632]
Discusses major principles characterizing the Whole Language philosophy of teaching and learning; assumptions of the mechanistic and relational paradigms; Whole Language practices such as the Shared Book Experience and Reading Recovery for helping students with reading difficulties; and the potential of Whole Language for developing readers, writers, and learners.

Weaver, Constance, and others, *Theme Exploration: A Voyage of Discovery*, Portsmouth, New Hampshire: Heinemann, 1993. [CS 011 327]
A conversation among three authors, offers strategies for theme exploration in Whole Language classrooms, focused on grades 1 and 4. Asserts that exploring a theme with students is the epitome of Whole Language teaching because students develop language and literacy best when they use language to gain understanding of a wide range of topics, themes, and concepts. The book's first section describes how a unit on robots became a journey of theme exploration; offers a definition of Whole Language principles and goals; describes one teacher's journey from a basal to a Whole Language approach. Details the development of a fourth-grade theme exploration project about improving the world by focusing on environmental, social, and technological issues. Outlines a first-grade theme exploration project titled Metaphors and Meteorology. The two final sections are retrospective assessments of both the fourth- and the first-grade projects. One of the appendices is titled "What Is Whole Language?"

Weaver, Constance, and others, "Understanding Whole Language: From Principles to Practice." (1990): 309 pp. [ED 326 847]
Introduces Whole Language philosophy; aims to demonstrate that Whole Language is indeed good education. Outlines research support of Whole Language education, how a Whole Language philosophy may be carried out in practice, and how to go about implementing a Whole Language philosophy in a school or a school system. Designed for a broad audience of teachers, teacher educators, curriculum supervisors, specialists, principals, superintendents, parents, and members of school boards. Chapter titles: (1) What Whole Language Is, and Why Whole Language (2) Defining and Redefining Literacy (3) Impetus for Revision and Reform (4) Developing Language and Literacy (5) What Does the Research Say? Research in Support of Part-to-Whole (6) What Does the Research Say? Research in Support of Whole-to-Part (7) Developing Phonics

Knowledge in Whole Language Classrooms (8) Developing Comprehension and Thinking in Whole Language Classrooms (9) Reconsidering Standardized Tests for Assessment and Accountability (10) Reconceptualizing and Reclaiming Assessment and Accountability (11) From Understanding to Implementing a Whole Language Philosophy.

Weaver, Constance, "Reading as a Whole," paper presented at the Annual Meeting of the National Council of Teachers of English (77th, Los Angeles, CA, Nov 20-25, 1987). [ED 290 132]
Underlying virtually all of the basal reading series available in the United States today is the assumption that learning to read is a skill-by-skill and word-by-word process. This part-to-whole approach to teaching reading is based on principles of behavioral psychology and "scientific management" developed a half century ago and treats meaning as merely an end to be attained after words are identified and sounded out. More recent research by Frank Smith, Kenneth Goodman (1973), and others indicates reading is a process of constructing meaning rather than merely obtaining meaning. Similarly, Jean Piaget and cognitive psychologists like Lev Vygotsky have advanced the concept that children learn best when what is to be learned is functional and concrete rather than dysfunctional and abstract, indicating that learning to read should be approached as a whole-to-part, Whole Language process which replaces dull and often frustrating drills with opportunities to develop an understanding of and pleasure in the written word. This approach has been adopted in New Zealand, in parts of Australia and Canada, and in a number of schools and classrooms in the United States.

Weaver, Connie, "Weighing Claims of "Phonics First" Advocates." (1990): 8 pp. [ED 334 557]
The question of whether research supports a "phonics first" approach to teaching reading is not entirely answerable by factual evidence or statistical data: the issue is partly a matter of values and opinion. The debate is over whether phonics should be taught and tested in isolation, as a prelude to reading texts (the phonics-first view) or whether phonics strategies should be developed more gradually, in the context of reading and writing materials that interest students. The debate has been fueled recently by federal legislative actions and by the distribution of a Senate Republican Policy Committee document entitled "Illiteracy: An Incurable Disease or Education Malpractice?" Misinformation abounds in the committee's document. It claims, for example, that there are only two ways to teach reading: phonics and "look and say," which the document incorrectly states is synonymous with "Whole Language." In addition, many of the studies cited in the document are deficient. Whole Language classrooms foster habits and attitudes of independent, self-motivated, lifelong readers and writers to a far greater degree than more traditional classrooms—especially those emphasizing phonics first.

Webb, Alice, and others, "Four Teachers Pilot a Whole Language Program," *Childhood Education 67*/3 (spr 1991): 155-60. [EJ 430 347]
Four K-3 teachers described their experiences using Whole Language programs. They had in common a child-centered attitude; an initial experience of frustration followed by encouragement from the children's excitement and involvement in learning; and an approach that began with the writing process and moved to literature-based instruction.

Weber, Joanne C., "Language Lab: A Pilot Project at R.J.D. Williams School for the Deaf, Saskatoon," *ACEHI Journal 18*/1 (1992): 43-50. [EJ 452 888]
The Language Lab was a pilot project which sought to develop communicative competence in deaf students with additional disabilities, through the use of the

bilingual-bicultural approach and the Whole Language approach. Discusses goals of the Language Lab, classroom strategies, administration, and student evaluation.

Wehmeyer, Lillian Biermann, "Partners: The Whole Language Teacher and the Library Media Specialist," *School Library Media Activities Monthly 9/5* (Jan 1993): 29-34. [EJ 456 157]

Discusses ways in which library media specialists can help teachers who are using the Whole Language approach. Topics addressed include reading aloud to children; wordless picture books; decoding; writing; core literature selections; automaticity in reading; independent reading; re-reading; reading across the curriculum; literature as content; and storytelling.

Weir, Beth, "A Research Base for Prekindergarten Literacy Programs," *Reading Teacher 42/7* (Mar 1989): 456-60. [EJ 385 144]

Examines current research concerning various instructional approaches for introducing print related concepts to preschool children. Discusses the nature of preschool literacy skills in light of research findings. Concludes that a Whole Language approach enhances initial print concepts and develops analytical reading related skills.

Weir, Beth, "Lessons from a French Class on Becoming Literate: A Personal Reflection," *Reading Horizons 31/1* (Oct 1990): 49-58. [EJ 418 015]

Draws a parallel between the experience of learning to read and write in a first and a second language. Notes that the experience of learning through an approach that permits talking, reading, and writing freely is satisfying whereas the experience with a text-based approach to learning is much less satisfactory.

Wepner, Shelley B., "Stepping Forward with Reading Software," *Journal of Reading, Writing, and Learning Disabilities International 5* (1989): 61-83 [EJ 397 845]

Presents an approach to using computers to meet the psychological, intellectual, and procedural needs of students with reading disabilities. A rationale is put forward for using Whole Language software packages to address these needs while facilitating reading and writing development; describes several software programs.

Wepner, Shelley B., "Holistic Computer Applications in Literature-Based Classrooms," *Reading Teacher 44/1* (Sep 1990): 12-19. [EJ 413 062]

Describes how computers, when cast in a holistic framework, can be a natural complement to students' literacy development. Discusses how six teachers use computers in holistic literacy instruction.

Westby, Carol E., and Linda Costlow, "Implementing a Whole Language Program in a Special Education Class," *Topics in Language Disorders 11/3* (May 1991): 69-84. [EJ 428 635]

A program for language learning-disabled students is described that uses a Whole Language philosophy to structure contexts that develop students' pragmatic, semantic, syntactic, graphophonemic, and metacognitive abilities underlying speaking, listening, reading, and writing. This paper describes the program environment, children, thematic contexts, contexts for literacy, and parent involvement.

Westby, Carol E., "The Role of the Speech-Language Pathologist in Whole Language," *Language, Speech, and Hearing Services in Schools 21/4* (Oct 1990): 228-37. [EJ 420 019]

Presents a framework for understanding the pragmatic, semantic, syntactic, text, and phonological aspects of language that underlie both oral and written communication. It gives suggestions for ways speech-language pathologists can assess children's language skills that are essential for success in a Whole Language program.

White, Joyce, and Mary Norton, "Whole Language: A Framework for Thinking about Literacy Work with Adults." (1991): 42 pp. [ED 332 051]
Describes the Whole Language approach to literacy education in the context of teaching adults. Information is drawn from literature and from interviews with teachers and literacy students. Topics covered include the following: Whole Language—a framework, learning language, learning through language, learning about language, what people said, people learning together, and learning how to be a Whole Language educator. Challenges for the Whole Language method are suggested. Three appendixes contain: (1) a discussion of providing adult literacy education in Canada; (2) acknowledgement of people quoted in the paper; and (3) views about reading and writing.

Whitmore, Kathryn F., and Yetta M. Goodman, "Inside the Whole Language Classroom," *School Administrator 49*/5 (May 1992): 20-26. [EJ 444 303]
The Whole Language movement is challenging educators to reconsider their early childhood programs and assumptions about children and learning. Explores four promises of Whole Language philosophy central to early childhood education (language, active learning, play, and home/school relationships), and explores some program implementation issues.

Whole Language and Integrated Language Arts. Special Collection Number 13." (Bloomington, Indiana: ERIC/RCS, 1991): 68 pp. [ED 334 570]
Contains seven ERIC Digests (brief syntheses of the research on a specific topic in contemporary education) and eight FAST Bibs (Focused Access to Selected Topics—annotated bibliographies with selected entries from the ERIC database), providing up-to-date information in an accessible format. The collection focuses on Whole Language, integrating the language arts, reading-writing relationships, literature and reading and writing, reader-response theory, communication skills, and creative dramatics. The material in the special collection is designed for use by teachers, students, administrators, researchers, policy makers, and parents.

Whole Language: A New Approach to Teaching and Learning. Special Report," *Teacher Magazine; v2*/9 (Aug 1991): 20-21. [EJ 433 792]
Introduces a special section on the Whole Language approach. The five articles discuss Whole Language's roots, Whole Language in the classroom, two schools that have embraced Whole Language, and Whole Language resources.

"**Why** Whole Language?" *Instructor 99*/9 (May 1990): 46-49. [EJ 417 468]
Several reading experts comment on the Whole Language approach to teaching reading and on the Whole Language debate. Topics include definitions of Whole Language, characteristics, justifications, shortcomings, and critiques.

Whyte, Sarah, "Whole Language Using Big Books." (1988): 73 pp. [ED 298 479]
Designed as thematic units around Wright Company Big Books, the lessons in this guide demonstrate ways that Big Books can be used in a Whole Language first grade program. Each lesson indicates skill focus, needed materials, procedures, and additional thoughts or suggestions about the lesson. Units consist of: "Bedtime" (five lessons); "Monsters and Giants" (five lessons); "Valentine's Day" (one lesson); "Houses" (two lessons); "Our Town" (four lessons); "Our Family" (four lessons); "Me" (one lesson); "Me (Feelings)" (three lessons); and "Me (Helping)" (one lesson). Discusses using African folk tales in the classroom; provides a list of African tales are provided. Includes a Whole Language and writing bibliography.

Wicklund, LaDonna K., "Shared Poetry: A Whole Language Experience Adapted for Remedial Readers," *Reading Teacher 42*/7 (Mar 1989): 478-81. [EJ 385 148]

Describes a shared-poetry exercise, combining Whole Language experiences with process writing techniques, that motivated remedial readers. Notes that this technique helps remedial readers achieve success in writing, build sight and meaning vocabularies, and improve reading fluency.

Wikstrom, Marilyn, "Whole Language for Disabled Readers," paper presented at the Annual Iowa Reading Conference (Des Moines, IA, Apr 5-7, 1990). [ED 325 808] Reading instruction for the middle-school disabled reader must vary from the way it has been taught in the student's past. Experiences using theme reading, poetry, scavenger hunt instruction cards, newspapers, and trade materials which form complete thought units prevent the reading task from becoming the isolated skills instruction of the past. Motivation will only develop if the student is interested in the material and if the content is new and not a repeat of earlier training. Reading material should be at the student's instructional level. Teachers will also be motivated by new and innovative content and the interest students demonstrate.

Williams, Sharon K., "Whole Language Resources," *Teacher Magazine 2/9* (Aug 1991): 46-47. [EJ 433 797]
Presents an annotated list of associations, organizations, publishing companies, children's bookstores, magazines, catalogues, and hot lines that can provide elementary and secondary teachers with more information on the Whole Language approach to teaching and learning.

Willing, Kathlene R., and Suzanne B. Girard, eds., "Learning Together: Computer-Integrated Classrooms," 109 pp. (1990). [ED 329 230]
Provides teachers with practical ideas for the use of computers to promote group interaction and cooperative learning. Includes (1) software webs to assist theme development, (2) pre-computer activities to motivate students, (3) computer activities to develop software competence, (4) post-computer activities to reinforce learning, (5) matrices and checklists to use as evaluation tools, (6) suggestions for initiating school projects and community events. Planned for teachers at the elementary level, grades 1-8, includes 11 chapters: (1) Cooperative Learning with Computers (2) Equipment and Materials (3) Human Factors (4) Using Software Across the Curriculum (5) Using Theme-Related Software (6) Integrating Computers with Whole Language (7) Graphics/Text Software and Whole Language (8) Word Processing Software and Whole Language (9) Simulation Software and Whole Language (10) Classroom Activities (11) Beyond the Classroom. Includes a glossary, a list of software, a list of software publishers, and an index.

Wilson, Marjorie S., "Helping Young Children Gain in Literacy: Implementing a Whole Language Approach in Prekindergarten," (1992): 75 pp. [ED 350 562]
A practicum was developed to assist prekindergarten teachers present a Whole Language approach in their already developmentally appropriate classes. Six teachers from three classrooms serving 63 four- and five-year-old children participated in on-site training and weekly consultations. The teachers were all experienced paraprofessionals with Child Development Associate (CDA) credentials. The children were admitted to the prekindergarten program based on income eligibility. The teachers attended five 2-hour workshops on how young children learn about reading and writing in a Whole Language approach classroom. The teachers learned about the use of predictable big books and ways to provide print experiences throughout the room. An attempt was made to involve parents through a meeting on the Whole Language approach, a book sale, and a lending library. The final checklist of each classroom documents a large increase in print opportunities, teacher encouragement and child

participation with print. Although the parent meetings were held and children's books sold, parents did not become active participants in the process. The teachers believed the parents needed more information about the program's parental expectations prior to the program's start.

Wilsted, Joy, *Now Johnny CAN Learn To Read.* (1987): 78 pp. [ED 315 752]
An an easy-to-read book intended for anyone involved in helping others learn to read. An initial section of the book focuses on how to make reading a socially stimulating, successful activity. In this section, viewpoints are shared from a child and a parent, and a reading specialist tells of the successes which reading specialists experience by giving children support as they learn to read. Contents: "Johnny's Story"; "Johnny's Mother's Story"; "Why Did Johnny Have Trouble Learning to Read?"; "A Specialist's Story"; "The Story of SUCCESS"; "Reading Is a Language Process"; "The Keys to SUCCESS in Reading: Modeling, Participating, and Interaction"; and "Why Use Whole-Language Strategies to Teach Reading?" The second section tells how to use the Five Success Reading Strategies, which will motivate students to become actively involved in the reading process. Chapter titles include: "What is SUCCESS?"; "Read-Spell-Read Games"; "Oral Reading Participation"; "Clozing Blanks and Riddling"; "Peer Questioning"; and "We Have Given Them Wings—Now Let Them Fly."

Winners, Diane, and Judith K. Cassady, "Teaching Reading and Writing in a Whole Language Atmosphere: The Teacher's Role," *Ohio Reading Teacher 24*/4 (sum 1990): 14-17. [EJ 432 604]
Discusses the Whole Language teacher's role in the development of children's writing, and establishing a positive writing environment in the classroom.

Winser, W. N., "Adult Readers' Problems: How a Language-Based Approach Can Help." (1992): 19 pp. [ED 355 410]
In order to help adult readers with problems, it is necessary to develop an approach to teaching them that is sensitive to language and that makes explicit reference to the way language works to make meaning in texts. A language-based approach requires teachers to become more aware of the relatively invisible language system that lies behind the text, as well as the social aspects of purpose and ideology that are always involved in making meaning through language. This approach suggests that teachers and students need to become more aware of the meaning-making powers of language as the basis for developing better teaching strategies. Some of the types of teaching strategies that may help adults with reading problems include the following: (1) cloze with discussion, focusing on chosen words; (2) modeling; (3) joint construction, encouraging students to gradually take on more responsibility; (4) building on students' field knowledge; and (5) use of the language experience approach for very low-level readers or with very anxious readers.

Wollman-Bonilla, Julie E., "Shouting from the Tops of Buildings: Teachers as Learners and Change in Schools," *Language Arts 68*/2 (Feb 1991): 114-20. [EJ 421 169]
Describes a collaborative professional development project designed to bring Whole Language knowledge to more classroom teachers. Discusses one staff developer's work with a second grade teacher. Argues that staff developers must (1) know and respect teachers; (2) provide ongoing support; and (3) link theory and practice. Concludes that staff development successes must be measured by teachers.

Wood, Peter, and others, "In Transition toward Whole Language Instruction," paper presented at the Annual Meeting of the International Reading Association (38th, San Antonio, Texas, Apr 26-30, 1993), Texas, 1993. [CS 011 335]
Reports a study in examination of 78 experienced Northwest Ohio elementary school

teachers' orientation toward Whole Language, teacher-made, and state-mandated tests. Reports the teachers' descriptions of their grading policies and distributions and their attitudes toward basal readers and phonics skills. The majority (56%) labeled themselves as over 50% "Whole Language" in their teaching of reading and language arts. Grade level taught and years of experience did not correlate with orientation toward Whole Language. Those with stronger orientation towards Whole Language tended to be more negative toward testing, the value of phonics skills, and the use of basal readers. Seatwork and tests appeared to dominate as sources for assignments of grades, followed by homework. Few, however, used information from portfolios as a source of grades. Most (81%) did assign A, B, C grades on report cards, but 46% reported skill levels on report cards, and 31% reported improvement grades or ratings. Major concerns include using portfolios to report to parents and other teachers, having to grade students, and learning more about Whole Language teaching. Few seemed to worry about the validity of their assessment procedures.

Wood, Margo, and Michael P. O'Donnell, "Directions of Change in the Teaching of Reading," *Reading Improvement 28/2* (sum 1991): 100-03. [EJ 448 346]
Discusses three trends in approaches to reading and literacy instruction: (1) the move from basal to literature-based instruction; (2) the move from emphasis on product to emphasis on process; and (3) the trend away from teacher as technician toward teacher as decision maker. States that these trends will result in profound and lasting changes in literacy instruction.

Woodley, John W., "Whole Language in the College Classroom: One Professor's Approach." (1988): 28 pp. [ED 295 125]
Teaching a course in content area reading instruction means that a professor will have students with a broad range of experiences and interests, all of which must be taken into account in the instructional process by providing many opportunities for choice and self-selection. The modeling of effective teaching is a strategy that can encourage students to consider actively the role of reading instruction in their content classes and to become aware of the broad range of options available to them as teachers. The use of Whole Language—a theory of instruction and learning based on knowledge of language learning and language use as well as knowledge of people of whatever age and however they learn—can help in selecting activities and materials, evaluating students' progress, and shaping the educational program in a classroom. Whole Language, at the college level, can be both possible and desirable—if the teaching approach is grounded on three beliefs: (1) language use is to be encouraged whenever possible; (2) language is to be kept whole and meaningful; and (3) each student learns as an individual. By carefully reviewing what is to be accomplished in the course and selecting instructional strategies, evaluation methods, and course content from a theoretical perspective consistent with Whole Language, the college teacher can conduct an effective Whole Language program.

Woodley, John W., "Reading Assessment from a Whole Language Perspective." (1988): 16 pp. [ED 296 309]
Several approaches to reading assessment, based on the Whole Language approach, can provide teachers with a frame of reference to guide them in making decisions about selecting and planning classroom activities. The more traditional approach to reading assessment, usually referred to as reading diagnosis, focuses on the final product (the test scores) and looks for symptoms of underlying reading disorders. Whole Language is a theoretical perspective which allows both teachers and students to focus on growth and development in language use and language learning rather than on instruction, conformity or a fixed curriculum. Approaches to reading assessment

within the Whole Language framework include a print awareness task, book handling task, patterned language task, reading interview, miscue analysis, and situational responses to reading. The observations made by teachers using these assessments provide a meaningful alternative to heavy reliance on standardized tests and lead to a more effective educational program for all.

Woronowicz, Stephanie A., and Brenda J. McInnis, "The Whole Language Approach to Reading and Writing Instruction. What We Know About." (1991): 44 pp. [ED 334 539]
Discusses the Whole Language approach to language instruction, which teaches students "from whole to part" through the integration of the language processes of reading, writing, speaking, and listening with an emphasis on meaning and purpose. The booklet explains what Whole Language is, describes its use in the teaching/learning process, summarizes the research related to its effectiveness, and discusses how it can be used appropriately in the teaching/learning process. The booklet's six sections are as follows: (1) What Is Whole Language? (discussing skills-based instructional approaches and a Whole Language approach to instruction); (2) Whole Language Strategies (the learning environment, instructional strategies, and phonics in Whole Language); (3) Whole Language Assessment (types of Whole Language assessment, and accommodating Whole Language assessment to standard grading requirements); (4) Research Relating to Whole Language Instruction (Whole Language studies, instructional strategies and grade levels, different learning styles, learning disabled students, at-risk first graders, disadvantaged students, and bilingual and culturally sensitive programs); (5) Implementing a Whole Language Program (the role of teachers and administrators, role of the school board, role of parents, and a combined approach to language instruction); and (6) Concluding Remarks.

Wray, David, "Reading: The New Debate," *Reading 23*/1 (Apr 1989): 2-8. [EJ 393 405]
Describes recent, major contributions to both sides of the debate between phonics instruction and the "meaning-based" approaches. Argues that it is too early to evaluate the debate, but that a tentative evaluation of the evidence favors meaning-based approaches.

Wright, Teresa A., "Improving Oral Language Skills in Kindergarten Students through the Use of the Whole Language Approach." (1990): 85 pp. [ED 323 503]
An instructional program was designed to improve the oral language skills of kindergarten students. The target group consisted of 10 students who, according to their scores on the Yellow Brick Road Language Battery, were in need of a strong language development program. The instructional plan was based on the Shared Book Experience and other components of the Whole Language Approach. Also included in the project was a parent involvement program. The Test of Language Development-Primary, an oral skills checklist, and a parental log were used to measure the effectiveness of the programs. Results of these measures indicated that exposure to the Whole Language Approach successfully improved the oral language skills of the target group. It was also concluded that exposure to a structured parent involvement program significantly increased the level of parent involvement.

Wyatt, Patricia B., "Improving Reading Comprehension in Grade 3 Using Whole Language Activities and the Computer." (1991): 53 pp. [ED 335 667]
A practicum was designed to improve reading comprehension in 50 third-graders over an 8-month period. The practicum's peripheral goal was to improve the efficient use of the microcomputer as a tool to supplement reading comprehension. The program included computer lab experiences to teach keyboarding skills, language arts software

use, and the use of a word processing program in combination with the Junior Great Books to promote discussion and interpretive evaluation skills along with other Whole Language activities. Pre- and post-tests of reading comprehension were administered to the students. In addition, their reading scores on the Comprehensive Testing Program taken during the practicum were compared to their scores in the previous year, and were also compared to the preceding third grade's second and third grade reading test scores. Results indicated that the general objective of the practicum to improve reading comprehension in grade 3 was successfully met. Analysis of the data revealed that the participants met the behavioral expectations.

Yates, Bill, "Changing Attitudes," *Canadian Journal of English Language Arts 12/1-2* (1989): 13-15. [EJ 390 383]
Describes different methods of giving parents information about changes that take place when a school system implements the Whole Language approach. Observes that the natural mistrust and uncertainty associated with change can be eliminated when students have positive attitudes toward their learning experiences.

Yellin, David, "Will Evaluation Kill Whole Language?" *Kansas Journal of Reading 7* (spr 1991):49-53. [EJ 428 333]
Outlines the main purposes of student evaluation. Suggests observation as an alternative to testing. Offers suggestions for keeping anecdotal records and a format for record sheets or class notebooks. Recommends that students keep records and maintain folders of their work. Cites an approach for teaching self-evaluation. Suggests helping students understand standardized tests.

Young, Robert D., "Risk-Taking in Learning, K-3. NEA Early Childhood Education Series." (1991): 78 pp. [ED 336 207]
Offers teachers suggestions for ways to help students become risk-takers. Five levels of risk-taking behavior are identified: the uninhibited risk-taker, the analytical risk-taker, the cautious risk-taker, the inhibited risk-taker, and the nonrisk-taker. The importance of risk-taking for problem solving, and the teacher's role in promoting risk-taking, are discussed. The type of classroom that promotes risk-taking is described, and suggestions for scheduling and encouraging affective and cognitive development are offered. Individual chapters on mathematics, science, and the language arts include discussion of educational practices in each of the subjects and a list of ideas and activities that can be used in the classroom to encourage risk-taking in learning the subjects. A final chapter offers further ideas and activities that can be used to integrate the content of the subject areas. The Whole Language approach is stressed.

Zarrillo, James, "Theory Becomes Practice: Aesthetic Teaching with Literature," *New Advocate 4/4* (fall 1991): 221-34. [EJ 432 477]
Asserts that there is a gap between theory and practice in literature-based reading programs. States that too often, these programs lack an underlying theory; they mimic methodology associated with basal programs. Describes the theoretical perspectives of Louise Rosenblatt, her principles of aesthetic teaching, examples from a fourth-grade classroom, and evaluation.

Zarrillo, James, "Literature-Centered Reading and Language Minority Students," paper prepared for the Institute on Literacy and Learning Language Minority Project, University of California (Santa Barbara, CA, Aug 24-25, 1987). [ED 299 541]
Argues that literature-centered reading programs, based on the perspective that reading is the process of bringing meaning to print, are in the best interest of the language minority students in the nation's elementary schools. After a review of basal reading systems and language-centered reading programs, the paper describes the problems

faced by language minority students and limited English proficient (LEP) students in traditional reading programs. Several case studies are presented in the development of second language literacy. Concludes with a model of a literature-centered reading program for language minority students which is built on the premises that reading and writing are processes acquired through use; that the ability to read and write competently in two languages is of value; and that elementary school children of the same chronological age differ widely in their interests and abilities. The model has three phases: (1) core book units, in which students are provided with a thorough experience with one book; (2) literature units, to allow students to learn about literary genres, themes, and selected authors; and (3) individualized reading and writing, in which students select the books to read and the genres and topics they wish to write about. Also discusses the Language Experience Approach and the use of predictable books, and stories, two special intervention programs for beginning readers, whether bilingual or monolingual.

Zola, Meguido, "The Tao of Whole Language," *Emergency Librarian 17*/2 (Nov-Dec 1989): 9-10,12,14-15. [EJ 405 654]
Uses the philosophy of Taoism as a metaphor in describing the Whole Language approach to language arts instruction. The discussion covers the key principles that inform the Whole Language approach, the resulting holistic nature of language programs, and the role of the teacher in this approach.

Zucker, Carol, "Using Whole Language with Students Who Have Language and Learning Disabilities," *Reading Teacher 46*/8 (May 1993): 660-70. [EJ 462 275]
Describes how the Whole Language philosophy undergirds the teaching approaches used in a non-traditional special- education program designed for students with language and learning disabilities.

More Resources on Whole Language

from ERIC® / EDINFO Press

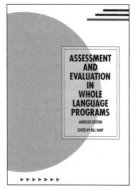

Assessment and Evaluation in Whole Language Programs
(Revised Edition) **edited by Bill Harp (1993)**

The first detailed examination of effective assessment and evaluation theory in current practice. Contributions by Jerry Harste, Dorothy Watson, Bill Harp, Yvonne Siu-Runyan, Jeanne Reardon, and others add up to a clear explanation and rationale for assessment and evaluation in a Whole Language context. Specific examples from primary, intermediate, bilingual, multicultural, and special-ed. classrooms.

Softcover, 6 ¾ x 10 in., 251 pp.
G44; $16.25

New Policy Guidelines for Reading: Connecting Research and Practice
by Jerome C. Harste (1989)

Encourages collaboration between researchers and teachers to improve the effectiveness of reading instruction. Evaluates the status of current practice and of current research. Challenges widespread assumptions about effective reading instruction.

Concludes with twenty policy guidelines—for administrators, teachers, researchers, and curriculum developers—to improve research and instruction in reading.

Copublished with the National Council of Teachers of English.

Softcover, 6 x 9 in., 81 pp.
G05; $9.95

Special
Collection
Number 13

**WHOLE
LANGUAGE AND
INTEGRATED
LANGUAGE ARTS**

ERIC ꟿINFO
PRESS

ERIC/REC's Special Collection: Whole Language and Integrated Language Arts

ERIC/REC's Special Collections are time-saving compilations for students, researchers, and practitioners. *Whole Language and Integrated Language Arts* is a collection of ERIC Digests and FAST Bibs offering educators summaries of scholarly research and annotated bibliographies of the most significant resources on Whole Language and integrated language arts instruction.

Digests
- Reading and Writing in a Kindergarten Classroom
- Book-Length Works Taught in High School English Courses
- Integrating Literature into Middle School Reading Classrooms
- Using Literature to Teach Reading
- Whole Language: Integrating the Language Arts—and Much More
- Schema Activation, Construction, and Application
- Creative Dramatics in the Language Arts Classroom

FAST Bibs
- Creative Arts in the Classroom: Readers' Theater, Drama, and Oral Interpretation
- Communication Skills across the Curriculum
- Whole Language in Secondary Schools
- Trade Books in the K–12 Classroom
- Reading-Writing Relationships
- Reading Material Selection
- Writing and Literature
- Reader Response

SC13; $7.95

For information on other Special Collections available from ERIC/REC, please call us at 1-800-759-4723.

Alternative Assessment of Performance in the Language Arts: What Are We Doing Now? Where Are We Going?
edited by Carl B. Smith (1991)

Leading researchers, theorists, educators, test publishers, and policy makers contribute to an analysis of the state of assessment in the language arts. A wide array of fundamental issues and questions are addressed.

Alternative Assessment of Performance in the Language Arts

What Are We Doing Now? Where Are We Going?

ERIC

PHI
DELTA
KAPPA

Issues

- Alternative vs. standardized assessment
- A national assessment vs. individualized instruction-driven assessment
- Multiple-choice tests vs. portfolios
- Whole Language theory vs. traditional reliability and validity
- Testing driven by instruction vs. instruction driven by testing

Questions

- Whom does assessment serve? How do teachers, schools, children, parents, and community benefit?
- What are the implications for instructional materials in alternative assessment?
- What are the connections between the theory and politics of alternative assessment?
- What are the implications for curriculum planning when implementing alternative assessment?
- How do society's concerns influence the development of alternative assessment?

Included are major presentations by educators Roger Farr and Kaye Lowe, Jerome Harste and William Bintz, Diane Bloom, Bert Wiser and Sharon Dorsey, as well as Don Ernst, education assistant to the Governor of Indiana, and Marilyn R. Binkley of the National Center for Education Statistics. Also represented are test developers and commercial publishers of assessment instruments.

Concludes with practical reports on portfolio assessment and literacy portfolios by participant Jerry L. Johns.

Copublished with Phi Delta Kappa.

Softcover, 6 x 9 in., 300 pp.
G22; $21.95

Celebrate Literacy!
The Joy of Reading and Writing

From the TRIED series—covers the full range of language-arts strategies and literature to turn your elementary school into a reading-and-writing carnival including literacy slumber parties, book birthdays, and battles of the books.

Softcover, 8 ½ x 11 in., 92 pp.
AT11; $14.95

The TRIED series from ERIC/EDINFO Press puts fresh and effective lesson ideas into your hands. Each TRIED is a collection of alternatives to textbook teaching designed and tested by your teaching peers. Assembled from entries in the ERIC database—the largest educational retrieval system in existence—TRIEDs make it easy to tap into the professional expertise and experience of the nation's finest educators

> *"The book suggests practical and creative teaching ideas for implementing reading skills in the elementary curriculum. Though no theory is specifically stated, a whole language approach is evident in the lessons. Basically* Celebrate Literacy! *emphasized the philosophy of the pleasure principle toward teaching reading."*
>
> —Joan Mento, Assistant Professor, Dept. of English, Westfield State College
> in "Book Reviews," JACA (*Journal of the Association for Communication Administration*) April, 1993: 53–54.

Peer Teaching and Collaborative Learning in the Language Arts
by Elizabeth McAllister (1990)

Six real-life scenarios illustrate how teachers have successfully implemented peer teaching and collaborative learning in the classroom. By sharing and cooperating, students gain more knowledge and sharpened skills, and they learn from one another how to learn.

Describes four ways of organizing a peer-teaching program, offers suggestions on how to train tutors and design tutoring lessons, and explains how to evaluate the effects of a program in cooperative learning.

Softcover, 8 ½ x 11 in., 65 pp.
G13; $15.95

ORDER FORM

Qty	Title	Price	Subtotal
____	Assessment and Evaluation in Whole Language Programs (G44)	$16.25	_____
____	New Policy Guidelines for Reading (G05)	9.95	_____
____	ERIC/REC's Special Collection: Whole Language and Integrated Language Arts (SC13)	7.95	_____
____	Peer Teaching and Collaborative Learning in the Language Arts (G13)	15.95	_____
____	Alternative Assessment and Performance in the Language Arts (G22)	21.95	_____
____	Celebrate Literacy! The Joy of Reading and Writing (T11)	14.95	_____

Please send your order to:

ERIC/REC
Indiana University
2805 E. 10th St.
Smith Research Center, Suite 150
Bloomington, IN 47408-2698

	Subtotal	_____
	Packing & Delivery	_____
	TOTAL Purchase	_____

Packing & Delivery
Please add 10% with a
minimum of $3.00.

Ship to:

**Order by phone: 1-812-855-5847, 1-800-759-4723,
or FAX 1-812-855-4220.**

_____
Name

_____
Title

_____
Organization

_____
Address

_____
City/State/Zip   Phone

Method of Payment

❑ check ❑ money order ❑ P.O.#_____

❑ MasterCard ❑ Visa

Cardholder_____

Card no._____Exp._____

Cardholder's signature_____